MAP IS NOT TERRITORY

MAP IS NOT TERRITORY

Studies in the History of Religions

BY

JONATHAN Z. SMITH

The University of Chicago Press
Chicago and London

Published by arrangement with E. J. Brill.

The University of Chicago Press, Chicago 60637
The University of Chicago Press, Ltd., London

Copyright 1978 by E. J. Brill, Leiden, The Netherlands
First published 1978.
University of Chicago Press edition 1993.
Printed in the United States of America

99 98 97 96 95 94 93   6 5 4 3 2 1

ISBN 0-226-76357-9 (pbk.)

Library of Congress Cataloging-in-Publication Data

Smith, Jonathan Z.
    Map is not territory : studies in the history of religions /
by Jonathan Z. Smith.
        p.   cm.
    Originally published: Leiden : E. J. Brill, 1978.
    Includes bibliographical references and indexes.
    1. Religion.   2. Religion—Study and teaching.
I. Title.
BL48.S595   1993
291—dc20   92-36231
                                                                CIP

♾ The paper used in this publication meets the minimum
requirements of the American National Standard for
Information Sciences—Permanence of Paper for Printed
Library Materials, ANSI Z39.48-1984

To my Mother
and
in loving memory of my Father

TABLE OF CONTENTS

Preface. IX
Acknowledgements XVII

I

I. The Garments of Shame 1
II. The Prayer of Joseph. 24
III. Wisdom and Apocalyptic. 67

II

IV. The Wobbling Pivot. 88
V. Earth and Gods. 104
VI. The Influence of Symbols on Social Change: A Place on Which to Stand 129
VII. Birth Upside Down or Right Side Up?. 147
VIII. The Temple and the Magician. 172
IX. Good News is No News: Aretalogy and Gospel. . . . 190

III

X. When the Bough Breaks 208
XI. *Adde Parvum Parvo Magnus Acervus Erit*. 240
XII. I am a Parrot (Red) 265

IV

XIII. Map Is Not Territory. 289

Index to Ancient Sources 311
   Bible; Jewish and Christian Apocrypha 311
   Other Ancient Sources 313
General Index 324

PREFACE

In his eloquent tribute to the Bureau of American Ethnology, Claude Lévi-Strauss made the shrewd observation that "anthropology is the science of culture as seen from the outside", that "anthropology, whenever it is practiced by members of the culture it endeavors to study, loses its specific nature and becomes rather akin to archaeology, history and philology."[1] The same principle, *mutatis mutandis*, has guided my understanding of the enterprise of History of Religions as well as the organization of the essays reprinted in this volume, more than half of which are devoted to Western religious materials.

It should, therefore, come as no surprise that those essays which are most narrowly focussed on specific texts from Late Antiquity (chapters 1-3) appear largely to surrender the characteristic stance of the historian of religions and seem more closely related to traditional exegetical procedures. Common to each of these essays is a comparative enterprise within closely adjacent historical, cultural or linguistic units which insists (in conscious distinction from the "parallelomania" that sometimes overwhelmed practitioners of the *Religionsgeschichtliche Schule*) that the comparison be between a total ensemble rather than between isolated motifs.

Such comparative endeavors have a double thrust. They seek both to situate a text within a "family of resemblances" and to clarify the complexity and limits of this "family" by examining a specific document. They are exercises in that most rudimentary, but also most basic, of scholarly procedures: classification.[2] I take seriously the oft-repeated remark that, in the history of a discipline, such a taxonomic enterprise is more indicative of a "natural history" than a "science"; indeed, as an *historian* of religions, I am content that this be so. The former stage appears to be the necessary precondition for achieving the latter.

---

[1] C. Lévi-Strauss, *Structural Anthropology* (New York, 1963-1976), Vol. II, p. 55.
[2] I intend a distinction between the enterprise of *classification* and that of *definition*. Definition is an essentially atemporal procedure that requires the specification of a unique principle of division thus resembling traditional, logical monothetic classification. Classification, in the sense I intend, is a polythetic grouping or clustering procedure which requires temporal specificity.

The three taxa that are being explored in chapters 1-3 are Gnosticism, Judaism and Apocalypticism. Each is a complex grouping term. That is to say, no single 'red thread' defines them; rather each is a constellation of characteristics in which judgements of relative *degree* may lead to judgements of differing *kind*. All three have most usually been treated as reified, substantive nouns (indeed, as proper names); I should like to reduce each to the status of qualifying adjectives.[3] There is no essence of Gnosticism, Judaism or Apocalypticism. Rather, there is a shifting cluster of attributes which, for a particular purpose and in terms of a given document, makes one or another of these labels appropriate. A specific instance (e.g. the *Apocalypse of Adam* [*C.G.* V.5]) may well be classified under all three headings—but the purpose will have shifted according to each label as well as those texts and associated religious and social phenomena with which it might be most usefully grouped. Therefore the strategy in each chapter has been to take a text which has been labeled on the basis of a single trait and explore the possibilities for reclassification on the basis of an internally coherent set of traits.

In the first two essays, the argument is essentially one of economy. The *Gospel of Thomas* is ostensively a Christian text; the *Prayer of Joseph* is ostensively Jewish. But both have been assigned other labels in the scholarly literature. Each essay seeks to demonstrate that there is no necessity to go beyond the ostensive identification. There is nothing in the text, when taken as a whole, that would prevent some type of Christian or some type of Jew from having written each detail in the text. This can be determined by careful comparison of each motif with Christian and Jewish materials. But the argument hinges on the identification of the "type" of Christian or Jew. This can only be determined by the *ensemble*. It is not enough that each isolated element be found within other members of the taxon, but that these elements be combined in a way that is similar to the text in question. Thus the *Gospel of Thomas* is located with respect to Syriac Christian baptismal practice; the *Prayer of Joseph*, to the Hellenistic Jewish "mystery of the Patriarchs" as elucidated (for all its problems) by Erwin Goodenough.

Both of these essays were written at a relatively early stage of my research. Today, I find them insufficiently historical. Chapter 3 is more representative of my current work. Borrowing the useful

---

[3] See my review of the Messina Colloquium's attempt to define Gnosis and Gnosticism in *Kairos*, X (1968), esp. p. 299.

term, "trajectory", from Koester and Robinson,[4] I have come to insist that it is not sufficient to merely name a text; rather, it is necessary both to locate a text within a history of tradition and to provide some sort of explanation for the processes of continuity and change. A central preoccupation of all my work has come to be the notion that, regardless of whether we are studying texts from literate or non-literate cultures, we are dealing with *historical processes of reinterpretation*, with *tradition*. That, for a given group at a given time to choose this or that mode of interpreting their tradition is to opt for a particular way of relating themselves to their historical past and social present.[5] It is for this reason alone that, as an historian of religions, the Hellenistic period and the religions of Late Antiquity have proved so interesting. While usually studied as "background" for the emergence of Christianity, such a perspective radically and illegitimately foreshortens the phenomena and, thus, radically distorts what is most illuminating. In almost no case, in this period, do we study a new religion. Rather almost every religious tradition has had a two thousand year history. We study archaic Mediterranean religions in their Hellenistic phase. To be able to trace the Eleusinian mysteries from their origin as a fourteenth century family cult to the gnosticization of their central myth in the *Naassene Sermon* in the third century (A.D.) is to be able to truly function as an historian of religions in contradistinction to the usual static comparison of isolated items such as the "raising" of Kore with the resurrection of Jesus or Adamas among the Naassenes with the Son of Man in the gospels or some generalized Anthropos myth.[6] Therefore, chapter 3 attempts to develop the history of apocalypticism in relation to wisdom traditions by tracing its trajectory from archaic Babylonian and Egyptian materials through late gnosticized texts and by correlating shifts in the literature with historical and social change.

The second set of essays (chapters 4-9) are related thematically and, therefore, have a somewhat different character. They have their origin in a theoretical issue: the adequacy of the description

---

[4] See H. Koester and J. M. Robinson, *Trajectories Through Early Christianity* (Philadelphia, 1971), esp. pp. 13-15.

[5] Compare J. Z. Smith, "The Social Description of Early Christianity," *Religious Studies Review*, I (1975), 19-25 and "A Pearl of Great Price and a Cargo of Yams," *History of Religions*, XV (1976), 1-19.

[6] For a general statement, see J. Z. Smith, "Native Cults in the Hellenistic Period," *History of Religions*, XI (1971), 236-249.

of sacred space as developed within the general History of Religions represented, preeminently, by the writings of Mircea Eliade (chapter 4). In each instance the model has been tested, either explicitly or implicitly, against Jewish materials in order to determine what the model can illuminate in the data and what alterations in the model are required to account for the data.

The model was first developed in its essential details by the Pan-Babylonian School and represented a conservative polemic against contemporary notions of evolutionary change.[7] It closely meshed with the *ideology* of the ancient Near Eastern texts which it sought to interpret by placing a high premium on conformity. In chapters 4, 6 and 7, I accept and elaborate this ideology, terming it a locative view of the world as elaborated by an imperial figure. Such a view is typical of early Near Eastern urban, agricultural, literate, hierarchical, bureaucratized, imperialist, slave cultures (including Israel). Its most persuasive witnesses are the production of priestly and scribal elites who had a vested interest in restricting mobility and valuing "place". The texts are by and large the production of royal courts and temples and provide their *raison d'être*. Scholars have been insufficiently attentive to the "hermeneutics of suspicion" with respect to the adequacy of this self-serving ideology for interpreting the *realia* of such societies; the model may not be extended, as it has by many historians of religions, to the hunting and gathering world of primitive man. Therefore I would insist, on both theoretical and methodological grounds, that the model is flawed with respect to those societies where it is applicable and illegitimate when it is universalized for all archaic or primitive societies.[8]

The locative model does provide a useful point of departure for understanding both ancient Israel's ideology of Holy Land and later Judaism's mythology of Exile (chapter 5). In my research, the phenomenon of exile proved to be particularly fruitful both for the understanding of the counter-locative elements of religious rebellion and incongruity which I term the utopian view of the world as organized by a salvific figure and for the particular interpretation of the history of Mediterranean religions during the Greco-Roman period in which the phenomenon of exile was characteristic of many religious traditions (chapters 4, 6 and 7).

---

[7] Compare my description of the morphological method in chapter 11, below.
[8] See further chapter 13, below.

To summarize and make more complex the model that underlies these various special studies:[9] Almost every religion in Late Antiquity occurred in both its homeland and in diasporic centers. With few exceptions, each of these religions, originally tied to a specific geographical area and people, had thousand year old traditions. In their homeland, they were inextricably tied to local loyalties and ambitions. Each persisted in its native land throughout Late Antiquity, frequently becoming linked to nationalistic movements seeking to overthrow Greco-Roman or Christian political and cultural domination. Indeed, many of these religions underwent a conscious archaicization during this period. Old texts in native languages were recopied (especially those which were related to such resistance themes as sacred kingship), national temples were restored and old, mythic traditions revived (especially those which contained such resistance themes as the creation battle of the national deity against the forces of chaos— now reinterpreted as the foreign dominators).[10] From Palestine to Persia one may trace the rise of Wisdom, Messianic and Apocalyptic traditions which reinterpret and maintain these central themes: the importance of the ancient, traditional lore; the saving power of kingship and the revival of myth.

Each of these native traditions likewise underwent, in their homeland, what might properly be called hellenization. This was frequently related to the establishment of a Hellenistic *polis*. Here, while the old, native religion continued uninterrupted in its traditional shrines (in some cases exhibiting a revival), the authority of the native priests remained unchallenged and the native language persisted (although in some instances being reduced to a learned or liturgical tongue), new religious practices and sensibilities were introduced. Sometimes the native and native-hellenistic forms remained apart; other times they mutually influenced one another, occasionally resulting in the discovery of genuinely new forms of an archaic deity. (Sarapis is the best documented example. His name and some of his functions antedate the Ptolemiac period; his iconography and much of his theology are novel).

Each native tradition also had diasporic centers which exhibited marked change during the Late Antique period. There was a noticeable

---

[9] See further, J. Z. Smith, "Hellenistic Religions." *The Encyclopaedia Britannica*, 15ed. (1974), Vol. 8, pp. 749-751 and "Native Cults," n. 6, above.

[10] See my review of M. Wakeman, *God's Battle with the Monster* (Leiden, 1973) in *Journal of Biblical Literature*, XCIV (1975), 442-444.

lessening of concern on the part of those in the diaspora for the destiny and fortunes of the native land and a relative severing of the archaic ties between religion and the land. Certain cult centers remained sites of pilgrimage or sentimental attachment, but the old beliefs in national deities and the inextricable relationship of the deity to particular places was weakened. Rather than a god who dwelt in his temple or would regularly manifest himself in a cult house, the diaspora evolved complicated techniques for achieving visions, epiphanies or heavenly journeys. That is to say, they evolved modes of access to the deity which transcended any particular place. Some traditions gave renewed emphasis to Protean deities, divinities who were interstitial in the older locative system, figures of uncertain form and habits subject only to their own inscrutable initiative.

Within diasporic religion, the chief religious figures were no longer priests or kings but rather god-men, saviors or religious entrepreneurs. The chief mode of religious activity shifted from celebration to initiation. Rather than being born into a divinely established and protected land whose glories one celebrated, one was initiated (reborn) into a divine protector who was tied to no land.

For the native religionist, homeplace, the place to which one belongs, was *the* central religious category. Ones self-definition, ones reality was the place into which one had been born—understood as both geographical and social place. To the new immigrant in the diaspora, nostalgia for homeplace and cultic substitutes for the old, sacred center were central religious values. For the thoroughly diasporic member, who may not have belonged to the deity's original ethnic group, freedom from place became *the* central religious category. Projecting the group's diasporic existence into the cosmos, he discovered himself to be in exile from his true home (a world beyond this world), he found his fulfillment in serving the god beyond the god of this world and true freedom in stripping off his body which belonged to this world and in awakening that aspect of himself which was from the Beyond. Diasporic religion, in contrast to native, locative religion, was utopian in the strictest sense of the word, a religion of "nowhere", of transcendence. Finally, I may note the existence of 'feedback' between these two points of view, especially in reaction to *the* central fact of Late Antique Mediterranean culture—the cessation of native kingship and sovereignty within the domains of Alexander's successors. If there was no native king, then even the homeland was in the diaspora. If the king is the divine center of the human realm just as the king-god is the center of the cosmos, but if the wrong king is sitting on the throne, what does this imply about the world and the deity?[11] In my later work, the implications of such a perception of radical incongruity have been expanded and made more complex both with respect to Late Antique (chapters 8 and 9) and primitive materials (chapter 13).

The third group of essays (chapters 10-12) are a set of methodological reflections. Three central problems are taken up which must preoccupy the historian of religions whatever his field of expertise: the possibility of developing a rigorous argument, methods of comparison and the issue of the truth and interpretation of religious statements. Each is a sample of the sort of historical "test case" that, I believe, is the prerequisite for the History of Religions becoming a responsible, academic discipline.

The final essay (chapter 13) which gives title to this collection, represents an attempt to sum up many of the themes in the previous papers and to suggest a new set of concerns with the incongruous which will preoccupy me in future research.

I have resisted the temptation to revise these essays and to add the numerous additional references accumulated since each was first published. I have welcomed my editor's suggestion that each essay, where appropriate, be provided with a brief afterword calling attention to the most important subsequent scholarship.

It is natural, in gathering together some of the scattered fruits of a decade of writing and study, to call to mind not only the specific occasion for each essay but also those institutions, teachers, colleagues, students, friends and loved ones who, in a multitude of ways, made them possible. But this would be only to hint at in public what has been and will continue to be said in private.

I would be remiss if I did not record my gratitude to Jacob Neusner, the editor of this series, for encouraging me to produce this volume as he has encouraged me at every stage of our long standing friendship and association and to the Max Richter Foundation for subsidizing the cost of the indexing.

It is with an intense sense of a debt that can never be discharged as well as with both joy and pain that I dedicate this volume to my parents: joy that they were both able to see these cold-print children of mine

---

[11] See below, chapter 3 and my further development of this theme with respect to both Gnosticism and Apocalypticism in "A Pearl of Great Price," n. 5, above.

from conception to original appearance, alongside of their sharing in my warm-blooded family of Elaine, Siobhan and Jason; pain in the fact that my father, my most faithful and enthusiastic supporter and collector, did not live to see them bound together in a form that would have given him pleasure and pride.

Chicago
June, 1976

JONATHAN Z. SMITH

ACKNOWLEDGEMENTS

The author thanks the following for permission to reproduce his papers in this book:

University of Chicago for "The Garments of Shame." *History of Religions*, Vol. 5, No. 2, Winter, 1966, pp. 217-238. © 1966 by The University of Chicago.

E. J. Brill for "The Prayer of Joseph." *Religions in Antiquity: Essays in Memory of Erwin Ramsdell Goodenough*, Edited by Jacob Neusner. Leiden, 1968: E. J. Brill, pp. 253-294. © 1968 by E. J. Brill.

Scholars Press for "Wisdom and Apocalyptic," *Religious Syncretism in Antiquity: Essays in Conversation with Geo Widengren*, Edited by Birger A. Pearson. Missoula, 1975: Scholars Press, pp. 131-156. © by Scholars Press.

University of Chicago for "The Wobbling Pivot." *The Journal of Religion*, Vol. 52, No. 2, April, 1972, pp. 134-149. © 1972 by The University of Chicago.

University of Chicago for "Earth and Gods." *The Journal of Religion*, Vol. 49, No. 2, April, 1969, pp. 103-127. © 1969 by The University of Chicago.

Liturgical Press for "The Influence of Symbols upon Social Change: A Place on Which to Stand." *Worship*, Vol. 44, No. 8, November, 1970, pp. 457-474. © 1970 by St. John's Abbey, Collegeville, Maryland.

University of Chicago for "Birth Upside Down or Right Side Up?" *History of Religions*, Vol. 9, No. 4, May, 1970, pp. 281-303. © 1969 by The University of Chicago.

University of Oslo for "The Temple and the Magician." *God's Christ and His People: Essays Honoring Nils Alstrup Dahl on the Occasion of his Sixty-fifth Birthday*. Edited by Jacob Jervell and Wayne A. Meeks. Oslo, 1976: Oslo Universitetsforlaget, pp. 233-247 © 1976 by The University of Oslo.

E. J. Brill for "Good News is No News: Aretalogy and Gospel." *Christianity, Judaism and Other Greco-Roman Cults: Studies for Morton Smith at Sixty*. Edited by Jacob Neusner, Leiden, 1975: E. J. Brill, Part One, New Testament, pp. 21-38. © 1975 by E. J. Brill.

University of Chicago for "When the Bough Breaks." *History of Religions*, Vol. 12, No. 4, May, 1973, pp. 342-371. © 1973 by The University of Chicago.

University of Chicago for "*Adde Parvum Parvo Magnus Acervus Erit*." *History of Religions*, Vol. 11, No. 1, August, 1971, pp. 67-90. © 1971 by The University of Chicago.

University of Chicago for "I am a Parrot (Red)." *History of Religions*, Vol. 11, No. 4, May, 1972, pp. 391-413. © 1972 by The University of Chicago.

University of Chicago for "Map is Not Territory." delivered as the inaugural lecture for the William Benton Professorship of Religion and the Human Sciences in the College, May, 1974. © 1976 by The College of The University of Chicago.

MAP IS NOT TERRITORY

CHAPTER ONE

THE GARMENTS OF SHAME

With the publication of the text of the *Gospel of Thomas* in 1956, a new period in the scholarly debate over the character of Gnosticism began. Controversy concerning the date of the Coptic text has reached a consensus at A.D. 350-400, but the problem of the sort of community which produced the document has not yet been resolved, nor will it yield to an easy solution.¹ At present it is possible only to insist that the traditions within the *Gospel* do not represent new creations but, rather, reflect a varied history. Oscar Cullmann, in the title of an essay published in the *Theologische Literaturzeitung* for 1960, has succinctly summarized the problem: "Das Thomasevangelium und die Frage nach dem Alter der in ihm enthaltenen Tradition."²

The question of the history of the various traditions within the *Gospel*, as well as the problem as to the Gnostic, semi-Gnostic, Encratite or Christian character of the text, may only be resolved after a detailed study has been made of each logion. Logion 37 (P. Labib, *Coptic Gnostic Papyri* [Cairo, 1956], I, pl. 87, 27-88, 1) has been identified as being "clearly Gnostic" and thus provides an excellent subject for examination.³

The saying, as it is given in the Coptic text, reads:

> His disciples said: When will you be revealed to us and when will we see you? Jesus said: When you unclothe yourselves without being ashamed⁴ and take off your clothes and put them under your feet as little children and tread on them, then [shall you see] the Son of the Living One and you shall not fear . . . .

---

¹ See esp. K. Grobel, "How Gnostic Is the Gospel of Thomas," *New Testament Studies*, VIII (1962), 367-73.

² *Theologische Literaturzeitung*, Vol. LXXXV (1960), cols. 321-24. English trans., *Interpretation*, XVI (1962), 418-38.

³ S. Giversen, *Thomas Evangeliet* (Copenhagen, 1959), p. 79 n.

⁴ There is a translation difficulty here. ⲉⲧⲉⲧⲛ̇ϣⲁⲕⲉⲕ ⲧⲏⲩⲧⲛ ⲉϩⲏⲩ ⲙ̇ⲡⲉⲧⲛ̇ϣⲓⲡⲉ "when you unclothe yourselves without being ashamed," may be rendered, as in some translations, "when you put off your shame" (A. Guillaumont, H-Ch. Puech, G. Quispel, W. Till, and Yassah 'Abd al Masih, *L'Évangile selon Thomas* [Paris, 1959], p. 23). The parallel in *P. Oxy.*, 655, ὅταν ἐκδύσηθε καὶ μὴ αἰσχύνθητε, is unambiguous and supports the former. See J. A. Fitzmeyer, "The Oxyrhynchus Logoi of Jesus and the Coptic Gospel of Thomas," *Theological Studies*, XX (1959), 546, n. 93.

It appears to be a fuller version of what was previously known in fragmentary form from the Greek Oxyrhynchus Papyrus 655 (frag. Ib):

> ... you? Who can add to your age? He himself will give you your garment. His disciples say to him: When will you be revealed to us and when shall we see you? He says: When you undress and are not ashamed ...

Far-ranging parallels have been suggested to logion 37, but no parallel or interpretation that I have seen accounts for four closely related elements within the passage: (1) the undressing of the disciples, (2) their being naked and unashamed, (3) their treading upon the garments, and (4) their being as little children. In the light of these, I would suggest that the origin of logion 37 is to be found within archaic Christian baptismal practices and attendant interpretation of Genesis 1-3.[5]

I. Nudity

Cultic nudity of various forms was widespread in the Greco-Roman world, occurring quite frequently in the initiation rites of the Mysteries.[6] More pertinent as a background for Christian baptismal

---

[5] Since first writing this paper, I have found that E. Segelberg ("The Baptismal Rite according to Some of the Coptic-Gnostic Texts of Nag-Hammadi," *Studia Patristica*, V [Berlin, 1962], 117-28) has noted on p. 127 that "The *Gospel of Thomas* ... has some few texts which with great care may be used as evidence for the ceremonial. We may be right in saying that it seems to support divesting-investing." Segelberg cites no texts in illustration of this, but as log. 21 and 37 are the only ones which mention undressing, it may be safely assumed that these are the ones to which he refers.

[6] For a cross-cultural survey see K. Weinhold, "Zur Geschichte des heidnischen Ritus," *Abhandlungen d. Kön. Akad. d. Wissenschaften zu Berlin 1896* (phil. -hist. Kl.), No. 1, pp. 1-50. For the Greco-Roman practice see the extensive collection of material in J. Heckenbach, *De nuditate sacrisque vinculis* (Giessen, 1911), esp. pp. 8-34. F. Pfister, "Nacktheit," in Pauly-Wissowa, *Real-Encyclopädie*, XVI, No. 2, cols. 1541-49, contains the classic exposition of the various theories concerning nudity. For material from the Mystery cults see Heckenbach, *op. cit.*, pp. 12-13, 61-63; G. Anrich, *Das antike Mysterienwesen* (Göttingen, 1894), pp. 200-5; H. Leisegang, "The Mystery of the Serpent," in J. Campbell (ed.), *Pagan and Christian Mysteries* (New York, 1955), pp. 3-69, esp. 45-50. The literary texts most often cited are Aristophanes, *Clouds*, ll. 498ff. and the scholion, l. 508. Phryne's famous nude bathing at the sea during the Eleusinian festival (Athenaeus xiii, 590), which is sometimes pointed to, appears to have been an isolated incident. Iconographically, see the nude initiant (?) in a relief from Eleusis (J. Leipoldt, "Darstellungen von Mysterientaufen," *Angelos*, I (1925), 46-47 and pl. 1) and the nude in the Mithraic fragments from the grotto at Capua (M. J. Vermaseren, *Mithras, the Secret God* [New York, 1963], Figs. 51-53). The nudity associated with the Mysteries appears to have continued in some Gnostic groups, esp. the Naassenes

nudity is its occurrence in post-biblical Judaism. Judaism, in the main, did not share with its Hellenistic neighbors the notion of sacral nudity; indeed, it was prudish to the highest degree. The cultic "horror of nakedness" (Exod. 20:26) was extended, in rabbinic literature, to a whole series of proscriptions against praying, reading the Torah, wearing the *tefillin*, etc. while nude.[7] The *Rule of the Qumran community* imposed a six months' penalty on one who went naked before his fellow (1QS 7.12) while, quite consistent with this general attitude, the Essenes required men to wear loin-cloths and the women robes while bathing (Josephus *Jewish Wars* II.161). This second practice was continued by later Palestinian groups, such as the Elchasaites in their purifying baths and the Mandaeans at baptism.[8] Within such a context, it appears all the more striking that the texts which describe Jewish proselyte "baptism" consistently suggest that the proselyte was nude.[9] We may assume that there was a deeper symbolic reason for this nudity beyond the halachic statement that it was essential that the water reach every part of the proselyte's body.[10]

(Hippolytus, *Ref.* v. 8.41ff.) and the Barbelo-Gnostics (Epiphanius *Pan.* xxvi,5). See, for contrast, the cultic text from P. Pariensis 43, "Leap into the river with your clothes on" (in A.D. Nock, *Early Gentile Christianity* [New York, 1964], p. 63) and the requirements for modesty in dress in the Andania inscription (W. Dittenberger, *Sylloge Inscriptionum Graecarum*, II, No. 653).

[7] b. *Ber.* 25b; *Shab.* 10a, 14a; *Sukka* 10b; Tosefta *Ber.* 2.14-15 (in L. Gulke-witsch, "Der Toseftatraktat Berakhoth," *Angelos*, III [1930], 159f.). Cf. Josephus *Jewish Wars* ii.148. See further various polemic texts against near-eastern cultic nudity, y. *AZ* 3.42; *Sanh.* 7.6; against the nude "barbarians" b. *Yeb.* 63b (cf. *Sifre* Deut. 320; *Yalkut* Deut. 945); and in general, *Pirke de R. Eliezer*, XXII: "R. Meir said: The generations of Cain went about stark naked, both men and women, just like beasts." Also see the polemics in *Jubilees* 3.30-32 against the nakedness of the Gentiles and the attacks against the gymnasium (I Macc. 1:13-14; II Macc. 4:12-14; Josephus *Antiquities* xii, 241) in which public nudity was standard (see V. Tcherikover, *Hellenistic Civilization and the Jews* [Philadelphia, 1949], pp. 27-28, 162-64, esp. 163).

[8] On the Elchaisite practice, see J. Thomas, *Le mouvement baptiste en Palestine et Syrie* (Gembloux, 1935), p. 148. For the Mandaeans, see E. S. Drower, *The Mandaeans of Iraq and Iran* (Oxford, 1937), p. 115. The attempt of E. Segelberg, *Maṣbūtā* (Uppsala, 1958), p. 126, to derive a Mandaean rite of divesting from the metaphorical description of the baptism of Johana, by Manda *d* Hayye in the *Right Ginza* v. 4 (M. Lidzbarski, *Ginzā* [Göttingen-Leipzig, 1925], p. 194, ll. 3-7) is unconvincing.

[9] By implication, M. *Gerim* 1.4 "A man is present at the immersion of a man; a woman at the immersion of a woman." Cf. the more extended description in b. *Yeb.* 47b; Maimonides *Mishneh Torah* "Issur Biah" 14; *Schulchan Aruch* "Yoreh Deah" 268 (see H. Löwe, *Schulchan Aruch* [2d ed.; Wien, 1896], II, pp. 295-97).

[10] b. *Pes.* 107a, "Nothing must interpose between his flesh and the water";

Whatever the Jewish understanding of "baptismal" nudity might have been, the custom was clearly carried over into early Christian practice. The early church shared Judaism's horror of nakedness (Rev. 3:18; 16:15)[11] but held that in baptism it was necessary.[12] Among the Coptic documents from Nag-hammadi, baptismal nudity is witnessed to in the *Gospel of Philip* 101 (Labib, pl. 123, 21-5).[13] Thus it is clear that, within a baptismal context, nakedness has a deep symbolic value and that the usual interpretation of nudity as sinfulness, as "ultimate insecurity and nothingness," requires correction by presenting its positive aspect.[14]

A clue to the positive symbolic value of nudity may be gained from a consideration of early Christian art. The reductionist suggestion that the presence of nudes in early Christian monuments is either a decorative use of mythological conventions or an imi-

---

cf. M. *Mik*. 10. 1-4 (cf. M. *Sabb*. 6.1; b. *BK* 82a, *Nidd*. 66a-b). If the passage in the fourth *Sibylline Oracle* (J. Geffcken, *De Oracula Sibyllina* [Leipzig, 1902], p. 100, l. 165) refers to Jewish proselyte "baptism," then it witnesses to a similar concept.

[11] For a typical example see the description of Mary in a Turin Papyrus: "For neither did she ever see the nakedness of her body, but when she was about to wear a garment, she would shut her eyes" (in F. Robinson, *Coptic Apocryphal Gospels* [Cambridge, 1896], p. 195).

[12] See, in general, H. Leclercq, "Nudité baptismale," *Dictionnaire d'archéologie chrétienne et de liturgie* (=*DACL*), XII, No. 2, cols. 1801-5. L. de Bruyne ("L'Imposition des mains dans l'art chrétien ancienne," *Rivista di archeologia christiana*, XX [1943], 113-298, esp. 239, 245) declares that, for the early church, water and nudity are the two requisite elements in baptism. One or the other might be absent, but one must be present. Among the texts that witness to baptismal nudity may be noted: Hippolytus *Apostolic Tradition* 21.3; *Acts of Xanthippe and Polyxena* 21; *Acts of Thomas* 121, 132-33, 157; Syriac *Didascalia apostolorum* 16; Cyril of Jerusalem, *Mystagogical Catecheses* 2; John Chrysostom *Catechesis* 2.24 and *Epistle to Innocent* (Migne, *Patrologiae Series Graeca* (=*MPG*), LII, 533); Theodore of Mopsuestia *Liber ad baptizandos*, Sermon 4; Narsai *Homily* 22; Pseudo-Dionysius *De ecclesiastica hierarchia* 2.2-3; Hippolytean *Canones* 114; John the Deacon *Epistle ad Senarius* 6; James of Edessa (text and translation in C. Kayser, *Die Canones Jacobs von Edessa* [Leipzig, 1886], p. 121); the Egyptian Church Order in P. de Lagarde, *Aegyptica* (Göttingen, 1883), p. 255; the *Testamentum Domini* ii, 8; and in the baptismal liturgies of the Byzantine, Armenian, Syro-Malabar, and Coptic rites.

[13] On the text from the *Gospel of Philip* see E. Segelberg, "The Coptic Gnostic Gospel according to Philip and Its Sacramental System," *Numen*, VII (1960), 189-200, esp. 193.

[14] I have taken the quotation from P. S. Minear, *Images of the Church in the New Testament* (Philadelphia, 1960), p. 58. This is not to deny that nakedness often does signify sinfulness. One need only think of the whole collection of Hebrew terms derived from the root ערם that are employed as synonyms for sin (i.e., of being stripped of virtue, of being exposed); this is a phenomonon also to be found in the metaphoric use of γυμνός.

tation of classical Greek painting must be rejected.¹⁵ Rather, there is a remarkable fixedness to those figures who are so represented. As one would expect, Adam and Eve in Paradise are naked. The only other Old Testament figures who are depicted nude are Jonah emerging from the mouth of the Great Fish, Daniel emerging from the Lion's Den, and the resurrected in the Vision of Ezekiel.¹⁶ It is hardly necessary to emphasize that these Old Testament scenes containing nude figures are precisely those which were held to be types of the resurrection.¹⁷ Among the New Testament illustrations, apart from baptismal scenes, there are nudes only in one representation of the

---

¹⁵ H. Leclercq, "Nu," *op. cit.*, cols. 1782-1801, esp. 1783.

¹⁶ This regularity has been noted by De Bruyne, *op. cit.*, pp. 207-8, and Leclercq, *loc. cit.* For a convenient collection of such figures, see J. Wilpert, *I Sarcofagi cristiani antichi* (Rome, 1932), Vol. II, pls. 112.2, 123.3, 156, 184.1, 194.4, 9, 204.7, 215.7, 219.1. In the Hellenistic Jewish Synagogue at Dura Europos, the Dead in the Vision of Ezekiel (C. H. Kraeling, *The Synagogue*, Final Report [New Haven, Conn., 1956], pls. 69-71; E. R. Goodenough, *Jewish Symbols in the Greco-Roman Period* [New York, 1963], Vol. XI, pl. 21) are depicted nude, as are the dead Egyptians in the scene of Moses Crossing the Red Sea (Kraeling, *op. cit.*, pl. 53; Goodenough, *op. cit.*, pl. 14). Kraeling, *op. cit.*, p. 83, n. 248, accepted by Goodenough (*op. cit.*, Vol. X, 126) has demonstrated the dependence of this detail upon midrashic tradition. In the Restoration of the Widow's Child (Kraeling, *op. cit.*, pl. 63; Goodenough, *op. cit.*, Vol. XI, pl. 8), the dead child is nude and the widow may be seminude, perhaps as a sign of mourning (Kraeling, *op. cit.*, p. 144; Goodenough, *op. cit.*, IX, p. 288). In these three representations, there would appear to be no symbolism beyond the convention that the dead are to be depicted nude. In a fourth, the Finding of the Infant Moses (Kraeling, *op. cit.*, pl. 67; Goodenough, *op. cit.*, Vol. XI, pl. 9), the Egyptian Princess is nude while drawing the child out of the water. Here there seems to be a deeper symbolism, although it defies precise explication. Kraeling contents himself with the minimal observation that it is striking that "the artists and the Jewish community which they serve [do not] show the slightest feeling that nudity would be improper in the pictorial decorations of a religious House of Assembly" (*op. cit.*, p. 176, n. 676). Goodenough attempts to relate the scene to the iconography of Anahita/Aphrodite (*op. cit.*, IX, 200-3) but does not explicate the significance of the nudity, except to state that the pose is typical of these goddesses. (In connection with his treatment, cf. the material on the symbolism of the nude with outthrust pudendum in M. Delcourt, *Hermaphrodite* [English trans., London, 1961], pp. 63f.). Surprisingly, the nude princess drawing Moses out of the water reappears in later Jewish and Christian illustrations. J. Gutmann ("The Haggadic Motif in Jewish Iconography," *Eretz-Israel*, VI [1960], English-French section, 16*-22*, esp. 18*, n. 5) points to its occurrence in a thirteenth-century Haggadah (BM Add., 27201), two fourteenth-century Sephardic Haggadahs (BM Or., 2884 and the Kaufmann Haggadah), as well as in three Christian miniatures (twelfth century, Morgan Library, 724; twelfth-thirteenth centuries, Paris, BN Lat. 8846; fourteenth century, Vatican, 3550).

¹⁷ See the material on Daniel in *DACL*, IV, No. 1, cols. 221-49, and on Jonah (who is already a *typos* of the resurrection in Matt. 12:39), *DACL*, VII, No. 2, cols. 2572-2631. Cf. De Bruyne, *op. cit.*, p. 207.

Raising of Lazarus and one representation of the Miracle at Cana.[18] On the basis of this iconographic evidence, nudity is clearly a symbol of new life as promised in the resurrection (cf. John 20:5-6 and Luke 24:12 in some MSS) and, when appearing in connection with baptism, must be interpreted as signifying sacramental rebirth.[19]

II. WITHOUT SHAME

Linked to the theme of the initiant's nakedness at baptism is the additional element that he be unashamed. In part, one may suppose, this is a practical requirement. Jewish proselyte "baptism" was one of self-immersion and thus, in the case of a woman, it was possible for the men to remain outside while she dipped herself in the water.[20] Christian ritual, however, made it necessary for an official to be present with the initiant, and this raised the question of the propriety of a man baptizing a nude woman.[21] In the third-century Syriac *Didascalia apostolorum* one finds:

> ... when women go down to the water, those who go down into the water ought to be anointed by a deaconess with the oil of anointing; *and where there is no woman at hand, especially a deaconess, he who baptizes*

---

[18] For the former, see Wilpert, *op. cit.*, pls. 233.3 and 235.7; for the latter, *idem.*, *op. cit.*, pl. 127.2. In Syrian tradition, the miracle at Cana is used as a type of the baptism (see P. Lundberg, *La typologie baptismale dans l'ancien Église* [Uppsala-Leipzig, 1942], pp. 19, 22-23). Cf. Tertullian *De baptismo* 9.

[19] Cf. De Bruyne, *op. cit.*, pp. 206-9.

[20] b. *Yeb.* 47b. See, in general, B. S. Easton, "Self-baptism," *Amer. Journal of Theology*, XXIV (1920), 513-18.

[21] It is difficult to establish beyond all challenge that this occurred. See, however, the narrative in John Moschus *Prat. spir.* 3, "Vita Cononis," Migne, *Patrologiae Series Latina* (= *MPL*), LXXIV, 124 (M.-J. Rouët de Journal [trans.], *Le Pré spirituel* [Paris, 1946], pp. 48-50). Here, in the monastery at Pethucla, the monk Conon is in charge of all baptizing, but he is embarrassed when he must baptize women, presumably because they are nude. One day a particularly beautiful Persian woman comes to be baptized, but Conon does not have the courage to anoint her. He flees the monastery but is stopped by a vision of John the Baptist, who makes the sign of the cross three times over Conon's genitals (thus symbolically castrating him). Conon returns to the monastery and baptizes the Persian woman "without even perceiving that she was a woman." He continues to perform this office for twelve years without "experiencing any movement of the flesh" (i.e., without erection) and without noticing the sex of those whom he baptized. Significantly, in this narrative, when the leader of the monastery thought to send for a deaconess to perform the rite on women, "he could not as it was not the custom." See further the Epitaph of Aquila which clearly depicts a nude girl being baptized by two men, in J. B. de Rossi, "Insigne vetro sul quale è effigiato il battesimo d'una fanciulla," *Bull. di archeologia cristiana*, ser. 3, I (1876), 7-14 and pl. 1. More surprisingly, "Les Grandes Heures" of the Duc de Berry (Paris, BN Lat., 919) depicts a nude couple in the baptismal basin.

must of necessity anoint her who is being baptized. But where there is a woman, and especially a deaconess, it is not fitting that women should be seen by men: but with the imposition of the hands do thou anoint the head only.[22] [Italics mine.]

The language of this passage clearly implies that when a deaconess is present she anoints the nude body of the woman while the man anoints the head; but when a deaconess is not available, the man is to perform the whole rite.

The biblical proof-text by which this was permitted is the account of Adam and Eve being "naked and unashamed" (Gen. 2:25). A fully developed baptismal typology based on this verse may be found in Cyril of Jerusalem (*ca.* A.D. 350), *Mystagogical Catechesis* II:

> Therefore, as soon as you entered in, you put off your garment which was an image of putting off the old man and his deeds ... What a marvel! They [i.e., the newly baptized] were naked before the gaze of all and did not become ashamed, because they were the image of the first created Adam who, in Paradise, was naked and not ashamed.[23]

---

[22] Syriac text in P. de Lagarde, *Didascalia Apostolorum* (Göttingen, 1911), pp. 70-71. I have followed the translation of R. H. Connolly, *Didascalia Apostolorum* (Oxford, 1929), pp. 146-47. Cf. F. X. Funk, *Didascalia et Constitutiones Apostolorum* (Paderborn, 1905), Vol. I, pp. 258-10. The order of a male anointing the woman's forehead and a woman anointing the rest of her body is illustrated in the Syrian *Acts of Thomas* 121 in the baptism of Mygdonia. The parallel passage in *Apostolic Constitutions* 3.15-16 lacks the implication that a male may perform the full anointing if a deaconess is not available. See L. Zscharnack, *Der Dienst der Frau in den ersten Jahrhunderten der christlichen Kirche* (Göttingen, 1902), p. 89; A. Kalsbach, *Die altchristlichen Einrichtung der Diakonissen bis zu ihrem Erlöschen* (Freiburg, 1926), pp. 26-27; and J. Ysebaert, *Greek Baptismal Terminology* (Nijmegen, 1962), pp. 360-62. Likewise the explicit injunction in the *Canons* of Christodulos (A.D. 1048) "Male and female shall not be baptized in the same baptism." (Bibl. Nat. Ms. Arab. 251 fol. 341ᵛ in O. H. E. Khs-Burmester, "The Baptismal Rite of the Coptic Church," *Bull. de la Soc. d'Arch. Copte*, XI [1945], p. 52, n. 1).

[23] *MPG*, XXXIII, 1078-80. Cf. Chrysostom *Homily ad Col.* 6.4 (*MPG* LXII, 342) and the text from *De Singularite clericorum* quoted by L. Duchesne, *Origines du culte chrétien* (5th ed.; Paris, 1909), p. 320, n. 2. This unashamed public nudity should be distinguished from (1) the nudity of protest practiced by groups such as the early Quakers (see E. C. Braithwaite, *The Beginnings of Quakerism* [London, 1912], pp. 89, 126, 148-49, and E. Russell, *The History of Quakerism* [New York, 1942], pp. 63-64, who refers to Isa. 20:2-3) and the present-day Doukhoborsti, who occasionally demonstrate in Canada to the delight of popular magazines such as *Life* (see G. Woodcock, "The Spirit Wrestlers," *History*, II [1960], 101-22, esp. p. 111); (2) the whole tradition of ascetic nudity (see, e.g., the narratives in H. Koch, *Quellen zur Geschichte der Askese und des Mönchtums* [Tübingen, 1933], pp. 118-20, and C. A. Williams, "Oriental Affinities of the Legend of the Hairy Anchorite," *Univer. of Illinios: Studies in Language and Literature* [1925], X, No. 2; [1926], XI, No. 4; (3) the nudity which indicates indifference to the

And likewise, in the baptismal homilies of Theodore of Mopsuestia (d., A.D. 428):

> You draw therefore near to the holy baptism and before all you take off your garments. As, in the beginning, when Adam was naked and was in nothing ashamed of himself, but after having broken the commandment and become mortal, he found himself in need of an outer covering.[24]

The association of Adam with baptism is an old tradition. In the complex *Vita Adae et Evae*, the primal pair, following their expulsion from the Garden, stand naked in the waters of the Jordan as an act of penance; but this is not baptism.[25] In the second-century (?) *Decensus Christi ad Inferas*, the baptism of Adam by Christ is a fully developed doctrine, as it is in the later Manichaean material; but I find no stress here on Adam and Eve recovering their lost innocent nakedness.[26] An understanding of this motif depends in part on the exegesis of the next two items.

III. Treading upon the Garments

That which definitely places logion 37 within the context of the Christian rite of baptism is the injunction to tread upon one's garments.[27] This, I would suggest, is an allusion to the prebaptismal exorcism of the catechumen while standing upon the *cilicium* known to us from Syrian, African, and Spanish sources.[28]

---

world, such as figures in the narrative of Serapion of the Girdle and the nun of Rome (*Historia Lausica* 37; Syriac recension, E. A. W. Budge, *The Paradise of the Holy Fathers* [London, 1907], I, p. 192) and in the famous incident of Fr. Ruffino and St. Francis appearing nude at the church in Assisi (*Fioretti* 30).

[24] A. Mingana, *Commentary of Theodore of Mopsuestia on the Lord's Prayer and on the Sacraments of Baptism and the Eucharist* ("Woodbrooke Studies" VI; Cambridge, Mass., 1933), p. 53; R. Tonneau and R. Devreesse, *Homélies catéchétiques de Théodore de Mopsueste* ("Studi e Testi" CXLV; Rome, 1949), p. 417, with slight variation.

[25] Their nudity is implied in the Slavonic recension 36.1 in R. H. Charles (ed.), *Apocrypha and Pseudepigrapha* (Oxford, 1913), II, p. 135.

[26] The *Decensus* legend has been most recently treated in E. C. Quinn, *The Quest of Seth for the Oil of Life* (Chicago, 1962), pp. 35-46. For the Manichaean material, see F. Cumont, "La cosmogonie manichéenne d'après Theodor bar Khoni," *Recherches sur le Manichéisme* (Brussels, 1908), I, p. 46-48; cf. G. Widengren, *Mesopotamian Elements in Manichaeism* (Uppsala, 1950), p. 123.

[27] For the rare word "to tread," see W. E. Crum, *A Coptic Dictionary* (Oxford, 1939), p. 743; *s.v.* ⲟⲩⲟⲡϣⲛ.

[28] For a general review see A. Hermann, "Cilicium," *Reallexikon für Antike und Christentum*, Vol. III (1957), cols. 127-36, esp. 131-32. My indebtedness to the articles of Fr. Quasten cited below (nn. 29, 42, 52) cannot be overstressed.

The most complete description of this rite is that found in the *Liber ad baptizandos* (Catechetical Homilies 12-14) of Theodore of Mopsuestia, first published by A. Mingana in 1933.[29] The existence of parallels would suggest that Theodore is a witness to the typical Syrian baptismal praxis consisting broadly of a four-stage ceremony: (1) the postulant lays aside his outer garments and is exorcized; (2) the postulant is signed with oil upon his forehead and, then, after removing all of his garments, is anointed on his entire body; (3) the postulant, now naked, is immersed; and (4) the newly baptized is clothed in white garments.[30]

In the Synopsis to the second chapter of his first homily, after a description of the roles of the godfather, registrar, and exorcist, Theodore declares that during the preliminary ceremony of questioning, while the godfather is answering for the initiant, the catechumen stands "with outstretched arms in the posture of one who prays, and you look downwards. This is the reason why you take off your outer garments and stand barefooted, and you stand also on sackcloth."[31] In the homily that follows, the significance of these details is explained. The silence and downward gaze of the catechumen is because he is still "in fear and dread" of Satan, unable to look at him "on account of the great injustice which he did to you and your

---

[29] See n. 24 above. Tonneau and Devreesse have published the photographs of the MS and a French translation. I have usually followed Mingana's rendering with some alteration of punctuation and have noted significant variations in Tonneau and Devreesse. On the rite in Theodore see J. Quasten, "Theodore of Mopsuestia on the Exorcism of the Cilicium," *Harvard Theological Review*, XXXV (1942), 209-19, B. Botte, "Le baptême dans l'Église syrienne", *L'Orient Syrien* I (1956), p. 143, and J. Daniélou, *Bible et liturgie* (Paris, 1958), pp. 32-36.

[30] Note the over-all parallelism in the *Homilies* of Narsai, Homily 22 is parallel to stages 1-2; Homily 21, to 3-4 (on this reversal of order see R. H. Connolly, *The Liturgical Homilies of Narsai* [Cambridge, 1909], p. xlvi) as well as that printed by A. F. J. Klijn, "An Ancient Syriac Baptismal Liturgy in the Syriac Acts of John," *Novum Testamentum*, VI [1963], 216-28. Cf. T. W. Manson, "Entry into Membership of the Early Church," *JTS*, XLVIII (1947), 25-30, who treats the significance of the prebaptismal anointing, and E. C. Whitaker, "Unction in the Syrian Baptismal Rite," *Church Quarterly Review*, CLXII (1961), 176-87, who strives to demonstrate that prebaptismal anointing is exorcistic and not a rite of confirmation. The growing scholarly consensus relating the *Gospel of Thomas* to Syriac Christianity is strengthened by the parallels adduced in this article relating logion 37 to Syrian baptismal praxis.

[31] Mingana, *op. cit.*, pp. 16-17. Cf. Narsai (Connolly, *op. cit.*, p. 39): "He bends his knees and bows his head and is ashamed to look aloft towards the judge. He spreads sackcloth and then he draws near to ask for mercy." Nudity and sackcloth figure also in the Syrian *Acts of John, Apocryphal Acts of the Apostles*, trans. W. Wright [London, 1871], II, pp. 39, 50; cf. Klijn, *op. cit.*, pp. 222, 227.

fathers ... through the punishment of death which he placed in your midst." The position of prayer is calculated to move the judge to mercy.[32] The removal of the outer garments is interpreted:

> You take off your outer garment and stand barefooted in order to show yourself in the state of cruel servitude in which you served the Devil for a long time according to the rules of captivity and in which you did all his work for him according to his requirements. Your aim in this posture is also to move the judge to mercy, and it is this picture of captivity that is implied in the words of God who spoke thus through the prophet Isaiah: As my servant Isaiah has walked naked and barefoot for three years as a sign and portent against Israel and Ethiopia, so shall the king of Assyria lead away the Egyptian captives and the Ethiopians, barefoot, both the young and the old, naked and barefoot.[33]

Here, the effect of the stripping during the "trial" of the catechumen prior to the administration of the baptism is clearly that of nakedness with shame. The text continues with an interpretation of the sackcloth as giving a hint of promise:

> You stand also on garments of sackcloth so that from the fact that your feet are pricked and stung by the roughness of the cloth you may remember your old sins and show penitence and repentance of the sins of your fathers ... and so that you may call for mercy on the part of the judge and rightly say: Thou hast put off my sackcloth and girded me with gladness.[34]

Here, the penitential symbolism of the *cilicium* is to the fore. One might propose that the two-stage movement from sackcloth to gladness in Ps. 30:11 is symbolic of the entire ritual.

The catechumen then advances to the priest, who is "clad in linen robes that are clean and shining", and pronounces an abjuration of Satan. Once again the Synopsis declares that the initiant's posture of prayer while standing on the sackcloth is symbolic of his servitude

---

[32] Mingana, *op. cit.*, p. 31. Cf. Narsai (Connolly, *loc. cit.*): "Naked he stands stripped before the judge, that by his wretched plight he may win pity to cover him."

[33] Mingana, *op. cit.*, p. 32. To the notion of baptism as a delivery from captivity should be compared the material collected in F. J. Dölger, "Der Durchzug durch das Rote Meer als Sinnbild der christlichen Taufe," *Antike und Christentum*, II (1930), 63-69. The motif of slavery is also present in Narsai (Connolly, *The Liturgical Homilies of Narsai*, p. 38), where the postulant appeals to the priest to "set him free from the subjection to the Evil One who took him captive. As an exile he stands naked and without covering." Cf. n. 23 above for the use of Isa. 20:2-3 among the Quakers.

[34] Mingana, *loc. cit.*

to Satan; but one additional and significant detail is given: "You recall in your memory your old tribulations in order that you may all the better perceive the nature of the things which you cast away and that of the things to which you will be transferred."[35] The mention of "things cast away" suggests the imagery of Col. 3:9—the garments removed are a putting off of the "old man and his deeds." Following this the priest signs the postulant with the chrism, and then his godfather clothes him:

> Immediately after your godfather, who is standing behind you, spreads an orarium of linen on the crown of your head and makes you stand erect. By your raising from your genuflection, you show that you have cast away your ancient fall... The linen which he spreads on the crown of your head denotes the freedom to which you have been called. You have before been standing naked[36] as this is the habit of the exiles and the slaves; but after you have been signed, he throws on your head linen, which is the emblem of the freedom to which you have been called.[37]

This concludes the references to the *cilicium* in Theodore. The sackcloth is expressive of penitence, the prebaptismal nudity is the nakedness of slavery (a symbolism based on Isa. 20:2-3). Prior to the actual immersion, however, there is an important passage which refers to the symbolism of nudity during the chrismation discussed above.

> You draw therefore near to the Holy Baptism and before all you take off your garments. As, in the beginning, when Adam was naked and was in nothing ashamed of himself, but after having broken the commandment and become mortal, he found himself in need of an outer covering—so you also, who are ready to draw near to the gift of Holy Baptism that through it you may be born afresh and become symbolically immortal, rightly remove your clothing which indicates your mortality... After you have taken off your garments, you are rightly anointed all over your body with the Holy Oil, a mark and sign that you will be receiving the covering of immortality which, through baptism, you are about to put on... And you are anointed all over your body as a sign that, unlike the covering used as a garment which does not always cover all the parts of the body, because,

---

[35] Mingana, *op. cit.*, p. 36. I prefer the rendering of the last phrase in Tonneau and Devreesse, p. 371: "Et vers quoi vous allez vous tourner." The notion of remembering your old tribulations is made more explicit in Connolly, *The Liturgical Homilies of Narsai*, p. 40: "That Fall which was in Paradise, he now recalls."

[36] This reading is given in the margin of Mingana's translation but is accepted into the text of Tonneau and Devreesse, *op. cit.*, p. 401.

[37] Mingana, *op. cit.*, p. 47.

although it may cover all the external limbs, it by no means covers all the internal ones.[38]

Following this symbolic undressing in which the postulant is reminded of the primal nudity of Adam and Eve and their subsequent clothing which was a mark of mortality, he is brought, still nude, to a pond where he is baptized in three immersions. Then, upon coming up from the water, he is clothed in a white garment that is "wholly radiant"[39] and is reminded that he has truly received a new life of which the baptism is a prefiguration: at the time of the resurrection, "such a garment will be wholly unnecessary, but since you do not now possess these things in reality, but only in types and signs, you are in need of garments."[40]

There are, thus, two different states of nakedness according to Theodore. The first is the nakedness of shame—of Adam and Eve after the Fall—a nakedness in which the postulant stands on the *cilicium* whose pricks remind him of his sinful state, a nakedness like that of a slave. The second state, which is like that of Adam and Eve before the Fall, is a nakedness without shame, a nakedness which will be fully realized by the believer only at the resurrection and for which a white shining garment is the anticipatory sign, a nakedness of transcendence.

The African-Spanish witnesses to the exorcism on the *cilicium* are less elaborate and, in what has survived, are more univocal in their symbolism. The earliest witness to the full rite is Augustine. In nine sermons (56-59; 212-16), as well as in *De catechizandis rudibus*, the Bishop of Hippo provides rich material for the study of the prebaptismal preparation of the catechumen in the African church.[41] The major passage treating the *cilicium* is Sermon 216.10:

---

[38] Mingana, *op. cit.*, pp. 53-54.

[39] There is no need to stress the widespread occurrence of the symbol of a white robe of immortality. See H. Reisenfeld, *Jesus transfiguré* (Copenhagen, 1947), Chap. viii, esp. pp. 120-24; F. Cumont, *Lux perpetua* (Paris, 1949), pp. 429-31, etc. For the equation of baptism with putting on a robe of immortality see, for example, *Apostolic Constitutions* 8.6.6; Gregory Naz. *Oratio* 40.4 (*MPG*, XXXVI, 361).

[40] Mingana, *op. cit.*, p. 68. The notion of a nude resurrection is denied in Jewish sources. See the discussion between Cleopatra and R. Meir, b. *Sanh.* 90b; cf. b. *Ket.* 111b; *Pirke de R. Eliezar* XXXIII.

[41] The classic treatment of Augustine's material on the catechumenate remains B. Busch, "De initiatione christiana secundum Sanctum Augustinus," *Ephemerides liturgicae*, LII (1938), 159-78; 385-483. Cf. I. Rodriguez, "Il Catecumenado en la disciplina de Africa segun San Agustin," *Contribución Española a una Misionología Agustiniana* ("Semanas Misionológicas de Burgos," Vol. VII [1955]), 160-74,

Being thus surrounded by enemies, clothe yourselves in goatskin and make your minds humble through fasting, for that is granted to humility which is denied to pride. It is true that you were not clothed in goatskin when rebukes in the name of the awesome Trinity were justly pronounced against him who incites flight and desertion; yet, with mystic meaning your foot stood upon it. So sin is trampled underfoot as is the goatskin.[42]

In the African rite, the catechumen is clothed in the goatskin (*"induite vos cilicio . . . non estis induti cilicio"*), a notion not found in Theodore[43]; and he does not merely stand upon the skin, he tramples

---

and A. Dondeyne, "La discipline des scrutins dans l'Église latine avant Charlemagne," *Rev. d'hist. ecclésiastique*, XXVIII (1932), 5-33, 751-87, esp. 15-16, who emphasizes the exorcistic character of the *scrutins*.

[42] *MPL*, XXXVIII, 1082. See J. Quasten, *op. cit.*, pp. 211-13, 217-18, and more recently his "Ein Taufexorzismus bei Augustinus," *Revue des études augustiniennes*, II (Memorial Issue: Gustave Bardy; 1956), 101-8, which is virtually a reprint of the former; Busch, *op. cit.*, pp. 434-40; and Rodriguez, *op. cit.*, pp. 172-73. I can see no sense in which Augustine's phrase *"non estis induti, sed tamen vestri pedes in eodem mystica constiterunt"* can be taken as a reference to Ps. 30:11 "in a negative sense," as Quasten maintains ("Theodore of Mopsuestia . . .," *op. cit.*, p. 217). This most likely refers to the "protoevangelium" of Gen. 3:15. Quasten's statement that the exorcistic use of the *cilicium* was unknown in Milan, Rome, and Gaul ("Ein Taufexorzismus . . .," *op. cit.*, p. 102) may be slightly qualified. There is a prebaptismal exorcistic rite of ashes on a goatskin in the Milanese *Ambrosian Manual* (M. Magistretti [ed.], *Monumenta veteris liturgicae Ambrosianae* [Milan, 1904], II, pp. 142-43) and in the rite of Beroldus (M. Magistretti [ed.], *Mediolanensis ecclesiae cicendelarii kalendarium et ordines*, [Milan, 1894], p. 92); a similar rite occurs in the *Ordo Romanus* (*MPL*, LXXVIII, 1023) within Roman tradition. Much work needs to be done on the interrelationship of penitence *in cilicio et cinere*, exorcism standing on the *cilicium*, and exorcism with ashes on the *cilicium*. See, in a preliminary manner, F. J. Dölger, *Der Exorzismus im altchristlichen Taufritual* (Paderborn, 1909), pp. 116-17; Dondeyne, *op. cit.*, p. 29. There is a slight possibility that the exorcistic rite of standing on the *cilicium* is implied in the *Bobbio Missal* 228 (ed. E. A. Lowe [London, 1920], p. 71) in the phrase, "the Devil, having been trodden under foot." But this most likely refers to Gen. 3:15. The relationship of the exorcism on the *cilicium* and the *protoevangelium* likewise requires further study. The prebaptismal Russian custom of placing an infant on a lambskin and feeding it bread and salt, and the child's subsequent baptism on the skin described by E. Samter, *Familienfeste der Griechen und Römer* (Berlin, 1901), pp. 63-64, is clearly not a parallel to the Syrian-African-Spanish rite of the *cilicium*, in contradistinction to the suggestion of W. Kroll, "Alte Taufgebräuche," *Archiv für Religionswissenschaft*, VIII (Beiheft, 1905), 27-38, esp. 37-38.

[43] In view of this, I wonder if the conjecture in Connolly's edition of Narsai (*op. cit.*, p. 37), "He spreads sackcloth [upon him]" (cf. p. xlvi where Connolly gives the picture of the initiant "kneeling down with a piece of sackcloth about him") should not be accepted. Quasten, "Theodore of Mopsuestia . . .," *op. cit.*, p. 212-13, has registered a strong protest, insisting that "the candidate does not spread the sackcloth 'upon him' but before himself on the floor in order to stand on it." In light of the Adamic typology discussed below (pp. 17-18), there might

it ("... *sed tantum vestri pedes in eodem mysticae constiterunt. Calcanda sunt vitia velleraque caprarum*"). This latter quotation introduces a suggestion of Adamic typology with the reference to the curses placed on the inciter, and it also contains an allusion to Gen. 3:15 in the notion of treading on sin. However, in Augustine, the exorcistic and penitential character of the *cilicium* have been merged, and the skin primarily takes on the aspect of a symbol of repentance. This is made explicit in Augustine's exegesis of the eleven veils of goatskin which hung in the Tabernacle (Exod. 26:7) in *De civitate Dei* XV.20.4:

> ... and in that goatskin there was a reminder of sins, because the goats were to be set on the left hand of the Judge; and therefore, when we confess our sins, we prostrate ourselves on goatskin as if we were saying what is written in the Psalm: My sin is ever before me.[44]

This penitential element is even more to the fore in the *De symbolo* II of Augustine's contemporary in Carthage, Quodvultdeus:

> What it is that in this night has happened about you that did not happen in past nights? That from hiding places you were brought forth one by one before the whole church, and then, with head held down that once was held too high, with humble feet upon the strewn goatskin, the proud Devil was exorcized and the lowly, most high Christ was called down upon you.[45]

The Spanish rite focuses exclusively on the *cilicium* as a symbol of penitence as witnessed to in *De cognitione baptismi* 14 of Hildefonse of Toledo (d. A.D. 669):

---

have been a two-part movement: the candidate strips off the garment and then tramples on it.

[44] Cf. *De consensu evangelium* 2.14.13 (*Corpus scriptorum ecclesiasticorum Latinorum* (=*CSEL*), XLIII, 99): "For who can question that the goatskin (in the Tabernacle) has a bearing on the expression of sin." In Jewish allegory, the goat's hair curtains have positive significance, for example, they are in remembrance of Jacob who obtained the blessing by means of the ruse of goatskin (*Midrash Shir ha-shirim* 2.4, in L. Ginzberg, *Legends of the Jews* (Philadelphia, 1955), Vol. V, p. 283, n. 88) or, in a more cosmic allegory in *Midrash Tadshe* 2, the eleven curtains correspond to the eleven upper heavens (Ginzberg, *op. cit.*, VI, p. 68, n. 347).

[45] *MPL*, XL, 637. This treatise was formerly attributed to Augustine; see D. G. Morin, "Pour une future édition des opuscules de S. Quodvultdeus évêque de Carthage au Ve siècle," *Rev. Bénédictine*, XXXI (1914-19), 156-62, esp. 156-57. Note that the beginning of this catechism given during the church's Pascha: "Quid est, quod hac nocte circa vos actum est, quod praeteritis noctibus actum non est" bears a striking resemblance to the opening of the "Four Questions" from the Jewish Passover celebration: "Why is this night different from all other nights?"

... as John himself said: I baptize in water unto repentance. For this reason the children are led by the priests to the anointing over a carpet of goatskin, that they may have a token of penitence, since because of their age, they cannot perform deeds of penance.[46]

In the Syrian, African, and Spanish texts presented, there are striking differences of liturgical setting. In the Syrian tradition there are apparently two exorcisms on the *cilicium*, one at an indeterminate time during the catechumenate, one on the eve of Easter immediately prior to baptism; the African-Spanish rite is administered only once, directly before baptism. Nonetheless, it has been possible to point to a general unity of symbolism throughout the tradition.

A previous generation of scholars attempted to trace the exorcistic rite of the *cilicium* to Hellenistic sources, leaving its penitential character within a Jewish milieu. The most frequently cited parallel is that of the Διὸς κῴδιον, the "Fleece of Zeus."[47]

The two major literary sources are the lexica of Hesychius and the *Suda*:

> (Hesychius) *The fleece of Zeus*: They use this expression when the victim has been sacrificed to Zeus and those who were being purified stood on it with their left foot.
>
> (*Suda*) *The fleece of Zeus*: ... they sacrifice to Meilichios and to Zeus Ktesios and keep the fleeces of these and call them Δία and they use

---

[46] *MPL*, XCVI, cols. 116-17. Cf. *ibid.*, col. 120 "If they are children, they are led by ministers to the priest over a carpet of goatskin in token of repentance." On this text see Sister Athanasius Braegelmann, *The Life and Writing of Saint Ildefonsus of Toledo* (Washington, 1942), pp. 69-70. A. Baumstarck (*Comparative Liturgy* [London, 1955; from 3d French ed.], p. 191) and others follow A. Helfferich in attributing this work to Justinian, Bishop of Valencia. This identification was decisively refuted by P. Glaue, "Zur Geschichte der Taufe in Spanien I," *Sitzungsberichte d. Heidelberger Akad.* (phil-hist. Kl.), IV, Abhandlungen 10 (1913), pp. 1-23; cf. Braegelmann, *op. cit.*, pp. 66f.

[47] For the Greek rite see W. H. D. Rouse, *Greek Votive Offerings* (Cambridge, 1902), p. 204; J. Harrison, *Prolegomena to a Study of Greek Religion* (2d ed.; Cambridge, 1908), pp. 23-27, 546-48; A. B. Cook, *Zeus* (Cambridge, 1914), I, pp. 422-28, cf. *ibid.*, III, p. 1081; Stengel, "*Dios kōdion*," in Pauly-Wissowa, *Real-Encyclopädie*, V, No. 1, col. 1084; P. Roussel, "L'initiation préalable et les symboles Éleusiniens," *Bull. Corr. Hell.*, LIV (1930), 58-65; M. P. Nilsson, *Greek Popular Religion* (reprint; New York, 1961), pp. 7, 49-50 and, most recently, G. Mylonas, *Eleusis and the Eleusinian Mysteries* (Princeton, 1961), pp. 205-8, 232, 242-43. For the relation of this rite to the exorcism on the *cilicium*, see G. Anrich, *Das antike Mysterienwesen* (Göttingen, 1894), pp. 204-5; F. J. Dölger, *Der Exorzismus im altchristlichen Taufritual*, pp. 114-16; W. Kroll, *op. cit.*, p. 38; P. Oppenheim, *Symbolik und religiöse Wertung des Mönchskleides im christlichen Altertum* (Münster, 1932), pp. 195-96; and Quasten, "Theodore of Mopsuestia ...," *op. cit.*, pp. 215-16.

them when they send out the procession in the month of Skirophorion, and the Dadouchos at Eleusis uses them, and others use them for purification by strewing them under the feet of those who are polluted.

There is also some ambivalent iconographic evidence, conveniently summarized in A. B. Cook's *Zeus*.[48] A careful examination of this material demonstrates that the Fleece was primarily employed during the Lesser Mysteries at Eleusis by the Torchbearer to purify those tainted with blood-guilt and that it was *not* employed as a general instrument of exorcism. Thus, the two practices are scarcely close parallels.

Rather, the symbolism of the rite is probably to be traced back to Jewish exegesis of Gen. 3:21, the clothing of Adam and Eve by God with "tunics of skins." Some rabbis interpreted this to mean that before the expulsion from Eden, Adam and Eve had bodies or garments of light, but that after the expulsion, they received bodies of flesh or a covering of skin. The full form of this *midrash* is found only in late sources such as the *Zohar*:

> Before, they were dressed in garments of light (כתנות אור), but after their trespass, in garments of skin (כתנות עור) which were of use only for the body, but not for the soul.[49]

The same word play occurs in a variant attributed to Rabbi Meir in *Bereshith Rabba* 20.12,[50] and the presence of a similar exegetical tradition regarding the bodies of light and skin in Samaritan, Christian,

---

[48] *Op. cit.*, I, pp. 423-28 and Figs. 305-9. See further the classic treatment of G. E. Rizzio, "Il sarcofage di Torre Nova," *Römische Mitteilungen*, XXV (1910), 89-167, and Mylonas, *op. cit.*, pp. 205-8.

[49] *Zohar*, I, 36b (Sperling-Simon, *Zohar* [London, 1931], I, p. 136, in a somewhat different rendering). See A. E. Waite, *The Holy Kabbalah* (reprint; New York, 1960), pp. 281-85 (which must be used with extreme caution); F. Cumont, *Lux Perpetua*, pp. 429-30; S. Aalen, *Die Begriffe 'Licht' und 'Finsternis' im alten Testament, im Spätjudentum und Rabbinismus* (Oslo, 1951), pp. 198-99, 265-66, 282-85, treats the theme of the *doxa* of Adam, and G. Scholem, "Die Vorstellung vom Golem," *Eranos Jahrbuch*, XXII (1953), pp. 255-56.

[50] *Ber. R.* 20.12: "In R. Meir's scroll of the Torah there was the reading כתנות אור; this alludes to the garments of Adam resembling the rue (לפיגס), wide below and narrow above." Theodor (in his ed. *Bereschit Rabba* [Berlin, 1912], I, 196, l. 5) reads a ב in place of the ג, thus reading לפנס, i.e., φανός. If this be accepted, R. Meir becomes an early witness to the tradition. Theodor's reading is followed in the Freedman-Simon translation, *Midrash Rabbah* (London, 1939), I, 171: "In R. Meir's Torah it was found written *garments of light*, this refers to Adam's garments which were like a torch (shedding radiance) broad at the bottom and narrow at the top." The interpretation of Gen. 3:21 in b. *Niddah* 25a, "This shows that the Holy One, blessed be He, does not prepare a skin for man until he is formed," may also imply knowledge of a similar tradition.

and Gnostic sources allows us to assume an early date and wide diffusion of this motif.⁵¹ Furthermore, working from quite different presuppositions, an analogous exegesis occurs in Philo, who seeks to interpet the χιτών δερμάτινος of Gen. 3:21.⁵² This he declares to be a symbol of our fleshly body,⁵³ which he calls upon man to cast off.⁵⁴

In Christian baptismal symbolism, the notion of rebirth merged with the exorcistic rite of the *cilicium* and with Adamic typology aided by passages such as the deutero-Pauline Col. 3:9; thus a nexus is established between the taking off of one's clothing at baptism, which symbolizes the unashamed nudity of the first pair, and the treading upon the goatskin, which signifies a triumph over the fleshly body with which the primal pair were clothed following the Fall.⁵⁵

An early witness to this nexus is Jerome's *Epistle to Fabiola* 19, which does not appear to involve a separate prebaptismal exorcism:

> And when ready for the garment of Christ, we have taken off the tunics of skin, then we shall be clothed with a garment of linen which has nothing of death in it, but is wholly white so that, rising from baptism, we may gird our loins in truth and the entire shame of our past sins may be covered.⁵⁶

---

⁵¹ For the Samaritans see J. MacDonald, *The Theology of the Samaritans* (London, 1964), p. 138; in Greek Christianity see Irenaeus, *Ref.* i.1.10, Origen *Contra Celsum* iv.40; for the Latin see Tertullian, *De resurrectione* 7 (cf. E. Evans, *Tertullian's Treatise on the Resurrection* [London, 1960], pp. 214-15), *De pudicitia* 9; for Syriac material see A. Levene, *The Early Syrian Fathers on Genesis* (London, 1951), p. 77, and the complex *Cave of Treasures* tradition in C. Bezold, *Die Schatzhöhle aus den syrisches Texte* (Leipzig, 1883), pp. 5-7; cf. E. A. W. Budge, *The Book of the Bee* (Oxford, 1886), pp. 52-53, 60, 107, and the Arabic recension *Kitāb al Magāll* 95b in Gibson, *Studia Sinaitica*, VIII (1901); and for the Gnostics, Clement Alex. *Excerpta ex Theodoto* 50, cf. Tertullian *Adv. valent.* 24, Irenaeus, *Ref.* i.5.5.

⁵² *QG* 1.53; 4.1; *LA* 2.56ff.; *Immut.* 56; *Det.* 159; *Post.* 137; *Gig.* 53; *Mig.* 192; cf. Empedocles fr. 126 where the soul is clothed "in the unfamiliar tunic of flesh." See J. Quasten, "A Pythagorean Idea in St. Jerome," *Amer. Journal of Philology*, LXIII (1942), 206-15, esp. 212-13.

⁵³ *QG* 1.53, extant only in Armenian. In Aucher's Latin rendering: *tunica pellicea symbolica est pellis naturalis, id est corpus nostrum* (*Philonis Opera* [Leipzig, 1829], VI, p. 276); cf. R. Marcus (*Philo*, ed. Loeb [Supplement I; London, 1953], p. 31), who attempts (note "m") a reconstruction of the Greek text.

⁵⁴ Esp. *Virt.* 76 and *QG* 2.69.

⁵⁵ I cannot determine how widespread was the tradition represented by R. Eleazar that the garments with which Adam and Eve were clothed by God were made of goatskins (*Ber. R.* 20.12), but this would supply a link in the chain of association.

⁵⁶ Epistle 64.19 (*CSEL*, LIV, 610). See J. Quasten, "A Pythagorean Idea in St. Jerome," p. 206 (cited in n. 52), whose translation I have followed. Quasten relates the Hellenistic notion of a linen garment being pure and incorruptible because it was made from a vegetable rather than an animal product to the passage.

The contrast between the *tunicae pelliceae*, which connotes both sin and death, and the white shining garment of Christ (the *veste linea nihil in se mortis habente*) is clearly based on the Adamic typology, now merged with imagery suggested by texts such as II Cor. 5:1-4.[57]

IV. As Little Children

There is no need to labor the point that the newly baptized are frequently referred to or conceived of as little children. This metaphor is present within the rites of Jewish proselyte "baptism," within the Hellenistic Mysteries, as well as in early Christian material.[58] The most obvious reference is to the baptism as new birth (a concept which employs such varied motifs as rites of adoption, the giving of a new name, feeding the newly baptized on milk and honey, the font as a womb etc.). But the Adamic typology also appears. The little child is a standard metaphor of innocence and sinlessness[59] like that of Adam and Eve before the Fall.[60] Their unashamed naked-

---

[57] R. M. Grant has called my attention to J. N. Sevenster, "Some remarks on the ΓΥΜΝΟΣ in II Cor. 5:3," *Studia Paulina in honorem Johannis de Zwaan* (Haarlem, 1953), pp. 202-14. Sevenster notes that while in the Hellenistic parallels adduced for this passage being naked at death is an ideal to be striven for, Paul, on the other hand, appears to shrink from this nudity. His explanation—that Paul's eschatological focus is not on the body that will be put off but on the heavenly body which will bring one into "closer communion with the Lord than ever would be possible here on earth"—is not convincing.

[58] For the rabbinic, see esp. b. *Yeb.* 48*b* (cf. b. *Yeb.* 22*a*, 62*a*, 97*b*; *Bek.* 47*a*). The debate over whether, with Rashi (ad b. *Sanh.* 57*b*), this should be explained as a juridical concept or whether a sacramental rebirth is implied continues. For representative Hellenistic material see M. P. Nilsson, *The Dionysiac Mysteries in the Hellenistic Roman Age* (Lund, 1957), pp. 106-15. For Christian examples see *Ep. Barnabas* 6.11; Clement Alex., *Prot.* 10 (84.2); cf. Matt. 18:3 and I Pet. 2:2 and the whole complex of material gathered by J. Schrijnen, "Milch und Honig in den altchristlichen Taufliturgie," *Collectanea Schrijnen* (Nijmegen-Utrecht, 1939), pp. 295-302.

[59] See, e.g., *Shepherd of Hermas* Sim. ix.29.1-3, etc. The innocence of little children is a common metaphor in Judaism (e.g., Tanhuma *Ber.* 7.10*a*) and in Hellenistic sources as collected by H. Herter, "Das unschuldige Kind," *Jahrbuch f. Antike u. Christentum*, IV (1961), 146-62.

[60] This is not to imply that *Thomas* does not draw on the Synoptic use of μικροί as a synonym for the true disciple (see, most recently, G. Bornkamm's excursus in G. Bornkamm, G. Barth, and H. J. Held, *Überlieferung und Auslegung im Matthäusevangelium* [Neukirchen, 1960], pp. 113-17). Nor is this to disagree with E. Haenchen's suggestion that in *Thomas* the little child is an "Ideal für die gnostische Askese" (*Die Botschaft des Thomas Evangeliums* [Berlin, 1961], p. 52)—both may well have roots in Adamic typology. Cf., without accepting the over-all structure imposed on the *Gospel*, Y. Janssen, "L'Évangile selon Thomas et son caractère gnostique," *Muséon*, LXXV (1962), 301-25, esp. 314-15,

ness (symbolically reproduced in the nudity of the initiant) is interpreted as being analogous to that of little children:

> With regard to *They were both naked*—it is implied that they were unaware of the shyness consequent on their nakedness as little children are [so unaware].[61]

With the exposition of these four elements (nudity, being unashamed, treading upon one's garments, and being as little children), it is possible to return to the exegesis of the *Gospel of Thomas*, logion 37. The logion is set in the context of an eschatological question: "When will you be revealed to us and when will we see you" (cf. *GT*, log. 51 and 113). In the *Gospel*, the language used to describe the disciple in relation to the fulfilled experience of the Kingdom is in terms which suggest a restoration of the ruptured relations following the Fall. The disciples shall not taste death (*GT*, logs. 1, 18, 19, and 85) nor see death (log. 111); they will be filled with light (log. 61) and they will reign over the All (log. 2). More generally, there is an over-all equation of Beginning and End (log. 18). While it is impossible and indeed illegitimate, as it is in the New Testament, to separate the "realized" and the "futuristic," the "anthropological" and the "cosmological" aspects of the eschatology of the *Gospel of Thomas*, it is clear that to some degree the disciple, insofar as he is saved, is a New Adam and that the cosmos, insofar as it is redeemed, will be a New Eden. Thus the disciple is called upon to transfigure himself, to appear naked and unashamed;[62] to transcend himself, trampling on the fleshly sinful garments of the Old Man; and to become reborn, to be as a little child. For all of these experiences (prior to the *eschaton*) baptism is, as in Theodore, a present sign. While there are many texts which witness to these transforming experiences in connection with either the rite of baptism or the prebaptismal exorcism, one of the most dramatic, because it includes all of these elements, is that of John the Deacon (*ca.* A.D. 500):

> They are commanded to go in *naked*, even down to their feet, so that [that may show that they have] *put off the fleshly garments of mortality* ...

---

who maintains that logs. 21, 22, 36, and 37 are united by "the fundamental concept ... that it is necessary to regain the innocence of little children, of Adam and Eve *before* the Fall."

[61] MS. Mingana 553, fol. 4*b* in A. Levene, *op. cit.*, p. 77.

[62] Thus Jesus at the Transfiguration, according to the *Acta Johannae* 110, is "not clothed but nude," A similar notion may be behind the action of Priscillian who prayed in the nude according to Sulpicus Severus, *Chron.* ii.50.8 (*CSEL* i. 1866).

> The church has ordained these things for many years with watchful care, even though the old books may not reveal traces of them ... [after the rite] They wear white garments so that though the tattered dress of ancient error has darkened the infancy of their *first birth*, the dress of their *second birth* should display the *raiment of glory* so that, clad in a wedding garment, he may approach the table of the heavenly bridegroom *as a new man*.[63] [Italics mine.]

Thus I would suggest that logion 37 is to be taken as an interpretation of this archaic Christian baptismal rite.

To logion 37 should be compared logion 21 (Labib, pls. 84.34-85.19):

> Mariham said to Jesus: Whom are your disciples like? He said: They are like little children camping in a field which is not theirs. When the owners of the field come, they will say: Leave to us our field. They [i.e., the discples] are naked before them [i.e., the owners] in order to leave it to them and give them back their field ...

A new dimension is added here to the symbolism we have been studying. Its background, I would suggest, is a pun between the Greek κόσμος meaning "the world" and κόσμος meaning "ornament" (i.e., to take off one's ornaments, one's dress, is to take off the world);[64] and between the Coptic ⲕⲱⲕⲁϩ, "to leave the world," and ⲕⲱⲕⲁϩⲏⲩ, "to be nude."[65]

---

[63] Mabillon-Germain, *Museum Italicum*, vol. I, No. 2 (Paris, 1687), pp. 71-72 (reprinted in *MPL*, LIX, 403). Cf. the critical ed. of A. Wilmart, *Analecta Reginensia* ("Studi e Testi" LIX; Vatican, 1933), pp. 174-75. Note the argumentative phrase with respect to the nudity of those who are being baptized: "Haec igitur aecclesiastica sollicitudo per successiones temporum cauta dispositione constituit, quamois horum vestigia vetus pagina non ostendat."

[64] I am tempted to venture the suggestion that the regulation requiring women to remove their *ornaments* before entering the baptismal waters so that "no *alien* thing would go down to the water with them" might possibly be a reflection of this pun. The study of C. F. Rogers, "How Did the Jews Baptize?" *Journal of Theological Studies*, XIII (1911-12), esp. p. 413, would support this suggestion. But see F. Gavin, "Rabbinic Parallels to Early Church Orders," *Hebrew Union College Annual*, VI (1929), esp. pp. 57-58. For the regulation see B. S. Easton, *The Apostolic Tradition of Hippolytus* (Cambridge, 1934), p. 45; cf. the Syrian *Testamentum Domini nostri Iesu Christi* (ed. E. Rahmani [Mainz, 1899]), p. 127; the Coptic, Ethiopian, and Arabic recensions in G. Horner, *The Statutes of the Apostles* (London, 1904), pp. 316, 243. The recent study of this rite by W. C. van Unnik, "Les cheveux defaits des femmes baptisées," *Vigilae Christianae* (1947), I, 77-100, does not treat the removal of the ornaments.

[65] This latter pun was suggested by R. Kasser, *L'Évangile selon Thomas* (Neuchâtel, 1961), p. 52, n. 2. Note that the image of Christians stripping like little children appears in Tatian's *Oration against the Greeks*; see R. M. Grant, "Tatian (Or. 30) and the Gnostics," *Journal of Theological Studies*, N.S., XV (1964), 65-69.

It is difficult to know to what extent one is permitted to allegorize the various elements in this parable. H. M. Schenke is certainly correct when he interprets the field as the cosmos and the owners as the *archontai*, but I find difficulty with his interpretation of the stripping as death[66] and with other suggestions that it is the body[67] or, more specifically, sexuality[68] that is stripped off. Certainly these motifs are present, but the text clearly correlates the act of stripping before the owners and the act of releasing the field back to them. I would suggest that the act of stripping is not merely a denial of the body but that it is a putting off of the "ornaments" of the "world," a transcendence of the world.[69] Without holding to a rigid separation of these elements, one may conclude that in logion 37 it is the anthropological dimension of the theology of baptism which is in the foreground; in logion 21, it is the cosmological.

A final passage that must be treated in this context is attributed to the "Gospel of the Egyptians" by Clement of Alexandria in his *Stromata* iii.91 (O. Stählin, *Die griechischen christlichen Schriftsteller*, XV [Leipzig, 1906], p. 238):

> When Salome asked when what she had inquired about would be known, the Lord said: When you have trampled on the garments of shame and when the two become one and the male with the female [is] neither male nor female.

The reference to trampling on the garment of shame (τὸ τῆς αἰσχύνης ἔνδυμα) suggests the possibility that this passage, in its original

---

[66] H. M. Schenke in Leipoldt and Schenke, *Koptischen-gnostische Schriften aus den Papyrus Codices von Nag-hammadi* (Hamburg-Bergstadt, 1960), p. 14, n. 2.

[67] R. M. Grant and D. N. Freedman, *The Secret Sayings of Jesus* (London, 1960), p. 134.

[68] H. C. Kee, "'Becoming a Child' in the Gospel of Thomas," *Journal of Biblical Literature*, LXXXII (1963), 312.

[69] I should not wish to imply a rigid separation of the notion of stripping off the world and stripping off one's body but, rather, their necessary correlation. For terms that can suggest both world and body in Gnostic literature see H. Jonas, *The Gnostic Religion* (rev. ed.; Boston, 1963), pp. 55-56; cf. K. Grobel, *The Gospel of Truth* (New York, 1960), p. 101, n. 239. For the stripping metaphor see C. R. C. Allberry, *Coptic Manichaean Psalmbook* (Stuttgart, 1938), Psalms 2 p. 19, ll. 26-28; 250, p. 59, l. 2; and 258, p. 99, ll. 27-30; M. Boyce, *The Manichaean Hymn Cycles in Parthian* (Oxford, 1954) where *fr'mwxt*, to "take off," occurs in three texts, all of which are unfortunately fragmentary (pp. 104, 169, 174); the *Odes of Solomon* 25.8 and *Corpus Hermeticum*, VII, 2 (cf. X, 18) on which see C. H. Dodd, *The Bible and the Greeks* (reprint; London, 1954), pp. 191-94, and A. D. Nock and A. J. Festugière, *Corpus Hermeticum* (2d ed.; Paris, 1960), I, pp. 82-83, n. 9. Sevenster, *loc. cit.*, and Quasten, "A Pythagorean Idea ...," *op. cit.*, pp. 213-14 give several parallels from Hellenistic literature.

setting, may have referred to the rite of the *cilicium* and that the abolition of sexual differentiation might refer to the unashamed baptismal nudity. As given in Clement, however, the text clearly has been reinterpreted as an antisexual polemic (the fragmentary citation does not allow one to determine whether by Julius Cassianus with whom Clement is debating, or by the author of the "Gospel of the Egyptians"). Similarly, in the somewhat parallel citation in II Clement 12:1-2, there is no reference to the garment of shame, all traces of baptismal context have been lost, and the emphasis is exclusively on the theme of the union of opposites.[70]

In this paper I have sought to place logion 37 of the *Gospel of Thomas* within a Christian baptismal context and to relate it to the attendant typology based on Genesis 1-3. I have argued that the four principle motifs within the logion—the undressing of the disciples, their being naked and without shame, their treading upon the garments, and their being as little children—are to be found joined together only within baptismal rituals and homilies. The nudity of the initiant—a feature shared by early Christianity with the initiation rites of the Hellenistic Mysteries and Jewish proselyte "baptism"—was found to be consistently related to the symbolism of new life or birth. Being naked and without shame is both a practical requirement stemming from the minister's anointing of nude women in a public ceremony and a typological return to the state of Adam and Eve before the Fall. The treading upon the garments I have held to be a specific reference to prebaptismal exorcism while standing on the *cilicium*. Although there is both a penitential and typological element to this rite, both refer ultimately to Adam and Eve. The pricks of the goatskin are to remind one of the sin of the first pair, while the treading on the garment, rather than being a Hellenistic rite of purification, is related to a rabbinic *midrash* on Adam and Eve being clothed with skins after the Fall. To take off these garments and tread on them is a renunciation of sin, flesh, and the world.

---

[70] Cf. further the thoroughly gnosticized tradition in the Naassene material preserved in Hippolytus *Ref.* v. 8.44, where the act of stripping and being sexually neuter appear to be correlated: "This is the gate of heaven and the house of God where the good God dwells alone; where no one impure enters, no psychic, no one fleshly. It is reserved for the *pneumatikoi* alone. When they come they cast away their garments and all will become bridegrooms having been made male by the virginal spirit," "Being made male" (ἀπηροσενωμένους) is most likely to be understood in light of the Naassene ideal of the castrated Attis, called to himself who was οὔτε θῆλυ οὔτε ἄρσεν, ἀλλὰ καινὴ κτίσις, καινὸς ἄνθρωπος, ὅς ἐστιν ἀρσενόθηλυς (v. 7.15).

And finally, "being as little children" refers to both the sacramental rebirth gained through baptism and the recovery of the lost innocence of the primal pair. In comparison to "more gnostic" parallel texts, logion 37 (and logion 21, which I have attempted to demonstrate relies on similar symbolism) must not be considered as distinct from representatives of the Christian homiletic tradition contemporary with it.[71]

AFTERWORD

To my knowledge, there has been no subsequent study of logion 37. The debate on the Syriac character of the *Gospel of Thomas* has continued with, for me, increasingly positive results. For the most balanced treatment of the state of the question, see H. J. W. Drijvers, "Edessa und das jüdische Christentum," *Vigiliae Christianae*, XXIV (1970), 4-33 and "Rechtgläubigkeit und Ketzerei im ältesten syrischen Christentum," in *Symposium Syriacum, 1972* ([*Orientalia Christiana Analecta*, vol. CXCVII] Rome, 1974), pp. 291-308 and the splendid introduction to R. Murray, *Symbols of Church and Kingdom: A Study in Early Syriac Tradition* (Cambridge, 1975), esp. pp. 4-38.

Some significant Patristic materials have been added. On Gregory of Nyssa, see J. Daniélou, "Les tuniques de peau chez Grégoire de Nysse," in *Festschrift E. Benz* (Leiden, 1967), pp. 355-367. On Chrysostom, see T. M. Finn, *The Liturgy of Baptism in the Baptismal Instructions of St. John Chrysostom* ([*Catholic University of America Studies in Christian Antiquity*, vol. XV] Washington, D.C., 1967), esp. pp. 77-80, 121-125, 137f., 147-149, 189-191, 191-197. An excellent comparison of Cyril, Chrysostom and Theodore of Mopsuestia on baptismal stripping is given in H. M. Riley, *Christian Initiation* ([*Catholic University of America Studies in Christian Antiquity*, vol. XVII] Washington, D.C., 1974), esp. pp. 159-189. These only serve to strengthen the position taken in this essay.

---

[71] This paper was first delivered as a lecture at Bryn Mawr College in February, 1963. I am indebted to several members of that audience, as well as to Professors C. Colpe, R. M. Grant, and J. Neusner, who have read the paper in its present form, for their helpful suggestions and criticisms.

CHAPTER TWO

THE PRAYER OF JOSEPH

In a period of renewed interest in non-canonical literature sparked by the discoveries in the Dead Sea area and at Nag-hammadi and in the remains of hellenistic Judaism so ably researched by E. R. Good-enough, it is imperative that there be a reexamination of the apocryphal literature of Judaism and Jewish-Christianity comparable in scope to Hennecke-Schneemelcher's *Neutestamentliche Apokryphen*.[1] Much of this literature has suffered from scholarly neglect, certainly none more so than the fragments of a Jewish apocryphon quoted by Origen under the title, *The Prayer of Joseph* (Προσευχὴ 'Ιωσήφ).[2]

---

[1] While the recent unrevised reprinting of R. H. Charles, *Apocrypha and Pseudepigrapha of the Old Testament* by the Oxford University Press was long overdue, an edition of texts on a scale comparable to Hennecke-Schneemelcher still remains a *desideratum*. The often artificial source-criticism of Charles', his emendations and faulty texts must be corrected by newer techniques of analysis. Likewise many of Charles' historical judgements are suspect in the light of our increased understanding of the diverse phenomena of post-Biblical Judaism. The many omissions (e.g. *Joseph and Asenath*, the *Testament* and *Apocalypse of Abraham*) as well as the failure to include representative Hebrew and Aramaic works of a similar character (such as those published by Jellinek in his *Bet ha-Midrash*) and the discovery of new material such as the so-called *Genesis Apocryphon* from Qumran render Charles inadequate for present use. The recently reprinted collection of P. Riessler, *Alt-jüdische Schrifttum ausserhalb der Bibel* 1ed. (Augsburg, 1928) has a wider selection of texts in translation but no critical commentary. See especially the programmatic essay of A.-M. Denis, "Les pseudépigraphes grecs d'Ancien Testament," *Novum Testamentum* 6 (1963), pp. 310-19 and two recently inaugurated series *Pseudepigrapha Veteris Testamenti Graece* and *Studia in Veteris Testamenti Pseudepigrapha*, eds. A. M. Denis and M. de Jonge.

[2] Henceforth cited as *PJ*. The major treatments of which I am aware are; R. Simon, *Histoire critique des principaux commentateurs du Nouveau Testament* (Rotterdam, 1693), Vol. II, pp. 238-42 ; J. Fabricius, *Codex Pseudepigraphus Veteris Testamenti* (Hamburg, 1722), Vol. I, pp. 761-71 ; Abbé Migne, *Dictionnaire des Apocryphes* (Paris, 1858), Vol. II, p. 419 n. 475 ; A. Dillmann, "Pseudepigraphen des Alten Testaments", in Herzog *et al.*, *Real-Encyklopädie für protestantische Theologie und Kirche* 2ed. (Leipzig, 1883), Vol. XII, p. 362 ; J. T. Marshall, "Joseph, Prayer of," in J. R. Hastings ed., *Dictionary of the Bible* (New York, 1899), Vol. II, col. 778b ; P. Batiffol, *Studia Patristica* (Paris, 1889), Vol. I, pp. 16-18 ; A. Resch, *Agrapha* (Leipzig, 1906), pp. 295-8 ; E. Schürer, *Geschichte des jüdischen Volkes*, 4ed. (Leipzig, 1909), Vol. III, pp. 359f. ; E. Norden, *Agnostos Theos* (Leipzig-Berlin, 1913), p. 300 ; A. von Harnack, *Der kirchengeschichtliche Ertag der exegetischen Arbeiten des Origines*

In the standard editions of Origen, the major fragment (A), preserved in the *Comm. in Ioann.* II, 31, occupies some fifteen lines of Greek encompassing eight periods. An additional fragment (B) is given in the *Philocalia* XXII, 15, but this adds only a single line. That this only constitutes a fraction of the whole work may be seen from the *Stichometry* of Nicephorus who reports that the *PJ* contained 1100 *stichoi*.

The fact that only so small a remnant remains, that testimonies to the work are sparse and quotations from it even rarer should not be allowed to obscure the interest or importance of the text.[3] The legend

---

(Leipzig, 1919), Vol. II, p. 48 cf. Harnack, *History of Dogma* (New York, 1958 rp.), Vol. I, pp. 102f. n. 2 and Harnack, *Geschichte der altchristlichen Literatur bis Eusebius* (Leipzig, 1958 rp.), Vol. I : 2, p. 853 ; L. Ginzberg, *Eine unbekannte jüdische Sekte* (New York, 1922), pp. 36f. ; Ginzberg, *Legends of the Jews* (Philadelphia, 1925), Vol. V, pp. 275 and 310f. ; H. Strack-P. Billerbeck, *Kommentar zum Neuen Testament aus Talmud und Midrasch* (Munich, 1924), Vol. II, pp. 340f. ; R. Cadiou, *La jeunesse d'Origène* (Paris, 1935), p. 79 ; W. L. Knox, *St. Paul and the Church of the Gentiles* (Cambridge, 1939), p. 49 and notes 5, 6 ; N. A. Dahl, *Das Volk Gottes* (Oslo, 1941), pp. 114f.; J. Ruwet, "Les 'Antilegomena' dans les oeuvres d'Origène", *Biblica*, 24 (1943), pp. 50f. ; Ruwet, "Les apocryphes dans les oeuvres d'Origène," *Biblica*, 25 (1944), p. 144 and pp. 368f. ; P. Winter, "ΜΟΝΟΓΕΝΗΣ ΠΑΡΑ ΠΑΤΡΟΣ", *Zeitschrift f. Religions- und Geistesgeschichte*, 5 (1953), pp. 351-2, 358, 361 ; R. P. C. Hanson, *Origen's Doctrine of Tradition* (London, 1954), pp. 135f. ; P. Winter, "Zum Verständnis des Johannes-Evangeliums", *Theologische Literaturzeitung*, 80 (1955), cols. 147f. J. Daniélou, *Théologie du Judéo-Christianisme* (Tournai, 1958), pp. 182-5 (abridged and revised in the English translation, *Theology of Jewish Christianity* Chicago, 1964, pp. 132-4) ; R. M. Grant, *Gnosticism and Early Christianity* (New York, 1959), pp. 18f. ; E. Schweizer, "Die Kirche als Leib Christi," *Theologische Literaturzeitung*, 86 (1961), cols. 167f.; D. S. Russell, *The Message and Meaning of Jewish Apocalyptic* (Philadelphia, 1964), p. 67 ; M. Smith, "The Account of Simon Magus in Acts 8", *Harry Austryn Wolfson Jubilee Volume* (Jerusalem, 1965), pp. 748f. The only relatively full studies of the *PJ* are those of M. R. James, *The Lost Apocrypha of the Old Testament* (London, 1920), pp. 21-31 and E. Stein, "Zur apokryphen Schrift 'Gebet Josephs' ", *Monatschrift f. d. Geschichte und Wissenschaft d. Judenthums*, 81 (1937), pp. 280-86. For general treatments of Origen's use of Jewish apocrypha see Harnack, *op. cit.*, Vol. I, pp. 34-50 ; Ruwet, *op. cit., Biblica*, 24 (1943), pp. 18-58 and *Biblica*, 25 (1944), pp. 143-66, 311-34 ; G. Bardy, "Les traditions juives dans l'oeuvre d'Origène", *Revue Biblique*, 34 (1925), pp. 217-52 esp. pp. 226f. ; and A. C. Sundberg, Jr., *The Old Testament of the Early Church* (Cambridge USA, 1964), pp. 134-8.

[3] Testimonies, besides the *Stichometry* of Nicephorus (in Th. Zahn, *Geschichte d. neutestamentlichen Kanons* [Erlangen-Leipzig, 1890] Vol. II : 1, p. 300) are : the list of "Sixty Canonical Books" (in Zahn, *op. cit.*, p. 292) ; the *Synopsis* of pseudo-Athanasius (in Zahn, *op. cit.*, p. 317) ; a list by the Armenian, Mechithar of Arivank (in Zahn, *Forschungen d. neutestamentlichen Kanons* [Leipzig, 1893], Vol. V, p. 109) ; Michael Glycas, *Annales* II.171 (ed. Bekker, *Corpus Scriptorum Historiae Byzantinae* xxvii [Berlin, 1836], p. 321) refers to a contest between Jacob and the angel Raphael (sic !) being found in an apocryphal

it narrates is unique. This, and the problem of determining the date and provenance of the apocryphon render its interpretation extremely difficult.[4] Within the scope of this paper, I can only discuss briefly the various motifs; at a later date I hope to publish a detailed commentary.

The text, as it has survived, appears to be a midrash on the Jacob narrative in Genesis (most particularly Gen. 32:24ff.). As such, it takes its place within an established literary tradition represented by works such as Jubilees, the pseudo-Philonic *Biblicarum antiquitatum*, the complex Testament-literature and the recently discovered "Genesis Apocryphon". The text bears definite verbal affinities to Genesis 48-49, especially in the Septuagint. Thus M. R. James concludes: "the book contained a dying speech of Jacob, of which we have a portion. I am tempted to think that it was addressed to Joseph and his sons Ephraim and Manasseh. The grounds are naturally slight: (a) We already have, in Genesis xlix, the full address of Jacob to the twelve; (b) there are coincidences of language with the episodes of Joseph's sons in Gen. xlviii."[5]

---

volume entitled προσευχὴ 'Ιωσήφ; Procopius of Gaza paraphrases fragment B of the *PJ* as being the *testimonium ab Jacobo dictum ex oratione Josephi* (*Comm. in I Gen.* 29, *MPG* LXXXVII: 1, cols. 95f.); the reference in the *Ascension of Isaiah* 4.22 to "the words of Joseph the just" have been taken by some critics to refer to the *PJ* (cf. A. Dillmann, *Ascensio Isaiae Aethiopice et Latine* [Leipzig, 1877], p. 69; R. H. Charles, *The Ascension of Isaiah* [London, 1900], p. 39; E. Tisserant, *Ascension d'Isaie* [Paris, 1909], p. 127n.; and G. H. Box-R. H. Charles, *The Ascension of Isaiah* [London, 1919], p. 41 n. 2); the question in Priscillian, *Liber de Fide et de Apocryphis* (ed. Schepss [Vienna, 1889], pp. 45f.) "Who ever heard of a prophecy of Jacob (*profetiam Jacob*) being included in the canon?" may well refer to the *PJ* where Jacob appears to be the chief speaker and possesses prophetic powers (so M. R. James, *The Testament of Abraham* [Cambridge, 1892], p. 13). Fabricius (*op. cit.*, Vol. I, p. 438) along with several other authorities, has misread the Gelasian list: *Liber qui appellatur Testamentum Job, apocryphus* as *Liber qui appellatur Testamentum Jacob, apocryphus* which has been interpreted as referring to the *PJ*; but this is manifestly an error. Fragment A is quoted only in Origen, *loc. cit.*; paraphrased in Origen's *Philocalia* XXIII.19; and alluded to in Glycas, *loc. cit.* Fragment B occurs in Origen, *Philocalia* XXIII.15,19; Eusebius, *Praep. evang.* VI.11.64 (ed. E. H. Gifford [Oxford, 1903] Vol. I, p. 373); and Procopius, *loc. cit.*

[4] The dating of Origen's *Commentary* prior to 231 provides the *terminus ad quem*. The parallelism of terminology and motifs between the *PJ*, Philo and other hellenistic Jewish material would suggest a possible first century dating and an Alexandrian provenance. M. Smith, *op. cit.*, p. 748 appears to suggest a Palestinian provenance and dates the *PJ* as being probably from the first century. P. Winter, "ΜΟΝΟΓΕΝΗΣ," p. 352 dates the *PJ* from "post-Valentinian times."

[5] James, *op. cit.*, p. 26.

However this would not explain the title Προσευχὴ Ἰωσήφ (although Joseph is mentioned in a context of prayer in Gen. 48:18; 50:5 and 50:25). From what has survived, one might well have anticipated the title being Προσευχὴ Ἰακώβ. This may, of course, simply be a problem of what has survived being unrepresentative of the whole, and James may be quite correct in assuming "that the book must have contained a prayer or prayers of considerable bulk uttered by Joseph (as *Asenath* contains a long prayer by Asenath). On what occasion it was offered, whether in the pit or in prison, or on his deathbed, there is no certainty."[6] I would suggest, as an alternative, the possibility that the *PJ* follows the format of the Testament-literature where, quite consistently, it is the previous patriarch who appears and speaks to the patriarch in the title, most usually at the point of the latter's death (e.g. Abraham to Isaac; Isaac to Jacob).[7] One might well expect heavy influence from Genesis 48-50 as well as Jacob's role as a heavenly figure within such a setting. However, it must be emphasized that the text does not permit final certainty on these questions.

Fragment A (Origen, *Comm. in Ioann.* II, 31)

If one accepts from the apocrypha presently in use among the Hebrews the one entitled "The Prayer of Joseph," he will derive from it exactly this teaching ... (namely) that those who have something distinctive from the beginning when compared to men, being much better than

---

[6] *Ibid.*

[7] E.g., W. E. Barnes, "The Testaments of Abraham, Isaac and Jacob" in M. R. James, *The Testament of Abraham* (Cambridge, 1892), pp. 133-161.

A possible connection between Joseph and a prayer of Jacob might be suggested by *T. Benj.* X,1 (ed. M. de Jonge, *Testamenta XII Patriarcharum* [Leiden, 1964], p. 84) which records that when Joseph was in Egypt, Benjamin longed to see him. Through the prayers of Jacob (δι' εὐχῶν Ἰακώβ), Benjamin has a vision of Joseph. (The suggestion of R. H. Charles, *The Testaments of the Twelve Patriarchs* [London, 1908], p. 212; *Apocrypha and Pseudepigrapha*, Vol. II, pp. 355 and 359 that this verse be emended and transferred to *T. Benj.* II,1 should be rejected). See further Jacob's role as the 'narrator' of Joseph's 'secret' in *T. Benj.* III,2-5 as reconstructed from the Armenian by R. H. Charles (*op. cit.* Vol. II, p. 355). The Armenian version, however, is probably not to be relied on (see M. de Jonge, *The Testaments of the Twelve Patriarchs* [Assen, 1953], pp. 23-34). This passage is lacking in the better Cambridge Univ. Library Ms. Ff 1,24 as edited by de Jonge (*op. cit.*, p. 80).

Further research needs to be done on the pattern of these patriarchal traditions within the *Testament* literature. With respect to my suggestion above "that the *PJ* follows the format of the Testament-literature where, quite consistently, it is the previous patriarch who appears and speaks to the patriarch in the title", see the valuable Appendix VI, "Valedictions and Farewell Speeches", in E. Stauffer, *New Testament Theology* (London, 1963), pp. 344-347.

other beings, have descended from the angelic to human nature. Jacob, at any rate, says: "*I, Jacob, who am speaking to you, am also Israel, an angel of God and a ruling spirit. Abraham and Isaac were created before any work. But I, Jacob, whom men call Jacob but whose name is Israel, am he who God (5) called Israel, i.e. a man seeing God, because I am the firstborn of every living thing to whom God gives life.*" And he continues:

"*And when I was coming up from Syrian Mesopotamia, Uriel, the angel of God, came out and said that I had descended to earth and I had tabernacled among (10) men and that I had been called by the name of Jacob. He envied me and fought with me and wrestled with me saying that his name and the name of him that is before every angel was to be above mine. I told him his name and what rank he held among the sons of God: 'Are you not Uriel, the eighth after me and I, Israel, (15) the archangel of the power of the Lord and the chief captain among the sons of God? Am I not Israel, the first minister before the face of God?'* And I called upon my God by the inextinguishable name . . . But we have made a lengthy digression in considering the matter of Jacob and using as evidence a writing not lightly to be despised to render more credible the belief concerning John the Baptist which maintains that he . . . being an angel, took a body in order to bear witness to the light.[8]

---

[8] In the editions of A. E. Brooke, (Cambridge, 1896), Vol. I, pp. 97f. and E. Preuschen, (Leipzig, 1903, *GCS*), pp. 88f. The standard English translation, unfortunately, remains that of A. Menzies in the *Ante-Nicene Fathers* (Grand Rapids, n.d.), Vol. X, pp. 340f. But see the English renderings in James, Ginzberg, Daniélou and Grant in their works cited above (n. 2).

There are several translation difficulties to be noted: (1) A, 7-10 ἐξῆλθεν Οὐριήλ . . . καὶ εἶπεν ὅτι κατέβην ἐπὶ τὴν γήν . . . καὶ ὅτι ἐκλήθην ὀνόματι Ἰακώβ. I have treated the whole as indirect discourse with the first ὅτι as introducing the reporting of Uriel's speech and the second ὅτι as a continuation of the quotation. (G. W. Lawell of the Yale Dept. of Classical Languages has made the suggestion that the second ὅτι be read as ὅτε. This is possible; but is not required). In both clauses, Uriel is the speaker and the behavior of Jacob-Israel is the subject of the discourse—the whole being reported by Jacob-Israel. Thus Jacob-Israel narrates that Uriel claims that Jacob-Israel has descended to earth, tabernacled among men and taken the name of Jacob. Daniélou (*Theology*, p. 133f.) treats the second ὅτι as the beginning of a new quotation and holds that both clauses refer to Uriel: "Uriel said: 'I have come down . . .' and: 'I am called by the name Jacob.'" This forces him to the conclusion that "each of the characters present claims the name of Jacob . . ." Father Daniélou informs me (in a letter of February 17, 1965) that he now believes "the terms κατέβην, κατεσκήνωσα and ἐκλήθη refer to the angel Israel and not to the angel Uriel" and withdraws his previous interpretation.

(2) A, 11-12 λέγων προτερήσειν ἐπάνω τοῦ ὀνόματός μου τὸ ὄνομα αὐτοῦ καὶ τοῦ πρὸ παντὸς ἀγγέλου. James (*op. cit.*, p. 22) suggests translating this as either "saying that his name (i.e. Uriel) should have precedence over my name and that of the angel that is before all" or "that his name and the name of the angel that is before all should have precedence over my name." This would introduce a third angelic actor (presumably a figure such as Michael or Metatron) who is the superior angel. This, however, would run contrary to the persistent emphasis in the *PJ* on the superiority of Jacob-Israel (A, 5,14-18). Schürer (*loc. cit.*) emends the text to read πρὸ τοῦ παντὸς ἀγγέλου but this is not required. Ginzberg

Fragment B (Origen, *Philocalia* XXIII, 15)

... like a book of God, in a manner of speaking, the whole heaven may contain the future. The saying of Jacob in the "Prayer of Joseph" should be understood in this manner: *For I have read in the tablets of heaven all that shall befall you and your sons.*[9]

(*Legends*, Vol. V, p. 310) believes the reference here is to the suffix -*el* which is frequently attached to the names of angels, referring to YHWH, and proposes to emend : "and the name of him who is after every angel." There is no justification for such a flagrant disregard of the given text. Daniélou (*Theology*, p. 133) suggests : "saying that his name which is the name of him that is before all the angels would prevail over mine." Either this has Uriel claiming YHWH's name, which is no where suggested in the text ; or, this translation is required by Daniélou's thesis that both Jacob and Uriel are claiming the name Israel which "is not the true name of either" (*op. cit.*, p. 134).

(3) A,13 καὶ πόσος ἐστιν ἐν υἱοῖς θεοῦ James (*op. cit.*, p. 22 n. 1) suggests emending πόσος to πόστος which is possible ; but not required. Fabricius (*op. cit.*, Vol. I, p. 766) erroneously reads : καὶ πρωτός ἐστιν ἐν υἱοῖς θεοῦ !

(4) A,18-19 καὶ ἐπεκαλεσάμην ἐν ὀνόματι ἀσβέστῳ τὸν θεόν μου. The problem is the relation of this clause to the preceding. All editors from Fabricius to Preuschen place the question mark after μου. This might suggest that a part of Israel's λειτουργία before YHWH was the utterance of the name and that Israel is here enumerating one more instance of his superiority (so James, *op. cit.*, p. 29). One would, however, have expected an imperfect of habitual action rather than the aorist ἐπεκαλεσάμην. The tense would seem to suggest that this should be treated as a new sentence, following Israel's address, in which the angel invokes the name of God. The question mark should then be placed after ὁ ἐν προσώπῳ θεοῦ λειτουργὸς πρῶτος (as Grant, *loc. cit* has translated). In A,18 the adjective ἄσβεστος has called forth some comment. I have treated it as a synonym for αἰώνιος. James (*op. cit.*, p. 29) remarks "the expression 'inextinguishable name' I have not found elsewhere, though I believe it to exist." For an occurrence of this term, see Esaias, *Oration* 4.9 (ed. Augustinos [Jerusalem, 1911], p. 26. Previously known only in Latin translation, cf. *MPG* XL, col. 1118B). However the context (a homily on Gen. 28) is quite different than the *PJ*, the name clearly referring to God's promise to Jacob, that his name would not be forgotten (vss. 13-15). Ginzberg (*Legends*, Vol. V, p. 310) suggests that a Hebrew idiom may be behind the expression and compares it to שמות שאינן נמחקין citing BT, *Shab.* 35a. This is scarcely a parallel. The reference in BT, *Shab.* 35a (cf. PT, *Rosh hash.* 1.56d etc.) "there are divine names that may be erased and such as may not be erased" refers to the ruling that, on a piece of paper, one may erase the attributes of YHWH but not His names (see further : M. *Sanh.* 7.8 ; Jastrow, *Dictionary*, Vol. II, pp. 763f. s.v. מחק; Levy, *Wörterbuch*, Vol. III, pp. 80f. s.v. *idem* ; J. Z. Lauterbach, "Substitutes for the Tetragrammaton," *Proceedings of the American Academy for Jewish Research*, 1930-1931, pp. 43f.). For a contrary opinion, see BT, *Shab.* 116a (on a writ of divorce "the Name, written in holiness, may be blotted out").

I should like to express my gratitude to Prof. Hiram J. Lester for his valuable criticism of my translation and this note.

[9] In the edition of J. A. Robinson, Cambridge, 1893, pp. 230f. The Greek text in Eusebius, *Praep. evang.* VI.11.64 is identical. The Latin version preserved in Procopius of Gaza, *Comm. in I Gen.* 29 reads : *Praetera, ut magis suam opinionem stabilant, adducunt illud testimonium ab Jacobo dictum ex oratione Josephi: Legi in*

Because of its importance for section III of this paper, I add also the paraphrase of Fragment A and quotation of Fragment B given in Origen's *Philocalia* XXIII, 19 :

> And moreover, Jacob was greater than man, he who supplanted his brother and who declared in the same book from which we quoted *I read in the tablets of heaven* that he was a chief captain of the power of the Lord and had, from of old, the name of Israel; something which he recognizes while doing service in the body, being reminded of it by the archangel Uriel.[10]

The "Prayer of Joseph", as it has survived, is dominated by (I), the lofty role of Israel who is called (1) 'Ιακώβ, (2) an ἄγγελος θεοῦ, (3) a πνεῦμα ἀρχικόν, (4) an ἀνὴρ ὁρῶν θεόν, (5) as being the πρωτογόνος παντὸς ζώου, (6) the ἀρχάγγελος δυνάμεως κυρίου, (7) the heavenly ἀρχιχιλίαρχος (8) and the λειτουργὸς πρῶτος ἐν προσώπῳ θεοῦ ; (II) the conflict between Jacob-Israel and Uriel, each claiming ascendency over the other and (III) the curious myth relating the descent to earth of Jacob-Israel. It is on these three elements that this paper will focus.

---

tabulis coeli quanta contigent vobis et filius vestris (*MPG* LXXXVII :1, cols. 95f.). The reference in Origen's *Comm. ad Ioann* I.31 to the γράμματα θεοῦ which the ἅγιοι may read and declare that they have read the future ἐν ταῖς πλαξὶ τοῦ οὐρανοῦ is too general to allow one to assume, as does Brooke (*op. cit.*, Vol. I, p. 41 margin) that this is a reference to Fragment B of the *PJ*. The image of the "tablets of heaven" is wide-spread in apocalyptic literature (e.g. it occurs some 20 times in *Jubilees* in a variety of contexts). Cf. H. Bietenhard, *Die himmlische Welt im Urchristentum und Spätjudentum* (Tübingen, 1951), ch. xi. and G. Widengren, *The Ascension of the Apostle and the Heavenly Book* (Uppsala-Leipzig, 1950), *passim*, and F. Nötscher, "Himmlische Bucher und Schicksalsglaube in Qumran," *Revue de Qumrân*, 1 (1958-9), 405-411. The reference in the *PJ* is most likely to Genesis 49 :1-2. Note that an almost exact parallel occurs in *Jubilees* 32.21 "And behold an angel descended from heaven with seven tablets in his hands, and he gave them to Jacob, and he read them and knew all that was written thereon which would befall him and his sons throughout all the ages." (Charles, Vol. II, p. 62).

[10] In Robinson, *op. cit.*, p. 208. Some scholars identify the unnamed *libellus* in Origen's *Hom. ad Num* XVII.4 (ed. W. A. Baehrens [Leipzig, 1921], p. 162 *GCS*) as the *PJ* : *sicut et in libello quodam legitur quia Iacob domus sit Istrahel, hoc est corpus eius Iacob dicatur et anima Istrahel*. There is nothing in the surviving lines explicitly quoted from the *PJ* to suggest that Jacob is considered the body and Israel, the soul. But this may represent an interpretation of the earthly Jacob and angelic Israel as given in the text. For the identification of this *libellus* with the *PJ*, see : Harnack, *op. cit.*, Vol. I, pp. 18f. ; Baehrens, *op. cit.*, p. 162 note ad line 1 ; A. Méhat, *Origène : Homélies sur les Nombres* (Paris, 1951), p. 351 n. 1 and Daniélou, *Théologie*, p. 183 n. 1.

I. The Titles

There is a remarkable consistency to the titles given Jacob-Israel in the *PJ*. Indeed, it is striking that many of Jacob-Israel's titles are applied by Philo to the *Logos*, by rabbinic literature to Michael, by Jewish mystical literature to Metatron and by Jewish Christianity to Jesus. This suggests, without arguing direct literary dependence, a community and continuity of tradition. It would appear that the center of this continuity must be located within hellenistic mystical Judaism as described by Erwin Goodenough in *By Light, Light* and in his magisterial *Jewish Symbols in the Greco-Roman Period*.[11] More specifically, I would suggest that in the *PJ* we are given a precious fragment of a mythology concerning the Mystery of Israel, a mythology which continues in the later Merkabah and Metatron speculation and which is presented in a 'de-mythologized' form in the writings of Philo.[12]

1. *Jacob*

In the *PJ*, the titles that are given apply exclusively to Jacob-Israel's heavenly nature. Indeed, it would appear that Jacob is his only earthly title, that by which he is known to men (A, 3 : ὁ κληθεὶς ὑπὸ ἀνθρώπων Ἰακώβ).[13] Although in Manichaean and hellenistic

---

[11] This does not imply an acceptance of Goodenough's tendency to postulate radical discontinuity between hellenistic Judaism and rabbinic circles of the time ; nor his portrait of "Pharisaic domination" of Palestinian Judaism which is the basis for his dichotomy. For a corrective to Goodenough at this point see M. Smith, "The Image of God : Notes on the hellenization of Judaism with especial reference to Goodenough's work on Jewish Symbols," *Bull. John Rylands Library*, 40 (1958), pp. 473-512, esp. pp. 488f. ; J. Neusner, "Notes on Goodenough's *Jewish Symbols*," *Conservative Judaism*, 17 (1963), esp. pp. 79-82 ; Neusner, "Judaism at Dura-Europos," *History of Religions*, 4 (1964), esp. pp. 95-101 and E. J. Bickerman, "Symbolism in the Dura Synagogue," *Harvard Theological Review*, 58 (1965), esp. pp. 129-135. Goodenough has only partially corrected his position in *Jewish Symbols*, Vol. XII, pp. 65-7 *et passim*.
[12] Goodenough's remarks on the angelology of Philo in comparison with that of the Sadduccees and Pharisees in *By Light, Light* (New Haven, 1935), pp. 79f. are to the point here.
[13] This is a standard feature of hellenistic revelation-literature. The heavenly revealer possesses a (secret) celestial name while being known on earth by another name. See already Homer, *Iliad* I, 403-4 "Ον βριάρεων καλέουσι θεοί, ἄνδρες δέ τε πάντες Αἰγαίων and XX, 74 "Ον Ξάνθον καλέουσι θεοί, ἄνδρες δὲ Σκάμανδρον. And compare Mandaean texts where Ptahil-Utra is named Gabriel : "He summoned Ptahil-Utra. He put names on him which are hidden and preserved on their place. He called him Gabriel, the apostle . . ." (*Right Ginza* III in M. Lidzbarski, *Ginza* [Göttingen-Leipzig, 1925], p. 98 :7ff. I have followed the English translation of G. Widengren, *The Ascension of the Apostle*,

sources there is an angel Jacob, in the *PJ* Israel is the name borne
by the angel; Jacob, by the man.¹⁴

---

p. 59. Cf. the parallels cited in K. Rudolph, *Theogonie, Kosmogonie und Anthropogonie in den mandäischen Schriften* [Göttingen, 1965], p. 198); and the catalogue of both the heavenly names and the names by which men call the five archons in *Pistis Sophia* 137 (C. Schmidt-W. Till, *Koptische-gnostische Schriften* [Berlin, 1962], Vol. I, p. 235, cf. A. D. Nock, "Greek Magical Papyri," *Journal of Egyptian Archaeology*, 15 [1929], p. 227 n. 5). Cf. the material collected in E. Norden, *Agnostos Theos* (Leipzig-Berlin, 1913), pp. 177-239 and, more recently, H. Becker, *Die Reden des Johannes-evangeliums und der Stil der gnostische Offenbarungsrede* (Göttingen, 1956), esp. pp. 14-41.

¹⁴ *Yākōb prēstag* (i.e. *ferestak*, see A. Ghilain, *Essai sur la langue Parthe . . . d'après les textes manichéens du Turkestan oriental* [Louvain, 1939], p. 98) "the angel Jacob" occurs in the Manichaean Turfan fragments M. 4 and M. 20 as edited and translated by F. W. K. Müller, "Handschriftenreste im Estrangeloschrift aus Turfan. Teil II," *Abhandlungen d. kön. Akad. d. Wissenschaften* Berlin, 1904 (Anhang, phil-hist, Kl. Abh. II). M. 4 (fol. 6) reads, in Müller's translation, "Ich verehre Gott, Jakob den Engel mit den 'Glorien', den 'Kraften', den guten Geistern, welche uns selbst beschützen mögen mit Kraft starkei. . . . Ich *bekenne in Freude die Kraft, die starke, Jakobs, des Engels, des Anführers der Engel . . . Neue Kraft komme von Jakob, dem Engel, neue (?) von allen Engeln . . ." (*op. cit.*, pp. 56f.) M. 20 contains a brief catalogue of angelic names: "der Dämon, Jakob der Engel, der Herr Bar Simus, Qaftinus, der mächtige. Raphael, Gabriel, Michael, Sarael, Narsus, Nastikus." (*op. cit.*, p. 45). For a detailed description of these two manuscripts and a guide to their secondary literature, see M. Boyce, *A Catalogue of the Iranian Manuscripts in Manichaean Script in the German Turfan Collection* (Berlin, 1960), pp. 2f. The occurrence of Jacob as an angelic name in these manuscripts was briefly noted by A. von Harnack and F. C. Conybeare, "Manichaeism," *Encyclopaedia Britannica* 11ed. (1911), Vol. XVII, p. 575; F. C. Burkitt, *The Religion of the Manichees* (Cambridge, 1925), p. 91 and H. Gressmann, *Die orientalischen Religionen im hellenistischen und römischen Zeitalter* (Berlin, 1930), p. 168. Its connection with the *PJ* was first suggested by T. Schneider, "Der Engel Jakob bei Mani," *Zeitschrift f.d. neutestamentliche Wissenschaft* 33 (1934), pp. 218f. and, more strongly, in Daniélou (*Theology*, p. 134 n. 146). It should be noted that *prēstag* carries the same force as the Hebrew מלאך and the Greek ἄγγελος i.e. it has the root sense of "messenger, one who has been sent" (see G. Widengren, *The Ascension of the Apostle and the Heavenly Book* [Uppsala, 1950], p. 37 cf. Widengren, *The Great Vohu Mana and the Apostle of God* [Uppsala-Leipzig, 1945], p. 30 and n. 4 and *Mesopotamian Elements in Manichaeism* [Uppsala-Leipzig, 1946], pp. 167-75; H. Corbin, *Avicenna and the Visionary Recital* [New York, 1960], p. 358 n. 1 cont'd.) For *angelos* as prophet-angel in hellenistic Jewish sources, see W. D. Davies, "A Note on Josephus, *Antiquities* 15.136", *Harvard Theological Review*, 47 (1954), pp. 135-140 and F. R. Walton, "The Messenger of God in Hecateus of Abdera", *ibid.* (1955), pp. 255-257. Cf. *sukkalmah* in Elam as the "exalted messenger" who can be either as prophet or an angel according to G. C. Cameron, *History of Early Iran* (Chicago, 1936), p. 71. Thus, *Yākōb prēstag* could, conceivably, be translated "the apostle James" (see: E. Waldschmidt-W. Lentz, "Der Stellung Jesu im Manichäismus," *Abhandlungen d. preuss. Akad. d. Wissenschaften* [Berlin, 1926], phil-hist. Kl. no. 4, pp. 8f. and H. H. Schäder, "Iranica 2: Fūlin", *Abhandlungen d. Gesellschaft d. Wissenschaften z. Göttingen* 1934, phil.-hist. Kl. F. 3, no. 10, p. 32 n. 3). However, the context

2. Israel, an angel of God

The angel Israel appears in several Jewish mystical documents such as the *Sefer Raziel*, but he possesses such a diffuse character in these

of both citations would clearly suggest the angel Jacob rather than the apostle James. Ginzberg, (*Legends*, Vol. V, p. 275 n. 35 cont'd) suggests that in the *PJ* "the patriarch Jacob is confounded with the Semitic god Jacobel mentioned in an Egyptian inscription. Many an angel is nothing more than a degraded god." I know of no such Semitic god. As is well known, *Ya'qob-el* occurs as a place name in the fifteenth century list of Thutmose III (in Pritchard, *ANET*, p. 242 cf. S. Yeiven, "Ya'qob'-el", *Journal of Egyptian Archaeology*, 45 [1959], pp. 16-18) which may be what Ginzberg is referring to. It is now suggested that *Ya'qob-el* is to be translated "May El protect" (so J. Bright, *A History of Israel* [London, 1960], p. 83) but the previous generation of scholars translated "Jacob is God" (e.g. Oesterley-Robinson, *History of Israel* [Oxford, 1932], Vol. I, pp. 52f. and 91). In addition to *Ya'qob-el*, see the name *Ia-ah-qu-ub-él* in an eighteenth century text cited by C. J. Gadd, "Tablets from Chagar Bazar and Tall Brak, 1937-38", *Iraq*, 7 (1940), p. 38.

'Ιακωβ occurs as the name of a supernatural being in the *Sword of Dardanus* (a charm which forms part of the Great Paris Magical Papyrus). To fashion the amulet, the user must take a magnetic stone, engrave on it a figure of Aphrodite and, under her, the figure of Eros. Under Eros must be engraved certain names including Adonai, Jacob and Iao. On the reverse of the amulet is to be carved the figures of Eros and Psyche embracing. Cf. the editions of C. Wessely, "Griechische Zauberpapyrus von Paris und London," *Denkschriften d. Akad. d. Wissenschaften* 36:2 (Vienna, 1888), p. 88, lines 1735-7 and K. Preisendanz, *Papyri Graecae Magicae* (Berlin, 1928) Vol. I, p. 126 (Papyrus IV, lines 1735-7). For a discussion of the significance of this amulet, see esp. A. D. Nock, "Magical Notes," *Journal of Egyptian Archaeology*, 11 (1925), pp. 154-8; M. Smith, "The Account of Simon Magus", p. 749 has related this text to the *PJ*. R. Mouterde, "Le Glaive de Dardanos : Objets et inscriptions magiques de Syrie," *Mélanges de l'Université Saint-Joseph* 15 :3 (1930), esp. pp. 56f. has discovered such an amulet with the fragmentary inscription [... ΧΛΑΔΩ ΝΑΙΕΒΑΣΜΑΧΑ... ΩΙΑ ΚΩΒΙΣΑΚΩ] which is to be restored, on the basis of the papyrus (line 1735) : [(Αχαπα) χ (α) (?) 'Αδωναῖε Βασμ(α)/χα/ (ραχ) ω 'Ιακωβ 'Ισακω (?)]. Another striking instance is an amulet (Newhall Collection No. 35) bearing on its obverse the inscription : ΙΑΚΩΒ/ΑΚΟΥΒΤΑ/ ΙΑΩ/ΒΕΡΩ/ published by H. C. Youtie, "A Gnostic Amulet with an Aramaic Inscription," *Journal of the American Oriental Society*, 50 (1930), pp. 214-20 (cf. C. Bonner, *Studies in Magical Amulets* [Ann Arbor, 1950], fig. 275 and pp. 171, 299) Youtie suggests that the text be read : Jacob/the likeness (עקובתא) /YHWH/ his son (ברו) and that there may be an attempt to derive an etymology of the name Jacob as the "image of God" IA (Ω) ΑΚΟΥΒ(ΤΑ). In his article (*op. cit.*, pp. 218f.), Youtie compares the notion of Jacob as the son of God with the description of Jacob in the *PJ*. The chief difficulty in Youtie's interpretation, of which he is well aware, is that עקובתא is a *hapax legomenon* in BT, *Sanh.* 96a (end) and is usually translated "buttocks" (e.g. Jastrow, *Dictionary*, Vol. II, p. 1105 and all translations that I am familiar with). Youtie, following Levy's *Wörterbuch* (Vol. III, p. 682) argues from an Arabic cognate that the word means "image". However, this must remain conjectural. Bonner (*op. cit.*, p. 171) suggests that ακουβτα and βερω may simply be *voces magicae*. Ganschinietz, in his article "Jacob" (Pauly-Wissowa, *Real-encyclopädie*, Vol. IX:1,

works that generalization is impossible.[15] In hellenistic sources, the name *Istraēl* is found in a wide variety of texts and may well represent a corruption of Israel.[16] In Justin's *Baruch* (Hippolytus, *Ref.* V,26,2),

---

cols. 623f.) notes the tendency to combine the name 'Ιακωβ with the divine name 'Ιαω (which might suggest a heavenly Jacob). He cites P. Paris 1736 'Ιακωβιαωη, P. Paris 1803 'Ιακωβ' ιαω, P. Paris 224 'Ιακουβιαι, P. Mimaut 'Ιωκουβια and P. Lugd. J. 384 'Ιαια 'Ιακουβια to which may be added the close association of these names in the material just discussed. Other possible occurrences of the name Jacob in a supernatural context are 'Ιακουβ as one of the *nomina sacra* in a love-charm (Preisendanz, *PGM* Vol. II, p. 29, line 649); 'Ιακουβια in P. London 121 (ed. Leemans [Leipzig, 1888], p. 51 line 715) which M. Schwab, *Vocabulaire de l'angelologie* (Paris, 1897), p. 291 translates as Jacob; 'Ιακωπ which is one of the παρέδρους τοῦ μεγάλου θεοῦ in the Great Paris Magical Papyrus (P. Paris 574 in Preisendanz, *PGM*, Vol. I, p. 118, line 1377); and Ιακου βαι on an engraved gem described in H. Carnegie, *Catalogue of Antique Gems formed by James, Ninth Earl of Southesk, K.T.* (London, 1908), p. 195 N84 (cf. Goodenough, *Jewish Symbols* Vol. II, p. 274 "It is hard to think which basis this word could have other than the name Jacob.") ιακογ ιδ appears as one of the Powers of Ialdabaoth, creating the right shoulder of man in *Apocryphon Johannis* 65.11 (ed. S. Giversen [Copenhagen], 1963, p. 79). ιακ which occurs as an angelic name in various Coptic magical papyri bears no relationship to the figure of Jacob and should not be confused with him. e.g. P. London 6795 (in M. Kropp, *Ausgewählte koptische Zaubertexte* [Brussels, 1931], Vol. II, p. 99, line 36 also C. D. G. Müller, *Die Engellehre der koptischen Kirche* [Wiesbaden, 1959], p. 297) and London Ms. Or. 6794 (in Kropp, *op. cit.*, Vol. II, p. 107, line 46 cf. Goodenough, *Jewish Symbols*, Vol. II, pp. 166-8 who treats this as a purely Jewish charm). Cf. Kropp, *op. cit.*, Vol. III, pp. 29f. and 45-7 for a discussion of this angel.

[15] ישראל appears as a conquering angel, lord of the seventh day of the week with dominion over the month of Shebat in *Sefer Raziel* (Amsterdam, 1701), f. 41b and is related to the sign of the Bull in *Sefer Raziel*, f. 4b (see M. Schwab, *op. cit.*, pp. 151f and T. Schrire, *Hebrew Amulets* (London, 1966), pp. 106f.). ישריאל is invoked, along with other angels, in the Hebrew *Sword of Moses* (M. Gaster, ed. *Studies and Texts in Folklore, Magic, Medieval Romance, Hebrew Apocrypha and Samaritan Archaeology* [London, 1928], Vol. III, p. 71, line 2. Cf. Gaster's translation, *op. cit.*, Vol. I, p. 314) and in M. Margalioth, *Sepher Ha-Razim* (Jerusalem, 1966), p. 97, line 19. The angel יוראל in *Sefer Raziel* f. 6b, who possesses dominion over fire and flame, may be a corruption of Israel (so Schwab, *op. cit.*, p. 146). Possibly an angelic Israel is implied in *Zohar* II. 4b (translation: J. de Pauly [Paris, 1908], Vol. III, p. 16): "the 'children of Israel' refers to the angels who are the children of the heavenly Israel."

[16] 'Ιστραήλ appears as an angelic name in the Greek manuscript of 1 *Enōch* 10:1 (R. H. Charles, *Apocrypha and Pseudepigrapha*, Vol. II, p. 193n.). He figures prominently in the Great Magical Paris Papyrus as part of the "Sword of Dardanus." The "sword" must be inscribed on a gold leaf along with the acclamation Εἷς Θουριὴλ Μιχαὴλ Γαβριὴλ Οὐριὴλ Μισαὴλ 'Ιρραὴλ 'Ιστραήλ. The gold leaf is to be swallowed by a partridge, the partridge is to be killed and the leaf recovered, a sprig of παιδέρως is to be inserted in the leaf and the whole hung around ones neck (Preisendanz, *PGM*, Vol. I, p. 128 esp. lines

one of the three *archai* is a female who is called Israel, a tradition which Resch suggests may be reflected in the *PJ*'s description of Israel as a πνεῦμα ἀρχικόν (an inference which is speculative at best and should be rejected).[17]

In Jewish mystical literature, the community of Israel chanting the *Kedusha* has become personified into a heavenly figure named Israel who leads (as does Michael or Metatron in parallel traditions) the celestial worship before the Throne. Thus, I would suggest, from the two-level action depicted in an anonymous *baraitha* in BT, *Hullin* 91b:

> Israel is beloved before the Holy One, blessed be He, even more than the ministering angels. For Israel repeats the song every hour while the ministering angels repeat it only once a day ... Furthermore the ministering angels do not begin the song above until Israel has started it below ...

1815f. cf. Nock, *op. cit.*, p. 157). 'Ιστραήλ also occurs in BM 46 (Wessely, *op. cit.*, p. 130, line 118); P. Oslo 36 (Preisendanz, *PGM*, Vol. II, p. 173, line 310 cf. Goodenough, *Jewish Symbols*, Vol. II, p. 199); in an inscription from Kodja-Geuzlar published by W. Ramsey, *The Cities and Bishophrics of Phrygia* (Oxford, 1897), Vol. I:2, p. 541 no. 404 and in an engraved gem (Palestine Archaeological Museum no. 36-1856) described in Goodenough, *Jewish Symbols*, Vol. II, pp. 275f. and Vol. III, fig. 1078. E. Peterson, "Engel- und Dämonennamen. Nomina barbara," *Rheinisches Museum*, 75 (1926), pp. 403f. declares that "*Istrael* appears *in der Namensform Israel* in the Prayer of Joseph," an opinion most recently put forth by J. Michl, "Engel, V", *Reallexikon f. Antike und Christentum*, Vol. V, cols. 217f. G. Scholem, *Jewish Gnosticism, Merkabah Mysticism and Talmudic Tradition* 2ed. (New York, 1965), pp. 95f. has suggested a possible connection between 'Ιστραήλ, 'Αστραήλ, and אסטר (*Aster*, in both Aramaic and Latin sources. See the literature cited by Scholem, *op. cit.*, pp. 89, 95n. 8 and 96n. 9). Ganschinietz, "Israel", Pauly-Wissowa, *Realencyklopädie*, Vol. IX:2, col. 2234 cites as further possible corruptions of the angelic name Israel 'Οσραήλ and Εσραήλ in P. Paris 3034, to which may be added 'Ιστρήλ which occurs in close proximity to 'Ιστραήλ in BM P. 46 (ed. Wessely, *op. cit.*, p. 129, line 112 and p. 130, line 118). Burkitt, *op. cit.*, p. 91 suggests that Sarael in Manichaean literature "appears to be a miswriting of Israel"—a suggestion with which I cannot concur. Whether there is a possible relationship between the Arabic archangel Izra'il or the angel of death Israfil and the angel Israel, I cannot determine. A. J. Wensinck's derivation of the former from אסריאל and the latter from Serafim appears unconvincing to me (*The Encyclopaedia* of *Islam* [London, Leiden, 1927], Vol. II, pp. 570-1 and 554).

Another probable occurrence of Israel as an angel occurs in London Ms. Or. 6796(4), line 21: "I am Israelel, the Dynamis of Iao Sabaoth, the great Dynamis of Barbaraoth", (in Kropp, *op. cit.*, Vol. I, p. 48; Vol. II, p. 58). *Istraēl* occurs as an angelic name in London Ms. Or. 5987, line 93 (in Kropp, *op. cit.* I, p. 25; II, p. 152). On Istrahel and the angel of death, see further, W. Bousset, *Des Religions d. Judentums*, 3ed. (Tübingen, 1926), pp. 328f.

[17] καλεῖται δὲ 'Εδὲμ αὕτη ἡ κόρη καὶ 'Ισραήλ. Cf. Resch, *op. cit.*, p. 298.

there developed a vision, in the *Pirke Hekhaloth*, of "the angel who bears the name of Israel standing in the center of heaven and leading the heavenly choir."[18] The antiquity and distribution of this tradition has recently been unexpectedly confirmed by the Coptic Codex II from Nag-hammadi which presents a description of the heavenly Throne. In this Merkabah text there stands, amidst Cherubim and Seraphim, near to Sabaoth, "a firstborn (ⲟⲩϣⲣⲡ ⲙ̄ⲙⲓⲥⲉ) whose name is Israel, the man who sees God (ⲡⲣⲱⲙⲉ ⲉⲧⲛⲁⲩ ⲉⲡⲛⲟⲩⲧⲉ)."[19] Here, in just one line, we find two of the major titles given Israel in the *PJ* (the firstborn and a see-er of God), set within the context of a celestial liturgy before the heavenly Throne.

Biblical and midrashic traditions concerning the Patriarch Jacob-Israel have likewise contributed to the *PJ*. Titles appropriate to the earthly Jacob have been attracted to the angel, Israel. The phrase in the *PJ* (A,3-4) "I, Jacob, whom men call Jacob, but whose name is Israel, am he who God called Israel" appears to be based on Genesis 32:29 where Jacob receives the name, Israel. The notion of Israel as an angel in the *PJ* may be based on an exegetical tradition which connects שרית עם אלהים, "you have striven with God" (Gen. 32:29) with שר "prince", and interprets the verse to mean "you are as a prince with God" i.e. as one of the angels.[20]

---

[18] G. Scholem, *Major Trends in Jewish Mysticism* (New York, 1954), p. 62 paraphrasing Jellinek, *BHM*, Vol. III, pp. 161-3. Cf. Ginzberg, *Legends*, Vol. V, p. 307 n. 253; Goodenough, *Jewish Symbols*, Vol. X, pp. 71-72. The pattern, in BT, *Hullin* 91b, of the angels not beginning their song above until Israel has begun it below is also found in the *Hekhaloth* material. See M. Smith, "Observations on *Hekhalot Rabbati*," in A. Altmann, ed., *Biblical and other Studies* (Cambridge, Mass., 1963), p. 143.

[19] A. Böhlig-P. Labib, *Die koptisch-gnostische Schrift ohne Titel aus Codex II von Nag Hammadi* (Berlin, 1962), plate 153, lines 23-5, pp. 52-5. Cf. J. Doresse, *The Secret Books of the Egyptian Gnostics* (New York, 1960), p. 167; P. Borgen, *Bread from Heaven* (Leiden, 1965), p. 177. Daniélou (*Theology*, p. 133 n. 43) was the first to relate this text to the *PJ*. Codex II has proved difficult to date with any security (see the review of Böhlig-Labib by G. Quispel, *Vigiliae Christianae*, 17 [1963], pp. 50-4). Böhlig-Labib (*op. cit.*, p. 54n.) compare to this passage the *Apocryphon of John* 30.7 (W. C. Till, ed., *Die gnostischen Schriften des koptischen Papyrus Berolensis* 8502 [Berlin, 1955], pp. 100f.) which narrates the birth of *Monogenēs*, the divine Self-born (ⲁⲩⲧⲟⲅⲉⲛⲏⲧⲟⲥ) and First Born (ϣⲣⲡ ⲙ̄ⲙⲓⲥⲉ) Son of All—which is not as relevant a parallel as the *PJ* which they fail to cite.

[20] In Jerome, *Liber Hebraicarum Quaestionum in Genesim* (*MPL* XXIII:1038): *Sarith* (שרית) *enim, quod ab Israel vocabulo derivatur, principium sonat. Sensus itaque est: Non vocabitur nomen tuum supplantator, hoc est, Jacob; sed vocabitur nomen*

Finally, we may relate the conflict motif in the *PJ* to a tradition that the mysterious figure with whom Jacob wrestled in Genesis 32 was an angel called Israel (or, in Jewish-Christian sources, was the *Logos* or the Christ who is named Israel). Thus, in the *Pirke de Rabbi Eliezer* 37 : "And the angel called his name Israel like his own name, for his name is called Israel."[21]

3. *A ruling spirit*

I am unable to account for the title πνεῦμα ἀρχικόν (A,2). It may well be related to astrological angelology in which the various angels are assigned planetary spheres of influence, days of the week, months, signs of the Zodiac, etc. (analogous to the hellenistic and Gnostic *archai*), but I have not been able to locate this particular phrase in any astrological text.[22] More probably, this title is to be related to the concept of a national angel. While it is usually Michael who is the angel of Israel, it may well be that in the *PJ*, Israel's ruling angel is himself named Israel.[23]

4. *A man seeing God*

This title has its biblical origin in Genesis 32:31 where Jacob after wrestling with the angel and receiving the name Israel, exclaims "I have seen God !" (ראיתי אלהים). However the interpretation of the

---

tuum princeps cum Deo, hoc est, Israel. Cf. the notes on this passage in L'Abbé Bareille, *Oeuvres complètes de Saint Jérome* (Paris, 1878), Vol. III, p. 549 and the discussion of Jerome's exegesis in Roger Bacon, *Opus Majus* III:6 (R. B. Burke, translation [Philadelphia, 1938], Vol. I, pp. 93-6). Cf. the medieval Jewish commentaries of Ibn Ezra, Gersonides and Hezekiah b. Manoa ad Genesis 32:29.

[21] G. Friedlander, *Pirke de Rabbi Eliezer* (London, 1916), p. 282 in an anonymous tradition. Cf. the Slavonic *Ladder of Jacob* (translated in M. R. James, *op. cit.*, p. 98) in which the archangel Sarakl says to Jacob after the vision at Bethel. " 'What is your name?' and I said, 'Jacob'. Then he said, 'Your name shall no longer be called Jacob, but your name shall be like my name, Israel.' " James, *loc. cit.* suggests that the *Ladder of Jacob* may contain "a dim reflection" of the *PJ*. For Christian interpretation of the wrestling narrative, where Christ who is called Israel gives his name to Jacob see esp. Justin Martyr, *Dial. c. Trypho* 125.5 and, more generally, Origen, *Comm. in. Ioann.* I.35 (40).

[22] It is not possible to maintain, as Resch (*op. cit.*, pp. 295-8) suggests, that this relates the *PJ* to the gnostic Archontic sect. Resch's thesis is rightly rejected by R. M. Grant, *op. cit.*, p. 190 n.36. Nor is it possible to accept Stein's attempt (*op. cit.*, p. 283 n.6) to derive the chronological force of ἀρχή from ἀρχικόν, and thus relate it to the *Logos* as ἀρχή in Philo.

[23] cf. *Jubilees* 35.17 "the guardian of Jacob is great and powerful and honored and praised more than the guardian of Esau." See below, pp. 47-49.

name Israel to mean "a man seeing God" (ἀνὴρ ὁρῶν θεόν = ראה אל איש) received its most massive development in Philo. This phrase occurs twenty-three times in the Philonic corpus and is expressed or implied in some twenty-six additional texts.[24] As the derivation rests on a Hebrew *jeu de mots* and as it is never argued but rather assumed by Philo, there is good reason to suggest that he is drawing upon an earlier tradition.[25] However, except for the *PJ*, Christian sources possibly dependent upon Philo, two Jewish(?) prayers and a late(?) Hebrew midrash—it occurs nowhere else.[26] The Philonic parallels to

---

[24] It should be noted that Philo nowhere employs the phrase ἀνὴρ ὁρῶν θεόν. For the phrase Ἰσραὴλ (ὁ) ὁρῶν (τὸν θεόν) in Philo see: *L.A.* II,34; III,186,212; *Sac.* 134; *Post.* 62,92; *Conf.* 56,72,146,148; *Mig.* 113,125,201; *Haer.* 78; *Cong.* 51; *Fug.* 208; *Somn.* I,173; II,44,173; *Abr.* 57; *Leg.* 4; *QG* III,49 and IV,233. Cf. *L.A.* III,15,172; *Plant.* 58,60 and *QE* II, 22 which mention vision in a context which suggests Israel. τὸ ὁρατικὸν γένος as a synonym for Israel occurs in *Immut.* 144; *Conf.* 91; *Mig.* 18, 54; *Mut.* 109,189,258; *Somn.* II,279 cf. *Somn.* II,44 where Judah is the king of the nation that sees. The substantivised forms ὁ ὁρῶν *Conf.* 159 and *QE* II,47 (in *Sobr.* 13 this may apply to either Moses or Israel. The former seems probable from *Agr.* 81) and οἱ ὁρατικοί *Plant.* 46f. and *QE* II,38 are also employed. Synonymous expressions applying other verbs of seeing and contemplation to Israel are θεορεῖν *Sac.* 120; *Heres.* 279; σκέπτομαι *Heres.* 279; βλέπω *Somn.* I, 114. Note further ὁρατικός plus some organ with reference to Israel: ψυχή *Ebr.* 111; διάνοια *Mig.* 14; νοῦς *Mut.* 209 (cf. *Somn.* II, 173) and ὀφθαλμός *Conf.* 92; *Mut.* 203. For a discussion of this etymology in Philo see esp. W. Michaelis, *TWNT* Vol. V, pp. 337-338 n.113 and, further, the penetrating treatment of the ideology contained in this etymology in P. Borgen, *op. cit.*, pp. 115-118, 175-179 esp. p. 177 where the "affinities" of this concept with Merkabah mysticism are suggested.

[25] So E. Stein, *op. cit.*, pp. 282f. Cf. Stein, *Die allegorische Exegese des Philo aus Alexandria* (Giessen, 1929), pp. 20f. There is no evidence for or against S. Baron, *A Social and Religious History of the Jews*, 2ed. (New York, 1952), Vol. I, pp. 182f. who assumes that the etymology in the *PJ* "antedates" Philo. While the Philonic derivation is to be rejected as having no linguistic claim, note that E. Sachsse, "Die Etymologie und älteste Aussprache des Names Israel," *Zeitschrift f. d. alttestamentliche Wissenschaft*, 32 (1914), p. 3 has suggested that Israel could be derived from a root שור "to behold." For a review of the present state of the discussion concerning the etymology of Israel, see G. A. Danell, *Studies in the Name Israel in the Old Testament* (Uppsala, 1946), pp. 22-8.

[26] Christian sources which may be presumed to be dependent upon Philo include the following forms: 1) ὁ ὁρῶν τὸν θεόν in Clement Alex., *Paed.* I,9 (*MPG* VIII,341); Origen, *Princ.* IV, 3 (*MPG* XI,395); Eusebius, *Praep. evang.* XI, 6 (ed. Gifford, 519b) etc. Cf. *Israhel est videre deum* in Jerome, *Heb. Quaest. in Lib. Gen.* ad Gen. 32:28-9 (*Corpus Christianorum*, LXXII,40f.) and Jerome (?), *Liber Interpr. Heb. Nom.*, Ex. (*idem*, 75); 2) νοῦς ὁρῶν τὸν θεόν in Macarius, *Hom.* XLVII, 5 (*MPG* XXXIV, 800); 3) ὁ τῷ ὄντι διορατικὸς in Clement Alex., *Strom.* I,5 (*MPG* VIII, 725). The alternative form ἀνὴρ ὁρῶν θεόν or ἄνθρωπος ὁρῶν τὸν θεόν in Hippolytus, *Contra Noetum*, 5 (*MPG* X, 809); Eusebius, *Praep. evang.* VII,8 (ed. Gifford, 525b) cf. Nag-hammadi

the *PJ* are far more extensive than this one point of contact. Indeed, as already suggested, the majority of the titles applied to Jacob-Israel in the *PJ* are applied to the *Logos* by Philo.²⁷ The most dramatic

---

Codex II quoted above (p. 36—a form *never* found in Philo, appears to represent a quite different strain of tradition, one perhaps closer to Hebraic sources depending upon the significant role of the heavenly איש in Genesis 32. Prof. Nils A. Dahl of Yale University has suggested, in a private communication, that this distinction may "support the view that the etymology in the *PJ* antedates Philo" as Stein (*loc. cit.*) held. Note that in Origin, *Hom. XI*,4 *in Num.* (*MPG* XII,648), the name Israel is applied to the angels who see God: *Nomen enim Istrahel pervenit usque ad angelicos ordines, nisi quia multo verius illi appellabuntur Istrahel, quanto verius illi sunt mens videns Deum; hoc enim Istrahel interpretatur.* On this theme in Origen, see M. Simonetti, "Due note sull' angelologia origeniana," *Rivista di cultura classica e medioevale*, 4 (1962), esp. pp. 165-79. Cf. Clement Alex., *Stromata* V,35,1-2 and *Excerpta ex Theodoto* 10-12 where the seven angelic πρωτόκτιστοι are those who see the face of God (on the relationship of this scheme to Origen, see Simonetti, *op. cit.*, p. 166; for its possible dependence upon Philonic tradition see W. Bousset, *Jüdischchristlicher Schulbetrieb im Alexandria und Rom* [Göttingen, 1915], pp. 231f. and R. P. Casey, *The Excerpta ex Theodoto of Clement of Alexandria* [London, 1934], pp. 105f. Cf. F. Andres, "Die Engel-und Dämonenlehre des Klemens von Alexandrien," *Römische Quartalschrift*, 34 [1926], p. 137). The phrase, in its Philonic form, appears twice in the *Constitutiones Apostolorum* VII, 36,2 τὸν ἀληθινὸν 'Ισραήλ... τὸν ὁρῶντα θεόν, and VIII, 15,7 ὁ θεὸς 'Ισραὴλ τοῦ ἀληθινῶς ὁρῶντος which Goodenough (*By Light, Light*, pp. 306-58 esp. 312, 330, 340), following W. Bousset, "Eine jüdische Gebetssamlung im siebenten Buch der apostolischen Konstitutionen," *Nachrichten von d.K. Gesellschaft d. Wissenschaften zu Göttingen* phil.-hist. Kl. 1915 (1916), pp. 435-85 esp. 444, quite rightly treats as prayers derived from hellenistic Judaism. The only occurrence of the etymology of Israel as a man seeing God in rabbinic sources appears to be a late midrash on Hosea 9.10 in *Seder Eliyyahu Rabbah* 27 (ed. Friedmann [Venice, 1900], pp. 138f.) אל תיקרי ישראל אלא איש ראה אל on which see Ginzberg, *Legends*, Vol. V, p. 307 n.253. I should like to express my debt of gratitude to Prof. N. A. Dahl who criticized this note in a previous draft and made several valuable suggestions which I have incorporated.

²⁷ (a) Jacob is not a title for the Logos in Philo (see E. R. Goodenough, *The Theology of Justin Martyr* [Jena, 1923], pp. 171-172); (b) Israel as a title for the Logos occurs, as cited above, in *Conf.* 146; (c) Logos as angel or archangel occurs in *L.A.* III,177; *Immut.* 182; *Haer.* 205; *Mut.* 87; *Conf.* 146; *Somn.* I,240 etc.; (d) πνεῦμα ἀρχικόν occurs nowhere in Philo, but one might compare the notion of the Ruling Power, especially in texts such as *Abr.* 125 τὴν ἀρχικήν, ἣ καλεῖται κύριος in the context of interpreting Abraham's vision of the Three (cf. Goodenough, *By Light, Light*, pp. 23-47 and *Jewish Symbols* Vol. X, pp. 87-96). See further *QE* II,64,66,68; (e) Logos as "the one seeing God" in *Conf.* 146; (f) to Israel as the "firstborn of all living things" compare the Logos as πρωτόγονος *Agr.* 51; *Conf.* 63 or as the πρεσβύτατος θεοῦ υἱός *L.A.* III,175; *Det.* 118; *Mig.* 6; *Conf.* 146; *Heres.* 205; *Somn.* I,230 and perhaps ἀρχή in *Conf.* 146 and *L.A.* I,43; (g) ἀρχιχιλιάρχος does not occur in Philo, but one may compare the Logos as ἡγεμών *Conf.* 174 (Goodenough, *By Light, Light*, p. 302 calls attention to the Logos being "recognizable as the χεὶρ καὶ δύναμις of God that fights with us as our ally" in *Somn.* II,265-7 and notes

instance, as has been noted by several scholars, occurs in *De confusione linguarum* 146 :

> God's first-born, the *Logos*, who holds the eldership among the angels, an archangel as it where. And many names are his for he is called: the Beginning and the Name of God and His Word and the Man after His Image and He that Sees i.e. Israel.

Jacob-Israel is likewise called in the *PJ* "firstborn" (A,5), an "archangel" (A,15) and Israel "a man seeing God" (A,4f.).[28]

5. *The first-born of every living thing to whom God gives life*

The claim ἐγὼ πρωτόγονος παντὸς ζώου ζωοποιουμένου ὑπὸ θεοῦ which bears such a striking resemblance to Colossians 1:15,17 πρωτότοκος πάσης κτίσεως ... καὶ αὐτός ἐστιν πρὸ πάντων[29] has its biblical origin in Exodus 4:22 where God declares that "Israel is my firstborn son" (Υἱὸς πρωτότοκός μου Ἰσραήλ cf. Ps. 89:27). While God is here clearly speaking of the Nation (cf. 4 *Ezra* 6:58), some rabbis interpreted the passage to refer to the Patriarch (e.g. R. Nathan in *Exodus R* 19:7). This concept was developed into the doctrine that the Patriarchs were formed before the Creation (a

---

that "in comparison to God, the Logos is only ὕπαρχος, lieutenant" citing *Somn.* I, 241); compare the Logos as *strategos* in the pseudo-Justin, *Oratio ad Graecos* 5. For the relationship of this text and title to Philo and hellenistic Judaism, see E. R. Goodenough, "The Pseudo-Justinian 'Oratio ad Graecos'," *Harvard Theological Review*, 18 (1925), pp. 194-195 and, further, P. Beskow, *Rex Gloriae* (Uppsala, 1962), pp. 209-210. ; (h) To Israel as the λειτουργός might well be compared Philo's Logos as ἱερεύς or ἀρχιερεύς *L.A.* III,82-88 ; *Spec.* I,230 ; *Gig.* 52 ; *Mig.* 102 ; *Fug.* 108-110 (see E. Käsemann, *Das wandernde Gottesvolk* [Göttingen, 1939], pp. 125-140) and perhaps ὑπηρέτης *Mut.* 87 ; *Immut.* 57.

[28] The correspondence has been noted by E. Stein, *op. cit.*, p. 283 and Daniélou, *Theology*, p. 133. Cf. the remarks on this passage in H. Wolfson, *Philo* (Cambridge, Mass., 1947), Vol. I, pp. 377-9.

[29] Especially in the Syriac Peshitta which reads "the first born of all creatures" rather than "of all creation" (see G. Widengren, *Mesopotamian Elements*, p. 23). M. R. James has failed to translate this passage but remarks (*op. cit.*, p. 26), "If Jacob is the first begotten of every living thing, is he the senior to Abraham and Isaac? One must doubt whether the author had thought this out." This is an all too typical example of the failure of scholars to appreciate the thought-forms of the material they are treating. One does not need to go beyond John 8:58 to see that the problem James poses was both raised and answered by first-century thought. In Christian material, see especially οἱ ἅγιοι ἄγγελοι τοῦ Θεοῦ οἱ πρῶτοι κτισθέντες in *Hermas*, Vis. III,iv,1. For a comparison between the *PJ* and Col 1.15, see H. Windisch, *Die göttliche Weisheit der Juden und die paulinische Christologie* (Leipzig, 1914), p. 225n. and, most recently, C. F. D. Moule, *The Epistles of Paul the Apostle to the Colossians and to Philemon* (Cambridge, 1962), p. 63.

tradition alluded to in the *PJ* A,2f 'Αβραάμ καὶ 'Ισαὰκ προεκτίσθησαν πρὸ παντὸς ἔργου[30] or that Israel (clearly the Nation, but capable of being interpreted as the Patriarch) was so formed.[31]

6. *The archangel of the power of the Lord*

This is one of the earlier occurrences of the term ἀρχάγγελος in hellenistic literature and appears here, especially with the qualifier δυνάμεως κυρίου to be a reflection of the traditional vocabulary associated with Michael as the שר הגדול (Dan. 12:1; Resh Lakish in BT *Hag.* 12b etc.)[32]

7. *Chief captain among the sons of God*

The title ἀρχιχιλίαρχος appears to be *hapax legomenon* in this document;[33] but it would seem to be parallel to Michael who is the

---

[30] προκτίζω is applied to Christ in a similar context in Christian literature. See Didymus Alex., *De Trinitate* III,4 (*MPG* XXXIX: 832) and Gelasius Cyz., *Historia concilii nicaeni* II,16 (*MPG* LXXXV:1257). Cf. the πρωτόκτιστοι in Jewish-Christian literature. See P. E. Testa, *Il Simbolismo dei Giudeo-Cristiani* (Jerusalem, 1962), pp. 61 *et passim*, and n. 29 above.

[31] In *Tanhuma* (ed. Buber) *Numbers, Naso* 19, the fathers of the world and Israel are among those created before the world; in *Midrash Tehillim* ad Psalm 93:3, Israel is pre-existent. Cf. Romans 11:2 οὐκ ἀπώσατο ὁ θεὸς τὸν λαὸν αὐτοῦ ὃν προέγνω. See the discussion by L. Blau, "Preexistence", *Jewish Encyclopedia*, Vol. X, pp. 182-4 esp. p. 182 and the convenient collection of texts in Strack-Billerbeck, *Kommentar*, Vol. III, pp. 256-8. See further: J. Jervell, *Imago Dei* (Göttingen, 1960), pp. 78-84 and further the discussion of the title "Firstborn" in P. Winter, "ΜΟΝΟΓΕΝΗΣ", pp. 335-365, and S. Buber, *Midrash Tehillim* (Wilna, 1892), p. 414 n.11. W. L. Knox, *op. cit.*, p. 49 n.6 raises the possibility that the notion of the preexistent patriarchs implies that the *PJ* also considers Abraham and Isaac to be angels. There is considerable debate as to the day on which the angels were created. The rabbinic view may be summarized in the dictum of R. Luliabi b. Tabri in the name of R. Isaac that "all agree that none were created on the first day" (*Gen. R.* 1.3 but see *Jubilees* 2.2. and the material collected in Ginzberg, *Legends*, Vol. V, pp. 20f. which represent "reminiscences of the old view according to which angels were created on the first day.") For the Christian discussion, see the material collected in G. W. H. Lampe, *Patristic Greek Lexicon* (Oxford, 1961), fasc. 1, p. 10 s.v. ἄγγελος sect. IIB,3-5. Note that Clement Alex. terms God's covenants with Adam, Noah, Abraham and Moses ἄγγελοι πρωτόκτιστοι *Ecl. proph.* 51 (*MPG* IX:722).

[32] See, on the occurrence of this term in the *PJ*, G. Kittell, "ἀρχαγγέλος", *TWNT* (English translation), Vol. I, p. 87.

[33] Sophocles, *Lexicon* s.v. ἀρχιχιλίαρχος cites only the passage in Origen which quotes the *PJ* as does Stephanus, *Thesaurus graecae linguae* Vol. I:2, col. 2128; D. Demetrakos, *Mega Lexikon tēs hellēnikēs Glōssēs* (Athens, 1936), Vol. II, p. 1023 and Lampe, *op. cit.*, fasc. 1, p. 241. Professor C. Bradford Welles of the Yale Department of Classical Languages informs me that he knows of no occurrence of this term in hellenistic papyri. I should like to acknowledge the

ἀρχιστράτηγος τῆς δυνάμεως κυρίου in hellenistic Jewish literature (Dan. 8:11 in the LXX and Theod.; 2 Enoch 22:6f. and 33:10f; 3 Baruch 11:1ff. etc.).[34]

8. The first minister before the face of God

It is possible that the angel Israel's service before the "face of God" (as well as the motif of his "seeing") may be based on the title *Peniel* conferred by Jacob upon the place of wrestling in Genesis 32:30. More particularly, in light of the tendency of the *PJ* to utilize for Israel titles frequently associated with Michael, Gabriel and Metatron (e.g. titles 1, 2, 6 and 7), ὁ ἐν προσώπῳ θεοῦ λειτουργὸς πρῶτος, is almost an exact translation of שר הפנים applied quite consistently to these figures in Jewish mystical literature.[35]

An examination of the various titles applied to Israel in the *PJ* has revealed that they all may be placed within a Jewish context. While some are derived from the Old Testament and its haggadic exegesis, some more frequent within circles of hellenistic and Merkabah mysticism as well as related Wisdom-theology, others more closely akin to Philo—no title requires that an extra-Jewish influence be postulated (e.g. from Christian, hellenistic or Gnostic tradition). This will be of crucial importance in investigating the second and third motifs: the

---

assistance of Professor Hardin Craig, Jr. of the Fondren Library, Rice University and Mr. Douglas Gunn of Yale University in attempting to further trace this word.

[34] Esp. in texts such as the *Assumptio Moysis* 10.2 *qui est in summo constitutus* (O. F. Fritzsche, ed., *Libri Apocryphi Veteris Testamenti* [Leipzig, 1871]. p. 719). Cf. the *Prayer of Joseph and Asenath* 14 where Michael appears to Asenath declaring: Ἐγὼ εἰμὶ ὁ ἀρχιστράτηγος κυρίου τοῦ θεοῦ, καὶ στρατιάρχης πάσης στρατειᾶς τοῦ ὑψίστου . . . In this version, Michael assumes the form of Joseph (καὶ ἰδοὺ ἀνὴρ ὅμοιος κατὰ πάντα τῷ Ἰωσήφ)! P. Batiffol, ed., *Studia Patristica* (Paris, 1889) Vol. I, p. 59, lines 11-16 cf. the Latin text, p. 101, line 31-p. 102, line 4 and Batiffol's discussion, pp. 32-4; M. R. James, *Joseph and Asenath* (London, 1918), p. 45. For Michael as warrior in Jewish tradition see the material collected in W. Luecken, *Der Erzengel Michael in der Überlieferung des Judentums* (Marburg, 1898), pp. 13-30. For Christ or the *Logos* as warrior see J. Barbel, *Christos Angelos* (Bonn, 1941), pp. 234f. (this tradition may reflect the LXX of Joshua 5:13 as well as assimilation to Michael). For Michael as warrior in Christian material see e.g. M. Bonnet, *Narratio de miraculo a Michaele archangelo* (Paris, 1890), p. 3.

[35] Note, however, that the occurrence of ἄγγελοι λειτουργοί in Philo (*Virt.* 73), οἱ λειτουργοῦντες... πρὸς κύριον (*T. Levi* 3.5) or λειτουργικὰ πνεύματα (Hebs. 1:14) as synonyms for angels suggests that this is an element in the general technical angelic vocabulary of hellenistic Judaism. On this possibility see C. Spicq, "L'Épître au Hébreux, Apollos, Jean-Baptiste, les hellénistes et Qumran," *Revue de Qumran*, 1 (1959), esp. pp. 377f.

combat of Jacob-Israel and Uriel and the myth of the descent of Jacob-Israel, for here scholars have suggested the presence of such influences.³⁶

In this section, I have resisted a univocal interpretation of any given title, preferring instead to suggest a variety of possible backgrounds within Jewish tradition. Nevertheless certain generalizations are possible. The majority of the titles seem to be drawn from material associated with the Patriarch Jacob, especially the narrative of Genesis 32 (i.e. titles: 1, 2, 4, 5, 8) or from material associated with Michael, Gabriel or Metatron (i.e. titles: 1, 2, 3?, 6, 7, 8). Secondly, some of the titles appear to be drawn from traditions concerning the celestial liturgy (i.e. titles: 2, 6, 7, 8 and Israel's calling upon the "inextinguishable name of God" in A,17f.). As will be noted below, the legend of Jacob wrestling with the angel, the figures of Michael, Gabriel and Metatron and the performance of the heavenly liturgy are combined in both hellenistic Jewish and rabbinic sources, thus strengthening the possibility of their mutual influence on the *PJ*.

II. THE CONFLICT

(1) The conflict between Jacob-Israel and Uriel is, without doubt, the most debated portion of the *PJ*. There have been five major approaches to its interpretation. The first may be represented by R. H. Charles who declares that "the work was obviously anti-Christian" and J. T. Marshall who detects "an anti-christian *animus*".³⁷ Or, more circumspectly, the opinion of M. R. James that

---

³⁶ Let me stress that I do not mean by this to imply an isolation of Judaism from its environment. Judaism, like Christianity, is to be treated within the context of the history of Mediterranean religions in the hellenistic period. I mean only to suggest that the *PJ* is representative of a type of Judaism, drawing upon specifically Jewish traditions as well as reflecting common hellenistic patterns such as the descent-ascent of a heavenly figure (see below pp. 60-64). It is only a reductionistic view of the complexity and diversity of Judaism within this period that requires "borrowings" to be postulated in order to explain a text such as the *PJ*.

³⁷ R. H. Charles, "Apocalyptic Literature," *Encyclopaedia Britannica* 11ed., Vol. II, p. 173; Charles, *The Ascension of Isaiah* (London, 1900), p. 39; J. T. Marshall, *loc. cit.* and, most recently, D. S. Russel, *The Method and Message of Jewish Apocalyptic* (Philadelphia, 1964), p. 67 who finds in the *PJ* "hints here and there of an anti-christian bias," and N. Turner, "Joseph, Prayer of" *The Interpreter's Dictionary of the Bible* (New York-Nashville, 1962), Vol. II, p. 979 who states, "The riddle of the book is not yet solved, but it must have been anti-Christian to some extent at least".

the text was Jewish and that the author "knew something of Christian theology and indulged in some side hits at it. Whether this was the main object of the book we cannot tell..."[38] The second interpretation takes the other extreme, as in the article of V. Burch who states that the text has an "anti-Jewish character".[39] A third position is held by J. Daniélou who suggests that the text is Jewish-Christian.[40] A fourth viewpoint, exemplified by R. M. Grant, maintains that the text, while Jewish, "is certainly proto-gnostic because of the rivalry between Jacob-Israel and Uriel".[41] The fifth, with which I would concur, accepts Origen's statement that the *PJ* is a Jewish text.[42]

For those who see an anti-Christian polemic in the work, Uriel must be equated with Christ and Jacob-Israel with a Jewish attempt "to claim for the three patriarchs the same sublime and supernatural characteristics as the Christians claimed for the Lord Jesus".[43] The identification of Uriel with Christ is not impossible as it occurs within at least two Ethiopian Christian documents.[44] And furthermore, within early Christian literature, the one who wrestled with Jacob is declared to be the *Logos*, the pre-existent Christ (e.g. Justin Martyr, Origen etc. see above n. 21). Thus by demoting Uriel, the status of Christ is attacked. This interpretation as advanced by

---

[38] James, *op. cit.*, p. 31.

[39] V. Burch, "The Literary Unity of the *Ascensio Isaiae*", *Journal of Theological Studies*, 20 (1918-19), esp. p. 21.

[40] Daniélou, *Théologie*, pp. 28,184; *Theology*, pp. 16f. In his contribution to J. Daniélou-H. Marrou, *The Christian Centuries* (New York, 1964), Vol. I, p. 76, Daniélou lists the *PJ* among "Jewish works, in particular some of Aramaic origin" which were re-written by the Jewish-Christians. Daniélou, *Message évangélique et culture hellénistique au IIe et IIIe siècles* (Tournai, 1961), pp. 451f. speculates that the text of the *PJ* may well reveal Christian influence. Though he has nowhere spelled this out in detail, this remark coupled with his note in Daniélou-Marrou, *op. cit.*, Vol. I, p. 76 appears to suggest that Daniélou is developing a complex redaction-history of the *PJ* involving a Jewish (Aramaic?) *Grundschrift* and one or more Christian redactions.

[41] Grant, *op. cit.*, p. 19. Cf. P. Batiffol, *op. cit.*, p. 17 who declares the *PJ* to be "*de la pure gnose juive.*"

[42] e.g. Fabricius, *op. cit.* ; Dillmann, *op. cit.* ; Schürer, *op. cit.* ; and Schweizer, *op. cit.*, esp. col. 167 who terms the *PJ* a "*reinjüdischen Apokryphon.*" (I am indebted to Prof. N. A. Dahl for this latter reference).

[43] Marshall, *loc. cit.*

[44] *Narrative of St. Clement*, translated by E. A. W. Budge, *The Contendings of the Apostles* (London, 1899), pp. 479f. and Urâ'el as a name of Christ in the Ethiopian *Lefâfa Sedek*, translated by E. A. W. Budge, *The Bandlet of Righteousness* (London, 1929), fol. 5a, p. 64. Only the former text has been cited by advocates of this identification.

Charles and Marshall is clearly secondary to their notion that the titles assigned to Jacob-Israel are conscious imitations of Christian titles already assigned to Jesus. It is this assumption which determines the identification of the two angelic actors. However, the *religionsgeschichtliche* inquiries of the past fifty years, the material quoted above from Philo, etc. would make it at least possible to reverse this chronology. Rather than the Jews imitating Christological titles, it would appear that the Christians borrowed already existing Jewish terminology. Thus this line of interpretation must be called into question.

The same objection may be brought against the view advanced by James. He cites as examples of familiarity with Christian theological terminology the pre-existence of the patriarchs, the notion of a heavenly figure "tabernacling among men", the "first born of every living thing" and the phrase "his name shall have precedence over mine"—each of which may be documented from Jewish sources (especially from Wisdom literature and Philo).[45] Furthermore, it is impossible to comprehend how Origen could declare of a presumed anti-Christian work that it is "a writing not lightly to be despised" (οὐκ εὐκαταφρόνητον γραφήν), unless one assumes that he had completely misunderstood the character of the text.

Burch's anti-Jewish theory is based on an alleged relation between the *PJ* and the *Testimonia adversus Iudaeos*. He declares the "chief theme" of the *PJ* to be "the surpassing of one angel appearance of the Christ by another—Uriel by Israel"; that, as in Cyprian's *Testimonia* so in the *PJ* "Jacob and Israel are as prototype and type of the Christ".[46] His argument hinges on the Ethiopian *Narrative of St. Clement* which contains the unique passage:

> And I (i.e. Peter) gave them commandments concerning circumcision according to the Law of Moses and God (i.e. Christ) appeared to me in the form of the angel Uriel and commanded me to do away the Old Law and to bring in the New.[47]

---

[45] For the pre-existence of the Patriarchs, see the material cited in n. 31 above; for "tabernacling among men" see, *Ecclus.* 24:8; *Baruch* 3:36-7; for the "first-born of every living thing" see Philo *Conf.* 146; *Agr.* 51; *Mig.* 6 and *L.A.* III,175 (cf. Goodenough, *By Light, Light*, p. 341 "the phrase πρωτότοκος πάσης κτίσεως seems only a variant of Philo's πρωτόγονος."); "his name shall have precedence over mine," see Philo *Conf.* 146.

[46] Burch, *op. cit.*, p. 20. Burch cites Cyprian's *Testimonia* I.20 as containing the view that "Jacob and Israel are as prototype and type of the Christ." I find no such typology in the text he cites.

[47] See n. 44 above.

But this text precisely reverses the direction Burch has assumed. Rather than Israel supplanting Uriel as would be required by Burch's thesis, the Ethiopian text portrays Uriel abolishing Israel's Law. Furthermore, it would be difficult to reconcile Origen's statement that the *PJ* was "in use among the Hebrews" (τῶν παρ' Ἑβραίοις φερομένων ἀποκρύφων τὴν ἐπιγραφομένην Ἰωσὴφ προσευχήν) with an alleged anti-Jewish bias.[48]

Daniélou's suggestion of a Jewish-Christian origin is based on two questionable premises. The first is an appeal to the researches of Resch as decisively demonstrating the *PJ*'s link with Jewish Christianity. However, Resch only maintained (on extremely slight evidence) that the origins of the *PJ* were to be sought among the *Archontikoi*, a group that does not fit Daniélou's usual definition of Jewish Christianity and, to my knowledge, is never so labeled by him.[49] The second is Daniélou's contention that Origen's location of the text παρ' Ἑβραίοις is not an argument against its Jewish Christian character, that Origen consistently calls Jewish Christians Ἑβραῖοι when he relates their traditions. However the texts Daniélou cites do not bear out this interpretation.[50] Daniélou's printed interpretation of the conflict is that Uriel (i.e. Jacob) tabernacles among men until he is contested by the true Israel (i.e. the *Logos*, Christ). However, Father Daniélou now informs me that he considers the verbs κατέβην, κατεσκήνωσα and ἐκλήθη to refer to Jacob-Israel and not Uriel, thus invalidating his exegesis.[51]

---

[48] Burch, *op. cit.*, p. 21 n.5 cites this text and declares, without offering any supporting argument, that it is not against the view that the *PJ* was anti-Jewish.

[49] Resch, *op. cit.*, pp. 295-8 ; Daniélou, *Théologie*, p. 184 n.2. See n. 22 above.

[50] In two of the texts Daniélou cites (*Théologie*, p. 185 n.1) *Hom. in Num.* 13.5 (ed. Baehrens, p. 114) and *Hom. in Jer.* 20.2 (*MPG* XIII:501) the reference is not to the general group of Ἑβραῖοι but to a specific individual (a Ἑβραῖος) who has converted from Judaism to Christianity. The third instance, *in Ezech.* 9:2 (*MPG* XIII:800), the context is not sufficiently clear to allow final security. On the use of the term Ἑβραῖος in these three passages cf. Bardy, *op. cit.*, pp. 221-3 and W. L. Knox, *op. cit.*, p. 49 n.5 who declares "There is no hint of Christianity in the fragments preserved by Origen who regards it as an orthodox Jewish work of an almost canonical character. But Origen's standard of orthodoxy is not high." Both the argument from Resch and the argument concerning the use of the term Ἑβραῖοι have been omitted from the English translation of Daniélou's work ; but Father Daniélou informs me that he should have allowed them to remain.

[51] *Théologie*, p. 184. Father Daniélou writes, in a letter of February 17, 1965; "... in fact the terms κατέβην, κατεσκήνωσα, and ἐκλήθη refer to the angel Israel and not the angel Uriel. The arguments that are developed in the paragraphs in question lose their foundation."

Grant's thesis as to the "proto-gnostic" character of the text appears to rest simply on the fact that there is rivalry between Jacob-Israel and Uriel. However, the mere presence of conflict or, for that matter, dualism is not in itself sufficient to term a text "gnostic."[52]

(2) On the basis of Jewish sources, I find that there are at least three possibilities of interpretation. The first approach would be to suggest that the *PJ*'s narration represents a projection of the conflict between Jacob and Esau. As presented in the biblical account, this struggle begins within Rebekah's womb (Gen. 25:22-6), continues through Jacob's acquisition of Esau's birthright (Gen. 25:29-34) and of the blessing (Gen. 27). Basing itself on texts such as Genesis 25:23, haggadic literature extended this conflict to the descendents of Esau and Jacob and to a final eschatological conflict between their sons and their guardian angels.[53]

The oldest strata of material which reveals this conflict may well be that which, basing itself on passages such as Genesis 36: 1, 8, 9, 43

---

[52] It must be admitted that the harshness of the rivalry between Jacob-Israel and Uriel is striking. If the *PJ* is employing a traditional scheme of either four, six or seven archangels—Jacob-Israel's taunt "Are you not Uriel the eighth after me?" (A,14) would appear to remove Uriel from the ranks of the chief hierarchs before the Throne. He has been excommunicated! (so Daniélou, *Théologie*, p. 134. The English translation is in error at this point and should read: "then the *former* does not fall..."). However if, as I believe, a scheme of eight heavens and principal angels is being employed, Uriel would remain within the hierarchy as the lowest of the seven archangels and Jacob-Israel would assume the role of the *Dynamis* of the eighth, highest and secret heaven (cf. Scholem, *Jewish Gnosticism*, pp. 65-71). On the motif of seven angels, see the classic paper of G. H. Dix, "The Seven Archangels and the Seven Spirits", *Journal of Theological Studies*, 28 (1927), pp. 233-250 and, further, G. Furlani, "I sette angeli del Yezidi", *Rendiconti della reale academia dei Lincei*, Ser. VIII, Vol. 2 (1947), pp. 141-161, esp. pp. 146-154. N.B. the similarity in angelological structure between the *PJ* and Clement of Alexandria's *Excerpta ex Theodoto* 10-12 (cf. *Stromata* V, 35,1-2 and n. 26 above) where there are three orders of angelic beings: (1) the Son who is the Face of God; (2) the seven πρωτόκτιστοι who behold the Face of God which is the Son and (3) the archangels. Jacob-Israel would appear to play a role in the *PJ* similar to the Son in Clement's scheme. See further the remarks of H. Corbin, *op. cit.*, pp. 65 and 287-88 n.14 comparing the Son and the seven πρωτόκτιστοι in Clement's *Excerpta* with the angelology of 3 *Enoch*. W. L. Knox (*op. cit.*, p. 49) suggests a seven-fold order of angels led by Jacob-Israel with a "rebellious hierarchy" of angels below, led by Uriel. See further, sect. III below.

[53] For the conflict between the descendants of Jacob and Esau, see esp. *Midrash Wa-Yissa'u* in *Yalkut* I,132 (ed. Jellinek, *BHM*, Vol. II, pp. 1-5 cf. Ginzberg, *Legends*, Vol. V, pp. 321f. n.317). Earlier fragments of this legend are preserved in *T. Judah* 9.4 and *Jubilees* 37-38.

identifies Rome as Esau, Edom, Seir etc.⁵⁴ and depicts conflicts between the guardian angel of Israel (i.e. Jacob) who is most usually Michael and the guardian angel of Rome (i.e. Esau) who is most usually Sammael.⁵⁵ Scholars agree that such identification is to be dated about the time of Herod the Idumean. The equation Esau-Rome was, at a later date than the *PJ*, transferred to the Christian (i.e. Roman) Church and produced polemic material which resembles in broad outline the conflict between Uriel and Jacob-Israel.⁵⁶

As one may expect, the various elements of the biblical narrative which tells of twin brothers struggling in the womb and throughout their lives (including the haggadic extension which has Esau finally slain by Jacob);⁵⁷ the distinctions of one being smooth, the other hairy; the one light, the other "ruddy" etc. lent themselves to dualistic symbolism. But this material is all late and does not appear to have influenced the *PJ*.⁵⁸

There is one biblical-midrashic tradition that does appear to be reflected in the *PJ*. The name Jacob is derived in Genesis 25:26 from עקב (the heel, one who takes by the heel i.e. the supplanter cf. Gen. 27:36; Hos. 12:3; עקוב in Jer. 17:9). This is continued in Philo who regularly assigns the title πτερνιστής to Jacob before he received the name, Israel.⁵⁹ This is one element in Uriel's charge against Jacob-Israel, that he has taken advantage of Uriel in descending to earth and unlawfully claiming precedence over him. I would suggest that this may be a reflection of Jacob's deception of blind Isaac, gaining Esau's blessing by putting on the goatskins. In light of the widespread metaphor which speaks of the incarnation of a heavenly soul as a putting on of garments (at times specifically

---

⁵⁴ e.g. strikingly in PT, *Ab. Z.* I.2 (2b) cited in H. Odeberg, *The Aramaic Portions of Bereshit Rabba* (Lund-Leipzig, 1939), Vol. II, p. 147.

⁵⁵ e.g. BT, *Yoma*, 38b ; *Gittin* 57b etc.

⁵⁶ See the collection of late texts illustrating the application of Esau, Edom, etc. to Christians in L. Zunz, *Die synagogale Poesie des Mittelalters* (Frankfurt a.M., 1920), pp. 437-52. For an earlier example of an anti-Christian polemic which contains the theme of illegitimate assumption and forcible expulsion see PT, *Nedarim* 38a where R. Aḥa declares in the name of R. Ḥuna : "Esau the wicked will put on his *tallith* and will sit with the righteous in the Garden of Eden in the time to come. But the Holy One, Blessed be He, will drag him out and cast him forth from there."

⁵⁷ *T. Judah* 9.3; *Jubilees* 38.1-4 cf. *Yalkut* I.132; *Midrash Tehillim* ad Ps. 18:159-60 and Ginzberg, *Legends*, Vol. V, pp. 321f.

⁵⁸ See especially the collection in *Yalkut Reubeni* ad Genesis 32:25-33.

⁵⁹ *L.A.* I,161; II,89; III,15,93; *Sac.* 42,135; *Mig.* 200; *Somn.* I,171; *Mut.* 81; *Heres.* 252.

garments of goatskins),⁶⁰ the legend in Genesis 27 would lend itself to such an interpretation. Note that in a late mythological fragment preserved in *Yalkut Reubeni* (ad Gen. 32:29), the angel Gabriel disguised as Esau appears before Jacob and accuses him of being an imposter in claiming to be Isaac's firstborn.⁶¹ It is possible that in the *PJ*, Uriel represents Esau and Israel, Jacob. However this identification of Uriel as the guardian angel of Esau would then be, to my knowledge, a unique instance in Jewish or Christian literature.

(3) While details of the conflict between Jacob and Esau might have influenced the tradition represented in the *PJ*, the most likely source of the setting of the conflict between Jacob-Israel and Uriel within our text is the wrestling of Jacob with the mysterious figure in Genesis 32:24ff. Indeed, several points of verbal contact between this text and the *PJ* may be noted. The dispute between Uriel and Jacob-Israel occurs when the latter is coming up from Μεσοποταμία τῆς Συρίας the standard Septuagint rendering of *Padan-aram*. The encounter by the Jabbok occurred as Jacob was journeying up from *Padan-aram* to rejoin his father in Canaan having fled from there to Laban's house to avoid Esau. Of the three-fold description of the conflict in the *PJ*, "he envied me and fought with me and wrestled with me" (A,10f), only the latter verb is to be found in the biblical account. The notion of envy supplies the motivation so strikingly lacking in the Genesis narrative.⁶²

Rabbinic literature tends to provide brief and fragmentary interpretations of the conflict. Usually it is held that the angel wrestled with Jacob in order to strengthen him for his struggle with Esau or to punish him for fearing Esau. Another view is that the angel fought with Jacob in order to remind him of his promise to tithe his possessions.⁶³ The identity of the mysterious heavenly combatant is

---

⁶⁰ See my article, "The Garments of Shame," *History of Religions*, 5 (Winter, 1965), pp. 217-238, esp. pp. 231f. and notes.

⁶¹ Paraphrased in Ginzberg, *Legends*, Vol. V, p. 310. *Yalkut Reubeni* cites as its source the *Pirke de R. Eliezer*, however it is not found in the present text of this midrash.

⁶² Compare, however, P. Winter's interpretation of the verb in "MONOΓΕΝΗΣ," p. 352. "Israel's rank in the order of existence is so high that Uriel, the angel of God, tries to impersonate him (ἐζήλωσε — he was jealous, he vied with, he emulated, he imitated) to maintain his superiority. But Israel tells him exactly where he stands...".

⁶³ For a convenient summary see Ginzberg, *Legends*, Vol. I, pp. 384-388 and the literature cited.

likewise controversial. I know of only one instance in a Jewish or Christian source where it is Uriel, and that is most probably dependent on the *PJ*.[64] Most usually he is identified as either Michael, Gabriel or Metatron. The view of R. Hama b. R. Hanina in *Genesis Rabbah* 77:3 and 78:3 that Jacob wrestled with Esau's guardian angel may be assumed to be a projection of the fraternal conflict. Nonetheless, incidental details in these *midrashim* reveal remnants of what must have been a rich combat tradition which may well have influenced the *PJ*. Thus a hint of a possible angelic contest

---

[64] L. Réau, *Iconographie de l'art chrétien* (Paris, 1956), Vol. II :1, p. 151 lists three traditional Christian identifications of Jacob's angelic combatant, concluding : "D'après une troisième tradition, ce serait l'Archange Uriel." As Réau gives no reference, I can only presume he is referring to the *PJ*. T. Schrire, *op. cit.*, p. 108 describes Uriel as "he who wrestled with Jacob". Schrire cites no source for this identification. The reference in a homily attributed to John of Jerusalem in Ms. Reims 427 (fol. 62): *Et pugnavit cum angelo Oriel* should, most likely, be assumed to refer to the conflict in the *PJ*. See G. Morin, "Le catalogue des manuscrits de l'abbaye de Gorze au XIe siècle. Appendix: Homélies inedites attribuées a Jean de Jerusalem," *Revue Bénédictine*, 22 (1905), p. 14 cf. James, *op. cit.*, pp. 24f. Several suggestions might be tendered as to the origin of this identification. Within the Ethiopian *Enoch* literature, Phanuel stands, at times, in Uriel's place in lists of the four arch-angels (1 *Enoch* 40:9; 54:6; 71:8, 9, 13). If this name can be related to the Peniel-Penuel of Gen. 32:30—as has been suggested by J. E. H. Thomson, *The Samaritans* (Edinburgh, 1919), p. 189 cf. A. Z. Aescoli, "Les noms magiques dans les apocryphes chrétiens des Éthiopiens," *Journal asiatique*, 220 (1932), p. 109—then this might be one link in the chain of identification. *Midrash Aggada* ad Exodus 4:5 (ed. Buber, p. 132) names Uriel as the one who attempted to slay Moses in the desert. Ginzberg suggests that this may be a parallel to the negative role of Uriel in the *PJ*. See *Eine unbekannte jüdische Sekte* (New York, 1922), p. 37 and *Legends*, Vol. V, p. 310 n.273. In the Falasha *Mota Muse* it is Suriel, the angel of death, who slays Moses (see the English translation by W. Leslau, *Falasha Anthology* [New Haven, 1951], pp. 107-111 esp. p. 109). As Ginzberg (*loc. cit.*) has noted, his suggestion is supported by this text in light of the widespread tendency to equate Suriel and Uriel. On this identification, see especially H. Malter, "Der Tod Moses in der aethiopischen Ueberlieferung," *Monatschrift f.d. Geschichte und Wissenschaft d. Judenthums*, 51 (1907), p. 711 n.3 ; J. H. Polotsky, "Suriel der Trompeter," *Muséon*, 49 (1936), pp. 231-43 esp. pp. 232-5 and cf. Peterson, *op. cit.*, pp. 418f. Note that in BT, *Ber.* 51a, Suriel is both a revealing angel and the prince of the Divine Face (see Scholem, *Major Trends*, p. 356 n.3). On the figure of Suriel, see further, G. Furlani, *op. cit.*, pp. 157f. A further suggestion of a negative role for Uriel is found in the tradition that he is the chief angel of the realm of the dead, especially within the Enoch-literature (see 1 *Enoch* 20:2; 33:3; 72:1; 74:2 etc.) and possibly in the *Testament of Solomon* 10 where the demon Ornias is an "offspring of Uriel, the power of God" (F. C. Conybeare, translation. *Jewish Quarterly Review*, o.s. 11 [1899], p. 17). For general treatments of Uriel, see especially P. Perdrizet, "L'archange Ouriel," *Seminarium Kondakorianum*, 2 (1928), pp. 241-276 and J. Michl, "Engel, IX", *Reallexicon f. Antike u. Christentum*, Vol. V, cols. 254-256.

between Uriel and Jacob might be seen in the narrative of R. Huna, a third century tradent:

> Eventually he (the angel) said to himself: Shall I not inform him with whom he is engaged? What did he do? He put his finger on the earth, whereupon the earth began spouting fire. Jacob said to him: Don't think you can terrify me with that! Why I am altogether of that substance! Thus it is written: AND THE HOUSE OF JACOB SHALL BE A HOUSE OF FIRE (Obad. 1:18).[65]

Uriel, according to at least one tradition, is derived from אוּר אֵל "the fire of God"—and the action of the angel in Huna's account would be thoroughly consistent with that role.[66] Jacob claims an equally exalted, if not superior, role. He is made wholly of fire and, hence, should probably likewise be understood to be claiming an angelic nature.[67]

(4) The content of Uriel's envy is the rank of Jacob-Israel among the heavenly host (A, 11f.). The notion, in apocalyptic literature, of a conflict between the angels of God and the "fallen" angels is familiar; but is not suggested in the *PJ*. Nor do we here have an example analogous to Satan's envy of the newly created Adam and his refusal to worship him. For though Israel has descended among men, both Israel and Uriel are clearly heavenly figures and their conflict is concerned with their relative position within the celestial hierarchy. The theme of one angel gaining domination over another is not unknown in Jewish sources, most particularly in political allegories which narrate the ascendency of one national angel over another.[68]

The theme of angelic rivalry before the Throne may be found in both hellenistic and Hebrew Merkabah literature.[69] Thus, in the

---

[65] *Gen. R.* 77:2, cf. *Midrash R. ad Cant.* 3.6.3. See further W. Bacher, *Die Agada der palästinensischen Amoräer* (Strassburg, 1899), Vol. III, p. 286.

[66] Isodore Seville, *Etym.* VII, 5 (*MPL* LXXXVII, 273) and L. Blau, "Uriel". *Jewish Encyclopaedia*, Vol. XII, p. 383. The text quoted from Obadiah 1.18 בית יעקב אש (ὁ οἶκος Ιακωβ πῦρ) would be sufficient to suggest a conflict between Jacob and the angel of fire (i.e. Uriel). The alternative etymology derives Uriel from אוּר אֵל "light of God."

[67] Cf. *Ex. R.* 15.6 "God compared Israel to the angels ... The angels are called fire because it is written THE FLAMING FIRE, YOUR MINISTERS (Ps. 104:4) and Israel is also so called, as it is written AND THE HOUSE OF JACOB SHALL BE A FIRE (Obad. 1:18)."

[68] See especially the narrative of Gabriel and Dubbiel in BT, *Yoma* 77a (omitted in most mss.) On this passage see E. Langton, *The Ministeries of the Angelic Powers* (London, n.d.), pp. 178f. and Ginzberg, *Legends*, Vol. VI, p. 434.

[69] Central to this tradition is Job 25:2, "Dominion and fear are with him; he makes peace in his heights." See R. Meir(?) *Num. R.* 11.7 "Great is peace,

early apocryphon, the *Apocalypse of Abraham*, which Scholem notes "more closely resembles a Merkabah text than any other in Jewish apocalyptic literature"[70] Jaoel (who plays the role assigned in Hebrew texts to Metatron) is the one "who hath been given to restrain, according to His commandment, the threatening attack of the living creatures of the Cherubim (i.e. the *ḥayyoth*) against one another" (ch. X), while in the vision of the Throne in chapter XVIII, Abraham sees that when the *ḥayyoth* have finished their singing:

> ... they looked at one another and threatened one another. And it came to pass when the angel who was with me saw that they were threatening each other, he left me and went running to them and turned the countenance of each living creature from the countenance immediately confronting him, in order that they might not see their countenances threatening each other. And he taught them the song of peace which hath its origin (in the Eternal One).[71]

---

for the name of the Omnipotent is called Peace as it says 'The Lord is peace' (Judges 6:24). Great is peace for the angels on high need peace as it says (Job 25:2)." cf. bar Kappara in *Lev. R.* 9.9 and, for *Shalom* as the name of God, see A. Mamorstein, *The Old Rabbinic Doctrine of God* (Oxford, 1927), Vol. I, pp. 104f. Cf. the angel סמוסלם in Scholem, *Jewish Gnosticism*, pp. 76 and 134. Frequently combined with Job 25:2 is a conflict between Michael as snow and Gabriel as fire (see esp. R. Simeon b. Laḳish in *Deut. R.* 5.15; R. Simeon b. Yohai in *Midrash R. ad Cant.* 3.11.1; R. Abib in *Num. R.* 12.8, *Midrash R. ad Cant.* 3.11.1. cf. Leucken, *op. cit.*, p. 55). Dependent on, or giving rise to this tradition is the notion of angels being composed half of snow and half of fire (cf. *Gedulath Moshe* 15 in Gaster, *Texts and Studies*, Vol. I, p. 129; *Midrash 'Asereth ha-dibberoth* in Jellinek, *BHM*, Vol. I, p. 66, translated in A. Wünsche, *Aus Israels Lehrhallen* [Leipzig, 1909], Vol. IV, p. 74). The whole complex may ultimately depend on cosmogonic imagery of creation as a mixture of fire and snow or water (see R. Yoḥanan BT, *Rosh hash.* 23b, *Gen. R.* 10.3, *Deut. R.* 5.12; R. Jacob of Kephar-chanin in *Peskita* 3a, PT, *Rosh.hash.* 58a. Cf. 2 *Enoch* 29:2; 3 *Enoch* 42:7 translation H. Odeberg [Cambridge, 1928], pp. 131f.) See, on aspects of this material, G. H. Box, *The Apocalypse of Abraham* (London, 1919), pp. 62f. n. 13 and p. 87 additional note ii. Of direct relevance to the *PJ* is the anonymous midrash on Canticles 3:11 in *Num. R.* 12.8 and *Midrash R. ad Cant.* 3.11.1. "Another explanation is that UPON KING SOLOMON means Upon the king who brought about peace between his handiwork and those who love him. He made peace between the fire and Abraham, between the knife and Isaac and *between the angel and Jacob*. Another explanation is that UPON KING SOLOMON means Upon the king who makes peace between his creatures. The hayyoth were of fire and the firmament of snow... Yet neither did the latter extinguish the former nor did the former consume the latter." [emphasis mine, J.Z.S.]

[70] Scholem, *Jewish Gnosticism*, p.23; cf. Box, *op. cit.*, pp. xxix-xxx.

[71] I have followed the translation of G. H. Box, *op. cit.*, pp. 47 and 63.

As G. H. Box has pointed out, this picture is paralleled by a text in *Tanḥuma, Bereshit* (ed. Buber, Vol. I, p. 10 with correction) which contains a midrash on Job 25:2 "Dominion and fear are with him, he makes peace in his high places". The text in *Tanḥuma* interprets "dominion" as Michael and "fear" as Gabriel and the latter part of the verse as God's action in keeping peace among the angels

> ... for even the heavenly ones need peace. The constellations rise, Taurus says 'I am first and I see what is before him'; the Gemini say 'I am first and I see what is before him' and so each one in his turn says 'I am first.'

It is perhaps significant that in the *Pirke Hekalot* the angel Israel has the function, as one of the *ḥayyoth*, of keeping order among the heavenly choir[72]—a role in close agreement with that of Jaoel in the *Apocalypse of Abraham*. The rivalry in the *PJ*, however, more closely resembles that depicted in *Tanḥuma*.

(5) What is most crucial to our understanding of the *PJ* is that in documents representing both hellenistic and rabbinic Judaism the motifs of Jacob's wrestling by the Jabbok and the theme of angelic rivalry before the Throne are combined. In a variety of midrashim, the angel with whom Jacob wrestled had to return at dawn (Gen. 23: 26a) in order to chant before the Throne. This Jacob prevented until he secured the angel's blessing or until he learned the angel's name (Gen. 32:26b-27).[73] This, coupled with a traditional etymology found in scattered texts of the name Israel as "trying to sing in the place of the angels"[74] suggests the possibility that there was a tradition of angelic rivalry between Jacob-Israel and the archangels similar to that reflected in the *PJ*. This supposition is strengthened, moreover, by the fact that in several sources YHWH not only keeps peace between the angels before His Throne but also between Jacob and the wrestling angel.[75]

---

[72] Jellinek, *BHM* Vol III, pp. 161-3.

[73] Pseudo-Philo *Biblical Antiquities* 18.5 (G. Kisch, *Pseudo-Philo's Liber Antiquitatum Biblicarum* [Notre Dame, 1959], p. 159); *Gen. R.* 78.2; *Midrash R. ad Cant.* 3.6.3; *Pirke de R. Eliezer* 37 and implied in BT, *Hullin* 91b. In *Pirke d. R. Eliezer* 37, Jacob appears to have successfully prevented the angel from returning above to sing at dawn.

[74] *Tanḥuma* (ed. Buber I,127). Ginzberg further cites *Haserot* in Wertheimer's *Batte Midrashot* Vol. III, p. 4 (*non vidi*. See Ginzberg, *Legends*, Vol. V, p. 307 n. 253). I can see no sense in which *Gen. R.* 78.2 may be interpreted as implying that Jacob attempts to sing instead of the angels as Ginzberg (*loc. cit.*) maintains.

[75] *Num. R.* 12.8 ; *Midrash R. ad Cant.* 3.11.1 See above n. 69.

Thus, while the conflict between Jacob-Israel and Uriel in the *PJ* gains its setting from the context between Jacob and the angel by the Jabbok in Genesis 32 (sect. II,3) and draws upon the narratives of Esau and Jacob for the content of the conflict (sect. II,2)—the text is more likely to be explained on the basis of the mystical theme of angelic rivalry before the Merkabah (sect. II,4,5). As in our study of the titles, so here in considering the conflict, we have found nothing that requires the postulation of non-Jewish influence (sect. II,1) and have once more located the *PJ* within circles of mystical Judaism.

III. The Descent Myth

(1) As M. R. James has noted:

> The leading idea of the principal fragment is that angels can become incarnate in human bodies, live on earth in the likeness of men, and be unconscious of their original state. Israel does so apparently in order that he may become the father of the chosen people. It is, I believe, a doctrine which is unique in Jewish teaching.[76]

Indeed it is remarkable! though not unique.[77] The paradigm that is employed here appears to be the Gnostic one of the descent of the heavenly soul, its incarnation in ignorant flesh and its recollection of its supra-mundane origin on encountering a heavenly revealer i.e., the familiar movement from λήθη and ἄγνοια to γνῶσις by means of ἀνάμνησις. The language of Origin's paraphrase of the *PJ* in *Philocalia* XXIII,19 quite strikingly employs the vocabulary of this Gnostic paradigm: καὶ ὄνομα κεκτημένος Ἰσραήλ. ὅπερ ἐν σώματι λειτουργῶν ἀναγνωρίζει, ὑπομιμνήσκοντος αὐτὸν τοῦ ἀρχαγγέλου Οὐριήλ. The simplest solution to the problem posed by this text would be to declare that the descent myth that is quoted from the *PJ* in Origin's *Commentary on John* (A,8-10) contains no suggestion of Jacob-Israel's forgetfulness nor of Uriel's positive role in reminding him of his former state. One might assume that, as the passage in the *Philocalia* is manifestly a paraphrase, Origen simply employs the Platonic language which was natural for him.[78] Or, as a variant to

---

[76] M. R. James, *op. cit.*, p. 30.

[77] M. Smith, in his recent contribution to the *Wolfson Festschrift* (*op. cit.*) has endeavored to demonstrate that "the belief that a particular individual might be a supernatural Power come down to earth and appearing as a man, was reasonably common in first century Palestine" (*op. cit.*, p. 749). He cites the examples of Dositheus, John the Baptist, Jesus, Simon Magus and Menander (p. 743) and includes Jacob-Israel in the *PJ* within this category (pp. 748f.).

[78] The standard treatment of this remains H. Koch, *Pronoia und Paideusis: Studien über Origines und sein Verhältnis zum Platonismus* (Berlin-Leipzig, 1932).

this approach, one might suggest that the sending of angels as revealers into the material world where they become incarnate as the Patriarchs of Israel is a theological motif within Origen's thought. Therefore it might be the case that Origen is here betraying his own interests rather than faithfully reporting the text.[79] So little of the *PJ* has actually survived that it is difficult to have confidence as to a judgement on the accuracy of Origen's report. But the fact that an analogous use of Platonic language and a mystical interpretation of the Patriarchs occurs in Philo leads me to assume that Origen had reason for employing the terms he did. It will be necessary to inquire whether extant Jewish sources contain material that would clarify this mythologoumenon.

(2) The language of the descent myth in the quotation from the *PJ* in Origen's *Commentary on John* clearly derives from the Jewish Wisdom-Shekinah theology that has been the preoccupation of many students of the Prologue to the Fourth Gospel since the pioneering researches of J. Rendel Harris : ὅτι κατέβην ἐπὶ τὴν γῆν καὶ κατεσκήνωσα ἐν ἀνθρώποις, καὶ ὅτι ἐκλήθην ὀνόματι Ἰακώβ (A,8-10). The two terms for descent καταβαίνω and κατασκηνόω are both witnessed to in pre-Christian Wisdom literature as well as in their New Testament adaptations. The clearest parallel to the *PJ* is *The Wisdom of Ben-Sira* 24.8 where Sophia, after wandering all over creation, is told by God who ὁ κτίσας με κατέπαυσεν τὴν σκήνην μου to Ἐν Ἰακὼβ κατασκήνωσον καὶ ἐν Ἰσραὴλ κατακληρονομήθητι. Here

---

M. Joel, *Blicke im die Religionsgeschichte zu Anfang des zweiten christlichen Jahrhunderts* (Breslau, 1880), Vol. I, pp. 118f. attempted to find a Jewish counterpart to the Platonic doctrine of *anamnesis* in the notion that the soul (or embryo) knows everything before it is born, forgets during life and is reminded of what it has known by an angel at death (R. Simlai in BT, *Niddah* 30b cf. the treatise *Seder Yezirat ha-Walad* in Jellinek, *BHM*, Vol. I, pp. 153-5 and the brilliant short story on this theme by I. B. Singer, "Jachid and Jechidah" in *Short Friday* [New York, 1964], pp. 81-90). The parallel is scarcely striking. The Platonic experience of recollection occurs during life; in the Jewish material it occurs at the point of, or after, death. It would appear that the Jewish tradition is secondary to the discussion of the purity of the soul before birth and debates concerning the point at which the *Yetzer ha-ra* is able to exercise influence on an individual.

[79] *De princ.* IV,3,12 etc. This theme employs the allegory of the descent into Egypt being a descent into the material world (cf. the interpretation of Genesis 46:3 in *Hom. ad Gen.* 15.5 etc.) an interpretation which is Philonic. See on this theme, J. Daniélou, *Origen* (New York, 1955), pp. 247-9; Daniélou, "Les sources juives de la doctrine des anges des nations chez Origène," *Recherches de Science Religieuse*, 38 (1951), p. 134; H. Crouzel, *Origène et la "connaissance mystique"* (*Museum Lessianum*, 1961), pp. 98-101, 305-12.

Sophia is identified with the Torah accepted by Israel after the other nations have refused it (cf. vs. 23 and *Baruch* 3.37f.). Likewise Israel's title in the *PJ*, πρωτόγονος as well as the notion that Abraham and Isaac προεκτίσθησαν πρὸ παντὸς ἔργου would appear to derive from speculation as to the role of Wisdom-Torah in the Creation.[80] But, as was noted above (see pp. 40f.), if theories as to the pre-existence of the Law and the nation Israel might be personified; so here, in the text from *Ben-Sira*, a mystical interpretation would read that Sophia became incarnate in the Patriarch, Jacob-Israel. This sort of mystical reading is represented by the Philonic model of a *hieros gamos* between the Patriarchs and Sophia, as elucidated by Goodenough.[81]

---

[80] Thus W. L. Knox (*op. cit.*, p. 112) explains the tradition in the *Assumptio Moysis* 1.14 *itaque excogitavit et invenit me, qui ab initio orbis terrarum praeparatus sum* (ed. Fritzsche, p. 703 cf. the Greek citation in Gelasius Cyz., *Comm. Act. Synodi. Nic.* II.18). "Firstborn" appears to be used as a title for Jacob by R. Nathan in *Ex. R.* 19.7.
Possibly there is some relation to the doctrine within heterodox Judaism of the world being created by an angel e.g. in the teachings of Simon Magus, Menander, Saturninus (cf. Grant, *op. cit.*, pp. 15-18); the doctrine of the Magharians (see L. Nemoy, "Al-Qirqisānī's Account of the Jewish Sects and Christianity," *Hebrew Union College Annual*, 7 [1930], pp. 363-4, H. A. Wolfson, "The Preexistent Angel of the Magharians and Al-Nahāwandi," *Jewish Quarterly Review*, 51 [1960], pp. 89-106.). Daniélou (*Theology*, p. 134) compares a Novatianist inscription first published by A. M. Calder, "Epigraphy of Anatolian Heresies," *Anatolian Studies presented to Sir William Mitchell Ramsay*, London, 1923, pp. 76f. no. 4: πρῶτον μὲν ὑμνήσω Θεὸν τὸν πάντει ὁρόωντα δεύτερον ὑμνήσω πρῶτον ἄγγελον ΟΣΤΙ ΣΑΙΤΡΣΙΝ (cf. H. Grégoire, "Epigraphie chrétienne," *Byzantion*, 1 [1924], pp. 699f. and idem., "Un nom mystique du Christ," *Byzantion*, 2 [1925]. pp. 449-53). Possibly, one might also relate the tradition which renders בראשית in Gen. 1:1 as ראשית and reads either "In the beginning God created a Son" or "In the Son, God created" which is found in several Jewish-Christian texts e.g. Jerome, *Quaest. Heb. in Gen.* 1.1: *in Altercatione Jasonis et Papisci scriptum est ... in Hebraeo haberi, in Filio fecit Deus caelum et terram*. (*MPG* V:1279 and notes 39, 40) Cf. Irenaeus, *Dem.* 43 (following J. P. Smith, "Hebrew Christian Midrash in Irenaeus," *Biblica*, 38 [1957], pp. 24-34); Tertullian, *Adv. Prax.* 5; Hilary of Poitiers, *Tract. Psalm.* II,2 and several polemic documents (see A. L. Williams, *Adversus Judaeos* [Cambridge, 1935], p. 29 n. 3) See further Harnack, *Evagrius' Altercatio Simonis et Judaei et Theophili Christiani* (Berlin, 1883), p. 130f. and Daniélou, *Theology*, pp. 167f. For a general survey on the relationship of Wisdom-Creation-Son traditions see J. R. Harris, *The Origin of the Prologue to St. John's Gospel* (Cambridge, 1917); Knox, *op. cit.*, ch. v; C. F. Burney, "Christ as the 'Ἀρχή of Creation," *Journal of Theological Studies*, 27 (1926), pp. 160-77; W. D. Davies, *Paul and Rabbinic Judaism*, 2ed. (London, 1958), ch. vii and Daniélou, *Theology*, pp. 166-72.

[81] Goodenough, *By Light, Light*, pp. 157-60, 164 *et passim*. I would agree with Goodenough that "the passages are not altogether satisfactory" in depicting a marriage between Jacob and Sophia but that it may be clearly inferred.

(3) The uniqueness of the decensus myth in the paraphrase of the *PJ* in Origen's *Philocalia* is that it is not the heavenly Sophia who incarnates herself or marries Jacob, but the heavenly Israel who becomes incarnate in his earthly counterpart, the Patriarch Jacob. Any speculation that is relevant to the *PJ* concerning descent-ascent must be related to the figures of the heavenly and earthly Jacob-Israel. The obvious point of focus about which such speculations would cluster is "Jacob's Ladder" in the vision at Bethel (Genesis 28:10-27). For here is a moment of contact, of entry and re-entry between the celestial and terrestrial realms as well as an explicit reference to angels "ascending and descending".

The biblical narrative presents the familiar picture of Jacob sleeping on the ground, the heavenly ladder with angels ascending and descending on it and, at its summit, the figure of YHWH. The *Targumim* provide a motivation for the angels' movement and, incidentally, attempt to explain why angels should first ascend, then descend:

> ... the angels who had accompanied him from the house of his father ascended to make known to the angels on high saying, Come, see Jacob the pious whose image is on the Throne of Glory and whom you have desired to see. And behold, the holy angels of the Presence of the Lord descended to look upon him.[82]

The tradition of the face of Jacob engraved on the Merkabah in early rabbinic sources most likely indicates a tendency to merge the Patriarchs with the *hayyoth*; but may also be a reflection of, or possibly the source of the tradition of the heavenly Israel.[83] Thus in a

---

[82] *Jerusalem Targum* ad Genesis 28:12, M. Ginsburger, ed., *Das Fragmententhargum* (Berlin, 1899), p. 16. I have adapted the translation of J. W. Etheridge, *The Targums of Onkelos and Jonathan* (London, 1862), Vol. I, pp. 252f.

[83] Cf. the anonymous Tannaitic *baraitha* in BT, *Hullin* 91b "They ascended to look at the image above and descended to look at the image below": *Gen. R.* 68:12; 78:3 etc. Joel, *op. cit.*, Vol. I, p. 117 unconvincingly attempts to provide a hellenistic parallel.

For the tradition that "the Patriarchs are the Merkabah" see R. Simeon b. Laķish in *Gen. R.* 47:6; 69:3; 82:6 (on this dictum see Scholem, *Major Trends*, p. 79; M. Smith, *op. cit.*, p. 507 and n. 3). Cf. *Zohar* I.173b (Sperling-Simon translation, Vol. II, p. 164) "AND GOD WENT UP FROM HIM IN THE PLACE WHERE HE SPOKE WITH HIM. R. Simeon said, From here we learn that Jacob formed the Holy Chariot together with the other patriarchs, further that Jacob constitutes the supernal Holy Chariot which will restore the full light of the moon and that he forms a Chariot by himself..." A reflection of the Jacob as the Merkabah tradition is to be seen in the interpretation of a saying of R. Simon b. Laķish (that God showed Jacob a three legged throne) by R. Levi, "Thou (i.e. Jacob) are the third leg" (*Gen. R.* 68:12). Abraham

remarkable passage in *Hekhaloth Rabbati* 9, God embraces, kisses and caresses the image of Jacob engraved on the Merkabah when Israel chants the Kedusha.[84]

The extended elaboration of this theme may be seen from a discussion between two first century Palestinian Amoraim, R. Ḥiyya and R. Yannai:

> R. Ḥiyya and R. Yannai differed (as to the meaning of בו in Gen. 28:12b), the one said: The angels ascended and descended on the ladder (בסולם); the other said: They ascended and descended on Jacob (ביעקב), they praised him and slandered him,[85] they ran about him, on him, sneered at him—for it is written, YOU, O ISRAEL, IN WHOM I WILL BE GLORIFIED (Is. 49:3),[86] that is said in the sense of: You are he whose image is engraved on high. They ascended on high and saw his image, they descended on earth and saw him sleeping. This is like a king who sits and judges; they ascend to his throne room and find him seated in judgement, they descend to his chamber and find him sleeping ... They (i.e. the angels) would have tried to harm him, but THE LORD STOOD BESIDE HIM. R. Simeon b. Laḳish said: If it were not thus written, it would have been impossible for us to say it. The Lord was like a father fanning his sleeping child to keep the flies away ...[87] R. Ḥiyya and R. Yannai differed (as to the meaning of עליו in Gen. 28:13a), the one said: The Lord stood beside the ladder; the other said: He stood beside Jacob ... R. Simeon b. Laḳish said: It shows that the Patriarchs form the Merkabah (i.e. taking על in the sense of "upon" and the masculine suffix to refer to Jacob).[88]

In the debate between Ḥiyya and Yannai and the interpolated comments of Simeon b. Laḳish, many of the motifs we have been con-

---

and Isaac are clearly the other two legs (cf. Goodenough, *Jewish Symbols*, Vol. IV, p. 183 n. 124). Cf. the mystical interpretation of YHWH standing "over" Jacob in the Bethel vision in the *Zohar* I. 150a (Sperling-Simon, Vol. II, p. 81) "the Lord was standing over him (i.e. Jacob) so as to form the Divine Chariot, with the community of Israel, embodied in Jacob, as the uniting link in their midst..."

[84] Jellinek, *BHM*, III, 90. Translated by P. Bloch in J. Winter - A. Wünsche, *Die jüdische Literatur seit Abschluss des Kanons* (Berlin, 1897) Vol. III, p. 238. I am indebted to Prof. N. A. Dahl for calling my attention to this important text.

[85] מעלים ומורידים בו might this be interpreted more literally "they raised him up and put him down"?

[86] This link between the hostility of the angels towards Jacob and the glorification of Israel may be paralleled in the midrashic elaboration of the refusal of the angels to glorify Adam, the "image" of God. See the sources in Ginzberg, *Legends*, Vol. V, pp. 69f. and M. Smith, "The Image of God", pp. 478-80 and 480 n. 1.

[87] R. Simeon b. Laḳish's dictum is attributed to R. Abbahu in BT, *Hullin* 91a and *Gen. R.* 63. 12.

[88] *Gen. R.* 68. 13-69. 3.

sidering are gathered together: the heavenly image of Jacob on the Throne, the contrast between the heavenly image of Jacob and the figure of the Patriarch sleeping below, the Patriarchs as constituting the Merkabah, the hostility of the angels toward Jacob-Israel and the ascent-descent of the angels. In addition, R. Yannai's interpretation of בו as ביעקב implies a mystical growth of Jacob to cosmic size, a theme present in the Fourth Gospel's allusion to the Ladder vision (ὄψεσθε τὸν οὐρανὸν ἀνεῳγότα καὶ τοὺς ἀγγέλους τοῦ θεοῦ ἀναβαίνοντας καὶ καταβαίνοντας ἐπὶ τὸν Υἱὸν τοῦ ἀνθρώπου Jn. 1:51)[89] and, perhaps, in the figure of Metatron as the personified Ladder of Jacob in late mystical literature.[90]

More crucially for the *PJ* and the question of the apparent Gnostic terminology in Origen's paraphrase in the *Philocalia* is the distinction between the image of Jacob on the Merkabah above and the sleeping figure below. Regardless of how the rabbis quoted may have understood the contrast, in view of the widespread metaphor of sleep as ignorance of God or of one's true self,[91] such a distinction may well have given rise to the picture in the paraphrase of the *PJ* of Israel's forgetfulness of his heavenly origin.[92]

---

[89] See C. F. Burney, *The Aramaic Origin of the Fourth Gospel* (Oxford, 1922), pp. 115f. and H. Odeberg, *The Fourth Gospel* (Uppsala-Stockholm, 1929), pp. 33-42. Some suggestion of this tradition may also be reflected in Philo's allegory of the Ladder in *Somn.* I,146f. My attention was first called to the notion of the soul growing to cosmic size as a motif distinct from the *Himmelreise der Seele* by Professor Carsten Colpe in his discussion of *Corpus Hermeticum* IV, 4f. and X. 25 (see the privately printed minutes of his seminar on the *Hermetica* at Yale University, 1963-1964, p. 18).

[90] See the texts cited in H. Odeberg, *3 Enoch* (Cambridge, 1928), "Introduction", p. 123.

[91] See the excellent collection of texts in H. Jonas, *The Gnostic Religion*, 2ed. (Boston, 1963), pp. 69f., 80-6, 92 *et passim*. (*idem.*, *Gnosis und spätantiker Geist* 3e. [Göttingen, 1964], Vol. I, pp. 113-15, 126-34 *et passim*.). Here the stress is upon the sleep of Adam. In addition see the striking text in *Corpus Hermeticum* I. 27 which most likely reflects Jewish background (see C. H. Dodd, *The Bible and the Greeks* [London, 1954], pp. 159f., 178f., 187f.). In Jewish literature, sleep is most usually the state in which the soul "wanders" from the body and may receive revelation by either vision or mystic ascent. These two notions of sleep as ignorance and precondition for revelation are not necessarily antithetical. See *Corpus Hermeticum* I. 1 where they are combined.

[92] H. Odeberg, *The Fourth Gospel*, pp. 37f. (accepted by R. Bultmann, *Das Evangelium des Johannes* [Göttingen, 1962], p. 74 n. 4 cf. his *Ergänzungsheft* [Göttingen, 1957] p. 19 *ad loc*. See further C. H. Dodd, *The Interpretation of the Fourth Gospel* [Cambridge, 1958], pp. 245f.) who argues from the passage in Gen. R. 68. 18: "The Divine utterance 'I will be glorified in thee' does not refer to Israel as he is in his earthly appearance (i.e. as Jacob) but to his ideal counterpart in heaven, his celestial appearance (i.e. as Israel properly). The

The one element not to be found in any Jewish source that I am familiar with is the notion that the celestial Israel descended or the terrestrial Jacob ascended,[93] but the ascent-descent of the angels on "Jacob's Ladder" would be, in itself, sufficient to provide the origin of this motif.

In this section, as in the preceding ones, I have sought to demonstrate that there is nothing in the *PJ* which is not explicable in terms of Jewish tradition. Specifically, with respect to the descent myth, I have attempted to defend the reliability of Origen's paraphrase in light of traditions surrounding Jacob's vision at Bethel.

(4) The *PJ* may be termed a myth of the mystery of Israel. As such it is a narrative of the descent of the chief angel Israel and his incarnation within the body of Jacob and of his recollection and ascent to his former heavenly state. This myth bears striking resemblance to a variety of traditions within the hellenistic Mediterranean world. The descent of a celestial being to earth, his forgetfulness of his previous state, his recollection upon meeting an angelic figure and his return (at times with combat) above fits well into what might be termed the common Gnostic pattern.[94] Whether we are to interpret the earthly Jacob-Israel as a thoroughly docetic figure (similar to the pattern of Cerinthus' Christ); as an appearance and incarnation of a heavenly

---

contrast obtaining between man's celestial and terrestrial appearance is thus emphasized by the dictum. In view of the simile used as illustration (the King in judgement contrasted with the King in sleep) there is not a doubt but that the celestial appearance is meant to be conveyed as the real man. Further, the 'sleep' is also, in all probability, taken in a mystical sense: the earthly man is, in regard to his real life, as one who sleeps." In a private communication (April 26, 1965) Professor Morton Smith has persuasively argued against Odeberg's interpretation of the simile. "Odeberg should have asked himself How can a King who sits and judges be in two places at once? The answer is, because in the judgement hall there is a statue representing him judging which can be seen even while the real King is at home asleep. So the image of Israel, as it should be, is on the throne while the real Israel is asleep below—and thus, the angels both praise and denigrate him."

[93] Indeed Jacob's ascent is specifically denied in the wide spread allegory of the guardians of the other nations partially ascending the Ladder while Jacob is afraid to do so—thus condemning his descendants to serve other nations. See *Sifre*, Numbers 119 ; *Midrash Tehillim* 78. 6 ; *Leviticus R.* 29.2. Cf. *Gen. R.* 68.14; *Pirke d. R. Eliezer* 35 and the late adaptation of this legend in the Slavonic *Ladder of Jacob* 4-5. However, compare R. Jacob in *Shir Ha-shirim Zuta* 1.4 on the phrase in Gen. 35:1 "ARISE, GO UP TO BETHEL. This teaches that the Holy One, blessed be He, showed him (i.e. Jacob) one level above another and showed him also the celestial realms"—clearly a fragment of an ascent-legend in connection with the Ladder vision.

[94] See above, p. 54.

power (analogous to Morton Smith's discussion of Dositheus, John, Jesus, Simon and Menander) or as a heavenly messenger (as elucidated in the works of G. Widengren) remains, for me, a moot question.[95] However it is characteristic of all of these patterns that the myth may be ritually appropriated by its believers, that the 'objective" narrative has a 'subjective' correlative. That which is accomplished by the paradigmatic figure of the Patriarch Jacob-Israel may, presumably, also be achieved by the "sons of Jacob". The pattern of this 'subjective' experience would be the ascent of the mystic to the Merkabah, an ascent fraught with peril from angelic adversaries, an ascent which results in a vision of the form of God on the celestial Throne.[96] The way of ascent for a son of Jacob, as I suspect it was for Jacob-Israel, is the *scala Iacobi* (significantly, such an interpretation is at least hinted at in Origen, *Contra Celsum* VI, 21).[97] Thus the *PJ* takes its place among a host of texts

---

[95] See especially G. Bardy, "Cérinthe", *Revue Biblique*, 30 (1921), 344-373; M. Smith, "The Account of Simon Magus", *Wolfson Festschrift* and G. Widengren, *The Great Vohu Manah and the Apostle of God; Mesopotamian Elements in Manichaeism; The Ascension of the Apostle and the Heavenly Book* and *Muhammed, the Apostle of God and his Ascension* (Uppsala-Wiesbaden, 1955). To the last two patterns might be compared the much discussed issue of angel-Christology. See, especially, A. Bakker, "Christ an Angel?", *Zeitschrift f. d. neutestamentliche Wissenschaft*, 32 (1933), 255-265; J. Barbel, *Christos Angelos* (Bonn, 1941); M. Werner, *Die Entstehung des christlichen Dogmas* (Leipzig, 1941), pp. 302-389 and cf. W. Michaelis, *Zur Engelchristologie im Urchristentum* (Basel, 1942). For a brief review of recent literature see M. Werner, *The Formation of Christian Doctrine* (London, 1957), p. 130 n. 1; J. Barbel, "Zur Engelchristologie im Urchristentum," *Theologische Rundschau*, 54 (1958), cols. 49-58, 103-112.

[96] See, in general, M. Smith, "Observations on Hekhalot Rabbati", in A. Altmann, ed., *Biblical and Other Studies* (Cambridge Mass., 1963), pp. 142-160 which effectively points to parallels between hellenistic and rabbinic ascent materials, a point already suggested in a preliminary way by W. Bousset, "Die Himmelreise der Seele", *Archiv für Religionswissenschaft*, 4 (1901), p. 153. See further, G. Scholem, *Jewish Gnosticism*, pp. 75-83. One might also profitably compare the mythologem of heavenly enthronement especially as elucidated by Scandinavian history of religions research. See G. Widengren, "Den himmelska intronisation och dopet", *Religion och Bibel*, 5 (1946), 28-61 especially p. 29; Widengren, "Baptism and Enthronement in some Jewish-Christian Gnostic Documents" in S. G. F. Brandon, ed., *The Saviour God: Comparative Studies in the Concept of Salvation presented to Edwin Oliver James* (New York, 1963), pp. 205-217; H. Reisenfeld, *Jesus transfiguré* (Copenhagen, 1947) and P. Beskow, *Rex Gloriae* (Uppsala, 1962), pp. 127-131, cf. pp. 103-106, 147-156.

[97] H. Chadwick, *Origen: Contra Celsum* (Cambridge, 1953), pp. 333f. See further, F. Cumont, *Afterlife in Roman Paganism* (New York, 1959), pp. 153f. and, especially, W. L. Knox, *Some Hellenistic Elements in Primitive Christianity* (London, 1944), p. 59 n. 1 who compares it with Aristides, *Hieroi Logoi* iii.48. This observation as well as others made in this paper renders imperative that a

witnessing to what I have come to believe is *the* fundamental pattern of hellenistic Mediterranean religions—an astrological mystery involving the descent-ascent of a heavenly figure, the *Himmelreise der Seele* of the believer through the astral-angelic spheres and magical-theurgic practices.[98] What distinguishes the *PJ* from other ascent-literature is the paradigmatic figure of Jacob-Israel, for, within Hebrew and Aramaic Merkabah texts, the Patriarch's play no normative role (save in Simeon b. Lakish's dictum that the "Patriarchs are the Merkabah" quoted above).[99]

---

careful study be made of the use of Gen. 25:10-17 in Jewish and Christian tradition. The only recent treatment that I am familiar with is C. A. Patrides, "Renaissance Interpretations of Jacob's Ladder", *Theologische Zeitschrift*, 18 (1962), pp. 411-418. While I think his interpretation excessive, note Goodenough's discussion of Exodus 19:4; Deut. 32:11 and *Assumption of Moses* (Charles, Vol. II, p. 422) as capable of being understood as referring to the astral ascent of Israel. Once again, what might be said of the Nation could be read as referring to the Patriarch. A further instance of Gen 28 understood as a ladder of mystical-initiatory ascent occurs in the Naassene exegesis of the Attis Hymn in Hippolytus, *Ref.* V. 8.81-91 in which Psalm 24:7,9; Gen. 28:17 and John 10:9 are correlated with the ascent of Anthropos.

[98] For general treatments of these motifs see W. Bousset, "Die Himmelreise der Seele", *Archiv für Religionswissenschaft*, 4 (1901), 136-169, 229-273 (reprinted Darmstadt, 1960); A. Dieterich, *Eine Mithrasliturgie*, 1ed. (Leipzig, 1903), pp. 179-212 (I regret that the two subsequent editions are not available to me at this writing); F. Cumont, "Le mysticisme astral dans l'antiquité", *Bulletin de l'Académie Royale de Belgique* 1909 (Classes des lettres), pp. 256-286; A-J. Festugière, *La révélation d'Hermès Trismégiste* Vol. I *L'astrologie et les sciences occultes*, 3ed. (Paris, 1950); M. Nilsson, "Die astrale Unsterblichkeit und der kosmischen Mystik", *Numen*, 1 (1954), pp. 106-119; J. Lewy, *Chaldean Oracles and Theurgy* (Cairo, 1956) and the works cited above, n. 96. Goodenough's treatment of this theme in *Jewish Symbols*, Vol. VIII, pp. 167-218 seems to me to be one of his weaker sections. From the perspective of History of Religions, the larger question must ultimately be raised as to the structural parallels between these Hellenistic and Jewish ascent and theurgic practices and other ecstatic initiatory procedures. See, in a preliminary way, the specialized study of J. W. Hauer, *Die Dhāraṇī im nördlichen Buddhismus und ihre Parallelen in der sogenannten Mithrasliturgie* (Stuttgart, 1927), esp. pp. 20-25 which is not, however, very satisfactory. More generally, see M. Eliade, *Shamanism* (New York, 1964), esp. pp. 375-403, 487-494.

[99] See n. 83, above. Also the traditions collected by M. Smith, "The Image of God", pp. 478-81 on the deification of the righteous through worship by being given the name of God. To the extent that this tradition is based on Genesis 33:20 where Jacob erects an altar at Shechem and called it ישראל אל אלהי it is still relevant to our text. Cf. BT, *Meg.* 18a "R. Aḥa said in the name of R. Eleazer: Where do we learn that the Holy One, blessed be He, called Jacob by the name of *El*? It is said (quoting Gen. 33:20)... this means AND JACOB WAS CALLED EL. Who called him thus? the God of Israel." Cf. R. Simeon b. Lakish in *Gen. R.* 79.8 "Jacob meant: Thou art the Lord of all heavenly things and I am the lord of all earthly things"; and *Zohar* I.138a. Note that

However, as Goodenough has demonstrated in *By Light, Light*, within hellenistic Judaism, the Patriarchs play just such a role.[100] Thus, without attempting a detailed demonstration, it should be noted that elements I find within the theology of the *PJ* appear reflected in Goodenough's discussion of the symbolism of the "great reredos" in the Dura Synagogue.[101] The reredos is dominated by the great Vine which is, in part, a ladder.[102] To one side, at the foot of the Vine, is the reclining figure of the Patriarch Jacob; in the branches is the figure of Orpheus, the heavenly singer; and, at the summit, is the Throne and the Powers. While the emphasis in the *PJ* is on the descent of Israel and, in Goodenough's exposition of the Dura fresco, on the ascent, the "value" remains similar:

> ... blessed at the bottom by the Patriarch wearing the white robe of a man of God on earth, Israel can go up to stand permanently beside the Throne with the Powers.[103]

A further parallel is found in a hellenistic Jewish spell entitled Προσευχὴ Ἰακώβ![104] Here the petitioner, after invoking God and his saving acts, prays:

> Fill me with wisdom, empower me, Master. Fill my heart with good things, Master, because I am an angel on earth, because I have become immortal, because I have received the gift from thee.

Here, in the name of Jacob (most likely, though not demonstrably, the Patriarch) we gain a picture of the 'subjective' experience of one who, receiving the "gift" of *sophia*, realizes that he is "an angel on

---

in *Gen. R.* 79.8, R. Huna rejects R. Simeon b. Lakish's exegesis (cf. *Sifre, Deut.* 355; *Midrash ha-Gadol* I,552f. etc.). A similar tradition is connected with the name *Jeshuran* e.g. R. Berekiah in the name of R. Simon, "There is none like unto God. Yet who is like God? Jeshuran which means Israel the Patriarch. Just as it is written of God AND THE LORD ALONE SHALL BE EXALTED (Is. 2:11) so also of Jacob AND JACOB WAS LEFT ALONE (Gen. 32:25)." in *Gen.* R. 77.1.

[100] Goodenough, *By Light, Light*, esp. chs. v and vi.
[101] Goodenough, *Jewish Symbols*, Vol. IX, pp. 78-123.
[102] *ibid.*, pp. 80 and n. 86. Cf. Vol. VIII, pp. 148-57 and M. Eliade, *Patterns in Comparative Religion* (New York, 1958), pp. 102-11.
[103] *ibid.*, p. 107.
[104] Berlin, P. gr. 13895 in Preisendanz, *PGM*, Vol. II, pp. 148f. It would be difficult to improve on the superb English rendering of this text in Goodenough, *Jewish Symbols*, Vol. II, p. 203 or to disagree with his conclusion that the *Prayer* is "quite unimpeachable as a product of hellenized Judaism ... the prayer seems to me to be one which Philo himself could have repeated from beginning to end, or could himself have written, since it is a prayer for transfiguration" (pp. 203f.).

earth" (ὡς ἄγγελον ἐπίγειον),[105] and has thereby "become immortal".

It is within such a circle of hellenistic Judaism which speaks of the ascent of the Patriarchs to the full reality of their heavenly (angelic) nature that the *PJ* is to be located. The Προσευχὴ Ἰωσήφ is the narrative of the "objective" mythology of the heavenly figure; the Προσευχὴ Ἰακώβ is the expression of the 'subjective' experience of this salvation within the individual believer.

The complete pattern might be illustrated by the figure of Enoch, especially as he appears in the Slavonic *Enoch* which contains much old tradition. Here Enoch was originally a man (I, preamble); ascends to heaven *and becomes an angel* (XXII,4-10 cf. 3 *Enoch* 10.3-4 and 48C); returns to earth as a man (XXXIII,5-10) and finally returns above to resume his angelic station (LXVII,2).[106]

I have attempted to demonstrate that the *PJ* must be placed within the environment of first or second century Jewish mysticism by examining the most striking elements in the text: the titles of the angel Jacob-Israel, the conflict between Jacob-Israel and Uriel and the descent of the heavenly Israel. In each instance I have sought to point to parallel traditions in available hellenistic Jewish and rabbinic documents.

The existence of an angel Israel is implies in both hellenistic (Jewish) magical papyri and in late Jewish mystical literature, in rabbinic material concerning the name of the angel with whom Jacob wrestled and in Hekhaloth literature which speaks of a heavenly Israel who leads the angelic liturgy before the Throne (sect. I,2). While the various titles given to Israel in the *PJ* are paralleled by those borne by Michael in rabbinic and apocalyptic texts, Metatron in Jewish mystical documents and Christ in Jewish-Christian authors (sect. I,2,3,6,7,8) as well as titles applied to Jacob-Israel within the Old Testament and its midrashim (sect.

---

[105] Cf. the material collected in H. Corbin, "Cyclical Time in Mazdaism and Ismailism" in J. Campbell, ed., *Man and Time : Papers from the Eranos Yearbooks III* (New York, 1957), pp. 114-172 esp. pp. 164,167 on "angelomorphosis" and in his *Avicenna* pp. 46, 71, 83, 90, 111, 114, 182 on the concept of *fereshtagī* i.e. "angelicity". See further the important summary statement on p. 21 on the "connection, little analyzed hitherto, between angelology and mysticism."

[106] The passages from Slavonic *Enoch* have been cited according to W. R. Morfill-R. H. Charles, *The Book of the Secrets of Enoch* (Oxford, 1896). In the new text and translation by A. Vaillant, *Le Livre des Secrets d'Hénoch* (Paris, 1952) XXII=IX (pp. 25-27); XXXIII=XI (p. 33); LXVII=XVIII (p. 65). See further H. Odeberg, "Foreställningarna om Metatron i äldre judisk mystik", *Kyrkohistorisk Årsskrift*, 27 (1927), 1-20 especially p. 6.

I,1,2,4,5,8)—the most striking parallels are to be found in those assigned to the *Logos* by Philo (esp. sect. I,4).

In considering the contest between Jacob-Israel and Uriel, I dismissed the arguments of previous scholars that this represents either anti-Christian or anti-Jewish polemic or that the conflict stems from Jewish gnosticism, maintaining that the *PJ* is a positive Jewish document (sect. II,1). Certain features appear to be drawn from the legends of conflict between Jacob and Esau (sect. II,2); but the setting is clearly to be traced to Jacob wrestling with the angel in Genesis 32 (sect. II,3). I sought to place the conflict within the context of angelic rivalry before the Throne of God as witnessed to in both hellenistic and rabbinic mystical literature (sect. II,4,5).

The problem of the gnostic language of the descent myth, especially as presented in Origen's paraphrase of the *PJ* in the *Philocalia*, was likewise to be interpreted on the basis of Jewish material (sect. III,1,2). I suggested that the mythologies of Israel's incarnation in Jacob and ignorance of his heavenly origin might be drawn from first century discussions of Jacob's Ladder with the angels ascending and descending between the image of Jacob on the Merkabah and the sleeping figure of the Patriarch below (sect. III,3). Finally, I pointed to two witnesses from hellenistic Judaism which appeared to give the 'subjective' correlative of the ascent-experience 'objectified' in the descent myth and suggested that the emphasis on the archetypical role of the Patriarch (an emphasis lacking in rabbinic Merkabah texts) most probably locates the *PJ* within the sphere of hellenistic mystical Judaism (sect. III,4).[107]

---

[107] I am deeply indebted to Prof. Nils A. Dahl, who first aroused my interest in the *PJ*, for his careful critical reading of the final draft of this paper and for graciously sharing with me his own unpublished lecture on the subject; though we disagree in our interpretation of the *PJ*, his comments, criticisms and suggestions have been a precious source of aid; to Professors H. Lester, W. Meeks, J. Neusner, M. Smith and K. Stendahl for reading this paper in various drafts and for their incisive criticisms and suggestions; to Père J. Daniélou for his courteous response to my questions; to Professors H. Craig, Jr., G. Lawell, G. Quispel, C. Bradford Wells and Mr. D. Gunn for suggestions and assistance on specific problems.

AFTERWORD

The fragments of the *PJ* have been conveniently edited by A.-M. Denis. *Fragmenta Pseudepigraphorum Graeca* ([*Pseudepigrapha Veteris Testamenti Graeca*, vol. III] Leiden, 1970), pp. 61f. and discussed by Denis in *Introduction aux pseudépigraphes grecs d'Ancien Testament* ([*Studia in Veteris Testamenti Pseudepigrapha*, vol. I] Leiden, 1970), pp. 125-127. I regret, when originally writing this essay, I had not seen H. Priebatsch, *Die Josephsgeschichte in der Weltliteratur: Eine legendengeschichtliche Studie* (Breslau, 1937), pp. iv-v, xvii, 8-14, 22f., 33f., 37-44 who offers a fantastic argument for a first century Essene provenance, and suggests that Philo knew the *PJ*! Of more significance is a personal communication from Professor Gershom Scholem which states that he has always believed the *PJ* to be a Jewish mystical text.

While I have added many more parallels, they only strengthen the position argued in the paper. I would call attention to the important article by G. Vermes, "The Archangel Sariel: A Targumic Parallel to the Dead Sea Scrolls," in J. Neusner, ed., *Christianity, Judaism and Other Greco-Roman Cults: Festschrift M. Smith* ([*Studies in Judaism in Late Antiquity*, vol. XIII] Leiden, 1975), Vol. III, pp. 159-166, which makes all but certain, without reference to the *PJ*, the antiquity and Palestinian provenance of the *PJ*'s combat tradition on the basis of the *Neofiti Targum* to Genesis 32:25-32 which identifies the angel with whom Jacob wrestled as Sariel "the chief of those who praise on high". As noted above (and expanded by Vermes) Suriel appears in place of Uriel in the Ethiopic version of I *Enoch* 9:1; in I *Enoch* 10:1 one Greek manuscript reads Uriel, another reads Israel and the Ethiopic reads Asreelyor. Likewise, Vermes' explanation of the identification strengthens my suggestion that "it is possible that the angel Israel's service before the 'face of God' (as well as the motif of his 'seeing') may be based on the title *Peniel* ... in Genesis 32:30." I shall make full use of this article in my forthcoming commentary on the *PJ* in the Duke-Doubleday edition of the Pseudepigrapha edited by J. Charlesworth.

CHAPTER THREE

WISDOM AND APOCALYPTIC

One of the more vexing problems in contemporary Biblical scholarship is that of determining the relationship between Wisdom and Apocalypticism. It is my hope that in this essay, writing as a historian of religions, I shall raise a set of questions which stem from presuppositions different from those frequently employed by specialists in Biblical research, and shall utilize as evidence a wider range of materials than those usually considered and thus achieve some modest progress towards a resolution of this problem. Therefore I shall not confine myself to questions such as the mythology of the figure of Wisdom in apocalyptic literature or the relationship of wisdom and apocalyptic literature to prophecy; rather, I shall take a more oblique approach and focus on materials removed from a Jewish or Christian provenance. I do so partly because I believe that such an examination may raise new questions and categories for further research and partly because of my own presuppositions as to the international character of many religious phenomena (including wisdom and apocalypticism) in the period of late Antiquity.[1] I should like to join with Hans Dieter Betz in arguing that "Jewish and, subsequently, Christian apocalypticism as well, cannot be understood from themselves or from the Old Testament alone, but must be seen and presented as peculiar expressions within the entire development of Hellenistic syncretism;"[2] although I differ from Betz in largely rejecting the explanatory utility of the concept of syncretism and by emphasizing the continuity of Hellenistic religious forms with the archaic.[3]

I agree with Betz and von Rad that apocalypticism cannot be reduced to a mere catalogue of elements such as secret or heavenly books, journeys to heaven by a sage, etc., as these motifs can be found within the archaic religions of the Near East and are typical

---

[1] See J. Z. Smith, "Native Cults in the Hellenistic Period," *History of Religions*, 11 (1971), esp. 236-239.

[2] H. D. Betz, "Zum Problem des religionsgeschichtlichen Verständnisses der Apokalyptik," *Zeitschrift für Theologie und Kirche*, 63 (1966), 409; English transl. *Journal for Theology and Church*, 6 (1969), 155.

[3] Smith, *op. cit.*

of all modes of Hellenistic religiosity.[4] What I should like to explore in this paper is the pattern of these elements in combination and their underlying social structure in the apocalyptic literature of Late Antiquity.

I

A valuable starting point for our inquiry may be gained by a consideration of the fragments from the *Babyloniaka* of Berossus.[5] A priest of Marduk in Babylon, he wrote his book c. 290-280 B.C. and dedicated it to Antiochus I, Sotēr.

The *testimonia* concerning Berossus divide into two categories. From Greco-Roman authors we learn that he was an astronomer, astrologer (Vitruvius, *De arch.* 9.6.2; Pliny, *N.H.* 7.123) and an apocalyptist related to the Babylonian Sibyl (Pausanias, 10.12.9; the *Suda*, s.v. *Sibulla Delphis*; cf. Moses Chorene, *Hist. armen* 1.6). From Jewish and Christian sources, we learn that he was a mythographer and historian (Josephus and Eusebius, both apparently dependent upon the excerpts from Berossus by Alexander Polyhistor). While these two types of *testimonia* clearly value different aspects of Berossus and put him to different uses, *taken as a whole* they reveal an overall pattern familiar to us from apocalypticism: a history of the cosmos and a people from creation to final catastrophe which is dominated by astrological determinism.

It is tempting to begin our consideration of Berossus by exploring the relationship between him and the Babylonian Sibyl, and the Babylonian Sibyl's relationship to the Jewish *Sibyllines*, especially, with respect to the redaction of *Oracula Sibyllina* III. 97-154, 809-829. But the tradition is extremely obscure, as witnessed by its oldest testimony in Pausanias: "The Hebrews who lived beyond Palestine had a prophetess called Sabbē (more recently corrected to Sambēthē or Sambathis) whose father they say was Berossus and mother Erymanthē; but some say she was a Babylonian Sibyl and others an Egyptian" (10.12.9; cf. pseudo-Justin, *Cohor. ad Graecos*, 37.3).[6]

[4] Compare G. Widengren, *The Ascension of the Apostle and the Heavenly Book* (1950) with G. von Rad, *Theologie des Alten Testaments*, 4 ed. (1965), Vol. II, p. 327 and Betz, *op. cit.* 392f. (135f.).

[5] See the edition of the fragments of Berossus in F. Jacoby, *Die Fragmente der griechischen Historiker* (1923-), Vol. IIIC, no. 680, pp. 364-397 and the older edition by P. Schnabel, *Berossos und die babylonisch-hellenistische Literatur* (1923), pp. 250-275. Schnabel's work is the only substantial monograph on Berossus.

[6] See, in general, A. Piretti, *La sibilla babilonese nella propaganda hellenistica* (1943)—especially pp. 215-301. For special studies, see J. Geffcken, "Die baby-

Barring further clarification on this point, I propose instead merely to refer to some elements in Berossus, setting aside the more usual questions as to the historical accuracy of the traditions he transmits.[7] The *Babyloniaka* describes the history of the world from its creation to its final destruction and offers a periodization of the history of Babylonia which stretches in between.[8] In the former, Berossos draws upon a learned mythic tradtion; in the latter, upon an equally learned chronicle tradition. A number of details are of interest as paralleling motifs in apocalyptic literature: the tradition of the antediluvian books of Oannes (F1, Jacoby) and the hidden books of Xisuthrus (F4) which contain cosmogonical and flood traditions clearly related to those represented by the *Atrahasis* epic, *Enuma elish* and *Gilgamesh*;[9] the correlation of the rule of foreign kings with the rise of idolatry and religious desecration (F11), etc. In the key apocalyptic fragment which has survived (F21), the beginning and the end are clearly correlated. All things will be consumed by fire and the world will be flooded and return to the watery chaos that existed in the beginning.[10]

Ionische Sibylle," *Nachrichten von der Akademie der Wissenschaften zu Göttingen*, Phil.-hist. Kl. (1900), 88-102; W. Bousset, "Die Beziehungen der ältesten jüdischen Sibylle zur chaldäischen Sibylle," *Zeitschrift für die neutestamentliche Wissenschaft*, 3 (1902), 23-49; K. Mras, " 'Babylonische' und 'ertryäische' Sibylle," *Wiener Studien*, 29 (1907), 25-49; E. Schürer, *Geschichte der jüdischen Volkes im Zeitalter Jesu Christi*, 4 ed. (1909), Vol. III, pp. 563-567; P. Schnabel, *Berossos*, pp. 69-93; H. C. Youtie, "Sambathis," *Harvard Theological Review*, 37 (1944), esp. 213-217; V. Tcherikover, *et al.*, *Corpus Papyrorum Judaicarum* (1964), Vol. III, pp. 47-52; A. M. Denis, *Introduction aux pseudépigraphes grecs d'Ancien Testament* (1970), esp. pp. 113f.; V. Nikiprovetsky, *La troisième Sibylle* (1970), pp. 88-122.

[7] For a recent example of such inquiries, see W. Spoerri, *Untersuchung zur babylonische Urgeschichte* (1961).

[8] While I reject genetic arguments as methodologically unsound when dealing with international religious phenomena such as apocalypticism, see H. Ludin Jansen, *Die Henoch-Gestalt* (1939), pp. 74-81 who claims Berossus as "das Vorbild der henochitischen Geschichtsübersicht" and compare, M. Hengel, *Judentum und Hellenismus* (1969), pp. 348-352.

[9] It may be noted that a major crux, the identification of the figure of Oannes, has been resolved by the discovery of his name on cuneiform lists as the "first, primeval sage." See W. Lambert, "Catalogues of Texts and Authors," *Journal of Cuneiform Studies*, 11 (1957), 73f.

[10] On this apocalyptic fragment, see J. Bidez, "Bérose et la grande année," *Mélanges P. Fredericq* (1904), pp. 9-19. P. Schnabel, "Apokalyptische Berechnung der Endzeiten bei Berossos," *Orientalische Literaturzeitung* (1910), 401f.; Schnabel, *Berossos*, pp. 94-109; W. Gundel in F. Boll-C. Bezold, *Sternglaube und Sterndeutung*, 4 ed. (1931), pp. 200-205 (compare the note in W. and H. G. Gundel, *Astrologumena* (1966), pp. 45-46, n. 14) and B. L. van Waerden, "Das grosse Jahr und die ewige Wiederkehr," *Hermes*, 80 (1952), 129-155.

What is of importance for us with respect to this book, which might be described as "proto-apocalyptic", is not an argument as to the nature of the work and the erection of some pan-Babylonian theory of the origins of apocalypticism[11] but an argument as to the nature of its author. Berossus was a learned Babylonian priest during the Seleucid period at a time when the Babylonian "Schools" were world-famous and the major activities of a Babylonian intellectual were astronomy, astrology, mathematics, historiography and the recovery of archaic ritual lore. These Babylonian intellectuals, for all the novelty of their speculation which would culminate in the rich literature of Greco-Egyptian astronomy and astrology and the rich philosophic school of Stoicism, stood in continuity with ancient Babylonian scribalism, an unbroken tradition from the Sumerian period to the sages of the Babylonian Talmud. It is to this scribalism that Berossus directs us for our first clue as to the interrelationship of wisdom and apocalyptic.

The scribes were an elite group of learned, literate men, an intellectual aristocracy which played an invaluable role in the administration of their people in both religious and political affairs. They were dedicated to a variety of roles: guardians of their cultural heritage, intellectual innovators, world travelers who brought about a cross-cultural flow of wisdom, lawyers, doctors, astrologers, diviners, magicians, scientists, court functionaries, linguists, exegetes, etc. Their greatest love was the study of themselves and they guarded and transmitted their teaching, wrote biographies and hagiographies of their lives and their ancestral prototypes, preserved and annotated one another's labors. They projected their scribal activities on high, on a god who created by law according to a written plan, on a god who was a teacher in his heavenly court. They hypostatized the scribe and scribal activities in the figure of Divine Wisdom. They speculated about hidden heavenly tablets, about creation by divine word, about the beginning and the end and thereby claimed to possess the secrets of creation. Above all, they talked, they memorized and remembered, they wrote.

The essence of scribal knowledge was its character as *Listenwissenschaft*, to use A. Alt's useful term.[12] It depends upon catalogues

---

[11] As has been by members of the classical pan-Babylonian School such as A. Jeremias and as may be found in attenuated form in Gunkel and Bousset.

[12] See A. Alt, "Die Weisheit Salomos," *Theologische Literaturzeitung*, 76 (1951), 139-144 and note the comments by von Rad, *Theologie*, Vol. II, pp. 317f. See

and classification; it progresses by establishing precedents, by observing patterns, similarities and conjunctions and by noting their repetitions. As such their basic faith was in the relevance of a limited number of paradigms to every new situation. Their goal—whether the scribe be called *dubshar*, *sopher*, "Chaldean" or *rabbi*—was nothing less than absolute perfection, the inclusion of everything within their categories. In the quest of this perfection, they developed complex hermeneutic and exegetical techniques to bridge the gap between paradigm and particular instance, between past and present.

This faith of the scribe may be most clearly seen in the great Babylonian omen series which are the major intellectual achievement of archaic Babylonia.[13] It permeates every other genre of literature as well, including the historiographic. For the scribe, if events have significance largely in terms of their precedent, then the same text may be used to describe two widely separated historical events so long as their pattern, their 'value' was perceived to be the same. For example, one of the great monuments of Sumerian literary composition is the "Lament over the Destruction of Sumer and Ur," a work composed c. 2100 B.C. bewailing the invasion of the Guti in 2500 B.C.

> For the misfortunes of Uruk, for the misfortunes of Agade, I am stricken.
> The Lady of Uruk wept, that departed was her might.
> The Lady of Agade wept, that departed was her glory ...
> Weep for Uruk, ravaging and shame has she received ...
> The throne of thy glory has been caused to pass away from me.
> The bridegroom, the husband of my well being, Marduk, has been taken away from me.

The same text was recopied in 287-286 B.C. bewailing the destructive acts of the Hellenistic monarch, Antigonus.[14] The same text is, at one and the same time, a Sumerian "original" religious expression and a Hellenistic Babylonian "original" religious expression. (The notion of "late copy" must be abandoned in such instances.) The

---

further, W. von Soden, "Leistung und Grenze sumerischer und babylonischer Wissenschaft," *Welt als Geschichte*, 2 (1936), 411-464, 509-557.

[13] On omens and oracles, see J. Nougayrol, *et al.*, *La divination en Mésopotamie* (1966); A. L. Oppenheim, *Ancient Mesopotamia* (1964), pp. 206-227.

[14] T. Pinches, *Historical Records and Legends of Assyria and Babylonia* (1902), pp. 477f. See now the translation of the Sumerian by S. N. Kraemer in the *Supplement* to J. B. Pritchard's *Ancient Near Eastern Texts Relating to the Old Testament*, pp. 611-619.

Guti invasion provided a pattern for interpreting all acts of foreign invasion and domination in Babylonian in the same way as the Hyksos invasion provided a pattern for the Egyptian.

This paradigmatic (or, if you prefer, typological) ideology leads to what I would term an *apocalyptic situation*, though not necessarily to apocalyptic literature. While many examples may be furnished from the so-called historical omens and from the various patterns in historiographic literature,[15] I prefer to call attention to a better known example—the Babylonian *Akitu* festival and its relation to the creation epic, *Enuma elish*.

As *Enuma elish* has been dated by some as early as 1600 B.C. (although a date around 1200 B.C. is more likely) and as there are early mentions of *Akitu* festivals, it has been almost universally assumed that the New Year festival which we reconstruct from Akkadian texts with its reading of *Enuma elish* and its ritual humiliation of the king is equally archaic (even though the ritual events in no way resemble the events described in the myth). It has rarely been observed that the Akkadian ritual texts, on which the Myth-Ritual School based their pattern of a Dying-Rising God and a Dying-Rising King (a pattern which, in fact, never existed in the Near East with the possible, but doubtful, exception of Dumuzi)[16] are not from the archaic period. Rather, they are Hellenistic Babylonian documents written during the period of Seleucid domination. They are clear witness to Hellenistic Babylonian religiosity and only possible witness to earlier practice. The Hellenistic Babylonian New Year festival is either a repetition of an earlier ritual typologically understood to describe the current situation of foreign domination, to have contemporary political as well as religious implications; or the text is a new, Hellenistic composition.

The ritual text begins by reminding the Lord Marduk of his protection of his sacred city and prays that he may return to his city and "establish the liberty of the peoples of Babylon." The priest

---

[15] See J. Nougayrol, "Note sur la place des 'présages historiques' dans extispicine babylonienne," *Annuaire de l'École pratique des Hautes Études* (1944-1945), 5-41 and the classic study by H. G. Güterbock, "Die historische Tradition und ihre literarische Gestaltung bei Babyloniern und Hethitern bis 1200," *Zeitschrift für Assyriologie* (1934), 1-91, 44 (1938), 45-149.

[16] This is not the context for an exhaustive bibliography on this growing consensus; see especially W. von Soden, "Gibt es ein Zeugnis dafür, dass die Babylonier an die Wiederauferstehung Marduks geglaubt haben?" *Zeitschrift für Assyriologie*, n. s. 17 (1955). 130-166.

then prays: "To your city, Babylon, grant release." It is impossible not to read contemporary nationalistic propaganda here—whatever may have been the original ritualistic understanding of the phrases. The king is then "dragged by the ears" before the statue of Marduk by the priest, struck on the cheek and stripped of his royal garments. He then offers a negative confession to the deity ("I have not sinned . . .") and his insignia are restored. Is this the 'ritual slaying' of a pious Babylonian king, or is this a threat (if you prefer, a nationalistic phantasy) of what will happen to the impious, foreign, Seleucid monarch? The confession of the king is decisive:

> I was not neglectful of the requirements of your lordship,
> I did not destroy Babylon;
> I did not command its overthrow.
> I [did not destroy] the temple Esagila,
> I did not forget its rites . . .
> [I watched over] Babylon,
> I did not smash its walls.

What native Babylonian king ever did? These were all acts committed by foreign rulers: during the period of Assyrian domination from 1360-1200 and 1116-990, under Sennacharib in 689, under Xerxes in 480-476 and finally under Antigonus in 316. As with Cyrus among the Israelites (whose promise to rebuild Jerusalem and its Temple concludes the Jewish version of the Hebrew Scriptures, 2 *Chronicles* 36.23) so too for the Babylonians—foreign kings could be pointed to who restored Esagila and Babylon: Tiglat Pileser III, Sargon II, Ashurbanipal, Nebuchadnezzar, Cyrus, Alexander, Seleukos I and Antiochus I and IV. The implication of the New Year's text is clear. If you act as the evil foreign kings have acted, you will be stripped of your kingship by the gods; if you act in the opposite manner, "the sceptre, and crown and the sword shall be restored to the king."[17]

This religious and nationalistic polemic is placed within a cosmic setting by the reading of *Enuma elish*. For this text is not simply a cosmogony. It is preeminently a myth of the creation of Marduk's city, Babylon and his temple, Esagila. Originally composed during the first period of Assyrian domination it correlates Marduk's king-

---

[17] I cannot here argue the thesis that the texts of the New Year ceremony break into two groups—an older, ambiguous collection which focus on the absence of Marduk from Babylon, all of which are of an Assyrian provenance and seem to be a parody on Babylonian ritual and belief; and the Hellenistic series which I have interpreted as reflecting anti-Seleucid propaganda.

ship with kingship in Babylon, the creation of the world with the building of Esagila. The opposite is likewise the case. Destroy Babylon or Esagila, neglect Marduk, and the world will be decreated, will return to its primeval watery chaos.

Examples such as this are what I have termed apocalyptic situations. All of the elements are present, but they have not yet been turned to the future orientation of apocalyptic literature. We may find the beginning of this turning in the proto-apocalyptic works of Hellenistic Babylonian authors such as Berossus and Abydenos.[18] But no native Babylonian apocalypse has survived.[19]

I would argue that wisdom and apocalyptic are related in that they are both essentially scribal phenomena. It is the paradigmatic thought of the scribe—a way of thinking that is both pragmatic and speculative—which has given rise to both. This initial perspective may be enlarged by examining Egyptian materials.

II

Egypt presents us with a variety of phenomena analogous to those in Babylonian. It is essentially a scribal culture dominated by *Listenwissenschaft*.[20] It has a learned historicistic tradition which, when paraphrased into Greek, may be described as proto-apocalyptic (e.g. Manetho).[21] It employs the paradigm of the Hyksos invasion, not only to interpret all acts of invasion and foreign domination, but also in apocalyptic materials.[22] Indeed, it uses this material in a thoroughly mythic fashion by identifying the Hyksos with the deity of confusion and chaos, Seth.[23] It has ritual texts written in a deliberately archaic style which parallel the apocalyptic

---

[18] On Abydenos, see Jacoby, *Fragmente*, Vol. IIIC, no. 685.

[19] I am discounting the Akkadian "prophecies" interpreted by Hallo as apocalypses, W. W. Hallo, "Akkadian Apocalypses," *Israel Exploration Journal*, 16 (1966), 231-242; cf. A. K. Gregson-W. G. Lambert, "Akkadian Prophecies," *Journal of Cuneiform Studies*, 18 (1964), 7-30. Nor am I including Babylonian material preserved in other apocalyptic works from *Sibylline Oracles* III and *Revelation* to Mani.

[20] See, for example, G. Maspero, "Manuel d'hiérarchie égyptienne," *Journal asiatique*, ser. VIII, 11 (1888), 250-280.

[21] See the Loeb edition of Manetho by W. G. Waddell (1940).

[22] On the Hyksos-pattern, see the classic work by R. Weill, *La fin du moyen empire égyptien* (1918), esp. pp. 22-68, 76-83 and 605-623 and the recent study by J. Yoyette, "L'Égypte ancienne et les origines de l'antijudaisme," *Revue d'histoire des religions*, 163 (1963), 133-143.

[23] J. G. Griffiths, "The Interpretation of the Horus-Myth of Edfu," *Journal of Egyptian Archaeology*, 44 (1958), 75-85.

situation described with respect to the *Akitu* festival (e.g. the *Book of Overthrowing Apophis* in P. Bremner-Rhind dated 310 B.C.).[24] However, in contradistinction to Babylonia, we have a variety of full blown apocalypses from Egypt, spanning a period of almost two millennia.[25] Thus it is possible, in the case of Egypt, to investigate not only the apocalyptic form but also the process of apocalypticization.

The materials available for analysis range from the hieratic apocalypse of Neferti (c. 1900 B.C.)[26] through demotic texts such as the so-called *Demotic Chronicle* (second century, B.C.)[27] and the *Curse of the Lamb* (beginning of the first century, A.D.)[28] to first century Greek materials such as the *Potter's Oracle*,[29] the apocalypse preserved in *Asclepius* (IX) 24-26 (now recovered in a Coptic recension from Nag Hammadi)[30] as well as the older Ptolemaic materials

---

[24] See the translation by R. O. Faulkner in the *Journal of Egyptian Archaeology*, 22 (1936), 121-140; 23 (1937), 10-16, 166-185; 24 (1938), 41-53.

[25] See the comprehensive treatment by C. C. McCown, "Egyptian Apocalyptic Literature," *Harvard Theological Review*, 18 (1925), 357-411 and J. Doresse, "Apocalypses égyptiennes," *La Table ronde*, 110 (1957), 29-39. The treatment by H. Gressmann, *Der Messias* (1929), pp. 417-445 should also be noted. For extremely archaic elements, which fall outside the scope of this paper, see S. Schott, "Altägyptische Vorstellungen vom Weltende," *Analecta Biblica*, 12:3 (1959) = *Studia Biblica et Oreintalia*, Vol. III, pp. 319-330 and G. Lanczkowski, "Eschatology in Ancient Egyptian Religion," *Proceedings of the IX International Congress for the History of Religions* (1960), pp. 129-134.

[26] See the translations of this text in Pritchard, *Ancient Near Eastern Texts*, 2ed. (1955), pp. 444-446 (to be cited as *ANET²*) and R. O. Faulkner, *et al.*, *The Literature of Ancient Egypt* (1972), pp. 234-240. See the study by G. Posener, *Littérature et politique dans l'Égypte de la XII dynastie* (1956), pp. 21-60, 145-157 for an argument as to the progandistic character of this work. Cf. W. Helck, *Die Prophezeihung der Nfr. tj* (1970).

[27] W. Spiegelberg, *Die sogenannte demotische Chronik des Pap. 215 der Bibliothèque Nationale zu Paris* (1914). There is a recent Italian translation in E. Bresciani, *Letteratura poesia dell'antico egitto* (1969), pp. 551-560. The classic study remains E. Meyer, "Ägyptische Dokumente aus der Perserzeit, I: Eine eschatologische Prophetie über die Geschichte Ägyptens in persischer und griechischer Zeit," *Sitzungsberichte der Preussischen Akademie der Wissenschaften*, Phil.-hist. Kl. (1915), 287-304.

[28] J. Krall, "Vom König Bokchoris," *Festgaben zu Ehren Max Büdingers* (1898), pp. 1-11; A. Moret, *De Bocchori Rege* (1903), pp. 35-49; J. M. A. Janssen, "Over Farao Bocchoris," in *Varia Historica aangeboden aan A. W. Byvanck* (1954), pp. 17-29.

[29] See now the edition by L. Koenen, "Die Prophezeiungen des 'Töpfers'," *Zeitschrift für Papyrologie und Epigraphik*, 2 (1968), 178-209 which supersedes all previous editions and cites all important secondary literature.

[30] See A. D. Nock-A. J. Festugière, *Corpus Hermeticum*, 2ed. (1960), Vol. II, pp. 322-335. On the Coptic Text (Nag Hammadi, VI:8), see M. Krause and P. Labib, *Gnostische und hermetische Schriften aus Codex II und Codex VI* (Berlin, 1971); J. Doresse, "Hermes et la gnose: À propos de l'Asclépius copte," *Novum*

recoverable from the *Sibylline Oracles* III.350-361, 367-380 (cf. III. 46-54, 75-92; V.512-632; XI.245-314).[31] In spite of the chronological range of some two thousand years which separate these texts, their varying language and situation, it is possible to construct a model Egyptian apocalypse by comparing these various documents.

(A) (1) The prophet came before the king and proclaimed to him all that he had asked concerning that which was to come. (2) And these are the words which he spoke on that occasion.

(B) (3) Behold the people are in confusion because there is disorder in the land. (4) Social relations have become reversed. (5) Religious obligations are ignored. (6) The natural cycle is overthrown. (7) Foreigners have appeared and are acting as if they were Egyptians. (8) The whole world is upside down, even the gods are affected. (9) The gods have abandoned Egypt. (10) The land of life has become a land of death.

(C) (11) But then shall come forth a great king sent by the gods. (12) The foreigners shall be driven out. (13) All relations will be restored. (14) All that is good will return to the people, the land and the gods and Egypt will again be a land of life.

(D) (15) Thus the prophet finished speaking before the king and was greatly renowned for the wisdom which he had spoken.

The overall structure is basically that of *Heils- und Unheilseschatologie* which shifts between a present and future set of woes and a future promise. There is an introduction (A) which serves as a narrative framework for the prophecy, usually an encounter between prophet and king. (B) The woes are perceived as a set of reverses affecting the people (3-5), the cosmos (6, 8, 10) and the gods (8-9)—the cause being identified as the intrusion of foreigners (7) who are homologized to the Hyksos pattern and interpreted in a mythical manner—parallel to the Old Testament's "enemies from the North."[32] This is followed by (C), a promise of restoration by a divine king (11) who will expel chaos (i.e., the foreigners (12)) and restore good order (13-14) and (D) a narrative conclusion.

It would be tempting to study all of these texts in detail noting their kinship with archaic Egyptian cosmogonies and kingship

---

Testamentum, 1 (1956), 54-69 and M. Krause, "Ägyptisches Gedenkengut in der Apokalypse des Asclepius," in *XVII Deutscher Orientalistentag, Vorträge* (1969) *Zeitschrift der Deutschen Morgenländischen Gesellschaft*, Supplementa 1), 48-57.

[31] See esp. W. W. Tarn, "Alexander Helios and the Golden Age," *Journal of Hellenic Studies*, 22 (1932), 135-160 for a study of this example of Ptolemaic propaganda.

[32] *Jeremiah* 4.6f.; 6.22f. See B. Childs, "The Enemy from the North and the Chaos Tradition," *J. of Biblical Literature*, 78 (1959), 187-198.

ideologies. Of particular relevance to our theme is the close parallels between the "woes" in these texts and social teachings which may be found in the rich Egyptian prophetic[33] and wisdom[34] traditions. As "woes" they resemble materials in such well known texts as *The Lamentations of Khakheperre-Soabe*, *The Admonitions of Ipu-Wer* and *The Dispute of a Man with his Ba* (esp. lines 103b-130a).[35] They reverse the instructions found in the widespread "Admonitions" and "Teachings" literature as well as in the well-known "Negative Confession" from the *Book of the Dead*, chapter 125—a text which, by the way, was translated into Greek.[36] However, I should like to focus attention on another set of problems, in consonance with my suggestion as to the centrality of scribalism for an understanding of the relationship of Wisdom and Apocalyptic.

The paradigmatic concerns of the scribes, whether expressed in the interpretation of oracles and omens, in legal rulings, in the hermeneutics of sacred texts or in their other manifold functions, led to the development of complex exegetical techniques devoted to the task of discovering the everchanging relevance of ancient precedents and archetypes. (These concerns also led, at times, to the fabrication of ancient precedents and archetypes). These exegetical techniques were international, being diffused throughout scribal centers in the Eastern Mediterranean world.[37] Texts are used and reused, glossed, interpreted and reinterpreted in a continual process of "updating" the materials.

---

[33] See the comprehensive survey by G. Lanczkowski, *Altägyptischer Prophetismus* (1960).

[34] See the rich bibliographical essay by J. Leclant, "Documents nouveaux et points du vue récents sur les sagesses de l'Égypte ancienne," in *La Sagesse du proche-orient ancien: Colloque du Strasbourg, 17-19 mai, 1962* (1963), pp. 5-26.

[35] For the most recent translation of these three texts, see Faulkner, *The Literature of Ancient Egypt*, pp. 230-233, 210-229, 201-209.

[36] *ANET*[2], pp. 34-36 and Ch. Maystre, *Les déclarations d'innocence: Livre des morts, chapitre 125* (1937). See the Greek translation by Euphantus, quoted in Porphyry, *De Abstinentia*, IV.10. For the possibility that the *Book of the Dead*, including ch. 125, was translated into Greek by Eudoxus, see J. G. Griffiths, "A Translation from the Egyptian by Eudoxus," *Classical Quarterly*, 15 (1965), 75-78.

[37] For an archaic example, see the wide diffusion of omen-series and commentaries which have been found in Akkadian in such widely dispersed sites as Susa, Nuzi, Hattusha, Qatna and Hazor and translated into Elamite and Hittite (see A. L. Oppenheim, *Ancient Mesopotamia*, p. 206). For a Hellenistic example, see the fundamental work of D. Daube, "Rabbinic Methods of Interpretation and Hellenistic Rhetoric," *Hebrew Union College Annual*, 22 (1949), 239-264.

This process of "updating" was particularly acute in prophetic oracular and apocalyptic traditions with their ambiguous messages and unfulfilled predictions. The various techniques of interpretations have been well explored for Jewish apocalyptic literature.[38] Each one of these have clear Egyptian parallels which demand close comparative investigation. For example, the *pesher* technique employed in the Qumran materials (1QpHab., 1QpMicah, 4QpNah, 4QpPs 37, 1QpPs 68, 1QpZeph, etc.) find an almost exact counterpart in the exegetical procedures of the *Demotic Chronicle*.[39]

The clarification of this process of "updating" is more difficult for us to accomplish in the Egyptian materials than it is in the Jewish and Christian because, in most instances, we do not have the various recensions of a tradition to compare (e.g. 4 Ezra 12 with Daniel 7). In the main we must rest content with the analysis of isolated motifs such as Hans Dieter Betz's intricate and convincing discussion of the tradition of the elements addressing the creator deity with prayer.[40] However there is one Egyptian text, the "Potter's Oracle" as interpreted in the pioneering researches of Ludwig Koenen,[41] that provides the possibility of perceiving the dynamics of tradition at work.

Koenen's work depends upon the fact that while the narrative framework of the prophecy is found in only one papyrus (P. Graf 29787), the actual prophecy is preserved in two recensions: P. Ranier 19813 and P. Oxyrhynchus 2332. This makes it possible to compare variants of the same tradition and determine redactional elements and interpolations.[42] Several further papyrus fragments have been tentatively identified as belonging to the "Potter" tradition.[43] While Koenen does not provide any detailed discussion of these, one

---

[38] E.g. D. S. Russell, *The Method and Message of Jewish Apocalyptic* (1964), pp. 183-187 *et passim*.

[39] I know of only one scholar who has studied these parallels, F. Daumas, "Littérature prophétique et exégétique égyptienne et commentaires esséniens," *Mémorial A. Gélin* (1961), pp. 203-211.

[40] Betz, "Zum Problem des religionsgeschichtlichen Verständnisses der Apokalyptik," 398-409 (= 138-154).

[41] L. Koenen, "Die Prophezeiungen des 'Töpfers' " (*supra*, n. 29); "The Prophecies of a Potter: A Prophecy of World Renewal Becomes an Apocalypse," in D. H. Samuel, ed., *Proceedings of the Twelfth International Congress of Papyrology* (1970), 249-254.

[42] See the detailed discussion in Koenen, "Die Prophezeiungen," 187-193. See the summary in E. Loebel-C. H. Roberts, *The Oxyrhynchus Papyri*, Vol. XII (1954), p. 89.

[43] See R. A. Pack, *The Greek and Latin Literary Texts from Greco-Roman Egypt*, 2ed. (1967), nos. 2488, 2639 and note 44, below.

(P.S.I.982) demonstrates additional interpretative possibilities by identifying the foreign, chaotic invaders as the Jews.[44]

The major discovery of archaic Wisdom was the paradigmatic figure of the sacred king. In the employ of the royal courts and shrines (whether in Babylonia, Egypt or Judea) the scribe discerned, developed, articulated and created the various ideologies and mythologies in which the king, through divine wisdom, was the center of social and cosmic order. In the archaic "proto-apocalyptic situation," the saving power of the king, his destruction of his enemies, the establishment of his rule and law were correlated with mythic traditions of the creation of cosmic and social order by a god in the beginning through his defeat of chaos. This pattern underlies a wide variety of materials from cosmogonies to New Year festivals, from royal praise hymns and chronicles to coronation rituals. In Egypt it is expressed in the two great patterns of kingship: the solar cycle of Amon-Re and the essentially chthonic cycle of Osiris-Horus. The former pattern, which depicts the new Pharaoh as the son of the deity, conceived by the Sun god who assumes the form of the ruling Pharaoh and has intercourse with the new Pharaoh's mother, presents a cosmogony where the Sun god is born on a primordial island, defeats the powers of chaos and establishes order and the cosmos. The Osiris pattern, which depicts every living Pharaoh as Horus, the son of Osiris, and every dead Pharaoh as Osiris, Lord of the Underworld, presents the primordial struggle as that between Osiris' brother, Seth and Osiris-Horus. Seth revolted against Osiris and slew him with cosmic and social consequences. Horus avenges his father's death by slaying Seth and restoring order.[45] In the complex royal ideologies, these two patterns are frequently combined. In "proto-apocalyptic" materials, these two kingship patterns yield corresponding patterns of woes. The Amon-Re ideology expresses chaos as an eclipse of the sun and violent storms; the Osiris pattern, while having signs of cosmic chaos such as the flooding of the Nile, expresses the chaotic primarily as rebellion or the invasion of foreigners. These two series of woes are likewise combined.

Archaic examples of these traditions in what I have termed "proto-apocalyptic situations" abound (e.g. the Hymns of Merenptah[46] and

[44] See the full discussion in V. Tcherikover et al., *Corpus Papyrorum Judaicarum*, Vol. III (1964), no. 520 (pp. 119-121).

[45] There is no "tradition-history" of the Amon-Re cycle comparable to J. G. Griffiths, *The Conflict of Horus and Seth* (1960).

[46] *ANET*^{2}, pp. 58 and 377.

Ramses IV[47]) and these elements persist into the Ptolemiac period. Perhaps the best known example is the Rosetta Stone decree of March 27, 196 B.C., celebrating the performance of the *Djed* festival for Ptolemy V:

> In the reign of the young one—who has received his royalty from his father—lord of crowns, glorious, *who has established Egypt* and is pious towards the gods, superior to his foes, *who has restored the civilized life of men* ... *a king like the Sun* ... *son of the Sun* ... *being a god sprung from a god and goddess* (*like Horus the son of Isis and Osiris who avenged his father Osiris*) ...

After these introductory praises, the text goes on to describe in paradigmatic fashion the central political and cosmic act of the foreign Ptolemaic king: the defeat of the rebels of Lycopolis. The king was first prevented from this by an inundation of the Nile, but this he controlled by "having damned at many points the outlets of the streams" and having accomplished this strategic (and cosmogonic) deed, he marched against Lycopolis, a city of "impious men ... who had done great harm to the temples and all the dwellers in Egypt," and "took the town by storm, and destroyed all the impious men in it, *even as Hermes and Horus, the son of Isis and Osiris formerly subdued the rebels in the same district.*"[48]

Texts such as these, associated with coronation, renewal of kingship or celebrating a victory, must be interpreted as political propaganda created by the scribe in service of his king. They represent the use of paradigms for typological ends—the presentation of a specific king as the fulfillment (or repetition) of the ancient patterns. These same propagandistic concerns, as Georges Posener has brilliantly demonstrated, yield the oldest surviving "apocalypse," that of Neferti in 1991 B.C. The narrative is cast in the form of a prophecy by the sage Neferti before King Snefru of the Fourth Dynasty; it is actually a piece of blatant propaganda in favor of the legitimacy of King Ammenemes I, the founder of the Twelfth Dynasty.

> Re must begin by recreating the land, which is utterly ruined, and nothing remains ... The sun is veiled and will not shine ... none will live when the (sun) is veiled (by) cloud ... Enemies have come into being in the east, Asiatics have come down into Egypt ... I will show you the land in calamity, for what has never happened before

---

[47] *ANET*², pp. 378f.
[48] I have followed the translation by E. Bevan, *A History of Egypt Under the Ptolemaic Dynasty* (1927), pp. 263-268. (Emphasis, mine).

has now happened ... Re has separated himself from mankind ...
A king of the South will come, Ameny by name ...[49]

Chaos will be subdued; Re's recreation of the world will have begun with his reign.

Such texts may be found in Egypt over a period of close to two millennia. Employing *vaticinia ex eventu*, the prophet describes the ascendency of a specific king as overcoming chaos (represented by eclipses, rebellions and foreigners) and establishing a new order, a new creation. While such texts "tend towards" apocalypticism, one does not find a full blown apocalypse until the prophecies and propaganda are disassociated from a specific king. This becomes possible for Egypt (as well as for Babylonia and, perhaps Judea) only in the Greco-Roman period when native kingship ceases. I am tempted to describe apocalypticism as *wisdom lacking a royal patron*. (A definition which will serve at least to question both the "lachrymose theory" of apocalypticism as growing out of a situation of general persecution and the popular recent theory that it reflects lowerclass interests.) In such contexts, the older models may become xenophobic nationalistic propaganda as in the case of some fragments of the "Potter's Oracle" where the woes have been reduced to anti-Hellenistic or anti-Jewish polemics—a prophecy against foreigners rather than in favor of a specific king. Or the king may be utterly cosmicized (a tendency always present in the various ideologies of divine kingship) in a thorough-going apocalypse. I find Koenen's work most interesting because he attempts to identify the various stages of this process at work in the different redactions of the "Potter's Oracle."

The narrative frame of the story (extant only in P. Graf 29787—2nd century A.D.) is pregnant with archaic significance:

> During the reign of king Amenhotep (18th Dynasty), a potter, at the command of Hermes-Thot, goes to the island of Helios-Re where he practices his art. But the people are upset by this sacrilegious action. They pull the pottery out of the oven, break it and drag the potter before the king. The potter defends himself by interpreting this action as a prophetic sign. Just as the pottery has been destroyed, so Egypt, and finally the city of the followers of the evil god Typhon-Set will be destroyed.[50]

---

[49] I have followed the translation in W. K. Simpson, *The Literature of Ancient Egypt*, pp. 234-240. See the literature cited above, note 26 and further, A. Volten, *Zwei altägyptische politische Schriften* (1945).

[50] Koenen, "The Prophecies of a Potter," 249.

The prophecies which then follow speak of the breakdown of cosmic and social order and the return of chaos. A savior-king (described in extraordinarily vague language) will come "from the sun" and reestablish order, Egypt and the cosmos.

The "Potter" is an epiphany of the ancient ram-headed deity Chnum who created the sun, the gods and man on his potter's wheel.[51] He is a traditional giver of royal oracles, including a number from the Hellenistic period that bear a close resemblance to themes in the "Potter's Oracle."[52] Thus his apocalyptic interpretation of the broken pottery goes far beyond the prophetic, symbolic actions of Jeremiah 19. For Chnum to have his pots broken is to plunge the world into total decreation and chaos. But the theme of re-creation is likewise suggested by the setting. The island of Helios-Re (in Egyptian, the Island of Flames) is the traditional birthplace of the solar deity and the scene of his defeat of the powers of chaos and darkness.[53] Thus the prophecy which predicts a destruction and restoration plays on a setting and a prophet who are inextricably related to both themes in archaic Egyptian mythology.

The frame story could have originally led to a set of historically identifiable woes and the prediction of a specific king who would set things right. If the text as we now have it is a translation of an Egyptian original and if (on the basis of the alleged similarity to P. Trinity College Dublin 192b) the original composition can be dated to the fourth or middle third centuries B.C.—this would be likely.[54] But I consider both of these suggestions to be extremely dubious. More likely is the suggestion that the text may have originally been produced at the time of the revolt of Harsiesis, c. 130 B.C. and promised his successful restoration of native rule.[55] However, this revolt was quickly crushed, and no native king did rise to overthrow the Ptolemies.

The text describes in vague terms (following the old Osiris-Horus pattern) the desolation of Egypt by the "Typhonians" and the

---

[51] The identification of the Potter and Chnum was first proposed by W. Struve, "Zum Töpferorakel," *Raccolta G. Lumbroso* (1925), 274 and has been followed by all subsequent commentators.

[52] See the examples in L. Kákosy, "Prophecies of Ram Gods," *Acta Orientalia Hungaricae*, 19 (1966), 341-358 esp. 343f.

[53] See the argument and the literature cited in Koenen, "Die Prophezeiungen," 184f. and esp. n. 12.

[54] Lobel-Roberts, *Oxyrhynchus Papyri*, XII, 92f.

[55] Koenen, "Die Prophezeiungen," 191.

eventual salvation (now combining both Solar and Horus patterns) brought by a king "who shall appear from the sun, established by the most great goddess Isis." But, as Koenen has remarked, this is divorced totally from any individual features and testifies to the Egyptians' awareness of their own weakness: "It is not he (the promised savior-king) who defeats the Greeks; the Ptolemies will destroy each other. Nor is he the destroyer of Alexandria; the destruction will result from the departure of the protective deity. And finally, he is not the one who recovers the statues of the gods which had been carried off; they will come back on their own ... The prophecies of the potter are not so much propaganda in favor of a specific king as propaganda directed against the Greeks."[56] The "Oracle" represents a characteristic apocalyptic shift necessitated by the cessation of native divine kingship—all decisive historical action and initiative has been transferred from the human to the divine realm.

However even this most general hope did not come true. The Ptolemies and Seleucids did not destroy each other; Alexandria endured. Hence the elite, scribal clergy of Chnum (to whom authorship of this oracle must be traced), introduced a learned set of interpolations designed to "update" the predictions. These may be isolated by the fortunate chance that P. Ranier 19813 (third century A.D.) and P. Oxyrhynchus 2332 (late third century A.D.) contain some forty-five lines of closely parallel material as well as many lines which reveal striking variations and interpolations.

The most significant of these interpolations for our purposes occurs in P. Oxyrhynchus 2332, lines 31-34. The prophecy, in both recensions, had assigned a reign of fifty-five years to the promised king. The later gloss now declares (if the editor's proposed reconstruction be accepted) that the fifty-five years do not refer to the good king's reign but rather to the period of evil which the Greeks will bring "as predicted by Bokcharis the Lamb."

The Prophecy of Bokcharis the Lamb (which is likewise a prophecy of the ram-headed potter deity Chnum) is extant both in a demotic papyrus from the first decade of the first century (A.D.) and is alluded to in Greco-Egyptian and Greco-Roman literature from Manetho to pseudo-Plutarch, Aelian and the *Suda*.[57] It predicts nine hundred years of woes for Egypt from the time of King Bok-

---

[56] Koenen, "The Prophecies of a Potter," 252.
[57] See the literature cited above, n. 28.

charis, before the promised restoration will begin. This period roughly corresponds to 790 B.C.-192 A.D. If one subtracts the fifty-five, years from this date by assuming that it refers to the last period of evil, one gets a date for the beginning of the turning towards a new world at 137 A.D. This date has already passed by the writing of P. Oxyrhynchus and hence the prophecy at first glance is a failure. However the date 137 is remarkably close to the beginning of the new Sothis cycle in 139 A.D. and thus Koenen argues, the prophecy is, in fact, greatly extended. The promised restoration will come at some point in the next cycle—a period which stretches from 139-1599 A-D.! "The potter's prophecy ... in which the idea of the concrete savior-king had virtually disappeared, was reshaped by historical reality. It became something new, namely, a prophecy of a new world cycle. What was originally a prophecy based upon the Egyptian concept of kingship was in the process of being transformed into an apocalypse."[58]

The fact that our surviving papyri indicate that the Oracle was circulated during the late third century and the fact that our latest copy (P. Oxyrhynchus) lacks both a narrative beginning and end suggests that the text had been divorced from all historical context and was being understood as a portrait of cosmic renewal rather than nationalistic restoration. In short, the "Potter's Oracle" by means of learned, scribal reinterpretation had become severed from its original Egyptian genre and had become an apocalypse. As in the case of the Babylonian Berossus, so in Egypt, the historical patterns of the scribal tradent were converted into a paradigm of cosmic history, a recurrent cycle of world creation, destruction and recreation. (One might compare Manetho's *Aegyptiaka* with the epistle of pseudo-Manetho accompanying the *Book of Sothis* for a close Egyptian analogue to Berossus).[59] In both the case of Babylonian and Egyptian tradition (and I would want to argue the same for the Jewish) it is necessary to see this development as an internal "trajectory" within Near Eastern scribalism for which it is unnecessary to postulate either Stoic or Iranian influence.

---

[58] Koenen, "The Prophecies of a Potter," 253, compare the fuller discussion in Koenen, "Die Prophezeiungen," 189f. The Sothic element was perceived, but wrongly interpreted, by U. Wilcken, "Zur Ägyptischen Prophetie," *Hermes*, 40 (1905), esp. 558f. and W. Struve "Zum Töpferorakel," 279. Cp. R. Reitzenstein-H. Schaeder, *Studien zum antiken Synkretismus* (1926), p. 42.

[59] On pseudo-Manetho, W. G. Waddell, *Manetho*, pp. 208-211 and compare the parallels in W. Scott, *Hermetica* (1926), Vol. III, pp. 491-493.

The pure apocalypse is, perhaps, best represented by the well-known apocalypse preserved in the Hermetic *Asclepius* 24-26 whose kinship with the "Potter's Oracle," especially with the woes, has long been recognized.[60] In *Asclepius* the woes are cosmicized and there is no longer any hint of salvation through a king. Rather the woes are characteristic of the "old age" of the world and when this has run its course at some unspecified time, God shall "recall the earth to its primeval form" and there shall be a "rebirth of the cosmos." The renewal of Egypt which was correlated with the Sothic cycle in the "Potter's Oracle" has become, in the *Asclepius*, a cosmic cycle correlated with the great World Year. In the Coptic recension from Nag Hammadi the cyclical character is more pronounced and the futuristic nature of the promised re-creation is more heavily emphasized.[61] A final transformation of the Potter tradition is represented by Book VII of Lactanius, *Divine Institutes*. Blending together quotations from the *Sibylline Oracles*,[62] the *Asclepius* apocalypse and the *Oracles of Hystaspes*—the cyclical character of destruction and re-creation has been altered, in a characteristically Christian redaction, into an eschatological vision of a final destruction, judgment and salvation.[63]

III

In this paper I have suggested that Wisdom and Apocalyptic are interrelated in that both are essentially scribal phenomena. They both depend on the relentless quest for paradigms, the problematics of applying these paradigms to new situations and the *Listenwissenschaft* which are the characteristic activities of the Near Eastern scribe. When these are applied to historiographic materials one may frequently discern proto-apocalyptic elements, though the genre apocalypse is lacking. When the historical patterns are correlated with cosmogonic and kingship traditions and when the attendant

---

[60] Reitzenstein-Schaeder, *Studien*, pp. 38-40; Nock-Festugière, *Hermès Trismégiste*, Vol. II, pp. 288, 379-381.

[61] J. Doresse, *The Secret Books of the Egyptian Gnostics* (1960), pp. 245-248; Doresse, "Apocalypses égyptiens," 34f.

[62] Note the parallels between elements in the Sibylline Oracles and the "Potter's Oracle" in E. Norden, *Die Geburt des Kindes* (1924), p. 55 and the discussion of parallels between the *Sibylline Oracles* and the *Asclepius* apocalypse in W. Scott-A. S. Ferguson, *Hermetica*, Vol. IV, pp. x-xvi, 416-419.

[63] For the relations between the *Oracle of Hystaspes*, the *Sibylline Oracles* and the *Asclepius* apocalypse, see H. Windisch, *Die Orakel des Hystaspes* (1929), esp. pp. 26-33, 44, 89.

structures of woes and promises are directed towards a condition of foreign domination, there is an apocalyptic situation—though again lacking the literary form of the apocalypse. Both protoapocalyptic literature and apocalyptic situations were present in Babylonian materials from the Hellenistic period and these materials stand in close continuity with archaic scribal traditions and activities.

In Egypt, these same elements were found to be present, intertwined with and alongside of literary apocalypses which bore close kinship to other Egyptian wisdom materials. Following Koenen's work on the "Potter's Oracle," we explored the twenty-five hundred year "trajectory" from Neferti to Lactantius, from political propaganda and prophecy to apocalypticism and eschatology emphasizing those techniques of interpretation and reinterpretation which provide the dynamics of scribal tradition.

In the course of this investigation, several characteristics of apocalypticism emerged on which I would insist. Apocalypticism is Wisdom lacking a royal court and patron and therefore it surfaces during the period of Late Antiquity not as a response to religious persecution but as an expression of the trauma of the cessation of native kingship. Apocalypticism is a learned rather than a popular religious phenomenon. It is widely distributed throughout the Mediterranean world and is best understood as part of the inner history of the tradition within which it occurs rather than as a syncretism with foreign (most usually held to be Iranian) influences.

It is tempting to continue in this vein, illustrating the movement within Near Eastern scribal tradition from historical precedent and propaganda to apocalypticism and exploring the variety of genres in which a single tradition may be found.[56] More research needs to be undertaken on the relationship of apocalypticism to archaic wisdom forms such as omens and Hellenistic wisdom forms such as astrology. Or we might press on to examine the radical interiorization of apocalyptic motifs in non-Christian gnostic and alchemical texts such as the *Hymn of the Pearl* and the *Visions of Zosimos*. But there is, within the world of academic discourse, a more definite and final *Endzeit* than has ever been dreamed of by the apocalypticist.

In this paper I have tried to illustrate the implications of adopting the perspective advanced by Peter Brown:

---

[64] An excellent example would be the complex Egyptian and Greco-Egyptian traditions surrounding Nectanebo, the last native king of Egypt.

There are two ways of approaching the way in which Manichaeism spread within the Roman Empire: the jig-saw puzzle and the Chinese boxes. The approach of the jig-saw puzzle sees Manichaeism exclusively as a product of religious syncretism. The scholar asks what pieces in the jig-saw of Manichaean beliefs appealed to what religious groups in the Roman world ... This approach has severe limitations. I would prefer the approach of the Chinese boxes. To become a Manichee or to favour the Manichee meant favoring a group. This group had a distinctive and complex structure.[65]

In a sense this is to return to the older social-functional understanding of syncretism as συν-κρητίζειν and to abandon the more recent biological interpretation of syncretism as συν-κεράννυμι.[66]

AFTERWORD

See my more extended treatment of the Babylonian materials in "A Pearl of Great Price and A Cargo of Yams: A Study in Situational Incongruity," *History of Religions*, XV (1976), 1-19. I have been much stimulated by R. Drews, "The Babylonian Chronicles and Berossus," *Iraq*, XXXVII (1975), 39-55 which offers a partial confirmation of the argument of this paper.

---

[65] P. Brown, *Religion and Society in the Age of Saint Augustine* (1972), p. 108.
[66] This paper was prepared under the auspices of the Rosenstiel Fellowship at the University of Notre Dame. I am grateful for the assistance and courtesies extended by the Notre Dame theological faculty.

CHAPTER FOUR

THE WOBBLING PIVOT[1]

In the course of a recent conversation, Professor Eliade reminisced about a French publisher who invited Eliade to contribute a book to a series he was editing. When Eliade asked him what the subject of his book should be the publisher responded, "On anything except sacred time or space." While this may well be the reaction to a paper which seeks to comment on aspects of Eliade's contribution to research on these two problems, it is also eloquent testimony to the centrality of these patterns in Eliade's thought and to the frequency with which he has returned to them in his published writings.

Certainly the three books which made Eliade's reputation in this country—The *Myth of the Eternal Return*, *Patterns in Comparative Religion*, (especially but by no means exclusively chapters X and XI), and *The Sacred and the Profane*—are centrally concerned with sacred space and time, as is *Myth and Reality*,[2] whose table of contents reveals the full, subtle range of Eliade's temporal vocabulary: Magic and the Prestige of Origins; Myths and Rites of Renewal; Eschatology and Cosmogony; Time Can Be Overcome; Mythology, Ontology, and History; Mythologies of Memory and Forgetting. Much of Eliade's prolific production has been related to these patterns of sacred space and sacred time, for example, his many articles on the notions of beginning (*ab origine, in illo tempore*), repetition, mythic, cyclical time in cosmogonic myths as opposed to history;[3] his remarks on the

---

[1] This paper was delivered as part of a symposium on the work of Professor Eliade at the University of Notre Dame, February 12, 1971. I have retained the style of the original, adding only brief footnotes.

[2] Mircea Eliade, *The Myth of the Eternal Return* (New York, 1954); *Patterns in Comparative Religion* (New York, 1958); *The Sacred and the Profane* (New York, 1959); *Myth and Reality* (New York and Evanston, 1963).

[3] Eliade, "Kosmogonische Mythen und magische Handlungen," *Paideuma*, VI (1956): 194-204; "La vertu créatrice du mythe," *Eranos Jahrbuch*, XXV (1957): 59-85; "The Prestige of Cosmogonic Myth," *Diogenes*, XXIII (1958): 1-13; "Structure et fonctions du mythe cosmogonique," in *La naissance du monde* (Paris, 1959), pp. 469-95; "Repetizione della cosmogonia," in E. de Martino, ed., *Magia e civiltà* (Milan, 1962), pp. 168-82; "Mythologie, ontologie, histoire," in E. Haberland, et al., *Festschrift für Ad. E. Jensen* (Munich, 1964), vol. I, pp. 123-33; "Archaic Man and Historical Man." *McCormick Quarterly*, XVIII (1965): 23-36;

prestige of origins;[4] his concern for the renewal of time or the abolition of profane time in New Year and initiatory scenarios;[5] his studies of recollection and memory,[6] and of eschatology and Paradise.[7] He has had, since his early writings, a special interest in Indian myths and philosophies of time, and this concern, joined with his perception of cosmic and spatial homologies, underlies his most creative studies of Yoga.[8] His numerous articles, perhaps influenced by Paul Mus's massive *Barabudur* which he reviewed in Romanian in 1937,[9] on the symbolism of the Center in cosmologies, rituals of orientation, temple and house construction, witness to a persistent theme.[10] In addition, one might point to other less obvious researches: his notion of the "speed up" of time in his studies of alchemy;[11] his concern for ascension symbolism and the transcendence of space and

---

"Cosmogonic Myth and Sacred History," *Religious Studies*, II (1967): 171-83. On the theme of history and cyclical time, see further "History and the Cyclical View of Time," *Perspectives*, V (1960): 11-14; and "Symbolism and History," in Eliade, *Images and Symbols* (London, 1961), pp. 151-78.

[4] Eliade, "Le mythe du bon sauvage ou les prestiges de l'origine," *Nouvelle revue française*, XXXII (1955): 229-49, (trans.) *Myths, Dreams and Mysteries* (New York, 1960), pp. 39-56; "The Quest for the 'Origins' of Religion," *History of Religions*, IV (1964), 154-69.

[5] New Year: Eliade, *The Myth of the Eternal Return*, pp. 62-73; "Nouvel An, peau neuve," *Le courier*, VIII (1955): 7-32. Initiation: Eliade, *Birth and Rebirth* (New York, 1958), pp. x-xv, 4-7 *et passim*.

[6] Eliade, "Mythologies of Memory and Forgetting," *History of Religions*, II (1963): 329-44.

[7] Eliade, "The Yearning for Paradise in Primitive Tradition," *Daedalus*, LXXXVIII (1959): 255-67; "Cosmic and Eschatological Renewal," in Eliade, *The Two and the One* (London, 1965), pp. 125-59; "Les Américains en Océanie et le nudisme eschatologique," *La nouvelle revue française*, VIII (1960): 58-74; "Cargo Cults' and Cosmic Regeneration," in S. L. Thrupp, ed., *Millennial Dreams in Action* (The Hague, 1962), pp. 139-43; "Paradise and Utopia: Mythical Geography and Eschatology," in F. E. Manuel, ed., *Utopias and Utopian Thought* (Boston, 1966), pp. 260-80.

[8] Eliade, "Time and Eternity in Indian Thought," in J. Campbell, ed., *Man and Time* (*Papers from the Eranos Yearbook*, Vol. III) (New York, 1957), pp. 173-200; "Symbolisme indien de l'abolition du temps," *Journal de psychologie*, XLV (1952): 430-38; "Mythes indiens du temps," *Combat* (March 13, 1952); *Yoga: Immortality and Freedom* (New York, 1958), *passim*.

[9] Eliade, "Barabudur, templul simbolic," *Revista Fundatiilor Regale*, IV (1937): 605-17 (*non vidi*).

[10] Eliade, "Centre du monde, temple, maison," in G. Tucci, ed., *Le symbolisme cosmique des monuments religieux* (*Serie orientale Roma*, XIX) (Rome, 1957), pp. 57-82; "Le symbolisme du centre," *Revue de culture européenne*, II (1952): 227-39; "Symbolism of the Center," in Eliade, *Images and Symbols*, pp. 27-56.

[11] Eliade, *The Forge and the Crucible* (New York, 1962), *passim*; "Alchemie und Zeitlichkeit," *Antaios*, II (1960): 180-88.

time in mysticism and ecstasy; the magical flight of shamans,[12] in the elucidation of the seven footsteps of the Buddha,[13] the Indian metaphor of "breaking the roof,"[14] or the Indian rope trick,[15] as well as in his exciting article on spatial and temporal bounds in his "The 'God Who Binds' and the Symbolism of Knots."[16] Finally, as many of the Romanian critics illustrated in Eliade's *Festschrift*, his novels are preoccupied with time and to a lesser degree with space.[17]

In this paper I propose to undertake two tasks. The first is a general discussion of Eliade's structures of sacred time and space with a few critical remarks. In making these, I feel acutely the stance of the pygmy standing on the giant's shoulders but without the attendant claim of having seen further (if one dares to so stretch this tortured phrase, fondly contracted as OTSOG, following Robert K. Merton's brilliant investigation of its history).[18] The giant, in this case, has taught all of us how and what to see; and, far more important, how to understand what we have learned to see. For as Marcel Proust has somewhere noted (a novelist equally obsessed with Eliade's problem of time): "One can place indefinitely in succession, in a description, the objects which appear . . . ; truth will not begin to appear until the moment when the writer will take two different objects and will place them in a relationship." Eliade has shown us the patterns and systems of these interrelationships (and thus differs, despite superficial similarities, from older catalogs of "objects" such as *The Golden Bough*). It is for us, his students, only to bring forth the questions, blurrings, and shadows which result from our more peripheral vision.

As a second task I should then like to offer some queries to and applications of Eliade's basic presuppositions. These queries arise for one who understands himself to be standing within Eliade's work as I confront the material that I am concerned with interpreting.

---

[12] Eliade, *Shamanism: Archaic Techniques of Ecstasy* (New York, 1964), pp. 477-82, *et passim* ; "Symbolisme du 'vol magique,'" *Numen*, III (1956): 1-13.

[13] See the articles collected in Eliade, *Myths, Dreams and Mysteries*, pp. 99-122.

[14] Eliade, "Briser le toit de la maison: Symbolisme architectonique et physiologie subtile," in *Studies in Mysticism and Religion: Festschrift G. Scholem* (Jerusalem, 1967), pp. 131-39.

[15] Eliade, "Ropes and Puppets," in *The Two and the One*, pp. 160-88.

[16] Eliade, *Images and Symbols*, pp. 92-124.

[17] See the contributions by V. Ierunca (esp. pp. 348-52), V. Horia (pp. 387-95), G. Uscatescu (pp. 397-406), and the article by G. Spaltmann (esp. pp. 375-85) in J. Kitagawa and C. Long, *Myths and Symbols: Studies in Honor of Mircea Eliade* (Chicago, 1969).

[18] R. K. Merton, *On the Shoulders of Giants: A Shandean Postscript* (Glencoe, Ill., 1965).

I. THE BASIC PRESUPPOSITIONS AND ELEMENTS OF ELIADE'S WORK REGARDING SACRED SPACE AND TIME

There is a basic opposition between the Sacred and the profane. At times the opposition in Eliade's presentation seems to resemble Durkheim's classic formulation in the opening chapter of *The Elementary Forms of the Religious Life*.[19] For Eliade, the Sacred, and sacred space and time in particular, is the extraordinary, the realm in which the Sacred paradoxically manifests itself through hierophanies, kratophanies, and the like. (Rudolph Otto will frequently be appealed to by Eliade in this connection.[20] Indeed one might suggest that part of Eliade's "strategy" has been to substitute Otto's language of the Holy for Durkheim's more neutral and positional Sacred while maintaining the dynamics of Durkheim's dualism.) The profane is the ordinary, the neutral, the realm of the adiaphora (to borrow a useful term from Lutheran theology). In other passages, Eliade appears to suggest that the Sacred is the Real, understood as Being, power, or creativity, as opposed to the profane, which is unreal, "absolute non-Being," or chaotic.[21] In accord with this formulation, which seems to me far more central to Eliade and to which I shall return, one might propose retitling Eliade's well-known book *The Sacred and the Chaotic*, or, adopting the title of Bernard W. Anderson's interesting study, *Creation versus Chaos*.

Since Kant it has been commonplace to define man as a world-creating being and human culture or society as a process of world construction. Taking their clue from the third *Kritik*, philosophers and social scientists have sought to elucidate the mechanisms of human creativity and to explore the limits of human possibility and freedom. Complex theories have been proposed—all starting from a fundamentally anthropological base ("man makes himself"). Eliade, at first glance, appears to continue this post-Kantian endeavor with his focus on the characteristic categories of time and space and in such pregnant formulations as, "*If the world is to be lived in* it must be *founded*"; in settling a territory "what is involved is *undertaking the creation of the world that one has chosen to inhabit*."[22] But, in fact, Eliade

---

[19] E. Durkheim, *Les formes élémentaires de la vie religieuse*, 4th ed. (Paris, 1960), pp. 50-56; English trans. J. S. Swain (London, 1915), pp. 37-41.

[20] See, for example, Eliade, "Power and Holiness in the History of Religions," in *Myths, Dreams and Mysteries*, pp. 123-54.

[21] Eliade, *The Sacred and the Profane*, pp. 62-65; *Myth of the Eternal Return*, pp. 9-11.

[22] Eliade, *The Sacred and the Profane*, pp. 22, 51.

implies a fundamental reversal. World creation and world founding are not anthropological categories expressive of human freedom. Rather, they are to be understood as ontological (perhaps even theological) categories.[23] Man's fundamental mode is not freedom and creativity but rather repetition. Or, perhaps more accurately, man's creativity is repetition.

Repetition is the human mode of articulating absolute Reality. It is expressive of man's "unquenchable ontological thirst," his desire to "found" his existence in "real existence," in "objective reality," in that which is not "illusory," which avoids the "paralysis" of "the never-ceasing relativity of purely subjective experiences."[24] This reality is *given* to man, it is autonomous, and it "s'impose à l'homme du dehors."[25] Yet man is no mere passive receiver; he must creatively appropriate it for himself. This he does primarily through repetition.

Eliade has several parallel languages for describing the givenness of Reality. At times he speaks of the "manifestation" of the Sacred which "ontologically founds the world."[26] Here a highly dramatic and dynamic language prevails of power breaking into and displaying itself within man's ordinary, profane, changing, and unreal world (his favorite term is "irruption"). In this category Eliade treats those "elementary manifestations" for which he is most famous— a set of terms founded on the root *phainō*: hierophanies, kratophanies, epiphanies. At other times he speaks of the symbol as "pointing toward" or "revealing" the Real.[27] Or he may speak of myths which, for him, reveal the inner dynamics of Reality expressed as the creative activity of the gods. "Myths describe the various and sometimes dramatic breakthrough [*irruptions* in the French original] of the sacred

---

[23] While I am appreciative of Peter Berger's attempt to reconcile Eliade's notion of *cosmos* with the sociological conception of *nomos* in *The Sacred Canopy* (Garden City, N.Y., 1969; reprint), chaps. I-II, his anthropological perspective reverses Eliade's presuppositions (see esp. pp. 25-27) in a creative and suggestive way. Likewise the important remark of C. Lévi-Strauss, that being in place is what makes a thing sacred, would precisely reverse Eliade's formulation (Lévi-Strauss, *The Savage Mind* [Chicago, 1966], p. 10; cf. J. Z. Smith, "Birth Upside Down or Right Side Up?" p. 148, n. 5, below.

[24] Eliade, *The Sacred and the Profane*, pp. 28, 64.

[25] Eliade, *Traité d'histoire des religions*, 2d ed. (Paris, 1964), p. 312.

[26] Eliade, *The Sacred and the Profane*, p. 21.

[27] Eliade, "Methodological Remarks on the Study of Religious Symbolism," in M. Eliade and J. Kitagawa, *The History of Religions: Essays in Methodology* (Chicago, 1959), pp. 86-107. For a valuable exposition and trenchant critique, see H. Penner, "Bedeutung und Probleme der religiosen Symbolik bei Tillich und Eliade," *Antaios*, IX (1967), esp. 134-42.

(or the 'supernatural') into the World. It is this sudden breakthrough [*irruption*] of the sacred that really *establishes* the World and makes it what it is today."²⁸ These myths of supreme creativity provide the blueprint for all creativity. Because they are an expression of the Real, their repetition in ritual or their paradigmatic use in all modes of human creativity confers reality on man and his world. This is the essence of the "primitive ontology" that Eliade has devoted a major portion of his scholarly life to elucidating: "an object or an act becomes real only insofar as it imitates or repeats an archetype. Thus, reality is acquired solely through repetition or participation; everything which lacks an exemplary model is 'meaningless,' i.e., it lacks reality."²⁹ Human reality thus depends upon participation in a given Reality and this is doubly "paradoxical." First, it is paradoxical that the Sacred should be manifested in something profane and limited. Eliade employs many synonyms to express this paradox: the "coming-together of sacred and profane, of being and non-being, absolute and relative, the eternal and the becoming ... the coexistence of contradictory essences: sacred and profane, spirit and matter, eternal and non-eternal, and so on." It is a "rupture of ontological levels"³⁰ which relentlessly leads toward the "reduction" and ultimately the "abolition" of the "spheres that are profane."³¹ Second, man's existence is paradoxical. "Human existence takes place simultaneously upon two parallel planes: that of the temporal, of change and illusion, and that of eternity, of substance and of reality."³² Man strives to be "real" and this results in his being swallowed by Being, in a loss of his "individuality." On the other hand, man asserts the value of his own creativity and thus, for Eliade, falls into a "flight from reality."³³ (It is in this sense that one must understand what has been, for me, Eliade's most shocking notion—that history and the historical mode of existence represents man's "second fall.")³⁴

In an uncharacteristic moment Eliade ventures a definition of the "principle function of religion" which grows out of these considerations. It is:

---
²⁸ Eliade, *Myth and Reality*, p. 6. Cf. the French original, *Aspects du mythe* (Paris, 1963), p. 15.
²⁹ Eliade, *Myth of the Eternal Return*, p. 34.
³⁰ Eliade, *Patterns*, pp. 29f.
³¹ *Ibid.*, p. 459.
³² *Ibid.*, p. 460.
³³ *Ibid.*, pp. 460f.; cf. *Myth of the Eternal Return*, pp. 34f., 158.
³⁴ See esp. *Myth of the Eternal Return*, pp. 154-62.

that of maintaining an "opening" toward a world which is superhuman, the world of axiomatic spiritual values. These values are "transcendent" in the sense that they are revealed by divine beings or mythical ancestors. They therefore constitute absolute values, paradigms for all human activity. The function of religion is to awaken and sustain the consciousness of another world, of a "beyond".... This other world represents a superhuman "transcendent" plane, that of absolute realities. It is this experience of the sacred, that is, the meeting with a transhuman reality, that generates the idea of something which *really* exists and, in consequence, the notion that there are absolute, intangible values which confer a meaning upon human existence. It is thus through the experience of the sacred that the ideas of *reality*, *truth* and *meaning* come to light, ideas which will later be elaborated and articulated in metaphysical speculations and which ultimately become the basis of scientific knowledge.[35]

For Eliade, the major problem man—especially modern, "historical" *homo faber*—confronts is that of relativism and subjectivism. Eliade faces the issue squarely by addressing the two categories which have been conceived as being relative and subjective *sans pareil*: space and time. Eliade revalues these categories by relating them to the manifestation of and participation in transhuman Reality. Both space and time are, for Eliade, modes of irruption and repetition. However, we may note that when Eliade speaks of sacred space, it is the irruptive element which predominates; when he speaks of sacred time, it is the repetitive. Both space and time are experienced by religious man as "non-homogeneous." Hence both reflect the experience of a breakthrough of the normal ontological levels, and this break allows the possibility of participation in Reality—of reifying or sacralizing the profane.

In sacred space it is this breakthrough, this "image of an opening," which is primary. "Every sacred space implies a hierophany, an irruption of the sacred that results in detaching a territory from the surrounding cosmic milieu and making it qualitatively different.... *Something* that does not belong to this world has manifested itself..." and this manifestation ontologically grounds (or "founds") human existence.[36] The sacred place is not merely the dramatic experience of the presence of the Sacred (Eliade's favorite example is the Bethel vision of Genesis 28:12-19); it is a point of communication, the "paradoxical point of passage from one mode of being to another,"

---

[35] Eliade, "Structures and Changes in the History of Religion," in C. H. Kraeling and R. M. Adams, eds., *City Invincible* (Chicago, 1960), p. 366.

[36] Eliade, *The Sacred and the Profane*, pp. 26f.

which is repeatable *by man*.³⁷ Here Eliade invokes his well-known image of the Center which is the experience of the break in homogeneous space par excellence, the place of passage and communication through all the planes of existence and the means of organizing and founding the world in which men live.³⁸ Eliade notes, by way of complicating this model, that one finds in the history of religions two basic attitudes toward this Center. The one emphasizes the accessibility of this Center to man, who may experience it in his cities, temples, and dwellings; the other emphasizes the inaccessibility of the Center, it is difficult to gain access to it, it is available only to an elite who have undergone ordeals and who possess sufficient merit so as to be worthy of its possession.³⁹ The repeatability of the Center experience, whether theoretically available to every man or only to an elite, and the notion that the Center founds and organizes the cosmos as real, leads Eliade to a second motif. As I have already suggested, Eliade postulates two coextensive, fundamental structures of reality: the irruption of the Sacred and the paradigmatic deeds of the gods in the beginning. Therefore the Center, which is revealed to man "from without," may also be "rebuilt" by him as a "reconstruction" of the world organized about the sacred Center by following the general model of creation provided by the cosmogonic myths. This is particularly the case in acts of human construction. Thus the space in which man dwells is reified by being ritually homologized to the sacred Center and is constructed according to the "true" laws of creation which are, as we have seen, the "inner dynamics" of the Sacred. "Every dwelling, by the paradox of the consecration of space and by the rite of its construction, is transformed into a 'centre.'"⁴⁰

Sacred time is likewise an "opening" to the transcendent which results in the radical discontinuities which are characteristic of the "irruptive" experience. Profane time is abolished and a new value-laden time intrudes. This sacred time is "indefinitely recoverable, indefinitely repeatable." Sacred time is not primarily the time of revelation; but rather the time of beginning. It is the time of cosmogony in its first, clear, pristine form. Hence Eliade's emphasis on the

---

³⁷ *Ibid.*
³⁸ *Ibid.*, pp. 36-47. See the literature cited in n. 10 above.
³⁹ Eliade, "The Symbolism of the 'Centre,'" in *Images and Symbols*, esp. pp. 54f.; and *Patterns*, pp. 382-85.
⁴⁰ *Patterns*, p. 379.

fact that sacred time differs from profane time in that it is "reversible," "circular," "cyclical." It is the time of festival, and particularly the time of myth and the occasion for the recovery of the realia narrated in the myths. It not only allows man to reexperience the time of creation which is the "supreme divine manifestation," "the stupendous instant in which a reality was for the first time fully manifested," but, by the cyclical character of creation-decreation (return to chaos)-recreation serves to strengthen and revivify the cosmos, society, and the individual.[41] The cosmos and its structures are understood to be "a living world—inhabited and used by creatures of flesh and blood, subject to the law of becoming, of old age and death. Hence it requires a periodical repairing, a renewing, a strengthening. But the only way to renew the World is to repeat what the Immortals did *in illo tempore*, is to reiterate the creation."[42] Thus Eliade would join with the distinguished Old Testament scholar, Sigmund Mowinckel, in insisting that every creation myth is soteriological as well as cosmogonical:

> That life is thus *created* through the cult means salvation from that death and destruction which would befall, if life were not renewed. For existence is an everlasting war between the forces of life and death, of blessing and curse. "The World" is worn out if it is not regularly renewed. ... Thus it is "the fact of salvation" which is actualized in the cult. ... The fact that the cult is a repetition and a renewed creation leads to the view that the salvation which takes place is a *repetition* of a *first salvation* which took place in the dawn of time.[43]

The faith of Eliade's "archaic man" is a profound faith in the "truth" of the cosmos as ordered in the beginning and a joyous celebration of the primordial act of ordering, as well as a deep sense of responsibility for the maintenance of that order through repetition of the myth, through ritual, and through norms of conduct.

II. Queries and Applications

Thus far I have tried to report as faithfully as possible what I understand the central theses of Eliade to be with respect to the categories of sacred space and time. To such a general understanding I have

---

[41] Eliade, *The Sacred and the Profane*, pp. 68-113, esp. pp. 69, 80, 85, from which I have taken the quotations.
[42] Eliade, *Myth and Reality*, p. 45.
[43] S. Mowinckel, *The Psalms in Israel's Worship* (Oxford, 1962), vol. I, pp. 18f. See further Mowinckel's more general statement in *Religion und Kultus* (Göttingen, 1953), pp. 70-80.

questions—some of which have effectively been spoken to by Eliade, although not necessarily in explicit form. Within the scope of this paper it is possible only to briefly state these before moving to a central problem which emerges for me out of my work in Hellenistic religions. Therefore I shall merely offer a set of interrelated questions for discussion and indicate where in Eliade's work I find the resources for their possible resolution.

1. Is chaos best understood as the equivalent of the profane, that which is neutral, that which is unreal? I would suggest that chaos is never profane in the sense of being neutral. It is not *chaos* in the archaic Greek meaning of the word: a "gap," "yawning hole," or "void."[44] Rather, chaos *only* takes a significance within a religious world view. Chaos is a sacred power; but it is frequently perceived as being sacred "in the wrong way." It is that which is opposed to order, which threatens the paradigms and archetypes but which is, nevertheless, profoundly necessary for the very creativity that is characteristic of Eliade's notion of the Sacred. Like the famous myth of the charioteer in Plato's *Phaedrus* (253-54), both horses are equally necessary. If one had only the white horse of decorum, temperance, and restraint, he would never reach heaven and the gods. If one had only the lawless black horse, he would rape the gods when he appeared before them. Without the black horse there would be neither motion nor life; without the white horse there would be no limits. Without such religious "black horses" as shamans and prophets, religious structures such as that of the High God might become so refined, so otiose, so transcendent, that they would run the risk of being irrelevant.[45] Thus chaos is never, in myths, finally overcome. It remains as a creative challenge, as a source of possibility and vitality over against, yet inextricably related to, order and the Sacred. For example, ancient Israel appears to share the common creation-by-combat mythology of the ancient Near East in which the warrior deity creates by dividing the chaotic waters. In later tradition the upper waters are male and the lower waters are female, and they cry out ceaselessly to be reunited. If they do come together, the world will be destroyed by flood, and chaos will have won. Yet once a year

---

[44] See the perceptive comments and the valuable collection of texts in F. M. Cornford, *Principium Sapientiae* (Cambridge, 1952), pp. 194f. (and notes).

[45] See the fundamental exposition of this pattern of the archaic otiose High Gods being replaced by younger fecundating deities in Eliade, *Patterns*, chap. II. See also the testing of Eliade's pattern in U. Oldenberg, *The Conflict between El and Ba'al in Canaanite Religion* (Leiden, 1969), esp. pp. 146-51.

(at the Feast of Water Drawing), the "stoppers" to the channels leading down to the subterranean dangerous waters were opened and the upper and lower waters were mingled while a general carnival atmosphere and sexual license prevailed in the Temple.[46] For my purposes it is essential only to emphasize that this was no descent into chaos so that chaos could be overcome through recreation; but rather a recognition of the power, the life-giving power, of chaos for insuring vitality and fecundity for the year to come. My sense is that on this issue, Eliade's discussion of water and water symbolism would provide a valuable corrective to the negative or neutral interpretation of chaos.[47]

2. Has not the illuminating category of the "Center" been too narrowly discussed in literalistic terms of geographical symbolism? Eliade has suggested, in works such as *Yoga*, the complexity of this symbol as equivalent to the *Grund* and has indicated the dimensions of this symbol in relation to interiority.[48] Yet most of his more general discussion has concerned midpoint on either a horizontal or vertical axis. I have attempted in a previous article to briefly sketch out the variety of ways in which Jerusalem served as the "Center": as an enclave against the forces of chaos, as the vertical and horizontal center of space, as the center of time and history, and as a center of value. The majority of relevant texts do not explicitly employ the kind of "Center" language Eliade has collected, yet they are frequently more eloquent testimony to the underlying ideology.[49] Furthermore, this focus on the explicit presence of the term "Center" leads Eliade at times to employ questionable interpretations of his material (e.g., the term given to Babylonian sanctuaries, *Dur-an-ki* [Bond of

---

[46] For the general pattern, the fundamental work remains H. Gunkel, *Schöpfung und Chaos in Urzeit und Endzeit* (Göttingen, 1895). See further, A. J. Wensinck, *The Ocean in the Literature of the Western Semites* (Amsterdam, 1918); O. Eissfeldt, "Gott und das Meer in der Bibel," in *Studia Orientalia Ioanni Pedersen* (Copenhagen, 1953), pp. 76-84; O. Kaiser, *Die mythischen Bedeutung des Meeres in Aegypten, Ugarit und Israel*, 2d ed., (Berlin, 1959); L. R. Fisher, "Creation at Ugarit and the Old Testament," *Vetus Testamentum*, XV (1965): 313-24; F. M. Cross, Jr., "The Divine Warrior in Israel's Early Cult," in A. Altmann, ed., *Biblical Motifs* (Cambridge, Mass., 1966), pp. 1-10. For the material on the Feast of Water Drawing, see R. Patai, *Man and Temple in Ancient Jewish Myth and Ritual* (London, 1947), chaps. II and III.

[47] Eliade, *Patterns*, chap. V.

[48] Eliade, *Yoga*, esp. pp. 115f., 219-27.

[49] J. Z. Smith, "Earth and Gods," see below, pp. 104-128. Compare Eliade's use of this article in "A Cosmic Territorial Imperative?" *Center Report*, IV: 2 (1971): 22-26.

Heaven and Earth], probably does not mean, as Eliade often implies, the place of intersection of the upper world with earth, but rather the scar, or navel, left behind when heaven and earth were forcibly separated in creation—it is the disjunctive rather than the conjunctive which is to the fore).[50] At other times it leads to him to ignore texts which *do* contain important elements of the "Center" pattern but never explicitly use the term (e.g., Eliade has not, to my knowledge, dwelt on the significance of the fact that the Babylonian creation epic, *Enuma elish*, is not so much a cosmogony as it is a myth of the creation of a temple).

As a second but related issue, directly informed by Eliade's work on the "Center," I would query whether one can pay such attention to the "Center" without giving equal attention to the periphery. I would note the anthropological work of Alfonso Ortiz, the theoretical paper of Edward Shils on "Center and Periphery," and my own concern for the category of exile as three examples of such use of Eliade.[51]

3. Are all mythic first times paradigmatic and to be ritually repeated, as the usual, but I think not accurate reading of Eliade would suggest? Many of the first times described in myth—particularly those dealing with the origin of death, sickness, illness, sin, and evil— may well be existentially repeated in the human condition itself; but they are neither celebrated nor ritually repeated. The myth is frequently utilized as a description of how the present cosmos was created in order that it may be uncreated, that creation may be reversed. This is particularly the case in myths concerning the destiny of man, and I find Eliade's 1967 article, "Cosmogonic Myth and 'Sacred History,' " a major advance in suggesting that there are two types of primordiality (the cosmogonic and the ancestral-anthropological) with differing modes of repetition.[52] In other traditions there are even more daring mythologies in which the whole of creation, the world, the gods, and the structures of order and destiny

---

[50] See the discussion of Dur-an-ki in Th. Jacobsen, *Toward the Image of Tammuz and Other Essays on Mesopotamian History and Culture* (Cambridge, Mass., 1970), pp. 112f.

[51] A. Ortiz, *The Tewa World* (Chicago, 1969), chap. II, *et passim*; E. Shils, "Center and Periphery," reprinted in *Selected Essays by Edward Shils* (Chicago, 1970), pp. 1-14; J. Z. Smith, "Earth and Gods," pp. 119-128, below. Mary Douglas, *Purity and Danger* (New York, 1966), and Victor W. Turner, *The Ritual Process* (Chicago, 1969), explore the relationship of center and periphery, but are not influenced by Eliade.

[52] Reprinted in Eliade, *The Quest*, pp. 72-87.

are judged to be evil or confining and must be reversed or destroyed. Although this has not been Eliade's major concern, he alludes to this possibility in his exegesis of the Indian metaphor of "breaking the roof" which, for him, "brings an end to the archaic idea that man can live only in a cosmos (i.e., territory, city, village, body), that is to say, in a 'world' which is sacred because it is patterned after the divine paradigm."[53] In my own research I have found reason to suggest that this pattern is just as fundamental as the category of a paradigmatic world and may well be just as archaic.

A related problem is suggested by questions one and three. It strikes me that historians of religion have been weakest in interpreting those myths which do not reveal a cosmos in which man finds a place to dwell and on which he found his existence, but rather which suggest the problematic nature of existence and fundamental tension in the cosmos. I have in mind such traditions as dualistic creation myths, Earth-diver traditions, Tricksters, or the complex narratives of Corn or Rice Mothers who create by "loathsome" processes (e.g., rubbing the dirt off their bodies, by defecation, secretion).[54] Clearly these mythologies, many of which are extremely archaic, point to a different spiritual horizon than that described by Eliade as the fundamental "archaic ontology."

4. Is the material Eliade describes best organized under the categories "archaic" and "modern"? If one accepts the basic dualism just described between those cultures which affirm the structures of the cosmos and seek to repeat them; which affirm the necessity of dwelling within a limited world in which each being has its given

---

[53] Eliade, "Structure and Change," in *City Invincible*, p. 366. See further the literature cited above, n. 14.

[54] Eliade has dealt with some of these traditions in "Mythologies asiatiques et folklore sud-est européen: Le plongeon cosmogonique," *Revue de l'histoire des religions*, CIX (1961), 157-212; "Dualism," *The Encyclopaedia Britannica* (1969), vol. VII, pp. 717f.; "Prolegomena to Religious Dualism: Dyads and Polarities," *The Quest*, pp. 127-75; "Le Diable et le Bon Dieu: Préhistoire de la cosmogonie populaire roumaine," in *De Zalmoxis à Gengis-Khan* (Paris, 1970), pp. 81-130. The Trickster has been dealt with from a History of Religions perspective in an exhaustive but inconclusive dissertation by M. L. Ricketts, "The Structure and Religious Significance of the Trickster-Transformer-Culture Hero in the Mythology of the North American Indians" (unpublished Ph. D. dissertation, University of Chicago, 1964), vols. I-II; see further, Ricketts, "The North American Indian Trickster," *History of Religions*, V (1966): 327-50. The theme of "loathsome" creation has been especially emphasized by G. Hatt, "The Corn Mother in America and Indonesia," *Anthropos* XLVI (1951), 853-914, who offers, however, no interpretation.

place and role to fulfill, a centrifugal view of the world which emphasizes the importance of the "Center" as opposed to those cultures which express a more "open" view in which the categories of rebellion and freedom are to the fore; in which beings are called upon to challenge their limits, break them, or create new possibilities, a centripetal world which emphasizes the importance of periphery and transcendence; in which, in Eliade's terms, one "has chosen not installation in the world but absolute freedom ... the annihilation of every conditioned world"[55]—ought one to suggest the periodization implied by the terms "archaic" and "modern"? In part this is a terminological problem. In my own writings I have toyed with the distinction centrifugal and centripetal, central and peripheral, considered adopting Bergson's classic distinction between the closed/static society and the open/dynamic one, or Eric Voegelin's contrast between a "compact" and "differentiated" experience of the cosmos.[56] With some hesitation I have settled for the present on the dichotomy between a *locative* vision of the world (which emphasizes place) and a *utopian* vision of the world (using the term in its strict sense: the value of being in no place). Whatever terminology is employed, we must be careful to preserve a sufficient sense of the experiential character of this dichotomy and resist imposing even an implicit evolutionary scheme of development "from the closed world to the infinite universe" (to borrow the title of Alexander Koyré's well-known work). This requires our resisting as well the frequent tendency to identify the centripetal-closed-locative view with primitive, archaic society and the centrifugal-open-utopian with the modern. Both have been and remain coeval existential possibilities which may be appropriated whenever and wherever they correspond to man's experience of his world. While in this culture, at this time or in that place, one or the other view may appear the more dominant, this does not effect the postulation of the basic availability of both at any time, in any place.

I have a sense that much will be learned from relating these cosmic views to the social worlds in which they are found. For example, my own appreciation of the locative and the rebellious has been

---

[55] Eliade, "Structure and Change," in *City Invincible*, p. 366.
[56] H. Bergson, *Les deux sources de la morale et de la religion* (Paris, 1932); E. Voegelin, *Order and History*, vol. I, *Israel and Revelation* (Baton Rouge, 1956), p. 5, and compare J. Z. Smith, ch. 7, below; Smith, ch. 6, below.

much enriched by reading works such as Louis Dumont's *Homo Hierarchicus*, and I would hope that historians of religion will pay more attention to these resources in the future.[57]

Although space forbids its development in this essay, the same question might be raised to the related distinction between cyclical-mythic time and linear-historical time, a distinction which is an inheritance from the pan-Babylonian school of Winckler and Jeremias. This dichotomy does not seem to do justice to the rich patterns of temporal significance which have been discovered in various cultures. Again, sociological works, such as Georges Gurvitch's *The Spectrum of Social Time*, may be of some use to the historian of religions.[58]

By way of conclusion, I should like to illustrate the coexistential conflict between what I have called the central-locative and the peripheral-utopian world views by two anecdotes told of Alexander the Great and his meeting with the naked sages of India. (The first, by the way, is the genesis of the title for this paper.)

> It was Calanus we are told who lay before Alexander the famous illustration of government. It was this. He threw down upon the ground a dry and shrivelled hide, and set his foot upon the outer edge of it; the hide was pressed down in one place, but rose up in others. He went all around the hide and showed that this was the result wherever he pressed the edge down, and then at last he stood in the middle of it, and lo! it was all held down firm and still. The similitude was designed to show Alexander that he ought to put most constraint upon the middle of his empire and not wander far away from it.[59]

> On the appearance of Alexander and his army, these venerable men stamped [the earth] with their feet and gave no other sign of interest. Alexander asked them through interpreters what they meant by this odd behavior, and they replied: "King Alexander, every man can possess only so much of this earth's surface as this we are standing on. You are but human like the rest of us, save that you are always busy . . . travelling so many miles from your home, a nuisance to yourself and to others."[60]

The dichotomy remains. On the one hand the structures of Center and conformity to place as represented by the Indian sages; on the

---

[57] L. Dumont, *Homo hierarchicus* (Paris, 1967); English trans. (Chicago, 1970).

[58] G. Gurvitch, *The Spectrum of Social Time* (Dordrecht, 1964).

[59] Plutarch, *Alexander*, LXV.4 (trans. B. Perrin, *Plutarch's Lives* [London, 1949], vol. VII, pp. 409, 411).

[60] Arrian, *Anabasis*, VII.i.6 (trans. A. de Sélincourt, *Arrian's Life of Alexander the Great* [Baltimore, 1958], pp. 225f.).

other, Alexander the world conqueror, the utopian, relentlessly and restlessly testing the boundaries of the cosmos and seeking to transcend all limits. The question of the character of the place on which one stands is *the* fundamental question as Eliade has taught us. The alternation, the discoveries and choices of and between these two views is, as again I have learned from Eliade, the history of man and the history of religions.

CHAPTER FIVE

EARTH AND GODS*

Among the many exciting developments in History of Religions research in the past few decades has been the elucidation of the category of sacred space. One might point to the general researches of Mircea Eliade (*The Sacred and the Profane*), Roger Callois (*L'homme et le sacré*), and, within specific traditions, the careful monographs of scholars such as P. Mus (*Barabudur*), G. Tucci (*Il simbolismo architettonico dei tempi di Tibet occidentale*), S. Kramrisch (*The Hindu Temple*), and others, as well as important conferences such as that held in Rome in 1955 on *Le symbolisme cosmique des monuments religieux*, in which Eliade, Daniélou, and Lévi-Strauss participated. However, there has been a relative lack of studies on sacred space within Jewish and Christian materials. The historian of religions working with Western religious traditions has had, for the most part, to confine himself to the old, though still valuable, monographs by W. H. Roscher on the *omphalos* (*Omphalos; Neue Omphalosstudien* and *Der Omphalosgedanke bei verschiedenen Völkern*), G. Klameth on *Die neutestamentlichen Lokaltraditionen Palästinas*, A. J. Wensinck on *The Idea of the Western Semites concerning the Navel of the Earth*, or J. Jeremias' study of *Golgotha*. More recently, there have been detailed studies such as the important treatment by Raphael Patai (*Man and Temple*) as well as monographs on particular aspects of the structure such as H. Sedlmayr's works on the cathedral, H. P. L'Orange on cosmic orientation, B. S. Childs' chapter on mythic and biblical space in *Myth and Reality in the Old Testament*, W. Müller's *Die heilige Stadt: Roma quadrata, himmlisches Jerusalem und die Mythe vom Weltnabel*, K. L. Schmidt's "Jerusalem als Urbild und Abbild" (*Eranos Jahrbuch*, XVIII [1950]), A. Haldar, *The Notion of the Desert in Sumero-Accadian and West-Semitic Religions*, and B. Goldman, *The Sacred Portal: A Primary Symbol in Ancient Judaic Art*. Additional resources, from quite another perspective, may be found in the contributions of phenomenologists such as Heidegger, Bachelard, Binswanger and Gurvitch, and in the important studies of phenomenological literary

---

* This paper was delivered as a lecture at the University of Chicago, February 12, 1968. I have retained the style of the original, adding only brief references.

critics such as Poulet and Richard on the categories of space, exile, and forgetfulness, which still have not been sufficiently appropriated by historians of religion.[1]

In recent years the recovery of the structure of sacred space has, especially within Judaism, become more than a merely academic enterprise. The repossession of the land of Israel in 1947 and the repossession of the site of the Temple in Jerusalem in 1967 have reawakened in an acute way the archaic language of sacred space and have reacquainted the modern Jew with a variety of myths and symbols which he had proudly thought he had forgotten, myths and symbols which he frequently boasted to others that he never had.

This is brought home with full force in Richard Rubenstein's *After Auschwitz*. One of the consistently repeated themes in Rubenstein's book is the notion that, for the contemporary Jew, the reestablishment of Israel, "marks the re-birth of the long forgotten gods of the earth within Jewish experience."[2] The issue that Rubenstein is raising is one that is ultimately far more significant than the alleged problem of Israelitic "syncretism": the question of the presence of Canaanite deities in, and their influence on, the cult of Israel (a problem which exists only for one who adopts a fundamentally unimaginative and simplistic view of the complexity of Israelitic religious traditions and experience and a correspondingly unimaginative and simplistic view of ancient Near Eastern religions), or the so-called resurgence of these deities under Jeroboam and among the Jews of Elephantine, the later renaissance of these figures in mystical and kabbalistic circles (as if they were ever dead!), or the whole debated question of the existence of Hebraic mother goddesses. Whether or not Rubenstein is aware of the vast literature and long scholarly debate on these issues, the thrust of his remarks seems directed to quite a different dimension. He claims that the "rediscovery of Israel's earth and the lost divinities of that earth" enables the Jews of today to "come in contact with those powers of life and death which engendered man's feelings about Baal, Astarte,

---

[1] See, for example, the impressive though slightly eccentric study of Heidegger by V. Vycinas, *Earth and Gods: An Introduction to the Philosophy of Martin Heidegger* (The Hague, 1961); W. Biemel's *Le concept de monde chez Heidegger* (Paris, 1950); and the essay by W. Kluback and J. T. Wilde, "An Ontological Consideration of Place," in their translation of M. Heidegger, *The Question of Being* (New York, 1958), pp. 18-26.

[2] R. L. Rubenstein, *After Auschwitz: Radical Theology and Contemporary Judaism* (Indianapolis, 1966), p. 130; cf. pp. 70, 122-26, 136.

and Anath. These powers have again become decisive in our religious life."[3] This, then, is not an issue of "origins" or "borrowings," but of religious experience and expression. Rubenstein (albeit indirectly) has performed as profound and radical a reversal of the usual mode of scholarly perception as that of Eliade when Eliade reminds us in a typically cryptic but pregnant sentence: "The drama of the death and resurrection of vegetation is revealed by the myth of Tammuz, rather than the other way about."[4] What Rubenstein appears to be suggesting (to phrase it in other terms) is that the recovery of the land of Israel has permitted Jews to rediscover what Charles Long calls a sense of "cosmic orientation" or what Theodore H. Gaster has termed the "topocosm" (i.e., "the entire complex of any given locality conceived as a living organism").[5]

The Israelitic cosmos as described by Rubenstein, as sung about in Israeli folksongs (especially some of the new songs growing out of the Six Days' War, e.g., "Yerushalayim shel Zahav," "Jerusalem of Gold"), or as celebrated by both her artists and politicians is a profoundly different cosmos than that experienced by generations of European Jews. One may express this radical shift in a number of ways: from a condition of an almost schizophrenic existence of living in a country but understanding one's true homeland to be somewhere else; from exile to return; in Robert Ardrey's brief examination of the Jew, from deterritorialization to reterritorialization. The result of this radical shift, to quote Rubenstein again, is that "Increasingly Israel's return to the earth elicits a return to the archaic earth religion of Israel. This does not mean that tomorrow the worship of Baal and Astarte will supplant the worship of Yahweh; it does mean that the earth's fruitfulness, its vicissitudes and its engendering power will once again become the central spiritual realities of Jewish life, at least in Israel."[6]

---

[3] *Ibid.*, p. 76. See further Rubenstein's clarification of his use of the terms "pagan" and "gods of the earth," with specific reference to Eliade, in his essay "Homeland and Holocaust: Issues in the Jewish Religious Situation," in D. R. Cutler (ed.), *The Religious Situation 1968* (Boston, 1968), pp. 39-64, 102-11, esp. pp. 41, 61, 105-6. Here Rubenstein explicitly declares, "What I refer to as pagan is very much the same religious type that Eliade calls archaic" (p. 41).

[4] M. Eliade, *Patterns in Comparative Religion*, trans. R. Sheed (New York, 1958), p. 426.

[5] C. H. Long, *Alpha: The Myths of Creation* (New York, 1959), pp. 18-19; T. H. Gaster, *Thespis: Ritual, Myth and Drama in the Ancient Near East* (2d ed.; Garden City, N. Y., 1961,) p. 17.

[6] Rubenstein, *After Auschwitz*, p. 7.

Merely compare this language of earth's "fruitfulness" and "engendering power" with the somewhat overdone and polemic, but nevertheless evocative, reconstruction of the world of the European ghetto Jew on the basis of an analysis of Yiddish vocabulary and literature written in 1943 by Maurice Samuel and you have the heart of the problem, a problem which, I would submit, can be best understood and interpreted by the historian of religions. A new world has been encountered, and a new mode of being must be assumed.

> Yiddish is a folk language, but unlike all other folk languages it has no base in nature. It is poor almost bankrupt by comparison with other languages in the vocabulary of field and forest and stream. ... Yiddish has almost no flowers ... the very words for the common flowers which are familiar to city dwellers everywhere are lacking in Yiddish. Yiddish is a world almost devoid of trees. ... The animal world is almost depopulated in Yiddish ... the skies are practically empty of birds. ... There is likewise a dearth of fish ... there are no nature descriptions to be found anywhere in Yiddish prose or poetry. ... All these expressions and perceptions were lacking because their material was withheld from the Jews. There were large areas of what we generally call folk self-expression to which the Jews were forever strangers.[7]

As symptomatic of the schizophrenia of exile, it may be noted that in general the ghetto Jew was far more expert on the flora and fauna of Palestine than he was of the neighboring fields in Poland.

What I propose in this essay is to undertake a brief examination of some Jewish texts and traditions from the standpoint of the History of Religion's category of sacred space, a category which involves the structures of "the center", of cosmic models, cosmogonic myths, and other elements familiar from works such as Eliade's.

It is to be regretted that there has been little solid work on Jewish and Christian materials using the discipline and categories of History of Religions, such as those found in Eliade's *Patterns in Comparative Religion*. Scholars have, in the main, either failed to subject these two religious traditions to the same methods of analysis, and thereby failed to employ the same categories and structures as they use to interpret other religious traditions, or, if they do employ the same methods and structures, they assert that in some unique way these do not exhaust the full reality of Judaism or Christianity (as if a historian of religions ever claimed or sought to exhaust the phenomenon he was interpreting)—that there is a "something more left over," a "some-

---

[7] M. Samuel, *The World of Sholom Aleichem* (reprint; New York, 1965), pp. 194-96.

thing more" which other traditions presumably do not possess, a "something more" which makes our Western traditions unique and true. Or, finally, a third posture is assumed by some scholars who do treat certain selected elements in Judaism and Christianity by the methods and structures of the History of Religions, but who claim that these either are survivals of a "pagan" past, foreign contaminations, or late accretions, or are the practice of a people on the fringes of the normative tradition (heresies, heterodoxies, popular or low-class practices). Each of these stances seems to me inadequate and, at heart, crudely apologetic.

The more I read in Jewish and Christian materials, the more I become convinced that many elements yield themselves far better to the sensitive historian of religions than to other disciplinary approaches. Elements such as the Old and New Testament as myth, the whole range of Jewish and Christian rituals and initiations, the liturgical year, etc., would profit from a careful examination in light of analogous structures in the History of Religions.

In the topic under discussion I shall claim the historian of religion's privilege of disregarding chronological and geographical considerations, of comparing and bringing together, as revealing, texts from widely different periods and contexts of Jewish history. And I shall use as my categories of interpretation the structures that emerge from the more general considerations of sacred space as it has been expressed within the History of Religions. This does not, however, mean that the Holy Land of Zion for the Jew is the same as the Dayak ancestral village studied by Hans Schärer. It does mean that the historian of Jewish traditions could well profit from an examination of Schärer's materials in order to be sensitized to certain categories and nuances of exile, of return to the ancestral land and primordial totality in moments of sacred time that he might otherwise miss in his studies. Likewise, a student of the sacred topography of Israel as set forth in Jewish and Christian pilgrim literature might do well to consider the fantastic elaboration of the primordial significance of each topographic feature on the sacred boulder of the Pitjandjara of Central Australia meticulously chronicled by Charles P. Mountford.[8]

---

[8] H. Schärer, *Ngaju Religion: The Conception of God among a South Borneo People* (The Hague, 1963), esp. pp. 94-97, conveniently anthologized in M. Eliade (ed.), *From Primitives to Zen: A Thematic Sourcebook on the History of Religions* (New York, 1967), pp. 170-72; C. P. Mountford, *Ayers Rock: Its People, Their Beliefs, and Their Art* (Honolulu, 1965), pp. 27-156, esp. p. 32, Fig. 3.

In this essay, I make no great claim to originality. I have deliberately confined myself to texts which have been translated into English in readily accessible volumes. There is nothing obscure about this material; it requires no elaborate field trips to collect. And yet, with the exception of Patai, I have not seen fruitful use made of this data either by scholars of Jewish traditions whose work usually remains uninformed by general History of Religions research, or by historians of religion who have, on the whole, exhibited a singular "failure of nerve" in incorporating Jewish and Christian materials into their works. I would further want to insist that it is only the historian of religions who is able to treat much of this material seriously.

I. THE ENCLAVE

The most archaic way Israel has of talking about her land may be described under a rubric borrowed from the war in Vietnam: Israel as an "enclave" or a "strategic hamlet." For the ancient Israelite, the wilderness or desert was not seen as neutral ground, but rather as sacred land—sacred in the "wrong way." It is the demonic land, the wasteland, the dangerous land. It is the land where thorns, nettles, and thistles grow. It is the haunt of the hawk, hedgehog, raven, owl, jackal, ostrich, hyena, and other wild-beasts. It is the place of demons and monsters, the place where the night hag shrieks. It is the land of confusion and chaos, the land that is waste and void as in the beginning (all of these descriptions from Isa. 34:9-15). It is a place of utter desolation, of cosmic and human emptiness, the "howling waste of the wilderness" (Deut. 32:10), the place called the "land not sown" (Jer. 2:2), the place "in which there is no man" (Job 38:26), the land of "no-kingdom-there" (Isa. 34:12).[9] The desert or wilderness is a place of strange, demonic, secret powers. It is a sacred land, a holy land in that it is a demonic realm; but it is not a place for ordinary men. It is not a place which is a homeland, a world where men may dwell.[10]

The world-for-man is a land which, in Eliade's terms, has been "founded." This may be expressed in a variety of ways: it is the land which has been given him by the deity; it is the land which has been

---

[9] I owe much in this section to J. Pedersen, *Israel: Its Life and Culture* (Copenhagen, 1926), I-II, 453-60, 467-80, 491-92.

[10] One must note the interrelatedness of the apparently contradictory notions of the desert or wilderness as a demonic land and Eden, the place of revelation and of purification. I am aware that the present discussion is one-sided at this point.

created for him by the deity; it is the land which man has established through his rituals; or it is the land which man has won by conquest.

In a sense (although space does not permit the elaboration of this suggestion) the Hexateuch, indeed the entire Old Testament, may be understood as a complex creation myth concerning the establishment of this land in which a man can be truly human and at home. In Israelitic terms, it is a myth of the establishment of Israel the land and the people of Israel.

It has become commonplace since the research of G. von Rad and M. Noth to speak of certain basic themes in the Hexateuch: the Patriarchs and the promise to the Patriarchs; the deliverance from Egypt and the crossing of the Sea of Reeds; the wilderness-wandering; the entry into or conquest of the land; the theophany at Sinai, and the primeval creation narrative. But, although a cultic *Sitz im Leben* is usually proposed for each of these traditions, the treatment they have received from biblical scholars has usually been overly theological or overly historicistic. Each theme is probably best understood as a creation myth; each takes its place in a mythic complex which narrates the myth of the origin of the land and its inseparable corollary, the myth of the creation of Israel.

If the Hexateuch is read from this perspective, several patterns emerge: (1) In order for land to be *my* land, one must live together with it. It is man living in relationship with his land that transforms uninhabited wasteland into a homeland, that transforms the land into the land of Israel. It is that one has cultivated the land, died on the land, that one's ancestors are buried in the land, that rituals have been performed in the land, that one's deity has been encountered here and there in the land that renders the land a homeland, a land-for-man, a holy land. It is, briefly, history that makes a land mine. In Old Testament terms it is the shared history of generations that converts the land into the land of the Fathers. (2) Alternatively, the land was not just there, at hand, to be granted willy-nilly by the deity. It was fought for and died for. The land was won. Though historians (rightly so) question the historicity of the biblical narrative of the sudden conquest of the land of Canaan, the religious-mythic reality of the tradition is beyond dispute. A holy land is a land that has been won. It is the fighting and, especially, the dying that renders the land uniquely mine. In the Old Testament, it is also the deity who has led one in battle for the land that confers upon the land its sacrality. (3) Or one may narrate a primordial charter to the land.

The land is Israel's land because Israel's god established it for her in the beginning. This view is implicit in the Old Testament and made explicit in the rabbinic traditions that Israel, Temple, and Torah were pre-existent, created by the deity before anything was brought into being.

The Old Testament presents one great initiatory saga of the death and rebirth of a people, their journey into a sacred land, their instruction there by the deity and the ancestors.

No matter how Israel's possession of the land is narrated, no matter what myth expresses the creation of the land, the possession of such a land is a responsibility, for the blessing of the land is a fragile thing. Whether the cosmography is expressed through the model of the sacred land as a mound in the midst of the raging desert or the world as a bubble of air in the midst of the dangerous cosmic waters which surround it, with the sacred land the highest point—the security of the blessing and the possession of the land is not guaranteed. The walls of the "hamlet" are always vulnerable to attack, and man must ceaselessly labor to sustain, strengthen, and renew the blessing, to keep the walls under repair. This he does (1) by the recitation of myth, by the performance of ritual repeating the new year myth of the creation of the land, the crossing of the Sea of Reeds or the River Jordan; (2) by remembering in solemn cultic recitation the mighty deeds of old, the shared history of the people and their land, the events associated with the ancestors who are buried in the land; (3) by the proper care of the land (e.g., the sabbath rest every seventh year); (4) by the way one lives on the land. The History of Religions is familiar with the widespread pattern of a close correspondence between conduct and blessing, between man's deeds and the maintenance of prosperity, fertility, and of creation itself. For the Israelite, the law provides a guaranty of the stability of the possession, the continuance of the land as my land, of its fertility and blessing: "You shall keep all my statutes and all my ordinances and do them in order that the land where I am bringing you to dwell may not vomit you out" (Lev. 20:22).

If man must labor to maintain the land as his land, so, too, the deity may be invoked to aid in the maintenance of the walls of the enclave. When David brings the ark up to Jerusalem in a great cultic ceremony, he is bringing up a powerful force (a force that can indeed kill) into the city. From the ark radiate out, in concentric circles, fields of force which maintain the city in blessing and fertility. Or, as an alternative expression, the traditions of the invulnerability of Zion: that YHWH will fight a holy war on behalf of his sacred city, at times against the Babylonians, and others at times against the mysterious "enemies from the North," which must be understood as demonic desert dwelling powers of chaos (especially Jer. 4:6-7; 6:22-23). For:

> Great is YHWH and much to be praised
> In the city of our God is his holy mountain;
> The most beautiful peak, the joy of all the earth.
> Mount Zion is the heart [i.e., the navel] of
> Zaphon,
> The city of the great King.
> God is her citadel, has shown himself her bulwark
> . . . .
> God will make her secure forever [Psalm 48].[11]

The structure of the Holy Land in the Old Testament is predominantly one of an enclave, a strategic hamlet walled against the demonic forces of evil and chaos, a land of blessing whose walls and blessing requires constant renewal.

The image of Jerusalem as the heart of Zaphon (itself an archaic image, compare *Baal and Anat 'nt* III:26-28: "In the midst of my mighty mountain Zaphon, on the holy mountain of my governance, on the beautiful hill of my dominion") introduces another structure little developed in the canonical Old Testament or the apocryphal books, but fully expressed in Josephus and rabbinic literature: the Holy Land as the Center of space and the Temple as the Center of the Holy Land.

II. The Center

The most famous and frequently cited rabbinic text illustrating this tradition reports that:

> Just as the navel is found at the center of a human being, so the land of Israel is found at the center of the world . . . and it is the foundation of the world. Jerusalem is at the center of the land of Israel, the Temple is at the center of Jerusalem, the Holy of Holies is at the center of the Temple, the Ark is at the center of the Holy of Holies and the Foundation Stone, is in front of the Ark, which spot is the foundation of the world.[12]

---

[11] I have followed here the translation of M. Dahood, *Psalms* (Garden City, N.Y., 1966), I, 288.

[12] Midrash Tanhuma, Kedoshim 10, as quoted in A. Hertzberg, *Judaism* (reprint; New York, 1963), p. 143.

It is for this reason that Jewish tradition speaks of its land with one voice from the rabbis in the Mishnah who declared: "The land of Israel is holier than all the other lands"[13] to east European Jews who observed in their travel letters home that Jerusalem is "particularly holy and the gate of heaven."[14]

For the Jew who journeys "up to Jerusalem" (and the journey to Jerusalem is always "up," though it stands only 2,200-2,310 feet above sea level and is surpassed in height by places such as Bethel and Hebron), he is undergoing what must be described as a mystical ascent. He is ascending to the center, to that one place on earth which is closest to heaven, to that place which is horizontally the exact center of the geographical world and vertically the exact midpoint between the upper world and the lower world, the place where both are closest to the skin of the earth, heaven being only two or eighteen miles above the earth at Jerusalem, the waters of Tehom lying only a thousand cubits below the Temple floor (in some traditions, the earthly Temple is connected to the heavenly sanctuary by an invisible tube and by shafts to the dangerous waters below). For the Jew to journey up to Jerusalem is to ascend to the very crucible of creation, the womb of everything, the center and fountain of reality, the place of blessing par excellence. It is, in Eliade's terms, to journey to the place which is pre-eminently real, a place which exhibits a "superabundance of reality," which may be expressed in a variety of ways (of which the following are only a small sample).

Emanating from the Center is an almost tangible power of holiness, of purity, which renders a magic quality to the land and insures its character as an enclave: "R. Yohanan said: 'Before the Temple was constructed evil spirits used to trouble the people in the world, but since the Tabernacle was built, the evil spirits have ceased from the world.' "[15] The land of Israel was supremely pure; Jerusalem was pre-eminently so. Thus, one reads in the Mishnah such observations as "any spittle found in Jerusalem may be deemed free from uncleanness"[16]; "there was no fly ever seen at the slaughter house in Jerusalem"[17]; or, more boldly, "He who lives in the land of Israel leads a

---

[13] M. Kelim I.6, in Hertzberg, *op. cit.*, p. 145.
[14] Letter of Isaac Hurwitz (d. 1630) in Hertzberg, *op. cit.*, p. 145.
[15] Num. R. XII.3, as quoted in R. Patai, *Man and Temple in Ancient Jewish Myth and Ritual* (London, 1947), p. 126.
[16] M. Shek. VIII.1, in H. Danby, *The Mishnah* (Oxford, 1933), p. 161.
[17] M. Aboth V.5, in Danby, *op. cit.*, p. 456.

sinless life."[18] This superabundance might be expressed in the almost automatic qualities of wisdom which adhere to those who inhabit the land. According to the rabbis, "the atmosphere of Israel makes men wise,"[19] "even the gossip of those who live in the land of Israel is *Torah*."[20] These two themes, the purity and wisdom inherent in the land and conferred on those who dwell within its boundaries, are magnificently joined together in the teaching of the eighteenth-century Ukrainian sage, Rabbi Nachman of Bratslav:

> His disciples have borne witness that all the life which he possessed came only from his having lived in the land of Israel. Every thought and every opinion which was his came only from the power of his having lived in the land of Israel for the root of all power and wisdom is the land of Israel. ... According to Rabbi Nachman, Israel is the starting place of the creation of the world, its foundation stone, and it is the source of the coming world in which everything will be good. It is the real center of the spirit of life and therefore of the renewal of the world by the spirit of life which will proceed from it. The spring of joy, the perfection of wisdom, the music of the world is in it ... the dust of the land of Israel has a magnetic power too: it draws men to holiness ... the earth can exert a healing influence on the man who settles on it and serves it by binding him to its indwelling holiness and then the spirit of man is supported, strengthened and borne by the power of the earth ... the pure and healing power of the earth is represented in the land of Israel.[21]

Indeed, so great is the magnetic attraction of this center that in a number of traditions the dead, buried in the Diaspora, are pictured as tunneling through the ground in order to reach their resting place in Israel.[22]

While these texts with their emphasis on purity and wisdom might (I believe wrongly) be judged a peculiar development of Jewish tradition, another complex which expresses this powerful superabundance is widespread in the history of religions: the land of Israel or the power of the land as concentrated in the Temple conceived as a center of fertility and fecundity. The vital power of the land and the Temple is expressed in a variety of ways, ranging from traditions

---

[18] BT Ket. 110*b*-111*a*, in Hertzberg, *op. cit.*, p. 143.
[19] BT Baba Bathra 158*b*, in Hertzberg, *op. cit.*, p. 144.
[20] Lev. R. XXXIV, in Hertzberg, *op. cit.*, p. 144.
[21] Hertzberg, *op. cit.*, p. 146; M. Buber, *The Tales of Rabbi Nachman*, trans. M. Friedman (reprint; Bloomington, 1962), pp. 207-8.
[22] A process known as *gilgul*. In some texts the dead burrow; in others, YHWH digs tunnels for them. See the convenient collection of texts in J. Zahavi, *Eretz Israel in Rabbinic Lore* (Jerusalem, 1962), pp. 99-100.

that so forceful was this creative power that even the gold representations of trees and vines in the Temple produced fruit which the priests ate, that even the dead wooden beams from which the Temple was constructed flowered and grew leaves,[23] to the observation that as Israel was the highest point in the world, it rains only in Israel, and the rest of the world is watered and fertilized by the run-off.[24]

This superabundance is apparent in the size of the animals and plants within the Holy Land, and the rabbis appear to vie with each other in outdoing the exaggeration. There are grapes as big as calves; cabbages so large that the stalk of one serves as a ladder; peaches so large that one-third of one feeds two men, one-third a herd of cattle, and the remainder is given away.[25]

More mysteriously, the land is the center of fertility, because heavenly beings engage in sexual intercourse in it, an intercourse at the heart of things which establishes and guarantees the fertility of the world. This may be expressed in some traditions by the belief that on top of the Ark in the Holy of Holies, the cherubim have been engaged in an act of unending intercourse since the beginning of time and if they should ever cease, the cosmos would collapse into chaos,[26] or by the tradition (quoted below) of YHWH having nightly intercourse with his bride on the "couch" of the site of the Temple in Jerusalem.

III. The Center of Time

The land of Israel is not only the enclave whose walls guard against the demonic powers of the chaotic desert or waters; it is not only the horizontal and vertical center of space, the focal point of purity, wisdom, blessing, and fertility—the land of Israel is understood to be the center of time as well.

In the Jewish traditions of the Holy Land, this has achieved a full mythic force which transcends the obvious fact that the important events in Israel's history, as recorded in the Bible, happened within the geographical confines of the land. Rather, the Center acts as a

---

[23] BT Yoma 21*b*, 39*b*; PT Yoma 41*d*; Tanhuma T'rumah 11; Tanhuma Ahare Moth 8, all in Patai, *op. cit.*, p. 90.
[24] BT Ta'anit 10*a*, in H. Malter, *The Treatise Ta'anit* (reprint; Philadelphia, 1967), pp. 134-36.
[25] See the collection of texts in Zahavi, *op. cit.*, pp. 51-52, 156.
[26] Patai, *op. cit.*, pp. 91-92; E. R. Goodenough, *Jewish Symbols in the Greco-Roman Period* (New York, 1954), IV, pp. 131-32.

magnet, attracting to itself, to the site of the Temple, all of the important creation events of Israel's traditions in a way similar to Golgotha in Christian legend and Mecca-Kaaba in Islamic lore. One might almost term the primeval stone, the Stone of Foundation which stands at the base of the Temple, a "dreaming" in the sense that the Australian aborigines use the term, that is, a track or sign left by a primordially significant being in mythic time.

At the Stone of Foundation, which stands at the exact center of the cosmos, the waters of Tehom were blocked off on the first day; it was upon this Stone that YHWH stood when he created the world; from out of this Stone, the first light came (this light was understood to still illuminate the Temple, which was constructed on the Stone; thus, the windows of the Temple were designed to let light out rather than in); from the surface of this Stone dust was scraped to create Adam; underneath this Stone Adam is buried; on this Stone Adam offered the first sacrifice; upon this Stone Cain and Abel offered their fateful sacrifice; from under this Stone the flood waters came and under this Stone the floodwaters receded; upon this Stone Noah's ark landed and on this Stone Noah offered the first sacrifice of the renewed cosmos; upon this Stone Abraham was circumcised and upon this Stone he consumed the mystic meal with Melchizedek; upon this Stone Isaac was bound for sacrifice; this Stone served as the "pillow" for Jacob in the ladder vision (that vision of a vertical center, a ladder connecting heaven and earth, a ladder which I suspect was either two or eighteen miles high, depending on the tradition followed); it was on this Stone that YHWH stood when he sent out and recalled the plagues from Egypt; it was this Stone which David discovered when he dug the foundations of the Temple, and, finally, it will be upon this Stone that the Messiah will announce the end of the present era and the creation of the new. With the exception of the Bethel vision and David's discovery of the Stone, each of these events is believed to have occurred during the festival of Passover, the cosmogonic feast par excellence.[27]

For the Jew who lives within this land, which is the vertical center of space, midpoint between the upper and lower world, the horizontal center of the earth, and the sacred center of his history, there is an awesome responsibility analogous to the common motif of perfection

---

[27] J. Jeremias, "Golgotha und der heilige Felsen," *Angelos*, II (1926), 74-128. This was reprinted as *Golgotha* ("Angelos: Archiv für neutestamentliche Zeitgeschichte und Kulturkunde," Suppl.), ed. G. Polster, I (Leipzig, 1926), 34-88.

in the performance of ritual in the history of religions. For there is a close correspondence between things which occur in the sacred land (especially within the Temple in Jerusalem) and actions in the heavenly Tabernacle. What is said anthropologically of Peter, the living Stone of Foundation in Christian tradition ("whatever you bind on earth shall be bound in heaven; whatever you loose on earth shall be loosed in heaven" [Matt. 16:19]) and of the Jewish magician Honi the Circledrawer, who ritually fashioned (mandala-like) a center in which he stood and commanded rain to fall ("You have decreed on earth below, now the Holy One, blessed be He, fulfils your word in heaven above"[28]) is said also of the relation of the action of the high priest at the earthly altar below to the archangel Michael, the heavenly high priest, in the celestial Tabernacle. Whatsoever the high priest does below shall be faithfully copied by the high priest above.[29] One may presume that if but a single error or alteration was made below, the cosmic liturgy itself would go awry. Small wonder a high priest who changed the ritual was pelted by the crowds at the Temple.[30] This sense of awesome responsibility, the requirement for ritual perfection and purity, was expressed forcefully centuries later by the Jewish folklorist S. Z. Rappoport in his famous play *The Dybbuk*:

> The holiest land in the world is the Land of Israel. In the Land of Israel the holiest city is Jerusalem. In Jerusalem the holiest place was the Temple, and in the Temple the holiest spot was the Holy of Holies. There are seventy peoples in the world. The holiest among these is the People of Israel. The holiest of the People of Israel is the tribe of Levi. In the tribe of Levi the holiest are the priests. Among the priests the holiest was the High Priest. There are 354 days in the year. Among these the holidays are holy. Higher than these is the holiness of the Sabbath. Among Sabbaths, the holiest is the Day of Atonement, the Sabbath of Sabbaths. There are seventy languages in the world. The holiest is Hebrew. Holier than all else in this language is the holy Torah, and in the Torah the holiest part is the Ten Commandments. In the Ten Commandments the holiest of all words is the name of God. And once during the year, at a certain hour, these four supreme sanctities of the world were joined with one another. That was on the Day of Atonement, when the High Priest would enter the Holy of Holies and there utter the name of God. And because this hour was beyond

---

[28] BT Ta'anit 23a, in Patai, *op. cit.*, p. 186; cf. Malter, *op. cit.*, p. 340.

[29] Seder'Arquim, in Patai, *op. cit.*, pp. 131-32.

[30] I am aware that this incident, recorded in M. Sukka III.16, Tosefta Sukka III.16, and BT Sukka 48b, is usually interpreted as a sociological-political-religious controversy; see, e.g., L. Finkelstein, *The Pharisees* (3d ed.; Philadelphia, 1962), II, pp. 700-708.

measure holy and awesome, it was the time of utmost peril not only for the High Priest but for the whole of Israel. For if in this hour there had, God forbid, entered the mind of the High Priest a false or sinful thought, the entire world would have been destroyed.[31]

The Temple as the Stone of Foundation, as the center of responsibility, is essential for the maintenance of the cosmos. This, again, may be expressed in a variety of ways. Rabbi Shmuel bar Nachman bluntly declares, "Before the Temple was built the world stood on a throne of two legs; but when the Temple was built, the world became firmly founded and stood solidly."[32] More allusively, the well-known dictum that "on three things the world stands: on the Law, on the Temple service, and on piety" was interpreted in a commentary to mean that *"the world rests on service* [and that] this is the service in the Temple. And so you find that all the time the service in the Temple was performed there was blessing in the world ... and the crop was plentiful, and the wine was plentiful and man ate and was satisfied, and the beast ate and was satisfied. ... When the Temple was ruined, the blessing departed from the world."[33] In these passages, the terms "the world stands" and "the world rests" should be understood within the context of their full mythic import. The Temple and its ritual serve as the cosmic pillars or the "sacred pole" supporting the world. If its service is interrupted or broken, if an error is made, then the world, the blessing, the fertility, indeed all of creation which flows from the Center, will likewise be disrupted. Like the Achilpa's sacred pole, which Eliade constantly reminds us of ("for the pole to be broken denotes catastrophe, it is like the end of the world, reversion to chaos"[34]), the disruption of the Center and its power is a breaking of the link between reality and the world, which is dependent upon the Sacred Land. Whether through error or exile, the severing of this relationship is a cosmic disaster.

For the Jew, the people, the land, the law as *derek eretz* ("the way of the land"), and YHWH are inseparable. And it is only in this context that one can understand the full, tragic force of the exile, which has

---

[31] J. C. Landis, *The Dybbuk and Other Great Yiddish Plays* (New York, 1966), pp. 51-52.

[32] Tanhuma Ex., in Patai, *op. cit.*, p. 121.

[33] M. Aboth, I.2, in Danby, *op. cit.*, p. 446; Aboth d. R. Nathan 4, in Patai, *op. cit.*, p. 123. Cf. J. Goldin, *The Fathers according to Rabbi Nathan* (New Haven, Conn., 1955), p. 33.

[34] M. Eliade, *The Sacred and the Profane*, trans. W. R. Trask (New York, 1959), p. 33.

been the characteristic mode of Jewish existence for 1,900 years.

While the exile is an event which can be located chronologically as after A.D. 70, it is above all a thoroughly mythic event: the return to chaos, the decreation, the separation from the deity analogous to the total catastrophe of the primeval flood.

IV. Exile

The category of exile is not an exclusively Jewish one. I have learned a great deal from studying the many texts expressing exilic traditions that may be found in the history of religions; and it is to be hoped that, along with the renewed interest in sacred space, some scholar in the near future will undertake a study of exile as it has appeared in the history of religions (a study which would include both texts which reflex an exile from a sacred land on earth and those which report an exile from a primeval or heavenly home).

Texts such as the following, recorded by R. P. Trilles from the Gabon pygmies after they had to leave their ancestral land, not only illuminates the general category of homeland and sacred space, but has proved to be specifically illuminating for an understanding of some Jewish expressions as well, sensitizing one to dimensions he might not have concerned himself with prior to reading it:

> The night is black, the sky is blotted out
> We have left the village of our Fathers,
> The Maker is angry with us ...
> The light becomes dark, the night and again night,
> The day with hunger tomorrow—
> The Maker is angry with us.
>
> The Old Ones have passed away,
> Their homes are far off, below,
> Their spirits are wandering—
> Where are their spirits wandering?
> Perhaps the passing wind knows.
> Their bones are far off below.
>
> Are they below, the spirits? Are they here?
> Do they see the offerings set out?
> Tomorrow is naked and empty,
> For the Maker is no longer with us—there,
> He is no longer the host seated with us at our fire.[35]

---

[35] R. P. Trilles, *Les Pygmées de la forêt équatoriale* (Paris, 1932), p. 503; Trilles, *L'ame du pygmée d'Afrique* (Paris, 1945), p. 96. English versions may be found in C. M. Bowra, *Primitive Song* (reprint; New York, 1963), pp. 137 and 262, and W. R. Trask, *The Unwritten Song* (New York, 1966), I, p. 62.

Perhaps this last phrase, "He is no longer the host seated with us at our fire," sums up best what has been for the Jew his experience of exile.

To be exiled is to be cut off from the land, from the blessing, from the ancestors, from history, from life, from creation, from reality, from the deity. It is to enter into a new temporal period, palpably different from that which has been before. It is to descend into chaos. Thus, in a phrase made famous several years ago by David ben Gurion, some rabbis lamented, "He who lives outside of the Land is in the category of one who worships idols,"[36] that is, he who lives outside of the land of Israel is as if he has no god. To be exiled is to be in a state of chaos, decreation, and death; to return from exile is to be re-created and reborn. For the Temple to have been destroyed is to experience the shattering of the Center, the breaking of the sacred pole. This has been expressed in a variety of ways, and it is an urgent task for some specialist in Jewish literature to collect and classify these expressions utilizing History of Religions categories, I give only four examples:

Jonathan Eibschutz, an eighteenth-century talmudist:

> If we do not have Jerusalem ... why should we have life?... Surely we have descended from life unto death. And the converse is true. When the Lord restores the captivity of Zion we shall ascend from death unto life.[37]

A Yiddish folksong:

> Forest O Forest how big you are,
> Bride O Bride how far you are.
> When the forest shall be taken away
> We shall come together one day.
>
> Exile O Exile how long you are,
> God O God how far you are.
> When the Exile has been taken away,
> We shall come together again some day.[38]

In 2 Baruch X:

> Husbandman—sow not again,
> And earth—keep locked within you the sweets of your bounty,
> And you, vine—why bother to give forth wine?
> For an offering will not be made again in Zion,
> Nor will first fruits again be offered.

---

[36] BT Ket 110b-111a, in Hertzberg, *op.cit.*, p. 143.
[37] Quoted in Hertzberg, *op. cit.*, p. 157.
[38] Translated in J. Leftwich, *The Golden Peacock: A Worldwide Treasury of Yiddish Poetry* (New York, 1961), p. 711.

> Heavens—withhold your dew,
> And do not open your treasure houses of rain,
> And you, sun—withhold the light of your rays,
> And you, moon—extinguish the radiance of your light.
> For why should light rise again,
> Where the light of Zion is altered?

And, finally, in most daring language, from the Zohar, a portion of the lament of Matrona, the bride of YHWH, at the Temple site:

> She sees that her dwelling place and her couch are ruined and soiled and she wails and laments ... she looks at the place of the Cherubim and wails bitterly and she lifts up her voice and says: "My couch, my couch, my dwelling place ... in it you came unto me, the Lord of the World, my husband. And He would lie in my arms and all that I wished for He would give me. At this hour He used to come to me. He left His dwelling place on high and came here and played between my breasts. My couch, O my couch. ..."[39]

With the exile and the destruction of the Temple the cosmic liturgy has ended and there has been a fragmentation of reality, of human *and* divine reality, as long as the exile persists. (Thus the tradition that when the Temple in Jerusalem was destroyed, the heavenly Temple fell also. "When that below is built anew; this one above will be built anew," says YHWH to Michael.)[40] This is *not* to suggest a historical judgment such as some apologetically motivated Christian authors have put forward, that Jewish existence, culture, and religion since A.D. 70 have been sterile and broken. Rather, as a historian of religions, I wish to point to a pervasive mythic and religious understanding of exilic existence.[41]

---

[39] Zohar Hadash, in Patai, *op. cit.*, pp. 92-93.

[40] Seder 'Arquim, in Patai, *op. cit.*, pp. 131-32.

[41] For an example of Christian apologetic distortion, see S. G. F. Brandon, *The Fall of Jerusalem and the Christian Church* (London, 1951), p. 167: "[The destruction] had a paralysing affect on the life of the Jewish people, and from it they only slowly recovered and settled to an essentially maimed existence, with their cherished religion bereft of much of its *raison d'être*." I am, in contradistinction to such an approach, attempting to interpret seriously such Jewish modes of self-expression as revealed in the following passage from Chaim Raphael's fascinating midrashic interpretation of the fall of Jerusalem (*The Walls of Jerusalem: An Excursion into Jewish History* [New York, 1968], pp. xv-xvi): "For Jews one historic event lay for nearly two thousand years in their memory—the loss of Jerusalem. It expressed everything: it accounted for everything.... They were now, behind every joy, a people of sorrows. But more than their own sorrows was at stake. It was not just the Jews who had been driven into exile: God himself was in exile. The world was out of joint. The Destruction was the symbol of it."

While the standard explanations and responses to the exile and the destruction of the Temple are well known—the traditional Jewish theodicy of punishment and or purification; the Christian understandign of a judgment against the Jew for rejecting Jesus; R. M. Grant's thesis of a gnosticism arising out of the frustration of Jewish apocalyptic expectations—there developed side by side with these explanations a daring new mythology of the exile, one which possibly harks back to such ancient Near Eastern myths as the lost eye of Horus, the missing genitals of Osiris, the dying-rising and disappearing gods, as well as certain common Mediterranean gnostic motifs. It is that the exile of Israel represents the exile of God as well (to reverse the famous Hermetic maxim, "as below, so above").

This is first stated in minimal terms by Rabbi Akiba in the first century: "Were it not written in Torah it would be impossible to say such a thing—whenever Israel was exiled, the Presence of God, as it were, went into exile with them. ... And when they return in the future, the Presence of God, as it were, will return with them."[42] What was stated so tentatively, "as it were," in the first century is stated boldy and unambiguously following the Jewish experience of expulsion from Spain in 1492 and the Marrano style of diasporic existence. In a daring myth, the land below is not homologized to sacred realities on high; but, rather, the exile of Israel is homologized to the exile of the deity. As Israel is in exile from the land and from reality, so YHWH is in exile from himself and from his plentitude. If Jewish existence is understood in this myth as broken, the divine totality is broken as well.

This language became, in a diversity of expressions, one of the dominant themes of European Jewry. It might be expressed semihumorously, as in the famous saying of Mendel Kotzkev: "Where does God dwell? Wherever he is not forced to move on!"[43] Or, far more seriously and poignantly, there developed under Isaac Luria and the sixteenth-century community at Safed a thoroughly mythic description and solution to the exile.

Space does not permit a detailed exposition of the creation myths of Lurianic kabbalah, which their greatest living interpreter, Gershom G. Scholem, has called "the deepest symbol of the exile that could be

---

[42] Mekilta, Visha 14, in Hertzberg, *op. cit.*, p. 149.

[43] One version of this quip is given in T. Reik, *Jewish Wit* (New York, 1962), p. 29.

thought of."⁴⁴ To barely summarize: God, in the process of withdrawing from himself in the beginning in order to provide room for the cosmos, in his first expansive sending forth of light which broke into countless sparks which have become trapped in the material world below, became broken, fragmented, and in exile from himself. It is man's awesome responsibility to rescue his deity and, in so doing, to rescue himself. Like the familiar new year pattern described by historians of religion—like the saved-saviors of gnostic traditions—as Israel rescues her deity from exile, she rescues herself.

The experience of exile on Israel's part is a participation in the divine pathos, and is itself, by a daring reinterpretation, a salvific experience. The exile of Israel is her initiation, is her experience of a death which will be followed by a rebirth, and hence it becomes necessary to experience death or exile in its fullest so that rebirth and restoration may more quickly come. When this cosmogony and eschatology was merged with the myth of the followers of Sabbatai Zevi (after his conversion to Islam in 1666 at the height of his messianic popularity), one finds the notion that Israel needs to press ever further into chaos and exile in order to gather the lost sparks of the deity and return the fragments of himself to him. Or, understood in terms of Israel, "This is the secret why Israel is fated to be enslaved by all the nations of the world. In order that she may uplift those sparks which have also fallen among them. . . . And therefore it was necessary that Israel should be scattered to the four winds in order to lift up everything."⁴⁵ When this language of the recovery of the lost sparks became identified as the central act of east European Hasidism, this myth became one of the dominant expressions of European Jewry.⁴⁶

That which is here expressed in a myth may be experienced and enacted in ritual. In several brilliant studies, Scholem has shown how the Jew of Safed underwent the rites of Rachel, where he mourned, participated, and became one with the exiled portion of the deity, and the rites of Leah, where, through mystical exercises and contemplation, he transformed his body into a chariot to lift on high the exiled fragments.⁴⁷

---

⁴⁴ G. G. Scholem, *Major Trends in Jewish Mysticism* (reprint; New York, 1954), p. 261. See Scholem's summary of the Lurianic kabbalah in *ibid.*, chap. vii.
⁴⁵ Sefer ha-Likkutim, in *ibid.*, p. 284.
⁴⁶ See M. Buber, *Hasidism and Modern Man*, trans. M. Friedman (reprint; New York, 1966), pp. 187-89; M. Buber, *Hasidism* (New York, 1948), pp. 7-8.
⁴⁷ G. G. Scholem, *On the Kabbalah and Its Symbolism*, trans. R. Manheim (London, 1965), pp. 148-50.

Most particularly, as is widespread in the history of religions, the exile may be overcome in moments of sacred time. For the Jew of the Lurianic community, as for later Hasidism, this especially occurred at the Sabbath.[48] On Friday afternoon the faithful, dressed in white, would go out into an open field which would be transformed through ritual into the "holy apple orchard." There they would solemnly await and escort into town the exiled and weeping Bride of God. Chanting the Song of Songs, the wedding liturgy of the broken "Old One" on high and the Bride trapped below, they would bring the Bride into their house to celebrate the nuptial feast.

Each dining room would be transformed through this ritual activity into, at one and the same time, the lost Temple of Jerusalem and the celestial Tabernacle. The angels from on high enter the room (or, does the room by performance of the ritual ascend on high?) and are pacified with a prayer. An extra Sabbath soul descends and enters the body of each Jew to strengthen him for the awesome sight he is about to witness and the daring ritual he is about to perform.

The room is decorated with myrtle, forming a marriage canopy for the intercourse of the deity and his bride, for the reuniting of the totality of the deity. The mother of the house is kissed in a ritual which Luria states has "deep mystical significance" and is homologized to the Bride of God through a recitation of Proverbs 31. She begins the ceremony by lighting the Sabbath candles, shielding her eyes from the light which shone on the first day (the light which was still visible in the Jerusalem Temple, the light which shattered into sparks in the kabbalistic myth).[49]

The leader of the house then chants the cosmogonic myth from Genesis 1, wine is sipped, and an invocation sung over the meal:

> Prepare the meal of the King,
> the meal of the field of holy apples
> of the Impatient One and the Holy Old One.

And then a fish meal is eaten, a fish which is believed to be both the food of rebirth and a proleptic taste of the flesh of the water dragon which YHWH defeated in the beginning and has preserved for a banquet in the Messianic age to come.

---

[48] I follow here Scholem's reconstruction, *ibid.*, pp. 139-46.

[49] Cf. Goodenough's ingenious intuition: "It seems to me no coincidence that the ancient ritualistic use of sex still survives in the old requirement that on the evening of a Sabbath or festival (that is, after the wife has lighted the lights), the husband must have intercourse with her. I should guess that it is with his wife as the Light of God that he has relations" (in *op. cit.*, IV, p. 98, n. 155).

Next, the one absolutely indispensable act of the Friday evening service is performed: the chanting of a hymn celebrating the *hieros gamos* of the deity on high and the exiled Bride, which takes place before the visionary eyes of the family—an act of intercourse which for one brief ritual moment reunites the shattered deity, which for a brief moment ends the exile and translates each home into the Center of blessing and fertility which stood in days of old.

> I sing in hymns to enter the gates of the field
> of apples of the holy ones.
>
> A new table we lay for her, a beautiful candelabrum
> sheds its light upon us.
>
> Between right and left the Bride approaches
> in holy jewels and festive garments.
>
> Her husband embraces her in her sexual organs,
> gives her fulfillment, squeezes out his strength.

It is a sexual act which produces a new creation:

> Torments and cries are past.
> Now there are new faces and souls and spirits.
>
> He gives her joy in twofold measure.
> Lights shine and streams of blessing.
>
> Bridesmen go forth and prepare the Bride
> victuals of many kinds and all manner of fish
> to beget new souls and new spirits. . . .
>
> All worlds are now formed and sealed within her,
> but all shine forth from the Old of Days.

And now this Center, this new creation, which for a brief moment is like the old, is explicitly related to both the old Temple and the heavenly shrine. The living room, the *hic et nunc*, is abolished, and once more the participants in the ritual "go up" to Jerusalem as in the days before the exile:

> To the southward set the mystic candlesticks,
> I make room in the north for the table with
> the loaves. . . .

That is, in the Tabernacle the candelabrum stood on the south side, the table with the bread of the Presence on the north (Exod. 26:35), but now through ritual the dining room table has become homologized with the Tabernacle and, further still, with the celestial shrine:

> With wine in beakers and boughs of myrtle
> to fortify the betrothed for they are feeble.
> Let the presence of the Bride be surrounded
> by six sabbath loaves,
> Connected on every side with the heavenly sanctuary.

The union is complete, and total integration of the deity, Israel, the family, and the temples on high and below has been achieved. Finally, since the exile is briefly ended, since one is living in the realm of sacred time, the chaos into which the Jew has been plunged is conquered:

> Weakened and cast out are the impure demons
> The menacing powers have now been chained.[50]

That night, there is required intercourse between husband and wife imitating and repeating the nuptials of God and his exiled Bride that have just been witnessed and celebrated.

Thus far we have seen the archaic biblical image of the Holy Land as an enclave; the later image of the Holy Land as a Center and the full force of the experience of exile from this Center, a descent into chaos, death and unreality; as well as the daring "solution" to this condition through myth and ritual.

The persistence of these themes in the many strata of Jewish tradition up to modern times is undeniable, although much careful and imaginative scholarship needs yet to be done before a full body of evidence is available.

Among Zionists, the successors to the mystical energies of kabbalism, Sabbatianism, and Hasidism, this language is predominant (as may be quickly seen by examining the writings of the most distinguished modern kabbalist, the passionate Zionist, and first chief rabbi of Palestine after the British mandate, Rabbi Abraham Isaac Kook).[51] Even among the so-called atheistic, secularist, deeply Marxist Zionists who founded the first *kibbutzim*, their religion of "land and labor" is a resurgence of the old language of a recovered center, of life shared with the land. Thus, for example, A. D. Gordan, understood by many to be the leader of the secular communitarians in the early twentieth century, describes their experience in a language resplendent with overtones of cosmic trees, world navels, and so forth:

---

[50] This poem is translated in Scholem, *On the Kabbalah*, pp. 143-44.

[51] Regarding Kook, see the brief selections from his largely untranslated writings in A. Hertzberg, *The Zionist Idea* (reprint; New York, 1966), pp. 416-31; see further the account of his life and thought by J. Agus, *Banner of Jerusalem* (New York, 1946), and the penetrating chapter in H. Weiner, *The Wild Goats of Ein Gedi* (reprint; Cleveland, 1963), pp. 159-84.

It is life we want, no more and no less than that, our own life feeding on our own vital sources, in the fields and under the skies of our Homeland.... We want vital energy and spiritual richness from this living source. We come to our Homeland in order to be planted in our natural soil from which we have been uprooted, to strike our roots deep into its life-giving substances and to stretch out our branches in the sustaining and creating air and sunlight of the Homeland.... It is our duty to concentrate all our strength on this central spot.... What we seek to establish in Palestine is a new re-created Jewish people.[52]

For the European Jew prior to World War II, the journey up to Jerusalem, the journey into the promised land, had about it all of the qualities of a mystic ascent and of a pilgrimage. As with any sacred space familiar in the general history of religions, the entrance into Israel was a process of initiation, of death to the old mode of exilic existence and rebirth to a new and real life. Abraham Kalisker, a Polish Jew writing from Tiberias in Palestine at the end of the eighteenth century, makes this unusually explicit:

Many a year passes before the days of his initiation are over, his initiation into true life. But then he will truly live in his native land and always before God.... Everyone who comes to the sanctuary must be born again in his mother's womb, be suckled again, be a little child again and so on, until he beholds the land face to face and until his soul becomes bound up with that of the land.[53]

But for the contemporary Jew, since World War II the situation appears to have changed. The chaos, the evil, the demonic dimension of exilic existence that was encountered in the Nazi era was of such a quality that no previous mythology has prepared the Jew of today to face it. For the majority of those who have survived, the naked horror is avoided with vague language of six million dead or the apocalyptic phrase "the holocaust." For others, like the brilliant and influential novelist Elie Wiesel, even the resources of the broken Lurianic deity are not sufficient. The God of the Jews, he insists, must be an evil, perverse, psychotic deity to have chosen a people for such an end. Wiesel has recovered the lost language of gnosticism, bereft, however, of the good though hidden deity.

The problem of Jewish existence "after Auschwitz" will, as Rubenstein has suggested, be the chief religious problem for the contemporary Jew. It is clear that the old language of theodicy, of purification,

---

[52] Translated in Hertzberg, *The Zionist Idea*, pp. 382-83.
[53] I have combined the translations of N. Glatzer, *In Time and Eternity* (New York, 1946), p. 218, and M. Buber, *The Tales of Rabbi Nachman*, p. 191.

preparation, and punishment, is no longer adequate. I suspect, however, that Paul Ricoeur is correct, that evil and the demonic, as that which resists order, will by its very nature forever elude philosophical and theological speculation. Only myth and symbol are adequate to describe it. And here the creative writers such as Wiesel and the historians of religions who remind Israel of myths and symbols she has forgotten must join hands and mutually fructify one another.

On the other hand, the re-establishment of Israel, what one scholar has called the "unexpected and thoroughly unmessianic event" of her restoration, poses, as Rubenstein has also suggested, a problem for which the old *heilsgeschichtliche* language is inadequate. Rubenstein calls for a "new paganism," and perhaps he is right. Once again the creative artist and the creative historian of religions must join hands in rediscovering old myths, in forging, perhaps, a new mythology.[54] For the recovery of the Center, as well as the agonizing encounter with the demonic, has opened up new possibilities of Jewish existence and expression, a new cosmos which has not yet been fully transformed into a world where man is at home.

AFTERWORD

Compare Mircea Eliade's use of this essay in "The World, The City, and The House," *Occultism, Witchcraft and Cultural Fashions* (Chicago, 1976), esp. pp. 27-30.

Of all of the essays printed in this volume, this one causes me the most difficulty. If I were to rewrite it, I would suggest that, along side of the mythology of exile discussed above, one should also note the positive response to the cessation of the archaic forms of worship. Indeed, I should want to go so far as to argue that if the Temple had not been destroyed, it would have had to be neglected. For it represented a locative type of religious activity no longer perceived as effective in a new, utopian religious situation with a concomitant shift from a cosmological to an anthropological view-point. To make such an argument, I would have to take history far more seriously than has been done in this paper (see my "Preface", above) and seek to describe the "trajectory" of the constellation of Holy Land and Temple. For a brief statement, see chapter 8, below.

---

[54] From quite a different perspective, see the suggestive review by R. Sanders, "Myth and Science at Masada," *Midstream*, XIII, No. 2 (1967), 72-75, esp. 74: "Archaeology in Israel not only serves to unearth the mythic heritage of place for a re-implanted people; it is itself a major element in the national myth-making process.... Digging is an act of major symbolic force in the modern history of Israel, and the now epic acts of communion between hands and soil that had been performed by the drainers of swamps, the builders of roads, and the founders of kibbutzim, have today been brought back to a reconciliation with the contemplative life by the digging of archaeologists."

CHAPTER SIX

THE INFLUENCE OF SYMBOLS
UPON SOCIAL CHANGE

A Place on Which to Stand*

I

The philosopher has the possibility of exclaiming with Archimedes: "Give me a place to stand on and I will move the world." The quest for this place finds paradigmatic expression in the almost initiatory scenario of Descartes *dans un poêle*. There is, for such a thinker, at least the possibility of a real beginning, even of achieving *the* Beginning, a standpoint from which all things flow, a standpoint from which he has clear vision.[1] The historian or the historian of religions has no such possibility. There are no places on which he might stand apart from the messiness of the given world. There is for him no real beginning, but only the plunge which he takes at some arbitrary point to avoid the unhappy alternatives of infinite regress or silence. His standpoint is not discovered; rather it is erected with no claim beyond that of sheer survival. The historian's point of view cannot sustain clear vision.

The historian's task is to complicate, not to clarify. He strives to celebrate the diversity of manners, the opacity of things, the variety of species. He is barred, thereby, from making a frontal assault on his topic. Like the pilgrim, the historian is obligated to approach his subject obliquely. He must circumambulate the spot several times before making even the most fleeting contact. His method, like that of Tristram Shandy, Gentleman, is that of the digression.

The historian's manner of speech is often halting and provisional. He approaches his data with that same erotic tentativeness expressed in the well-known colloquy from the "Circe" episode of Joyce's *Ulysses*:

> You may touch my . . . .
> May I touch your?
> O, but lightly!
> O, so lightly![2]

---

* This essay has been reprinted, in slightly revised form, in J. D. Shaughnessy, *The Roots of Ritual* (Grand Rapids, 1973), pp. 121-143.
[1] Cf. M. Foss, *Abstraktion und Wirklichkeit* (Bern, 1959), ch. I, esp. pp. 5-7.
[2] J. Joyce, *Ulysses* (New York, 1934), p. 561.

And having shyly addressed and momentarily touched the object, he must let it go and return it to its place, unexhausted and intact.

The historian in his work detects clues, symptoms, exemplars. He provides us with hints that remain too fragile to bear the burden of being solutions. He is a man of insights; not, preeminently, a man of vision.

II

He was a most curious Frenchman, Seigneur de Saint-Évremond, who was born in Normandy and buried in the Poet's Corner of Westminster Abbey—a distinguished soldier, brigadier general in the army of Louis XIV, political critic of strong monarchy, fugitive and exile, sceptic, *philosophe*, Epicurean, friend of Hobbes and Spinoza, defender and author of English comedy, wit and "Freethinker triumphant."[3] About 1678, writing his *Dissertation sur le mot de Vaste* addressed to the Academy, he maintained:

> The *vast* and the dreadful have a great affinity to one another.... *Vasta solitudo* is not one of those solitudes which offer the sense of charming repose... (rather) it is a wild solitude where we are afraid of being alone.... A *vast* house offers something ghastly to the sight. *Vast* apartments never tempt anyone to live in them. *Vast* gardens lack both the amenities which are the result of art and those graces which Nature bestows. *Vast* forests frighten us; the sight loses itself in looking across *vast* plains.... Savage lands that are uncultivated, landscapes ruined by the desolation of war, lands forsaken and abandoned— all partake of the quality of *vastness* which gives rise to a sense of secret horror within us.... *Vast* is almost the same thing as laid waste, spoiled and ruined.... The most common meaning of *vastus* is too extended, too great, immoderate.... We never say '*vast* enough' because 'enough' implies something fitting and reasonable; whereas as soon as a thing is *vast*, there is an excess, it is too much [*de trop*].[4]

Such a sense of almost Sartrean nausea before the vast, the *de trop*, is, as R. Ternois, Saint-Évremond's most recent editor, has pointed out, in sharp contrast with definitions of *vaste* in contemporary French

---

[3] See the fine, brief account of Saint-Évremond in P. Hazard, *The European Mind* [*1680-1715*] (New York, 1963; reprint), pp. 120-130. I have borrowed the phrase, "Freethinker triumphant" from p. 127.

[4] *Oeuvres meslées de Mr. de Saint-Évremond* 2 ed. (Paris, 1697), pp. 90, 92, 94. See further the excellent critical edition by R. Ternois, *Saint-Évremond: Oeuvres en prose* (Paris, 1966), vol. III, pp. 380f, 382, 383. Compare the rendering above with the original English translation by P. Des Maizeaux, *The Works of Monsieur de St. Évremond Made English from the French Original* (London, 1714), vol. II, pp. 98, 100, 101.

lexica. In dictionaries such as those of P. Richelet (1680) and A. Furetière (1690), *vaste* carries the meaning of free, expansive, imaginative.[5] It is this positive sense which led de Tocqueville to use *vaste* or a synonym nine times in the first three pages of his enthusiastic physical description of America. Indeed, it has been a characteristic description of America—it peoples the pages of material collected in Henry Nash Smith's classic, *Virgin Land*; it lies behind such characteristic American expressions as Frederick Jackson Turner's well-known "Frontier thesis." It is a curious, and possibly significant detail, that the three great powers in today's world are those most frequently described in traveler's reports as vast, open, almost limitless realms: America, Russia and China.

The ambivalence here expressed in relation to the notion of vastness may be seen in analogous concepts. For example, in classical sources the nomadism (and hence the openness and vastness) of the Scyths is both idealized and abjured. On the one hand, their mobility makes them shiftless, barbaric, frightening, perpetual exiles; on the other hand, they are free, uncontaminated, wise, lords of all the earth they so casually roam.[6] (A similar dichotomy may be seen in the varying assessments of the period of wilderness-wandering in the biblical texts.[7])

The difference between these two standpoints—horror in the face of the vast, and enthusiasm for expanse and openness—is not merely a matter of aesthetic sensibility. A total world-view is implied and involved in assuming these postures, one that has to do with a culture's or an individual's symbolization of the cosmos and their place within it. There have been many ways of naming these two basic structures of human symbolization and experience. One might speak of a centripetal and a centrifugal viewpoint. One might adopt the

---

[5] R. Ternois, *Saint-Évremond*, vol. III, p. 384n. Cf. the discussion of the word *vaste* in the works of Baudelaire, in G. Bachelard, *La Poétique de l'espace* (Paris, 1957), pp. 174-181.

[6] See the material collected in A. Riese, *Die Idealisierung der Naturvölker des Nordens in der griechischen und römischen Literatur* (Leipzig, 1875); A. O. Lovejoy-G. Boas, *Primitivism and Related Ideas in Antiquity* (Baltimore, 1935), vol. 1, pp. 315-344; G. Boas, *Essays on Primitivism and Related Ideas in the Middle Ages* (Baltimore, 1948), pp. 135-137.

[7] Following the magnificent traditio-historical investigations of G. W. Coats, *Rebellion in the Wilderness: The Murmuring Motif in the Wilderness Traditions of the Old Testament* (Nashville, 1968), it is no longer possible to speak of a simple dichotomy between positive wilderness traditions dependent upon a alleged "nomadic ideal" and negative ones.

language of Bergson and speak of the closed/static society and the open/dynamic one. Or one might follow the fruitful lead of Eric Voegelin and point to the contrast between a "compact" and "differentiated" experience of the cosmos.[8]

Whatever terminology is employed, we must be careful to preserve a sufficient sense of the experiential and symbolic character of this dichotomy, and resist imposing an evolutionary scheme of development "from the closed world to the infinite universe" (to borrow the title of Alexandre Koyre's well-known history of science). And we must resist as well the frequent tendency to identify the centripetal-closed with primitive or archaic society, and the centrifugal-open with the modern. Both have been and remain existential possibilities which may be appropriated whenever and wherever they correspond to one's experience. We might recall that in Greece the period of the development of the *polis*, with its characteristically bounded understanding of the world, coincided exactly with the rise of Greek colonization, with its correspondingly expansive view. Or we might point to our contemporary society with its growing reinterest in community and in rediscovery of one's roots in the earth, on the one hand, and its fascination with space exploration, on the other. Nevertheless, and bearing this caveat firmly in mind, we can point to the oscillation in human history between these viewpoints, with one and now the other giving a dominant complexion to a people or an age. The adoption of one or the other of these symbolic systems has the most profound implications for the question of social change.

III

In the Mediterranean and Near Eastern world, for some 2,000 years man's faith was predominantly informed by what Cornelius Loew (following the researches of Frankfort, Jacobsen, Voegelin and others) has termed "a cosmological conviction," that is, "the conviction that the meaning of life is rooted in an encompassing cosmic order in which man, society and the gods all participate." Loew goes on to specify five facets of this conviction: 1) there is a cosmic order that permeates every level of reality; 2) this cosmic order is the divine society of the gods; 3) the structure and dynamics

---

[8] H. Bergson, *Les deux sources de la morale et de la religion* (Paris, 1932; English trans. London, 1935); E. Voegelin, *Order and History*, vol. 1, *Israel and Revelation* (Baton Rouge, 1956), p. 5: "the history of symbolization is a progression from compact to differentiated symbols."

of this society can be discerned in the movements and patterned juxtapositions of the heavenly bodies; 4) human society should be a microcosm of the divine society; 5) the chief responsibility of priests and kings is to attune human order to the divine order.[9]

This pattern of affirming and celebrating the order of the cosmos is exemplified in the typical creation myth of the Mediterranean—Near Eastern world, a creation by combat between the forces of order and chaos. Order is something won by the gods and it is this primordial act of salvation which is renewed and reexperienced in the cult. For example, in the famous Babylonian creation myth, *Enuma elish*, Marduk the king-god and his forces are victorious over the powers of watery chaos. In victory, Marduk seals the tablets of destiny (IV.121f.), sets bounds, limits and guards over the chaotic waters (IV.139f.), creates stations for the gods, establishes their signs in the zodiac (V.1f.), and their laws and destinies (VI.78; VII.144). Man's response to these activities, slave of the gods though he may believe himself to be, is that he "rejoice in Marduk ... [for] reliable is his word, unalterable his command; the utterance of his mouth no god whatever can change" (VII.149,151f.).[10]

There may be periods of tension (such as the myth of the theft of the tablets of destiny by the Zu bird or the imprisonment of Marduk during the New Year festival), but the "reliable" and "unalterable" structures of destiny will ultimately win out. They will be victorious because they are real, having been established by the gods. They will be victorious because they have been annually renewed and strengthened in the great double ceremony of the fixing of the divine and human destinies which concluded the Akitu festival.

Man's responsibility becomes one of discovering, of knowing his place. The man of wisdom is the sage—the one who can discern the pattern of things and aid the king and people in fulfilling their appointed role. Man is charged with the task of harmonizing himself with the great rhythms of cosmic destiny and order. If he does rebel (as in the case of Gilgamesh, who seeks to overcome the structures of destiny and death which are the common human lot) he will learn that he "cannot rise above his human characteristics ... and after a brief time of despair, he squares his shoulders and goes back to face reality."[11]

---

[9] C. Loew, *Myth, Sacred History and Philosophy* (New York, 1967), pp. 5, 13.
[10] I have followed the translation of A. Heidel, *The Babylonian Genesis*, 2 ed. (Chicago, 1951).
[11] Th. Jacobsen, "The Epic of Gilgamesh," in J. Neusner, ed., *Report of the*

Indeed, it might be suggested that one of the characteristic epic figures in societies of "cosmological conviction" is what I would term the hero-that-failed. Like the Polynesian culture hero, Maui, or the Greek Orpheus, the hero-that-failed was *not* successful in overcoming death or his humanity; rather, through rebellion against order, he was initiated into, discovered and assumed his humanity. By his hard-won affirmation of both the human and cosmic structures of destiny, he became a model for his fellow men.[12]

This locative vision of man and the cosmos is revealed in a variety of descriptions of the places in which men may stand. The world is perceived as a bounded world; focusing on the etymological roots, the world is felt to be an *envir*on*ment*, an *ambi*ance.[13] That which is open, that which is boundless is seen as the chaotic, the demonic, the threatening. The desert and the sea are the all but interchangeable concrete symbols of the terrible, chaotic openness. They are the enemy *par excellence*. To battle against the power of the waters a "divine warrior" is required: Baal versus Prince Sea (*Zabul Yam*) or the seven-headed water dragon, *Lotan*; Marduk versus Apsu and Tiamat; Yahweh against Leviathan, Rahab or the Sea (*Yam*); Ninurta against Kur. Victory establishes those two inseparable companions: divine kingship and cosmic order. Order is produced by walling, channeling, and confining the waters.[14]

1965-1966 Seminar on Religions in Antiquity: Dartmouth College Comparative Studies Center (Hanover, 1966), p. 18. Cf. Jacobsen in H. Frankfort *et al.*, *Before Philosophy* (Harmondsworth, 1949), pp. 223-227.

[12] For the tradition concerning Maui and death, see the text conveniently reprinted in M. Eliade, *From Primitives to Zen* (New York, 1967), pp. 142-144.

[13] W. Pax, "Sprachvergleichende Untersuchungen zur Etymologie des Wortes *amphipolos*," *Wörter und Sachen*, 18 (1937), 1-88, esp. 16-26. See further: K. Michaëlsen, "Ambiance," *Studia Neophilologica*, 12 (1939-40), 91-119; L. Spitzer, "Milieu and Ambiance," *Philosophy and Phenomenological Research*, 3 (1942-43), 1-42, 169-218, reprinted in Spitzer, *Essays in Historical Semantics* (New York, 1948), pp. 179-316.

[14] For the general pattern, the fundamental work, to which new texts have been brought, remains H. Gunkel's classic, *Schöpfung und Chaos in Urzeit und Endzeit* (Göttingen, 1895). See further: A. J. Wensinck, *The Ocean in the Literature of the Western Semites* (Amsterdam, 1918); O. Eissfeldt, "Gott und das Meer in der Bibel," in *Studia Orientalia Ioanni Pedersen* (Copenhagen, 1953), pp. 76-84; O. Kaiser, *Die mythische Bedeutung des Meeres in Aegypten, Ugarit und Israel*, 2 ed. (Berlin, 1959); L. R. Fisher, "Creation at Ugarit and in the Old Testament," *Vetus Testamentum*, 15 (1965), 313-324. The important notion of the "divine warrior" is brilliantly discussed in F. M. Cross, Jr., "The Divine Warrior in Israel's Early Cult," A. Altmann, ed., *Biblical Motifs* (Cambridge, Mass., 1966), pp. 1-10.

> The Lord [Marduk] rested, examining her dead body, ...
> He split her open like a mussel [?] into two [parts];
> Half of her he set in place and formed the sky [therewith] as a roof.
> He fixed the crossbar [and] posted guards;
> He commanded them not to let her waters escape.[15]

> [Yahweh] shut in the sea with doors ... put bounds upon it,
> Set up bars and doors,
> Saying, 'Thus far come, but no more.
> Here your wild waves halt.'[16]

Ninurta, after slaying Kur, had to set up a heap of stones over the body and form a great wall of stones in front of the land: "These stones hold back the 'mighty waters' and as a result the waters of the lower regions rise no longer to the surface of the earth. As for the waters which had already flooded the land, Ninurta gathers them and leads them into the Tigris...."[17]

The same stratagem will be employed against the desert.[18] It is defeated by the erection of walls and boundaries. This is why the *Epic of Gilgamesh* begins and ends with the same set of injunctions: praising the king's building:

> He built the wall of Uruk, the enclosure
> Of holy Eanna, the sacred storehouse.
> Behold its outer wall, whose brightness is like [that of] copper!
> Yea, look upon its inner wall, which none can equal!
> Take hold of the threshold ....
> Climb up upon the wall of Uruk [and] walk about;
> Inspect the foundation terrace and examine the brickwork,
> If its brickwork be not of burnt bricks,
> [And] if the seven [wise men] did not lay its foundation! ...
> One *shar* is city, one *shar* orchards, one *shar* prairie;
> [then there is the] uncultivated land [?] of the temple of Ishtar.
> Three *shar* and the uncultivated land [?] comprise Uruk.[19]

Although this repetition may be explained as simply an example of epic "ringcomposition," I would suggest something more profound

---

[15] *Enuma elish* IV. 135-140; in A. Heidel, *The Babylonian Genesis*, p. 42.
[16] Job 38:8-11, in M. Pope, *Job* (Garden City, L.I., 1965), p. 247.
[17] S. N. Kramer, *Sumerian Mythology*, 2 ed. (New York, 1961), p. 81.
[18] J. Pedersen, *Israel: Its Life and Culture* (London—Copenhagen, 1926), vol. I-II, pp. 453-60, 467-80, 491f; A. Haldar, *The Notion of the Desert in Sumero-Accadian and West-Semitic Religions* (Uppsala, 1950); S. Talmon, "The 'Desert Motif' in the Bible and in Qumran Literature," in A. Altmann, ed., *Biblical Motifs* (Cambridge, Mass., 1966), pp. 31-63; J. Z. Smith, "Earth and Gods," chapter 5, above.
[19] *Gilgamesh* I.9-19; XI.303-307, in A. Heidel, *The Gilgamesh Epic and Old Testament Parallels*, 2 ed. (Chicago, 1949), pp. 16f, 93.

is at stake.[20] Although Gilgamesh is a hero-that-failed, although he has not been able to overcome death and bring back for his people the wondrous plant "old-man-becomes-youth-again," he can, as king, win a limited security from destruction by maintaining the walls. The walled city is a symbolic universe which serves (to borrow a term from the Vietnam war) as an "enclave," a "strategic hamlet" against the threat of the boundless, chaotic desert. The desert, which is a place of utter desolation, of cosmic and human emptiness—the place called "the howling waste of the desert" (Dt. 32:10), the "land not sown" (Jer. 2:2), the land of "no-kingdom-there" (Is. 34:12), the place "in which there is no man" (Jb. 38:26)—is an active threat, constantly seeking to breach the walls.

The possession of such an "enclave" is a responsibility; the security won, a fragile thing. Whether the cosmography is expressed through the model of the inhabited land as a bubble of air in the midst of the dangerous cosmic waters, which surround it, or as a walled mound in the midst of the raging desert, safety is not guaranteed. The walls of the "hamlet" are always vulnerable to attack, and man and the gods must ceaselessly labor to sustain, renew and strengthen the power, to keep the walls under repair. If they fail, the vision of destruction will be fulfilled:

> I saw the earth—lo, chaos primeval!
> The heavens—their light was gone.
> I saw the mountains—and lo, they were quaking,
> And all the hills rocked to and fro.
> I looked—and behold, no human was there,
> And the birds of the skies had all flown.
> I looked—and behold, the tilled land was desert,
> Its cities all lying in ruins . . . .[21]

In such a cosmos lines must be clearly drawn. Civic officials may physically set up and maintain boundary stones with inscriptions proclaiming, "I am the border."[22] Cartographers may draw maps which show the boundaries of the world *polis*, with border peoples (Scyths, Indians, Celts and Ethiopians) who are not like us, their strangeness expressed in either their idealization as "noble savages"

---

[20] See W. A. A. van Otterlo, *De ringcompositie als opbouwprincipe in de epische gedichten van Homerus* (Amsterdam, 1948).

[21] Jeremiah 4:23-26, in J. Bright, *Jeremiah* (Garden City, L.I., 1965), pp. 30f.

[22] See the border stones described and figured in R. E. Wycherley, *The Athenian Agora*, vol. III, *Literary and Epigraphical Testimonia* (Princeton, 1957), p. 218.

or their denigration as monsters.[23] Great brazen walls (such as the one constructed by Alexander the Great to confine the peoples of Gog and Magog) may be pictured as bulwarks against chaotic forces.[24] But the concern for limits, borders and boundaries is a far more subtle and pervasive thing than these.

One need only refer to Mary Douglas' already classic work, *Purity and Danger: An Analysis of Concepts of Pollution and Taboo*, to see a total interpretation of religious and social mores in the light of these concerns. "Holiness is exemplified by completeness. Holiness requires that individuals shall conform to the class to which they belong. And holiness requires that different classes of things shall not be confused."[25] Hence no hybridization and no "mingling of seeds," no animals are to be eaten which are on the borderline with respect to their class (i.e., the bat which is neither animal nor bird), marital regulations of both exogamy and endogamy, the polluting capacities and magic utilization of nails, hair, excrement, mucus, etc., which come from the boundary, and hence most vulnerable parts of the human body. Or, as Claude Lévi-Strauss has noted:

> A native thinker makes the penetrating comment ... 'All sacred things must have their place.' It could even be said that being in their place is what makes them sacred for if they were taken out of their place, even in thought, the entire order of the universe would be destroyed. Sacred objects therefore contribute to the maintenance of order in the universe by occupying the places allocated to them. Examined superficially and from the outside, the refinements of ritual can appear pointless. They are explicable by a concern for what one might call 'micro-adjustment'—the concern to assign every single creature, object or feature to a place within a class.[26]

Such a locative view of the cosmos seems foreign to our tendency to idealize openness and mobility. When we confront a total system of boundaries, limits and places such as the caste system of India, we

---

[23] See R. Wittkower, "Marvels of the East: A Study in the History of Monsters," *Journal of the Warburg and Courtauld Institutes*, 5 (1942), 159-197; R. Bernheimer, *Wild Men in the Middle Ages* (Cambridge, Mass., 1952).
[24] A. R. Anderson, *Alexander's Gate, Gog and Magog and the Enclosed Nations* (Cambridge, Mass., 1932).
[25] M. Douglas, *Purity and Danger* (New York, 1966), p. 53.
[26] C. Lévi-Strauss, *The Savage Mind* (Chicago, 1966), p. 10. I am appreciative of Lévi-Strauss' reversal: it is not the sacred which gives things their place; but being in their place which makes things sacred. However his "native thinker," as quoted in A. C. Fletcher, "The Hako: A Pawnee Ceremony," *Twenty-Second Annual Report of the Bureau of American Ethnology* (Washington, D.C., 1904), Part 2, p. 34, does not imply this.

find it difficult to conceive of it as anything but constricting and shackling. Yet *homo hierarchicus*[27] enshrines a notion of cosmic responsibility, of the unique and precious value of each individual's keeping his place. This sense of significance is often lacking among societies possessing a more egalitarian view. Indeed, it might be suggested that if lack of freedom appears to be the "sin" of a locative world view, meaninglessness is the "sin" of the open. It is the power of the vision that has made the locative understanding of the cosmos and man's role within it, along with its associated complex of symbols and social structures, one of the two basic existential options open to man.

IV

As Mircea Eliade has pointed out in his important and imaginative essay, "The 'God Who Binds' and the Symbolism of Knots," there is a multivalence and a depth to such symbolisms of limit-situations.[28] There is the language of the "great chain of being" into which all things are bound and in which all things, distinct as they are, share. One might talk of the affirmation of one's place, the place on which one stands; or seek to be unbound, to be liberated. Both are experiential possibilities and postures. The symbolizations and expressions flow from the situation in which a man finds himself.

In the Mediterranean world we have been describing, in the Hellenistic period, such a radical revaluation of the cosmos occurred.[29] Suffering from what might be termed "cosmic paranoia" man sees danger and threat everywhere. Looking up at the heavens, at the stars and the motions of the heavenly bodies, he no longer sees the signs and guarantors of order, the guardians of a good cosmic and human destiny, the positive limits placed on the chaotic powers above and below and on the span of human existence; but rather a grim system of aggressors, an openly hostile army which seeks to chain him. He finds himself in a world surrounded and hemmed in by powers, powers one dares do no more than name in terrifying titles such as the following:

[27] I utilize the title of Louis Dumont's brilliant book on this theme, *Homo Hierarchicus* (Paris, 1967).

[28] M. Eliade, "Le 'dieu lieur' et le symbolisme des noeuds," *Revue de l'histoire des religions*, 134 (1947-8), 5-36; English trans. in *Images and Symbols* (London, 1961), pp. 92-124.

[29] Cf. H. Jonas, *The Gnostic Religion*, 2 ed. (Boston, 1963), esp. pp. 5-7, 241-265; J. Z. Smith, "Birth Upside Down or Right Side Up?" chapter 7, below.

O mighty, majestic, glorious Splendors; holy and earth-born, mighty arch-daimons; compeers of the great god; denizens of Chaos, of Erebus and of the unfathomable Abyss; earth-dwellers, haunters of sky-depths, nook-infesting, murk-enwrapped; scanners of the mysteries, guardians of the secrets, captains of the hosts of hell; kings of infinite space, terrestrial overlords; globe-shaking, firm-founding, ministering to earthquakes; terror-strangling, panic-striking, spindle-turning ... tempest-tossing Lords of Fate, dark shapes of Erebus, senders of Necessity; flame-fanning fire-darters, snow-compelling, dew-compelling, gale-raising, abyss-plumbing, calm-bestriding air spirits; dauntless in courage, heart crushing despots; chasm-leaping iron-nerved daimons; wild-raging, unenslaved; watchers of Tartarus; delusive Fate-phantoms; all-seeing, all-hearing, all-conquering, sky-wandering vagrants.[30]

In such a world-view, the structures of order are perceived to have been reversed. Rather than the positive limits they were meant to be, they have become oppressive. Man is no longer defined by the degree to which he harmonizes himself and his society to the cosmic patterns of order; but rather by the degree to which he can escape the patterns. Rather than the hero-that-failed of the locative world-view, the paradigm here is the hero-that-succeeded, succeeded in escaping the tyrannical order. Every man is called upon to be such a hero. The man of wisdom is no longer the sage but the savior—he who knows the escape routes.

To escape from the despotism of this world and its rulers, exemplified in the seven planetary spheres described in brutal archaic language, becomes the goal:

> The foes, the foes—seven are they, seven are they; evil are they, evil are they; seven are they, seven are they. Seven gods, seven evil gods .... Seven demons of oppression. On high they bring trouble, below they bring chaos .... Falling in rain from the sky, issuing from the earth, they penetrate the strong timbers, the thick timbers; they pass from house to house. Doors do not stop them; locks do not stop them. They glide in at doors like serpents; they enter by the windows like the wind. Seven are they—they grind the land like grain. Knowing no mercy they rage against man. Roaring above, gibbering below, they—the seven—they are the voices which cry and pursue mankind.[31]

---

[30] [Invocation to] the All-powerful Might of the Constellation of the Great Bear," from the Great Paris Magical Papyrus (Bibl. Nat. suppl. Gr. 574, f.15ᵛ) in K. Preisendanz, *Papyri Graecae Magicae* (Leipzig—Berlin, 1928), vol. I, p. 118 (lines 1345-80). I have followed, with minor alterations, the translation by E. M. Butler, *Ritual Magic* (Cambridge, 1949), p. 9.

[31] I have adapted the rendering of R. C. Thompson, *Semitic Magic* (London, 1908), pp. 47-50.

To ascend to another world of freedom and openness becomes the aim of Hellenistic man and the chief concern of his religion. Hellenistic man discovered himself to be an exile from his true home, a home beyond the borders. He strives to return to the world-beyond-this-world which is his true place; to the god-beyond-the-god-of-this-world who is the true god; to awaken the part of himself which is from the beyond and strip off his body which belongs to his present constricted realm.

> I no longer have trust in anything in the world
> In father and mother;
> I have no trust in the world
> In brothers or sisters;
> I have no trust in the world . . . .
> After my soul alone I go searching about,
> which is worth more to me than generations or worlds.
> I went and found my soul . . . .
> I went and found Truth where she stands,
> at the outermost rim of the world.[32]

As Paul in Romans 7 was to discover about the Law of Yahweh, that it was good *once*, but that it had been captured by the Powers and turned upside down so that "the very commandment which promised life proved to be death to me" (Rom. 7:10), so each locative culture was to discover that its cherished structures of limits, the gods that ordained and maintained these limits, and the myths which described the creation of the world as an imposition of limits were perverse. Each culture rebelled against its locative traditions, developing a complex series of techniques for escaping limitation, for achieving individual and cosmic freedom now.

V

It is tempting to continue along these lines, offering yet further examples which might add subtlety to the extremely broad strokes with which we have painted our portrait. We might point to the cosmogonic conflict in Indian mythology between the Restrainers (Vritras or Daityas) and the Non-Restrainers (Adityas) with its complex dialectic of positive and negative closure and openness. We might point to constellations of symbols which associate spaciousness, openness and freedom in a far more positive way than the Hellenistic

---

[32] M. Lidzbarski, *Ginza: Der Schatz oder Das Grosse Buch der Mandäer* (Göttingen, 1925), pp. 390f; English trans. in Jonas, *The Gnostic Religion*, pp. 90f.

model we have dwelt on.³³ We might point to the idealization of social mobility so rampant in this country which has lead S. E. Morison to preface his *Oxford History of the American People* with the following quotation from Oliver Wendell Holmes: "I find the great thing in this world is not so much where we stand as in what direction we are moving." We might point to the more recent mythology of conflict between these two versions of the world, the cowboy versus the homesteader, the one with his cry of "Ride on" and "Don't fence me in," the other with his barbed wire and language of roots.³⁴ Or we might point to an older incarnation of the same duality: Alexander the Great and the naked sages of India.

> On the appearance of Alexander and his army these venerable men stamped [the earth] with their feet and gave no other sign of interest. Alexander asked them through interpreters what they meant by this odd behavior, and they replied: 'King Alexander, every man can possess only so much of this earth's surface as this we are standing on. You are but human like the rest of us, save that you are always busy ... travelling so many miles from your home, a nuisance to yourself and to others.'³⁵

But the basic dichotomy remains. The question of the character of the place on which one stands is *the* fundamental symbolic and social question. Once an individual or culture has expressed its vision of its place, a whole language of symbols and social structures will follow.

While it is beyond the scope of this paper to catalogue and explicate the variety of social forms and expressions associated with either of these basic human stances, perhaps one small but significant example will suffice. We have all learned that money is symbolic; but, symbolic of what? In an expansive, open culture money becomes an important means of expressing transcendence of place. Through the acquisition of money, social mobility is made possible for the individual or culture group. One may rise above his station, class or place. Similarly, the acquisition of wealth with its attendant phenomena of conspicuous consumption and waste is, at least in part, an expression of trans-

---

³³ For example, J. F. A. Sawyer, "Spaciousness: An Important Feature of Language about Salvation in the Old Testament," *Annual of the Swedish Theological Institute*, 6 (1968), 20-34.

³⁴ I owe this example to my colleague, Professor Charles H. Long of the University of Chicago.

³⁵ Arrian, *Anabasis* VII.i.6; English trans. A. de Sélincourt, *Arrian's Life of Alexander the Great* (Baltimore, 1958), pp. 225f.

cendence of finitude. One is no longer bound to the limits, the necessities of life. One may waste freely.

On the other hand, in a locative culture money, or more properly, exchange, serves to establish and re-enforce a sense of place. Since the work of Marcel Mauss on *The Gift*, we have been accustomed to perceive the total symbolic universe implied in the structures of reciprocity which lie behind the gift and exchange process.[36] In its Melanesian form a complex notion of not transgressing bounds is involved. To cite a recent report:

> The ideal is equivalence, neither more nor less, neither 'one-up' nor 'one-down' . . . . All transgression in Tangu may be seen as attacks on equivalence . . . . The accepted, public device for finding and maintaining equivalence is the *br'ngun'guni* . . . and a series of feasting exchanges . . . . In the best of all possible worlds, since all exchanges would be equivalent and true amity reign over all, there would no longer be any need to make exchanges.[37]

Exchange, the acquisition of foodstuffs or other wealth, is ultimately a means to the keeping of one's place. By way of an aside, we may note that it is in these very same Melanesian exchange cultures that the so-called "Cargo-cults" flourish. Within these highly charged, intensively studied recent examples of the phenomena of social change, great emphasis has been placed on "Cargo" as symbolic of European technology, culture, colonial power, etc. The native discovers himself to be deprived in confrontation with the white man's material wealth and seeks to obtain these goods for himself. Insufficient attention has been paid in these accounts to "Cargo" as disruptive of equivalence and place, and the requirement of some system of exchange in order to rectify this situation. Indeed, in a recent essay K. Burridge has suggested that the conflict caused by the introduction of the open-money world view into a society which has a locative-exchange view is one of the four basic scenarios leading to the widespread phenomenon of contemporary millenarianism.[38]

---

[36] M. Mauss, "Essai sur le don: Forme et raison de l'échange dans les sociétés archaïques," *L'Année Sociologique*, n.s. 1 (1925), 30-186; English trans. I. Cunnison, *The Gift* (London, 1967). Cf. C. Lévi-Strauss, *Les Structures élémentaires de la parenté*, 2 ed. (Paris, 1967), ch. 5.

[37] K. Burridge, *Mambu* (London, 1960), pp. 82-85. Cf. the older classic accounts of B. Malinowski, *Argonauts of the Western Pacific* (London, 1922), chs. 3, 6; R. Firth, *Primitive Economics of the New Zealand Maori* (New York, 1929); Firth, *Primitive Polynesian Economy* (London, 1939).

[38] K. Burridge, *New Heaven, New Earth: A Study of Millenarian Activities* (New York, 1969), pp. 143-149.

VI

In the conclusion to his well-known study, *Social and Economic History of the Roman Empire*, Professor Rostovtzeff passed under review the variety of theories which had been suggested to account for the decline of the Roman Empire. After settling on a psychological explanation, he concluded by observing that a change in a people's outlook on the world was one of the most potent factors in social, economic and political change, and that further exploration of change in outlook was one of the most urgent tasks in the field of ancient history.[39] Several scholars have taken up Rostovtzeff's challenge, most notably M. P. Nilsson, "The New Conception of the Universe in Late Greek Paganism," *Eranos*, 44 (1946); and E. R. Dodd's brilliant Wiles Lectures, *Pagan and Christian in an Age of Anxiety* (Cambridge 1965). This paper is intended as a modest continuation of these studies.

The implication of these observations would be that *social change is preeminently symbol or symbolic change*. At the heart of the issue of change are the symbolic-social questions: what is the place on which I stand? what are my horizons? what are my limits? I have suggested that there are two basic answers to these questions, that these two provide the description of a social or individual center of value and meaning, and that from such a center all other symbolizations derive their meaning. Thus when one adopts one or the other of these two basic stances, one adopts a whole symbolic universe which is, for the individual or culture, *the* Universe. To change stance is to totally alter one's symbols and to inhabit a different world. And finally, I have suggested that these two stances ought not to be looked upon as stages in social (or individual) evolution or growth, with maturity or modernity associated with the open or limitless. Rather I have insisted that these two stances are coeval possibilities. From this perspective, place (whether in an open or closed structure) ought not to be viewed as a static concept. It is through an understanding and symbolization of place that a society or individual creates itself. Without straining the point, this active sense is crystallized in the expression "to take place" as a synonym for "to happen," "to occur," "to be." It is by virtue of its view of its place that a society or an individual (that history or biography as the description of a society

---

[39] M. Rostovtzeff, *Social and Economic History of the Roman Empire* (Oxford, 1926), p. 486.

or individual) takes place. The insight of the poet Mallarmé may be extended as the exhaustive description of history or biography: "Nothing shall have taken place but place."[40]

It is this sense of happening, of things taking place, that allows us to conjoin the notion of symbol and social change or history. For both of these are characteristic human activities. Both are forms of human creativity. Both are means by which man expresses the truth of what it is to be human (be it a limited or infinitely open view), establishes and discovers his existence, invents and participates in human culture—"the creation by man of a world of meaning in the context of which human life can be significantly lived."[41] For with Cassirer we would hold:

"We cannot define man by any inherent principle which constitutes his metaphysical essence, nor can we define him by any inborn faculty or instinct which may be ascertained by empirical observation. Man's outstanding characteristic, his distinguishing mark, is not his metaphysical or physical nature, but his work. It is this work, it is the system of human activities, which defines and determines the circle of 'humanity.' "[42]

From this point of view—and joining with those anthropologists and sociologists who have defined man as a symbol-producing animal and society or culture as a symbol-system—we may say, by way of tautology, social change is symbol change. Furthermore, as has already been stressed, society or culture is preeminently the construction of significance and order through symbolic activity. Social change may then be specified as the discovery or creation of new modes of significance and order.

In the preceding remarks we have deliberately introduced an ambivalence. Man, we have said, "establishes and discovers"; "invents and participates in"; "discovers or creates" the world. This reflects our conviction that one of the consistent failures in discussions of symbol and history has been to reify and value one of these terms at the expense of the other. Most usually in Western discussions it has been the symbol that has been so valued. The symbol, while possessing no ontological status of its own, has quite consistently been held to be "transparent" to the realm of being, of ultimate value.

---

[40] Quoted in G. Poulet, *The Interior Distance* (Baltimore, 1959), p. 281.

[41] T. F. O'Dea, *The Sociology of Religion* (Englewood Cliffs, 1966), p. 5. I have omitted one word from Professor O'Dea's definition of culture.

[42] E. Cassirer, *An Essay on Man* (New Haven, 1944), p. 68.

The world, and hence history as the world-process, is deficient in reality (profane) until status is conferred on it through the symbol.[43] More recently we have seen, in historicism, this locus of values reversed.

In the works of some contemporary social scientists, much has been accomplished to overcome these unfortunate bifurcations. Thus scholars such as Peter Berger speak of three moments in the dialectic of society: externalization, which is the "outpouring of human being into the world"; objectification, the cultural processes by which the products of human externalization attain a "reality that confronts its original producers as a facticity external to and other than themselves"; and finally, internalization, "the reappropriation by men of this same reality."[44] This fruitful development out of the tradition of Marx and Durkheim provides a "double-objectivity" for the symbolic process which grows out of the activity of the process rather than some external locus. Man creates his place in the world as he creates his world; man discovers his place as he encounters the world in which he finds himself.[45] Social change, symbolic change of the sort we have been describing, occurs when there is disjunction, when there is no longer a "fit" within all the elements of this complex process.

Each society has moments of ritualized disjunction, moments of "descent into chaos," of ritual reversal, of liminality, of collective anomie. But these are part of a highly structured scenario in which these moments will be overcome through the creation of a new world, the raising of an individual to a new status, or the strengthening of community.[46] Change—in the strongest sense of the word, a society's conversion—is required when such moments meld into history. When the world is perceived to be chaotic, reversed, liminal,

[43] See particularly the trenchant critique of H. Penner, "Bedeutung und Probleme der religiösen Symbolik bei Tillich und Eliade," *Antaios*, 9 (1967), 127-143.
[44] P. L. Berger, *The Sacred Canopy: Elements of a Sociological Theory of Religion* (Garden City, L.I., 1969, reprint), p. 4.
[45] See C. Geertz, "Ethos, World-View and the Analysis of Sacred Symbols," *Antioch Review* (Winter 1957-8), 421-437; Geertz, "Religion as a Cultural System," in M. Banton, ed., *Anthropological Approaches to the Study of Religion* (London, 1966), pp. 1-46; and especially Berger, *The Sacred Canopy*, chs. 1-2, to which I am particularly indebted.
[46] See the important work in progress of V. Turner, in particular, "Betwixt and Between: The Liminal Period in *Rites de Passage*," in Turner, *The Forest of Symbols: Aspects of Ndembu Ritual* (Ithaca, 1967), pp. 93-111.

filled with anomie. Then man finds himself in a world which he does not recognize; and perhaps even more terrible, man finds himself to have a self he does not recognize. Then he will need to create a new world, to express his sense of a new place. For man: "can adapt himself somehow to anything his imagination can cope with; but he cannot deal with Chaos .... Therefore our most important assets are always the symbols of our general *orientation* in nature, on the earth, in society and in what we are doing: the symbols of our *Weltanschauung* and *Lebenanschauung*."[47]

[47] S. Langer, *Philosophy in a New Key*, 4 ed. (Cambridge, Mass., 1960), p. 287. This paper was first presented on April 30, 1970 at a colloquium, "Man and Symbol" sponsored by The Institute for Ecumenical and Cultural Research.

CHAPTER SEVEN

BIRTH UPSIDE DOWN OR RIGHT SIDE UP?

> All things have their place, knew we how to place them.
> George Herbert.
> Tout, dans les représentations humaines, ou du moins tout l'essentiel, est système.   Georges Dumézil.

One of the most exciting and profound developments in recent years in the study of archaic cultures, myths, and rituals has been the increased focus on structural elements, on systems of logic, order, and classification. This has been the outgrowth of the rejection of older theories of a primitive *Urdummheit*, a repudiation of statements such as Frazer's that "haziness is the characteristic of the mental vision of the savage. Like the blind man at Bethsaida, he sees men like trees and animals walking in a thick intellectual fog."[1]

The beginning of this new perspective might be dated from the early part of this century with the works of the French Sociological School, especially the essay by Durkheim and Mauss on primitive classification[2] and Hertz's study of symbolic forms of classification associated with the dualism left/right.[3] More recently, one might point to the researches of Dumézil and his followers, the work of some of the contemporary British Social Anthropologists and studies by American Ethnoscientists.[4] Research in this direction

---

[1] J. G. Frazer, *Totemism and Exogamy* (London, 1910), vol. IV, p. 61. See F. R. Lehmann, "Der Begriff 'Urdummheit' in der ethnologischen und religionswissenschaftlichen Anschauungen von K. Th. Preuss, Ad. E. Jensen und G. Murray," *Sociologus*, II (1952), 131-45.

[2] E. Durkheim and M. Mauss, "De quelques formes primitives de classification: contribution à l'étude des représentations collectives," *L'Année sociologique*, VI (1901-2), 1-72; English translation: *Primitive Classification* (Chicago, 1963).

[3] R. Hertz, "La prééminence de la main droite: étude sur la polarité religieuse," *Revue philosophique de la France et de l'étranger*, LXVIII (1909), 553-80; English translation: *Death and the Right Hand* (London, 1960), pp. 89-113 [text], 155-60 [notes].

[4] See the detailed introduction by R. Needham to Durkheim and Mauss, *Primitive Classification*, esp. pp. xxxii-xli which reviews the later influence of the French Sociological School. For the new discipline of Ethnoscience, see the survey article by W. C. Sturtevant, "Studies in Ethnoscience," *American Anthropologist*, LXVI (1964), 99-131.

has culminated, for the present, in the theoretical works of Claude Lévi-Strauss, Mary Douglas, and Victor Turner.

Much of Lévi-Strauss's extremely provocative work may be understood as an attempt to lay bare the various taxonomies, typologies, and logical systems of archaic myths, rituals, and social structures. As he has noted in an important paragraph:

> A native thinker makes the penetrating comment that "All sacred things must have their place."[5] It could even be said that being in their place is what makes them sacred for if they were taken out of their place, even in thought, the entire order of the universe would be destroyed. Sacred objects therefore contribute to the maintenance of order in the universe by occupying the places allocated to them. Examined superficially and from the outside, the refinements of ritual can appear pointless. They are explicable by a concern for what one might call "micro-adjustment"—the concern to assign every single creature, object or feature to a place within a class.[6]

Mary Douglas in her already classic work, *Purity and Danger: An Analysis of Concepts of Pollution and Taboo*, and Victor Turner in his on-going studies of liminality[7] have examined precisely those persons, objects, creatures, and places which do *not* have a place, which are out of place, betwixt and between. Starting with an analysis of Leviticus 11 and Deuteronomy 14 and using a wealth of comparative material, Douglas demonstrates, that "holiness is exemplified by completeness. Holiness requires that individuals shall conform to the class to which they belong. And holiness requires that different

---

[5] Quoting A. C. Fletcher, "The Hako: A Pawnee Ceremony," *Twenty-Second Annual Report of the Bureau of American Ethnology* (Washington, D.C., 1904), Part II, p. 34. Although I am extremely appreciative of Lévi-Strauss's interpretation (i.e., "it could even be said that being in their place is what makes them sacred")—the actual context for this remark in Fletcher's report gives a somewhat different implication: "The first act of a man must be to set apart a place that can be made sacred and holy, that can be consecrated to Tira'wa ... a place where a man can put his sacred articles, those objects which enable him to approach the powers ... We are now to set aside a place where we shall put the sacred articles. ... The sacred fire must come in a place set aside for it. All sacred things must have their place. Kataharu is the place set apart for the sacred fire, where it can come and bring good to man" (Fletcher, pp. 33f). It is not, in this account, being-in-their-place which *confers* sacrality as Lévi-Strauss suggests.

[6] C. Lévi-Strauss, *The Savage Mind* (Chicago, 1966), p. 10.

[7] See esp. V. Turner, "Betwixt and Between: The Liminal Period in *Rites de Passage*," *Proceedings of the American Ethnological Society* (1964), reprinted in Turner, *The Forest of Symbols: Aspects of Ndembu Ritual* (Ithaca, 1967), pp. 93-111; cf. Turner "Myth," *International Encyclopedia of the Social Sciences* (New York, 1968), Vol. X, esp. p. 580.

classes of things shall not be confused."⁸ She then brilliantly (and, to me, quite convincingly) applies this general thesis to the Israelitic prohibitions:

> The farmer's duty was to preserve the blessing. For one thing, he had to preserve the order of creation. So no hybrids . . . either in the fields, or in the herds, or in the clothes. . . . Cloven hoofed, cud chewing ungulates are the model of the proper kind of food for a pastoralist. If they must eat wild game, they can eat wild game that shares these characteristics and is therefore of the same species . . . [Those that do not conform are held to be unclean, for example] animals which are cloven-hoofed but not ruminant, the pig and the camel. Note that this failure to conform to the two necessary criteria for defining cattle is the only reason given in the Old Testament for avoiding the pig [Deut. 14:6,8; Lev. 11:3,7]; nothing whatever is said about its dirty scavenging habits. . . . I suggest that originally the sole reason for its being counted as unclean is its failure as a wild boar to get into the antelope class. . . . In general the underlying principle of cleanness in animals is that they shall conform fully to their class. Those species are unclean which are imperfect members of their class, or whose class itself confounds the general scheme of the world. To grasp this scheme we need go back to Genesis and the creation. Here a three-fold classification unfolds, divided between the earth, the waters and the firmament. Leviticus takes up this scheme and allots to each element its proper kind of animal life. In the firmament two-legged fowls fly with wings. In the water scaly fish swim with fins. On the earth four-legged animals hop, jump or walk. Any class of creatures which is not equipped for the right kind of locomotion in its element is contrary to holiness. . . . Thus anything in the waters which has not fins or scales is unclean [Lev. 11:10-12]. Nothing is said about predatory habits or of scavenging. The only sure test for cleanness in a fish is its scales and its propulsion by means of fins. Four-footed creatures which fly [Lev. 11:20-26] are unclean. . . . If penguins lived in the Near East I would expect them to be ruled unclean as wingless birds.⁹

Though the elements which are out of place are dangerous and unclean, they are also extremely potent and thus may be voluntarily crossed over into at significant moments in the life of an individual, culture, or the cosmos. In this connection, one may think of the well-known phenomenon of the suspension of taboos for initiates following initiation; the deliberate eating of unclean food (e.g., Isa. 65:3-5) or cultic transvestism by magicians, shamans, and practitioners of Tantra; the saturnalia and other periods of license

---
⁸ M. Douglas, *Purity and Danger: An Analysis of Concepts of Pollution and Taboo* (New York, 1966), p. 53.
⁹ Douglas, *Purity and Danger*, pp. 54-56.

and chaos preceding or following New Years; or the punctuation of the liturgical year with cultic acts of obscenity or burlesque (e.g., the *Festum Asinorum* or the *Purimspiele*). But in general, these interstructural activities and liminal situations (like other similar phenomena, e.g., ecstasy) are punctual, limited experiences which form part of a highly structured scenario of existence, of birth and rebirth, of creation, order and chaos.

That which gives shape to the whole, which provides the boundaries within which a person or thing obtains its class as well as providing a map for those who would venture outside their station, is, as Mary Douglas intimated with her reference to the opening chapter of Genesis, the cosmogonic myth. It has been the consistent emphasis of Mircea Eliade that the cosmogonic myth functions as an exemplary model, a paradigm which reveals and describes not only the structure of the cosmos as it was in the beginning but also its structure as it is experienced in the here and now. Eliade goes on to point out that the cosmos and its structures are understood to be "a living world—inhabited and used by creatures of flesh and blood, subject to the law of becoming, of old age and death. Hence it requires a periodical repairing, a renewing, a strengthening. But the only way to renew the World is to repeat what the Immortals did *in illo tempore*, is to reiterate the creation."[10] If this repairing and repetition were not accomplished, the structures would dissolve and the cosmos would return, permanently, to primordial chaos.

> That life is thus *created* through the cult means salvation from that distress and destruction which would befall, if life were not renewed. For existence is an everlasting war between the forces of life and death, of blessing and curse. "The World" is worn out if it is not regularly renewed. ... Thus it is the "fact of salvation" which is actualized in the cult. ... The fact that the cult is a repetition and a renewed creation leads to the view that the salvation which takes place is a *repetition* of a *first salvation* which took place in the dawn of time.[11]

One finds in many archaic cultures a profound faith in the cosmos as ordered in the beginning and a joyous celebration of the primordial act of ordering as well as a deep sense of responsibility for the maintenance of that order through repetition of the myth, through

---

[10] M. Eliade, *Myth and Reality* (New York, 1963), p. 45.
[11] S. Mowinckel, *The Psalms in Israel's Worship* (Oxford, 1962), Vol. I, pp. 18 f. Cf. Mowinckel, *Religion und Kultus* (Göttingen, 1953), pp. 70-80.

ritual, through norms of conduct, or through taxonomy. But it is equally apparent that in some cultures the structure of order, the gods that won or ordained it, creation itself, are discovered to be evil and oppressive. In such circumstances one will rebel against the paradigms and seek to reverse their power, frequently employing (with the effect of a Black Mass) the very same ritual techniques which had maintained the original order. Such a phenomenon may be seen in India where the yogi utilizes the structures of the archaic Brahmanic sacrifices—sacrifices designed to maintain and renew the order of the cosmos—in order to escape the cosmic restraints of order and destiny. A similar rebellion occurred in the Mediterranean world during the hellenistic period. Here the all-pervasive structure of gnosticism[12] judged the cosmos, its gods, the human condition, and all structures of order to be evil and oppressive and sought to liberate man by annihilating or reversing these structures. It is with one particular example of this rebellion, the tradition of the upside-down crucifixion of the Apostle Peter as recorded in the *Acts of Peter* that the remainder of this paper is concerned.

The Acts of Peter

The apocryphal *Acts of Peter* is one of the earliest extant examples of this genre of literature, composed most probably between A.D. 180-190 in either Asia Minor or Rome. Originally in Greek (although only ninth- to eleventh-century manuscripts survive), our prime source is a Latin translation found at Vercelli. While this manuscript dates from the sixth or seventh century, it is dependent on a translation from Greek into Latin produced in the third, or, at the latest, fourth century.[13]

The *Acts of Peter* may be easily divided into two main sections: the first narrates the conflict between Simon Magus and Peter; the

---

[12] My understanding of gnosticism is that it is a structural possibility within a number of religious traditions in the hellenistic-Mediterranean world, that it is not a new religion, or a Christian heresy, but rather a structure analogous to mysticism or asceticism.

[13] For these details, see the classic studies of C. Schmidt, "Studien zu den alten Petrusakten," *Zeitschrift für Kirchengeschichte*, XLIII (1924), 321-48; XIV (1927), 481-513; Schmidt, "Zur Datierung der alten Petrusakten," *Zeitschrift für die neutestamentliche Wissenschaft und die Kunde des Urchristentums*, XXIX (1930), 150-55. See further, C. H. Turner, "The Latin Acts of Peter," *Journal of Theological Studies*, XXXII (1931), 119-33; W. Schneemelcher, "The Acts of Peter," in E. Hennecke, W. Schneemelcher, and R. McL. Wilson (eds.), *New Testament Apocrypha* (London, 1965), Vol. II, pp. 259-75.

second, with which we are concerned, is a lengthy account of Peter's martyrdom (chaps. 33-41 in Codex Vercellenses). This latter section was widely circulated as may be seen from surviving texts or fragments in Coptic, Syriac, Armenian, Arabic, Ethiopic, and Old Slavonic.[14]

The earliest datable reference to the upside down motif is in Eusebius, *Ecclesiastical History* (III.i.2) where it is reported that Origen, in the third book of his commentary on Genesis, had written of Peter: "At the end he came to Rome and was crucified head downwards, for so he requested to suffer."[15] Usually this upside-down crucifixion has received a moralistic interpretation:

> He [Peter] had the happiness to end his life on the cross. His Lord was pleased not only that he should die for his love, but in the same manner [he] himself had died for us, by expiring on the cross which was the throne of his love. Only the apostle's humility made a difference in desiring to be crucified with his head downwards ... for he was not worthy to suffer in the same manner as his divine master. ... His master looked toward heaven ... [but Peter] judged that a sinner formed from dust, and going to return to dust, ought rather in confusion to look on the earth as [he was] unworthy to raise his eyes to heaven.[16]

This understanding of Peter's reversed crucifixion has been the leading interpretation since the ninth century; but I would propose that it is a distortion, both of the explicit words of the narrative and of the meaning of the upside down motif. Rather than dealing with an exercise in humility, we have here an *act of cosmic*

---

[14] For these traditions, see the superb edition of L. Vouaux, *Les Actes de Pierre* (Paris, 1922), pp. 1-22.

[15] K. Lake, *Eusebius: The Ecclesiastical History* (London, 1926), Vol. I, pp. 190 [text]-191 [translation]. I am not interested, within the limits of this paper, in the vexed question of the historicity of Peter's residence and martyrdom in Rome. See the classic treatments of H. Lietzmann, *Petrus und Paulus in Rom*, 2d ed. (Berlin and Leipzig, 1927); O. Cullmann, *Peter: Disciple, Apostle and Martyr* (Cleveland, 1958 reprint) and the new archeological researches summarized by M. Guarducci, *The Tomb of Saint Peter* (New York, 1960). The latter remain controversial (see the excellent bibliography prepared by A. A. de Marco, *The Tomb of Saint Peter* [Leiden, 1964]). On June 26, 1968 "the Vatican has conclusively determined that the mortal remains found under St. Peter's Basilica are those of the Apostle" (Associated Press Dispatch—further details are not available to me at this writing). Both partisans and detractors of the Roman tradition agree that "Peter was crucified in Rome with his head downwards scarcely has historical value" (Cullmann, *Peter*, p. 117).

[16] A. Butler, *Lives of the Eminent Saints*. I cite an edition published in Boston, 1880, p. 235.

audacity consistent with and expressive of a Christian-gnostic understanding and evaluation of the structures of the cosmos and of the human condition. Thus, while Morton Scott Enslin declares of the description of the crucifixion of Peter in the *Acts of Peter* that "even this narrative is clogged by a lengthy explanation as to why he wished thus to be crucified,"[17] I would insist, to the contrary, that in this explanation we have one of the more overt texts illustrating one type of Christian mystery.

> Then when he had approached and stood by the cross, he began to say: "O name of the cross, mystery that is hidden, O inexpressible grace that is spoken in the name of the cross! O nature of man that cannot be separated from God! O love unspeakable and inseparable that cannot be revealed through unclean lips! I seize you now, having come to the end of my release from here. I will declare you, what you are; I will no longer conceal the mystery of the cross that has long been shut in and hidden from my soul. For you who hope in Christ, do not let the cross be this thing that is visible: for [my death] like the passion of Christ is something other than a visible thing. And now, above all, since you who are able to hear can hear from me who is at the last final hour of my life—pay attention! withdraw your souls from every outward sense, from all that appears but is not truly real; close your eyes! shut your ears! cease actions outwardly seen! and you shall know all that concerns Christ and the whole secret of your salvation. Let this much be said to you who hear—[but] remain as if it were unspoken. But now it is time for you, Peter, to surrender your body to those who are taking it. Take it then, you whose function it is. I request, O executioners, that you crucify me head downwards, in that position and in no other. And the reason [for this] I will tell to those who hear."[18]

Thus far we have been given an exhortation by one-who-knows, who possesses *gnosis*, to an initiated circle of listeners. It is not, I think, to go beyond the meaning of the text to understand Peter here as speaking as one possessed, in ecstasy. It is the inner voice, the pneumatic voice of Peter that we are hearing; and we are invited to hear him with our inner, pneumatic ears. Peter can dissociate himself from his body and can address his fleshly, visible form: "It is time for you, Peter, to surrender your body"; for Peter is

---

[17] M. S. Enslin, "Peter, Acts, of," *The Interpreter's Dictionary of the Bible* (Nashville, 1962), Vol. III, p. 758.

[18] Text: R. A. Lipsius and M. Bonnet, *Acta Apostolorum Apocrypha* (Leipzig, 1891; reprinted Hildesheim, 1959), Vol. I, pp. 90-93. English translations: M. R. James, *The Apocryphal New Testament* (Oxford, 1955 reprint), p. 334; R. Schneemelcher and G. C. Stead in Hennecke, Schneemelcher and Wilson, *New Testament Apocrypha*, Vol. II, p. 319.

one at the threshold of death, at the moment of truth, about to experience the great initiation. He is at the "last final hour" of his life, at the moment when he is about to put off the old man and put on the new. At the moment when, what he declares will no longer be spoken with "unclean lips"; when what he utters will be supremely true for the impediments of his life-long earthly existence, impediments which have resulted heretofore in the "mystery of the cross" being "shut in and hidden from his soul," are about to be stripped away. Peter is here speaking in the traditional language of the mystery cults and inviting a select audience to participate in the mystery with the classic formula: Let him who has ears, hear!

Peter's discourse from the cross, as the text continues, is a revelation of the mystery of Christ, a mystery which repeats the most ancient mystery of all: creation.

> And when they had hanged him in the way which he had requested, he began to speak again, declaring: "Men, whose right it is to hear pay attention to what I shall tell you at this moment that I am hanged! You must know the mystery of all nature and the beginning of all things, how it came about. For the first man, whose likeness I bear in my appearance, in falling head downwards displayed a manner of birth that was not once—for it was dead, without motion. He, being drawn down—he who also cast his first beginning down to the earth—established the whole of the cosmic system as an image of his creation [or, vocation]. Upside down as he was, he showed what is on the right hand as on the left, and those on the left as on the right, and changed the signs of all their nature so as to consider fair those things which were not beautiful and those things which were really evil to be good. Concerning this the Lord says in a mystery: *Unless you make what is on the right hand as what is on the left and what is on the left hand as what is on the right and what is above as what is below and what is behind as what is before—you will not have knowledge* [or recognize, or look upon] *of the Kingdom.* This thought then I have declared to you; and the form in which you now see me hanging is the representation of that man who first came to birth. You then, my beloved, both those who hear me now and those that shall hear in time, must leave your former error and turn back again; for you should come up to the cross of Christ, who is the Word stretched out, the one and only, of whom the Spirit says: For what else is Christ but the World, the sound of God. So that Word is this upright tree on which I am crucified; but the sound is the crosspiece, the nature of man; and the nail which holds the cross-piece to the upright in the middle is the conversion and repentence of man.[19]

---

[19] Text: Lipsius and Bonnet, *Acta Apostolorum Apocrypha*, Vol. I, pp. 94-97. English translations: James, *Apocryphal New Testament*, pp. 334f.; Hennecke,

After giving this revelation of the mystery, Peter concludes his discourse with a lengthy doxology and dies.

The theme of Peter's upside down crucifixion is common in the complex apocryphal Petrine corpus. At times it is found in a setting similar to that quoted above, with a lengthy mystagogic discourse by Peter on the significance of the Cross (e.g., Pseudo-Linus, *Martyrium beati Petri apostoli*, XII);[20] more commonly as in the complex *Acts of the Holy Apostles Peter and Paul*, which are widely diffused in medieval manuscripts and apparently cannot be dated earlier than the ninth century, the moralistic interpretation is given:

> And Peter, having come to the cross said: "Since my Lord Jesus Christ, who came down from heaven to earth, was raised upright upon the cross, and since he has been gracious enough to call me to heaven who is from the earth—my cross ought to be set up head downwards so as to direct my feet towards heaven, for I am not worthy of being crucified like my Lord."[21]

The motif of the upside-down crucifixion of Peter is widely disseminated in works of art as well, one of the earliest representations being found in a ninth-century manuscript of Gregory Nazianzus (Parisinus 510, fol. 32ᵛ), the most famous probably being the painting of Giotto in the Sala del Capitolo of St. Peter's in the Vatican.[22]

There is only one other major tradition which narrates the upside down crucifixion of an apostle—that of Philip.[23] The *Acts of Philip* were composed in the fourth or fifth century and are clearly dependent upon the *Acts of Peter*. Unfortunately this apocryphon has survived only in Greek and Syriac fragments. In these, Philip, like Peter, is crucified head downwards; unlike Peter, he does not

---

Schneemelcher and Wilson, *New Testament Apocrypha*, Vol. II, pp. 319f. See further the valuable French translation of the whole discourse in Vouaux, *Les Actes de Pierre*, pp. 442-50.

[20] Lipsius and Bonnet, *Acta Apostolorum Apocrypha*, Vol. I, p. 14.

[21] *Acts of the Holy Apostles Peter and Paul*, LX in Lipsius and Bonnet, *Acta Apostolorum Apocrypha*, Vol. I, pp. 170f. The various recensions of this composite work are given in Lipsius and Bonnet, Vol. I, pp. 118-34.

[22] The miniature from Parisinus 510 is conveniently reproduced in the *Dictionnaire d'archéologie chrétienne et de liturgie*, Vol. VI:2, fig. 5414. For a convenient catalogue of representations of Peter's crucifixion, see L. Réau, *Iconographie de l'art chrétien* (Paris, 1959), Vol. III:3, pp. 1096-99.

[23] I have omitted from consideration the occurrence of upside-down crucifixion or hanging in martyrological traditions (e.g., St. Calliopius). In a recently published tenth-century Arabic manuscript, Paul is crucified in a horizontal position, see S. Pines, *The Jewish Christians of the Early Centuries of Christianity according to a New Source* (Jerusalem, 1966), p. 28.

appear to have requested this mode of execution. His explanation of his posture is similar to the opening lines of Peter's discourse:

> Do not grieve that I hang in such a manner, for in so doing I bear the form of the first man who was brought to earth head downwards and by the tree of the Cross was made alive, [saved] from the death of his transgression. In this manner I fulfil a rule, for the Lord said to me. . . .

In the various Greek manuscripts of this apocryphon there are three versions of the dominical saying:

a) Unless you make your below the above and the left the right—you will not enter my kingdom.
b) Unless you make the left right and consider the dishonorable honorable—you will not be able to enter the kingdom of heaven.
c) Unless you turn the below into the above and the above into the below and the right into the left and the left into the right—you will not enter the kingdom of God.

And finally Philip gives a dogmatic formulation which is a major key to this upside-down tradition: "Imitate me in this, for all the world is turned the wrong way and every soul that is in it."[24]

Upside Down

What can the historian of religions say about this curious tradition? What does it mean to be upside down? Its most basic sense is to be nonhuman. As the phenomenological psychiatrist E. W. Straus has argued in his brilliant essay, "The Upright Posture," the vertical standing position is characteristic of being human, involving man in a unique world of experience.[25] To reverse this posture, to be upside down or to walk on one's hands is an annihilation of humanity as profound as that experienced by Nebuchadnezzar when he, on all fours like an animal, was "driven from among men" and ate grass "like an ox" (Dan. 4:25,32f.; 5:21).[26] To walk on one's hands is, to use the terminology of Lévi-Strauss and Mary Douglas, to violate one's class by overturning the usual mode of locomotion, to become unclean, to be "driven from among men." *To be upside down is to be other-than-human*, is to have adopted a system

---

[24] Lipsius and Bonnet, *Acta Apostolorum Apocrypha*, Vol. II:2, pp. 74f.
[25] E. W. Straus, *Phenomenological Psychology* (New York, 1966), pp. 137-65.
[26] A characteristic of asceticism is often the desire to annihilate specifically human characteristics. Thus one should compare the dehumanizing of Nebuchadnezzar with the Christian "browsers" of Egypt, Syria, Palestine, and Ethiopia. See the summary account in J. Lacarrière, *Men Possessed by God* (Garden City, N.Y., 1964), pp. 154-57.

of spatial relationships from a nonhuman world. *To be upside down is to be alien.*

In Western tradition, the general symbolism of being upside down is most commonly associated with the *antipodes*, a continent in which men walk upside down in relation to the known Western world and which takes on the character of a "never-never land."[27] Such a world is totally alien to our own, as a third-century critic of the antipodal theory suggests in his scoffing inquiry:

> How is it with those who imagine that there are antipodes opposite to our footsteps?... Is there anyone so senseless as to believe that there are men whose footsteps are higher than their heads? or that things which with us are in a recumbent position, with them hang in an inverted direction? that crops and trees grow downwards? that the rains and snow and hail fall upwards to the earth?[28]

The notion of a reversed world is found in non-Western cultures as well[29] and persists in science-fiction novels such as Austin Hall and Homer Flint's, *The Blind Spot.*

This nonhuman, alien, or even antihuman characteristic of being upside down may be expressed in a variety of ways. It may symbolize a time when a man was not yet (or a time when man is no longer) a man. Thus in some Jewish traditions it is held that in Paradise men walked on their hands, Isaac being the only figure to retain this unique mode of locomotion after leaving Paradise.[30] Alternatively, in a number of cultures, the dead are depicted as walking upside down.[31] The hostile, antihuman, threatening aspect of being upside

---

[27] See A. Rainaud, *Le continent austral* (Paris, 1893); J. E. Wright, *Geographical Lore at the Time of the Crusades* (New York, 1925), pp. 55-57, 157-60.

[28] Lactantius, *Divinae institutiones*, III.24; translation by W. Fletcher, *The Ante-Nicene Fathers* (Grand Rapids, Mich., n.d.), Vol. VII, p. 94.

[29] See, e.g., C. Hentze, "Cosmogonie du monde dressé debout et du monde renversé," in *Le symbolisme cosmique des monuments religieux* (Rome, 1957), pp. 91-117, esp. pp. 106f.; J. Batchelor, *The Ainu and their Folklore* (London, 1901), p. 58, cf. J. Kitagawa, "Ainu Bear Festival," *History of Religions*, I (1961), 125f.

[30] L. Ginzberg, *Legends of the Jews* (Philadelphia, 1925), Vol. V, p. 263 n. 301; S. Lieberman, "Some Aspects of Afterlife in Early Rabbinic Literature," in the *Harry Austryn Wolfson Jubilee Volume* (Jerusalem, 1965), esp. pp. 498f.

[31] EGYPTIAN: J. H. Breasted, *Development of Religion and Thought in Ancient Egypt* (New York, 1912), pp. 283f.; J. Zandee, *Death as an Enemy according to Egyptian Conceptions* (Leiden, 1960), pp. 75-78. JEWISH: Ginzberg, *Legends of the Jews*, Vol. IV, p. 70 and Vol. VI, p. 236 n. 75; S. Lieberman, *Harry Austryn Wolfson Jubilee Volume*, pp. 498f. AFRICAN: A. B. Ellis, *The Yoruba Speaking Peoples of the Slave Coast of West Africa* (London, 1894; reprinted Chicago, 1964), p. 245; R. Needham, "Introduction," Durkheim and Mauss, *Primitive Classification*, p. xxxix; compare as a literary motif the dead who walk backwards in A.

down may be seen in the widespread belief that witches walk upside down[32] as well as in practices such as among the Lugbara who invert "hostile or suspect neighbours."[33]

In some traditions such as Yoga where, as Eliade has noted, "the yogin undertakes to 'reverse' normal behavior completely," the upside-down posture (the *Shīrshāsana* or the *Ūrdhvapadmāsana*) is part of a complex repertory of ritual techniques to annihilate one's manhood, to become nonhuman.[34]

In certain transitional or liminal periods such as initiations or New Years, there is a deliberate dehumanizing of the novice or society through ritual activity. In some societies this includes juggling and other acrobatic stunts featuring, among other things, an upside-down position.[35] Likewise in myth, the figure of the Trickster, himself a liminal figure, occasionally appears in an upside-down position.[36] Perhaps a continuation of this motif may be seen in the

---

Tutuola, *The Palm-Wine Drinkard and his Dead Palm-Wine Tapster in the Dead's Town* (New York, 1953), pp. 97, 100. Tutuola writes: "everything they [the dead] were doing there [in Dead's Town] was incorrect to alives and everything that all alives were doing was incorrect to deads too" (p. 100). The same motif is utilized by Tutuola to describe ancestral time when men were not yet men (see above n. 30): "in the olden days when the eyes of all human-beings were on our knees, when we were bending down from the sky because of its gravitiness and when we were walking backwards and not forwards as nowadays" (p. 75). GREEK: The same symbolism appears to lie behind the tradition that in consulting the oracle at Trophonius—a procedure which clearly involves a descent to the Underworld and a return—one entered a hole in the ground right side up, but "the return upward is the reverse of the descent ... the feet being pushed out first" (Pausanias IX.39.1), i.e., one returned in the posture of a dead spirit. FINNO-UGRIAN: R. Karsten, quoted in I. S. Wile, *Handedness Right and Left* (Boston, 1934), p. 297, cf. H. Ostermann, *K. Rasmussen's Posthumous Notes* (Copenhagen, 1939), pp. 102-4. See in general, S. Thompson, *Motif-Index of Folk Literature* 2d ed. (Copenhagen and Bloomington, Ind., 1955-8), F167.4 and F167.4.1.

[32] S. Eitrem, *Papyri Osloenses* (Oslo, 1925), Vol. I, p. 67 "even now-a-days we come across the belief that witches bend down and look at the landscape backwards between their legs," Eitrem refers to an article by him on the subject in *Kunst og kultur* (1923), 78 (*non vidi*); R. Needham, "Introduction," Durkheim and Mauss, *Primitive Classification*, p. xxxix.

[33] Needham, p. xxxix.

[34] M. Eliade, *Yoga: Immortality and Freedom* (New York, 1958), p. 362; E. Wood, *Yoga* (Baltimore, 1959), p. 114.

[35] See, in general, W. Deonna, *Le symbolisme de l'acrobatie antique* (Berchem and Brussels, 1953). See further the ritual role of clowns especially in North American Indian traditions, e.g., J. G. Neihardt, *Black Elk Speaks* (Lincoln, 1961), p. 192, "in the heyoka ceremony everything is backwards."

[36] P. Radin, *The Trickster* (New York, 1956), p. 98 (I am certain more convincing examples may be cited). Note that Peter, who in gospel traditions is some-

somewhat "tricksterish" figure of Father William in Lewis Carroll's *Alice in Wonderland*:

> "You are old, father William," the young man said,
> "And your hair has become very white;
> And yet you incessantly stand on your head—
> Do you think, at your age, it is right?"

As that which is unhuman, the upside-down posture is often associated with shame, that is, it is unnatural. While to be hung or crucified upside down has rarely been employed as a legal form of execution (it was a practice in Rome),[37] "to be hung by the heels" is frequently an extralegal form of derision, usually after the individual has been slain (e.g., Mussolini).[38]

For Peter to *request* to be crucified upside down was to deliberately dehumanize himself, to reverse the natural order, and to make of his death an act of rebellion against his manhood and the cosmos. Paradoxically, *it was also an act of birth*. It was a commonplace in hellenistic scientific literature that birth takes place in an upside-down position: "It is the due order of nature that men should enter the world with the head first and be carried to the tomb in a contrary fashion."[39] It is within this context, so typical of the general mood of hellenistic religions, of a destruction of one's humanity which is at the same time one's birth, that the upside-down crucifixion of Peter must be interpreted.

---

what of a simpleton, in folk literature often functions as a trickster figure. Thus in one tale containing the widespread motif of transposed heads or resuscitation with misplaced head (Thompson, *Motif-Index* E34 cf. A1371.1), Peter attempts to create a man but places his head on backwards (cited in A. Aarne and S. Thompson, *The Types of the Folktale* [Helsinki, 1964], 774A).

[37] Seneca reports: "I have seen crosses of many kinds ... and some hung with their heads downwards" (*Consolatio ad Marciam* 20); W. Aston, "Crimes and Punishments: Japanese," J. Hastings (ed.), *Encyclopedia of Religion and Ethics*, Vol. IV, p. 286 cites examples of upside-down crucifixion from Japan.

[38] I have omitted from consideration hanging upside down as a form of torture, since the physiological consequences would be more to the fore; however in sadistic and bondage literature, hanging upside down is frequently featured— here the sense of shame and the unnatural is clearly present.

[39] Pliny, *Historia naturalis* VII.6. It is noteworthy that it is only in archaic medical literature that the notion of being upside down has positive connotations. Thus in Jewish tradition, at birth a male child issues from the womb headfirst, a female, feetfirst (BT *Sotah*, 11b; *Ber. R* XVII.7; *Sh. R* I.13-14; J. Trachtenberg, *Jewish Magic and Superstition* [Cleveland, 1961 reprint], p. 188). Likewise the description of man found in a number of old Jewish and Christian manuals: *hominem esse arborem inversam* (see C.-M. Edsman, "Arbor inversa," *Religion och Bibel*, III [1944], esp. 32f.; C. G. Jung, *Alchemical Studies* [New York, 1967], pp.

The Mythic-Cosmic Setting

Peter's mood and that of the group who first established the *Acts of Peter* tradition may be described, in Albert Camus's phrase, as that of "metaphysical rebellion . . . the movement by which man protests against his condition and against the whole of creation."[40] How is this mood to be accounted for?

In the Mediterranean and Near Eastern world, for some 2,000 years man's faith was informed by what Cornelius Loew (following the researches of Frankfort, Jacobsen, Voegelin, and others) has termed "a cosmological conviction . . . [i.e.] the conviction that the meaning of life is rooted in an encompassing cosmic order in which man, society, and the gods all participate." Loew specifies five facets of this conviction: "(1) there is a cosmic order that permeates every level of reality; (2) this cosmic order is the divine society of the gods; (3) the structure and dynamics of this society can be discerned in the movements and patterned juxtapositions of the heavenly bodies; (4) human society should be a microcosm of the divine society; and (5) the chief responsibility of priests and kings is to attune human order to the divine order."[41] This archaic pattern of affirming and celebrating the order of the cosmos (see above, pp. 147-51) is exemplified in the typical creation myth of the Mediterranean-Near Eastern world, a creation by combat between the forces of order and chaos. Order is something won by the gods, and it is this primordial act of salvation which is renewed and re-experienced in the cult. For example, in *Enuma elish*, Marduk, the king-god, and his forces are victorious over the powers of watery chaos. In victory, Marduk seals the tablets of destiny (IV.121f.), fixes bounds, limits, and guards over the chaotic waters (IV.139f.), creates stations for the gods and establishes their signs in the zodiac (V.1f.), and establishes their laws and destinies (VI.78; VII.144). Man's response to these activities, slave of the gods though he may believe himself to be, is that he "rejoice in Marduk . . . [for] reliable is his word, unalterable his command; the utterance of his mouth no god whatever can change" (VII.149, 151f.).[42] There may be periods

---

311f.). This cannot be treated apart from the general symbol of the Inverted Tree (see M. Eliade, *Patterns in Comparative Religion* [New York, 1958], pp. 273-276 and the literature cited).

[40] A. Camus, *The Rebel* (New York, 1956), p. 23.

[41] C. Loew, *Myth, Sacred History and Philosophy* (New York, 1967), pp. 5, 13.

[42] I have followed the translation of A. Heidel, *The Babylonian Genesis*, 2d ed. (Chicago, 1951).

of tension (such as the myth of the theft of the tablets of destiny by the Zu bird, or the imprisonment of Marduk during the New Year festival) but the structures of destiny will ultimately win out. They will be victorious because they are real, having been established by the gods. They will be victorious because they have annually been renewed and strengthened in the great double ceremony of the fixing of the destinies which concluded the Akitu festival.[43] Man's responsibility is to accord with, to harmonize himself to, the great rhythms of cosmic destiny and order. If he does rebel (as in the case of Gilgamesh), he will learn that he "cannot rise above his human characteristics ... and after a brief time of despair, he squares his shoulders and goes back to face reality."[44] Gilgamesh is one example of the widespread pattern of the hero-that-failed. Like Maui or Orpheus, he was not successful in overcoming death or his humanity; but rather through rebellion he was initiated into, discovered and assumed his humanity, and affirmed both the human and the cosmic structures of destiny. In sum, he became an *upright* man. I have focused on Babylonian materials, partly because they persisted into the hellenistic period. The same general pattern is to be found in nearly every Mediterranean and Near Eastern culture.

During the hellenistic period, there was a "radical revaluation" (Hans Jonas's phrase) of this all-pervasive "cosmological conviction," a revaluation which has led classicists such as Gilbert Murray to speak of a "failure of nerve," E. R. Dodds to describe the period as "an age of anxiety," and Eric Voegelin to formulate a shift from a "compact experience of the cosmos" to a "differentiated experience of existential tension."[45] Hellenistic man suffers from what might be termed cosmic paranoia. He experiences himself to be naked and helpless; he sees danger and threat everywhere. Looking up at the heavens, at the stars, and the motions of the heavenly bodies, he no

---

[43] Compare the similar picture of the Egyptian world view in C. J. Bleeker, *Egyptian Festivals: Enactments of Religious Renewal* (Leiden, 1967), esp. pp. 6-8, 21f.

[44] Th. Jacobsen, "The Epic of Gilgamesh," in J. Neusner (ed.), *Report of the 1965-1966 Seminar on Religions in Antiquity* [Dartmouth College Comparative Studies Center] (Hanover, 1966), p. 88. Cf. Jacobsen in H. Frankfort *et al.*, *Before Philosophy* (Harmondsworth, 1949), pp. 223-27.

[45] H. Jonas, *The Gnostic Religion*, 2d ed. (Boston, 1963), p. 250; G. Murray, *Five Stages of Greek Religion* 3d ed. (Garden City, N.Y., 1955 reprint), pp. 119f.; E. R. Dodds, *Pagan and Christian in an Age of Anxiety* (Cambridge, 1965), p. 3 *et passim*; E. Voegelin, "Immortality," *Harvard Theological Review* LX (1967), esp. 277.

longer sees the guarantors of order, the guardians of a good cosmic and human destiny, the positive limits placed on the chaotic powers above and below and on the span of human existence; but rather a grim system of aggressors, an openly hostile army which seeks to chain him. He lives in a world surrounded and hemmed in by powers, powers one dares do no more than name in terrifying titles such as the following:

> O mighty, majestic, glorious Splendors; holy, and earth-born, mighty arch-daimons; compeers of the great god; denizens of Chaos, of Erebus and of the unfathomable Abyss; earth-dwellers, haunters of sky-depths, nook-infesting, murk-enwrapped; scanning the mysteries, guardians of secrets, captains of the hosts of hell; kings of infinite space, terrestrial overlords, globe-shaking, firm-founding, ministering to earthquakes; terror-strangling, panic-striking, spindle-turning; snow-scatterers, rain-wafters, spirits of the air; fire-tongues of summer-sun, tempest-tossing lords of fate; dark-shapes of Erebus, senders of Necessity; flame-fanning fire-darters; snow-compelling, dew-compelling, gale-raising, abyss-plumbing, calm-bestriding air-spirits; dauntless in courage, heart-crushing despots; chasm-leaping, overburdening, iron-nerved daimons; wild-raging, unenslaved; watchers of Tartaros; delusive Fate-phantoms; all-seeing, all-hearing, all-conquering, sky wandering vagrants.[46]

The structures of order have become reversed; rather than the positive limits they were meant to be, they have become oppressive. Man is no longer defined by the degree to which he harmonizes himself and his society to the cosmic patterns of order; but rather by the degree to which he can escape the patterns. Rather than the archaic hero-that-failed, the savior, the paradigm of the hellenistic world is the hero-that-succeeded, succeeded in escaping a tyrannical order. Every man is called upon to be such a hero. To escape from the despotism of this world and its rulers, exemplified by the seven planetary spheres, and to ascend to another world of freedom, or of creative limits, becomes the aim of hellenistic man and the chief concern of his religion. Hellenistic man experiences himself to be an exile from his true home, the Beyond, and he constantly seeks for ways to return. He strives to return to the world-beyond-this-world which is his home, to the god-beyond-the-god-

---

[46] "[Invocation to] the All-powerful Might of the Constellation of the Great Bear" from the Great Paris Magical Papyrus (Bibl. Nat. suppl. Gr. 574, f.15ᵛ) in K. Preisendanz, *Papyri Graecae Magicae* (Leipzig and Berlin, 1928), Vol. I, p. 118 (lines 1345-80). I have followed, with minor alterations, the translation by E. M. Butler, *Ritual Magic* (Cambridge, 1949), p. 9.

of-this-world which is the true god, to awaken that part of himself which is from the beyond and to strip off his body which belongs to this world.

> I no longer have trust in anything in the world
> In father and mother;
> I have no trust in the world
> In brothers or sisters;
> I have no trust in the world . . .
> In what is made and created,
> In the whole world and its works;
> I have no trust in the world.
> After my soul alone I go searching about
> which is worth more to me than generations and worlds.
> I went and found my soul . . .
> I went and found Truth where she stands,
> at the outermost rim of the world [beyond the
> seven planetary spheres].[47]

Many attempts have been made to account for this shift in world view, most persuasively H. Jonas's argument that man felt rootless after the conquest of Alexander because the old structure of the *polis* was broken down and man was understood to be a *cosmopolitan*, a citizen of the entire cosmos, and this was too big. Man was "no longer a part of anything *except the universe*."[48] I would rather eschew the quest for origins and insist that the world was seen by hellenistic man in this manner because this *was* the way he had discovered his world to be. The world was experienced as a prison, as a constellation of reversed values. It was experienced this way objectively; and this experience was reenforced by the testimony of those figures who, in this period, had ascended beyond the planetary spheres and had brought back a report of what they had seen and experienced. As Paul in Romans 7 was to discover about the Law of YHWH, that it was good *once*, but that it had been captured by the powers of Sin and turned upside down so that "the very commandment which promised life proved to be death to me" (Rom. 7:10), so each culture was to discover that its cherished structures of Fate, the gods that ordained and maintained the structure of Fate, and the myths which described the establishment of the world according to these cosmic patterns were perverse, were upside down. And each culture rebelled against

---

[47] M. Lidzbarski, *Ginza: Der Schatz oder Das Grosse Buch der Mandäer* (Göttingen, 1925), pp. 390f. English translation in H. Jonas, *Gnostic Religion*, pp. 90f.

[48] Jonas, *Gnostic Religion*, esp. pp. 5-7, 241-65. The phrase quoted is from p. 247.

these archaic traditions, developed a complex series of techniques for escaping destiny and for "righting" the world, and discovered a new set of myths which described the origins of the sort of world in which they now found themselves living.

It is in such a world, a world already seen by the Egyptian prophet Nefer-Rohu (c. 1850 B.C.) ("I show thee the land topsy-turvey ... I show thee the undermost on top")[49] that the motif of the reverse crucifixion of the apostle has its setting. It is a world which is "arsey-turvey" (to use a delightful idiomatic expression from John Barth's *Sotweed Factor*); "The World's Turned Upside Down" (to use the title of the tune played by the British Army band when Cornwallis surrendered). In such a world, *to be upside down is in fact to be rightside up*; or, as Philip declared in explaining his reverse crucifixion: "Imitate me in this, for all the world is the wrong way and every soul that is in it." Likewise, the Cynic, Diogenes, who requested to be buried face downwards "because in a little while, down will be converted into up" (Diogenes Laertius, VI.32).

The origin of this perverse world is the establishment of the astral and planetary *archons*' rule over the cosmos (e.g., *Apocryphon of John* 72:4):

> They brought Fate into being and through measure, periods and seasons they imprisoned the gods of the heavens, the angles, the demons and men, so that all would come into its [Fate's] fetters and it [Fate] would be lord of all—an evil and perverse plan.[50]

Salvation may be effected by a cosmic reversal enacted by a cosmic savior (e.g. Jesus in *Pistis Sophia*, XV-XVI):

> And the Fates and the sphere over which they rule, I have changed and brought it to pass that they shall spend six months turned to the left and accomplish their influences and that six months they face to the right and accomplish their influences. [Previously, they had been] facing the left at every time and accomplishing their influences and deeds.[51]

---

[49] Translation by J. A. Wilson, in J. B. Pritchard, (ed.), *Ancient Near Eastern Texts Relating to the Old Testament*, 2d ed. (Princeton, 1955), p. 455. Cf. A. Erman, *The Ancient Egyptians: A Sourcebook of their Writings* (New York, 1966 reprint). p. 115, who translates: "I show thee the land in lamentation and distress ... I show thee how the undermost is turned to uppermost." A remarkably similar text of "prophetic complaint" may be found from Niassan: "The earth is all twisted and turned, The world is upside down.... It is like an areca nut turned inside out: The kernel is where the rind was" (translated in W. R. Trask, *The Unwritten Song: Poetry of the Primitive and Traditional Peoples of the World* [New York, 1966], Vol. I, pp. 164f.
[50] Translated by R. Grant, *Gnosticism: An Anthology* (London, 1961), p. 84.
[51] Translated by G. R. S. Mead, *Pistis Sophia*, 2d ed. (London, 1921), pp. 19f.

It is this sort of cosmic reversal wrought by a savior such as Jesus which would give to circles of his devotees their mood of "freedom now" and the confidence to assert: "We are exalted above Fate and in place of the planetary daimons we know but one ruler of the cosmos"[52]; "Now there are no more horoscopes and there is no longer such a thing as Fate";[53] "the birth of the Savior released us from becoming and from Fate ... until baptism, they say, Fate is real, but after it the astrologers are no longer right."[54]

This reversal of the cosmic-astrological pattern of destiny may be understood as an eschatological version of the myth of the cosmic cycles in Plato's *Statesman* (269-274) where, after a period, God relinquishes his control over the revolution of the cosmos "and then Fate and innate desire reversed the motion of the world." In the Hellenistic myth, unlike Plato, the deity or his representative once more reverses the revolution and frees the cosmos from Fate. In this tradition, what is usually taken as signs of cosmic disorder heralding the end of the world (e.g., the sun shining by day, the moon by night; the stars altering their orbits; the seasons disturbed) is taken as a positive sign that the astral powers have been dethroned, that the rulers of this world have been overthrown.

Through this cosmic reversal the world has been quite literally converted (*epistrephein; convertere*), that is, turned about, and by being so converted has been saved.[55] In *Pistis Sophia*, Jesus' power to reverse the astral spheres is one sign of his lordship over the cosmos. It is

---

Cf. C. Schmidt and W. Till, *Koptisch-gnostische Schriften* Bd. I, *Pistis Sophia*, 3d ed. (Berlin, 1962), pp. 15f. The parallel between this text and the upside-down crucifixion of Peter was, to my knowledge, first drawn by Mead in his *Fragments of a Faith Forgotten* 1st ed. (London, 1900); I cite the 3d ed. (London, 1931; reprint New York, 1960), p. 449. See further, H. Jonas, *Gnosis und spätantiker Geist* (Göttingen, 1934), Vol. I, pp. 193f.; H. Leisegang, *La Gnose* (Paris, 1951), pp. 253f.; H.-Ch. Puech, "Gnosis and Time," in J. Campbell (ed.), *Man and Time: Papers from the Eranos Yearbooks*, (New York, 1957), pp. 60f.; J. Doresse, *Les Livres secrets des gnostiques d'Egypte* (Paris, 1959), Vol. I, pp. 77-82; Vol. II, pp. 211-16 (partially translated in Doresse, *The Secret Books of the Egyptian Gnostics* [New York, 1960], pp. 67f.).

[52] Tatian, *Oratio adversus Graecos* IX (in D. R. Bueno, *Padres apologistas griegos* [Madrid, 1954], Vol. II, p. 584).

[53] Methodius, *Symposium* VIII.15, 16 (N. Bonwetsch, *Opera* [Leipzig, 1917], p. 103).

[54] Clement Alexandrinus, *Excerpta ex Theodoto* 76, 78 (in R. P. Casey, *The Excerpta ex Theodoto of Clement of Alexandria* [London, 1934], pp. 87-89).

[55] See the valuable monograph by P. Aubin, *Le problème de la 'conversion': étude sur un terme commun a l'hellénisme et au christianisme des trois premiers siècles* (Paris, 1963), esp. pp. 50-55, 93-104.

a power analogous to the Egyptian magician who proclaimed: "I shall let the earth fall ... so that the south becomes north and the earth turns around";[56] analogous to Isaiah's power to invoke YHWH to reverse the sun's course before the astonished eyes of Hezakiah;[57] to Zeus' intervention on behalf of Atreus when: "Helios, already in mid-career, wrested his chariot about and turned his horses' heads towards the dawn. The seven Pleiades, and all the other stars, retraced their courses in sympathy; and that evening, for the first and last time, the sun set in the East."[58] By turning this perverse cosmos upside down, Jesus, according to this Christian-gnostic understanding, had, in fact, righted it. By his descent from on high (a reversal) when, in the words of the *Odes of Solomon*, "the head went down to the feet"[59] or by his death on the cross which reversed death, turned it about, and brought forth life from it (1 Cor. 2:8; 15:12-57), Jesus had in birth and death been upside down; but in being thus reversed, he had converted the world and men to being right side up. By violating a false and perverse order, he established (or perhaps reestablished) a true and upright order where all present relationships will be inverted, where "the last will be first and the first, last" (Matt. 19:30; Matt. 20:16; Luke 13:30).[60]

The First Man

In interpreting the reverse crucifixion of the apostle in the *Acts of Peter*, much depends on how one interprets the mysterious figure of the First Man (*ho prōtos anthrōpos; primus homo; prior homo*—in the various recensions) whose downward fall Peter imitates in his upside

---

[56] P. Mag. Harris VII.1 in F. Lexa, *La magie dans l'Égypte antique de l'ancien empire jusqu'à l'époque copte* (Paris, 1925), Vol. II, p. 39. See further, S. Eitrem, *Papyri Osloenses* (Oslo, 1925), Vol. I, pp. 65-70.

[57] 2 Kings 20:8-11; Isa. 38:7f.

[58] I have quoted the summary of R. Graves, *The Greek Myths* (Baltimore, 1955), Vol. II, p. 45. See the text in Apollodorus, *Epitome* II.12 (translation: J. G. Frazer, *Apollodorus: The Library* [London, 1921], Vol. II, p. 165) and the scholion on Iliad II.106 (translation: A. B. Cook, *Zeus* [Cambridge, 1914], Vol. I, p. 405).

[59] *Odes of Solomon* 23.16a (in W. Bauer, *Die Oden Salomos* [Berlin, 1933], p. 49).

[60] On this motif (Thompson, *Motif-Index* E758; Aarne and Thompson, *Types of the Folktale*, 802), see the illuminating comments of H. Schwarzbaum, *Studies in Jewish and World Folklore* (Berlin, 1968), p. 157 who notes: "According to Talmudic legend [*Baba Batra* 10b and *Pesahim* 50a] Joseph, the son of Rabbi Joshua, who, during his sickness falls in a trance is asked by his father after his recovery: 'What vision did you have?' He replied: 'I saw a topsy-turvy world in which the upperclass or the rich were below, whereas the lower class or the poor were above'."

down posture. Is he Adam? a gnostic, fallen Anthropos-Demiurge? Christ? The identification remains problematic and a matter of controversy among the various scholars who have treated the text.[61]

---

[61] Among the major treatments of the text, J. Daniélou (*Theology of Jewish Christianity* [Chicago, 1964], p. 282) apparently despairs of identifying the figure and speaks simply of "the fall of the first man." J. Doresse, *Les livres secrets des gnostiques d'Égypte* (Paris, 1959), Vol. II, p. 208 sees the figure as symbolic of Adam and his Fall into sin. W. Bousset ("Platons Weltseele und das Kreuz Christi," *Zeitschrift für die neutestamentliche Wissenschaft*, XIV [1933], 276) seeks to relate the figure to an inverted cosmic Chi-cross (see *Timaeus* 36b-c; cf. E. Stommel, "Sēmeion ekpetaseōs," *Römische Quartalschrift*, XLVIII [1953], 21-42) and finds the figure of the inverted *Urmensch* and the inverted apostle a "groteske Phantasie." R. Reitzenstein (*Poimandres* [Leipzig, 1904], p. 243 and n. 1) simply relates the figure to the First Man who was identified with Osiris, Hermes, and Korybas but fails to account for the upside-down motif. H. Rahner (*Greek Myths and Christian Mystery* [London, 1963], p. 55) combines all of these possibilities into a diffuse syncretistic portrait: the upside-down crucifixion of Peter "is a symbol of the fall of the first man before the creation of the world, for he falls into sin headlong, which means, according to Gnostic belief, that he fell into physical existence. There is a mixture here of Platonic stuff with some of the myths of human origins we find in the *Poimandres* and Hippolytus' Naassene sermon. Yet, through it all we catch a gleam of the Christian belief concerning the sin of Adam which was wiped out by the Cross." Father Antonio Orbe (in his chapter "El misterio de la cruz en los Acta Petri," in *Los primeros herejes ante la persecucion* [Rome, 1956], pp. 176-212) offers the most complex and radical interpretation. While the Primordial Man is a widespread figure in gnostic traditions, in the Acts of Peter he is the Christ (p. 181 n. 3). Rather than a description of Adam's Fall, the text describes the "crucifixion of the Primal Man" which should be related to the Valentinian doctrine of the crucifixion of the Upper Christ (esp. pp. 187f.; 188 n. 29). However, there is no instance of primal inversion in the Valentinian texts, the closest being the myth of Sophia Achamoth in the system of Ptolemaeus as reported by Irenaeus where, in response to the plight of the banished Sophia below: "The Christ above took pity on her and was extended through the Cross ([*anō*] *Christon kai dia tou Staurou epektathenta* = *Superiorem Christum, et per crucem extensum*) to form her shape by his own power" (Irenaeus, *Adversus haereses* I.iv.1; text: W. Völker, *Quellen zur Geschichte der christlichen Gnosis* [Tübingen, 1932], p. 102; translation: R. Grant, *Gnosticism: An Anthology* [London, 1961], p. 170; see further Orbe, *Los primeros herejes*, pp. 161-75, esp. pp. 168-70, and F. M.-M. Sagnard, *La gnose valentinienne et le témoignage de saint Irénée* [Paris, 1947], pp. 244-49).

Two further parallels have been noted. The first is in the *Poimandres* where the heavenly Anthropos "bent through the composite framework of the spheres, having torn off the covering, and showed to downward tending Nature the beautiful form of God" (text: A. D. Nock and A. J. Festugière, *Corpus hermeticum* 2d ed. [Paris, 1960], Vol. I, p. 11; translation: Grant, *Gnosticism*, p. 214). It is possible to see this act of looking down (*parakuptein*), followed by a fall of the primordial Man into the realm of Nature as a parallel to the First Man in the *Acts of Peter*: "being drawn down—he who also cast his first beginning down to earth." *Parakuptein* in *Poimandres* 14 seems to me a more convincing parallel than does its use in a Hermetic fragment (Cyril, *Contra Iulianum* 552d in Nock and Festugière, Vol. IV, pp. 133f. [fragment 28]) cited by Reitzenstein, *Poimandres*, p. 243 n. 3.

Regardless of what final decision be made as to the origins and *Sitz im Leben* of the portrait of the fall of the Primal Man head downwards in the *Acts of Peter*, it is clear that his action effected a cosmic reversal so that "upside down as he was he showed what is on the left hand as on the right, and changed the signs of all their nature so as to consider fair those things which were not fair and take those things which were really evil to be good." Depending upon how one interprets this reversal (and this is where a determination of the original setting of the myth would be a priceless aid), either this inversion has a positive value (i.e., the Primal Man reversed the influence of the astral powers on his descent much as did Jesus in *Pistis Sophia*) or it had negative value (i.e., through his fall the First Man reversed the good order of the good creator deity and is responsible for the world's present evil condition). In either case, man is called upon to imitate the upside-down posture if he has *gnosis*; but the effect of this imitation will differ according to the interpretation of the myth. If the inversion be seen as positive, man by standing upside down, by reversing all values, will liberate himself from Fate and from astral determinism and will gain freedom. If the inversion be understood as negative, man, by standing on his head, is actually standing on his feet since the world has been reversed following the Fall of the First Man. In either case, to be upside down is to be upright, to be converted.

The second is from the Naassene commentary on the Attis Hymn preserved by Hippolytus: "This man is called Korybant by the Thracians ... and the Phrygians give him a similiar name, because from the top of the head [*koryphe*] and from the unimprinted brain he begins his descent and passes through all the elements of the lower parts. We do not know how or in what way he comes down" (text: Hippolytus, *Refutatio* V.viii.13 in Völker, *Quellen*, p. 19; translation: Grant, *Gnosticism*, p. 108). The parallel was first suggested by Reitzenstein, *Poimandres*, p. 243 n. 1; cf. R. Reitzenstein and H. Schaeder, *Studien zum antiken Synkretismus aus Iran und Griechenland* (Berlin, 1926), pp. 168 n. 1, 191f. A number of the other motifs present in the description of the Primal Man in the *Acts of Peter* are likewise present in the Naassene text (e.g., the First Man was "dead without motion" in the former parallels the Naassene text where Adam after his creation "lay without breath and motionless and immovable, like a statue"), and the motif of reversal is perhaps implied in one description of the Anthropos in the Naassene text: "The Phrygians also call him Goatherd [*Aipolos*], not because he feeds goats ... but because he is ever-turning [*aei-polos*], i.e., always turning and circulating and impressing the whole universe with turning motion. For to turn [*polein*] is to circulate and alter matters ... he turns about and goes around.... Thus the Phrygians call *Aipolos* the one who always turns things in every direction and tranfers them to his own domain" (*Refutatio* V.vii.44 in Völker, *Quellen*, p. 22; translation: Grant, *Gnosticism*, pp. 111f.).

The call of Philip to "imitate me in this, for all the world is turned the wrong way and everything that is in it" is thus a gospel of rebellion and liberation (though the object of this rebellion and liberation must, unfortunately, remain ambiguous). To those on the outside it might appear, as it did to the Jews of Thessalonica, that such a movement of rebellion and liberation was destructive, that the members of such a movement were "men who have turned the world upside down" (Acts 17:6); to those on the inside, to those who possessed the saving knowledge, the rebellion restored the world to an upright posture.[62]

In this paper I have attempted to reflect on certain structures of order and chaos from the perspective of the discipline of History of Religions. I began with the notion current in contemporary anthropological circles that order consists primarily in keeping one's place, a place that is appropriate to one's species. This place is given in the cosmogonic myth, established by the gods in the beginning. Within this place which serves as a "strategic hamlet" against the incursions of chaos, each thing finds its home. The walls, the boundaries of one's place, must be periodically renewed or chaos will win out. Thus, in a tribe of California Indians studied by A. L. Kroeber and E. W. Gifford in their important monograph, *World Renewal: A Cult System of Native Northwest California*, the celebrant, at the end of the year, performs a complex set of rituals repeating the actions of the Immortals in primeval times, employing formulas such as, "This world is cracked, but when I pick up and drag the stick, all the cracks will fill up and the earth will become solid again"; and, approaching a sacred stone and setting it carefully upright: "the earth which has been tipped will be straight again"; and, sitting on the stone: "When I sit on the stone the earth will never get up and tip again."[63] In such an archaic culture employing such structures, there are liminal periods, but these are only the symbolization and ritual expression of chaos which will be overcome through the repetition of the cosmogony.

---

[62] A full interpretation of this tradition would need to take account of the ritual dimension of rebellion in this tradition, especially the baptismal interpretation of the dominical sayings in the *Acts of Peter* and *Acts of Philip*. An investigation of this problem will be reserved for a later date.

[63] A. L. Kroeber and E. W. Gifford, *World Renewal: A Cult System of Native Northwest California* (Berkeley, 1949), p. 15. See further the discussion of this in M. Eliade, "Renouvellement cosmique et eschatologie," *Eranos Jahrbuch*, XXVIII (1959), esp. pp. 256-64; Eliade, *Myth and Reality*, pp. 41-47.

Within some cultures, however, the faith in the good order of the cosmos and its ability to confer reality—in short, a culture's "cosmological conviction"—is shattered. Rather than renewing the creation, reestablishing the patterns of destiny, the patterns are seen to be fundamentally perverse. It is the chaotic, demonic powers themselves which control the structures of order. Against this *mésalliance* man is challenged to rebel, to "tip over" the world. Reality is discovered to lie not within the cosmos as ordered through creation but above the world, beyond it, and the aim of existence is seen to be to escape the constricted confines of one's place. In an Indian metaphor elucidated by Eliade, one seeks to *break through the roof*: "The image of breaking through the roof means that one has now abolished every 'situation' and has chosen not installation in the world but the absolute freedom which implies . . . the annihilation of every conditioned world."[64] In a world experienced in this way, liminality becomes the supreme goal rather than a moment in a rite of passage.

I have intended this paper to be a contribution to the theme of order and chaos by focusing on one dimension of both cosmic and human rebellion. The phenomenology of rebellion has not yet been fully studied (although one might point to works as diverse as Camus's, *The Rebel* and Sartre's, *Saint Genet* on the one hand, E. J. Hobsbawm's, *Social Bandits and Primitive Rebels* and Cunha's, *Os Sertões* on the other, as providing a starting point for such an endeavor). It is my conviction that such a study is long overdue and, in our present situation, might be of more than strictly academic relevance. Perhaps we shall someday clarify the structures which lie behind the refrain in William Butler Yeat's poem of the Irish Rebellion ("Easter 1916"):

> All changed, changed utterly
> A terrible beauty is born.
> . . . .
> He too has been changed in his turn
> Transformed utterly:
> A terrible beauty is born.

---

[64] M. Eliade, "Structures and Changes in the History of Religion," in C. H. Kraeling and R. M. Adams, *City Invincible* (Chicago, 1960), pp. 365f. Cf. Eliade, "Centre du monde, temple, maison," in *Le symbolisme cosmique des monuments religieux* (Rome, 1957), pp. 78-80; Eliade, "Briser le toit de la maison: symbolisme architectonique et physiologie subtile," *Studies in Mysticism Presented to Gershom G. Scholem* (Jerusalem, 1967), pp. 131-39.

When we do, we shall be better able to answer the question which has motivated this paper: Is the act of rebellion an act of birth which is upside down, or is it, in reality, a birth right side up?[65]

[65] This paper was presented at the Fellows Meeting of the Society for Religion in Higher Education, August 1968, to the group on "Order and Chaos" established and chaired by Professor Paul Kuntz. I am grateful to my colleagues at this conference for their comments and criticism.

CHAPTER EIGHT

THE TEMPLE AND THE MAGICIAN

One of the most precious texts for an understanding of the religious life of Late Antiquity is the second century autobiography of Thessalos, the magician. Although this text has been commented upon by several scholars, its significance has not been exhausted. It is, therefore, a pleasure to dedicate this brief study of *Thessalos* to Nils A. Dahl who has well taught those of us who were privileged to be his students to value a non-Christian text not as mere "background" but as a *document humain*.

Thessalos exists in two major versions, both serve as prefaces to a complex herbal: a Byzantine Greek manuscript, copied in 1474, now in Madrid (Codex Matritensis Bibl. nat. 4631 [old number 110], f.75-79^v) and a fourteenth century Latin translation which is now part of the medical library at Montpellier (Codex Montepessulanus Fac. méd. 227, f.31-35^v). The Greek text was first described in 1769 in a catalogue of the manuscripts in the Royal Library of Madrid prepared by Juan Iriarte;[1] and was 'rediscovered' and edited by Charles Graux in 1878.[2] It received wider circulation and discussion following its publication, in 1912, by Pierre Boudreaux in the eighth volume of the *Catalogus codicum astrologorum graecorum*.[3]

The Madrid manuscript attributed authorship of the autobiography to Harpokration, the alleged tradent of the *Kyranides*, a Hermetic magico-medical, astrobiological collection.[4] But, as the earliest editors perceived, there is a problem with such an attribution.

---

[1] J. Iriarte, *Regiae Bibliothecae Matritensis codices Graeci* (Madrid, 1769), Vol. I, p. 435. The catalogue contains an extract of some fifteen lines.

[2] Ch. Graux, "Lettre inédite d'Harpokration à un Empereur publiée d'après un manuscrit de la Bibliotheca naçional de Madrid," *Revue de Philologie*, II (1878), 65-77. This should be considered the *editio princeps*.

[3] P. Boudreaux, *Catalogus codicum astrologorum graecorum* (henceforth cited, *CCAG*), Vol. VIII: iii, esp. pp. 134-139, 16.

[4] See M. Stephan, "Harpokration," in Pauly-Wissowa, *Realencyclopädie der klassischen Altertumswissenschaft* (henceforth cited, *RE*), Suppl. vol. VI, cols. 102-104. For an excellent summary of the complex *Kyranides* tradition, see A-J. Festugière, *La révélation d'Hermès Trismégiste* (Paris, 1949), Vol. I, pp. 201-216; for its relation to *Thessalos*, see M. Wellmann, *Marcellus von Side als Artz und die Koiraniden des Hermes Trismegistos* (Leipzig, 1934), pp. 12f.

Although there is a close connection between the treatise on astral botany which the autobiography introduces and the *Kyranides*, tradition is unanimous that Harpokration was born in Alexandria. The author of the autobiography unambiguously asserts his birth place to have been Asia Minor and describes, with excitement, his later journey to Alexandria.[5]

A clue as to the identity of the author was gained in 1906 with the publication of a fourteenth century Byzantine manuscript which contained an extract from the astral treatise of the Madrid manuscript and named its author as "Thessalos the Astrologer".[6] The name Thessalos did, in fact, occur in the Madrid manuscript in direct address to the author by the god, Asclepius, but it had been garbled by the scribe.[7]

Franz Cumont recalled the title of an unedited Latin text on the mystical-magical nature of plants entitled, *Thessalus philosophus de virtutibus herborum* and intuited a connection.[8] Examining the text, which was part of an extensive manuscript containing a collection of occult documents, he determined that Codex Montepessulanus Fac. med. 227 was, in fact, a close Latin translation of the Greek. He announced his discovery in 1918[9] and, subsequently, edited the Latin version for the *Catalogus*[10] declaring that the claim of Thessalos' authorship had been established "with a certainty which is rarely attained in researches into literary paternity".[11] His judgement has

---

[5] Graux, "Lettre inédite," 66 and note 5; Boudreaux, *CCAG*, Vol. VIII: iii, p. 136, n. 1.

[6] Codex Vaticanus Graecus 1144, f. 243, first published in the *Mélanges de l'École de Rome*, XXVI (1906), 351, and noted by Boudreaux in *CCAG*, Vol. VIII: iii, p. 134.

[7] See Graux, "Lettre inédite," 75, n. 61 "Il y a là quelque alteration grave, probablement une lacune" and compare, Boudreaux, *CCAG*, Vol. VIII: iii, p. 137 *ad* line 9.

[8] *Thessalus philosophus* had been noted by title, but left unedited, in *CCAG*, Vol. VII, p. 231, n. 1 and in H. Diels, *Die Handschriften der antike Ärzte* (Berlin, 1906), Vol. II, p. 107. Note that L. Thorndike, *A History of Magic and Experimental Science* (New York, 1923), Vol. II, p. 234 calls attention to a mention of *Tesalus in secretis de XII herbis* in Jacobus de Dondis, *Aggregatio Medicamentorum* (1355).

[9] F. Cumont, "Écrits hermétiques (II): Le médecin Thessalus et les plantes astrales d'Hermès Trismégiste," *Revue de Philologie*, XLII (1918), 85-108. Compare, Cumont, "Lettre de Thessalus," *Comptes rendus de l'Académie des inscriptions*, 1918, 225f.

[10] F. Cumont, *CCAG*, Vol. IV: iv, esp. pp. 254-258, 16.

[11] Cumont, "Le médecin," 102. Although not cited by Cumont, further proof of this identification is provided by the well known Codex Laurentinus 75.1,

remained unchallenged, although debate continues as to whether the Thessalos of the autobiography is to be identified with the infamous physician, Thessalos of Tralles.[12] Recently, the entire manuscript, autobiography and herbal, has been reedited by Hans-Veit Friedrich.[13]

The autobiography is couched in the form of a letter to a king from the magician—a convention well known from both Hermetic revelation literature and medical materials—which serves to introduce and authenticate the herbal which constitutes the major part of the manuscript.[14] It narrates the author's perseverance through a set of

---

f.143 which names *Thessalus ex Nechepso*, a relationship explicated by the autobiography. See M. Wellmann, "Zur Geschichte der Medicin in Altertum," *Hermes*, XXXV (1900), 370 who, lacking the autobiography, finds the relationship inexplicable. For the identification, see H. Diller, "Thessalos," *RE*, Vol. VIA, col. 181; R. Reitzenstein, *Die hellenistischen Mysterienreligionen*, 3ed. (Leipzig, 1927), p. 129.

[12] See the summary of the life and teachings of Thessalos of Tralles by H. Diller in *RE*, Vol. VIA, cols. 168-180 and the autobiography, cols. 180-182. While I doubt the identification, the *vita* of Thessalos of Tralles would be an apt illustration of the sociological thesis of this article. Born in Lydia, the son of a weaver, he followed his father's trade and, with little formal education, emigrated to Rome during Nero's reign, and established himself as a physician of the school of the *Methodikoi*, famous for his violent curative techniques (*metasynkrisis*). According to his critics (chiefly Galen), he was vain and boastful, claiming that he was the greatest of physicians who, reversing the Hippocratic maxim that "the art is long," maintained that he could teach the whole of medicine in six months. He was buried on the Via Appia; his tomb bore the inscription ὁ 'Ιατρονίκης—" the conqueror of physicians".

[13] H.-V. Friedrich, *Thessalos von Tralles*, Beiträge zur klassischen Philologie, XXVIII (Meisenheim am Glan, 1968), esp. pp. 43-54. See further his valuable comparisons between the Greek and Latin versions, pp. 17f. and 21f.

[14] Compare *Corpus Hermeticum* XVI, Ἀσκληπιοῦ πρὸς Ἄμμωνα Βασιλέα; Lactantius, *Div. inst.* II.15.6, *Asclepius . . . in illo sermone perfecto quem scripsit ad regem* and the materials cited in Th. Hopfner, *Griechisch-ägyptischer Offenbarungszauber* (Leipzig, 1924), Vol. II, par. 36 and Festugière, *La révélation*, Vol. I, pp. 324-332 (not all of which are relevant). See below, n. 34. For medical material see, for example, A. Nelson, "Zur pseudohippokratischen Epistula ad Antiochum," in *Symbolae Philologicae Dicatie O. A. Danielson* (Uppsala, 1937), pp. 203-217. F. Boll, "Das Eingangsstück der Pseudo-Klementinen," *Zeitschrift für die neutestamentliche Wissenschaft*, XVII (1916), 141 compares the epistle to that introducing the pseudo-Clementines—which is impossible. But see Boll's valuable excursus (II), "Könige als Offenbarungsträger," in his *Aus der Offenbarung Johannis* (Leipzig, 1914), esp. pp. 136-142 for shrewd comments on the genre.

For the purposes of this essay, the precise identification of *Germanico Claudio regi et deo eterno* (the Latin ms. preserves the better reading) is not crucial. The general consensus is that it is either Tiberius or Nero. See Cumont, "Le médecin," 98f. and *CCAG*, VIII: iv, p. 254; Festugière, "L'expérience religieuse du médecin Thessalos", p. 155, n. 52 (originally published in the *Revue Biblique*, XLVIII [1939], 45-77 and reprinted in Festugière, *Hermétisme et mystique païenne* [Paris,

trials in seeking "miraculous" knowledge "beyond the boundaries of human powers" and begins with a description of an 'upwardly mobile' young man. Born of wealthy parents in Asia Minor, Thessalos studied with the local rhetoricians and then set out for the 'culture capital' of Alexandria to prove his mettle.[15] There he studied both grammar and "dialectical medicine" and soon became famous among his contemporaries. One day, while searching through a library, he came upon an astrological treatise "by Nechepso which described twenty-four ways of treating the whole body and every illness according to each sign of the Zodiac along with stones and plants".[16] Overcome with the power the book promised, he tried every one of the cures and recitations (especially the preparation of the "helic pill"),[17] but all were futile. "I failed in every one of my attempts to cure sickness". Overcome with shame, he could neither face his friends in Alexandria nor return home to his parents in Asia Minor as he had boasted to both of his abilities. Therefore he began to wander about Egypt, vowing to commit suicide unless he received some communication from the gods "whether by vision in my dreams or by an inspiration from on high".[18]

1967], pp. 141-180 which pagination I follow); Friedrich, *Thessalos*, p. 45 *ad* line 1.

[15] I see no sign, in this narrative, of the traditional aretalogy of the *sophos*—his excellence in studies in his homeland and his journey to a foreign center of learning in order to measure the *sophia* of its wise men, as Festugière claims ("L'expérience," p. 156, n. 56). There is no mention of miraculous speed of learning in Thessalos' homeland (which is *the* aretalogical convention) nor are the *sophoi* of Alexandria being put to the test by Thessalos (for example, by dialogue which is *the* aretalogical convention). Rather the text offers a realistic portrait of a young, wealthy, provincial intellectual journeying to a capital for advanced studies in the hope of securing fame and fortune; a life which may be found in many a biography from Late Antiquity. As I shall argue below, traditional aretalogical motifs appear to be reversed by this account.

[16] *Thessalos*, 6. For a general treatment of such works, see A. Delatte, *Herbarius: Recherches sur le cérémonial usité chez les anciens pour la cueillette des simples et des plantes magiques*, 3ed. (Brussels, 1961), esp. pp. 64-69 and compare the important review of the first edition by F. Pfister in *Byzantinische Zeitschrift*, XXXVII (1937), 381-390. See further, Pfister, "Pflanzenaberglaube," *RE*, Vol. XXXVIII, cols. 1446-1456. It is just such a book which makes up the bulk of the Thessalos manuscript (see Friedrich, *Thessalos*, pp. 60-273) on which see Cumont, "Le médecin" and Festugière, "L' expérience".

[17] *Thessalos*, 7: τροχίσκον ἡλιακόν—*trociscum heliacum*. The recipe has not been further identified.

[18] *Thessalos*, 11. On the request for a dream or vision, see Festugière, "L'expérience", 143-146. Most of the materials cited are not direct parallels. Far better is A. D. Nock's collection of visions which resolve religious doubts or questions in "A Vision of Mandulis Aion," *Harvard Theological Review*, XXVII (1934) re-

This narrative conceals a stunning reversal of traditional Greco-Egyptian revelatory *bioi*. There is no more common theme in these materials than the quest for ancient, hidden books of wisdom. This *topos* depends on an earlier apologetic *topos* of an ancient (frequently antediluvian) book which is miraculously rediscovered (in fact, having been recently forged). In older materials, this *topos* occurs either in inner-directed apologetics in which a king (or his representative) rediscovers a holy book which legitimates a religious innovation[19] or in outer-directed apologetics in which it becomes part of the general Hellenistic debate over autochthony and heurmatismatics, becoming a means of legitimating the cultural age of a people.[20] In Greco-Egyptian magical, alchemical and astrological literature, it became a special convention in works such as the *bios* of (Bolos-) Demokritos, the "Emerald Tablet of Hermes" and the "Book of Krates".[21] This tradition is continued in Thessalos by

---

printed in Z. Steward, ed., *A. D. Nock: Essays on Religion and the Ancient World* (Cambridge, Mass., 1972), Vol. I, esp. pp. 368-374 referring, in passing, to Thessalos (pp. 372f.).

[19] Certainly the most complex libretto for the 'rediscovery' of such a forgery is the account in 2Kings 22-23; 2Chron. 34. The oldest, unambiguous Egyptian example is the Shabaka stone (in J. Pritchard, ed., *Ancient Near Eastern Texts Relating to the Old Testament*, 2ed. [Princeton, 1955], p. 4). The best, late example would be the Demotic tale of the discovery of the "Book of Breathings" in P. Louvre 3284 (edited and translated by W. Erichsen, "Eine neue demotische Erzählung," *Abhandlungen der Akademie der Wissenschaften und der Literatur zu Mainz*, Geistes- und sozialwissenschaftliche Kl., 1956:2). Whether the same is the case for the well known rubric to chapter XXX of the *Book of the Dead* (with variants) is unclear. For an example of a 'rediscovery' that failed, see the "Books of Numa" in Livy XL.29 and Plutarch, *Numa*, XIII.87 and the study by A. Delatte, "Les doctrines pythagoriciennes des livres de Numa," *Bulletin de l'Academie Royale Belgique*, XXII (1936), 19-40. The same *topos* can, of course, be used in revelation literature to authenticate radically new teachings as in the complex books or stelae of Seth traditions in the various Nag Hammadi codices (see esp. *Gospel of the Egyptians* [*C.G.* III.2 and IV.2] in J. Doresse, *The Secret Books of the Egyptian Gnostics* [New York, 1960], p. 180).

[20] This tradition most certainly may be traced back to early fifth-century Greco-Egyptian apologetics concerning Thot as the inventor of writing (for a useful overview, see C. Froidefond, *Le mirage égyptien dans la littérature grecque* [Aix-en-Provence, 1971], pp. 279-284 *et passim*.). It becomes standard in Hellenistic Near Eastern literature which paraphrases archaic traditions in Greek (e.g. Philo of Byblos, Berossus, Manetho, Josephus).

[21] The narrative of (Bolus-) Demokritos journeying to Egypt to study with Ostanes and the miraculous discovery of the hidden books of Ostanes' father in a column of a temple would be the classic example (ps. Demokritos, *Physika*, 3 in J. Bidez-F. Cumont, *Les mages hellénisés* [Paris, 1938], Vol. II, pp. 317f.). The best collection of examples is in Festugière, *La révélation*, Vol. I, pp. 319-324 and the brief note by Cumont, *CCAG*, Vol. VIII: iv, pp. 102f. It is of interest to note

linking the unexpectedly discovered book to the renowned figure of royal wisdom, Nechepso.[22] While most often cited, in Greco-Roman tradition, as an astronomical authority in an occult chain of tradition,[23] he is well known as a lithicist and designer of amulets.[24] In Greco-Egyptian tradition, he is, as king, the recipient of a number of revelatory epistles, most usually from the sage Petosiris.[25] From a later tradition, closely linked to the *Kyranides*-Thessalos type of astrology, there is a report that: "We have composed this moon book (σεληνοδρόμιον) by putting two books together: one is in the hand of the sacred scribe, Melampous, addressed to Nechepso, King of Egypt; the other has been found in Heliopolis in Egypt, in the temple, in the holy of holies, engraved in hieroglyphics under King Psammetichus."[26] But, in the autobiography, this tradition has been radically altered. Rather than the setting of the discovery being a temple, it is a βιβλιοθήκη. Rather than the book being a true revelation of hidden, archaic wisdom, it is a collection of erroneous information which lacks power. Rather than resulting in triumphal enlightenment, mastery of its contents produces despair.[27]

In his depression, Thessalos vows to wander Egypt in quest of a revelation or, barring this, to kill himself. His journey takes him to

---

that Harpokration, the alleged author of the *Kyranides*, claimed to have translated his work from an ancient column (L. Delatte, *Textes latins et vieux français relatifs aux Cyranides* [Lièges-Paris, 1942], pp. 13 and 15; Festugière, *La révélation*, Vol. I, pp. 322f.).

[22] On Nechepso, see the classic dissertation by E. Riess, *Nechepsonis et Petosiridis fragmenta magica* (Bonn, 1890) conveniently reprinted in *Philologus*, Supplementband VI:1 (1891-3), pp. 325-394; W. Kroll, "Nechepso," *RE*, Vol. XVI, cols. 2160-2167 and W. Gundel-H. G. Gundel, *Astrologumena* (Wiesbaden, 1966), pp. 27-36.

[23] Perhaps the best known passage is Firmicus Maternus, *Math.*, IV, *praef.* 5: (= Riess, T.7) "[I have transcribed] all that Hermes and Anubis have revealed to Asclepius, all that Petosiris and Nechepso have set out in detail, all that Abraham, Orpheus and Kritodemus have written as well as that set forth by other men learned in astronomy."

[24] Perhaps the best known passage is Galen, *De simpl.* X.19 (in the translation by C. Bonner, *Studies in Magical Amulets* [Ann Arbor, 1950], p. 54): "Some also set it in a ring [a green jasper stone] and engrave on it the radiate serpent, just as King Nechepso prescribed in his fourteenth book. I myself have made a satisfactory test of this stone ...".

[25] Collected in Riess, *Nechepsonis*, fragments 37-41, see Festugière, *La révélation*, Vol. I, p. 327.

[26] P. Parisin. 1884, f.150ᵛ in *CCAG*, Vol. VIII: iv, p. 105, 1-4 (see Festugière, *La révélation*, Vol. I, pp. 207 and 230). The 'second', Heliopolitan book appears the object of a separate tradition (see *CCAG*, Vol. VII, p. 63).

[27] See below, pp. 178, 181-85, for a further set of negative characterizations of the book.

Thebes (Diospolis), "the most ancient capital of Egypt, possessing many temples . . . priests, philosophers and sages".[28] In this portion of the narrative, another convention is being employed—the journey to an archaic center of learning to gain a revelation of Oriental *gnosis*—but, once again, the pattern is altered.[29] The Thebes described by Thessalos is not the 'golden city', the center of wealth and wisdom imagined by most writers of this genre. It is rather a realistic portrait of the city in Late Antiquity, such as we find in Strabo, a shadow of its former glory, with a handful of religious specialists inhabiting a few ruined temples.[30] It is a *necropolis* rather than a *diospolis*, and the

---

[28] *Thessalos*, 12.

[29] For this widespread theme, see, among others, Festugière, *La révélation*, Vol. I, pp. 19-44. F. Boll, "Das Eingangsstück der Ps.-Klementinen," 139-148 suggests a specific adaptation of this theme. He compares the parodic structure of Lucian, *Nekyomanteia*, esp. 3, 4, 6 (we may set aside the thorny question of the relationship of Lucian to Menippus [compare, Horace, *Satires* II.5] and the equally complex question as to what religious tradition is being satirized as set forth in the classic debate between R. Helm, *Lucien und Menipp* [Leipzig, 1906], esp. pp. 17-62 and B. M. McCarthy, "Lucian and Menippus," *Yale Classical Studies*, IV [1934], 3-58); *Thessalos* and the pseudo-Clementines (*Hom.* I.1, 3, 5-8, 10, 13-15; *Recog.* I.1, 3, 5-6) noting a variety of common themes in the lives and journeys of the protagonists (Boll, 142f.). The parallels have some validity; but are not overwhelming. His attempt to find structural (Boll, 141) and verbal (Boll, 143f.) parallels with *Thessalos* is unconvincing. A. D. Nock, *Conversion* (Oxford, 1933), pp. 107-109 follows and paraphrases Boll without demurral. Festugière, "L'expérience," p. 142, n. 7 offers some further parallels.

[30] For the traditional view of the wonders of Thebes, see texts such as Diodorus Siculus I.45.4-50.7 which presents a portrait of the magnificence of the "most prosperous city, not only of Egypt, but of the whole world", the wealth of its monumental and temple architecture and records the Theban propaganda that: Οἱ δὲ Θηβαῖοί φασιν ἑαυτοὺς ἀρχαιοτάτους εἶναι πάντων ἀνθρώπων, καὶ παρ' ἑαυτοῖς πρώτοις φιλοσοφίαν τε εὑρῆσθαι καὶ τὴν ἐπ' ἀκριβὲς ἀστρολογίαν (I.50.1). For the journey-initiation motif, see the characteristic advice of Thales to Pythagoras in Iamblichus, *Vita Pyth.* II. 12.

On the decay of native Egyptian temples, the reduction of the sacred centers to cities of old priests, see the remark of A. Bataille who, quite correctly, observes that, by the Roman period, Thebes was a "ville musée" ("Thèbes gréco-romaine," *Chronique d'Égypte*, XXVI [1951], 346). See the description of Thebes in Strabo, XVII.1.46 (816) as possessing only "traces" of her former glory, being now only a "collection of villages" with a few ruined temples, although once fabled for its wealth and for the wisdom of its priests who were "philosophers and astronomers". Compare the portrait of Heliopolis (Strabo, XVII.1.27-29 [805f.]): "The city is now entirely deserted, it contains the ancient temple constructed in the Egyptian manner [now ruined] . . . I also saw large houses in which the priests *had* lived, for it is said that this place in particular was, in ancient times, a settlement of priests who studied philosophy and astronomy; but both this organization and its pursuits have now disappeared. At Heliopolis, in fact, no one was pointed out to me as presiding over such pursuits, but only those who performed the sacrifices and explained to strangers what pertained to the

priests that Thessalos encounters are described as a group of timid old men who are shocked by the "rashness" of Thessalos' query as to whether the "energizing power of magic still exists."[31] While most scholars have interpreted the priests' distress as fear of the Greco-Roman laws against magic,[32] such an understanding, I believe, falls wide of the mark. The προπετεία of Thessalos does not consist in his inquiry into a forbidden subject which, if exposed, might make the priests liable to prosecution; rather it is his faith in the continued efficacy of magic itself—a faith which the priests had evidently lost.[33] Only one of the priests, a person of great dignity and age, gives Thessalos the "assurance" (a term which makes sense only if the interpretation of Thessalos' audacity just offered be accepted) that he has the power to produce a vision through lekanomancy.[34]

---

sacred rites" (translation: H. L. Jones, *The Geography of Strabo* [London, 1935], Vol. VIII, pp. 79, 83).

[31] *Thessalos*, 13: τι τῆς μαγικῆς ἐνεργείας. That Egyptian temples were considered to be sites of magical, alchemical and astrological activities and their priests, the chief initiators into such mysteries, is well documented from many types of materials. See F. Cumont, *L'Égypte des astrologues* (Brussels, 1937), pp. 163-168 *et passim* and the materials cited above, n. 21. On the Asclēpion in Thebes, see W. Otto, *Priester und Tempel im hellenistischen Aegypten* (Leipzig, 1908), Vol. I, pp. 135f.

[32] Graux, "Lettre inédite," 67f.; Cumont, "Le médecin Thessalos," 92; Cumont, *L'Égypte des astrologues*, p. 164; Festugière, "L'expérience," p. 159, n. 70.

[33] Compare the Latin at this point which garbles the question but aptly paraphrases the priests' reaction: *querebam ab eis, si aliquod opus divinandi erat in civitate eorum et quidam eorum faciebant ridiculum de me* (Friedrich, *Thessalos*, p. 50, 10f.). See further, Festugière's useful note on the difficult Greek, "L'expérience," p. 159, n. 71.

[34] See "Hydromanteia," *RE*, Vol. XVII, cols. 79-86 and "Lekanomanteia," *RE*, Vol. XXIV, cols. 1879-1889. To the bibliography cited in these articles should be added the rich study, largely devoted to medieval materials, by A. Delatte, *La catoptromancie grecque et ses dérivés* (Liège-Paris, 1932), pp. 8-11, 147f., 168-170 *et passim*. For the study of *Thessalos*, the most important parallel text is P. Bibl. Nat. suppl. gr. 574 in K. Preisendanz, *Papyri Graecae Magicae* (Leipzig, 1928-31), P.IV, 155-285 (Vol. I, pp. 77-81)—henceforth cited as *PGM*. This portion of this great *Theban* manuscript is in the *form of a letter* from Nephōtēs to King Psammētichos. It offers a procedure for self-divinization by uniting the practitioner with the sun (see the splendid translation of this "recipe" in M. Smith, *Clement of Alexandria and A Secret Gospel of Mark* [Cambridge, Mass., 1973], p. 221) and a gloss on this "theurgic" experience describing a lekanomantic procedure (see on this procedure, A. Abt, *Die Apologie des Apuleius von Madaura und die antike Zauberei* [Giessen, 1908], pp. 171-173; Th. Hopfner, *Griechisch-ägyptischer Offenbarungszauber*, Vol. II, pars. 241-244; M. Ninck, *Die Bedeutung des Wassers im Kult und Leben der Alten* [Leipzig, 1921], pp. 51f. and Festugière, "L'expérience," pp. 159f., n. 72 who provides a partial translation). This "Letter" is followed, in this complex compendium, by a Βοτανήαρσις (pp. 81.286-83.295). Thus, in overall form, it is quite parallel to *Thessalos*. (See further, Delatte, *Herbarius*, pp. 64-100, esp. pp. 64f., 81f.).

Thessalos has an interview with this venerable priest in the "most desolate part of the city" during which, with tears and swoons, he reiterates his decision to either have a vision of a deity or to die. The priest promises him a vision and instructs him to undertake a preparatory fast of three days.[35] After this period, Thessalos is brought, at dawn, by the priest to a specially prepared οἶκός and there is given the choice of communicating with either "the soul of a dead man or a god". Thessalos chooses the later and requests to see Asclepius, "alone, face to face".[36] Although the priest is unnerved by this demand, he agrees, locks Thessalos in the οἶκός after having him sit on a chair opposite a throne on which the deity will manifest himself, and invokes Asclepius with "powerful mysterious words". The priest then leaves and Thessalos experiences the vision.[37]

This description of the *praxis*, though brief, is remarkable in several respects. Despite what we have been led to expect, it is not a lekanomantic procedure, even though the priest's initial question as to whether Thessalos wished to speak with a soul or a god may be taken as such.[38] Lekanomancy is always an indirect vision—a reflection;[39] Thessalos demanded to speak with the god μόνος πρὸς μόνον—a phrase especially characteristic of neo-Platonic, "theurgic" materials.[40] But, in these circles, the experience almost always implies

---

[35] Fasting is the most widespread means of preparation for visions; the three day period is common. See, for example, in various traditions: *PGM* III, 304 (Vol. I, p. 44); Iamblichus, *De Mysteriis*, III.11; Philostratus, *V.Apollonii*, II.37; Philo, *Contemp*. 34; *Canon Muratori*, lines 10f.; *Actus Petri cum Simone* [Codex Vercellensus], 1 and 17; Tertullian, *De ieiunio*, 7. For a general statement with respect to magical praxis, see A. J. Festugière, *L'idéal religieux des grecs et l'évangile* (Paris, 1932), pp. 298f., n. 2 and Th. Hopfner, *Griechisch-ägyptischer Offenbarungszauber*, Vol. II, par. 169. For a recent study, see R. Arbesmann, "Fasting and Prophecy in Pagan and Christian Antiquity," *Traditio*, VII (1949-51), 1-71 esp. 9-32, 52-71. Compare the earlier works by Arbesmann, "Fasten im antiken Zauber, " *Blätter zur bayrischen Volkskunde*, XI (1927), *non vidi* and *Das Fasten bei den Griechen und Römern* (Giessen, 1929), pp. 63-70 *et passim*.

[36] *Thessalos*, 21f.

[37] *Thessalos*, 23.

[38] For the union (or confusion) of lekanomancy with nekromancy, see Varro *apud* Apuleius, *Apologia*, 42 and Augustine, *Civ. Dei*, VII.35 (on which see, *RE*, Vol. XI, col. 884; Delatte, *Catoptromancie*, pp. 23 and 148) and the "Letter of Nephōtēs to Psammētichos," *PGM* IV, 220f. (Vol. I, p. 78). Compare the "nekromantic" invocation of Asclepius in Origen, *Contra Haer.* IV.32 in E. J.-L. Edelstein, *Asclepius* (Baltimore, 1945), Vol. I, pp. 167f., (testimony, no. 328).

[39] See above, n. 34.

[40] See, for example, Plotinus, *Enneads*, I.6.7, V.1.6, VI.7.34, VI.9.11; Porphyry, *De abstinentia*, II.49; Proclus, *In Tim*. I.212, 24; Numenius (Thedinga, fr. 10) *apud* Eusebius, *Praep. Evang.* XI.22. For these texts, and their relationship to

the ascent of the adept, as in the well known conclusion of Plotinus, *Enneads* VI.9.11: φυγὴ μόνου πρὸς μόνον. In *Thessalos*, to the contrary, an autophany is described in archaic Temple language. The deity Asclepius (no doubt, originally, the Egyptian Imḥotep-Imouthes)[41] descends and enthrones himself in a kratophanic display: "for no human speech could adequately describe the features of the [god's] face or the beauty of the ornaments that adorned it. The god lifted his right hand and greeted me ..."[42]

Once more a traditional pattern has been altered. The vision does not take place in a temple but rather in an οἶκός. Although this term could refer to a temple, it is difficult not to understand the word as designating either an ordinary dwelling which has been specially prepared and purified (thus, simply, a room); or, less likely, but more tempting, a special construction for the occasion.[43] On either inter-

---

Thessalos, see F. Cumont, "Le culte égyptien et le mysticisme de Plotin," *Monuments Piot*, XXV (1921-2), esp. 87f. and E. Peterson, "Herkunft und Bedeutung der *Monos pros Monon*-Formel bei Platon," *Philologus*, LXXXVIII (1933), 30-41. The formula μόνος πρὸς μόνον stands in some relationship to the older formula μόνος μόνῳ as "private" or "secret" (see the texts cited by Peterson, *op. cit.*, 34f.); but see Philo, *V.Mosis*, II.163 where it approaches the force of the mystic formula.

[41] On Imhotep-Imouthes-Asclepius, see O. Weinreich, "Imhotep-Asclepius und die Griechen," *Aegyptus*, XI (1931), 17-22; and K. Sethe, *Imhotep der Asklepios der Aegypter* (Leipzig, 1902), esp. p. 23.

[42] *Thessalos*, 24. Compare Festugière's attempt to locate the vision in Hopfner's typology (*Griechisch-ägyptischer Offenbarungszauber*, Vol. II, pars. 70-75) in "L'expérience," pp. 175-180.

[43] Festugière reversed his earlier interpretation of οἶκός as a room in an ordinary house ("L'expérience," pp. 160f., 175-179)—quoting with some justification the account in Hippolytus, *Ref.* IV.32—and now argues: "Le mot [οἶκός] est courant au sens de 'chambre sacrée' dans un temple, de 'chapelle' dans un témenos ou encore de 'tombe' ... Mais je croirais volontiers qu'il s'agit ici d'une cabane construit exprès pour la circonstance (il faut qu'elle n'ait jamais servi encore pour être parfaitement 'pure'), car un manuel de magie hellénistique conservé en Arabe (*Ghāyat al-ḥakim*, 'But du sage') et traduit en latin sous le nom de *Picatrix* contient, à la lettre, la même formule: 'Mache dich auf am Donnerstag, wenn Jupiter im Bogenschützen ... steht und *baue ein* sauberes Haus (οἶκος καθαρός!) und stelle es aus so schön wie du nur kannst, das ist der Tempel, und gehe hinein allein ...'" cf. H. Ritter, *Picatrix, ein arabisches Handbuch hellenistischer Magie* (Vorträge, d. Bibl. Warburg, 1922), p. 23 du tiré à part ... Voir aussi Blochet, *Gnosticisme musulman*, 1913, p. 52, n.1: dans l'Égypte arabe les *berba* (mot égyptien) étaient des édifices où l'on faisait de la magie: ainsi la magicienne Tadoura construit à Memphis un *berba* sur les ordres se la reine Dalouka." (*La révélation*, Vol. I, pp. 57f., n. 3).

While I am tempted by Festugière's intuition, the evidence he presents is far from conclusive, being far removed from *Thessalos* by centuries—indeed, it all but evaporates under careful examination. Festugière did not have available to him the recent translation of *Picatrix* and therefore relied on a contextless quotation in Ritter's early article. The passage he quotes (*Picatrix*, III.9) is alleged,

pretation, the locus of religious experience has been shifted from a permanent sacred center, the temple, to a place of temporary sacrality sanctified by a magician's power. The mode of the autophany, a throne vision,[44] is likewise associated with the royal temple cultus as

by the author of *Picatrix*, to be taken from the pseudo-Aristotelian, *Kitāb al-Isṭamāṭis* of which other Arabic manuscripts and versions are extant. According to the critical apparatus, these manuscripts and versions read "prepare the clean room" rather than "build a pure house" and the editor notes that by "house is clearly meant only a room" (H. Ritter-M. Plessner, *Picatrix : Das Ziel des Weisen von pseudo-Maǰrīti* [London, 1962], p. 248, n. 5). There is a closely parallel instruction, most likely also from the *Kitāb al-Isṭamāṭis*, in *Picatrix*, III.6: "go into a pure room" (Ritter-Plessner, *Picatrix*, p. 200, 3f.); the same reading appears in the fifteenth century Latin version of *Picatrix*, III.6 (unfortunately as yet unedited, but see the paraphrase, in L. Thorndike, *History of Magic and Experimental Science* [New York, 1923], Vol. II, p. 819). Thus the same ambiguity: house, temple, room, special construction—is, at least, continued, with the last option the least likely. The same ambiguity may be found with respect to Festugière's notice of the term, *berba*. It is derived from the Egyptian, *pr*, meaning house, temple or tomb. It carries over into the Coptic ⲡⲣⲉ, usually restricted to temple and, as a Coptic loan-word with the article (ⲧⲉⲡⲣⲉ), is found as the Arabic *berbe* or *barbā* (W. Spiegelberg, *Koptisches Handwörterbuch* [Heidelberg, 1921], p. 102; W. E. Crum, *A Coptic Dictionary* [Oxford, 1939], p. 298). *Barbā* is the general word for the ruins of ancient Egyptian temples and, by extension, of any pagan temple or ancient building. It is almost always used in texts describing magical practices—presumably being carried on at these ancient sites (C. H. Becker, *The Encyclopaedia of Islam* [Leiden, 1913], Vol. I, p. 655; G. Wiet, *The Encyclopaedia of Islam*, 2ed. [Leiden, 1960], Vol. I:2, pp. 1038f.). See, for example, its use in an Arabic hermetic text describing a throne vision and the revelation of a hidden book in an underground *barbā* (A. Siggel, "Das Sendschreiben *Das Licht über das Verfahren des Hermes* . . .," *Der Islam*, XXIV [1937], 301 and n. 2).

It is possible to find many examples of temporary cultic houses in archaic Egyptian materials—see W. B. Kristensen, *De loofhut en het loofhuttenfeest in den Egyptischen cultus* (Amsterdam, 1923)—as well as elsewhere in the Near East—see the material collected in H. Riesenfeld, *Jésus transfiguré* (Copenhagen, 1947), pp. 146-205—but none of these seem relevant.

[44] For the archaic language of throne epiphanies, see the materials assembled in H. P. L'Orange, *Studies on the Iconography of Cosmic Kingship in the Ancient World* (Oslo, 1953), pp. 18-37 *et passim*. For θρόνος in the praxis or visions of the magical papyri, see *PGM* I, 333 (Vol. I, p. 18); II, 160, 165 (p. 29); V, 31, 35, 36, 44 (p. 182); VII, 737 (Vol. II, p. 33). R. Reitzenstein, *Die hellenistischen Mysterienreligionen* 3ed. (Leipzig-Berlin, 1927), pp. 129f. compares the vision in *Thessalos* to traditions of the revelation of a hidden book by a figure seated on a throne in alchemical literature (see above, n. 21) as in "The Book of Krates" (M. Bertholet, *La chimie au moyen âge* [Paris, 1873], Vol. III, p. 46; J. Ruska, *Tabula Smaragdina* [Heidelberg, 1926], p. 113) and an alchemical manuscript edited by Reitzenstein (*loc. cit.*). See further, the later alchemical parallels quoted by C. G. Jung, *Psychology and Alchemy* (New York, 1953), pp. 237f., n. 7 and fig. 128. In his interpretation of Hermas, *Vis.* I.2.2, E. Peterson offers a brilliant comparison with *Thessalos* and quotes much of the above cited material ("Beiträge zur Interpretation der Visionen im Pastor Hermae," in *Miscellanae G. de*

is the general homology of the appearance of the god with the first rays of the sun[45] and the raising of the deity's right hand.[46] But, in *Thessalos*, this language has been displaced. Thessalos and his "room" have replaced the archaic complex of king, priest and temple.

The vision is set in the context of an oracle[47] with three parts: (1) a salutation: "O blessed Thessalos"; (2) a promise of divinization: "today a god greets you ... later men will greet you as a god" and (3) an invitation to ask a question, the question and the god's response.[48] Such a structure would appear to be a pattern in some archaic literary oracles[49] as well as in some magical "recipes for immortality".[50] But, unlike the latter, there is relatively little interest in Thessalos' divinization; but great interest in the god's response. Once again, a surprising element is introduced. The oracle consists of a denigration of the legendary powers and wisdom of King Nechepso.[51] Thessalos asks why the recipes in Nechepso's book failed and receives the answer: "King Nechepso, although a wise man and a

---

Jerphanion [Rome, 1947], rp. in Peterson, *Frühkirche, Judentum und Gnosis* [Freiburg, 1959]—which edition I cite—esp. pp. 254-258). A caution should be given against his understanding of the epithet θρονομάντις as applied to Harpokrates (R. Harder, *Karpokrates von Chalkis und die memphitischer Isis-propaganda* [Berlin, 1944], p. 8). While many translate this as "divining by throne" (Peterson, "Beiträge," p. 256, n. 17; A. D. Nock, *Essays on Religion in the Ancient World*, Vol. II, p. 702), perhaps thinking of the mantic throne of Apollo (e.g. Euripides, *Iphig. Taur.*, 1254, 1282; Aeschylus, *Eum.*, 616), the *Supplement* to the Liddell-Scott *Lexicon* (Oxford, 1968), p. 72 renders "diviner by θρόνον, magic herbs".

[45] One needs do no more than call attention to the solar orientation of many temples in the Mediterranaen world, especially in Egypt and to the equally widespread tradition of revelation at dawn, as in our text (see Arbesmann, "Fasting and Prophecy," 30f.).

[46] See H. P. L'Orange, *Studies*, pp. 139-197 and Peterson, "Beiträge," p. 258, n. 25.

[47] See above, n. 18, for such "theological" oracles.

[48] *Thessalos*, 25-27. The macarism is defective in the Greek (see above, n. 7) and was first restored on the basis of the Latin: *o beate Thessale* by Cumont, "Le médecin," 90. It should be noted that at this point (*Thessalos*, 25), the textual tradition becomes more complex. In addition to the Madrid Greek manuscript which attributed authorship to Harpokration and the Latin Montpellier text which attributed authorship to Thessalos, there is a third group of Herbals which begin with the conclusion of the narrative and attribute authorship to Hermes Trismegistus under the general title περὶ ἱερῶν βοτανῶν καὶ χυλώσεως. See Friedrich, *Thessalos*, pp. 55-60 for these texts and variant readings—none of which alter the sense of the passage under discussion.

[49] The oldest example I know is the Pythian prophetess' response to Lykurgos in Herodotus, I.65.2. For other examples of macarisms in oracles, see G. L. Dirichlet, *De veterum macarismis* (Giessen, 1914), pp. 60f.

[50] See the materials quoted in Festugière, "L'expérience," p. 146 and n. 27.

[51] See above, p. 177.

possessor of great magical powers, had not received from a divine voice the secrets you have requested. Endowed with natural wisdom he had grasped the affinities of stones and plants with the stars; but he did not know the times or places where the plants must be gathered . . . ." While this may be interpreted, in part, as a polemic against a rival astral-botanical system,[52] it is a stunning reversal of Nechepso's claim that, during a nocturnal ecstasy, he had ascended through the air and heard a "heavenly voice"[53] and the claim of his companion, Petosiris, to have journeyed together with gods and

[52] Thus, F. Boll in Boll-C. Bezold-W. Gundel, *Sternglaube und Sterndeutung*, 4ed. (Berlin, 1931), p. 140, compare p. 97. For an alternative understanding of the text as polemic, see Cumont, "Le médecin," 94f. Note that F. H. Cremer, *Astrology in Roman Law and Politics* (Philadelphia, 1954), p. 123 has entirely missed the polemic elements.

[53] E. Riess, *Nechepsonis et Petosiridis*, fr. 1: ἔδοξε δέ μοι παννύχον πρὸς ἀέρα < . . . > καὶ μοί τις ἐξήχησεν οὐρανοῦ βοή (*apud* V. Valens, *Anth.* VI, *praef.* ed. W. Kroll [Berlin, 1908], p. 241, 16-18). Riess joined this fragment to the *Thessalos* text which he printed as frs. 35-36. R. Reitzenstein, *Poimandres* (Leipzig, 1904). pp. 4-7 argued that this was a hellenized Egyptian literary form. Other examples, mostly of revelation from a heavenly body, are given in Reitzenstein, *loc. cit.*; Boll-Bezold-Gundel, *Sternglaube*, pp. 96-99 [the best collection] and Boll, *Offenbarung Johannis*, pp. 4-8. Festugière, *L'idéal religieux*, p. 123, n. 1 and 2, relates the Nechepso fragment to the general theme of an ἀνάβασις εἰς οὐρανόν but his texts all lack the crucial element of a heavenly or divine voice. In *La révélation*, Vol. I, pp. 104, 313-315, Festugière does print some proper parallels: *Poimandres*, 4 (see A. D. Nock-A. J. Festugière, *Corpus Hermeticum*, 2ed. [Paris, 1960], Vol. I, pp. 7f., n. 2); the claim, in the herbal Περὶ τῆς Παιωνίας, that botanical knowledge was given directly by God to Hermes Trismegistos (*CCAG*, vol. VIII: i, p. 190, 31—see the brilliant French translation of this text by Festugière, "Un opuscule hermétique sur la pivoine," *Vivre et penser*, II [1942], rp. in Festugière, *Hermétisme et mystique païenne*, pp. 181-201, esp. p. 192) and the logion attributed to Hermes Trismegistos: "I spoke to Zeus and Zeus spoke to me" (*CCAG*, vol. V: i, p. 149, 27). One might also compare the "Ὅρασις of Kritodemos (see Boll, *RE*, Vol. XI, col. 1928). It should be noted that W. Burkert, *Lore and Science in Ancient Pythagoreanism* (Cambridge, Mass., 1972), p. 357, n. 6 attempts to relate the "heavenly voice" of Nechepso, fr. 1 to the tradition of hearing the music of the heavenly spheres rather than to a revelation-discourse.

Attention should also be called to the horoscope (dated 137-138 A.D.) in P. Salt (= P. Louvre 2342) which suggests a revelatory chain: "After examination of many books as they have been handed down to us [ὡς παρεδόθη ἡμεῖν] from ancient wisemen, that is, the Chaldeans, and Petosiris, and, especially, king Necheus [*scil.* Nechepso—see the early argument on this in Lauth, "König Nechepsos, Petosiris und die Triakontaëteris," *Sitzungsberichte* . . . *München*, 1875, phil.-hist. Kl. Vol. II, esp. pp. 96-109], just as they themselves consulted with [ὥσπερ καὶ αὐτοὶ συνήδρευσαν ἀπὸ. . .] our Lord Hermes and Asclepius, that is, Imouthes son of Hephaistos". The συνεδρεία suggests a situation of face to face (revelatory) discourse. This text has been much commented on. See Riess, *Nechepsonis*, fr. 6; Kroll, *RE*, Vol. XVI, col. 2160; and, especially, Cumont, *CCAG*, Vol. VIII:iv, pp. 95 and 121 and O. Neugebauer-H. B. van Hoesen, *Greek Horoscopes* (Philadelphia, 1959), pp. 39-45 with bibliographies, to which add: Gundel, *Astrologoumena*, pp. 26 and n. 38, 29.

angels.⁵⁴ It is, above all an utter revaluation of the archaic Egyptian kingship ideology that the Pharaoh was divine and spoke, himself, with a "divine voice". Such a revaluation would only be possible in Late Antiquity. Thessalos, as the recepient of a "divine voice", has made the pilgrimage from natural wisdom to revealed knowledge analogous (although with a quite different end) to Philo's allegory of the migration of Abraham.⁵⁵ The content of the revelation is knowledge of the καιροί καί τόποι,⁵⁶ the complex herbal which follows this narrative in the manuscript, and, ultimately, Thessalos' divinization and immortality.⁵⁷ But it is, above all, to have met Asclepius face to face, to have won through from a state of death-like despair, to have 'come home'.⁵⁸ Thessalos accomplished through his horizontal journey from Asia Minor to Diospolis what Plotinus' *Enneads* were designed to accomplish through vertical ascent—φυγή μόνον πρὸς μόνον.⁵⁹

In describing the text of *Thessalos*, I have used the term "reversal" or the phrase "the pattern has been altered" to describe every major

---

⁵⁴ Riess, *Nechepsonis*, fr. 33 (*apud*. Proclus, *in Rem* ed. W. Kroll [Leipzig, 1899-1901], Vol. II, p. 345, 3).

⁵⁵ Philo, *Abr.* 60-62, 68-80; *Mig.* 176-196; *Somn.* I.41-60, 68-71; on which see E. Bréhier, *Les Idées philosophiques et religieuses de Philon d'Alexandrie* 2 ed. (Paris, 1925), pp. 56-61, esp. p. 56, n. 6 and A. Wlosok, *Laktanz und die philosophische Gnosis* (Heidelberg, 1960), pp. 81-114, esp. pp. 81-84. I find this a more convincing parallel than that proposed by Nock, *Conversion*, p. 109 who refers to the "rabbinic type of true proselytes, Joshua, Naaman and Rahab . . ."

⁵⁶ On the importance of the "proper time and place" in astral botany, see Delatte, *Herbarius*, pp. 39-72 ("Temps propice à la récolte"). See further the theurgic materials discussed by G. Wolff in his edition of Porphyry, *De philosophia ex oraculis haurienda* (Berlin, 1856), pp. 195-205 and H. Lewy, *Chaldean Oracles and Theurgy* (Cairo, 1956), pp. 228-244 *et passim*. See especially the complex "Chaldean" ritual described in Psellus, *Peri daimonen* (Migne, *PG*, vol. CXXII, p. 881 B-C; Bidez-Cumont, *Les mages hellénisés*, Vol. II, p. 172, n. 2 and compare J. Bidez in *Catalogue des manuscrits alchimiques grecs* [Brussels, 1928], Vol. VI, p. 218).

One might also compare the overall structure of *Asclepius* 37-38 which invokes Imhotep as the *medicinae primus inuentor . . . omnia etiamnunc hominibus adiumenta praestans infirmis numine nunc suo, quae ante solet medicinae arte praebere* and goes on to describe the theurgic doctrine of the *di terreni: Constat, o Asclepi, de herbis, de lapidibus et de aromatibus* and see the valuable note *ad* Iamblichus, *de Myst.*, V.23 in the edition of E. des Places (Paris, 1966), pp. 178f., n. 3.

⁵⁷ *Thessalos*, 25 and compare the conclusion to the Latin text of the Herbal, II, *epil.* 12-14 (Friedrich, *Thessalos*, p. 271 and parallels [pp. 272f.]).

⁵⁸ I have omitted discussion of the initiatory scenario of Thessalos twice being brought to the point of death in the narrative, especially during his complex and dramatic interview with the aged priest (*Thessalos*, 15-20).

⁵⁹ Plotinus, *Enn.* VI.9.11 and compare *Orac. chald.* 213 with the note in the edition of E. des Places, *Oracles chaldaïques* (Paris, 1971), p. 151 (*ad.* 213.1).

episode. And it is precisely this unexpected character of the document that makes it such a precious witness to the religious life of Late Antiquity.

In a series of articles, I have set forth several correlative models of religious persistance and change in the Mediterranean world in Late Antiquity: native/diaspora; locative/utopian; celebration/rebellion.[60] For most, the diasporic, utopian, rebellious world-view has been taken as characteristic of Late Antiquity. This is the case, I would want to argue, largely due to the almost total cessation of native kingship and sovereignty in the domains of Alexander's successors. Or, to phrase it differently, if there is no native king, then even the homeland is in the diaspora.[61] But I believe that a more complex model is called for—one that might better account for a large class of cultic phenomena that exhibit characteristics of mobility, what I would term religious entrepreneurship and which represent both a reinterpretation and a reaffirmation of native, locative, celebratory categories of religious practice and thought.[62]

To develop this model fully, it would be necessary to undertake a careful study of the various fortunes of temples throughout the Mediterranean world during this period: those that continue, those that are newly founded, those that are restored, those that are re-dedicated or otherwise altered, those that are destroyed and those that are neglected. While a final proposal would have to await the assemblage of this vast quantity of data, *Thessalos* may allow one to advance some tentative suggestions.

I am particularly interested in the shift so brilliantly depicted by Peter Brown with his image of Simeon Stylites:

> The idea of the holy man holding the demons at bay and bending the will of God by his prayers came to dominate Late Antique society. In many ways, the idea is as new as the society itself. For it places a man, a 'man of power', in the centre of people's imagination ... Ancient religion had revolved round great temples ... their ceremonies assumed a life in which the community, the city, dwarfed the individual. In the fourth and fifth centuries [A.D.], however, the individual, as a

---

[60] See J. Z. Smith, "Birth Upside Down or Rightside Up?," chapter 7, above; "A Place on Which to Stand," chapter 6, above; "Native Cults in the Hellenistic Period," *History of Religions*, XI (1971), 236-249; "The Wobbling Pivot," chapter 4, above.

[61] It is the great merit of S. K. Eddy, despite the many faults of his work, to have emphasized this element in *The King is Dead* (Lincoln, 1961).

[62] For other aspects of this model, see "Wisdom and Apocalyptic," chapter 3, above and "Good News is No News: Aretalogy and Gospel" chapter 9, below.

'man of power', came to dwarf the traditional communities ... Simeon the Stylite, gloriously conspicuous on his column, sifting lawsuits, prophesying, healing, rebuking and advising the governing classes of the whole eastern empire not far from the deserted temple of Baalbek, was the sign of a similar change. In the popular imagination, *the emergence of the holy man at the expense of the temple marks the end of the classical world.*[63]

We would disagree only as to date. The sociological niche that the holy man, in Brown's sense of the term,[64] would later fill was already being occupied by entrepreneurial figures as early as the second century (B.C.).[65]

One way of stating this shift is to note that the cosmos has become anthropologized. The old, imperial cosmological language that was the major mode of religious expression of the archaic temple and court cultus has been transformed.[66] Rather than a city wall, the new enclave protecting man against external, hostile powers will be a human group, a religious association or secret society. Rather than a return to chaos or the threat of decreation, the enemy will be described as other men or demons, the threat as evil or death. Rather than a sacred place, the new center and chief means of access to divinity will be a divine man, a magician, who will function, by and large, as an entrepreneur without fixed office and will be, by and large, related to "protean deities" of relatively unfixed form whose major characteristic is their sudden and dramatic autophanies. Rather than celebration, purification and pilgrimage, the new rituals will be those of conversion, of initiation into the secret society or identification with the divine man. As a part of this fundamental

---

[63] P. Brown, *The World of Late Antiquity* (London, 1971), pp. 102f. (emphasis mine). Compare Brown, "The Rise and Function of the Holy Man in Late Antiquity," *Journal of Roman Studies*, LXI (1971), 80-101, esp. 100.

[64] Brown uses the term "holy man" in conscious distinction to the "divine man" and "magician" of, for him, an earlier period (Brown, "Rise and Function," 92f.).

[65] See, already, Joseph son of Tobias as described by V. Tcherikover, *Hellenistic Civilization and the Jews* (Philadelphia, 1959), pp. 133f.

[66] For a brief description of the archaic cultus, see J. Z. Smith, "Earth and Gods," chapter 5, above. The perspective of this article requires correction in light of the above. While from an archaic point of view, exile and the destruction of the Temple was a "descent into chaos", elements in Judaism had, before these two traumatic events, responded to the new religious and social situation in a manner characteristic of the religions of Late Antiquity. In the synagogue, Judaism found its secret society; in the rabbi, its magician. Through the magic of words it attempted, in the great rabbinic legal enterprise, to construct a mythical cosmos, a portable homeland in which any Jew might dwell.

shift, the archaic language and ideology of the cult will be revalorized—only those elements which contribute to this new, anthropological and highly mobile understanding of religion will be retained.[67]

In previous scholarship, some of these elements have been recognized and subsumed under the formula: "the spiritualization of the cult",[68] held to be a "prophetic" protest against the "automatic" and "magical" efficacy of archaic practices such as sacrifice.

Such an interpretation contains a modicum of truth, but it is formulated in a way that requires demurral. It is clearly evolutionary in form, a modification of the Victorian chain from "magic" to "religion" and owes much to Reformation polemics against "Paganopapism". It emphasizes the "compulsive", "automatic", *ex opere operato* character of the archaic rituals and denigrates these as "magical" as opposed to the "petitionary", "inward" and "ethical" activities labeled "religious". Although such a dichotomy was proposed by figures in Late Antiquity,[69] this must be taken, not as evidence that such a view is correct, but rather that the religious horizon had shifted from that of the archaic period.[70]

The most serious consequence of the *Spiritualisierung* interpretation is that it permits us to overlook the creativity of magic in Late Antiquity. Indeed, although this theme has been as yet insufficiently explored, the only major set of materials from Late Antiquity which continue to employ sacrificial structures and terminology, which continue to reinterpret their meaning and reapply the rituals are the so-called magical papyri, theurgic and alchemical treatises.[71]

---

[67] One might note the concentration upon mobile elements from the Jewish cultus, e.g. the *shekînāh*, *kābôd* and ark rather than the "house" (see K. Baltzer, "The Meaning of the Temple in the Lukan Writings," *Harvard Theological Review*, LVIII [1965], 263-277 which requires extension); the image of the temple as the community of believers and the "body" of the divine man (see, among others, B. Gärtner, *The Temple and the Community in Qumran and the New Testament* [Cambridge, 1965], pp. 16-46 *et passim.*); etc., in early Christianity as examples of this revalorization which may be paralleled throughout the religious traditions of Late Antiquity.

[68] For the classical formulation, see H. Wenschkewitz, "Die Spiritualisierung der Kultusbegriffe: Tempel, Priester und Opfer im Neuen Testament," *Angelos*, IV (1932), 71-230. Cp. N. A. Dahl, *Das Volk Gottes* (Oslo, 1941), pp. 70 *et passim.*

[69] Much of this material is collected in J. Bernays, *Theophrasts Schrift über Frommigkeit* (Berlin, 1866) and J. Haussleiter, *Der Vegetarismus in der Antike* (Berlin, 1935). See further, F. W. Cremer, *Die Chaldäischen Orakel und Jamblich de Mysteriis* (Meisenheim am Glan, 1969), pp. 123-130.

[70] See the useful note by M. Smith, *Clement of Alexandria and a Secret Gospel of Mark*, p. 222, n. 8 *ad* Iamblichus, *Myst.* III.18.

[71] Perhaps the best study, to date, is H. Riesenfeld, "Remarques sur les hymnes

Thessalos provides a direct witness to this shift. The ancient books of wisdom, the authority—indeed the divinity—of the priest-king, the faith of the clergy in the efficacy of their rituals, the temple as the chief locus of revelation—all of these have been relativized in favor of a direct experience of a mobile magician with his equally mobile divinity. This experience allows Thessalos to revalorize the archaic wisdom of plants, stones and stars,[72] to transform the archaic practices of sacrifice into a salvific event.

It is revealing that the Hebrew Scriptures, in the two great traditions that cherish them, do not end, in their present Late Antique redactions, with the same passage. The Jewish collection ends with the promise of 2Chronicles 36.23 of a rebuilt Temple and restored cultus. The Christian collection ends with the promise of Malachai 4.5 of the return of the *magus* Elijah—a promise fulfilled in the figure of John the Baptist who reinterprets an archaic water-ritual of purification into a magical ritual that saves. The Temple and the Magician were one of the characteristic antinomies of Late Antique religious life; the tension between them contributed much to its extraordinary creativity and vitality.

---

magiques," *Eranos*, XLIV (1946), 153-160 but this is insufficient. A study of these phenomena remains a prime need. Some useful material, with respect to the astral-botanical tradition represented by *Thessalos*, may be gleaned from Delatte, *Herbarius*, pp. 148-163 who notes a variety of "transformations" of sacrificial procedures in the magical, herbal *praxis*.

[72] For a careful delineation of such archaic wisdom as *Listenwissenschaft*, see the important article by A. Alt, "Die Weisheit Salomos," *Theologische Literaturzeitung*, LXXVI (1951), 139-144; see also, J. Z. Smith, "Wisdom and Apocalyptic," chapter 3, above.

CHAPTER NINE

GOOD NEWS IS NO NEWS: ARETALOGY AND GOSPEL

> Crito: In what way shall we bury you?
> Socrates: In any way that you like, if you can catch me and I don't elude you.   (*Phaedo* 115C)

In recent years, sparked largely by the works of Morton Smith, Dieter Georgi, Hans Dieter Betz and Helmut Koester there has been a revival of interest in the question of the possible relationship between Greco-Roman aretalogies and Christian gospels. While others have made more extensive contributions to the implications of this relationship for the understanding of particular New Testament texts, Morton Smith, through his invaluable *Heroes and Gods* and his sophisticated and fulsome essay on the history of scholarship and the current state of the question, has provided the parameters for much of the current discussion.[1] However, I believe that further progress can be made only if we question two presuppositions that have shaped much of this research: that the aretalogy functions primarily as a model to be imitated and that the essential character of the aretalogy is that of a collection of miracle stories.[2]

I have taken my clue from a little noticed séance of the nineteenth century French magician, Eliphas Lévi. On July 24, 1854 as the culmination of a three week period of preparation, Lévi invoked the spirit of Apollonius of Tyana:

> The mirror which was behind the altar seemed to brighten in its depth, a wan form was outlined therein which increased and seemed to approach by degrees. Three times, and with closed eyes, I invoked Apollonius. When again I looked forth there was a man in front of me, wrapped from head to toe in a species of shroud, which seemed more grey than white. He was lean, melancholy and beardless, *and did not altogether correspond to my preconceived notion of Apollonius* ...

---

[1] M. Hadas and M. Smith, *Heroes and Gods: Spiritual Biographies in Antiquity* (London, 1965); M. Smith, "Prolegomena to a Discussion of Aretalogies, Divine Men, the Gospels and Jesus," *Journal of Biblical Literature*, XC (1971), 174-199.

[2] See, for example, D. L. Tiede, *The Charismatic Figure as Miracle Worker* (Missoula, 1972) who distinguishes between the aretalogy of the sage (model) and the aretalogy of the miracle worker (chapter 1, *passim*).

After the evocation I have described, *I re-read carefully* the Life of Apollonius ... and I remarked that towards the end of his life he was starved and tortured in prison. This circumstance, which perhaps remained in my memory without my being aware of it, may have determined the unattractive form of my vision.[3]

While there are many elements in the elaborate description of Lévi's ritual which are worthy of comment by an historian of religions, in the context of this article I would call attention only to the function of the *Vita Apollonii* in Lévi's account. The narrative of Apollonius' life in the *Vita* inspired Lévi with the desire to 'meet' and gain wisdom from Apollonius. The ritual he employed was, he believed, a faithful repetition of one devised by Apollonius.[4] Yet Lévi's 'experience' of Apollonius did not accord with his expectation. This drove Lévi to a reexamination of the *Vita* in the light of his experience and to a new understanding of his experience in the light of his reconsideration of the *Vita*.

I should like to suggest that this experience of discrepancy provides an important corrective to our usual understanding of aretalogies as models to be imitated by disciples. The devotee does not passively reenact or imitate. Rather he has an experience which *both validates and challenges* the model proposed by the "Life" and through a process of double-reflection, his understanding of both his experience and the "Life" requires reinterpretation. There is an interplay between text and experiential context and both are mutually challenged by this process. I would further argue that this sense of discrepancy, this interplay, is a major function of the aretalogy which is best expressed as the interplay between understanding and misunderstanding. In this paper, I shall explore this interplay in the *Vita Apollonii* by Philostratus and in the complex *Vita Pythagorae* tradition as represented by Iamblichus.

I

In his important study of the use of the terms "magician" and "sorcerer" in Western European literature, Robert-Léon Wagner

---

[3] E. Lévi, *Transcendental Magic*, A. E. Waite, transl. (London, n.d.), pp. 154-157 (emphasis, mine). Compare the use of this séance in W. Somerset Maugham's novel, *The Magician* (New York, 1909), pp. 81-86. E. M. Butler, *Ritual Magic* (Cambridge, 1949), pp. 283-293 is the only scholar I have seen who calls attention to the importance of Lévi's evocation.

[4] Lévi, esp. pp. 500f. Compare the recent occult interpretation of this document by J. van Rijckenborgh, *Het Nuctemeron van Apollonius van Tyana* (Haarlem, 1968).

noted the pains which his sources took to distinguish "les deux magiciens: le sincère et le roué."[5] This is, in fact, a far more significant and pervasive mode of division than the frequently employed functional typology which distinguishes a variety of forms of magic by the substance utilized or the action performed.[6]

There have been many suggestive theoretical contributions to the understanding and definition of magic.[7] One of the more important insights was brought forth by the French Sociological School which argued that magic was not different in essence from religion, but rather different with respect to social position. In Durkheim's pithy formulation: *"There is no Church of magic . . . A magician has a clientele and not a Church . . . Religion, on the other hand, is inseparable from the idea of a Church."*[8] It is thus possible only to speak of the magician not of magic and to characterize his social and religious role as one of *mobility* (frequently expressed theologically by the charge that the magician is heterodox or politically by the charge that he is a foreigner or a subversive). The recent work of Peter Brown and Morton Smith has allowed us to describe this mobility with more precision.[9]

Both Smith and Brown have focussed attention on the one, universal characteristic of magic—it is illegal; within the Greco-Roman world it carried the penalty of death or deportation.[10] Smith concentrates on the implications of this for the magician and his disciples; Brown

---

[5] R.-L. Wagner, *"Sorcier" et "Magicien": Contribution à l'histoire du vocabulaire de la magie* (Paris, 1939), esp. pp. 26-35.

[6] For a classic, and utterly unoriginal, example of this sort of functional typology, see Isidore of Seville, *Etymologies* VIII.9, *De Magis*.

[7] See the recent review article by M. and R. Wax, "The Notion of Magic," *Current Anthropology*, IV (1963), 495-518.

[8] E. Durkheim, *The Elementary Forms of the Religious Life* (London, 19 4), p. 44 (original italics). Compare, M. Mauss, *A General Theory of Magic* (London, 1972), esp. p. 24 and H. Hubert's classic article, "Magia." in Ch. Daremberg and E. Saglio, *Dictionnaire des antiquités grecques et romaines* (Paris, 1873-1919), Vol. III: 2 (1904), cols. 1494-1521, esp. 1494-1496.

[9] P. Brown, "Sorcery, Demons and the Rise of Christianity from Late Antiquity into the Middle Ages," in M. Douglas, ed., *Witchcraft: Confessions and Accusations* (London, 1970), pp. 17-45 (reprinted in P. Brown, *Religion and Society in the Age of St. Augustine* [New York, 1972], pp. 119-146); M. Smith, *Clement of Alexandria and a Secret Gospel of Mark* (Cambridge, Mass., 1973), esp. 220-237.

[10] See, in general, E. Massonneau, *Le crime de magie dans la droit romain* (Paris, 1933) and the Christian material collected by F. Martroye, "La répression de la magie et les cultes des gentils au IVe siècle," *Revue historique du droit français et étranger*, Sér. IV, IX (1930), 669-701.

(influenced by contemporary anthropological theory) concentrates on the magician's accusers. Smith emphasizes that the terms magician, Θεῖος ἀνήρ and son of god all refer to "a single social type", that magician is the term applied to the figure by his "enemies", that "sceptical but reverent" admirers would use Θεῖος ἀνήρ and that his "believers" would call him son of god.[11] Brown emphasizes another distinction common in the literature, that between philosopher and magician,[12] and insists that these terms refer to a conflict for power. Both figures are competing for a 'place at the table' of "vested" Imperial-traditional power by claiming access to "inarticulate" non-traditional power, in particular the claim to possess an enlightened soul and powerful words. Thus the rhetor may bring a charge of magic against a religious adept or, himself, be charged with magic.[13]

These observations have a number of important implications for our understanding of the religions of Late Antiquity.[14] In this essay, I should like to focus only on their relevance to the way in which we read gospels and aretalogies. They suggest that for those figures for whom an ultimate religious claim is made (e.g. son of god), their biographies will serve as apologies against outsiders' charges that they were merely magicians and against their admirers' sincere misunderstanding that they were merely wonder-workers, divine men or philosophers. From Iamblichus' *De mysteriis Aegyptiorum* and Apuleius' *Apologia* to the Gospel of Mark (following T. J. Weeden and L. Keck),[15] the characteristic of every such religious biography (and associated autobiographical and dogmatic materials) of Late Antiquity is this double defense against the charge of magic—against the calumny of outsiders and the sincere misunderstanding of admirers.

---

[11] For a contemporary example, see Don Juan in C. Castaneda, *The Teachings of Don Juan: A Yaqui Way of Knowledge* (Berkeley-Los Angeles, 1968) who is at pain to distinguish himself as a "man of knowledge" from the *brujo*. *Brujos* are shot according to Yaqui law (see R. L. Beals, *The Contemporary Culture of the Cáhita Indians* [Washington, 1945], p. 197).

[12] See the collection of terms in R. MacMullen, *Enemies of the Roman Order* (Cambridge, Mass., 1966), pp. 320f., n. 16.

[13] Examples in Brown, *loc. cit.* which may be multiplied, for example the rhetor Adrian οὕτω τι εὐδόκιμος, ὡς καὶ πολλοῖς γόης δόξαι in Philostratus, *Vita Sophisti* 590.

[14] See "The Temple and the Magician," chapter 8, above.

[15] T. J. Weeden, "The Heresy that Necessitated Mark's Gospel," *Zeitschrift für die neutestamentliche Wissenschaft*, LIX (1968), 145-168; *Mark: Traditions in Conflict* (Philadelphia, 1971); L. Keck, "Mark 3.7-12 and Mark's Christology," *Journal for Biblical Literature*, LXXXIV (1965), 341-358.

The solution of each group or individual so charged was the same: to insist on an inward meaning of the suspect activities. The allegedly magical action, properly understood, is a sign. There is both a transparent and a hidden meaning, a literal and a deeper understanding required. At the surface level the biography appears to be an explicit story of a magician or a *Wundermensch*; at the depth level it is the enigmatic self-disclosure of a son of god.

The *double-entendre* character of the traditions extends from the most trivial detail to the most major incident. Every word, every gesture of the figure is pregnant with *possible* significance. The discipline, the reader, is obsessive and insane if he attempts to interpret every word and gesture as having a deeper meaning; he is a blind man and a fool if he fails to detect the deeper meaning.

This play between appearance and reality is not to be understood merely as an apologetic strategm to avoid unpleasant legal consequences. Code, the *double-entendre*, is the very essence of these figures. Whether revealed in a characteristic form of spells: "You are this, you are not this, you are that" "It is I, it is not I, it is so and so who says this" or in the equally characteristic use in the biographical tradition of riddle, aporia, joke and parable, these figures depend upon a multivalent expression which is interpreted by admirers and detractors as having univocal meaning and thus invites, again by admirers and detractors alike, misunderstanding. The function of the narrative is to play between various levels of understanding and misunderstanding, inviting the reader to assume that both he and the author truly do understand and then cutting the ground out from under this confidence. The figure for whom the designation son of god is claimed characteristically plays with our seriousness and is most serious when he appears to be playing. This is a sign of his freedom and transcendence, the *sine qua non* of a religious figure of Late Antiquity worthy of belief.

This toying with the reader's confidence is especially prominent in traditions surrounding the chief disciples of the son of god. It raises for the reader the problem of the refraction of the figure through the reports of those who do not understand and those who misunderstand as, in both the case of the Gospels and the aretalogies, it is these same not quite understanding disciples who are the major source of our knowledge of their master. For example, Philostratus' *Vita Apollonii* is alleged to be chiefly based on the "Memoirs" of Damis. The reader is presented with the claim (again as in the Gospels) of a retrospective understanding by the disciples which is relativised by their evident lack of understanding while their master was yet alive.[16] Philostratus introduces Damis with the revealing comment: "There was a man named Damis who was by no means stupid" (I.3)[17]; he was also, as the text repeatedly demonstrates, by no means wise! Damis lasts three hundred and twelve chapters of intimate acquaintance with Apollonius before he "first really understood the true nature of Apollonius, that is, that it was divine and more than human" (VII.38)—or, Jesus' plaint to his disciples, "Do you still not understand" (Mt. 16.9 etc.).

Like Peter in Mark's Gospel (especially in the "Confession" of chapter 8) reversals with respect to the understanding and misunderstanding of the chief disciples are characteristic of the Greco-Roman *Vitae*. For example, in Philostratus I.18, Apollonius' disciples refuse to accompany him on his travels. He answers them:

> I have taken the gods into counsel and have told you of their decision; and I have made a trial of you to see if you are strong enough to undertake the same things as myself. Since you are so soft and effeminate, I wish you very good health so that you may go on with your philosophy; but I must depart whither wisdom and the gods lead me.

Three lines later he meets Damis who answers Apollonius immediately: "Let us depart, Apollonius, you following the gods and I [following] you." Damis thus appears to be the model of the true and understanding disciple in contradistinction to the previous group; but just as swiftly he reveals that he too does not truly understand. He offers to be of service to his master in that he knows many of the languages of the peoples they will encounter on their journey. Apollonius replies: "I understand all languages, though I never learned a single one ... I also understand all the secrets of human silence". Rather than comprehending, even now, Apollonius' rebuke, that the journey was not to be a tour and that Apollonius

---

[16] Compare the attempts to understand (in a literal fashion) the characteristic riddle-speech of Apollonius in III.15 (cp. VI.11), IV.24 (cp. V.7) and IV.43 and the glosses by Damis and others in III.15, VI.32 etc. This material has been collected and discussed (without, I think, perceiving its central significance) by G. Petzke, *Die Traditionen über Apollonius von Tyana und das Neue Testament* (Leiden, 1970), pp. 111-116.

[17] I have cited Philostratus, *Vita Apollonii* according to the text in the Loeb edition by F. C. Conybeare (London, 1912) and have followed, with slight modifications, his translation. Attention should be called to the superb, lively translation by C. P. Jones in the Penguin Classics series (Harmondsworth, 1970) which is, unfortunately, abridged.

did not require the services of a guide, that the discussions they would have required no translation because human speech was inadequate for the matters to be discussed—Damis misunderstands Apollonius to be claiming *daimonic* status and "worshipped him".

Throughout the *Vita*, Damis functions like Peter in Mark's Gospel, the first and most cherished of the disciples who nevertheless consistently misunderstands. Like Peter, the last scene we have of Damis is a betrayal (VII.15)—and, like Peter, we have only the tradition that later reflection led to his final understanding.

What then is there to be understood about a figure such as Apollonius? It is here that the title of this essay's play on *euangelion* becomes *à propos*. The *Vita Apollonii* begins with a set of conflicting birth-stories, an aretalogical convention which apparently originated with Neanthes of Cyzicus (fl. 200 B.C.). After providing a series of portents, each of which testifies to Apollonius' divinity, but each of which reflects a different understanding of that divinity, Philostratus concludes: "The people of the country say that Apollonius was the son of this Zeus, but the sage called himself the son of Apollonius" (I.6). Regardless of the possible historical truth of the tradition that Apollonius' father bore the same name as his son, I find it impossible not to read a further meaning here. Apollonius is his own father, he is *sui generis*, he is himself, himself alone. All other definitions are inadequate.

From this introductory chapter where Apollonius is introduced as a new epiphany of Proteus ("the god of ever changing form, defying capture" I.4) to the last words of Apollonius, the Pythagorean, which relativise the central Pythagorean doctrine of the immortality of the soul (VIII.31), we are presented with a portrait of a powerful figure who muddles all models. The disciples (and his later readers) are incapable of being like him, even of truly understanding him, because he is fundamentally not like us. He is himself. He is an Other.

As is the case with John the Baptist or Jesus in the Gospels, there is a bewildering assortment of models projected upon Apollonius in Philostratus' account. But none of these is who he truly is. He is, as he constantly reiterates, Apollonius and it is up to disciple and reader to make what poor sense of that as they can. The disciple and the reader remain in the paradigmatic stance of the Babylonian satrap who asks Apollonius the question "From where have you come and who sent you?" (a question pregnant with possible meanings) and is toyed with for three times before the *egō eimi* pronouncement: "I am Apollonius of Tyana" (I.21).

Apollonius, as he functions in his *Vita*, remains opaque. He is a cipher. He has no teachings of his own. His philosophy, as represented by Philostratus, consists of neo-Pythagorean and Stoic commonplaces that may be found in any doxographical handbook. His own characteristic mode of speech appears to have been the riddle, the paradox or silence (see the programmatic statement in VI.11). Commanding enough to secure initial attention, he does not announce a new doctrine but rather seems to become invisible in any given situation. He is an αὐτοσχεδιαστής in the positive sense of the word (VII.30).

His opacity is equalled by his transparency. Neither providing a model nor a saving message, he does not overshadow a situation but rather dissolves from view. Every encounter is similar to that with the Emperor—he simply vanishes (VIII.15). He is able to step inside of every situation because he is, himself, outside of every situation. His biography as biography is not important. His message is given only in his free, playful and utterly transcendent intervention in specific situations which allow for a moment the possibility of another point of view. The narrative of these situations could have been either immeasurably compressed or expanded, for each situation is essentially nonrepeatable. There can be no "Life" of Apollonius. He lives whenever and wherever a Lévi encounters him and can say "He did not altogether correspond to my preconceived notion" and reflect on this incongruity.

II

The traditions concerning Pythagoras are more complex, but the same general pattern may be discerned. Within the scope of this essay, I shall focus on the theme of understanding and misunderstanding within Iamblichus', *Vita Pythagorica*.[18]

The text begins with the declaration that "this book concerns the divine Pythagoras" (1, pg. 5,2). A declaration that demonstrates that, as in the case of the superscription in Mark 1.1, the purpose

---

[18] I have cited Iamblichus according to the text edited by L. Deubner, *De Vita Pythagorica liber* (Leipzig, 1937). Compare the rather free, English translation by T. Taylor, *Iamblichus' Life of Pythagoras* (London, 1818). For the purpose of this paper, I have ignored a number of critical source problems in Iamblichus. Of special interest would be the vexed question of the degree to which Iamblichus is dependent upon an alleged biography of Pythagoras by Apollonius of Tyana!

of the work is not the gradual revelation of the divine nature of the protagonist—this is presumed from the beginning; but rather that its function is to play between a true and false understanding of this announcement on the part of *both* disciple and opponent.

The opening chapters, as in the *Vita Apollonii*, are given over to a set of conflicting birth stories.[19] Iamblichus presents a moralistic interpretation which stands, at times, in marked tension to the traditions he preserves. The progenitor of Pythagoras "it is said, was conceived by Zeus" which Iamblichus glosses "this was said either because of his virtues or his greatness of soul" (3, pg. 6, 5-7). It was "said" that Pythagoras was "conceived by Apollo" and it was because of this "nobility of birth" that a Samian poet refers to "Pythagoras whom Pythias bore to Apollo" (5, pg. 7, 5-8). He was educated in a way that made him "like a god". Although still young when his father died, he was reverenced by his elders because of his virtues—therefore "it was reasonable to call him the son of a god". His "divine nature" was exhibited in his virtues: his piety, his lack of anger and other violent emotions, his rational self-discipline. Hence it may be said that he lived at Samos as an ἀγαθὸς δαίμων (10, pg. 8, 20-30).

In offering these moralistic glosses on the traditions concerning Pythagoras as a son of god, Iamblichus is combatting what he considers to be the misunderstanding of Epimenedes, Eudoxus and Xenocrates that Apollo had sexual intercourse with Pythagoras' mother (7, pg. 7, 22-24). The text reveals considerable tension and is probably deliberately ambiguous (5, pg. 7, 9-23). The story is a version of the well-known literary motif and cultic fact of a childless couple visiting the oracle at Delphi and the subsequent birth of a *Wunderkind*.

Mnesarchus went to Delphi, in Iamblichus' version, on a business trip accompanied by his wife who was not aware that she was pregnant. He asked the Pythia about the success of his commercial travels to Syria. He received the prophecy that his venture would be successful and the additional oracle that his wife was now pregnant and would bear a wonderful child of surpassing beauty and

---

[19] Note that Diogenes Laertius (VIII.1,4) has organized his collection of traditions concerning Pythagoras' birth in a manner which more closely resembles that found in the *Vita Apollorii*—a set of conflicting birth-stories followed by an enigmatic self-testimony. I would take the intrusive material (VIII.2f.) to be the result of his editorial breaking of the form.

wisdom. When Mnesarchus reflected on the fact that the Pythia, without being asked, had volunteered the prediction that he would have a son possessing divine gifts, he named the child Pythagoras (i.e. "announced by the Pythia" ἀγορεύων τὸν Πύθιον)[20] and changed his wife's name from Parthenis (i.e. "virgin") to Pythais in honor of the oracle. Iamblichus hastened to add that one is not to think of physical intercourse.

Those whom he is combatting take the alternative understanding of the story. Pythagoras' mother was not pregnant at the time of the visit to Delphi. She became so as a result of the virgin having intercourse with Apollo (Παρθενίδι ... μιγῆναι τὸν 'Απόλλωνα). For Iamblichus, such an understanding is crude superstition and is a misunderstanding of the true nature of Pythagoras' divinity. It is to be rejected as was the reverence paid by superstitious sailors with whom Pythagoras travelled who took him for a god, built an altar to him and offered sacrifices (15-17, pp. 11, 24-12, 26; compare Acts 14:11f.). It is to such a misunderstanding that Iamblichus juxtaposes a euhemeristic or moralistic interpretation. Pythagoras was called divine because of his virtues and conduct.

If Iamblichus is concerned to combat this outsider's misinterpretation, he is equally concerned with the misinterpretation of the insider, one who belongs to that outer circle of disciples whom he calls the *Akousmatikoi* and to whom he denies the title of "true Pythagoreans".[21] Two themes predominate in their interpretation, both of which are strikingly parallel to elements in the lives of other sons of god such as Jesus and Apollonius: a variety of titles which are projected upon the figure in an attempt to 'locate' him and an interpretation of his divinity in terms of wonders and miracles.

The multiple titles play an analogous role to the multiple birth-stories. A chain of conflicting or competing testimony is capped by an enigmatic identification or self-testimony (compare John 1:19-23).

> Some of them [the *Akousmatikoi*] spoke of him as the Pythian [Apollo], others as the Hyperborean Apollo, others as [Apollo] Paean. Still others thought him to be one of the *daimons* who inhabit the moon, others considered him to be one of the Olympian gods who sometimes appear to men in human form. (30, pg. 18, 12-17)

[20] See the discussion in M. Delcourt, *L'oracle de Delphes* (Paris, 1955),pp. 235-239.

[21] Within the scope of this paper, it is not necessary to discuss the vexing question of the relationship between the *Akousmatikoi* and the *Mathēmatikoi*—on which, see W. Burkert, *Lore and Science in Ancient Pythagoreanism* (Cambridge, Mass., 1972), pp. 192-208. I have followed Iamblichus' polemical interpretation.

To such speculations, Iamblichus juxtaposes the insiders' interpretation—one of the traditions of the *Mathēmatikoi* or "true Pythagoreans" as preserved by Aristotle:

> Aristotle relates in his work on Pythagorean Philosophy that the following division was preserved by the Pythagoreans as one of their greatest secrets—that there are three kinds of rational, living creatures: gods, men and beings like Pythagoras (31, pg. 18, 12-16 = Aristotle, Fragment 192 [Rose]).[22]

Pythagoras, rightly understood, is *sui generis*, he is in a class by himself. It is a misunderstanding to classify Pythagoras either as a man (especially as a mere "magician") or as a god. Rather he is the mysterious 'included middle'. The history of the misunderstanding of Pythagoras could be written, in Iamblichus' view, from the same perspective as a history of Christian heresy, i.e., the emphasis on either the godhood or the manhood of the son of god and the failure to assert the *tertium quid*.

There are those who exhibit one pole of this misunderstanding and relate Pythagoras to a variety of deities as an epiphany; there are those who focus too much upon the other pole and, conceiving of him as a man, narrate his miracles and thus run the risk of preceiving him as a magician and a fraud.[23]

The miracles of Pythagoras form a somewhat fixed catalogue which is capable of an independent, contextless circulation in paradoxographical collections such as Apollonius, *Historia thaumasiai* 6 or Aelian, *Varia historia* II.26 and IV.17.[24] The most commonly recurring motifs are: (1) At the same hour Pythagoras was seen in two cities; (2) he had a golden thigh; (3) he told a Crotanite that in a previous existence he had been King Midas; (4) a white eagle permitted him to stroke it—in other versions, he converted a wild bear to vegetarianism or persuaded an ox to abstain from eating beans; (5) a river greeted him, "Hail, Pythagoras!"; (6) he predicted that a dead man would be found on a ship which was just then enter-

---

[22] Compare Iamblichus 144, pg. 80, 25f. "[they say that] man, bird and another third thing are bipeds—and the third thing is Pythagoras"; a play on the "man is a featherless biped" tradition, and the Scholion in Homer, Il. A.340 (G. Dindorf, *Scholia graeca in Homeri Iliadem* [Oxford, 1875-1877], Vol. III): "The Pythagoreans posited alongside God and Man a distinct third class (τρίτον γένος) in their reverence for the King or Wise Man."

[23] See Lucian, *Alexander* 4.

[24] For an excellent discussion and rich bibliography, see Burkert, pp. 141-147. The collection apparently derives from Aristotle's lost work on the Pythagoreans.

ing the harbor; (7) when asked for a sign, he predicted the appearance of a white bear before a messenger reached him bearing the news; (8) he bit a poisonous snake to death—in a more rationalistic version, he drove out a snake from a village. These stories are all presented without interpretation or explanation. They hint at the divine, the numinous, the ability to control the animal, the power of transcending space and time. But they do not define Pythagoras' divinity. "There is always something enigmatic about the meaning of these miracles ... explicitness is avoided".[25] They are hints; but they do not serve to prove or to demonstrate. Indeed, in a manner analogous to the ending of the Fourth Gospel (Jn. 20.30f.), Iamblichus relativises their importance. They are outsiders' stories, they speak only περὶ τἀνδρός:

> Ten thousand other more divine and more wondrous things than these are related concerning the man by every source such as the prediction of earthquakes, the expelling of plagues and violent winds and the calming of rivers and seas so that his disciples may more easily pass over them. And similar wonders are narrated of others such as Empedocles, Epimenedes and Abaris ... But these [that I have narrated] are sufficient as an indication of his piety (135, pp. 76, 19-77, 13).

and immediately Iamblichus turns to a 'higher' mode of discourse, characteristic of the *Mathēmatikoi*, which includes a complex discussion of the modes of reality in mythological and miraculous tales (138-140, pp. 78, 14-79, 12).

While the details of this discussion are not germane to this paper, two anecdotes, each of which Iamblichus narrates *twice* during the course of this section on wonders, are revealing of the point of view of the "true" Pythagoreans towards signs and miracles.

> A shepherd feeding his flock near a tomb heard someone singing; but the Pythagorean to whom this was told was not at all incredulous, but asked what harmonic mode the song was in.
>
> Pythagoras, himself, was asked by a young man what was the significance of the fact that he had, while asleep, conversed with his dead father. Pythagoras said that "it signified nothing, for neither is anything signified by your talking to me". (Compare 139, pp. 78, 20-79, 3 and 148, pp. 83, 24-84, 7).

The miraculous is to be accepted as ordinary[26]; it has, in itself, no meaning unless it leads to insight or higher speculation. Each miracle

---

[25] Burkert, p. 144.
[26] Compare Aristotle, Fragment 193 [Rose], "The Pythagoreans marvelled at any city-dweller who said that he had never seen a *daimon*".

is unimportant if interpreted univocally as a sign of divinity; its value comes from the perception that it is a *double-entendre*.

The true understanding of Pythagoras is only hinted at by Iamblichus in a *double-recension* of the epiphany of Pythagoras. The first version (140-143) begins with one of the classic *akousmata*: "Who is Pythagoras? They say that he is the Hyperborean Apollo" (pg. 79, 13f.). In this version, which appears to be derived from Aristotle's rather credulous reporting of Pythagorean miracle-tales, "this is supposed to be proven" by two separate incidents: by Pythagoras accidentally showing his thigh while watching a dramatic performance and by his theft of the magic, gold arrow of Apollo from Abaris. The rest of the miracle-chain, discussed above, then follows. In this tradition, Pythagoras is the Hyperborean Apollo as demonstrated by his deeds.

Iamblichus' rejection of this understanding of Pythagoras depends upon his distinction between the *Akousmatikoi* and the *Mathēmatikoi* where the former are the outer circle of disciples, left with a set of enigmatic sayings (*akousmata*) and therefore lacking in true grounds for their beliefs.[27] It is from this outer circle that this misunderstanding derives. The nature of Pythagoras, for the *Mathēmatikoi*, cannot be disclosed or demonstrated from his miraculous deeds.

The second recension (90-94) is attributed by scholars to Nichomachus, who was a critic of "mere" miracle-stories. It is representative of the interpretation of the *Mathēmatikoi*. Far more complex than the previous tradition, it joins in a free composition the episode of the golden thigh and the encounter with Abaris. Both the accidental nature of the disclosure in the theatre and the crude power-play of Pythagoras' theft are eliminated in favor of a dignified self-disclosure by Pythagoras. It is the transfiguration of Pythagoras before an equally divine witness who will not misunderstand. (It is thus parallel to the role of the heavenly witnesses at Jesus' transfiguration in contradistinction to the disciples who misunderstand).

The relationship between Pythagoras and Abaris in this version is one of immediacy. At first sight, Abaris immediately recognizes Pythagoras' true nature. Even though Abaris is not learned in the Greek philosophical tradition, Pythagoras sets aside his usual lengthy

---

[17] Compare *Vita* 81-89 (pp. 46, 22-52, 19) with Iamblichus, *De communi mathematica scientia* 25 (N. Festa, editor [Leipzig, 1916], pp. 76, 16-78, 8), and see above, note 21.

regimen and "immediately considered him capable" of learning his most esoteric doctrines. Abaris mastered them within the smallest possible space of time (pg. 53, 4-7).

To summarize the narrative: While travelling through Italy on his return to the North, Abaris, a priest of the Hyperborean Apollo, "immediately on seeing Pythagoras thought him like the god (εἰκάσας τῷ θεῷ) whose priest he was. And believing that Pythagoras was none other than the god himself, that no man was like him, but that he was truly Apollo (καὶ πιστεύσας μὴ ἄλλον εἶναι, μηδὲ ἄνθρωπον ὅμοιον ἐκείνῳ, ἀλλ' αὐτὸν ὄντως τὸν 'Απόλλωνα)" Abaris gave him his golden arrow.[28] When Pythagoras received the miraculous arrow, he did not seem surprised nor did he inquire about it, but immediately, "as if he were the god himself (ὡς ἂν ὄντως ὁ θεὸς αὐτὸς ὤν)", he took Abaris aside and privately showed him his golden thigh as an indication that Abaris was not mistaken and that he had truly recognized him. Pythagoras declared that he had come on a mission of *therapeia* "and that it was for this reason that he had assumed human form (διὰ τοῦτο ἀνθρωπόμορφος) in order that men would not be disturbed by the strangeness of his transcendence (ἵνα μὴ ξενιζόμενοι πρὸς τὸ ὑπερέχον ταράσσωνται)". He then taught Abaris the esoteric, mathematical knowledge; but these things must remain secret (pp. 53, 10-54, 15).

For mere mortals, a figure like Pythagoras must remain a cipher. They will be "disturbed by his strangeness" but they cannot overcome it. They will either be reduced to misunderstandings or dark riddles or complex and paradoxical theories such as that offered by Iamblichus:

> No one can doubt that the psyche of Pythagoras was sent from the kingdom of Apollo, though whether [he is related to the deity] as an attendant (συνοπαδόν) or through a more direct interpenetration (συντεταγμένην) we cannot know. (8, pp. 7, 29-8, 1)

The only possible means of obtaining true knowledge is through the principle of like knowing like. Thus Abaris and Pythagoras; or, in the Fourth Gospel, the Father and the Son. But even in these cases, what has been recorded by men is opaque and doubtless has been misunderstood.

What an Apollonius, a Pythagoras, a Jesus reveals in the narratives concerning them, is their own enigmatic nature, their *sui generis*

---

[28] On the shamanistic elements in the Pythagoras-Abaris story, see M. Eliade, *Zalmoxis: The Vanishing God* (Chicago, 1972), pp. 21-75.

character. What was said by one of these sons of god might have been said by the others: "You will seek me and you will not find me, where I am you cannot come" (Jn 7:34)—a saying which was *misunderstood by opponent and disciple alike* (compare Jn 7:35f. with 13:33 and, even, the spurious Jn 21:18f. where it is reinterpreted, indeed misinterpreted, as a Passion-prediction of the disciples' suffering).

III

As I have already noted, conclusions quite similar to these have already been reached with respect to the lives of Jesus.[29] Mark, it has been suggested, is concerned with combatting a θεῖος ἀνήρ christology which focussed on Jesus' miracles; the disciples are represented as misunderstanding Jesus as being merely a divine man. The genre "gospel" is in the process of being redefined as a "reverse aretalogy".[30] I have tried to demonstrate that an analogous process is at work in Philostratus and Iamblichus. If we reserve the term "aretalogy" for those collections of model hagiographies and paradoxographies which are so widespread in the period of Late Antiquity, then I would want to reserve the term "gospel" for those works in which the adequacy of a magical or divine man interpretation of a son of god, in which the portrait of a life which can be imitated and the demonstration of divinity through miracles is relativized by the motif of misunderstanding and through the depiction of the protagonist as *sui generis*, as enigmatic and estranged. *A "gospel" is a narrative of a son of god who appears among men as a riddle inviting misunderstanding.* I would want to claim the title "gospel" for the *Vitae* attributed to Mark and John as well as for those by Philostratus and Iamblichus.

I would likewise relate my discussion of the content of the knowledge of the son of god transmitted by these "gospels" to the pioneering researches of Wayne Meeks on John. His description of the function of speech in the Fourth Gospel applies as well as to the materials studied in this paper:

---

[29] See above, note 15. However there remains in the New Testament discussion some lingering notion that this is unique, i.e. that the theme of misunderstanding represents a Christian correction of a hellenistic mode of understanding Jesus. I would want to insist that the juxtaposition of the enigma of the son of god with misunderstandings is precisely characteristic of all hellenistic "gospels".

[30] I have taken this notion from an unpublished paper by Norman Peterson, Jr., "So-called Gnostic Type Gospels and the Question of the Genre 'Gospel'," manuscript page 66: "a gospel is a sub-type of Aretalogy, perhaps a polemical parody [of an aretalogy]." Compare Bertolt Brecht's notion of *Gegenentwurf*.

The dialogue with Nicodemus and its postscript connected with John the Baptist constitute a virtual *parody* of a revelation discourse. What is 'revealed' is that Jesus is incomprehensible ... The forms of speech which would ordinarily provide warrants for a particular body of information or instruction are here used in such a way that they serve solely to emphasize Jesus' strangeness. Yet it is not quite accurate to say with Bultmann that Jesus reveals only that he is the revealer. He reveals rather that he is the enigma ... [Only the initiate] can possibly understand its double entendre and abrupt transitions. For the outsider—even for the interested inquirer (like Nicodemus)—the dialogue is opaque.[31]

While the theme of hostility to the world and the dualism heaven/world is not as pronounced in the Greco-Roman *Vitae* as it is in the Christian, this description would hold as well for Apollonius and Pythagoras. In both the Greco-Roman and the Christian "gospels" we encounter an essentially contentless revelation, we encounter a figure who speaks and acts in a *sui generis* manner which breaks all previous cosmic and social structures. The Christian "gospels" appear to shrink from the full consequences of this enigmatic disclosure by introducing the category of the future when all will be clear and when the disciple and the son will be reunited. The Greco-Roman materials relativise the enigma by placing it within a context of public, philosophical rhetoric. But both require on the part of their readers a perception of discrepancy between their understanding and the protagonist's self understanding.

IV

I should like to conclude with one further set of reflections lest what I have written be misunderstood in a manner characteristic of New Testament theologians. I am not describing a shift from myth (i.e. "aretalogy") to *kerygma* or a process of existential demythologization. I would want to insist, as an historian of religions, that what I have attempted to describe is thoroughly consistent with a proper understanding of myth. I should like to affirm some 'hard-nosed' statements about myth—that it is a "category mistake" (Ryle) and that it is "that which gives wordly objectivity to that which is otherworldly" (Bultmann)—and reject some 'softer' statements such as those associated with the Frankfurt School which seek to maintain a distinction between the primal moment of myth as *Ergriffenheit*

---

[31] W. Meeks, "The Man from Heaven in Johannine Sectarianism," *Journal of Biblical Literature*, XCI (1972), 44-72. I have taken the quotation from page 57.

and a secondary application. I would propose that there is no such category as "pristine" myth but only application and that this application derives from the character of myth as a self-conscious category mistake. That is to say that the discrepancy of myth is not an error but the very source of its power.

My understanding of the nature of application has been much influenced by recent anthropological studies of divination. The diviner, by manipulating a limited number of objects and by rigorously interrogating his client in order to determine his "situation" arrives at a description of a possible world of meaning which confers significance on his client's question or distress. The diviner offers a plausibility structure, he suggests a possible "fit" between the structure he offers and the client's situation and both the diviner and his client delight in exploring the adequacy, the possibilities and implications of the diviner's proposal.[32]

Myth as narrative, I would suggest, is an analogue to the limited number of objects manipulated by the diviner. Myth as application represents the complex interaction between diviner, client and "situation". There is delight and there is play in both the 'fit' and the incongruity of the 'fit', between an element in the myth and this or that segment of the world that one has encountered. Myth, properly understood, must take into account the complex processes of application and inapplicability, of congruity and incongruity. Myth shares with other genres such as the joke, the riddle and the "gospel" a perception of a possible relation between two different 'things' and it delights in the play in-between.

We have need of a rhetoric of incongruity which would explore the range from joke to paradox, from riddle-contest to myth and the modes of transcendence, freedom and play each employs. The "gospel" as I have described it stands in the closest relation to the joke which has been recently described by Mary Douglas as:

> A play upon form. It brings into relation disparate elements in such a way that one accepted pattern is challenged by the appearance of another which in some way was hidden in the first ... The joke affords opportunity for realizing that an accepted pattern has no necessity. Its excitement lies in the suggestion that any particular ordering of experience may be arbitrary and subjective. It is frivo-

---

[32] For example, V. Turner, *Ndembu Divination: Its Symbolism and Techniques* (Manchester, 1961).

lous in that it produces no real alternative, only an exhilarating sense of freedom from form in general.[33]

Given the religious situation which confronted the man of late antiquity, which described a world in which the archaic structures of order and destiny were discovered to be evil, confining and untrue, in which man strove to be free from being 'placed', such frivolity is, in fact, transcendence.[34]

---

[33] M. Douglas, "The Social Control of Cognition: Some Factors in Joke Perception," *Man*, n.s. III (1968), 365.

[34] See J. Z. Smith, "Birth Upside Down or Rightside Up?" chapter 7, above; "The Wobbling Pivot," chapter 4, above; "The Influence of Symbols upon Social Change: A Place on Which to Stand," chapter 6, above.

CHAPTER TEN

WHEN THE BOUGH BREAKS

> I was about to observe when I lost my way in this parenthesis....
> J. G. Frazer, January 26, 1927

One of the most famous modern deathbed scenes is that reported of Gertrude Stein when she raised herself up from her bed and asked her faithful companion, Alice B. Toklas, "What is the answer?" When Toklas responded, "There is no answer," Stein sank back and murmured, "Then there is no question!" There is a compelling logic to this exchange. We have become accustomed, as scholars, to perceiving the degree to which the questions we ask predetermine our answers. But Stein has raised another sort of issue: If there are no answers, then there have been no questions. Perhaps the most massive illustration of the "Stein principle" is James George Frazer's, *The Golden Bough*.[1]

It is no simple task to isolate the "questions" Frazer sought to "answer" in *The Golden Bough*, as there was a steady expansion of the number of questions and an enlargement of his understanding of the scope of his work in each successive edition.

In the first edition of *The Golden Bough*, published in 1890, Frazer set a fairly limited "question". He wrote that "for some time I have been preparing a general work on primitive superstition and religion," that his attention was caught by "the hitherto unexplained rule of the Arician priesthood," and that he had decided to attempt to account for this institution and "propose an explanation of the rule in question." Thus the first edition was conceived by Frazer as an answer to the question of "the meaning and origin of an ancient Italian priesthood" and not as a general discussion of primitive religion. He had "resolved to develop it fully and, detaching it from my general work, to issue it as a separate study. This book is the result."[2] In accord with this modest view of the scope of his work,

---

[1] I have used the following abbreviations for the various editions of *The Golden Bough*: GB^1, 1st ed. (London, 1890), Vols. I-II; GB^2, 2d ed. (London, 1900), Vols. I-III; GB^3, 3d ed. (London, 1911-1915), Vols. I-XII; GB^a, abridged ed. (London, 1922).

[2] GB^1, "Preface," reprinted in GB^3, Vol. I, pp. xi-xii.

Frazer entitled the first edition, *The Golden Bough: A Study in Comparative Religion*.

The first edition was conceived as a study of one religious institution and attempted to answer two questions: "Why had the priest of Nemi (Aricia) to slay his predecessor? And why, before doing so, had he to pluck the Golden Bough?"[3] It was in answer to these two questions that the four chapters of closely packed comparative material which comprise the first edition of *The Golden Bough* were written.[4]

With the publication of the second edition in 1900, Frazer expanded the material covered while retaining the original format of four chapters. The work was issued in three volumes, and most of the additions were new examples rather than new interpretations or hypotheses. One significant change was made. The work was now entitled *The Golden Bough: A Study in Magic and Religion*.[5] Frazer still maintained that he has set out to perform a limited task:

> As the scope and purpose of my book have been seriously misconceived by some courteous critics, I desire to repeat in more explicit language what I had vainly thought I had made quite clear in my original preface, that this is not a general treatise on primitive superstition, but merely the investigation of one particular and narrowly limited problem, to wit, the rule of the Arician priesthood, and that accordingly only such general principles are explained and illustrated in the course of it as seemed to me to throw light on that special question.[6]

Frazer continued to hold out hope for the completion of the "general work" alluded to in his first edition, but there is the clear implication that he may never finish it.[7] Again Frazer offered the same two questions—why the priest at Aricia had to slay his predecessor and why he first had to pluck the golden bough—as the central questions he has sought to answer.[8]

The third edition of *The Golden Bough* was announced in a prospectus published in 1907, although parts of the new edition were

---

[3] GB^1, Vol. II, p. 223.

[4] The four chapters of the original edition constitute the "core" of *The Golden Bough* in all its forms: "The King of the Wood," "Taboo and the Perils of the Soul," "Killing the God," and "The Golden Bough."

[5] Frazer had become convinced of the distinction between magic and religion and introduced a new section to the first chapter in which he developed the dichotomy (GB^2, Vol. I, pp. 7-128). The distinction, for which Frazer is most famous, is, in fact, a digression from his announced theme.

[6] GB^2, "Preface," reprinted in GB^3, Vol. I, p. xxi.

[7] *Ibid.*

[8] GB^2, Vol. III, p. 201.

already published in 1905. In 1911-1915, the familiar twelve-volume set was issued. In the third edition, Frazer's understanding of his purpose had radically shifted:

> When I originally conceived the idea of the work ... my intention merely was to explain the strange rule of the priesthood or sacred kingship of Nemi and with it the legend of the Golden Bough. ... But I soon found that in attempting to settle one question I had raised many more: wider and wider prospects opened out before me; and thus step by step I was lured on into far-spreading fields of primitive thought. ... Thus the book grew in my hands, and soon the projected essay became in fact a ponderous treatise, or rather a series of separate dissertations loosely linked together by a slender thread of connexion with my original subject. With each successive edition these dissertations have grown in number and swollen in bulk by the accretion of fresh materials, till the thread on which they are strung at last threatened to snap under their weight. Accordingly, following the hint of a friendly critic,[9] I have decided to resolve my overgrown book into its elements, and to publish separately the various disquisitions of which it is composed.[10]

The Arician priesthood and the reason for entitling his work *The Golden Bough* have receded into the background: "Should my whole theory of this particular priesthood collapse ... its fall would hardly shake *my general conclusions as to the evolution of primitive religion and society*."[11] The third edition of *The Golden Bough* had become the "general work on primitive superstition and religion" mentioned in the "Preface" to the first edition.

While Frazer repeated the same two questions as to the reason for the priest slaying his predecessor and his need to pluck the golden bough,[12] they are no longer of importance. The question of the interpretation of a puzzling ritual had become a question of style and literary tactics:

> But while I have thus sought to dispose my book in its proper form as a collection of essays on a variety of distinct, though related, topics, I have at the same time preserved its unity, as far as possible, by retaining the original title for the whole series of volumes, and by pointing out from time to time the bearing of my general conclusions on the particular problem which furnished the starting point of the enquiry.

---

[9] The "friendly critic" is most probably Joseph Jacobs who reviewed GB^1 in a collective review, "Recent Researches in Comparative Religion," *Folk-Lore*, I (1890), 393f.
[10] GB^3, Vol. I, pp. vii-viii.
[11] GB^3, Vol. I, p. ix (emphasis mine).
[12] GB^3, Vol. X, p. 1.

> It seemed to me that this mode of presenting the subject offered some advantages which outweighed certain obvious drawbacks. By discarding the austere form, without, I hope, sacrificing the solid substance of a scientific treatise, I thought to cast my materials into a more artistic mould and so perhaps to attract readers. ... Thus I put the mysterious priest of Nemi, so to say, in the forefront of the picture ... because the picturesque natural surroundings of the priest of Nemi among the wooded hills of Italy, the very mystery which enshrouds him, and not least the haunting magic of Virgil's verse, all combine to shed a glamour on the tragic figure with the Golden Bough, which fits him to stand as the centre of a gloomy canvas.[13]

Three years later, when Frazer penned the "Preface" to the final volume of the third edition, the priest of Nemi was removed finally and inalterably from even the diminished status granted him at the beginning of the work:

> Balder the Beautiful in my hands is little more than a stalking-horse to carry two heavy pack-loads of facts. And what is true of Balder applies equally to the priest of Nemi himself, the *nominal hero* of the long tragedy of human folly and suffering which has unrolled itself before the readers of these volumes, and on which the curtain is now about to fall. He, too, for all the quaint garb which he wears and the gravity with which he stalks across the stage, *is merely a puppet*, and it is time to unmask him before laying him up in the box. To drop the metaphor, *while nominally investigating a particular problem of ancient mythology, I have really been discussing questions of more general interest which concern the gradual evolution of human thought from savagery to civilisation.*[14]

As this remarkable confession explicitly states, what appeared to be the question of *The Golden Bough* was, in fact, not the question.

Nevertheless, in 1922 when Frazer issued his abridged edition of *The Golden Bough*, he ignored this reversal. He noted that the original work had grown from two to twelve volumes, which had led him to discuss "certain more general questions" but, he insisted, "the primary aim of this book is to explain the remarkable rule which regulated the succession to the priesthood of Diana at Aricia."[15]

In 1936, in *Aftermath: A Supplement to the Golden Bough*, Frazer returned to the sentiments of the third edition: "When I first put pen to paper to write *The Golden Bough* I had no conception of the magnitude of the voyage on which I was embarking; I thought only to explain a single rule of an ancient Italian priesthood. But

---

[13] *GB*³, Vol. I, pp. vii-ix.
[14] *GB*³, Vol. X, p. vi (emphasis mine).
[15] *GB*ᵃ, p. v.

insensibly I was led on, step by step, into surveying, as from some specular height, some Pisgah of the mind, a great part of the human race."[16] In this apocalyptic mood, the concern for Nemi was transcended and is mentioned only once in the subsequent pages.[17]

This brief survey of the fortunes of the priest of Nemi within the various editions of *The Golden Bough* has shown that he is alleged to be the chief concern of the work in the first, second, and abridged editions; he is no longer an important concern in the third edition and in *Aftermath*. But, whether or not the Arician priesthood is claimed to be the central topic, Frazer began and ended each edition of *The Golden Bough* with the same two questions and claimed that the data set forth was relevant to their answer: "Why had the priest of Nemi (Aricia) to slay his predecessor? And why, before doing so, had he to pluck the Golden Bough? The rest of this book will be an attempt to answer these questions."[18] It is with the priesthood at Nemi and these two questions that one must start in attempting to determine (regardless of Frazer's own varying estimate) whether or not Frazer sought to answer a "real" question.

THE PORTRAIT OF THE PRIEST

In its original form, Frazer's study of the priesthood of Nemi was probably intended as one of a series of articles Frazer wrote between 1887 and 1893 in which he took a curious custom or a puzzling line from classical sources and attempted to elucidate it with cross-cultural parallels. Although occasionally longer, these were usually one- or two-page notes. Indeed, the initial presentation of Nemi's priest in the first and second editions of *The Golden Bough* occupied only six pages; by the third edition, the section had grown to forty-three pages.[19] We are introduced to Nemi by one of Frazer's verbal

---

[16] J. G. Frazer, *Aftermath* (London, 1936), p. vi.
[17] *Ibid.*, pp. 309f.
[18] GB^1, Vol. I, p. 6, Vol. II, p. 223; GB^2, Vol. I, p. 6, Vol. III, p. 201; GB^3, Vol. I, p. 44, Vol. X, p. 1; GB^a, pp. 9, 592. The version in GB^3, Vol. I, p. 44, is more complex and attempts to outline the entire work: "The questions which we have set ourselves to answer are mainly two: first, why had Diana's priest at Nemi, the King of the Wood, to slay his predecessor? second, why before doing so had he to pluck the branch of a certain tree which the public opinion of the ancients identified with Virgil's Golden Bough? The two questions are to some extent distinct, and it will be convenient to consider them separately. We begin with the first, which, with the preliminary enquiries will occupy this and several following volumes. In the last part of the book I shall suggest an answer to the second question."
[19] GB^1, Vol. I, pp. 1-6; GB^2, Vol. I, pp. 1-6; GB^3, Vol. I, pp. 1-43.

landscape portraits with eerie, Gothic elements: "In antiquity this sylvan landscape was the scene of a strange recurring tragedy" where there was practiced a custom "which seems to transport us at once from civilisation to savagery," a scene of "dark crimes which under the mask of religion were often perpetrated there."[20] Frazer's description of the principals in this "crime" has become justly famous as a masterful example of Victorian purple prose:

> In the sacred grove there grew a certain tree round which at any time of the day, and probably far into the night, a grim figure might be seen to prowl. *In his hand he carried a drawn sword, and he kept peering warily about him as if at every instant he expected to be set upon by an enemy. He was a priest and a murderer; and the man for whom he looked* was sooner or later to murder him and hold the priesthood in his stead. Such was the rule of the sanctuary. A candidate for the priesthood could only succeed to the office by slaying the priest, and having slain him, he retained office till he was himself slain by a stronger or a craftier.
>
> The post by which he held this precarious tenure carried with it the title of king; but surely no crowned head ever lay uneasier or was visited by more evil dreams than his. For year in and year out, in summer and winter, in fair weather and in foul, he had to keep his lonely watch, and whenever he snatched a troubled slumber it was at the peril of his life. The least relaxation of his vigilance, the smallest abatement of his strength of limb or skill of fence, put him in jeopardy; gray hairs might seal his death warrant. His eyes probably acquired that restless, watchful look which, among the Esquimaux of Bering Strait, is said to betray infallibly the shedder of blood; for with that people revenge is a sacred duty, the manslayer carries his life in his hand. To gentle and pious pilgrims at the shrine, the sight of him might well seem to darken the fair landscape, as when a cloud suddenly blots out the sun on a bright day. The dreamy blue of Italian skies, the dappled shade of summer woods, and the sparkle of waves in the sun, can have accorded but ill with that stern and sinister figure. Rather we picture to ourselves the scene as it may have been witnessed by a belated wayfarer on one of those wild autumn nights when the dead leaves are falling thick and the winds seem to sing the dirge of the dying year. It is a sombre picture—set to melancholy music—the background of the forest showing black and jagged against a lowering and stormy sky, the sighing of the wind in the branches, the rustle of withered leaves underfoot, the lapping of the cold water on the shore, and in twilight and now in gloom, a dark figure with a glitter of steel at the shoulder whenever the pale moon, riding clear of the cloud-rack, peers down at him through the matted boughs.[21]

---

[20] *GB³*, Vol. I, pp. 1, 8.
[21] *GB³*, Vol. I, pp. 8-10 (emphasis mine).

This portrait, consisting of four hundred and sixty-six words, has been retained with little variation in all editions of *The Golden Bough*.[22] It is a remarkable "imaginary portrait." More than half of the description is romantic nature prose-poetry derived entirely from Frazer's fancy. The mimetic art of the narrator is such that the reader is lulled into believing that Frazer has actually glimpsed the furtive figure. One forgets Frazer's own hypothetical language— "*we picture to ourselves* the scene as *it may have* been witnessed," "he kept peering about . . . *as if* . . . he expected to be set upon," "his eyes *probably* acquired that restless watchful look," "the sight of him *might well seem* to darken the fair landscape"—and fails to ask how Frazer knew this "grim figure's" dreams and emotions.

Frazer's sole reference for this lengthy description is Strabo *Geography* V.3.12, which is a model of verbal economy, consisting of only seventeen words in the Greek original: "He is appointed priest who, being a runaway slave, has managed to murder the man who was priest before him; he is always armed with a sword, keeping watch against attacks and ready to ward them off."[23] Strabo can be held responsible for only a tenth of Frazer's portrait (italicized in the quotation above), the remainder is Frazer's own imaginative reconstruction ("we picture to ourselves") without any textual or historical warrant.

Three motifs are present in Frazer's initial description: (1) A runaway slave becomes priest by slaying the previous priest and then remains on guard against being attacked and slain by his successor. (2) The priest guards a tree or circles around it. (3) The priest receives the title of king. The first motif is largely explicit in Strabo's account. The second and third motifs of tree and king are not even hinted at in Strabo.

---

[22] *GB*[1], Vol. I, pp. 2f.; *GB*[2], Vol. I, pp. 2f.; *GB*[a], pp. 1f. In *GB*[1, 2] the Eskimo analogy is omitted. In J. G. Frazer, *Lectures on the Early History of Kingship* (London, 1905), p. 16, a shorter version is given. The *Lectures* may be considered a "first draft" of portions of *GB*[3], Vols. I-II.

[23] I have followed the translation of H. L. Jones, *The Geography of Strabo* (London, 1949), Vol. II, pp. 422f. In *GB*[3], Vol. I, p. 9, n. 1, and *Lectures*, p. 16, Frazer appears to consider Strabo to have been an eyewitness to the Nemi scene. There is one ambiguity in the text. The "attacks" (*epitheseis*) may be read as (1) attacks against the priest from which he was protecting himself; or (2) that the priest was protecting the grove against trespassers or sacrilege (see J. Fontenrose, *The Ritual Theory of Myth* [Berkeley-Los Angeles, 1966], pp. 38-44). Frazer's interpretation appears to be more likely.

The Tree and the Bough

On the page following his initial description, Frazer acknowledged his additional sources.[24] The only Greek or Latin reference to the tree which plays such a major role in Frazer's description is the same source which provided Frazer with his only evidence for the identification of this tree with Virgil's golden bough—a scholion by the fourth century (A.D.) writer, Servius (*ad Aeneid* VI.136).

> In the shady tree the gold [branch] lays hidden. Although those [people] who are said to have written about the sacred things of Proserpine assert concerning this branch that it is something related to the mysteries, nevertheless a common notion has it that Orestes, after the slaying of king Thoas, fled into the Tauric region with his sister Iphigenia, as we have said above, and, not very far from Aricia, erected the statue of Diana carried from there. After the rite of the sacrifice had been changed, there was a certain tree in this temple from which it was forbidden to break off a branch. However a power was granted to fugitives so that if anyone were able to carry away a branch from that place, he would contend with the fugitive-priest in a duel—for there was a fugitive-priest there before the image of the ancient flight. The office of fighting was given, however, as a sort of substitution of the ancient sacrifice. Now therefore, it took from here this shade of meaning and it was inevitable that the branch would be the cause of the death of someone: hence it immediately connects with the death of Misenus, and one was not able to approach the sacred [rites] of Proserpine without the carried-away branch. Moreover to celebrate the sacred [rites] of Proserpine means this: to go down to the Underworld. However, concerning the return of the soul, there is this: we know that Pythagoras of Samos divided human life in the form of the letter Υ because the first period [of life] is undetermined and is given to neither vices nor virtues. The juncture point of the letter Υ begins at youth, at which time men either follow vices (i.e., the left part) or virtues (i.e., the right part). Hence Persius says that he guides troubled minds at the meeting point of the branches. Therefore he says that by the branch, which is the imitation of the letter Υ the virtues are to be striven for. This [branch] lays hidden in the forest because, in fact, virtue and integrity lay concealed in the confusion of this life in the greater part of vices. Others say that the underworld is sought by means of the golden branch because mortals easily perish in riches. Tiberianus [says]: Gold by which bribe the thresholds of wealth are opened.[25]

---

[24] *GB*³, Vol. I, p. 11, n. 1.

[25] G. Thilo-H. Hagen, *Servii Grammatici qui feruntut in Vergilii carmina commentarii* (Leipzig, 1881; reprinted Hildesheim, 1961), Vol. II, pp. 30f. As to my knowledge there has been no previous translation of this passage, I have striven for a literal rather than literary translation. It is significant that this text, which is crucial for Frazer's argument, is one of the few classical texts which he fails to translate.

In this passage, Servius records four interpretations of the golden bough in the *Aeneid* VI.136-138. (1) A cultic interpretation which relates the branch to the mysteries of Proserpine by maintaining that Aeneas' entry into the Underworld is equivalent to initiation into the rites of Proserpine. None enters these rites without a branch, hence Aeneas is given a sacred bough.[26] (2) The second interpretation is described by Servius as a "common notion" (*publica opinio*),[27] which reports that near Aricia there was a statue of Diana and, within her precinct, a sacred tree from which no branch could be broken. The only exception to this regulation was that if a fugitive could break off a branch, he could challenge the "fugitive-priest" to a duel. This combat substituted for the older rites of human sacrifice characteristic of Diana. (3) The third interpretation is a Pythagorean allegory on the letter Υ, its fork being understood as the two ways of virtue and vice which confront an individual after passing through the innocence of childhood. (4) The fourth interpretation is a moralistic one—men are brought to death (i.e., Proserpine's door) by riches. All of these interpretations are simply recorded by Servius without accepting any of them. His *own* interpretation of the golden bough was offered at an earlier point in his commentary—it is a *figmentum poeticum*.[28]

---

[26] That the sixth book of the *Aeneid* is initiatory has been held by a number of scholars, most famously by W. F. Jackson Knight, *Cumaean Gates: A Reference of the Sixth Aeneid to the Initiation Pattern* (Oxford, 1936), cf. K. Kerenyi, "Zum Verständnis von Vergilius Aeneis Buch VI," *Hermes*, LXVI (1931), 413-441; M. Bodkin, *Archetypal Patterns in Poetry* (Oxford, 1934), pp. 122-136, among others. It was brought into close association with the Eleusinian mysteries more than two centuries ago by W. Warburton, *The Divine Legation of Moses* (London, 1738), Vol. I, p. 182, and more recent scholars have suggested the parallel between the golden bough and the branches of myrtle or olive carried by the Eleusinian initiates (see F. Lenormant, "Eleusinia," in C. Daremberg-E. Saglio, *Dictionnaire des antiquités grecques et romaines* [Paris, 1873-1919], Vol. II, p. 570; E. Norden, *P. Vergilius Maro Aeneis Buch VI*, 2d ed. [Leipzig-Berlin, 1926], pp. 171-173).

[27] There has been some controversy as to the meaning of this term. Frazer rendered *publica opinio* as "the public opinion of the ancients" (*GB³*, Vol. I, pp. 11, 44). "the general or popular view" (*GB³*, Vol. XI, p. 284, n. 3), "the general opinion of antiquity" (*ibid.*), or "Italian tradition" (*GB³*, Vol. XI, p. 285, n. 2). R. S. Conway, *Harvard Lectures on the Vergilian Age* (Cambridge, Mass., 1928), p. 42, strongly objected and insisted on the translation "a common notion" (cf. Fontenrose, *The Ritual Theory of Myth*, p. 42). While I accept the Conway-Fontenrose translation, it should be noted that *publicus* carries the same nuances as *volgaris/volgatus* and may well bear Frazer's translation in the strict sense, though certainly not his implication of a well-known universal tradition.

[28] Servius, *ad Aeneid* III.46 (Thilo-Hagen, Vol. I, p. 344), cf. Cornutus in Macrobius, *Saturnalia* V.19.2.

Frazer chose only one of these interpretations (the second) and failed to mention the other three. He chose the only interpretation that has no explicit connection in Servius with the golden bough. This Frazer appears to recognize in his first mention of Servius' text: "The custom of breaking the branch and its *supposed connection* with the Golden Bough of Vergil, are recorded by Servius alone."[29] However, in all subsequent allusions to the tradition, the equation is baldly assumed. The Virgilian golden bough has completely replaced the mysterious "branch of a certain tree" and it is accepted, without argument, that the branch at Nemi was the golden bough of *Aeneid* VI.[30] There is no warrant for this in Servius or any other classical authority (indeed, Servius' phrase, *arbor quaedam de qua infringi ramum non licebat*, appears to apply to any branch on the forbidden tree; it clearly makes no mention of a golden bough).

The title, *The Golden Bough*, is a misnomer.[31] Frazer's massive work may, perhaps, be seen as an interpretation of the curious customs surrounding the priesthood at Nemi. It has nothing to do with the golden bough of the *Aeneid*. Indeed, Frazer's earlier "draft" of the third edition of *The Golden Bough*, his *Lectures on the Early History of Kingship* (in my opinion a far more successful work than its more famous successor), treats all of the data relevant to Nemi and cites most of Frazer's best anthropological parallels without once mentioning the Virgilian golden bough or the alleged identification of this bough with a branch of the tree at Nemi in Servius.

THE KING OF THE WOODS

Frazer's description of the scene at Nemi contained three motifs: (1) A runaway slave becomes priest at Nemi. As priest, he remains on guard against attacks by would-be successors. (2) The priest guards a tree or circles around it. (3) The priest bore the title of king. The first motif is based on Strabo and is confirmed by Pausanias' description of Aricia.[32] The presence of a tree has been deduced

---

[29] *GB*³, Vol. I, p. 11, n. 1 (emphasis mine).
[30] *GB*³, Vol. I, pp. 11, 44; Vol. X, pp. 1f.; Vol. XI, pp. 284f., 302f., 309.
[31] This was already stated by two of Frazer's earliest reviewers, A. B. Cook, "The Golden Bough and the Rex Nemorensis," *Classical Review*, XVI (1902), 380; and O. Gruppe, [Review of *GB*³, Parts I-II], *Berliner Philologische Wochenschrift*, XXXII (1912), 745.
[32] Pausanias II.xxvii.4 in the translation by W. H. S. Jones, *Pausanias' Description of Greece* (London, 1959), Vol. I, pp. 392f.: "[Aricia] where, down to my time, prizes of single combat are the victor's service to the goddess as priest; the contest is not open to any free men, but to slaves who have run away from

from Servius. Frazer's picture of the priest circling warily around the tree without sleep is based solely on Frazer's imagination, as is his notion that there was a particular bough (let alone, the golden bough!) which must be broken off by a challenger. Frazer offers five texts which he believed supported the fact that the *sacerdos* at Nemi bore the title *Rex* (or, more crucial for his argument, *Rex Nemorensis*).[33] One text clearly refers to the *Rex Nemorensis*;[34] three of the texts are brief, poetic allusions to a *Regis* in Aricia who gains his office by combat[35] and are thus analogous to the material cited from Strabo

their masters." The aetiological myth in Pausanias differs from that in Servius. Rather than Orestes being the founder of the practice after slaying Thoas as in Servius, Pausanias records that after Hippolytus was raised from the dead by Asclepius, he refused to forgive his father and departed to Aricia. There he became king and consecrated a temple to Artemis, whose priesthood was won by combat as in the quoted text. This story is widely known (e.g., Virgil *Aeneid* VII.761-782). Both are clearly late aetiologies and have little to do with the Arician practice as Andrew Lang already noted in his early review of *The Golden Bough* in *The Fortnightly Review*, n.s. LXXIII (1901), 236, and *Magic and Religion* (London, 1901), pp. 209, 218. Neither Orestes nor Hippolytus was a fugitive slave; Hippolytus never killed a predecessor; and Orestes' slaying of Aigisthos is scarcely a parallel.

[33] *GB*³, Vol. I, p. 11, n. 1.

[34] Suetonius *Caligula* 35 in the translation by J. C. Rolfe, *Suetonius* (London, 1913), Vol. I, pp. 458f.: "In short, there was no one of such low condition or such abject fortune that he [Caligula] did not envy him such advantages as he possessed. Since the King of the Grove at Nemi (*Nemorensi regi*) had now held his priesthood for many years, he hired a stronger adversary to attack him." I have altered Rolfe's translation of *Nemorensi regi* as "King of Nemi" to "King of the Grove at Nemi" as a happier version than Frazer's standard rendering "King of the Wood" (*GB*³, Vol. I, pp. 1, 40, 42, *passim*.) For a discussion of the translation of this title, see A. B. Cook, "The Golden Bough and the Rex Nemorensis," 379f.; and G. Wissowa, *Religion und Kultus der Römer*, 1st. ed. (Munich, 1902), p. 199, n. 3. For a recent discussion of the passage in Suetonius, see A. Bernardi, "L'interesse di Caligola per la successione del rex Nemorensis e l'arcaica regalità nel Lazio," *Athenaeum*, n.s. XXI (1953), 273-287.

[35] (*a*) Ovid *Fasti* III.263f., 271f., in the translation by J. G. Frazer, *Ovid Fasti* (London, 1931), pp. 138-141: "In the Arician vale there is a lake begirt by shady woods and hallowed by religion from of old.... The strong of hand and fleet of foot do there reign kings, and each is slain thereafter even as himself had slain." See further Frazer's note (pp. 403-405) here and in his large edition (*The Fasti of Ovid* [London, 1927], Vol. III, pp. 72-87) which recapitulates the argument of *The Golden Bough*. The lines of Ovid are the source for the well-known passage in Macaulay's *Lays of Ancient Rome* which Frazer used as a frontispiece for *The Golden Bough*: "From the still glassy lake that sleeps/Beneath Aricia's trees—/Those trees in whose dim shadow/The ghastly priest doth reign./The priest who slew the slayer,/And shall himself be slain." (*b*) The brief allusion in Ovid *Ars amatoria* I.259f. to the "temple of woodland Diana" where "the assassin and priest carries the sword in his hand." (*c*) The brief reference to the violent proceedings at Aricia in Valerius Flaccus *Argonautica* II.305.

and Pausanias; one text most likely has nothing to do with the custom.³⁶

In the opening chapter of *The Golden Bough*, Frazer painted a lengthy verbal portrait of the proceedings at Nemi. He cited nine classical authorities as his sources. In the first description (printed above) only Strabo was utilized, and this accounted for only a tenth of Frazer's reconstruction. The remainder was solely the product of Frazer's imagination. In a second, briefer, description, Frazer was less imaginative. He closely paraphrased four authors (Servius, Ovid, Suetonius, and Pausanias) in order to produce a composite portrait:

> *Within the sanctuary of Nemi grew a certain tree of which no branch might be broken. Only a runaway slave was allowed to break off, if he could, one of its boughs. Success in the attempt entitled him to fight the priest in single combat* and IF HE SLEW HIM, HE REIGNED IN HIS STEAD WITH THE TITLE KING OF THE WOOD (Rex Nemorensis). *According to the public opinion of the ancients the fateful branch was that Golden Bough which, at the Sibyl's bidding, Aeneas plucked before he essayed the perilous journey to the world of the dead. . . . This rule of succession by the sword was observed down to Imperial times;* for amongst his other freaks CALIGULA, THINKING THAT THE PRIEST OF NEMI HAD HELD OFFICE TOO LONG, HIRED A MORE STALWART RUFFIAN TO SLAY HIM, and a Greek traveller, who visited Italy in the age of the Antonines, remarks that *DOWN TO HIS TIME THE PRIESTHOOD WAS STILL THE PRIZE OF VICTORY IN A SINGLE COMBAT.*³⁷

As these observations suggest, in the opening pages of *The Golden Bough* Frazer was able to establish the custom of a violent succession to the priesthood at Nemi (Strabo, Servius, Pausanias, Ovid, Suetonius) and the use of the title "king" for the priest (Suetonius, Ovid, Valerius Flaccus). He was not successful in establishing any connection between the golden bough and the priesthood at Nemi. The bulk of his description was imaginative reconstruction without textual warrant.³⁸ The question that must be answered is why Frazer

---

[36] The reference in Statius *Silvae* III.i.55f. which refers to the grove of Diana in Aricia as a place suited for fleeing/fugitive/wandering/banished kings (*profugis cum regibus aptum*) most probably does not refer to the succession-combat but rather to the Arician legend that Orestes and Hippolytus found refuge there.

[37] *GB*³, Vol. I, p. 11. I have indicated the different sources used with different type: *Servius*, OVID, SUETONIUS, and *PAUSANIAS*.

[38] Frazer did not cease his invention of Arician details with the penning of the portrait of the priest at Nemi (see his imaginative interpretation of details on the double herm excavated in 1885 at Nemi in "The Leafy Bust at Nemi," *Classical Review*, XXII [1908], 147-149).

insisted on the identification of the golden bough of Virgil with the branch plucked from the tree at Nemi. In what sense was *The Golden Bough* actually concerned with the golden bough? Or, as already argued, was the title a misnomer? Was not, in fact, his work actually an attempt to explain the succession-combat of the *Rex Nemorensis*? We have already noted that Frazer's *Lectures on the Early History of Kingship* is *The Golden Bough in nuce* but that this work does not contain a single mention of Virgil's golden bough. The *Lectures* are, in their entirety, an attempt to interpret the succession-combat at Nemi through the use of anthropological parallels and utilize all of the characteristic Frazerian structures (e.g., the distinction between magic and religion, the evolution of the king from the magician and the god from the king, vegetation deities, and sacral regicide). The *Lectures* begin with the description and question of Nemi and end with a description of the violent contest for kingship in Calicut: "This is an Indian parallel to the priest of Nemi."[39] Even in *The Golden Bough* Virgil's bough plays little role, being mentioned only in the opening and closing chapters of the work.[40] In the period since the publication of *The Golden Bough*, a few scholars have accepted the identification,[41] most have flatly rejected it.[42] Ironically, a number

---

[39] Frazer, *Lectures*, p. 297.

[40] *GB*³, Vol. I, pp. 1-44; Vol. XI, pp. 284-309, 315-320. The golden bough is mentioned in passing in Vol. I, p. 123; Vol. II, p. 379; and Vol. X, p. 1.

[41] Most recently, the last of the Frazerians, E. O. James, *The Tree of Life* (Leiden, 1966), p. vii. The greatest Italian scholar of Aricia, L. Morpurgo, "Nemus Aricinum." *Monumenti antichi pubblicati delle Reale Accademia dei Lincei*, XIII (1903), esp. 364-366, rejected Frazer's interpretation but agrees that Servius did record a local custom identifying the golden bough with the branch at Nemi. (See further, F. Fletcher, *Virgil: Aeneid VI* [Oxford, 1941], p. 46: "Servius unaccountably associates it [the golden bough] with Aricia and Lake Nemi.... This suggestion, while of no value as a comment on Virgil, is of interest as having afforded a starting-point for Sir James Frazer's great anthropological work, *The Golden Bough*"; and H. J. Rose's confused article, "Nemi and the Golden Bough," in G. E. Daniels, *Myth or Legend* [London, 1955], pp. 117-125, esp. pp. 121-124, which accepts the identification and appears to accept much of Frazer's interpretation).

[42] For example, in O. Gruppe, *Berliner Philologische Wochenschrift*, XXXII (1912), esp. 746—the golden bough is a poetic figure; in E. Norden, *Aeneis Buch VI*, pp. 163-174, esp. p. 164, n. 1—a poetic figure; in R. S. Conway, *Harvard Lectures on the Vergilian Age*, pp. 41-45—a complex symbol of faith; in L. Herrmann, "Le rameau d'or et l'empereur Auguste," *Mélanges J. Bidez* (Brussels, 1934), pp. 487-494, esp. p. 487—a political symbol; in M. Bodkin, *Archetypal Patterns in Poetry*, pp. 129-136, esp. p. 130, 132—a symbol of mysterious power like *mana*; in G. Martin, "Golden Apples and Golden Boughs," *Studies Presented to D. M. Robertson* (Saint Louis, 1953), Vol. II, pp. 1191-1197, esp. p. 1191—a complex symbol (there is a relationship between Juno's golden apples as a means

of classicists have accepted one of Servius' interpretations—that the golden bough has something to do with the mysteries of Proserpine—an interpretation which Frazer completely ignored.[43]

THE ARGUMENT AND THE PARASITE

The clue to why Frazer so stubbornly insisted on his identification of the golden bough with the branch at Nemi is found in the *Aeneid* VI.205-211:

---

of entry into the upper world and a sign of the reign of the heavenly Juno and the golden bough as a means of entry into the lower world and a sign of the reign of Proserpine, *Juno infernae* [*Aeneid* VI.138]. She compares the combination of golden apples and golden tree in the underworld vision in Claudian, *De raptu Proserpinae* II.277-293); in L. Herrmann, "L'arbre aux rameaux d'or," *Mélanges G. Smets* (Brussels, 1952), pp. 400-406—a symbol not of death and resurrection but of the eternal succession of the Caesars; in R. A. Brooks, "*Discolor aura*: Reflections on the Golden Bough," *American Journal of Philology*, LXXIV (1953), 260-280, esp. 260, 269, 274f.—a complex symbol of tensions and antitheses. J. G. Préaux, "Virgile et le rameau d'or," *Hommages à G. Dumézil* (Brussels, 1960), pp. 151-167, calls attention to the magical and ritual uses of plants in quests for immortality (cf. A. K. Michels, "The Golden Bough of Plato," *American Journal of Philology*, LXVI [1945], 59-63, and R. Einarson, "Plato in Meleager's Garland," *Classical Philology*, XXXVIII [1943], 260f.). C. P. Segal, "*Aeternum per saecula nomen*: The Golden Bough and the Tragedy of History," *Arion*, IV (1965), 617-657; V (1966), 34-72, is a rich, symbolic analysis maintaining that the golden bough is a symbol which spans opposites, a paradoxical union of contradictions, a place between worlds (cf. the interpretation of Brooks, cited above). J. Fontenrose, *The Ritual Theory of Myth*, extremely critical of Frazer, offers no interpretation; C. P. Segal, "The Hesitation of the Golden Bough: A Reexamination," *Hermes*, XCVI (1968), 74-79, responds to J. H. D'Arms, "Vergil's *cunctantem (ramum)*," *Classical Journal*, LVI (1964), 265-267; and in W. T. Avery, "The Reluctant Golden Bough," *Classical Journal*, LXI (1966), 269-272, it is a magical token of mythic reality; in C. Kresic, "Le rameau d'or chez Virgile," *Classical News and Views*, XII (1968), 92-102, an excellent review of some previous theoreis and a symbolic interpretation.

T. H. Gaster, *The New Golden Bough* (New York, 1959), p. 668, offers a blunt but confused criticism: "The golden bough at Aricia has nothing whatsoever to do with that borne by Aeneus on his journey to the underworld." It is curious that Gaster seems to accept the fact that the branch at Nemi was a golden bough! Moreover, Gaster's criticism is in error: "Frazer has misunderstood the comment of Servius, the third century commentator on Vergil, who says that the bough of Aeneus was of the same color as that of Aricia." Servius says no such thing. He states that there was a custom at Aricia of slaying the priest, involving the breaking of a bough, and that from this custom Virgil may have taken the suggestion (*istum colorem sumpsit*) for his bough, hence it is appropriate that the death of Misenus followed. *Colorem* here has nothing to do with the hue of the bough!

[43] See esp. A. Buse, "De Vergilii ramo aureo," *Eos*, XXXIII (1930), 171-176; K. Kerenyi, "Zum Verständnis von Vergilius *Aeneis* Buch VI," *Hermes*, LXVI (1931), 413-441; H. Wagevoort, "De gouden tak," *Hermeneus*, XXXI (1959), 46-52, 72-79.

> Perched on the double tree, where the off-color
> Of gold was gleaming golden through the branches.
> As mistletoe, in the cold winter, blossoms
> With its strange foliage on an alien tree,
> The yellow berry gilding the smooth branches,
> Such was the vision of the gold in leaf
> On the dark holm-oak.[44]

It is the mistletoe which, in a cut designed by J. H. Middleton, has adorned the cover of each successive edition of *The Golden Bough*. It is the mistletoe which is, in fact, the botanical leitmotiv of the entire work.[45]

Frazer's earliest dated interest in mistletoe was in September 1889, one year before the publication of the first edition of *The Golden Bough*. Frazer had contributed one of his many brief reports on folk customs to the *Folk-Lore Journal*, this one concerning the practice of rolling Easter eggs, and concluded his note with the request that "the undersigned would be glad to hear of any superstitions, customs or beliefs about parasitic plants, especially the mistletoe."[46] In *The Golden Bough* the mistletoe served as the connecting link between all of these various elements in Frazer's theory. It is the one, indispensable assumption in the work. If the golden bough of Virgil is not mistletoe and if it is not to be identified with the branch at Nemi, *The Golden Bough* is shattered.[47]

The central thesis of Frazer's work was summarized in the "Preface" to *Balder the Beautiful*:

> If I am right, the Golden Bough over which the King of the Wood, Diana's priest at Aricia, kept watch and ward was no other than a branch of mistletoe growing on an oak within the sacred grove; and as the plucking of the bough was a necessary prelude to the slaughter of the priest, I have been led to institute a parallel between the King of the Wood at Nemi and the Norse god Balder. . . . On the theory

---

[44] R. Humphries, *The Aeneid of Virgil* (New York, 1951), p. 150.

[45] Perhaps this was subconsciously realized by the painter, G. F. Watts. While he was working on Alfred Lord Tennyson's portrait, the poet had read to him the first edition of *The Golden Bough*. "It is noticeable that the background of the portrait bears a pattern of mistletoe" (R. A. Downie, *James George Frazer: Portrait of a Scholar* [London, 1940], p. 20).

[46] J. G. Frazer, "May Day Customs," *Folk-Lore Journal*, VII (1889), 265.

[47] As A. Lang, *Magic and Religion*, p. 213, had already realized: "That Virgil's branch of gold was mistletoe, that the tree of Aricia was an oak, that the bough to be plucked . . . was mistletoe, seems (if I follow Mr. Frazer accurately) to be rather needful to the success of the solution of his problem which he finally propounds."

here suggested both Balder and the King of the Wood personified in a sense the sacred oak of our Aryan forefathers, and both had deposited their lives or souls for safety in the parasite.[48]

The main argument which led Frazer to this conclusion (eliminating the excurses which, in fact, occupy the bulk of the eleven volumes of *The Golden Bough*) consists of three main stages, each employing a number of conjectural equations, which may be outlined as follows:

Stage I
1. The golden bough of Virgil = the branch at Nemi
2. The golden bough of Virgil = mistletoe
3. Therefore the branch at Nemi = mistletoe
4. The tree in Virgil on which the golden bough grew = an oak
5. Therefore the tree at Nemi = an oak

Stage II
1. Before slaying the priest, the challenger at Nemi plucked a sacred branch (which, following the syllogism of Stage I, was mistletoe)
2. Balder was killed by a shaft of mistletoe
3. Therefore, the slaying of Balder = the slaying of the priest at Nemi

Stage III
1. Balder = the tree-spirit residing in the oak, his external soul resided in the mistletoe
2. The *Rex Nemorensis* = a personification of the oak-spirit
3. Both Balder and the *Rex Nemorensis* embody the vitality of plant life and must be slain before they grew old and this vitality became dissipated.[49]

Each stage of the argument must be considered in order.

I.1. On the first identification, that of Virgil's golden bough with the branch at Nemi, there is (as has already been demonstrated) no evidence. Frazer has gone far beyond the sense and context of Servius' commentary which was his sole support for this identification. With the rejection of this equation, *The Golden Bough* is broken.

---

[48] GB^3, Vol. X, p. v.

[49] Frazer offers two explanations of the parallelism of Balder and the priest of Nemi. (*a*) "As an oak-spirit, his life or death was in the mistletoe on the oak and so long as the mistletoe remained intact, he, like Balder, could not die. To slay him, therefore, it was necessary to break the mistletoe, and probably, as in the case of Balder, to throw it at him" (GB^2, Vol. III, p. 450; GB^3, Vol. XI, p. 285). There is no evidence for Frazer's conjecture that the branch was thrown at Nemi. (*b*) In GB^3 Frazer altered his interpretation, although he allowed his previous interpretation to stand (this palimpsest effect is characteristic of Frazer's writings). The mistletoe is not the "external soul" of Balder or the *Rex Nemorensis* but rather of the Aryan celestial Sky God (GB^3, Vol. X, p. x; Vol. XI, pp. 298-303).

I.2. On the second identification, that of Virgil's golden bough with mistletoe, it is undeniable that Virgil *compares* the bough with mistletoe in *Aeneid* VI.205-211 (quoted above). The question is whether an analogy can be understood as a statement of identity. Frazer held that the golden bough was not simply like mistletoe, it was mistletoe. Lacking any evidence for this bold identification, Frazer was unusually cautious. "It is not a new opinion that the Golden Bough was the mistletoe. True, Virgil does not identify but only compares it with mistletoe." Nevertheless, he argued, Virgil's comparison should be interpreted as an identification based on the popular belief that at times the mistletoe "blazed out in a supernatural golden glory." "The inference is almost inevitable that the Golden Bough was nothing but the mistletoe seen through the haze of poetry or of popular superstition."[50] Frazer modestly disclaims originality for his thesis that the golden bough and mistletoe are identical and cites several previous authorities which are not convincing.[51] The verdict of scholarship, with which I concur, may be summarized by Andrew Lang's brutally simple objection, "A poet does not compare a thing to itself."[52]

---

[50] *GB*³, Vol. XI, pp. 284f.

[51] Frazer quotes (*GB*³, Vol. XI, p. 284, n. 3) three sources: J. Sowerby, *English Botany* (London, 1805), Vol. XXI, p. 1470; the "author" of the *Lexicon mythologicum* appended to *Edda Rhythmica seu Antiquior vulgo Saemundina dicta* (Copenhagen, 1828), Vol. III, p. 513, n.; and C. L. Rochholz, *Deutscher Glaube und Brauch* (Berlin, 1867), Vol. I, p. 9. Sowerby was a well-known botanical illustrator and collector of marine fossils. The reference is scarcely more than a literary allusion: "The Misseltoe is celebrated in story as the sacred plant of the Druids, and the golden bough of Virgil." The "author" of the *Lexicon* was the poet, Ossian scholar, and runologist, Finnur Magnússon, who sought, in his *Lexicon*, to compare the *Edda* with Greek, Sanskrit, and Persian mythology. His reference is a passing comment that the golden bough "is mistletoe glorified by poetic license." Rochholz merely refers in passing to Magnússon.

[52] A. Lang, *Magic and Religion*, p. 212. The question of the relevance of folk beliefs concerning mistletoe to Virgil's golden bough was, to my knowledge, first raised by H. Keck, "Zu Vergilius Aeneis," *Jahrbucher für klassische Philologie*, CXVII (1878), 792-794—though Keck does not identify the bough with mistletoe. Jacob Grimm, in *Deutsche Mythologie*, independently put forth the suggestion, though carefully noting: "In Virgil's descr. of the sacred bough, Aen VI ... this aureus fetus is merely *compared* to (not ident. with) the croceus fetus of this mistletoe" (English translation by J. S. Stallybrass, *Teutonic Mythology by Jacob Grimm* [London, 1888], Vol. IV, p. 1675; emphasis in the text). The fullest discussion of the comparison of mistletoe and Virgil's bough is in E. Norden (*Aeneis Buch VI*, pp. 164-168) who concluded that a study of the folklore of mistletoe does not aid in the elucidation of Virgil and stressed that the juxtaposition of mistletoe and the golden bough is merely a *Vergleich*.

The most complete study of mistletoe is by the plant parasitologist, K. F. von

I.3. With the collapse of the first and second identifications, the third, that the forbidden branch at Nemi was mistletoe, is left without foundation. Frazer never argued this identification, but simply asserted its truth as following logically from the two preceding equations.[53]

I.4. That the tree on which the golden bough grew was an oak (*Quercus ilex*) is explicit in the *Aeneid* VI.209.

I.5. But it does not follow from this that the sacred tree at Nemi was likewise an oak, as Frazer consistently maintained.[54] Frazer's argument is intricate. (*a*) Because of the identity of the golden bough with the branch at Nemi, what is true of one is true of the other. If the golden bough grew on an oak, then the branch of Nemi must be an oak. (*b*) The oak was the sacred tree, par excellence, of the Aryans, hence any important, sacred tree was most probably an oak.[55] (*c*) The goddess Diana at Nemi was called Vesta, and this suggests the maintenance of a sacred fire in her sanctuary (even though there is no evidence for a Vestal fire at Nemi).[56] The Vestal fire at Rome was

---

Tubeuf, in *Monographie der Mistel* (Munich-Berlin, 1923), esp. pp. 11-87 which contain valuable contributions by H. Neckel on mistletoe in the sagas (pp. 20-27), and by G. H. Marzell on folkloristic materials (pp. 23-36, 84-87). See further, G. H. Marzell, "Mistel," *Handwörterbuch des deutschen Aberglaubens* (Berlin-Leipzig, 1934-1935), Vol. VI, cols. 381-393, and n. 68 below.

[53] *GB³*, Vol. XI, p. 285.

[54] E.g., *GB³*, Vol. I, p. 42; Vol. X, p. v.

[55] The theory of the sacred oak was extremely popular when Frazer wrote. See *GB³*, Vol. II, pp. 349-375; and further, P. Wagler, *Die Eiche in alter und neuer Zeit* (Würzen-Berlin, 1891), Vols. I-II; H. M. Chadwick, "The Oak and the Thunder God," *Journal of the Royal Anthropological Institute*, XXX (1900), 22-42; A. B. Cook, "Zeus, Jupiter and the Oak," *Classical Review*, XVII (1903), 174-186, 268-278, 403-421; *ibid.*, XVIII (1904), 75-89, 325-328, 360-375 (on the latter, see W. M. Fowler, *The Religious Experience of the Roman People* [London, 1911], p. 143, n. 60: "We must, however, remember that Mr. Cook is, so to speak, on an oak-scent and his keenness as a hunter sometimes leads him astray").

[56] On Diana, see H. Dessau, *Corpus Inscriptionum Latinarum* (Berlin, 1887), Vol. XIV, n. 2213: "*Diana nemorensi Vestae sacrum dict. imp. Nerva Traiano Aug. Germanico.*" This establishes a title, not the existence of a Vestal fire. There has been discovered, at Aricia, a circular "basement" which A. B. Cook ("The Golden Bough and the Rex Nemorensis," 376) suggested, following Frazer's article ("The Prytaneum, the Temple of Vesta, the Vestals, Perpetual Fire," *Journal of Philology*, XIV [1885], 145-172), was the site of the hearth, but this is an unconfirmed conjecture. Frazer, who lacked this hypothesis in *GB²* (Vol. I, p. 5), eagerly seized on it in *GB³* (Vol. I, p. 13 and n. 5).

On *Diana Nemorensis*, see G. Wissowa, *Religion und Kultur der Römer*, 2d ed. (Munich, 1912), pp. 247-252; N. Turchi, *La religione di Roma antica* (Bologna, 1930), pp. 140-143; F. Altheim, *Griechische Götter im alten Rom* (Giessen, 1930), pp. 93-135 (see, contra, A. E. Gordon, "On the Origins of Diana," *Transactions of the American Philological Association*, LXIII [1923], 177-192); A. E. Gordon, *The Cults of Aricia* (Berkeley, 1934), pp. 4-13; K. Latte, *Römische Religionsge-*

fed with oak wood: "hence *it is reasonable to conclude* that wherever in Latium a Vestal fire was maintained, it was fed, as at Rome, with the wood of the sacred oak. *If this was so at Nemi, it becomes probable* that the hallowed grove there consisted of a natural oak wood, and that *therefore* the tree which the King of the Wood had to guard at the peril of his life was itself an oak."[57] As this quotation indicates, the argument is mere conjecture. Even less convincing are Frazer's hypotheses that (*d*) the *Rex Nemorensis* was the successor of the Alban dynasty of the Silvii who were crowned with oak leaves,[58] and (*e*) that the double-herm excavated at Nemi depicts a figure crowned with oak.[59] Even if these identifications are correct (i.e., that the King of the Woods was the successor of the Silvii and that the double-herm depicts the *Rex Nemorensis*—both of which are dubious), it is difficult to see how this crown establishes that the tree at Nemi was an oak. The equation of the tree at Nemi with an oak has not been established.[60]

BALDER

II.1-3. In the second stage of his argument, Frazer prepared for the identification of the Norse god Balder with the *Rex Nemorensis*. The crucial point of comparison is the motif of the "pulling of the mistletoe" as a prelude to the slaying of Balder, which Frazer maintained was a close parallel to the plucking of the branch (according to Frazer, of mistletoe) as a prelude to the duel with the *Rex Nemoren-*

---

schichte (Munich, 1960), pp. 169-173; A. Alföldi, "Diana Nemorensis," *American Journal of Archaeology*, LXIV (1960), 137-144; Alföldi, *Early Rome and the Latins* (Ann Arbor, 1963), pp. 47-56, 85-88; G. Dumézil, *Archaic Roman Religion* (Chicago, 1970), Vol. II, pp. 407-412.

[57] *GB*³, Vol. II, pp. 378f. (emphasis mine).

[58] *GB*³, Vol. II, pp. 178-194, 379 n. 4, following A. B. Cook, "Zeus, Jupiter and the Oak," 363f.; Cook, "The European Sky God," *Folk-Lore*, XVI (1905), 227f.

[59] *GB*³, Vol. I, pp. 40f. The fullest discussion of the hypothesis that the leaves are oak is L. Morpurgo, "La rappresentazione figurata di Virbio," *Ausonia*, IV (1909), 109-127. Other scholars have identified the leaves as water plants, vervain, or one of the nettles.

[60] While most scholars have rejected Frazer's identification, A. B. Cook, *Zeus* (Cambridge, 1914-1940) Vol. II:1, pp. 417-422 attempted to support Frazer's identification by references to eighteenth-century reports of a large oak tree on the shore of Lake Nemi which tradition held went back to the days of Augustus: "It occurred to me at once that the tree in question might be the successor of the tree guarded by the rex Nemorensis." However the tree was at Genzano, on the opposite side of the lake from the Nemi sanctuary. Cook argued, "As Diana's temple at Nemi was duplicated by Diana's temple at Aricia, so *ex hypothesi* the oak at Nemi was duplicated by the oak at [Genzano]." This is even more conjectural than Frazer!

sis. There are several difficulties with this comparison. (*a*) The "pulling of the mistletoe" is scarcely a central theme in the Balder myth, especially when the different versions are taken into account. (*b*) If *mistilteinn* is understood to be a plant, it is apparently not, in the Icelandic sources, the familiar parasite (*Viscum album*) with which Frazer identified it. (*c*) There is the possibility, seriously defended by several scholars, that *mistilteinn* does not refer to a plant but to a weapon. (*d*) The parallelism depends on the identification of both Virgil's golden bough and the branch at Nemi as mistletoe. This has already been demonstrated to be groundless.

Frazer began by citing the familiar twelfth-century version of the myth from the *Gylfaginning* section of the prose *Edda* of Snorri Sturlson.[61] This complex narrative contains a number of motifs (e.g., Balder's dream of his own death; his invulnerability save to one thing, the treachery of Loki; the transformation and capture of Loki, *Ragnarök*) of which Frazer isolated two—Loki's "pulling up of the mistletoe" and the cremation of Balder.

The brief notice that Loki "took hold of the plant and pulled it up" (*En Lóki tok mistiltein ok sleit upp*) conceals a problem which Frazer ignored. One does not think of pulling *up* mistletoe, but rather of pulling it *down* or *off* its host tree. Nor would one describe mistletoe as a small, young, slender bush or tree (*viðarteinungar*). Snorri's description of the characteristics of *mistilteinn* does not accord with the usual portrait of mistletoe.[62]

The same problem recurs in one of Snorri's sources, the Sibyl's prophecy in the *Voluspa* which forms part of the poetic *Edda*:

> I saw Balder, the bloody victim
> The son of Odin, his destiny established.
> Growing [there], stands over the fields
> Slender and beautiful, the *mistilteinn*.
> From the branch that seemed so slender
> Came a harmful shaft, that Hodr shall hurl.[63]

---

[61] *Snorra Edda*, 49-50 in the edition by A. Holtsmark-J. Helgason, *Snorra Edda* (Copenhagen, 1950), pp. 62-68; the standard translation in English is A. G. Brodeur, *The Prose Edda by Snorri Sturlson* (New York, 1929), pp. 70-77; J. I. Young, *The Prose Edda of Snorri Sturlson* (Berkeley-Los Angeles, 1964), pp. 80-86 is the most recent.

[62] See R. Much, "Balder," *Zeitschrift für deutsches Altertum und deutsche Literatur*, LXI (1924), 104; E. J. Gras, "Mistilteinn," *Neophilologus*, XVII (1932), 293; J. Hanssen, "Mistelteinen i Norge," *Nyt magazin for naturvidenskaberne*, LXXII (1932), 290f.

[63] *Voluspa*, 31-32 in F. Jónsson, *De gamle Eddadigte* (Copenhagen, 1932), p. 10; and L. M. Hollander, *Seven Eddic Lays* (Austin, 1945), p. 64 (see the standard English translation by H. A. Bellows, *The Poetic Edda* [New York, 1926], pp. 14f.).

The phrase, *stoð um vaxinn, vǫllum hæri ... mistilteinn* may mean that the plant was growing above the ground on its host tree, or it may imply that the *mistilteinn* was a tall shrub.[64] Likewise, the brief line in *Baldr's draumar*: "Hodr is bearing the tall branch of fate"— if it refers, as likely, to the *mistilteinn*—supports the picture of a large, tall plant quite unlike the familiar parasite.[65] Within these sources, there is, at least, considerable ambiguity as to what plant is referred to as the agent of Balder's death.

In the other major source cited by Frazer (Saxo Grammaticus, *Historia Danica*), the motif of Balder being slain by the *mistilteinn* is lacking. Rather he is killed by the sword of Mimingus.[66]

---

[64] Frazer argued that the reference is to the height at which the plant grew and quoted a private communication from H. M. Chadwick in support of this interpretation (*GB*³, Vol. X, pp. 102 and 103, n. 2 continued). He is probably correct (see, among others, E. J. Gras, "Mistilteinn," 293); but see A. Kabell, *Balder und die Mistel* (Helsinki, 1965), pp. 9f.

[65] *Baldr's draumar* 9.1-2 in Jónsson, *De gamle Eddadigte*, p. 140: "hǫðr berr hóvan hróðrbaðm þinig."

[66] Saxo Grammaticus *Historia Danica* III.ii in the edition by P. Herrmann-C. Knabe (Copenhagen, 1931), Vol. I, pp. 63-67 (see the standard English translation by O. Elton, *The First Nine Books of the Danish History of Saxo Grammaticus* [London, 1894], pp. 83-93). The myth is radically altered in Saxo (see in general, G. Dumézil, *Du mythe au roman* [Paris, 1970] and pp. 157-172 on Balder).

A. B. Rooth has argued (*Loki in Scandinavian Mythology* [Lund, 1961], pp. 129-133) that Saxo's motif of the sword of Mimingus and the *mistilteinn* in Snorri and the *Voluspa* are linked by the sword called Mistilteinn in the *Hrómundar saga Greipssonar* (see the text in C. C. Rafn, *Fornaldarsögur Norlanda* [Copenhagen, 1829], Vol. II, pp. 363-380; V. Asmudarson, *Fornaldarsögur Nordlanda* [Reykjavik, 1886], Vol. II, pp. 323-336; G. Jónsson, *Fornaldarsögur Nordlanda* [Reykjavik, 1954], Vol. II, pp. 407-422; and the study by A. L. Andrews, "Studies in the Fornaldarsögur Norlanda," *Modern Philology*, VIII [1910-1911], 527-544, IX [1911-1912], 371-397, X [1912-1913], 601-630). I see *no* basis for this linkage. The sword, Mistilteinn, was won by Hrómundar in a battle with the ghostly guardian of a barrow treasure, Thrain (*Hrómundar saga Greipssonar*, IV), and taken with him on his exploits. There was rivalry between Hrómundar and the king's two evil advisers, Bildr and Voli (esp. V) which some scholars have suggested are variants of Balder and Vali; but this is dubious (see the effective arguments of Andrews, "Studies," X, 610). The sword, Mistilteinn, does not cause either Bildr or Voli's death. Bildr is slain by the invading Swedish army (VI); Voli is slain by Hrómundar, after Voli magically blows the sword out of Hrómundar's hand, by having his neck broken on the ice (VII). On the significance of the *Hrómundar saga Greipssonar* in relation to the Balder myth see, among others, A. Olrik, *Sakses Oldhistorie* (Copenhagen, 1894), Vol. II, pp. 26f.; F. Kauffmann, *Balder: Mythus und Sage* (Strassburg, 1902), pp. 74-76; G. Neckel, *Die Überlieferungen vom Gotte Balder* (Dortmund, 1920), pp. 89f.; P. Herrmann, *Erläuterungen zu den ersten neun Büchern der dänischen Geschichte des Saxo Grammaticus*, Vol. II: *Kommentar: Die Heldensagen des Saxo Grammaticus* (Leipzig, 1922), pp. 234-236; E. J. Gras, "Miltiltein," 295-298; G. Dumézil, *Loki* (Darmstadt, 1959), pp. 34f.; A. B. Rooth, *Loki*, pp. 129-133. See below, n. 81, for Mistilteinn as a sword name.

There would appear to be two quite separate traditions surrounding the death of Balder. In one, he is killed by a shaft of a plant called *mistilteinn* (Snorri, *Voluspa* and probably *Baldr's draumar*). The description of the plant, while ambigious, does not accord with the parasite mistletoe. In the other tradition, Balder is killed by a sword (Saxo). Neither of these traditions supports strongly Frazer's thesis that Balder was killed by "pulling up" mistletoe and hurling it at the god, nor does either support Frazer's identification of the killing of Balder with the duel of the *Rex Nemorensis*.

Although the standard dictionaries identify *mistilteinn* as mistletoe (*Viscum album*),[67] many scholars have puzzled over this identification.[68] All are agreed that the European mistletoes do not grow in Iceland, the home of the sagas. Therefore it has been argued: (1) the motif of the mistletoe has been imported into the myth from another area where the plant is found (England, Norway, Sweden); (2) some other

---

[67] For example, H. Gering, *Glossar zu den Liedern der Edda* (Paderborn-Munster, 1887), p. 114; J. Fritzner, *Ordbog over det Gamle Norske Sprog*, 2d ed. (Kristiania, 1891), Vol. II, p. 717; G. T. Zoëga, *A Concise Dictionary of Old Icelandic* (Oxford, 1910), p. 300; A. Jóhannesson, *Isländisches etymologisches Wörterbuch* (Bern, 1956), pp. 470f.; R. Cleasby-G. Vigfusson-W. Craigie, *An Icelandic-English Dictionary*, 2d ed. (Oxford, 1957), p. 432; J. de Vries, *Altnordisches etymologisches Wörterbuch*, 2d ed. (Leiden, 1962), p. 389.

[68] Among the special studies which have been devoted to this subject, see esp. E. J. Gras, "Mistilteinn," *Neophilologus*, XVII (1932), 293-298; J. Hanssen, "Misteleinen i Norge," *Nyt magazin for naturvidenskaberne*, LXXII (1932), 283-339, esp. 288-291; A. Hvidfeldt, "Mistilteinn og Baldr's død," *Aarbøger for nordisk Oldkyndighed og Historie*, (1941), 169-175; I. M. Boberg, "Baldr og Mistiltenen," *Aarbøger*, (1943), 103-106; A. Kabell, *Balder und die Mistel*. See also the special historical-botanical studies by H. Jensen-Tusch, *Plantenavne i forskellige europeiske sprog*, Vol. I: *Nordiske plantenavne* (Copenhagen, 1867), esp. pp. 147, 232; C. Jessen-G. Pritzel, *Die deutschen Volksnamen der Pflanzen*, 2d ed. (Leipzig, 1882), p. 442; A. Lyttkens, *Svenska växtnamn* (Stockholm, 1915), Vol. III, pp. 1174-1180; J. Hoops, *Reallexikon der germanischen Altertumskunde* (Strassburg, 1916), Vol. III, p. 230, cf. Hoops, *Waldbaume und Kulturpflanzen im germanischen Altertum* (Strassburg, 1905), p. 606; I. Teirlinck, *Flora magica* (Antwerp, 1930), pp. 65-67 *et passim*; N. von Hofsten, *Eddadikternavs djur och växter* (Uppsala, 1957), p. 47.

Among the many studies of Balder's death, the following have proved especially useful on this problem: S. Bugge, *Studien über die Entstehung der nordischen Götter- und Heldensagen* (Munich, 1889), pp. 45-48; V. Rydberg, *Undersökningar i germanisk Mytologi* (Stockholm, 1889), Vol. II, pp. 203-352; F. Kauffmann, *Balder*, pp. 250-255 *et passim*; F. Niedner, "Baldrs Tod," *Zeitschrift für deutsches Altertum und deutsche Literatur*, XLI (1897), 305-334; R. Much, "Balder," *Zeitschrift für deutsches Altertum*, LXI (1924), 93-136; G. Neckel, *Überlieferungen vom Gotte Balder*, esp. pp. 88-96, 175-199; E. J. Gras, *De noordse Loki-mythen in hun onderling verband* (Haarlem, 1931), esp. p. 84; J. de Vries, "Der Mythos von Balders Tod," *Arkiv för nordisk Filologi*, LXX (1955), 41-60; de Vries, *Altgermanischer Religionsgeschichte*, 2d ed. (Berlin, 1957), Vol. II, pp. 223-226; G. Dumézil, *Les dieux des Germains* (Paris, 1959), pp. 78-105; A. B. Rooth, *Loki*, pp. 133-139.

plant than mistletoe is being described; (3) *mistilteinn* did not originally refer to a plant, but rather to a weapon.

Comparative folklore has yielded a number of apparent parallels to the Balder-*mistilteinn* tale, and these have been used by scholars in an attempt to locate the story's original provenance. Much depends on what motifs are isolated for the comparison. The motifs of flawed invulnerability, of a hero with an "Achilles Heel" (S. Thompson, *Motif-Index*, Z 311) or vulnerable to only one weapon (Z 312) or to only one person (Z 313) as well as the varied motifs of accidental death (N 320, 330) are too widespread to be of aid in such an attempt.[69] Thus, I am not convinced by the alleged parallels of the death of Balder to the accidental shooting of Herebald by Haeðcyn in Beowulf (4861-4875);[70] to the killing through the ruse of a mock sacrifice of King Vikar in *Gautreks Saga* (although this tale does contain the motif of a reed stalk becoming a spear);[71] to the slaying of the invulnerable Esfandiyār by Rostam (in the *Shah Nameh*) who shoots him in the eye with a tamarisk branch;[72] to the slaying of the invulnerable Lemminkäinen by a reed stalk driven through his heart in the *Kalevala*;[73] or to the hanging of Jesus on a cabbage stalk in the

---

[69] See J. de Vries, *Heroic Song and Heroic Legend* (London, 1963), p. 215. Rooth (*Loki*, p. 105) has attempted to take the whole narrative rather than an isolated motif into account and has identified the Balder tale as a variant of "The Oedipus Tale, or the King and his Prophesied Death" (A. Aarne-S. Thompson, *Types of the Folktale*, 931).

[70] C. L. Wrenn, *Beowulf* (London, 1953), p. 159. It has been suggested that Herebald and Haeðcyn are linguistically related to Balder and Hodr. See the excellent bibilography on the *Beowulf*-Balder comparison in A. Kabell, *Balder und die Mistel*, pp. 5f., n. 1, continued. For an early statement on the problem of the British Balder, see J. Grimm, *Teutonic Mythology*, Vol. I, pp. 220-223; more recently, see E. O. G. Turnville-Petre, *Myth and Religion of the North* (New York, 1964), pp. 120-122.

[71] Text in G. Jónsson, *Fornalder sögur Nordlanda*, Vol. IV, pp. 30f.; translation in H. Pálsson-P. Edwards, *Gautrek's Saga and Other Medieval Tales* (London, 1968), p. 40.

[72] Translation in R. Levi, *The Epic of Kings* (Chicago, 1967), pp. 206-211.

[73] Translation in J. M. Crawford, *The Kalevala* (Cincinnati, 1898), Vol. I, pp. 143-223. The story contains several motifs which have been employed in the comparison. Lemminkäinen, in order to obtain the woman he desired, had to perform three difficult tasks. The third was to obtain a swan from the underground river of Tuonela. On the bank of the river he was shot by a blind herdsman with a reed or shaft of cow bane. The herdsman dismembered the body and threw it into the river. After a long search, his mother collected all of the pieces, joined them together, and, by magic, restored Lemminkäinen to life. This story, which closely resembles the Isis-Osiris tale and has therefore been used by those who would argue an original Near Eastern or "Oriental" provenance for the Balder

medieval Jewish polemic version of the Gospel narrative, the *Tol^edot Ješu*.[74] I am equally unconvinced by more "pattern"-conscious

myth (see below, n. 75, and V. Vikentiev, "La légende d'Osiris à travers le monde," *Bulletin of the Faculty of Arts: Fouad I University*, XV [1953], 15-36), in fact resembles Balder only in the motif of the blind assailant and the reed. There is no hint of a restoration of Balder until Ragnarök; nor is his body dismembered (see the older comparisons of Lemminkäinen with Balder by K. Krohn, "Lemminkäinens Tod < Christi > Balders Tod." *Finnisch ugrische Forschungen*, IV [1904], 83-138; and V. J. Mansikka, "Balder und Lemminkäinen," *ibid.*, VIII [1908], 206-217).

The magical practice employed by Lemminkäinen's mother to restore him does resemble the magical practice used to restore the sprained foot of Balder's horse in the second Merseburg charm—this is scarcely a significant parallel especially in light of the fact that the praxis, joining "bone to bone, blood to blood, limb to limb" has wide distribution (e.g., *Atharva-veda* IV.12; see F. Schröder, "Balder und der zweite Merseburger Spruch," *Germanisch-romanische Monatschrift*, XXXIV [1953], 161-183). There is considerable debate as to whether *balderes* in this charm is the proper name of Balder, the Norse god, or an appelative, "lord" (see the excellent, brief discussion in D. H. Green, *The Carolingian Lord* [Cambridge, 1954], pp. 14-17).

[74] The text, in the *Tol^edot Ješu*, reads in the Strassburg manuscript (VII): "When they [had brought him forth] to hang him on the tree, it broke, for the Secret Name of God was with him. Now when the foolish ones saw that the trees had broken under him, they explained this as being due to his righteousness. Then they brought for him the stalk of a cabbage.... For by uttering the Secret Name of God he had brought it to pass that no tree should be able to bear him, but over the cabbage stalk he had not uttered the Name, because it is no tree but a plant" (see the text in S. Krauss, *Das Leben Jesu nach jüdischen Quellen* [Berlin, 1902], p. 45 and Krauss' German translation, p. 58; the other recensions summarized or printed in Krauss [pp. 28, n. 1, 80, 106, 120, 126, 148]; and the important Yiddish version published by E. Bischoff, *Ein jüdisch-deutsches Leben Jesu* [Leipzig, 1895], p. 40). Most scholars who discuss the question either refer to the quotation from Krauss in O. Dähnhardt, *Natursagen* (Leipzig-Berlin, 1909), Vol. II, pp. 209f., or to the similar text type in J. A. Eisenmenger, *Entdecktes Judentum* (Königsberg, 1700), Vol. I, p. 173 (text), p. 180 (translation).

On the motif of the trees, see the Haggadic accounts of the hanging of Haman in which either the trees compete for the honor of bearing him or refuse to do so (L. Ginzberg, *Legends of the Jews* [Philadelphia, 1928], Vol. VI, p. 479, n. 184). In some versions, Judas brings the cabbage stalk from his garden. The motif of a large cabbage is found elsewhere in rabbinic materials (e.g., b. *Ketuvot* 116b: "R. Simeon b. Tachlifa related, our father left us a cabbage stalk and we ascended it and descended it by means of a ladder") and needs to be related to the general theme of wondrous growth and deeds in the Holy Land (see R. M. Dorson "Jewish-American Dialect Stories on Tape," *Studies in Biblical and Jewish Folklore* [Bloomington, 1960], p. 116; J. Z. Smith, "Earth and Gods," chapter 5, above, p. 115). No scholar of the *Tol^edot* or of the Balder tradition appears to have noted that the specific reason for the cabbage stalk being employed, "because it is no tree but a plant," is a traditional problem in both rabbinic and Greco-Roman taxonomy (see the discussion in *jKil'aim* V [end], 30a, in M. Schwab, *Le Talmud de Jerusalem* [Paris, 1878] Vol. II, p. 281, and Theophrastus, *Historia plantarum* I.3.4, in the edition and translation by A. Hort [London, 1916], Vol. I, pp. 26f., where the cabbage is termed a "tree-plant [*dendrolachanon*]." See further, S.

interpretations which have placed emphasis on the mistletoe as an ambiguous symbol of life and death in connection with a ritual experience of birth-death-rebirth (pointing to alleged parallels such as the golden bough in the *Aeneid* or the plant of life in *Gilgamesh*) and have interpreted the slaying of Balder as the killing of a king to insure fertility or as an initiatory ritual.[75] Each of these comparisons has the common flaw that it compares only one detail in the complex Balder myth (usually relying on only one version) or that it cannot adequately account for the transmission of the motif from its presumed point of origin to the Nordic saga and must rely on the vague language of diffusion.

The most impressive set of parallels that have been adduced are from British and Celtic folklore of the general type: "Accidental death through misdirected weapon" and the subtype: "Blind (man) accidentally kills friend."[76] As mistletoe is common in England and

Lieberman, *Hellenism in Jewish Palestine* [New York, 1950], pp. 180f.). It is possible that both Snorri and the *Tol^{e}dot* are reflecting Christian legends about various trees refusing to be made into the Cross and bear Jesus and the treachery of one tree (usually an aspen) which agrees to become the tree (Thompson Z 352, cf. A 2721.2.1). See A. de Gubernatis, *La mythologie des plantes* (Paris, 1882), Vol. II, p. 85; T. F. Thiselton Dyer, *The Folklore of Plants* (New York, 1889), pp. 256-258; A. S. Rappoport, *Medieval Legends of Christ* (New York, 1935), pp. 191-193, and compare the Jewish Haman legends cited above and Christian legends about the Judas tree (in I. Teirlinck, *Flora diabolica* [Antwerp, 1924], esp. pp. 157f.). This tradition is quite independent from the well-known legend of the Rood-tree (see E. C. Quinn, *The Quest of Seth for the Oil of Life* [Chicago, 1962]; and M. Overgaard, *The History of the Cross-Tree Down to Christ's Passion: Icelandic Legend Versions* [Copenhagen, 1968]).

The comparison between the *Tol^{e}dot* and Balder was first proposed by C. Hofmann ("Zum Mythus von Baldurs Tod," *Germania*, II [1857], 48) and raised to prominence by S. Bugge (*Studier over de nordiske Gude- og Heltesagns Oprindelse* [Kristiania, 1880], pp. 45f.) and K. Krohn (*Skandinavisk Mytologi* [Helsinki, 1922], pp. 121-134) and depended upon the identification of Balder as the "White Christ" (see G. Stephens, *Professor S. Bugge's Studies on Northern Mythology* [London, 1883], pp. 326-330). See further, Dähnhardt, *Natursagen*, Vol. II, pp. 209-214; Kaufmann, *Balder*, pp. 163f.; Dumézil, *Loki*, pp. 110f.; Rooth, *Loki*, pp. 101-103.

[75] E.g., Neckel, *Die Überlieferungen vom Gotte Balder*, pp. 132-220; F. R. Schröder *Germanentum und Hellenismus* (Heidelberg, 1924), pp. 39-153; J. de Vries, "Der Mythos von Balders Tod," *Archiv för nordisk Filologi*, LXX (1955), 41-60.

[76] This has been most extensively argued by Rooth, *Loki*, pp. 110-129. Perhaps the closest parallel is from *Silva Gadelica* 2: "And where was Ferchis MacComain the poet killed? It was the shot of a hardened holly [*aquifolium*] javelin which ... Ael, son of Dergdubh delivered at a stag, but with the same slew Ferchis unwittingly" (in S. H. O'Grady, *Silva Gadelica* [London, 1892], p. 129 and R. Thurneysen, *Die irische Helden- und Königsage* [Halle, 1921], p. 576). Cf. T. P. Cross, *Motif Index of Early Irish Literature* (Bloomington, 1952), N 337. For the magical powers of *aquifolium*, see K. Meyer, "The Irish Mirabilia in the Norse *Speculum Regale*," *Folk-Lore*, V (1894), 303.

Ireland, it has been argued that Anglo-Saxon and Celtic literature "have influenced the Scandinavian tradition,"⁷⁷ but the lines of influence remain obscure. There is no definite evidence for the existence of the Balder cult in England or Ireland; none of the stories adduced as parallels contain mistletoe as the weapon which causes the death—and, thus, the conjecture that the *mistilteinn* motif in the Balder myth is due to Anglo-Saxon or Celtic influence remains unproven.

A Norwegian provenance for the *mistilteinn* motif has been eliminated by scholars on philological grounds. While mistletoe is known in Norway, it is consistently called *ledved*, which will not easily yield the forms common to the saga traditions.⁷⁸ Sweden, on the other hand, provides a host of similar forms: most commonly *mistel* or *mistelten*, but also *misteltein*, *mesterjene*, *mistiltenn*, *mispel*, *mespel*, *vispel*, and *verspelten*. However, this is the only group in which plant names end in *-ten*. As the name for mistletoe (*Viscum album*), it occurs in scholarly post-Eddic commentaries and in learned herbals or pharmacopoeia. When *mistelten* does occur as a popular plant name, it is almost always with reference to some plant other than the mistletoe: most frequently ivy (*Hedera helix*) or the Medlar (*Mespilus germanica*; Old French, *mesle/medle*; German, *mispel*); more rarely, other plants such as the Cotoneaster (*C. vulgaris*).⁷⁹ Thus it is possible, on the basis of the Swedish evidence and in light of the fact that the physical description of the *mistilteinn* in the Balder materials does not accord with mistletoe, to conjecture that *mistilteinn* refers to a plant other than mistletoe.⁸⁰

A final possibility is to note that the ending *-teinn* is frequently associated in the saga literature with the names of swords (e.g., *benteinn*, *bifteinn*, *eggtein*, *hjorteinn*, *mordteinn*, *sarteinn*, *valteinn*) and that in several sagas and poetic gloss, *mistilteinn* occurs as a sword name.

---

⁷⁷ Rooth, *Loki*, p. 241, cf. pp. 138f.
⁷⁸ See K. Krohn, "Lemminkäinens Tod," 121; J. Hansen, "Mistilteinen i Norge," 330; Rooth, p. 138.
⁷⁹ See esp. A. Lyttkens, *Svenska vaxtnamn*, pp. 1174-1180; and Rooth, *Loki*, p. 137 and n. 71. For *mistelten* as ivy, see Rooth, p. 135. For *mistelten* as medlar, see J. Grimm, *Teutonic Mythology*, Vol. III, p. 1207; J. Hoops, *Waldbaume*, p. 606; H. Janssen-Tusch, *Plantenavna*, p. 67; H. Marzell, ed., *Wörterbuch der deutschen Pflanzennamen* (Leipzig, 1965), Vol. III:2, cols. 184-190. For *mistelten* as cotoneaster, see Janssen-Tusch, p. 67.
⁸⁰ It is perhaps of significance in light of the fact that the height of *mistilteinn* appeared as a motif in the Icelandic material and seemed to contradict the usual picture of mistletoe, to note that a similar tradition exists in Sweden (Grimm, *Teutonic Mythology*, Vol. III, p. 1205).

This, together with the motif of Balder being killed by the sword of Mimingus in Saxo, has led to the suggestion that *mistilteinn* is not a plant but a weapon.[81]

The second stage of Frazer's argument is in question. The identification of the killing of the priest of Nemi preceded by a plucking of the mistletoe and the killing of Balder preceded by a plucking of the mistletoe is dubious. Frazer's identification of the branch at Nemi as mistletoe is sheer conjecture. The identification of the *mistilteinn* in the Balder myth as mistletoe is, at the very least, problematic.[82]

The External Soul

In the third stage of his argument, Frazer sought to establish that Balder and the *Rex Nemorensis* personified the oak, that their external soul was bound up in the mistletoe, that their strength and life sustained the vegetative world, and that when their vitality waned they were slain. These elements were introduced early in *The Golden Bough* and preoccupied Frazer throughout his work. In *The Magic Art and the Evolution of Kings* he had introduced the notion of sacred kingship, figures who were identified with the powers of nature and whose continued vitality was necessary to the maintenance of these powers in the cosmos. In *Taboo and the Perils of the Soul* he

---

[81] This was the early suggestion by V. Rydberg, *Undersökningar i germanisk Mythologi*, Vol. I, pp. 292f. On -*teinn* in sword names and *mistilteinn* as a sword name, see H. Falk, *Altnordisches Waffenkunde* (Leipzig, 1914), p. 56, n. 97; E. J. Gras, "Mistilteinn," 295-298. Three hypotheses have been advanced: (*a*) *mistilteinn* was first a plant name, but because the plant was unknown in Iceland and because it was identified with Balder's death, it was transferred to the name of a powerful sword (F. Ström, *Loki*, [Göteborg, 1956], p. 159; A. Kabell, *Balder und die Mistel*, pp. 7f., and cf. F. Detter, "Die Baldrmythus," *Beiträge zur Geschichte der deutschen Sprache und Literatur*, XIX [1894], 498; G. Neckel, *Überlieferungen vom Gotte Balder*, pp. 89-96, cf. Neckel, "Mistel," *Reallexikon der germanischen Altertumskunde*, Vol. III, p. 230); (*b*) *mistilteinn* was originally a plant name rationalized into a sword name when the original narrative was judged incredible (Turville-Petre, *Myth and Religion of the North*, pp. 115f.); (*c*) the sword name was prior, its identification as a plant is a secondary folkloristic motif (F. Detter, "Der Baldermythus," 495-516; W. Golther, *Handbuch der germanischen Mythologie* [Leipzig, 1895], p. 379; F. Niedner, "Baldrs Tod," 305, 310; J. A. MacCulloch, *Eddic Mythology* [Boston, 1930], p. 136; A. Hvidfeldt, "Mistilteinn og Baldrs død," 169-175; I. M. Boberg, "Baldr og Misteltenen," 103-106).

[82] A recent, Frazerian interpretation has been proposed by A. V. Ström, "King God and Sacrifice in Old Norse Religion," in C. J. Bleeker, ed., *La regalità sacra: The Sacral Kingship, Contributions to the Central Theme of the VIIIth International Congress for the History of Religions* (Leiden, 1959), esp. pp. 706f., which depends on a parallel between the Norse *blauttein* and the Iranian *barzman*.

focused on the restrictions which surround and protect these kingly figures so that their health and strength are maintained. In *The Dying God* he attempted to demonstrate that when these figures grew sick, aged, or impotent, they were slain by their community in order to prevent their souls from becoming "enfeebled" and to prevent a corresponding "enfeeblement" of the power and vitality of the cosmos. In *Adonis, Attis and Osiris* he argued that this ideology was represented by the great Oriental fertility deities. The seasonal drama of the growth and decay of vegetation, of the birth and death of all things, is reflected in the drama of the lives of these royal gods. In *Spirits of the Corn and of the Wild* he maintained the presence of this pattern in Western traditions, not only in great deities such as Dionysus, but also in European folk belief. The spirit of vitality is absorbed by the community through a sacramental eating of the young Corn Maiden (or first fruits); the death of the spirit of vitality is ritually represented by beating the last sheaf (Corn Mother) or by killing a human representation. In *The Scapegoat* Frazer explored the ritual of ridding a community of evil by transferring it to a surrogate which was then killed or expelled. This was compared to the killing of the king or god in order to preserve the cosmos from degeneracy. With this ideological background established, Frazer announced that *Balder the Beautiful*, the concluding volumes of *The Golden Bough*, would contain the solution to the two questions he had proposed at the outset of his work.

III.1. In the first volume of *The Golden Bough*, Frazer promised to demonstrate "later on" that the *Rex Nemorensis* "embodied" the life of the tree which he represented and that this tree was an oak.[83] One hundred and fifty-eight pages later he mentioned a belief found among the Queensland aborigines, the Battas of Sumatra, and the Norsemen that "the afterbirth or navel string [is considered] a seat of the external soul," and promises a treatment of the external soul in a "later part of this work."[84] Three thousand and thirty-one pages later, less than two hundred and fifty pages from the end of the massive eleven-volume work, Frazer finally returned to this topic.[85] What was written in between were the major motifs of *The Golden Bough* (as summarized above). In a strict sense these are tangential to the two questions Frazer claimed to be answering; and yet, in a

---

[83] *GB³*, Vol. I, p. 42.
[84] *GB³*, Vol. I, pp. 200f.
[85] *GB³*, Vol. XI, p. 95.

thematic way, they are not irrelevant. The test will be whether Frazer could apply them to the specific questions he had proposed.

III.2. Frazer began by attempting to establish that "the invulnerable Balder is neither more nor less than a personification of a mistletoe-bearing oak" and that "the mistletoe was viewed as the seat of the life of the oak" so that "the pulling of the mistletoe was thus at once the signal and the cause of his [Balder's] death."[86] Lacking any text, Frazer created his own myth:

> we might tell how the kindly god of the oak had his life securely deposited in the imperishable mistletoe which grew among the branches; how accordingly so long as the mistletoe kept its place there, the deity himself remained invulnerable; and how, at last *a cunning foe, let into the secret of the god's invulnerability tore the mistletoe* from the oak, thereby killing the oak-god and afterwards burning his body in a fire which could have made no impression on him so long as the incombustible parasite retained its seat among the boughs.[87]

With his "solution" so near at hand, Frazer, quite characteristically, launched into a digression. Fearing that "the idea of a being whose life is thus, in a sense, outside himself, must be strange to my readers," Frazer cataloged instances of "external souls" for one hundred and eighty-three pages. Then, without warning, he abruptly finished the sentence interrupted by his digression: "Thus the view that Balder's life was in the mistletoe is entirely in harmony with primitive modes of thought."[88]

Frazer's conclusion cannot be criticized because no grounds for his assertion were offered. Frazer could not offer any Scandinavian myth or tradition which suggested that Balder was an oak god, a spirit of an oak, or that his "external soul" was contained in the mistletoe—he could only offer his own myth which owed but fourteen words to Scandinavian texts.[89] Balder is not a god of the oak; his life was not deposited in the mistletoe; there is no suggestion in the Balder myth that the mistletoe was imperishable; Balder was not invulnerable so long as the mistletoe remained on the tree (rather he was invulnerable to everything save a projectile made of *mistilteinn*); Balder was not killed by plucking the *mistilteinn* from the tree but by having it hurled at him; it was not his assailant who burned Balder's body in the fire but rather the Asa gods who honorably

---

[86] *GB*[3], Vol. XI, pp. 93f.
[87] *GB*[3], Vol. XI, p. 94.
[88] *GB*[3], Vol. XI, pp. 94-279.
[89] Italicized in the above quotation.

cremated him in this fashion. I can think of no other passage of less than one hundred words in the work of any other scholar which contains a comparable number of errors of fact and interpretation.

Frazer's only evidence for his identification of the oak and mistletoe with the life of Balder is an alleged parallel: "the analogy of a Scottish superstition. Tradition had it that the fate of the Hays of Errol ... was bound up with the mistletoe that grew on a certain great oak."[90] Even if Frazer's interpretation of the Scottish tradition was correct (and it is not; the life of the family is bound up with the fate of "Errol's aik" not the mistletoe),[91] the analogy is not close enough to be of value in interpreting the medieval Icelandic Balder tradition. Frazer's crucial argument depends wholly on parallels which are usually no more than superficially similar and are almost always geographically and chronologically remote.[92]

III.3. Frazer's thesis that Balder is a tree spirit residing in an oak with his external soul protected within the mistletoe has broken down for lack of evidence, and with it his inference that Balder (or his surrogate) was killed to prevent a waning of the powers of fertility and fecundity. With the collapse of this hypothesis (one is tempted to write "balderdash," but, alas, the word has nothing to do with the Norse deity) falls, likewise, the thesis that the *Rex Nemorensis* was a tree spirit whose external soul was protected in the mistletoe and who was slain when his powers of vitality waned. For this thesis, which was Frazer's answer to his question, he can offer no evidence other than an analogy with Balder: "And what we have said of Balder in the oak forests of Scandinavia *may perhaps, with all due diffidence in a question so obscure and uncertain, be applied* to the priest of Diana, the King of the Wood, at Aricia in the oak forests of Italy."[93]

---

[90] *GB*³, Vol. XI, p. 283.

[91] In the traditional verses ascribed to Thomas the Rhymer there is a slight ambiguity, but the vitality of the oak, not the mistletoe, is to the fore. It is a good omen when "the mistletoe bats on Errol's aik,/And that aik stands fast"; it is an ill omen when "the root of the aik decays,/And the mistletoe dwines on its withered breast" (see J. B. Pratt, *Buchan*, 2d ed. [Edinburgh, 1859], p. 342). In the prose version of the legend, as given in J. H. Allen, *The Bride of Caölchairn* (London, 1822), pp. 337f., there is no ambiguity. The fate of the oak is intertwined as a "life-token" with the fate of the family. The only function of the mistletoe in this version is in the making of a charm against witchcraft and as a signal of success in battle.

[92] Cf. Frazer's treatment of the motif of blindfolded violence (*GB*³, Vol. XI, pp. 279f., n. 4) with the careful treatment of the same motif in Rooth (*Loki*, pp. 110-129; see n. 76, above).

[93] *GB*³, Vol. XI, p. 302 (emphasis mine).

No Answers, No Questions

Frazer appears to have answered his two questions, although we may judge his answers to be failures. As already recognized by his earliest critics, each conjecture put forth by Frazer which directly bears on the problem of the priesthood of Nemi was without foundation.[94] The original purpose of the book was not accomplished.[95] But the final denouement has yet to be revealed. Frazer boldly declared to his "indulgent readers" that he had known this all along. What had been alleged to be the purpose of *The Golden Bough* was, in fact, not its purpose.

> Though I am now less than ever disposed to lay weight on the analogy between the Italian priest and the Norse god, I have allowed it to stand because it furnishes me with a pretext for discussing not only the general question of the external soul in popular superstition, but also the fire-festivals of Europe.... Thus Balder the Beautiful in my hands is little more than a stalking-horse to carry two heavy packloads of facts. And what is true of Balder applies equally to the priest of Nemi himself, the nominal hero of the long tragedy of human folly and suffering which has unrolled itself before the readers of these volumes, and on which the curtain is now about to fall. He, too, for all the quaint garb he wears, is merely a puppet, and it is time to unmask him before laying him up in the box.[96]

---

[94] For example, A. Lang, *Magic and Religion*, pp. 217f.; and A. B. Cook, "The Golden Bough and the Rex Nemorensis," 371f., 376, 380.

[95] See Frazer's first letter to Macmillan proposing *The Golden Bough* (dated November 8, 1889) in C. Morgan, *The House of Macmillan* (New York, 1944), pp. 168-170; and S. Nowell-Smith, *Letters to Macmillan* (New York, 1967), pp. 223-225; as well as the passages from the various editions of *The Golden Bough* cited above in n. 18.

[96] *GB*³, Vol. X, pp. v-vi. It is to be regretted that Frazer left this denouement out of the abridged edition of *The Golden Bough* (as did T. H. Gaster in *The New Golden Bough*) so that countless readers who have read the work in this edition have not been "in on the joke." See the comments of R. R. Marett on this passage in his review of *GB*³: "The long suspected cat is now out of the bag" (reprinted in Marett, *Psychology and Folklore* [London, 1920], p. 178) and his 1927 Frazer Lecture: "I know nothing in the history of science more dramatic ... than the *peripeteia* that awaits one in the third edition [of the Golden Bough]" (reprinted in W. R. Dawson, *The Frazer Lectures: 1922-32* [London, 1932], p. 177), as well as that by R. A. Downie, Frazer's faithful secretary and biographer: "It would be presumptuous to say so, had we not the author's word for it, but the main thesis, the investigation of the priesthood at Nemi, is hardly the most important part of the work" (Downie, *James George Frazer: Portrait of a Scholar*, p. 36). The alert reader should catch a further "reversal" which abandons the crucial argument of the work: Frazer rejected the "solution ... I have advocated in the text, namely that Balder was a mythical personification of a mistletoe-bearing oak" (*GB*³, Vol. XI, p. 315) which was buried in an appended note.

The "Stein principle" has been perfectly fulfilled. There have been no answers because there were no questions.

It is not possible to agree with an assessment of Frazer's work that holds: "If here and there he was mistaken, if on this doubtful detail or the other his guess has been discarded, the substance of his argument stands erect among the noblest scientific monuments of a century that knew how to build in the grand manner."[97] The *Bough* has been broken and all that it cradled has fallen. It has been broken not only by subsequent scholars, but also by the deliberate action of its author.

AFTERWORD

I had originally intended a companion piece to this essay accounting for the reasons that Frazer chose to make his central work a joke. It was to argue that Frazer, in his researches, encountered the Savage which put the axe to his Victorian confidence in Progress and, in his studies of dying gods and kings, was brought up short before the absurdity of death. The history of mankind became, for him, the attempt to transcend that which cannot be transcended—namely death, "no figurative or allegorical death, no poetical embroidery thrown over the skeleton, but the real death, the naked skeleton" (GB^3, Vol. VII, p. vi). And, in the face of this "real death", one can only act absurdly, or, to put it another way, all action is a joke. "Man has not always been willing to watch this momentous conflict [between life and death]; he has felt that he has had too great a stake in its issue to stand by with folded hands while it is being fought out; he has taken sides against the forces of death and decay—has flung into the trembling scale all the weight of his puny person, and has exulted in his fancied strength when the great balance has slowly inclined towards the side of life, little knowing that for all his strenuous efforts he can as little stir that balance by a hair's breadth as can the primrose on a mossy bank in spring or the dead leaf blown by a chilly breath of autumn" (GB^3, Vol. IX, p. 241). However, I have decided to defer this piece until the publication of Robert Ackerman's promised psycho-historical biography of Frazer appears.

I would not wish "When the Bough Breaks" to be misunderstood. Frazer, for me, becomes the more interesting and valuable precisely because he deliberately fails.

---

[97] H. N. Brailsford, "The Golden Bough," *New Statesman and Nation* (1941), 501, reprinted in *Turnstile One* (London, 1948), pp. 28-31.

CHAPTER ELEVEN

ADDE PARVUM PARVO MAGNUS ACERVUS ERIT

The process of comparison is a fundamental characteristic of human intelligence. Whether revealed in the logical grouping of classes, in poetic similes, in mimesis, or other like activities—comparison, the bringing together of two or more objects for the purpose of noting either similarity or dissimilarity, is the omnipresent substructure of human thought. Without it, we could not speak, perceive, learn, or reason. Instances of comparison are presumably as old as mankind itself and may be found in our earliest literary documents.[1] It is unfortunate that relatively little work has been done on the history of the use of comparison in scholarship and that deeper questions of method and the underlying philosophical implications of comparison have been ignored by many disciplines[2] including History of Religions.[3] That comparison has, at times,

---

[1] For the literary use of comparison in archaic literature see S. N. Kramer, "Sumerian Similes," *J. of the American Oriental Society*, LXXXIX (1969), 1-10; J. Gonda, *Remarks on Similes in Sanskrit Literature* (Leiden, 1949); and H. Fränkel, *Die homerische Gleichnisse* (Göttingen, 1921). For its use in early Greek philosophical thought, see W. Kranz, "Gleichnis und Vergleich in der frühgriechischen Philosophie," *Hermes*, LXIII (1938), 99-122 (special reference to Empedocles); K. Riezler, "Das homerische Gleichnis und der Anfang der Philosophie," *Die Antike*, XII (1936), 253-271; A. Rivier, *Un emploi archaïque de l'analogie* (Lausanne, 1952) (special reference to Heraclitus); B. Snell, "From Myth to Logic: The Role of the Comparison," in Snell, *The Discovery of the Mind* (Cambridge, Mass., 1953), pp. 191-226; G. E. R. Lloyd, *Polarity* and *Analogy* (Cambridge, 1966).

[2] There have been relatively few philosophical studies devoted to the significance of comparison and similarity; see esp. H. Hoffding, *Der Begriff der Analogie* (Leipzig, 1924); P. Schwarz, "Zur Ontologie der Vergleichungssachverhalte," *Jahrbuch für Philosophie und phenomenologische Forschung*, X (1929), 451-483; R. W. Church, *An Analysis of Resemblance* (London, 1952); P. Butchvanov, *Resemblance and Identity: An Examination of the Problem of Universals* (Bloomington, 1966), esp. ch. II.

[3] The most recent study is B. Mazlish, "Historical Analogy: The Railroad and the Space Program," in Mazlish, ed., *The Railroad and the Space Program* (Cambridge, Mass., 1965), esp. pp. viii-x, 1-12. Mazlish laments the lack of an adequate theoretical study (p. 2 and n. 3). See further, L. Davillé, "La comparaison et la méthode comparative, en particulier dans les études historiques," *Revue de synthèse historique*, XXVII (1913), 4-33, 217-257; XXVIII (1914), 201-229 (unfinished), which Mazlish has overlooked. W. F. Albright, *Archaeology, Historical Analogy and Early Biblical Traditions* (Baton Rouge, 1966) is not useful.

led us astray there can be no doubt; that comparison remains *the* method of scholarship is likewise beyond question. As Samuel Butler recorded in his notebook: "Though analogy is often misleading, it is the least misleading thing we have."[4]

Robert Redfield, in his important essay, "Primitive World View," suggested that a world view of any people consisted essentially of two pairs of binary oppositions: MAN/NOT-MAN and WE/THEY.[5] Both of these pairs imply comparison; it is the latter which underlies most forms of *cultural comparison*. When one encounters another, a place must be found for the other within or without one's cosmos.

There have been a number of important recent studies by British and American anthropologists on the comparative method, e.g., A. R. Radcliffe-Brown, "The Comparative Method in Anthropology," *J. of the Royal Anthropological Institute*, LXXXI (1951), 15-22; I. Schapera, "Comparative Method in Social Anthropology," *American Anthropologist*, LV (1953), 353-361; F. Eggan, "Social Anthropology and the Method of Controlled Comparisons," *American Anthropologist*, LVI (1954), 743-763; E. H. Ackerknecht, "On the Comparative Method in Anthropology," in R. F. Spencer, ed., *Method and Perspective in Anthropology* (Minneapolis, 1954), pp. 117-125; O. Lewis, "Comparisons in Cultural Anthropology," in *Yearbook of Anthropology 1955* (New York, 1955), pp. 259-292; M. J. Herskovits, "On Some Modes of Ethnographic Comparison," *Bijdragen tot de Taal-, Land-, en Volkenkunde*, CXII (1956), 1-20; G. P. Murdock, "Anthropology as a Comparative Science," *Behavioral Science*, II (1957), 249-254; F. W. Moore, *Readings in Cross-Cultural Methodology* (New Haven, 1961); M. Ginsberg, "The Comparative Method," in Ginsberg, *Essays in Sociology and Social Philosophy*, Vol. III, *Evolution and Progress* (New York, 1961), pp. 194-207; R. Needham, "Notes on Comparative Method and Prescriptive Alliance," *Bijdragen tot de Taal-, Land-, en Volkenkunde*, CXVIII (1962), 160-182; W. J. McEwen, "Forms and Problems of Validation in Social Anthropology," *Current Anthropology*, IV (1963), 155-183; W. Goldschmidt, *Comparative Functionalism: An Essay in Anthropological Theory* (Berkeley-Los Angeles, 1966); C. S. Ford, ed., *Cross-Cultural Approaches: Readings in Comparative Research* (New Haven, 1967). These, as well as important programmatic essays on the comparative method in History of Religions, lack methodological rigor in answering the fundamental question: "When is a parallel a true parallel?" There have been a number of criticisms of allegedly false parallels (e.g., H. J. Rose, *Concerning Parallels* [Oxford, 1934]; H. Frankfort, *The Problem of Similarity in Ancient Near Eastern Religions* [Oxford, 1951]; B. M. Metzger, "Considerations of Method in the Study of Mystery Religions," *Harvard Theological Review*, XLVIII [1955], 1-20; S. Sandmel, "Parallelomania," *J. of Biblical Literature*, LXXXI [1962], 1-13) but little positive criteria. Perhaps in the future we may learn from other disciplines concerned with classification, e.g., library science (see A. Broadfield, *The Philosophy of Classification* [London, 1946], esp. ch. I) or biological taxonomy (see the extremely stimulating recent work of E. Mayr, *Principles of Systematic Zoology* [New York, 1969]).

[4] H. F. Jones, ed., *The Notebooks of Samuel Butler* (New York, 1912), p. 94.

[5] R. Redfield, "Primitive World View," *Proceedings of the American Philosophical Association*, XCVI (1952), 30-36, reprinted in Redfield, *The Primitive World and its Transformations* (Ithaca, 1953), pp. 84-110. Passage quoted, p. 92.

Four specifications of the WE/THEY duality have been employed: (1) They are LIKE-US, (2) They are NOT-LIKE-US, (3) They are TOO-MUCH-LIKE-US (Robert Frost's "Good fences make good neighbors"), or (4) We are NOT-LIKE-THEM (expressions and polemics concerning "uniqueness"). This primary sense of comparison depends upon the living contact between two peoples, whether this contact be through travel, invasion, or trade. It is the attempt to "place" one another.

A second major class of comparison is that of *historical comparison*, whether of the popular *exemplum* type[6] or in more complex hermeneutic discussions by scientific and philosophical historians. Here the question is not communication between two living representatives of differing cultures and their mutual positioning, but between the present and the past. The question has become: are the individuals and cultures of the past LIKE-US or NOT-LIKE-US? If they were LIKE-US why should we want to know about them? If they were NOT-LIKE-US how can they be comprehended? These questions are to the fore in Dilthey's description of the hermeneutic task: "Interpretation would be impossible if [past] expressions of life were completely strange. It would be unnecessary if nothing strange were in them. It lies, therefore, between these two extremes."[7] History in general, and historical study of religion in particular, is caught between these tensions. Comparison, the existence of similarity, is the inescapable presupposition of historical research. On the one hand the historian recognizes the truth of Toynbee's remark that "this word 'unique' is a negative term signifying what is mentally inapprehensible. The absolutely unique is, by definition, indescribable."[8] On the other hand, he recognizes that he is dealing with a subject so value laden (whether it be an individual's biography or religion) as to elicit from his subject a self-consciousness of importance and uniqueness. In a shrewd passage, which I recall each time I hear the historian of religions insist on the *sui generis* character of religions, William James put the matter with precision: "The first thing the

---

[6] See J. Th. Welter, *L'Exemplum dans la littérature religieuse et didactique du moyen âge* (Paris, 1927), and the recent motif index to this complex literature by F. C. Tubach, *Index Exemplorum* (Helsinki, 1969).

[7] W. Dilthey, *Gesammelte Schriften* (Stuttgart, 1926, rp. 1958), Vol. VII, p. 255. Translated in H. P. Rickman, *Pattern and Meaning in History: Thoughts on History and Society by Wilhelm Dilthey* (New York, 1962), p. 77.

[8] A. J. Toynbee, *A Study of History* (Oxford, 1961), Vol. XII, p. 11. See further, C. B. Joynt and N. Rescher, "The Problem of Uniqueness in History," *History and Theory*, I (1960-1961), 150-162; and the symposium edited by L. Gottschalk, *Generalization in the Writings of History* (Chicago, 1963).

intellect does with an object is to class it along with something else. But any object that is infinitely important to us and awakens our devotion feels to us also as if it must be *sui generis* and unique. Probably a crab would be filled with a sense of personal outrage if it could hear us class it without ado or apology as a crustacean, and thus dispose of it. 'I am no such thing,' it would say: 'I am *myself, myself alone.* ' "[9] This tension between the subject's sense of the unique and the methodological requirement of the analogous generates both the excitement and the problematics of historical research.

The third great class of comparison is, in part, a combination of the first two. It is, at one and the same time, both observation and theory. It is the noting of similarity (LIKE-US) and the accounting for this similarity in terms of a process of *assimilation, diffusion, or borrowing* (i.e., they are LIKE-US because they ARE-US, they have COME-FROM-US, we are RELATED-TO-THEM). It is to introduce a temporal, historical framework with high value placed on priority in time. While not always displaying the hostility of early Christian theories of "demonic plagiarism,"[10] there is a clear sense of higher value and authenticity attached to the source and a sense of second-handedness, of imitiation, and even of fraud attached to the alleged borrower.[11] Furthermore, there is frequently a strong sense of in- and out-groups, of peoples from whom it is all right to have borrowed and peoples from whom one ought not. The pedigree, being "of good stock," is all-important.[12] Such diffusionist theories have remained the prime mode of accounting for similarity since the writings of Herodotus.[13]

---

[9] William James, *The Varieties of Religious Experience* (New York, 1929: Modern Library edition), p. 10.

[10] The earliest example of the demonic theory of plagiarism is Justin Martyr, I *Apology*, LXVI.4. See further the recent study by S. Grill, *Vergleichende Religionsgeschichte und die Kirchenvater* (Horn, 1960).

[11] Cf. M. Eliade, "The Quest for 'Origins' of Religion," *History of Religions*, IV (1964), 154-169, reprinted in Eliade, *The Quest: History and Meaning in Religion* (Chicago, 1969), pp. 37-53.

[12] This concern for pedigree is particularly to the fore in biblical scholarship in attempting to relate and distinguish either the Old or New Testament from its environment. See, for example, the interview with Theodore Gill, president of the San Francisco Theological Seminary: "In his own education, Dr. Gill added, the Jew as opposed to the ancient Greek, the Gnostic or the mystery religionist was the 'good guy' " and hence one focused on the Jewish background of the New Testament (quoted in the *New York Times* [May 29, 1966], Section E, p. 7). On the methodological question of "borrowings," see the articles by Metzger and Sandmel cited above, n. 3, and the older essay by R. M. Meyer, *Kriterien der Aneignung* (Leipzig, 1906).

[13] Herodotus, presumably repeating Egyptian propaganda, accounts for the

The fourth great class of comparison is *comparison as a hermeneutic device*. Here the meaning and function of a particular motif, symbol, or custom in one culture may be used as a key to interpret a similar motif, symbol, or custom in another culture by moving from what is known to what is unknown. The rationale given for this procedure may take three forms: an atemporal argument that both elements are manifestations of a common archetype or reflections of the psychic unity of mankind; a broadly temporal argument for the validity of comparing similar stages of human development (e.g., the comparisons between the Australian aborigines and certain Paleolithic religious structures); or an argument that presupposes some temporal sequence (e.g., the hermeneutic use of the notion of survivals).[14]

It will be my contention in this paper that these four great classes of comparison, when applied to religious and cultural data, have involved four modes or styles of comparison: the ethnographic, the encyclopaedic, the morphological, and the evolutionary. The remainder of this paper will be concerned with a brief characterization, history, and evaluation of these in the belief that most of the procedures and specific instances of comparison may best be understood as an application of one or more of these styles or modes.

The Ethnographic

The earliest extant example of comparative religions occurs in the well-known fragment of Xenophanes (*ca.* 570-475 B.C.): "The Ethiopians say that their gods are snub nosed and black; the Thracians say that their gods have light blue eyes and red hair."[15] However,

---

similarity between Greek and Egyptian customs by insisting that the "younger" Greeks had borrowed from the "older" Egyptians (e.g., II.4, 43, 49, 50, 57, 58, 81, 82); on the other hand he maintains that the Egyptians, being the oldest people, are dependent on no one for their customs and borrow no foreign practices (II.79, 91). The Persians, objects of scorn for both Greek and Egyptian, borrow from everyone: "No people are so ready to adopt foreign ways as are the Persians" (I.135). The subject of borrowing and diffusion on the one hand and autochthony on the other is a key factor in ethnic propaganda in the Hellenistic world; see esp. E. J. Bickerman, "Origines gentium," *Classical Philology*, XLVII (1952), 65-81.

[14] It is the notion of survivals that first gives rise to comparison as a hermeneutic device in the history of religious studies. Space forbids the demonstration of this thesis in this paper. To date the best (though sadly inadequate) study remains M. T. Hodgen, *The Doctrine of Survivals: A Chapter in the History of Scientific Method in the Study of Man* (London, 1936).

[15] H. Diels and W. Kranz, *Die Fragmente der Vorsokratiker* 5th ed. (Berlin, 1934), fr. 16 (B). See the discussion of this text by R. Pettazzoni, "Alle origini della scienza delle religioni," *Numen*, I (1954), 136f.

the text is too brief to permit one to determine the sorts of traditions which lie behind this observation or to permit one to elucidate the method of comparison being employed. The development of procedures of comparison between religions is first displayed in the writings of Herodotus (484-424 B.C.) who, in addition to his usual title, *Pater historiae*, may be accurately termed the Father of Anthropology and the Father of History of Religions.[16] Herodotus sums up the ethnography of the Ionian School of historians, and his work and procedures remain the model for the ethnographic style.[17] Central to this enterprise was the use of comparison. As M. T. Hodgen has noted: "the most significant bequest made by Herodotus to subsequent thought was his use of comparison, and his recognition, even in the fifth century B.C., of some of the problems which have emerged whenever the comparison of cultures has revealed either similarities or differences."[18] A hint as to the basis for cultural com-

---

[16] On Herodotus as the Father of Anthropology, see J. L. Myres, "Herodotus and Anthropology," in R. R. Marett, ed., *Anthropology and the Classics* (Oxford, 1908), pp. 121-168 esp. p. 125; E. E. Sikes, *The Anthropology of the Greeks* (London, 1914), p. 7; C. Kluckhohn, *Anthropology and the Classics* (Providence, 1961), p. 5. A. Grassl, *Herodot als Ethnologe* (Munich, 1903), p. 71 calls Herodotus the first comparative ethnologist. J. Réville, *Les phases successives de l'histoire des religions* (Paris, 1909), p. 48 terms Herodotus the "father of History of Religions"; A. B. Cook, *Zeus* (Cambridge, 1914), Vol. I, p. 437 calls him "the first student of comparative religion."

[17] On Greek anthropology in general, see E. E. Sikes, *The Anthropology of the Greeks*, esp. pp. 1-24; the indispensable monograph by K. Trüdinger, *Studien zur Geschichte der griechisch-römischen Ethnographie* (Basel, 1918); A. Schröder, *De ethnographiae antiquae locis quibusdam communibus observationes* (Halle, 1921); and K. Merz, *Forschungen über die Anfange der Ethnographie bei den Griechen* (Zurich, 1923). For later sources, see A. Dihle, "Zur hellenistischen Ethnographie," in M. Reverdin, ed., *Grecs et barbares* (Geneva, 1962), pp. 205-223. See the treatment of ethnographic stereotypes in classical sources by L. Vedja, "Traditionelle Konzeption und Realität in der Ethnologie," in E. Haberland, ed., *Festschrift für Ad. E. Jensen* (München, 1964), Vol. II, pp. 759-790.

For Herodotus as an anthropologist, see J. L. Myres, "Herodotus and Anthropology," in R. R. Marett, *Anthropology and the Classics*, pp. 121-168 and A. Grassl, *Herodot als Ethnologe*. For Herodotus as a historian of religions, see E. Wessling, *Prolegomena zu Herodots Nachrichten über die Religionen kulturarmer Völker* (Bonn, 1925); I. M. Linforth, "Greek Gods and Foreign Gods in Herodotus," *University of California Publications in Classical Philology*, IX:1 (1926), 1-25; Linforth, "Named and Unnamed Gods in Herodotus"; *ibid.*, IX:7 (1928), 201-243; and the brief discussion in W. Schmidt, *Geschichte der griechischen Literatur* (Munich, 1934, rp. 1959), Vol. II, pp. 611-615. An excellent survey of the state of Graeco-Roman knowledge concerning other religions may be gleaned from the series edited by C. Clemen, *Fontes historiae religionum ex auctoribus Graecis et Latinis collectos* (Bonn-Berlin, 1920-1939), Vols. I-VII, which merits reprinting.

[18] M. T. Hodgen, *Early Anthropology in the Sixteenth and Seventeenth Centuries*

parison may be found in Herodotus' report of the reply of the Athenians to the Spartans when they refused to break with the common Greek cause. Here we are given the four criteria Herodotus had for determining a cultural unity: common descent, common language, common religious practices, common customs and world view (VIII.144).[19] It will be the presence of one or more of these features in common that will allow Herodotus to make cross-cultural comparisons.

In Ionian ethnography as represented by Herodotus we find *historia* in the most literal sense of the word, "a narrative of what one has learned by inquiry," and it would appear that there was a fixed form of inquiry, a questionnaire, employed by Herodotus in his researches. The topics may be discerned in the stereotyped form Ionian ethnography followed for the presentation of its data.[20]

> I. *The Land*: (*a*) borders, measurement, shape; (*b*) nature and character of the land; (*c*) rivers; (*d*) climate; (*e*) animals, trees etc.
> II. *People—History and Customs*: (*a*) number of population; (*b*) their antiquity; (*c*) their habits (e.g., dress, food); (*d*) customs (*nomoi*). The subdivisions of this category may be best illustrated by the Scythian material in Book IV (1) gods (*theoi*, IV.59); (2) sacrifices (*thusiē*, IV.60); (3) war customs (*ta es polemon*, IV.64); (4) oracles (*manties*, IV.67); (5) oaths (*horkia*, IV.70); (6) burial practices and tombs (*taphai*, IV.71); (7) foreign customs (*zeinika nomaia*, IV.76).
> III. *Wonders and Marvels* (*thaumasia*).

What is being collected under these headings for some fifty cultures is basically a set of traveler's impressions. Something other has been encountered, and it is surprising either in its similarity or dissimilarity to what is familiar "back home." In such a context,

---

(Philadelphia, 1964), p. 25. See further, A. Grassl, *Herodot als Ethnologe*, pp. 70-74; E. E. Sikes, *Anthropology of the Greeks*, pp. 7, 16f.

[19] J. L. Myres, "Herodotus and Anthropology," in R. R. Marett, ed., *Anthropology and the Classics*, pp. 134-159 discusses these four elements. He notes that they constitute "for the first time, a reasoned scheme of ethnological criteria.

[20] The existence of this pattern was first noted by F. Jacoby in his programmatic essay, "Über die Entwicklung der griechischen Historiographie und den Plan einer neuen Sammlung der griechischen Historikerfragmente," *Klio*, IX (1909), 80-123, esp. 88-96 (reprinted: H. Bloch, ed., *Abhandlungen zur griechischen Geschichtschreibung von Felix Jacoby* [Leiden, 1956], pp. 16-64, esp. pp. 26-34), cf. Jacoby, "Herodotus," in Pauly-Wissowa, *Realencyclopädie*, Suppl. II, esp. cols. 330-332 (reprinted: Jacoby, *Griechische Historiker* [Stuttgart, 1956], esp. pp. 69f.). The stereotyped form was most extensively developed and discussed by K. Trüdinger, *Studien zur Geschichte der griechisch-römischen Ethnographie*, pp. 14-37. See further the useful chart of these formulae in W. Aly, *Formprobleme der frühen griechischen Prosa* (Leipzig, 1929), esp. p. 48.

comparison becomes primarily a means of overcoming strangeness. Geographical features, political structures, customs, and religious practices—these are at one and the same time the most ethnically distinct and humanly similar features that would attract the eye of the traveler.[21] Only rarely is the truly unique met and recorded (e.g., "The Magi are indeed a unique race [*kechōridatai pollon*] different entirely from the Egyptian priests and indeed from all other men" [I.140]); more often the differences are relativized by means of comparison.

This reliance on the traveler's eye relates Herodotus and the Ionian ethnographic tradition to ethnography as it is practiced today. Not only does the outline of *topoi* look very much like a table of contents for a contemporary fieldworker's report, but other characteristics are shared as well. Without pressing the point too far (and thus continuing the fallacious tradition in popular works on classics for finding Greek antecedents for contemporary theories such as evolution and atomic structures) there is a marked functionalism to these ancient accounts. As each culture encountered is presented largely in its own terms (the *interpretatio graeca* notwithstanding), the individual items are given in the complexity of their interrelationships and not excised from their context. They are given as they appear to the observer's vision without apparent analytical mediation. In the case of religious material, it is striking how rarely Herodotus introduces a description of a people's god or their mythology for its own sake. Of the thirteen peoples whose religion is discussed, in only one case, that of the Scythians, do the gods occupy first place in Herodotus's account. In the other twelve, priority is given to cultic institutions, and their gods or theology are only introduced insofar as it is required to comprehend the cult which has been seen by the observer. Thus in the Egyptian material, the fullest presentation of religion in Herodotus and one which clearly derives from his own travel experience, the material is not arranged as in present-day handbooks, by deities, but by animals sacred to the gods or utilized in their cult. The individual gods are only introduced as excurses under the heading of the appropriate animals.[22] The same pattern

---

[21] E.g., *Geographical features*: II.10; IV.44, 99. *Rivers*: I.202; II.10, 29, 33; IV.53. *Soils*: I.149; II.12; IV.198. *Climates*: I.142, 149; III.106; IV.198. *Political structures*: I.134, 149. *Customs*: I.74, 94, 140, 195, 198, 202, 215; II.80, 105, 167; IV.17, 23, 61, 104, 105, 168, 170, 171, 172, 186. Not only similarities but *dissimilarities* are noted: I.140, 173; II.35-38, 70; III.20; IV.109, 187.

[22] (*a*) II.35-37: General introduction to Egyptian customs. (*b*) II.38-41 *Cattle*:

may be noted in Herodotus's use of myth. He only narrates seven myths, and these he tells with extreme economy.[23] Two of them (the births of Herakles [II.43-45] and of Pan and Dionysos [II.142-146]) are told for their importance in establishing a chronological detail; five are cult aetiologies [II.42, 63, 146; VII.26; VIII.55).[24] Consistently, for Herodotus, it is the descriptions of the cultic institutions as they are seen which calls forth a discussion of the gods and not vice versa.

Herodotus's cultural comparisons are likewise dependent upon what happens to have been seen and what catches his fancy:

> Oaths are taken by these people the same way as by the Greeks except that they make a slight flesh wound in their arms.(I.74)
> The Lydians have very nearly the same customs as the Greeks except that they do not raise their girls in the same way. (I.94)
> [The Babylonian's] shoes are peculiar; not unlike those worn by the Boetians. (I.195)
> In their dress and mode of living, the Massagetae resemble the Scythians. (I.215)
> The Thracians, Scyths, Persians, Lydians and almost all other barbarians hold the citizens who practice trades in no less repute than the rest. ... These ideas prevail also in Greece, particularly among the Lacedaemonians. Corinth is the place where handicrafts are least despised. (II.167)

The difficulties with these comparisons are the same difficulties encountered in specific cultural ethnography today (as Lévi-Strauss has brilliantly argued with respect to Boas and Malinowski).[25] Such comparisons are idiosyncratic, depending upon intuition, a chance

---

"Male cattle are considered to belong to Epaphus." Discussion of Epaphus and Isis-Io. (c) II.42-46 *Sheep and Goats*: "Such Egyptians as possess a temple to the Theban Zeus ... offer no sheep in sacrifice but only goats." Discussion of Zeus Amon, Herakles, and Pan-Mendes. (d) II.47-64 *Swine*: "The pig is regarded among them as an unclean animal." Discussion of Dionysos. (e) II.65-76 *Wild animals*: "Egypt is not a region abounding in wild animals." Discussion of sacred crocodile, ibis, etc. See the brief discussion of this pattern in I. M. Linforth, "Greek Gods and Foreign Gods in Herodotus," *U. of Calif. Publ. in Classical Philology*, IX:1 (1926), 9.

[23] There are a number of mythological allusions; but these are mainly incidental, e.g., I.131, 193; II.13, 43, 123; III.8, 37, 111, 124, 125; IV.45, 59, 79, 180, 198; V.80; IX.51. This is not the context for discussion as to the degree that this economy reflects Herodotus's alleged "rationalism."

[24] See I. M. Linforth, "Named and Unnamed Gods in Herodotus," *U. of Calif. Publ. in Classical Philology*, IX:7 (1928), 207-210 where the same observation is utilized to argue a different conclusion.

[25] C. Lévi-Strauss, "History and Anthropology," in *Structural Anthropology* (New York, 1963), pp. 1-27, esp. pp. 11-16.

association, or the knowledge one happens to have at the moment of another culture. There is nothing systematic to such comparisons, they lack any basis, and so, in the end, they strike us as uninteresting, petty, and unrevealing. In Lévi-Strauss's critique, such comparison "loses the means of distinguishing between the general truths to which it aspires and the trivialities with which it must be satisfied."[26] Finally, the ethnographer is driven to generalizations which are platitudes (such as Herodotus's famous dictum, quoting Pindar, "custom is king over all" [III.38]) or to the tautologies of functionalism.[27]

Herodotus has bequeathed to us the rich tradition of culture-specific ethnography; he has bequeathed to us also the problems of such a procedure. Whether in Greco-Roman texts or in the more recent arguments concerning *Kulturkreislehre*, historicism, fieldwork, limited comparison, or functionalism—the ethnographer cannot escape generalization and comparison and thus cannot escape the problem of the basis for such generalization and comparison, its criteria, its extent, and meaning.[28]

The Encyclopaedic

The ethnographic tradition begun by the Ionian school continues with varying fortune to the present day. In Greco-Roman writers such as Ctesias on the Persians and Indians, Megasthenes on the Indians, Poseidonius on the Celts, Tacitus on the Germans, or the nationalistic ethnologies compiled by figures such as Alexander Polyhistor, the device of presenting a set group of *topoi* concerning the culture of a specific people remained a major scholarly option. Dependent as it was upon travel and first-hand acquaintance, it flourished in periods of travel and trade and declined in periods of isolation. In the West, with only an occasional pilgrim's *itinerarium* as an exception, there is little new ethnography until the *Ystoria Mongalorum* of John of Pian del Carpine in the thirteenth century.[29]

[26] Lévi-Strauss, *op. cit.*, p. 14.

[27] Compare the important critique of the tautological character of functionalist explanation by C. G. Hempel, "The Logic of Functional Explanation," in L. Gross, ed., *Symposium on Sociological Theory* (Evanston, 1959), pp. 271-307.

[28] Note that Herodotus does attempt to account for most of his comparisons by appeal to diffusion and borrowing.

[29] For editions, translations and commentaries, see esp.: *Ctesias*: J. W. McCrindle, *Ancient Indian as Described by Ktesias* (London, 1882); R. Henry, *Ctésias: La Perse, l'Inde: Les sommaires de Photius* (Paris, 1947). *Megasthenes*: E. A. Schwanbeck, *Megasthenes Indika* (Bonn, 1846: reprint, Amsterdam, 1966); J. W. Mc-

From this point on there has been, with few gaps, a relatively unbroken tradition of ethnographies.

The encyclopaedic tradition was not limited by external circumstances. Rather than the presentation of *topoi* for a single culture which has been encountered by the author as was characteristic for the ethnographic mode, the encyclopaedic style offered a topical arrangement of cross-cultural material (arranged either by subject matter or alphabetically) culled from reading.[30] It is the style of the "armchair" anthropologist rather than the fieldworker.

The tradition began with Hellanicus in the fifth century. He produced a variety of ethnographies reminding us of the works of the Ionian school (*Aegyptiaca, Persica, Scythica*) but distinguished from them by being entirely derived from reading other men's works. He also produced a set of general, topical collections with titles such as *On Peoples* (*Peri ethnōn*), *On the Foundings of Cities and Peoples* (*Ktiseis ethnōn kai poleōn*), and *Foreign Customs* (*Barbarika nomima*).[31]

Crindle, *Ancient India as Described by Megasthenes* (London, 1877, rp. 1926); on the *interpretatio graeca* in Megasthenes, see the curious work by A. Dahlquist, *Megasthenes and Indian Religion* (Uppsala, 1962), see contra, S. S. Hartman, "Dionysos and Heracles in India according to Megasthenes: A Counter-Argument," *Temenos*, I (1965), 55-64. *Poseidonius*: J. J. Tirney, "The Celtic Ethnography of Poseidonius,' *Proceedings of the Royal Irish Academy*, LX (1959), section C, pp. 189-275. *Tacitus*: E. Koestermann, *Tacitus* (Leipzig, 1964), Vol. II.2; M. Hutton, *Tacitus: Germania* (London, 1963). *John of Pian del Carpine*: A. van den Wyngaert, *Sinica Franciscana* (Quaracchi-Florence, 1929), Vol. I, pp. 27-130; C. Dawson, ed., *The Mongol Mission* (New York, 1955), pp. 3-72.

[30] There are, regrettably, no good histories of the encyclopaedic form. The best overview is by P. A. Lyon, "Encyclopaedia," in the *Encyclopaedia Britannica* 9th ed. (1875-1889), Vol. VIII, pp. 190-204 (reprinted in a less satisfactory abbreviated form in subsequent editions). See further, B. Wendt, *Idee und Entwicklungsgeschichte der enzyklopädische Literatur* (Wurzberg, 1941) (most useful as a checklist) and H. J. de Vleeschauwer, *Encyclopédie et bibliothèque* (Pretoria, 1956). On classical encyclopaedias, see O. Jahn, "Über römische Encyclopädien," *Berichte d. kön. sächsischen Gesellschaft d. Wissenschaften* (1850), phil.-hist. Kl. II:4, pp. 263-287; H. Nettleship, *Lectures and Essays on Subjects Connected with Latin Literature and Scholarship* 1st series (Oxford, 1885), esp. pp. 205f., 283-286; F. della Corte, *Enciclopedisti latini* (Genoa, 1946). On Christian medieval encyclopaedias see the standard works of C. V. Langlois, *La connaissance de la nature et du monde au moyen âge* (Paris, 1911) (revised as *La vie en France au moyen âge* [Paris, 1927], Vol. III); and L. Thorndike, *A History of Magic and Experimental Science* (New York, 1926), Vol. II. See further, M. de Bouard, "Encyclopédies medievales," *Revue des questions historiques*, CXII (1930), 258-304; and M. Hodgen, *Early Anthropology in the Sixteenth and Seventeenth Centuries* (Philadelphia, 1964), pp. 49-77 (must be used with caution; Hodgen has read no texts not in English translation).

[31] On Hellanicus, see L. Pearson, *Early Ionian Historians* (Oxford, 1939), ch. V.

If one stream of the encyclopaedic tradition descends from these sort of collections, the other stream focuses on the contents of these collections. The third group of data given in the Ionian scheme was that of wonders. While frequently these take the form of points of interest which the traveler must see, at times they express what is different about a culture, how they are NOT-LIKE-US. Thus Herodotus provides, in II.35-37, an antipodal account of Egypt: "Not only is the climate different from that of the rest of the world, and the rivers unlike any other rivers, but the people also, in most of their manners and customs, exactly reverse the common practice of mankind."[32] A similar description is given of the Scyths (IV.28). Occasionally other sorts of marvels are narrated (e.g., the Phoenix [II.73]; flying snakes [II.75], or the ants who dig up gold [III.102, 105]) but Herodotus is careful to insist that he has never seen these things but was "told" about them.

With the development of the paradoxographical tradition associated in its origin with the poet Callimachus (*fl.* 270 B.C.), these materials began to be collected in works reminiscent of more recent books such as Charles Fort's *Book of the Damned* or Robert Ripley's series, *Believe It or Not*. The encyclopaedic tradition became inextricably wedded to the quest for the exotic, the marvelous, the anomalous, the strange. Callimachus's works—*Customs of Foreign Peoples* (*Barbarika nomima*), *Curiousities Collected All Over the World according to Place* (*Thaumatōn tōn eis hapasan tēn gēn kata topous sunagōgē*)— as well as those of his descendants—the pseudo-Aristotelian (?), *De mirabilibus*, Antigonus of Carystas, *Collection of Wonderful Stories* (*Historiōn paradoxōn sunagōgē*), Phlegon of Tralles, *On Marvels and Long Lived Peoples* (*Peri thaumasiōn kai makrobiōn*)—stand in direct relationship to such later works as Frazer's *The Golden Bough*.[33] The

---

[32] This antipodal account of Egypt is traditional (cf. Sophocles, *Oed. Col.*, 337f.; Diodorus Siculus, I.27; Ammianus Marcellinus, XXII.16). On the Herodotus text, see E. Wiedemann, *Herodots zweites Buch* (Leipzig, 1890), pp. 147-149; and K. Trüdinger, *Studien zur Geschichte der griechisch-römischen Ethnographie* (Basel, 1918), pp. 34-37. On the theme in general, see C. Préaux, "Les raisons de l'originalité de l'Egypte," *Museum Helveticum*, X (1953), 203-221, esp. 204.

[33] Most of the classical paradoxographical texts are conveniently edited by A. Giannini, *Paradoxographorum graecorum reliquiae* (Milan, 1965). See further Giannini's study of the tradition, "Studi sulla paradossografia greca (I): Da Omero a Callimaco. Motivi e forme del meraviglioso," *Instituto Lombardo di scienza e lettere, Rendiconti classe di lettere*, XCVII (1963), 247-266; "Studi sulla paradossografia greca (II): Da Callimaco all'età imperiale. La letteratura paradossografia," *Acme*, XVII (1964), 99-140.

encyclopaedic tradition, fused with paradoxographical and teratological traditions, became *cabinets de curiosités*, contextless lists of strange things done by strange peoples in strange lands. Characteristic of this entire tradition is relatively little interest in explicit comparison. The material is NOT-LIKE-US, it is inhuman, monstrous, primitive, exotic. It possesses, by its very nature, no comparability with civilized or cultured men. Nor, with its interest in the unique, does the encyclopaedia compare the data in its lists. They simply cohabit within some category, inviting comparison by their very coexistence; but providing no explicit clues as to how this comparison may be undertaken.

The sheer density of the "factual" material presented—whether it be Pliny's claim to have read two thousand books by four hundred and seventy three authors and to have excerpted some twenty thousand items for his *Historia Naturalis XXXVII* or the even grander enterprise of Frazer—the almost epic quality of the lists tends to dull one's critical faculties. The data are accepted as being overwhelmingly and massively there. Interpretation and comparison are simply not asked for. Similarly it is the aesthetic of the catalogue or list to present largely a surface appearance. Depth, the problematics, are eliminated (much as in a Robbe-Grillet novel) in favor of the "hard" enumeration of things.[34] When one does begin to ask depth questions, when one inquires into the context of the material, the principles of internal order governing the lists, or asks for some evaluation of the significance of the material (other than that it is exotic and hence intrinsically interesting), the surface cracks apart. Franz Steiner, in his important book *Taboo*, has caught a classic instance in Frazer: "Burial grounds were taboo; and in New Zealand a canoe which had carried a corpse was never afterwards used, but was drawn on shore and painted red. Red was the taboo colour in New Zealand; in Hawaii, Tahiti, Tonga and Samoa it was white. In the Marquesas a man who had slain an enemy was taboo for ten days: he might have no intercourse with his wife and might not meddle with fire; he had to get some one to cook for him. A woman engaged in the preparation of cocoa-nut oil was taboo for five days or more."[35]

---

[34] See the excellent discussion of the aesthetics of the list and catalogue in H. Kenner, *Flaubert, Joyce and Beckett: The Stoic Comedians* (Boston, 1962), esp. pp. 1-4, 50-66, 70-74, 76-92, and 104-106.

[35] J. G. Frazer, "Taboo," *Encyclopaedia Britannica* 9th ed., Vol. XXIII, p. 16 (column a).

Extending Steiner's analysis, I would suggest that five different verbal associations make up this extract: (1) General thesis—burial grounds are taboo, that is, the place where the corpse was laid. This leads to the example of the New Zealand canoe in which a corpse was laid because it was taboo. (2) This canoe was painted red; this leads to the report, irrelevant to the subject of burial taboos, that in New Zealand red is a taboo colour. (3) On the order of the familiar test question, "If I say black, what do you think of?" Frazer continues a chain of association. If red is the taboo color on one Pacific island, white is taboo for four other Pacific islands. (4) Having noted color taboos on Pacific islands, Frazer recalls the taboos on Marquesa, another Pacific island, regarding a man who has slain his enemy. This report, while having nothing to do with colors or burial grounds, has at least the virtue of having something to do with death. (5) One of these Marquesan taboos involves cooking, which leads Frazer to speak of another cooking taboo in some unnamed location (presumably another Pacific island) having to do with the preparation of cooking oil. And so, on and on. After carefully working through a passage like this, which is by no means unique to Frazer or any other encyclopaedist, one can only echo Steiner's conclusion: "This is the rhetoric of association. The more clearly it stands out, the less trustworthy the scholarship of the author appears."[36]

The unfortunate link of the use of contextless lists held together by mere surface associations rather than careful, specific, and meaningful comparisons with the interest in exotic content has plagued the encyclopaedic tradition until the present time. Malinowski's charge to his anthropological colleagues likewise remains in force: "We can only plead for the speedy and complete disappearance from the records of fieldwork of the piecemeal items of information, of customs, beliefs and rules of conduct floating in the air. . . . With this [disappearance] the theoretical arguments of Anthropology will be able to drop the lengthy litanies of threaded statement which make us anthropologists feel silly and the savage look ridiculous."[37]

THE MORPHOLOGICAL

In his seminal essay on the sociology of knowledge, Karl Mannheim introduced a valuable distinction which bears directly on the question

---

[36] F. Steiner, *Taboo* (New York, 1956), p. 92.

[37] B. Malinowski, *Crime and Custom in Savage Society* (Paterson, 1964: reprint), p. 126.

of the logic of comparison as well as having profound implications for discussions of reductionism. Mannheim distinguished between "right-wing" and "left-wing" methodologies: "Early nineteenth century German conservatism ... and contemporary conservatism too, for that matter, tend to use morphological categories which do not break up the concrete totality of the data of experience, but seek rather to preserve it in all its uniqueness. As opposed to the morphological approach, the analytical approach characteristic of the parties of the left, broke down every concrete totality in order to arrive at smaller, more general, units which might then be recombined through the category of causality or functional integration."[38] Extending Mannheim's observation, the following methodological clusters emerge as possibilities:

"Right Wing": Morphological / Synthetic / Structural / Synchronic / Phenomenological.[39]

"Left Wing": Evolutionary / Analytic / Functional / Diachronic / Historical.

Each cluster has its legitimate types of tasks, questions, and procedures. Reductionism is an inherent danger for either group (although the conservative approach, by its very nature, *appears* less likely to be reductionistic than the radical; an observation not sufficiently recognized in many discussions of reductionism). A more serious problem arises when, to borrow a pun from a recent anthropological symposium, there is a muddle instead of a model, when elements from the two clusters are carelessly combined. It is this muddle, as I shall discuss below, which produced the dismay with late nineteenth and early twentieth-century use of The Comparative Method.

The rise of the "science" of Comparative Religions cannot be separated from nineteenth-century scientific thought in general. When, in 1905, Louis H. Jordan defended the legitimacy of Comparative Religion to claim for itself the title of a "science," he pointed to analogies in the field of Comparative Anatomy and Comparative

---

[38] K. Mannheim, *Ideology and Utopia* (New York, n.d.: reprint), p. 274.

[39] I use the term "phenomenological" only in the loose sense currently employed by historians of religions. For an important critique and major constructive statement, see H. Penner, "Is Phenomenology a Method for the Study of Religion?" *Bucknell Review*, XXXVIII (1970), 29-54. Penner's paper is the most suggestive and sophisticated methodological contribution by a historian of religions in the past decade.

Philology.⁴⁰ It is often forgotten how decisive a role the successes of Comparative Anatomy played in the development of the various comparative disciplines. Beginning with Buffon and continued by his great disciple, Cuvier, and as an independent development the more speculative researches of Goethe and St.Hilaire, the anatomists consistently insisted that comparison was *the* scientific method. Buffon declared that "comparison was the sovereign key to the discovery of general laws in zoology"; Goethe insisted that "natural history is basically comparison."⁴¹

As is well known, in early literature the term "anthropology" was almost exclusively limited to what is today termed "physical anthropology,"⁴² and most of the important early cultural anthropologists were themselves medical men (e.g., A. Bastian, D. Livingstone, K. von den Steinen, W. H. R. Rivers, C. G. Seligman, P. Rivet). Thus it is not surprising that Anthropology was swift to

---

⁴⁰ L. H. Jordan, *Comparative Religion, Its Genesis and Growth* (Edinburgh, 1905), *passim*.

⁴¹ Buffon is quoted in J. C. Greene, *The Death of Adam* (New York, 1961: reprint), p. 173; Goethe in W. E. Meuhlmann, *Geschichte der Anthropologie* (Bonn, n.d.), p. 69; and E. H. Ackerknecht, "On the Comparative Method in Anthropology," in R. F. Spencer, ed., *Method and Perspective in Anthropology* (Minneapolis, 1954), p. 119. Goethe's influence, while significant in cultural studies in the nineteenth century mainly in works which reflected the influence of either Schelling's *Naturphilosophie* or Spengler's cultural morphologies, has become more important in several fields of comparative studies today. It clearly underlies Eliade's use of such terms as *morphologie* and *homologie* and is explicitly acknowledged as a major influence in the works of the great Russian folklorist, V. Propp. See Propp, "Struttura e storia nello studio della favola," in G. L. Bravo's Italian translation of Propp, *Morfologia della fiaba* (Turin, 1966), esp. pp. 205-209. I do not know how to assess the comment by I. Levin, "Vladimir Propp: An Evaluation on his Seventieth Birthday," *Journal of the Folklore Institute* IV (1967), 33: "Perhaps Propp would have become a botanist, had he not felt more strongly the calling to botanize in the not less flowery fields of folk literature. Already in his early works on the 'morphology' of the folktale ... Propp established himself as a hard-working researcher and penetrating synthesizer in the tradition of Linné." The failure to sufficiently realize the influence of Goethe's morphology on Propp has undercut several recent treatments of his work, e.g., C. Lévi-Strauss, "La structure et la forme: réflexions sur un ouvrage de Vladimir Propp," *Cahiers de l'Institut de Science economique appliqué*, No. XCIX (1960), 3-36 (= Lévi-Strauss, "L'analyse morphologique des contes russes," *International Journal of Slavic Linguistics and Poetics*, III [1960], 3-36); and B. Nathhorst, *Formal or Structural Studies of Traditional Tales* (Stockholm, 1969). I regret that I have not been able to obtain a copy of V. Erlich, *Russian Formalism: History and Doctrine* (The Hague, 1955).

⁴² See J. Dieserud, *The Scope and Content of the Science of Anthropology* (Chicago, 1908) for a chronological bibliography of publications in Anthropology from the sixteenth century to 1900 which will reinforce this observation.

adopt the comparative (anatomical) method both for its treatment of physical and cultural data.[43] Likewise in Linguistics, the second great nourishing stream of the Comparative Religions method, Jacob Grimm, Friedrich Schlegel, and William von Humboldt all confessed themselves to be deeply influenced by Comparative Anatomy.[44] The same was the case for the equally influential philosophical sociologists, A. Comte and H. Spencer.[45]

The discipline of Comparative Anatomy in the eighteenth and nineteenth centuries underwent two main stages of development: first, the morphological approach; then, the evolutionary. Comparative Religions, naively reflecting this development, was basically an illegitimate and unreflective combination of the older morphological approach to the problems of comparison with the newer evolutionary frame of reference.

Linnaeus had proposed that his taxonomy represented a closed immutable system which reflected the world of nature conceived as a fixed order of permanent structures. Goethe, who first coined the word "morphology," while recognizing variability, nevertheless arranged his material serially in a hierarchy of increased organization and complexity. One series illustrated the gradations from the simplest herb to the most complex tree; another series illustrated the sequence of individual organs within the same plant from cotyledon to leaf to corolla to fruit. In no case was a temporal schema employed. The progression was one of logical-formal sequence, not growth and development in time. Goethe's scheme, despite the claims of some of his later admirers, was never evolutionary; it was a typological series that was fundamentally ahistorical while employing the most complex dialectic between the universal and the

---

[43] See Ackerknecht, "On the Comparative Method," pp. 120f., who emphasizes the significance of this point.

[44] See the quotations from Grimm, Schlegel, and von Humboldt in the important study by E. Rothacker, *Logik und Systematik der Geisteswissenschaften* (Bonn, 1948), pp. 93, 95. There are some brief but shrewd observations on the interrelationship of Humboldt to Goethe's morphological studies and an even briefer comment on Schlegel in N. Chomsky, *Cartesian Linguistics* (New York, 1966), pp. 23f., 26, and 89, n. 46.

[45] Spencer's own biological researches are well known; his constant use of anatomical and morphological analogies to illustrate and interpret social processes are found throughout his works, e.g., *The Study of Sociology* 2nd ed. (London, 1874), p. 331; *The Principles of Sociology* (London, 1876), Vol. I, pp. 469, 616-618 for important theoretical statements (compare their biological parallels in *The Principles of Biology* [London, 1864], sects. 37, 40). A. Comte was particularly influenced by the anatomist, H. M. D. de Blainville. A. Comte, *The Positive Philosophy*, H. Martineau, transl. (New York, n.d.), pp. 313-319, 329f., 336-338, 478-485.

particular, between ideal and experience, between idea and appearance, between Being and history.[46]

The constellation of terms used by Goethe to describe the status of the *Urpflanze*—it is a concept (*Begriff*), supersensible, beyond the vicissitudes of time, symbolic, a self-revealed mystery (*das offenbare Geheimnis*), visible to the mind alone—has led some interpreters to overemphasize the idealistic character of the morphology and to fail to take into account the dialectic between the type and history. The type is by definition ahistorical, yet it stands in a complex relationship to the historical. "Time is governed by the oscillations of a pendulum; the moral and scientific worlds, by oscillations between ideas and experience."[47] This "oscillation" has profound implications for the comparative enterprise. Meditation on concrete plants or animals may reveal the archetype which they manifest; meditation upon the type will reveal the vitality of the individual variations. The morphological enterprise is "to recognize living forms as such, to see in context their visible and tangible parts, to perceive them as manifestations of something within and thus to master them to a certain extent in their wholeness through a concrete vision (*Anschauung*).[48] (I note parenthetically that this seems closer to what

---

[46] Goethe's writings on the subject are conveniently available in the edition by A. B. Wachsmuth, *J. W. Goethe: Schriften zur Botanik und Wissenschaftslehre* (Munich, 1963). For the interpretation given above, see esp. R. Magnus, *Goethe as a Scientist* (New York, 1949), pp. 41f., 58-60, 116-118. See further, E. Rotten, *Goethes Urphänomen und die platonische Idee* (Giessen, 1913); E. Cassirer, *Idee und Gestalt* (Berlin, 1921), cf. Cassirer, *The Problem of Knowledge* (New Haven, 1950), pp. 118-216, esp. pp. 137-150; R. Steiner, *Goethe's Conception of the World* (London, 1928); A. Liebert, *Goethes Platonismus zur Metaphysik der Morphologie* (Berlin, 1932); R. Bertholet, *Science et philosophie chez Goethe* (Paris, 1932); A. Arber, *The Natural History of Plant Form* (Cambridge, 1942); Arber, *Goethe's Botany* (Waltham, 1946); M. Hocquette, *Les fantasies botaniques de Goethe* (Lille, 1946); E. Heller, *The Disinherited Mind* (New York, 1959), pp. 3-34; M. Marache, *Le symbole dans la pensée et l'oeuvre de Goethe* (Paris, 1960); E. M. Wilkinson, "Goethe's Concept of Form," in E. M. Wilkinson and I. A. Willoughby, *Goethe: Poet and Thinker* (London, 1962), pp. 167-184; E. Mendelsohn, "The Biological Sciences in the Nineteenth Century: Some Problems and Sources," *History of Science*, III (1964), 39-59; A. B. Wachsmuth, *Geeinte Zweinatur: Aufsätze zu Goethe's naturwissenschaftlichen Denken* (Berlin-Weimar, 1966).

[47] Quoted in Cassirer, *The Problem of Knowledge*, p. 145. I have followed his interpretation (pp. 143-147) in the above remarks.

[48] J. W. von Goethe, "Vorwort zur Morphologie," in E. von der Hellen, *et al.*, *Goethes Samtliche Werke* (Jubiläums-Ausgabe), (Stuttgart-Berlin, 1902-), Vol. XXXIX, *Schriften zur Naturwissenschaft*, Vol. I, p. 251: "die lebenden Bildungen als solche zu erkennen, ihre äussern sichtbaren, greiflichen Teile im Zusammenhange zu erfassen, sie als Andeutungen des Innern aufzunehmen und

historians of religion mean when they invoke phenomenology than the technical procedures of the philosophical phenomenological movement.) But, as in Plato, the upward path requires the downward for its fulfillment. "The particular always underlies the universal; the universal must forever submit to the particular."[49] Comparison may thus occur between the individual and the archetype; comparison may also occur between analogous members of an atemporal series (X is homologous to Y).[50] In either case, neither temporal nor causal conclusions may be drawn from such comparison, that is, X is simpler than Y, it is logically and formally prior but not necessarily prior in time.

In cultural studies, this morphological perspective might be illustrated by J. F. McLennan in 1896, when he advocated the study of the "least-developed races" which he defined as "the lowest and simplest," reminding his readers that "in the science of history old means *not old in chronology but in structure.*"[51] It is massively and masterfully illustrated in Mircea Eliade's *Patterns in Comparative Religion.* Thus when I read in Eliade his numerous and central references to *un système cohérent* behind the various manifestations and hierophanies; when he arranges a series of hierophanies from the most elementary to the most complex; when he insists that this *système* nowhere exists but that the archetypes preexist any particular manifestation, that the *systèmes* "manifest more clearly, more fully and with greater coherence what the hierophanies manifest in an individual, local and successive fashion"—I am reminded of such classic statements of the morphological enterprise as Goethe's letter to Herder (Naples, May 17, 1787).[52] The failure to recognize this

---

so das Ganze in der Anschauung gewissermassen zu beherrschen." I have followed the translation by E. Heller, *The Disinherited Mind*, p. 14.

[49] Goethe, *Maximen und Reflexionen*, No. 199 in *Goethes Samtliche Werke*, Vol. XXXIX, p. 92; see Cassirer, *Problem of Knowledge*, p. 146, and compare the text quoted on p. 144.

[50] I do not use the terms "analogy" and "homology" in the strict sense as defined by Richard Owen. Homology properly understood requires the postulation of an evolutionary development which would be inappropriate in the above discussion. (See the excellent brief description of these two terms by L. H. Hyman, *Encyclopaedia Britannica* [1969 ed.], Vol. XV, p. 838.)

[51] J. F. McLennan, *Studies in Ancient History*, 2d series (London, 1896), p. 16. (Emphasis mine, JZS.)

[52] M. Eliade, *Patterns in Comparative Religion* (New York, 1958), esp. pp. 7-10, 26, 448-451, 461f. Compare Goethe's letter to Herder: "I must confess to you that I am very close to discovering the secret of the creation and organization of plants .... The *Urpflanze* is to be the strangest creature in the world—Nature

ambience has been responsible for significant misinterpretation of the role of history and the status of the patterns in Eliade's work.

Such a morphology does have one crucial presupposition, the scientific analogue to which was clearly stated by Kant in his *Critique of Judgement*: "All such comparison presupposes this: that in respect to her empirical laws nature has observed a certain economy that to our judgement appears fitting, and an understandable uniformity, and this presupposition as a principle of *a priori* judgement must precede all comparison."[53] Whether in the strict morphology of Eliade (or the looser works of Jung or Goodenough on symbols) this "fitting economy" is assumed. There can only be a relatively limited number of systems or archetypes, though there may be an infinite number of manifestations. Comparison, while global in scope, nevertheless remains strictly limited in procedure. One may only compare within the system or between the pattern and a particular manifestation. Comparisons within the system do not take time or history into account; comparisons between the pattern and manifestation are comparisons as to the degree of manifestation and its intelligibility and do not take historical, linear development into account. If a series is proposed, it will deal with the movement from the simple to the complex, from the perfect manifestation to the fractured—in Goethe's term, with metamorphosis (compare Eliade on degradation, infantilism, etc., in *Patterns*, chapter XIII).

THE EVOLUTIONARY

In what I have termed the second stage of development of scientific theory, the comparative anatomists introduced the temporal dimension. Buffon, Cuvier, Lamarck, and Darwin drew the implication that an increased complexity reflected a process of growth, adaptation, and evolution. In so doing, they abandoned the atemporal presuppositions of their predecessors and concentrated more and more on the variability, the internal history of *individual* species. One might claim that with the introduction of a temporal frame of ref-

---

herself shall be jealous of it. With such a model ... it will be possible to invent plants *ad infinitum*. They will be strictly logical plants—i.e., even though they may not actually exist they could exist—they would not be mere picturesque or poetic shadows or dreams but would possess an inner truth and necessity. And the same law will be applicable to everything alive," in *Goethes Samtliche Werke*, Vol. XXVII, *Italienische Reise*, p. 5 (transl. in Heller, *op. cit.*, p. 10).

[53] I. Kant, *Kritik der Urteilskraft*, in E. Cassirer, ed., *Immanuel Kants Werke* (Berlin, 1913), Vol. V, p. 194.

erence, the comparative method, in the strict sense, was abandoned.[54] As I have suggested, Comparative Religion as it was practiced in the nineteenth and early twentieth centuries was essentially an illegitimate combination of the older morphological approach to comparison and the newer evolutionary frame of reference. As among the older comparative morphologists, the comparative religionists held that structures were to be studied and compared without regard to chronology and geography (or speciation, for that matter); but rather as to an increased order of complexity. However this was linked by the anthropologists and comparative religionists to an overall evolutionary frame of reference. The analyses of structure and the taxonomic classifications were employed to demonstrate a chronological chain of religious and cultural evolution on a global scale. Paradoxically (and impossibly), the newer evolutionary and temporal perspective was linked to the older ahistorical methodology. The detection of simplicity now yielded historical origins (e.g., "the primitive") rather than "logical" *Urformen*.[55]

The cultural evolutionists wedded this hybrid method to the encyclopaedic style of presenting data. The dynamics of this mode (as discussed above), its contextless lists, its lack of depth, its "hard" surface made this style ideal for avoiding the implications arising from this combination of methods. As was the case in the encyclopaedic style, a careful examination of the works of the cultural evolutionists will reveal no principles of organization or comparison. The meticulous arrangement of series, the micromovements and variations so essential to the biological evolutionists' work, were totally lacking in the studies of their cultural counterparts.

The problems inherent in this combination are displayed with clarity in the introduction to E. B. Tylor's classic work, *Primitive*

---

[54] It is significant that in both the ninth and eleventh editions of the *Encyclopaedia Britannica* the only listing under Comparison or Comparative is "Comparative Anatomy." In the ninth edition (1875-1889) it is fulsomely praised. In the eleventh edition (1910-1911) we are informed that "the term is now falling into desuetude, and lingers on practically only in the .itles of books or in the designation of university chairs. The change in terminology is chiefly the results of modern conceptions of zoology" (Vol. VI, p. 803). Thus, not atypically, the cultural disciplines adopted Comparative Anatomy as a "norm" about the same time as it was losing its status in the biological sciences.

[55] Cf. G. Widengren, "Evolutionism and the Problems of the Origin of Religion," *Ethnos*, X (1945), 57-96. The concept of "survivals," the use of geological terms such as "strata" and "fossils," certain developments in Comparative Philology, all contributed to this shift; but examination of these details will be reserved for a future publication (see n. 14, above).

Culture (1871). Tylor begins with a rather confused attempt to apply the Linnaean category of species to cultural phenomena: "What [the ethnographer's] task is like may be almost perfectly illustrated by comparing these details of culture with the species of plants and animals as studied by the naturalist. To the ethnographer the bow and arrow is a species, the habit of flattening children's skulls is a species, the practice of reckoning numbers by tens is a species. The geographical distribution of these things and their transmission from region to region, have to be studied as the naturalist studies the geography of his botanical and zoological species."[56] This attempt to answer the question of what in culture corresponds to the morphologist's organism or the evolutionist's species remains unconvincing in Tylor as well as in later theorists. As Lévi-Strauss shrewdly observed, "The historical validity of the naturalist's reconstructions is guaranteed, in the final analysis, by the biological link of reproduction. An ax, on the contrary, does not generate another ax."[57]

As Tylor continued to articulate his methodological presupposition, it became clear that he was dependent upon the combination of evolution with an ahistorical methodology. The purpose of his scheme of classification is that of demonstrating "how the phenomena of culture may be classified and arranged, stage by stage, in a probable order of evolution."[58] But in so doing Tylor claimed, as had the older comparative morphologists, the privilege of ignoring chronology and geography: "Little respect need be had in such comparisons for date in history or for place on the map; the ancient Swiss lake-dweller may be set beside the Medieval Aztec, and the

---

[56] E. B. Tylor, *Primitive Culture* (London, 1871: reprint, New York, 1958), Vol. I, p. 8.
[57] C. Lévi-Strauss, *Structural Anthropology*, pp. 4f.
[58] Tylor, *Primitive Culture*, Vol. I, p. 6. There has been in recent years a renewed appreciation of Tylor's evolutionary hypotheses by anthropologists. See I. L. Murphree, "The Evolutionary Anthropologists," *Proceedings of the American Philosophical Society*, CV (1961), 265-300; G. W. Stocking, Jr., "Matthew Arnold, E. B. Tylor and the Uses of Invention," *American Anthropologist*, LXV (1963), 783-799; J. W. Burrow, "Evolution and Anthropology in the 1860's," *Victorian Studies*, VII (1963), 137-154; M. Opler, "Cause, Process and Dynamics in the Evolutionism of E. B. Tylor," *Southwestern Journal of Anthropology*, XX (1964), 123-144; G. W. Stocking, Jr., "'Cultural Darwinism' and 'Philosophical Idealism' in E. B. Tylor," *Southwestern Journal of Anthropology*, XXI (1965), 130-147; J. W. Burrow, *Evolution and Society: A Study in Victorian Social Theory* (Cambridge, 1966), pp. 228-259 *et passim*. This latter study by Burrow is the most significant contribution to the study of this theme.

Ojibwa of North America beside the Zulu of South Africa. As Dr. Johnson contemptuously said when he had read about the Patagonians and South Sea Islanders in Hawkesworth's Voyages, 'one set of savages is like another.' How true a generalization this really is, any Ethnological Museum may show."[59] Comparison and the recognition of parallels, in such a program, might be divorced from historical studies and considerations. Similarities were to be explained on the basis of their reflecting similar "logical stages" of human development and cultural evolution (the *Urmensch* corollary to the *Urpflanze*) though, again impossibly, chronological implications were to be drawn.[60] This hypothesis and its relationship to theories drawn from comparative anatomy was clearly formulated by J. G. Frazer in the "Preface" to the concluding part of *The Golden Bough*: "If there is one general conclusion which seems to emerge from this mass of particulars, I venture to think that it is the essential similarity in the working of the less developed human mind among all races, which corresponds to the essential similarity in their bodily frame revealed by comparative anatomy."[61]

These two legacies from biological theories—the linkage of the comparative method to evolutionary presuppositions and its a-historical method—combined in a motley hybrid, when brought over into the cultural realm and religious scholarship came swiftly under attack. Perhaps the most significant critic was the doyen of American anthropology, Franz Boas, in his article first published in 1896 entitled "The Limitations of the Comparative Method of Anthropology."[62] In this paper (which had great impact when

---

[59] Tylor, *Primitive Culture*, Vol. I, p. 6. Compare M. Eliade, *Patterns*, pp. 461f. I would insist that what is a legitimate method for Eliade as a morphologist is illegitimate for Tylor as an evolutionist.

[60] This assumption of the psychological unity of mankind runs counter to the assumption, from Herodotus to the present, that similarity may be explained by postulating diffusion and culture contact. The debate between these two points of view (parallel development of similar minds and diffusion) makes up the dullest part of Victorian anthropological speculation for the modern reader. See the precise formulation of the issue in Tylor, *Researches into the Early History of Mankind and the Development of Civilisation* 3rd ed. (London, 1878: reprinted, P. Bohannan, ed., Chicago, 1964), pp. 3f. For a useful review of the arguments for each position, see A. J. Toynbee, *A Study of History* (Oxford, 1962: reprint), Vol. I, pp. 424-440 (Appendix to I. C. [iii] [b]).

[61] J. G. Frazer, *Balder the Beautiful* (London, 1935), Vol. I, p. vi.

[62] F. Boas, "The Limitations of the Comparative Method of Anthropology," *Science*, n.s. IV (1896), 901-908: reprinted in Boas, *Race, Language and Culture* (New York, 1940), pp. 270-280.

published, even though its argument seems slight today), Boas insisted that "the same phenomena may develop in a multitude of ways" and "demanded" that "comparisons be restricted to those phenomena which have been proved to be the effects of the same cause"⁶³—thus attempting to introduce an analogue of "the biological link of reproduction" (Lévi-Strauss). It needs to be stressed that Boas did not reject comparison *per se*, as this point was immediately misunderstood by some of Boas's American and British colleagues. Indeed, as late as 1938, he called for "a cultural *morphology* founded on comparative studies of similar *forms* in different parts of the world."⁶⁴ He sought rather to improve the method, to tighten up the criteria by which similarities were determined and on the basis of which comparisons might be made. He did so by introducing the temporal dimension so important to the biological researches of his time. Boas suggested the employment of what he termed "the historical method"; "Historical inquiry must be considered the critical test that science must require before admitting facts as evidence. By means of it, the comparability of the collected material must be tested, and uniformity of processes must be demanded as proof of comparability."⁶⁵

The results of this article were unfortunate. Boas had linked comparison to naïve evolutionary theory and had juxtaposed what he termed historical method to this combination, thus setting off a conflict which continues to the present day (Boas's historical method, it may be noted, seems no less naïve today).⁶⁶ With the general loss of faith in social Darwinism and theories of progress, with the rising dominance of historicistic and positivistic thinking in the social sciences, Boas's article could be and was used as the excuse for jettisoning the comparative enterprise and for purging one's work of all but the most limited and specific comparisons.⁶⁷

---

⁶³ Boas, *op. cit.*, 903f. (= *Race*, p. 275). However Boas is not usually sanguine about the possibility of demonstrating like causes; see Boas, "The Occurrence of Similar Inventions in Areas Widely Apart," *Science*, IX (1887), 485f.

⁶⁴ F. Boas, *General Anthropology* (New York, 1938), p. 675. (Emphasis mine, JZS.)

⁶⁵ Boas, "Limitations," 907 (= *Race*, p. 279).

⁶⁶ For an attack on the historical presuppositions of Boas, see P. Radin's cranky work, *The Method and Theory of Ethnology* (New York, 1933), pp. 24-60 and the brief but brilliant critique of Lévi-Strauss, *Structural Anthropology*, pp. 1-27, esp. pp. 6-14.

⁶⁷ The method of limited comparison advocated by Boas has become almost a dogma in American anthropological circles, frequently stated in naïve form,

As Paul Mercier noted in his recent history of Anthropology, Boas's article represented the end of an era.[68] The problem for History of Religions today is that a new era has not yet arrived to take its place. And thus we need to reflect on our own history, for: "If anthropology returns to the comparative method, it will certainly not forget what it has learned meanwhile in general and what it has learned about the limitations of the method in particular. It will return only in that spiral like movement, so characteristic of scientific thought, arriving after half a century at the same point but at a higher level. It will know better how and what to compare than it knew fifty years ago."[69] This applies to our discipline as well.

AFTERWORD

The discussion of general methodological principles for comparison has not advanced since the original publication of this essay. See, among others, the excellent reviews of the state of the question by Gopāla Śaraṇa, *The Methodology of Anthropological Comparisons: An Analysis of Comparative Methods in Social and Cultural Anthropology* ([*Viking Fund Publications in Anthropology*, Number LIII] Tucson, 1975) and Ulrich Weisstein, *Comparative Literature and Literary Theory: Survey and Introduction* (Bloomington, 1973) both of which contain rich bibliographies.

Note should be taken of the careful specification of eight modes of comparison within a limited area by Morton Smith, *Tannaitic Parallels to the Gospels* ([*Journal of Biblical Literature Monograph Series*, Volume VI] Philadelphia, 1951) and its effective application by Jacob Neusner, *Aphrahat and Judaism: The Christian-Jewish Argument in Fourth-Century Iran* ([Studia Post-Biblica, Vol. XIX] Leiden, 1971) esp. pp. 187-195. If latitude be still permitted on the wider cross-cultural comparisons, surely this much ought to be required of any historian of religions working within a particular cultural context.

---

e.g., E. Sapir, *Time Perspective in Aboriginal American Culture: A Study in Method* (Ottawa, 1946), p. 50 who maintains that comparison "needs to be restricted to the bounds set by at most a continent or adjacent parts of two continents." The method of limited comparison falls under the strictures suggested above in the section on the ethnographic mode.

[68] P. Mercier, *Histoire de l'anthropologie* (Paris, 1966), pp. 29f.

[69] E. H. Ackerknecht, "On the Comparative Method in Anthropology," in R. F. Spencer, ed., *Method and Perspective in Anthropology* (Minneapolis, 1954), pp. 124f.

CHAPTER TWELVE

I AM A PARROT (RED)

The primitive Brazilian Indian can accept without thought of contradiction anything whatsoever that is told him.
H. Baldus, 1931.

There are some animals which have played so decisive a role in the history of the history of religions that they may truly be seen as emblems (if not totems!) of our discipline. One might recall Saint Nilus and his camel which so animated discussions of sacrifice in the early quarter of this century (see now the major review of this tradition by J. Henninger)[1] or, more recently, the pangolin in the important researches of Mary Douglas on taboo, dirt, and systems of order[2] (see further the splendid parallel study by Ralph Bulmer, "Why Is a Cassowary Not a Bird?").[3] However the most notable creature of our time is, perhaps, the Brazilian parrot in the traditions of the Bororo tribe, which serves as the *"mythe de référence"* for the three published volumes of Lévi-Strauss's *Mythologiques* despite formidable competition from jaguars, armadillos, and the like.[4] Perhaps this is due not only to the central role of the bird among the Bororo,[5] but also because the bird has a "prehistory"— historians of religion have met the Bororo and their parrots before in an ethnographic report which has continued to fascinate scholars from its first mention in 1894 to the present.

The report is given in the narrative of the second Brazilian expedition of Karl von den Steinen (1887-1888), *Unter den Natur-*

---

[1] J. Henninger, "Ist der sogenannte Nilus-Berichte brauchbare religionsgeschichtliche Quelle?" *Anthropos*, L (1955), 81-148.

[2] M. Douglas, "Animals in Lele Religious Thought," *Africa*, I (1957), 46-58 (reprinted in J. Middleton, ed., *Myth and Cosmos* [Garden City, L.I., 1967], pp. 231-247); M. Douglas, *Purity and Danger: An Analysis of Concepts of Pollution and Taboo* (New York, 1966), *passim*.

[3] R. Bulmer, "Why Is the Cassowary Not a Bird? A Problem of Zoological Taxonomy among the Karam of the New Guinea Highlands," *Man*, II (1967), 5-25.

[4] C. Lévi-Strauss, *The Raw and the Cooked* (New York, 1969), pp. 35-37 *et passim*.

[5] C. Albisetti-A. J. Venturelli, *Enciclopédia Bororo* (Campo Grande, 1962), Vol. I, pp. 725-730; Lévi-Strauss, *The Raw and the Cooked*, esp. p. 47.

völkern Zentral-Brasiliens (first edition, 1894; second edition, 1897).[6] Von den Steinen, after noting that in order to understand the native "we must put totally out of our minds the boundaries between man and the animal,"[7] goes on to report that "the Bororos boast of themselves that they are red parrots (Araras)." This, he insists, is not merely to claim that after death the Bororo become parrots or that parrots have been transformed into men. The Bororo conceive of themselves simultaneously as birds and men: "They think of themselves as parrots";[8] "the red parrots are Bororo, indeed the Bororo go even further as we have already noted and say 'we are parrots' [*wir sind Araras*]."[9] On the other hand, von den Steinen does introduce metamorphic imagery: the Bororo call themselves parrots "as a caterpillar says that he is a butterfly";[10] and more explicitly (and in apparent contradiction to his previous remarks), "the Bororo are parrots because their dead transform themselves into parrots,"[11] "[their] belief is that the Bororo man or woman after death becomes a red parrot."[12]

No study of the Bororo listed in H. Baldus' definitive bibliography of the ethnology of Brazilian tribes that I have seen independently confirms von den Steinen's claim that the Bororo flatly assert: "*Die roten Araras sind Bororo . . . wir sind Araras.*"[13] Where it has continued to be repeated and discussed is in books on "primitive mentality" where it takes its place in what Malinowski termed "the lengthy litanies of threaded statement which make us anthropologists feel silly and the savage look ridiculous."[14] Thus we learn from a Frazer or a Cassirer that the Trumai of North Brazil

[6] K. von den Steinen, *Unter den Naturvölkern Zentral-Brasiliens* (Berlin, 1894), esp. pp. 352f.; 2d ed. (Berlin, 1897), esp. pp. 305f. (In this paper I cite the 1st ed.) See further the translation by E. Schaden with a valuable introduction to von den Steinen's work by H. Baldus, *Entre os aborígenes do Brasil Central* (São Paulo, 1940), esp. pp. 452f. There is an evaluation of von den Steinen's material on the Bororo (largely philological) by M. Cruz, "Em tôrno do livro 'Entre os aborígenes do Brasil Central' de von den Steinen," *Revista do Arquivo municipal*, LXXXIV (1942), 163-172.

[7] Von den Steinen, *Unter den Naturvölkern*, p. 351.
[8] *Ibid.*, pp. 352f.
[9] *Ibid.*, p. 512.
[10] *Ibid.*, p. 353.
[11] *Ibid.*, p. 353.
[12] *Ibid.*, p. 511.
[13] H. Baldus, *Bibliografia crítica da etnologia Brasiliera* (São Paulo, 1954), s.v. Bororo.
[14] B. Malinowski, *Crime and Custom in Primitive Society* (Paterson, 1964: rp.), p. 126.

say that they are aquatic animals, the natives of Mabuiag think of themselves as cassowaries, the headman of the Dieri tribe was thought to be a seed-bearing plant—and that the Bororo say that they are red parrots.[15]

This paper will consider a number of representative examples of the use and interpretation of this particular utterance, "We are red parrots," in the history of the discussion of "primitive mentality." I intend by this study not only a chapter in the history of our discipline, but also a beginning attempt to clarify a thorny methodological question: How should the historian of religion interpret a religious statement which is apparently contrary to fact? The Bororo is not a parrot—as one psychiatrist noted, presumably applying the ultimate test of speciation, "he does not try to mate with other parakeets"[16]—and any interpretation of von den Steinen's report must begin with this primary fact.

Alfred Hitchcock has demonstrated that it does not spoil a mystery to give away the solution at the beginning, so let us start with what the Bororo intended to communicate and then work our way backward. The Bororo never said that they were red parrots in the sense that von den Steinen and the majority of his later commentators understood them. They declared several times, according to von den Steinen's own account, that when they are dead they will become red parrots, and thus they may speak of themselves as being red parrots in the present "as a caterpillar says that he is a butterfly." The identification is quite specific. Only the Bororo will become red parrots. When pressed, they speculated with von den Steinen that members of other tribes will become other species of birds, that Negroes will become black vultures and the white man would probably become a white heron.[17] This belief in the transformation of the Bororo after death into red parrots is well attested in the ethnographic literature, for example, Lévi-Strauss: "As for the ani-

---

[15] E.g., J. G. Frazer, *The Golden Bough*, 3d ed. (London, 1911-15), Vol. VIII, pp. 206-208; E. Cassirer, *An Essay on Man* (New Haven, 1944), pp. 82f.

[16] W. Percy, "The Symbolic Structure of Interpersonal Process, *Psychiatry*, XXIV (1961), 39-52. This quote is on p. 48, n. 47.

[17] Von den Steinen, p. 512. The 'solution' was already unambiguously recognized by É. Durkheim and M. Mauss in their famous essay on classification (1901-2): "The Bororo sincerely imagines himself to be a parrot; at least, though he assumes the characteristic form only after he is dead, in this life he is to that animal what the caterpillar is to the butterfly" (Durkheim-Mauss, *Primitive Classification* [Chicago, 1963], pp. 6f.).

mals, some belong to the world of men—birds and fish, above all—
and some, as in the case of certain terrestrial animals, to the physical
universe. The Bororo consider, therefore, that their human shape is
transitory: midway between that of the fish (whose name they have
adopted for themselves) and the *arara* (in whose guise they will
complete the cycle of their transmigrations)."[18] This belief in transmigration into birds needs to be distinguished from the kind of
phenomena we have usually termed "totemic" and, more particularly,
from the notions of animal guardians, nagualism, the alter ego, and
visionary animal transformations (such as the widely read report
of Carlos Castaneda 'becoming' a black crow)[19] which are common
in the Americas, especially in association with shamanistic traditions.[20] Such beliefs are likewise found among the Bororo, who

---

[18] C. Lévi-Strauss, *Tristes Tropiques* (New York, 1964), p. 219. Cf. Lévi-Strauss, *The Raw and the Cooked*, p. 47: "The Bororos believe in a complicated system of transmigration of souls: the latter are thought to be embodied for a time in the macaws." For other reports, see T. Koch-Grünberg, *Zum Animismus der südamerikanischen Indianer* (Leiden, 1900), pp. 10-19, esp. pp. 12, 14; A. Tonelli, "Il nome dei vivi e dei degunti (aroe) presso gl'Indi Orari (Bororo Orientali) del Matto Grosso," in *Festschrift P. W. Schmidt* (Vienna, 1928), pp. 734-739, esp. pp. 738f.; A. Colbacchini and C. Albisetti, *Os Boróros Orientais* (São Paulo-Rio de Janeiro, 1942), p. 87; M. Cruz, "O cemitério dos Bororos," *Revista do Arquivo Municipal*, XCVIII (1944), 127-130; G. Mussolini, "Os meios de defensa contra a moléstia e a morte en duas tribos brasileiras: Kaingang de Duque de Caxias e Boróro oriental," *Revista do Arquivo Municipal*, CX (1946), 7-152, esp. 67, 69f., 100; C. Albisetti and A. J. Venturelli, *Enciclopédia Bororo*, Vol. I, pp. 100-104, esp, p. 102. But note, as well, the Bororo tradition that they have *descended from caterpillars*. While this tradition may be a wordplay (*aororo/aroro*), it might as well explain the metamorphic inagery quoted above and discussed below. See A. Colbacchini, *A Tribu dos Bororos* (Rio de Jainero, 1919), p. 51 and Albisetti and Venturelli, *Enciclopédia Bororo* Vol. I, p. 175.

[19] C. Castaneda, *The Teachings of Don Juan: A Yaqui Way of Knowledge* (Berkeley-Los Angeles, 1968), pp. 90-94, 128f. See the remark of Don Juan: "Am I a man or a bird? I'm a man who knows how to become a bird " (p. 45). For the relationship of crow, "wizard" and animal transformations among the Yaqui, see R. L. Beals, *The Contemporary Culture of the Cáhita Indians* (Washington, D.C., 1945), pp. 196-198.

[20] For a general theoretical discussion, see the curious study by O. Falsirol, *Il totemismo e l'animalismo dell'anima* (Naples, 1941). On the complex subject of animal guardians, nagualism, and the alter ego (even further distinctions are required, see C. Wisdom, "The Supernatural World and Curing," in S. Tax, editor, *Heritage of Conquest* [Glencoe, 1952], p. 122) see the comprehensive monographs by R. Benedict, *The Concepts of the Guardian Spirit in North America* (Menasha, 1923); G. Foster, "Nagualism in Mexico and Guatemala," *Acta Americana*, II (1944), 85-103; and J. Haeckel, "Die Vorstellung vom Zweiten Ich in den ameri-kanischen Hochkulturen," *Wiener Beiträge zur Kulturgeschichte und Linguistik*, IX (1952), 124-188. Of particular interest are the studies by H. Baldus, "Super-natural Relations with Animals among Indians of Eastern and Southern Brazil,"

believe their shamans to be capable of assuming animal forms to perform a variety of functions—including becoming parrots to gather fruit.[21]

Von den Steinen appears to have realized the possibility of this solution. With one exception, no commentator on the Bororo tradition has noted that, following his report, von den Steinen speculated that the formula "we are birds" is a later, secondary form. The original formula, he suggested, was "I become a bird" or "I have a [soul] bird."[22] However, this history of the concept does not remove the difficulty of the saying, "We are araras." This, von den Steinen continued to believe, rests on the inability of the Indian to distinguish animals from men.

On both internal and external grounds, we are justified in concluding that von den Steinen fundamentally misinterpreted the Bororo's intention. His own account predominantly witnesses to a postmortem belief in the transformation of the Bororo into a parrot, and he offers a theory of the original form of the saying which requires this future understanding of the statement. The postmortem identification among the Bororo is independently confirmed by other ethnologists, the present identification of the Bororo as parrots is not. The

---

Proceedings of the 30th International Congress of Americanists (São Paulo, 1955), pp. 195-198; and O. Zerries, "Die Vorstellung zum Zweiten Ich und die Rolle der Harpye in der Kultur der Naturvölker Südamerikas," *Anthropos*, LVII (1962), 889-914. Though concerned with a different culture area, see the perceptive remarks by E. Z. Vogt, "Human Souls and Animal Spirits in Zincantan," in *Échanges et communications: Mélanges offerts à Claude Lévi-Strauss* (The Hague, 1970), Vol. II, pp. 1148-1167.

[21] For general material on South American shamanism, see the various articles by A. Métraux, esp. "Le shamanisme chez les indiens de l'Amérique du Sud tropicale," *Acta Americana*, II (1944), 197-219, 320-341; and "Religion and Shamanism," in *Handbook of South American Indians* (Washington, D.C., 1949), Vol. V, 559-599. The Bororo material, with its complex distinctions between the *bari* and *aroettowarare*, has been discussed by Colbacchini and Albisetti, *Os Boróros Orientais*, pp. 87-133; A. Tonelli, "Alcune notizie sui Baere e sugli Aroettawarare 'medici-stregoni' degli indi Bororo-Orari del Matto Grosso," *Atti del XXII Congresso Internazionale degli Americanisti: Roma, 1926* (Rome, 1928), Vol. II, pp. 395-413; R. Lowie, "The Bororo," *Handbook of South American Indians* (Washington, D.C., 1946), Vol. I, pp. 432f.; G. Mussolini, "Os meios de defesa contra a moléstia e a morte," 74-93 *et passim*; Albisetti and Venturelli, *Enciclopédia Bororo*, Vol. I, pp. 115-120, 239-253; and Lévi-Strauss, *Tristes Tropiques*, pp. 222-224. For the detail about becoming parrots, see Colbacchini and Albisetti, p. 131; and Lévi-Strauss, *The Raw and the Cooked*, p. 318.

[22] Von den Steinen, pp. 512f. Cf. N. W. Thomas, "Transmigration (Primitive)," in J. Hastings, ed. *Encyclopaedia of Religion and Ethics* (New York, 1922), Vol. XII, p. 429.

theory which von den Steinen offers to account for the present identification, that the Bororo cannot distinguish between men and animals, is patently false even on the basis of von den Steinen's own report and owes more to his reading of contemporary anthropological theory than to field observation.[23]

I know of only two later scholars who have brought this Bororo belief in transmigration directly to bear on von den Steinen's report: Rafael Karsten, the Finnish anthropologist, in *The Civilisation of South American Indians* (1926) and, more fully, in his posthumous volume, *Studies in the Religion of the South American Indians East of the Andes* (1964), and the Dutch historian of religions, Th. P. van Baaren, in a brief review of the von den Steinen tradition published in 1969.[24] Karsten, in his later monograph, provides a rich comparative framework for his thesis that the notion of the transmigration of souls into animals and plants is one of the key elements in South American Indian religion. While much of his material is drawn from late nineteenth- and early twentieth-century ethnography, his evidence is strikingly confirmed by more recent studies, such as Otto Zerries's work among the Waika and Gerardo Reichel-Dolmatoff's rich report on the Desana.[25] Karsten claims: "All animals have once been men, or all men animals. This seems to be a tenet explicitly or implicitly held by all [South American] tribes."[26] However, his evidence for this assertion is an unconvincing mixture of animal clan names, food taboos, alter ego traditions, and nagualism, along with well-documented beliefs in transmigration.[27] It is within this framework

---

[23] See below, note 32.

[24] R. Karsten, *The Civilisation of the South American Indians* (London, 1926); R. Karsten (A. Runeberg and M. Webster, editors), *Studies in the Religion of the South American Indians East of the Andes* (Helsinki, 1964), esp. pp. 50-74; Th. P. van Baaren, "Are the Bororo Parrots or Are We?" in *Liber Amicorum: Studies in Honor of Professor Dr. C. J. Bleeker* (Leiden, 1969), pp. 8-13.

[25] O. Zerries, "Die Vorstellungen der Waika-Indianer des oberen Orinoko (Venezuela) über die menschliche Seele," *Proceedings of the Thirty-second International Congress of Americanists: Copenhagen, 1956* (Copenhagen, 1958), pp. 105-113; Zerries, *Waika: Die kulturgeschichtliche Stellung der Waika-Indianer des oberen Orinoco im Rahmen der Völkerkunde Südamerikas* (Frankfurt am Main, 1964), Vol. I, pp. 237-284, esp pp. 256-264; G. Reichel-Dolmatoff, *Amazonian Cosmos: The Sexual and Religious Symbolism of the Tukano Indians* (Chicago, 1971), pp. 63-65, 192f. *et passim*.

[26] Karsten, *Civilisation*, p. 294, cf. p. 435; *Studies*, p. 70.

[27] Karsten's material in *Studies* from the Ona (p. 51), Toba (p. 54), Gurani (pp. 55f.), Itonama (p. 56), Gayacatazes (p. 61), Piaroa (p. 62), and Auracanian (p. 69) tribes appears to reflect some doctrine of transmigration. His material from the Auracanian (pp. 51f.), Juris (p. 61), Vainumá (pp. 61f.), Gonjiros, and

of "the doctrine of metempsychosis" that Karsten places the Bororo tradition. Almost every important animal is "regarded as the temporary or permanent abode of a disembodied human soul. Thus the Bororo identify themselves with red macaws: the Bororo are macaws and the macaws are Bororo. The souls of both men and women are believed to transmigrate into this bird."[28] His report on the Bororo, derived entirely from von den Steinen, is unfortunately marred by combining transmigration motifs with food taboos, hunting rituals, magical transformations, etc.[29] Nevertheless, he has under-

---

Awawaks (pp. 62-64, 73f.) seems only to reflect the presence of animal clan names. His general discussion (pp. 52f.) and material from the Jibaro (pp. 56-59, 64f.), Caribs and Arawaks (pp. 65f.), Checo (p. 67), Quichan (pp. 67f.), and some Ecuadorian tribes reflects nagualism and related themes of magical transformation. His material on pp. 71-73 clearly pertains to alter-ego beliefs. (N.B. I have only reviewed the material *as given* in Karsten. I have neither checked the accuracy of his summary of the ethnography nor checked his original sources against more recent reports.)

[28] Karsten, *Studies*, p. 59. Compare the placing of the Bororo material within a similar context, without however providing Karsten's theoretical framework, in H. Baldus, *Indianerstudien im nordöstlichen Chaco* (Leipzig, 1931), p. 81.

[29] Karsten, *Studies*, pp. 59-61, provides a summary account of the Bororo entirely derived from von den Steinen. With respect to his interpretative framework, several details may be noted: (*a*) The plucking of the feathers of the tame parrots and the painting of the plucked spots with a sap that turns them yellow is not a "precaution against its spirit" (pp. 59, 61). It produces yellow feathers which are highly prized in ornamentation (Lowie, *Handbook*, Vol. I, p. 424). The same practice among the Desana involves solar symbolism (Reichel-Dolmatoff, *Amazonian Cosmos*, p. 187); this may be the case among the Bororo. (*b*) The "blessing" of a slain animal (von den Steinen's term) by the *bari* does not seem to be related to a "totemic" concept (*Studies*, p. 60), but rather is a propitiation of the animal's guardian spirit (O. Zerries, "Primitive South America and the West Indies," in W. Krickenberg, et al., *Pre-Columbian American Religions* [New York, 1968], p. 270, who follows Karsten's earlier understanding of the ritual in Karsten, *Civilisation*, p. 484). For other interpretations and descriptions of the ritual, see R. Waehneldt, "Exploração da Provincia do Matto Grosso," *Revista trimensal do Instituto historico y geographico do Brasil*, XXVI (1864), 216; von den Steinen, pp. 491-493; V. Frič and P. Radin, "Contributions to the Study of the Bororo Indians," *Journal of the Royal Anthropological Institute*, XXXVI (1906), 392; M. Cruz, "O exorcismo da caça, do peixe e das frutas entre os Borôro," *Revista do Arquivo Municipal*, LXXXIX (1943), 151-156; Lévi-Strauss, *Tristes Tropiques*, p. 204. This needs also to be related to the complex rituals surrounding the *mori* hunt and to the portions of any hunt set aside for the *bari* as *mori* (see Colbacchini and Albisetti, *Os Bororos Orientais*, pp. 83f.; Lowie, *Handbook*, Vol. I, p. 428; Albisetti and Venturelli, *Enciclopédia Bororo*, Vol. I, pp. 245-248, 803f.; and Lévi-Strauss, *Tristes Tropiques*, pp. 219-221). (*c*) For the *bari's* tranformation into animals—a belief which ought not be combined with a general notion of transmigration—see the material cited in n. 23 above. (*d*) The animal clan names cannot be confused with food taboos in order to suggest a "totemic" system. As Lévi-Strauss has noted, among the Bororo the clan species are freely killed and

stood the Bororo claim as it was intended. Professor van Baaren, confining himself to a close reading and analysis of von den Steinen's text (and in apparent ignorance of Karsten's work) argues a similar conclusion: "According to the Bororo, man and arara are two different manifestations of one and the same entity. Man is potentially an arara; this, however, is quite a different thing from stating that he is one actually, here and now. Man and arara are not identical in the sense that a man is here and now at the same time an arara: as long as he is a man he is only potentially an arara. The comparison of caterpillar and butterfly leads us to conclude that the arara is a form in which man manifests himself after a transformation, after death."[30]

I should not like to suggest that the correction of von den Steinen's present interpretation of the identification and the substitution of a postmortem understanding does any more than shift the problem (although, prima facie, it *seems* less difficult). For us, the meaning of the phrase "we will become parrots after death" remains as problematic as "we are now parrots" and, apparently, just as contrary to fact. But the exploration of the meaning of this future identification may be set aside for future study. For now it suffices to say that, for me, the key to exegesis lies in Lévi-Strauss's observation of the Bororo differentiation between aquatic, terrestrial, and aerial realms and the animals associated with them: the Bororo were fish, they are now men, they will become birds.[31]

Leaving this question aside, it is possible to perform a "thought experiment." What if we did not have this apparent tension in von den Steinen between realized and futuristic parrothood and the supporting evidence of transmigration beliefs culled from later scholars? *What if we only knew that the Bororo insist that they are men and parrots at one and the same time?* The majority of scholars who have quoted von den Steinen have assumed that this was the case, and they have followed von den Steinen's mistaken lead in assuming that the key to exegesis lay in the fact that the Bororo cannot distinguish between animals and men or between different species of animals.[32]

---

eaten (Lévi-Strauss, "Contribution a l'étude de l'organisation sociale des indiens Bororo," *Journal de la Société des Américanistes*, XXVIII [1936], 298), while the most rigid food taboos pertain to the deer, a "non-totemic species" (Lévi-Strauss, *The Savage Mind* [Chicago, 1966], p. 99).

[30] Van Baaren, p. 12.
[31] See above, note 18.
[32] The statement in von den Steinen (p. 351) admits no qualification: "Wir müssen uns die Grenzen zwischen Mensch und Tier vollständig wegdenken."

The earliest use of the Bororo tradition, and one that remains dominant in the literature, is as an illustration of the alleged inability of primitive man to make distinctions. It is all but impossible to recover the origins of this regnant notion.[33] Certainly its most sophisticated nineteenth-century form was represented by Tylor's argument that the origins of magic are to be found in a misapplication of the Laws of Association of Ideas familiar from the writings of British and Scottish empiricists (especially Locke, Hume, and Mill).[34] This led Tylor to proclaim that "the sense of an absolute psychical distinction between man and beast, so prevalent in the civilised world, is hardly to be found among the lower races."[35] An early use of the Bororo material to illustrate this thesis is found in the works of Frazer. For Frazer, "haziness is the characteristic of the mental vision of the savage. Like the blind man at Bethsaida, he sees men like trees and animals walking in a thick intellectual fog."[36] Totemism was a central illustration of this "haziness," and it is in this connection that Frazer introduces the Bororo material, closely paraphrasing von den Steinen. Frazer notes, however, that "this curious identification of themselves with the birds does not of itself constitute totemism, though it may be said to be totemic in principle."[37] Although most scholars are certain that totemism is

---

This thesis is patent nonsense, as demonstrated by von den Steinen's own anecdote about the differing transformations of three "species" of men into three species of birds quoted above. The later work of the Salesians and Lévi-Strauss have revealed the presence of a complex system of Bororo taxonomies. Similarly, his claim of the lack of distinction between animals and men can be refuted by von den Steinen's observation, in the same passage (p. 351) that "the animal has no bow and arrow or maize pestle" although he insists that, for the Bororo, this constitutes a "mere minor difference." Nevertheless, von den Steinen's statement continues to be quoted as characteristic of primitive thought in works by anthropological amateurs, e.g., W. Shumaker, *Literature and the Irrational: A Study in Anthropological Backgrounds* (New York, 1960: rp. 1966), p. 93.

[33] For an excellent collection of articles tracing the notion of 'primitive,' see A. Montagu, ed., *The Concept of the Primitive* (New York, 1968). Fr. Golz, *Der primitive Mensch und seine Religion* (Gütersloh, 1963), provides a shrewd review of the major theories, far superior to E. E. Evans-Pritchard, *Theories of Primitive Religion* (Oxford, 1965). See further the valuable article by F. R. Lehmann, "Der Begriff 'Urdummheit' in der ethnologischen und religionswissenschaftlichen Anschauungen von K. Th. Preuss, Ad. E. Jensen und G. Murray," *Sociologus*, II (1952), 131-145.

[34] E. B. Tylor, *Primitive Culture*, 3d ed. (London, 1891: rp. New York, 1958), Vol. I, p. 116.

[35] *Ibid.*, Vol. II, p. 53.

[36] J. G. Frazer, *Totemism and Exogamy* (London, 1910), Vol. IV, p. 61.

[37] *Ibid.*, Vol. III, p. 576; cf. Vol. I, p. 119. Frazer also cites the Bororo material

not present among the Bororo, the totemic interpretation of the identification has persisted, occurring most recently in Jensen's *Myth and Cult*.[38]

It was the publication, in 1910, of L. Lévy-Bruhl's *Les fonctions mentales dans les sociétés inférieures* which won for the Bororo a secure place in literature. Lévy-Bruhl's most famous postulate was the *loi de participation* which he defined: "In the collective representations of primitive mentality objects, beings, phenomena can be, though in a way incomprehensible to us, both themselves and something other than themselves [*à la fois eux-mêmes et autre chose qu'eux-mêmes*]."[39] His first, and hence normative, example of this "law" was the Bororo:

> For instance, "the Trumai (a tribe of Northern Brazil) say that they are aquatic animals.—The Bororo (a neighboring tribe) boast that they are red araras (parakeets)." This does not merely signify that after their death they become araras, nor that araras are metamorphosed Bororos, and must be treated as such. It is something entirely different. "The Bororos," says von den Steinen, who would not believe it but finally had to give in to their explicit affirmations, "give one rigidly to understand that they are araras *at the present time*, just as if a caterpillar declared itself to be a butterfly." It is not a name they give themselves, nor a relationship that they claim. What they desire to express by it is actual identity. That they can be both the human beings they are and the birds of scarlet plumage at the same time, Von den Steinen regards as inconceivable, but to the mentality that is governed by the law of participation there is no difficulty in the matter.[40]

Immediately after this passage, Lévi-Bruhl introduces for the first time the term "prelogical," of which the Bororo are again to be seen as the normative example.

The citation in Lévy-Bruhl is quite close to von den Steinen's original. Lévy-Bruhl has added the detail that von den Steinen "could

---

in *The Golden Bough*, 3d ed. (n. 15 above), Vol. III, p. 34; Vol. VIII, pp. 207f. It does not appear in the previous editions.

[38] A. Jensen, *Myth and Cult among Primitive Peoples* (Chicago, 1963), p. 148. For earlier totemic interpretations, see E. Reuterskiöld, *Die Entstehung der Speisesakramente* (Heidelberg, 1912), pp. 47-49, 82f.; and "Der Totemismus," *Archiv für Religionswissenschaft*, XV (1912), 1-26, esp. 11, 18; E. S. Hartland, "Totemism," in J. Hastings, ed. *Encyclopaedia of Religion and Ethics*, Vol. XII, esp. pp. 405, 407. The presence of totemism among the Bororo is maintained chiefly by Colbacchini-Albisetti, *Os Boróros Orientais*, p. 33.

[39] L. Lévy-Bruhl, *Les fonctions mentales dans les sociétés inférieures*, 6th ed. (Paris, 1922), p. 77. I quote the translation by L. A. Clare, *How Natives Think* (New York, 1926: rp. New York, 1966), p. 61.

[40] Lévy-Bruhl, *Les fonctions*, p. 78; *How Natives Think*, p. 62.

not believe it" and has made one significant alteration in direct quotation. Von den Steinen had asserted that the Bororo understood themselves to be araras just as a caterpillar may speak of himself as a butterfly. Lévy-Bruhl's version omits the ambiguity between present and future (or the Aristotelian actuality and potentiality) in order to emphasize the element of participation. In his translation, the Bororos insist that "they are araras *at the present time.*" (Compounding the misrepresentation, Lévy-Bruhl italicized his addition of *actuellement.*)[41] The mischief done by this cannot be overemphasized. It is Lévy-Bruhl and not von den Steinen's original report (no matter what the footnote may cite) which will be used by most subsequent writers as an illustration of primitive mentality. For example, G. van der Leeuw, writing about the "instability" of the primitive notion of person as being indefinitely extendable, declared: "[The primitive believes] I am simultaneously made up of several beings and these beings are 'me.' I can be a man and, at the same time, a panther or a monkey. We need only recall the famous example of von den Steinen, quoted by Lévy-Bruhl, concerning the South American Bororo who are, at the same time, araras."[42] Lévy-Bruhl's version and interpretation dominates the literature. It is only recently that books on "primitive mentality" have begun to dispense with the example of the Bororo.[43]

---

[41] See van Baaren, p. 10.

[42] G. van der Leeuw, *De primitieve mens en de religie,* 2d ed. (Groningen, 1952), p. 40. Cf. van der Leeuw, "La structure de la mentalité primitive," *Revue d'histoire et de philosophie religieuses,* VIII (1928), 8, for a more extensive paraphrase of von den Steinen which he already terms "un exemple qui est devenu presque classique." Van der Leeuw appears inclined to go as far, if not further, than Lévy-Bruhl: "La symphatie est un relation, tandis qu'ici il y a identification ... il a dû se rendre a l'assertion pure et simple des Bororo qu'ils *sont* effectivement des *arara,* en dehors de toute interprétation symbolique ou métaphorique."

[43] E.g., the valuable survey by G. Guariglia, *Il mondo spirituale dei primitivo,* Vol. I, *Le categorie mentali* (Milan, 1967), who discusses Bororo totemism (p. 174) and traditions concerning the destiny of the soul (pp. 195f.) but omits the *arara* report. It is perhaps significant that the unjustly neglected monograph by H. Werner, *Comparative Psychology of Mental Development* (New York, 1940)—an expanded translation of Werner, *Einführung in die Entwicklungspsychologie* (Leipzig, 1926)—while quoting copiously from von den Steinen and devoting a section to the primitive notion of person (in which he argues, like Lévy-Bruhl, that "no essential differences are thought to exist between man and animal") which quotes the sentences immediately preceding and following the *arara* report, fails to quote the identification (*Comparative Psychology,* pp. 419f., 426f.; *Einführung,* pp. 301, 303f.). Compare his more general statement, *Comparative Psychology,* p. 16; *Einführung,* pp. 16f.

Lévy-Bruhl's use of the Bororo identification of themselves with parrots had two crucial effects on all subsequent use of this tradition. First, it separated out the ambiguities of von den Steinen's original report and suppressed the transmigration-metamorphosis motif in favor of a totally present understanding of the identification. (Indeed, reversing von den Steinen's conjectural history of the saying [see above, p. 269], Lévy-Bruhl gloomily concludes his book by declaring that when the primitive collective breaks down in transition to "higher mental types" and "individualism" asserts itself, then "the Bororo tribesmen will no longer declare that they *are* araras. They will say that their ancestors were araras, that they are of the same substance as araras, that they will become araras after death.")[44] From this point on, those who cite the Bororo-*are*-parrots tradition omit the metamorphosis; those who cite the Bororo-*will-become*-parrots tradition omit the identification.[45] It is the present rather than the futuristic understanding of the identification that will preoccupy scholars. That a man should think of himself as simultaneously a man and a bird seems absurd, primitive, and hence worthy of comment. That a man should think of himself as becoming a bird after death seems "normal'" by comparison (whether because for positivistic scholars, all statements concerning life after death are incapable of empirical verification and hence equally nonsense or, for religious scholars, because they are used to the notion of Christians becoming angels). The present identification is exotic and thereby revelatory of primitive mentality; the future is not. Second, by driving an absolute wedge between "primitive" and "civilized" thought and by insisting that each had its own laws, Lévy-Bruhl set the stage for the consideration of the Bororo as profoundly alien, so different that they made no sense. Either they were representative of a different

---

[44] Lévy-Bruhl, *How Natives Think*, p. 328. Given his severe criticisms of British speculative anthropology, Lévy-Bruhl would, no doubt, be justified in rejecting von den Steinen's conjectural history.

[45] Examples of the former are given throughout this paper; for the latter, see the material cited above, in n. 20 and general works such as A. E. Crawley, *The Idea of the Soul* (London, 1909), p. 162. More tellingly, when Frazer cites the present identification (*The Golden Bough*, Vol. VIII, pp. 207f.) he omits the metamorphosis; when he cites the metamorphosis (*The Golden Bough*, Vol. III, p. 34), he omits the identification. Some scholars who perceive that the transformation is one that will occur after death, utilize an interpretation that depends on the present identification, e.g., H. Kelsen's fascinating study, *Vergeltung und Kausalität: Eine soziologische Untersuchung* (The Hague, 1941), pp. 83f., which declared that this illustrates the fact that "the difference between men and animals, self-evident for civilized man, has no meaning at all for primitive man."

species of man or they were insane, and one might be tempted to add the Bororo to the lists of parallels between primitives and schizophrenics such as that compiled by Alfred Storch.[46] (It need not be emphasized that this was antithetical to Lévy-Bruhl's intention and that he later altered his position on the absolute dichotomy of primitive and civilized.)

Following Lévy-Bruhl, scholars utilizing the Bororo tradition had several options. They could uncritically repeat the identification as a classic example of *participation mystique*[47] or offer minor variations on Lévy-Bruhl's interpretation.[48] They could uncritically reject Lévy-Bruhl without providing a cogent alternative interpretation.[49] They could overturn Lévy-Bruhl's basic thesis and show that the primitive tradition was not discontinuous with modern expressions.[50] They could reject this intention and seek to demonstrate that the Bororo identification was logically explicable, that is, it was capable of being intelligible to modern man (usually by invoking the logic of naming).[51] They could make fools of themselves in putting forth rival hypotheses such as C. R. Aldrich's suggestion "that the Boróros consider that they are araras is hardly more incomprehensible than that a mother feels that her new-born child is

---

[46] A. Storch, *Das archaisch-primitive Erleben und Denken der Schizophrenen* (Berlin, 1922).

[47] E.g., van der Leeuw (see above, n. 42); E. Cassirer, *The Philosophy of Symbolic Forms* (New Haven, 1955), Vol. II, pp. 65, 184, and *An Essay on Man* (New Haven, 1944), pp. 82f.; E. Neumann, *The Origins and History of Consciousness* (New York, 1954), p. 105.

[48] E.g., J. Murphy, *Primitive Man: His Essential Quest* (Oxford, 1927), pp. 107f. E. Reuterskiöld's thesis, while in respects similar to that of Lévy-Bruhl, is independent of it (see above, n. 38).

[49] E.g., O. Leroy, *La raison primitive: Essai de réfutation de la théories du prélogisme* (Paris, 1927), pp. 68f.; S. G. Moelia, *Het primitieve denken in de moderne wetenschap* (Groningen, 1933), pp. 46f., 147f.; J. Cazeneuve, *La mentalité archaïque* (Paris, 1961), pp. 13f. I regret that the excellent review of criticism of Lévy-Bruhl by R. Eysink, *Collectieve voorstellingen in het denken der natuurvolken* (Utrecht-Nijmegen, 1946) does not treat the Bororo tradition.

[50] E.g., Michael Polanyi's wry comment: "What the Boróros mean by identifying themselves with red parrots may be difficult to fathom, but I see no reason to say that it is anymore absurd than the view of many scientists and philosophers that they are machines." I have taken this quote from a recent lecture by Polanyi, "Myths: Ancient and Modern" (1970), manuscript p. 12. Compare a quite similar ploy by H. Bergson, who compares "totemic" identification with animals to Pascal's dictum, "Man is a reed that thinks" in *The Two Sources of Morality and Religion* (New York, 1935: rp. Garden City, L.I., 1954), pp. 183f.

[51] E.g., J. J. Fahrenfort, *Dynamisme en logies denken bij natuurvolken* (Groningen, 1933), esp. pp. 49-53.

herself. Primitive tribes rarely move away from their own territory, unless they are driven out of it, so that in all probability the Boróros have no memory of ever living in a land that was not inhabited by araras; they have not yet become sufficiently conscious to discriminate between themselves and the red feathered inhabitants of their country."[52] The relationship between the three theses in this passage, I might add, would boggle even a "prelogical" mind!

However, modifications and alternative approaches to Lévy-Bruhl began to be expressed. The first caution was a linguistic one, that is, the precise sense in which the identification, "we *are* parrots" was to be understood. The problem was already realized by Lévy-Bruhl, although he did not develop it. In *Les fonctions*, after comparing Spencer and Gillen's report on Australian totemism with von den Steinen's Bororo identification, he declared: "The verb 'to be' (which moreover is non-existent in most of the languages of undeveloped peoples) has not here the ordinary copulative sense it bears in our languages. It signifies something different, and something more."[53] Henri Bergson shrewdly pushed this observation further, while criticizing Lévy-Bruhl on totemic identifications:

> Let us take the commonest case, that of an animal, a rat or kangaroo, for example, which serves as a "totem," that is to say a patron for the whole tribe. The most striking thing is that the members of the clan assert that they are one with it; that they *are* rats, they *are* kangaroos. True, it remains to be seen in what sense they use the word. To conclude straightaway that there is a specific logic, peculiar to "primitive man" and exempt from the principles of contradiction, would be somewhat overhasty. Our verb "to be" carries meanings that we have difficulty in defining for all our civilization: how can we reconstitute the meaning given by primitive man in such and such a case to a similar word, even when he supplies us with explanations? These explanations would possess an element of precision only if he were a philosopher, and even then we should have to know all the fine shades of his language to understand them.[54]

For our purposes we may set the specific question aside. I am not competent in Bororo linguistics, and an examination of the available grammars has not proved illuminating. Furthermore, even if the service of a specialist were available, it would be of no assistance.

---

[52] C. R. Aldrich, *The Primitive Mind and Modern Civilization* (New York, 1931), p. 79. Note that this fantastic book contains laudatory prefaces by both B. Malinowski and C. G. Jung!
[53] Lévy-Bruhl, *How Natives Think*, p. 75.
[54] H. Bergson, *The Two Sources of Morality and Religion*, p. 183.

Von den Steinen provided only a German translation of the Bororo sentence (if, indeed, he was not himself relying on a translator), and thus the recovery and assessment of the Bororo original is impossible. The conditions of Bergson's more general critique are likewise impossible to fulfill in this case (and, I suspect, in any other) and would have the practical consequence of reducing all hermeneutics to silence.

Beyond this question, the interpretation of Lévy-Bruhl and his successors was based on a literal understanding of the sentence. The identification made sense, even though it is false, because the Bororo lack a logic of distinction. I may note, parenthetically, that the futuristic interpretation is equally literal, although it assumes that the Bororo do possess distinctions between actuality and potentiality and that this "Aristotelianism" is the key to exegesis. Whether this implicitly invokes the argument about the characteristic lack of distinction among primitives remains a question. Men do not, in fact, become birds in strict analogy to the acorn becoming an oak or the caterpillar a butterfly. (As a subquestion, I would like to know who suggested this analogy, the Bororo or von den Steinen?) Either one must assume that the Bororo ignore or are ignorant of the fact that men and birds are not the same species (in contradistinction to the acorn and oak and the caterpillar and the butterfly which are) or one must assume that for the Bororo man, bird, oak, acorn, butterfly, caterpillar, each constitutes a separate species which can transfer itself into another species at will (*scil. participation mystique*). In either case, the von den Steinen—Lévy-Bruhl interpretation appears to be maintained.

More recent interpretations have sought to set aside a literal understanding of the sentence, usually by invoking either the notion of the symbolic or the functional. This change in perspective was signaled in 1934 by E. E. Evans-Pritchard in his critical and appreciative lecture on Lévy-Bruhl: "An object may be perceived in different ways according to different affective interests, interests which in their turn are evoked by different situations. Hence it comes about that a savage can be both himself and a bird."[55] In subsequent writings, Evans-Pritchard was able to supply two parallel instances from his fieldwork among the Nuer. The closest analogue to the

---

[55] E. E. Evans-Pritchard, "Lévy-Bruhl's Theory of Primitive Mentality," *Bulletin of the Faculty of Arts, Cairo University*, II (1934), 1-36. This quote is from p. 32 and was generally endorsed by Lévy-Bruhl in "A Letter to E. E. Evans-Pritchard," *British Journal of Sociology*, III (1952), 117-123.

Bororo tradition is the Nuer assertion that "a twin is not a person, he is a bird"; but Evans-Pritchard has also explored the processes of identification in his report that when the Nuer utilize a cucumber in sacrifice, they call it an ox.[56]

In his interpretation of the Nuer twin-bird identification, Evans-Pritchard, in conscious dialogue with Lévy-Bruhl, introduced three important elements: (1) he eschewed the contextless catalogues of primitive customs found in the early anthropologists in favor of a detailed study of the language and ideology of the particular people who made the identification; (2) he saw the identification as relational and classificatory, that is, particular aspects of twins = particular aspects of birds in syllogistic fashion (this point has been brilliantly developed by Lévi-Strauss in his comments on Evans-Pritchard's report); (3) he saw the identification as occasional, called into consciousness only by particular situations and thus representative of a particular point of view.

---

[56] See Evans-Pritchard, "Customs and Beliefs Relating to Twins among the Nilotic Nuer," *Uganda Journal*, III (1936), 230-238; "A Problem of Nuer Religious Thought," *Sociologus*, IV (1954), 23-41 (rp. J. Middleton, editor, *Myth and Cosmos, Readings in Mythology and Symbolism*, [Garden City, L.I., 1967], pp. 127-148); "A Problem" appears as chap. 5 of Evans-Pritchard, *Nuer Religion* (Oxford, 1956), esp. pp. 128-132. Note that this latter article is framed with explicit reference to Lévy-Bruhl. For comments on Evans-Pritchard's twin/bird, ox/cucumber reports, see esp. E. Gellner, "Concepts and Society," *Transactions of the Fifth World Congress of Sociology* (London, 1962), Vol. I, pp. 153-183 reprinted in Emmet and A. MacIntyre, *Sociological Theory and Philosophical Analysis* (New York, 1970), pp. 115-149, esp. pp. 131-137 and B. R. Wilson, editor, *Rationality* (Oxford, 1970), pp. 18-49, esp. pp. 34-39; C. Lévi-Strauss, *Totemism* (Boston, 1963), pp. 78-83 (cf. *The Savage Mind*, p. 224); J. Beattie, *Other Cultures* (London, 1964), pp. 68f.; A. MacIntyre, "Is Understanding Religion Compatible with Believing?" in J. Hicks, editor, *Faith and the Philosophers* (London, 1964), reprinted in B. R. Wilson, ed., *Rationality*, esp. pp. 65f.; S. Lukes, "Some Problems about Rationality," *Archives européennes de sociologie*, VIII (1967), reprinted in Wilson, *Rationality*, esp. pp. 205f.; A. Hayley, "Symbolic Equations: The Ox and the Cucumber," *Man*, n.s. III (1968), 262-272; S. Runciman, "The Sociological Explanation of 'Religious' Beliefs," *Archives européennes*, X (1969), esp. 155-157. The most complete review of the material, with excellent comparative material, is R. Firth, "Twins, Birds and Vegetables: Problems of Identification in Primitive Religious Thought," *Man*, n.s. I (1966), 1-17. See the comments on this article by E. E. Evans-Pritchard, R. Needham, E. Leach, and the rejoinder by Firth in *Man*, I (1966), 398f., 557f. (Leach's position draws on his important article, "Anthropological Aspects of Language: Animal Categories and Verbal Abuse," in E. H. Lenneberg, editor, *New Directions in the Study of Language* [Cambridge, Mass., 1964], pp. 23-62 which considers another kind of animal/human identification. Cf. J. Buxton, "Animal Identity and Human Peril: Some Mandari Images," *Man*, n.s. III [1968], 35-49; G. Wijeyewardene, "Address, Abuse and Animal Categories in Northern Thailand," *Man*, n.s. III [1968], 76-93.)

It seems odd, if not absurd to a European when he is told that a twin is a bird as though it were an obvious fact, for Nuer are not saying that a twin "is like" a bird but that "he is" a bird. There seems to be a complete contradiction in the statement, and it was precisely on statements of this kind recorded by observers of primitive peoples that Lévy-Bruhl based his theory of the prelogical mentality of these peoples, its chief characteristic being, in his view, that it permits such evident contradictions—that a thing can be what it is and at the same time something altogether different. But, in fact, no contradiction is involved in the statement, which, on the contrary, appears quite sensible, and even true, to one who presents the idea to himself in the Nuer language and within their system of religious thought. He does not then take their statements about twins any more literally than they make and understand them themselves. They are not saying that a twin has a beak, feathers and so forth. Nor in their everyday relations with twins do the Nuer speak of them as birds or act towards them as though they were birds. They treat them as what they are, men and women.[57] But in addition to being men and women they are of a twin birth, and a twin birth is a special revelation of Spirit; and the Nuer express this special character of twins in the "twins are birds" formula because twins and birds, though for different reasons, are both associated with Spirit.... The formula does not express a dyadic relationship between twins and birds but a triadic relationship between twins, birds and God. In respect to God twins and birds have a similar character.[58]

A somewhat similar formulation was proposed by Evans-Pritchard's student and colleague, Godfrey Lienhardt, in interpreting the Dinka assertion that there are men who can transform themselves into lions and there are lions existing in the form of men. This, Lienhardt maintains, is neither contradiction nor metaphor but rather a mode of expression between the figurative and the literal. Man/lion represents "two possible ways of viewing the same being."[59]

Without explicit reference either to Evans-Pritchard or Lienhardt,

---

[57] For a more explicit formulation of what I have termed "the occasional nature of the identification," compare Evans-Pritchard, "Customs and Beliefs Relating to Twins," p. 238: "the Nuer belief that twins are birds is only a conscious notion in certain situations. They are not always aware of the bird-quality of a twin but only on some occasions, for normally they speak of, and act towards, twins as they speak of and act towards other persons."

[58] Evans-Pritchard, "A Problem" (in Middleton, pp. 136f. = Evans-Pritchard, *Nuer Religion*, p. 131). Within the context of this paper it is not necessary to argue the question of the validity of Evans-Pritchard's evidence and interpretation (see Firth, pp. 3-8) or to offer alternative hypotheses such as Hayley's ("Symbolic Equations") unconvincing psychoanalytic interpretation.

[59] G. Lienhardt, "Modes of Thought," in E. E. Evans-Pritchard, *The Institutions of Primitive Society* (London, 1954), pp. 97-99. (The quote occurs on p. 98). See Lienhardt's later formulation in *Divinity and Experience: The Religion of the Dinka* (Oxford, 1961), p. 117.

the type of interpretation they propose has been applied to the Bororo in two recent treatments: W. Percy (1961) in a rather confused attempt to delineate the various modes of identification that might be present in the statement, "I am a parrot," through an exercise of what he terms "qualitative phenomenology";[60] and Clifford Geertz (1966) who, taking Percy as a point of departure, utilizes the Bororo identification to establish a central element of religion in his well-known essay, "Religion as a Cultural System."

> It would seem necessary to see the sentence [I am a parrot] as having a different sense in the context of the "finite province of meaning" which makes up the religious perspective and of that which makes up the common-sensical. In the religious, our Bororo is "really" a "parakeet," and given the proper ritual context might well "mate" with other "parakeets"—with metaphysical ones like himself not commonplace ones such as those which fly bodily about in ordinary trees. In the common-sensical perspective he is a parakeet in the sense—I assume—that he belongs to a clan whose members regard the parakeet as their totem, a membership from which, given the fundamental nature of reality as the religious perspective reveals it, certain moral and practical consequences flow. A man who says he is a parakeet is, if he says it in normal conversation, saying that, as myth and ritual demonstrate, he is shot through with parakeetness and that this religious fact has some crucial social implications—we parakeets must stick together, not marry one another, not eat mundane parakeets, and so on, for to do otherwise is to act against the grain of the whole universe. It is this placing of proximate acts in ultimate contexts that makes religion, frequently at least, socially so powerful. It alters, often radically, the whole landscape presented to common sense, alters it in such a way that the moods and motivations induced by religious practice seem themselves supremely practical, the only sensible ones to adopt given the way things "really" are.[61]

---

[60] W. Percy, "The Symbolic Structure of Interpersonal Relations," *Psychiatry*, XXIV (1961), 39-52, esp. 48: "The quasi-identification events of symbolic behavior can be grasped only by a qualitative phenomenology. This qualitative scale must take account not only of true-or-false-or-nonsense statements ... but also of various modes of magical identification. It does not suffice, for example, to say that the assertion of a Bororo tribesman of Brazil, 'I am a parakeet,' is false or nonsense. Nor is it adequate to say that it is false scientifically but true mythically. It is necessary to understand the particular mode of identification of a particular language-event. Sentences exhibiting the same syntactic and semantic structure may be asserted in wholly different modes of identification." A good example of Percy's contention would be President Kennedy's famous dictum "I am a Berliner" which poses no interpretive problem within a specific, historic context. The Bororo sentence, however, is of a different order and cannot be relieved by context.

[61] C. Geertz, "Religion as a Cultural System," in M. Banton, editor, *Anthropological Approaches to the Study of Religion* (London, 1966), pp. 37f.

The solution to the Bororo's seeming plurality of beings, advocated since Evans-Pritchard, is the assumption of a plurality of languages and, by implication, a plurality of truths.

It is now time to withdraw our experiment and reflect on its results. We have been engaged in tracing the history of an error—no less revealing for being a mistake.[62] In the history of interpretation of the Bororo, there has been a noticeable shift from *surface* to *depth*, from the placing of the Bororo within a contextless catalogue of illustrations of a *general* theory of primitive mentality to a depth analysis of the underlying principles of a *particular* culture.[63] In this process, the statement, "I am a parrot," has shifted from being an absurdity to be explained away or a puzzle to a serious statement, the truth of which might be empathetically entertained by a non-Bororo (e.g., Lienhardt's remark that "as anthropologists we have to give at least a temporary assent to such ways of thinking.... Only by such suspension of criticism can one learn gradually how thought of this sort, in its context, is a representation of experience which at least is not obviously, self-contradictory; and which can satisfy men no less rational, if less rationalizing, than ourselves").[64] The statement, "I am a parrot," has come to be seen as revealing a truth rather than being the result of a peculiar process of thought. By utilizing terminology such as "mode" or "symbolic," it has been possible to affirm both the humanness and the parrotness of the Bororo without allowing one to subsume the other. Historians of religion will presumably be attracted by this anthropological approach which bears so close a resemblance to Eliade's well-known paradox of sacrality: "By manifesting the sacred, any object becomes *something else*, yet it continues to remain itself."[65] Yet we must be cautious at this point, for the relativism of the anthropologist is not shared by Eliade. While I hear Pirandello's "*cosí è (se vi pare)*" in the background of the anthropologists' treatments, I hear, rephrased, Ivan Karamazov's famous dictum: only "if God does not

---

[62] See the fascinating history of error and miscitation by R. K. Merton, *On the Shoulders of Giants: A Shandean Postscript* (Glencoe, 1965). More germane to our discipline would be the classic study, *Totemism*, by Lévi-Strauss.

[63] See my remarks on "surface" and "depth" in the history of the history of religions in Smith, "Adde Parvum Parvo Magnus Acervus Erit," Chapter 11, above.

[64] Lienhardt, p. 98.

[65] M. Eliade, *The Sacred and the Profane* (New York, 1959), p. 12.

exist then everything is possible" as the rejoinder from the other. For the one, a functionalist criterion of truth is employed; for the other, an ontological. Both possess problems in yielding specific explanations and interpretations.

Some of these questions have been raised with explicit reference to Evans-Pritchard's treatment of the Nuer bird/man identification by Ernest Gellner, whose critique of functionalism ranks with the theoretical study by C. Hempel and its application to religious theories by H. Penner.[66] Gellner charges most functionalists with a "too charitable" interpretation of conceptual statements that used to be dismissed by earlier anthropologists as illogical, noting the inevitable circularity of the more recent approach. The functionalists insist that "people cannot mean what at one level (e.g., implicitly, through their conduct) they also know to be false or absurd." Thus, since the Bororo do not try to mate with parrots, the Nuer do not "act towards" twins "as though they were birds," they cannot be guilty of contradiction in stating that men are simultaneously birds. But no sane conduct, especially societal conduct which must endure over a long period, can be, by definition, self-contradictory. Therefore it becomes an *a priori* assumption of the functionalist that no society may hold absurd beliefs. The task of interpretation becomes only that of casting about for a sufficient context to account for a belief one already knew was not absurd. Gellner advances a number of criticisms of Evans-Pritchard and others in light of this proposition, arguing that the contextual theory appears to have as a major function "to enable us to attribute meaning to assertions which might otherwise be found to lack it." His most telling formulation for our problem is the following:

> I am not arguing that Evans-Pritchard's account of Nuer concepts is a bad one. (Nor am I anxious to revive a doctrine of pre-logical mentality *à la* Lévy-Bruhl.). What I am anxious to argue is that contextual interpretation, which offers an account of what assertions "really mean" in opposition to what they seem to mean in isolation, does not by itself clinch matters. It cannot arrive at determinate answers (concerning "what they mean") without doing a number of things which may in fact prejudge the question: without delimiting just which context is to

---

[66] E. Gellner, "Concepts and Society," reprinted in D. Emmet, and A. MacIntyre, *Sociological Theory and Philosophical Analysis*, pp. 115-149. Cf. C. G. Hempel, "The Logic of Functional Analysis," in L. Gross, editor, *Symposium on Sociological Theory* (Evanston, 1959), pp. 271-307; H. Penner, "The Poverty of Functionalism,' *History of Religions*, XI (1971), 91-97.

be taken into consideration, without crediting the people concerned with consistency (which is precisely what is *sub judice* when we discuss, as Evans-Pritchard does, Lévy-Bruhl's thesis) or without assumptions concerning what they can mean (which, again, is precisely what we do not know but are trying to find out) . . . nothing is more false than the claim that, for a given assertion, *its use is its meaning*. On the contrary its use may depend on its lack of meaning, its ambiguity, its possession of wholly different and incompatible meanings in different contexts, *and* on the fact that, at the same time, it as it were emits the impression of possessing a consistent meaning throughout.[67]

The debate between Gellner and Evans-Pritchard is part of a continuing discussion that has exercised British anthropology for more than a decade following the publication of Peter Winch's *The Idea of a Social Science* (1958). Some of the key articles in this controversy have been collected in Bryan R. Wilson's anthology, *Rationality*. The discussion centers about the problems of meaning, intelligibility, and rationality. As summarized by Steven Lukes, the problem is: "When I come across a set of beliefs which appear *prima facie* irrational, what should be my attitude towards them? Should I adopt a critical attitude, taking it as a fact about the beliefs that they *are* irrational, and seek to explain how they came to be held, how they manage to survive unprofaned by rational criticism, what their consequences are, etc? Or should I treat such beliefs charitably: should I begin from the assumption that what appears to me to be irrational may be interpreted as rational when fully understood in its context? More briefly, the problem comes down to whether or not there are alternative standards of rationality."[68] Thus in the case of the Bororo identification, one approach has been to take the statement literally, judge it by our standards, and conclude that it is false, an error or a misapplication of our normal, rational procedures. This is the approach of Tylor and Frazer. The question of the meaning of the assertion, "I am a parrot," is not nearly as important to this view as an account of its genesis. A second approach, represented by Lévy-Bruhl, takes the statement literally but holds that our standards do not apply. It contravenes our laws of logic but follows intelligible rules of its own. The statement, "I am a parrot," is a

---

[67] Gellner, pp. 123, 136, 138, 143.
[68] S. Lukes, "Some Problems about Rationality," *Archives européennes de sociologie*, VIII (1967), 247, reprinted in Wilson, *Rationality*, p. 194. Lukes's paper (*Archives*, pp. 247-264; Wilson, *Rationality*, pp. 194-213) is the most suggestive item in this debate and I have drawn on it in the discussion which follows.

different statement than it appears to us to be. What appear to function as the subject, copulative, and predicate noun in this sentence are none of these in our understanding of the terms. The question of meaning, in such a view, is likewise held in suspense, despite the many specific interpretations offered. If a characteristic of the "logic" of "primitive mentality" is that it is not constrained to avoid contradictions, how may we interpret the statement by invoking a logic of identification which, for us, is but the concomitant of noncontradiction? If the statement is really different than it appears to be and if our standards do not apply, how can we ever hope to understand it? Are we not driven to accept the full consequences of Elsdon Best's statement quoted approvingly by Lévy-Bruhl before he introduces the Bororo example? "We hear of many singular theories about Maori beliefs and Maori thought, but the truth is that we do not understand either, and, what is more, we never shall."[69] It is this problem which ultimately drove Lévy-Bruhl to the uncertainties, ambiguities, and retractions represented by *Les Carnets*. A literal understanding of "I am a parrot" has lead to two consequences: they mean it and they are wrong, or they mean it, but we can never understand what they mean.

In an attempt to escape the horns of this dilemma, anthropologists turned to a variety of nonliteral interpretations: the statement functions as expressive in certain situations. The principles of rationality are upheld and the problem becomes one of finding the situation in which the statement will function in a noncontradictory way. Stated in this blunt fashion, this view ignores the question of truth as irrelevant to the interpreter's task. The best one can say, and this appers to be Geertz's point, is that it functions as if it were true. But what possible meaning can inhere in the word "truth" in such a view? And will not the functional interpretation of the statement, "I am a parrot," remain forever empty? The fourth approach, exemplified by Evans-Pritchard, adds to this view the notion of a contextually determined truth. A statement which appears at first glance to be untrue or irrational can be shown to be true or rational by the depth analysis of the criteria for truth or rationality held by a particular culture. This departs from the Frazerian notion of error and the functionalist insistence on the irrelevance of truth. It resembles most closely the approach of Lévy-Bruhl, but appears

---

[69] E. Best, "Maori Medical Lore," *Journal of the Polynesian Society*, XIII (1904), 219 quoted in Lévy-Bruhl, *How Natives Think*, p. 55.

to differ from him by substituting a culturally relativistic notion for his hypothesis of a universal "primitive mentality" and by suggesting, although with considerable ambiguity, that those contextually determined criteria for truth bear at least formal resemblance to our own and are thus, at least in theory, fully intelligible to us. Such an approach, while not affirming that the Bororo are in fact parrots (arguing, indeed, that the Bororo know they are not), seeks to make intelligible the reasons for holding the belief, "I am a parrot." This approach begs only the question as to whether there are universal, contextually invariable principles of logic, rationality, and truth in addition to contextual ones. It is the suggestion that there are which makes Lévi-Strauss's exegesis of the Bororo statement so intriguing to me, and for this reason I shall return to it in a later publication.

The history of the exegesis of the Bororo statement has driven us to raise the question of truth from which, as historians of religion, we have largely abstained. When confronted with experiences and statements which appear contrary to fact, we have most usually bracketed the question of veracity prompting acidulous criticisms from our more historically minded colleagues; while, at the same time, making grandiose, metaphysical claims, such as "myth is true," which have irritated our philosophical colleagues.[70] In other instances, we have simply repeated or paraphrased a tradition as if this offers self-evident truth (Professor van Baaren's witty title is apropos: "Are the Bororos Parrots or Are We?").

The discussion of this issue has become a lively one in both philosophical hermeneutics and anthropology, and it is essential that historians of religion join in this debate both to learn and to contribute. But the price of admission, to reverse the Steppenwolf formula, is the use of our mind. We must submit ourselves to the kinds of rigorous questions Hans Penner and Edward Yonan have been raising about our principles of intelligibility.[71] If we fail to do so, then it is we rather than the Bororo who are unable to make distinctions and who remain in the dilemma of the ancient Chinese philosopher:

---

[70] For an example of bracketing, see M. Eliade, *Shamanism* (New York, 1964), p. 255 n. 120 *et passim*, which has drawn the somewhat naïve but pointed criticism of M. Smith, "Historical Method in the Study of Religion," in J. S. Helfer, editor, *On Method in the History of Religions* (*History and Theory*, Beiheft 8 [Middletown, 1968]), pp. 8-16, esp. pp. 14f.

[71] See H. Penner and E. Yonan, "Is a Science of Religion Possible?" *Journal of Religion*, LI (1972), 107-133.

"I don't know whether Chuang Chou dreamed he was a butterfly, or a butterfly is dreaming that he is Chuang Chou!"[72]

AFTERWORD

The theoretical issues raised by this essay remain unresolved. For an example of the practical, interpretative questions which require a theory of truth, see the closely related report from the Machiguengas of the Amazon who believe that various birds are incarnate "spiritual tribes". For example, concerning the "tribe", Shiguríite: "Some of them descend here in the form of birds, and those are which the Machiguengas call *shiguíri* . . . Although they are seen as birds, they are people; and although their nests appear as nests, they are large houses like those of the Machiguengas. They are hunted and eaten because, although they are people, they appear as birds. After they raise their chicks, which also are people, they prepare to return [to their celestial river home] with all their children . . . When they arrive [on high] they take their old form again, and their children also receive human form." See S. García, "Mitología Machihuenga," *Misiones Dominicanas Perú*, XVIII (1936), esp. pp. 173-179. I have taken the quotation from p. 176.

I have not been able to obtain the unpublished paper by J. Christopher Crocker, "My Brother, the Parrot," delivered at the American Anthropological Association Symposium on "The Social Use of Metaphor" (San Diego, California).

---

[72] J. R. Ware, *The Sayings of Chuang Chou* (New York, 1963), p. 28.

This paper was presented as part of a symposium on "Theory in the Study of Religion" at the 1971 Annual Meeting of the American Academy of Religion. I have retained the oral style of the original and its necessary brevity. I am especially grateful to Prof. Hans Penner for his detailed critique of an earlier draft. The research for this paper was begun in 1968 with the aid of a fellowship from the Institute of Religious Studies, University of California, Santa Barbara.

CHAPTER THIRTEEN

MAP IS NOT TERRITORY*

Due to the present fuel crisis, it has not been possible for me to thoroughly repeat the Cartesian initiatory scenario and cogitate on this lecture in a stove heated room. Yet, despite the chill, it seemed appropriate to seize the occasion of this address as an opportunity for self reflection.

Without advocating some odd breed of nominalism, the first item this process of introspection yielded was the pattern of conjunctions that follows the listing of my name in the Faculty Directory: Religion and the Human Sciences, Religion and the Humanities, History of Religions. Each of these terms, taken by themselves, are difficult to define and controversial. Joined together, the difficulties are compounded. Yet such a series of pairings is, I trust, not accidental. It is symptomatic of a direction in contemporary scholarship about religion, a direction which my own work seeks to advance and affirm. Therefore it seemed appropriate to begin by exploring some of the implications of these conjunctions.

I take the terms "Human Sciences", "Humanities" and "History" to function synonymously and to serve as limiting perspectives on my understanding of religion. They play the same rôle as that stubborn stone in Doctor Johnson's fabled retort to Bishop Berkeley, that is, as boundaries of concreteness over against which to judge more speculative and normative inquiries in religious studies. As I have written in another context, the philosopher or the theologian has the possibility of exclaiming with Archimedes: "Give me a place to stand on and I will move the world". There is, for such a thinker, the possibility of a real beginning, even of achieving The Beginning, a standpoint from which all things flow, a standpoint from which he may gain clear vision. The historian has no such possibility. There are no places on which he might stand apart from the messiness of the given world. There is, for him, no real beginning, but only the

---

* This paper was delivered as my inaugural lecture upon receiving a chair as the William Benton Professor of Religion and the Human Sciences in the College of the University of Chicago in May, 1974. I have retained the oral style of the original and added a minimum number of references.

plunge which he takes at some arbitrary point to avoid the unhappy alternatives of infinite regress or silence. His standpoint is not discovered, rather it is fabricated with no claim beyond that of sheer survival. The historian's point of view cannot sustain clear vision.

The historian's task is to complicate not to clarify. He strives to celebrate the diversity of manners, the variety of species, the opacity of things. He is therefore barred from making a frontal assault on his topic. Like the pilgrim, the historian is obliged to approach his subject obliquely. He must circumambulate the spot several times before making even the most fleeting contact. His method, like that of Tristram Shandy, Gentleman, is that of the digression.

The historian's manner of speech is often halting and provisional. He approaches his data with that same erotic tentativeness expressed in the well known colloquy from the "Circe" episode in Joyce's *Ulysses*:

> You may touch my ...
> May I touch your?
> O, but lightly!
> O, so lightly!

And having shyly addressed and momentarily touched the object of his attention, he must let it go and return it to its place, unexhausted and intact.

The historian provides us with hints that remain too fragile to bear the burden of being solutions. He is a man of insights: not, preeminently, a man of vision.[1]

The second implication that I derive from the limiting effect of these conjunctions is that religion is an inextricably human phenomenon. In the West, we live in a post-Kantian world in which man is defined as a world-creating being and culture is understood as a symbolic process of world-construction. It is only, I believe, from this humane, post-Enlightenment perspective that the academic interpretation of religion becomes possible. Religious studies are most appropriately described in relation to the Humanities and the Human Sciences, in relation to Anthropology rather than Theology.

What we study when we study religion is one mode of constructing worlds of meaning, worlds within which men find themselves and in which they choose to dwell. What we study is the passion and drama

---

[1] I have taken these paragraphs, in slightly revised form, from the beginning of my article, "The Influence of Symbols upon Social Change: A Place on Which to Stand," chapter 6, above.

of man discovering the truth of what it is to be human. History is the framework within whose perimeter those human expressions, activities and intentionalities that we call "religious" occur. Religion is the quest, within the bounds of the human, historical condition, for the power to manipulate and negotiate ones 'situation' so as to have 'space' in which to meaningfully dwell. It is the power to relate ones domain to the plurality of environmental and social spheres in such a way as to guarantee the conviction that ones existence 'matters'. Religion is a distinctive mode of human creativity, a creativity which both discovers limits and creates limits for humane existence. What we study when we study religion is the variety of attempts to map, construct and inhabit such positions of power through the use of myths, rituals and experiences of transformation.

Allow me to illustrate these reflections with a story. A number of years ago, in preparation for entering an agricultural school, I worked on a dairy farm in upstate New York. I would have to rise at about a quarter to four and fire up the wood burning stove, heat a pan of water and lay out the soap and towels so that my boss could wash when he awoke half an hour later. Each morning, to my growing puzzlement, when the boss would step outside after completing his ablutions, he would pick up a handful of soil and rub it over his hands. After several weeks of watching this activity, I finally, somewhat testily, asked for an explanation: "Why do you start each morning by cleaning yourself and then step outside and immediately make yourself dirty?" "Don't you city boys understand anything?", was the scornful reply. "Inside the house it's dirt; outside, it's earth. You must take it off inside to eat and be with your family. You must put it on outside to work and be with the animals." What my boss instinctively knew is what we have only recently discovered through reading books such as Mary Douglas', *Purity and Danger*, that there is nothing that is inherently or essentially clean or unclean, sacred or profane. There are situational or relational categories, mobile boundaries which shift according to the map being employed. As my boss used to observe: "There's really no such plant as a weed. A rose bush, growing in my cornfield, is a weed. In my flower garden—thistles, mullen and goldenrod—make right smart plants, if you keep them under control."

My boss' remarks, which I jotted down at the time in a diary we were required to keep, returned to me vividly during the process of introspection that has led to this address. They have been in the background of my work for the last fifteen years. And while he is no longer alive to render an undoubtedly caustic judgment on what follows, my subsequent teaching and research has represented the attempt of a city boy to understand.

There was nothing 'natural' about my farmer's activities. Rather, he had created a world by gestures and words in which he, his family and farm gained significance and value. There were certain 'givens' which limited his creativity and there were elements of freedom—even of arbitrariness—in his creation.

The world of the home and the world of animals and plants were perceived as being intersecting realms. Each had its own ordering principles, rules of conduct, boundaries and relations of exclusivity and inclusivity. My boss, as homemaker and as organizer of his farm's world of domesticated plants and animals, was required to determine and map the given limits and structures of each domain. As homemaker, he had to adhere to the rules of social intercourse which constituted the community of Holland Patent, New York. As husbandman, he was not free to violate the seasonal rhythms in deciding when to plant his crops or breed his animals. What he established within the walls of his house and within the fences that surrounded his farm was the carving out of a space which was separate from other spaces and yet in harmony with his perception of the larger social and natural environments. By limiting the space over which he had dominion, he strove to maximize all of the possibilities of that space. He sought to create, in both his home and farm, a microcosm in which everything had its place and was fulfilled by keeping its place. If his ordering grid was of sufficiently tight mesh, all anomalous elements would be forced to the periphery (for example, the garbage dump which stood on his property line, the weeds which were allowed to grow beneath his fences). My boss had achieved power through his skill in compartmentalization. He had dispensed power by allowing each being within his realm the freedom to fulfill its assigned place. He conferred value upon that place by his cosmology of home and farm and by the dramatization of his respect for the integrity of their borders.

I would term this cosmology a locative map of the world and the organizer of such a world, an imperial figure. It is a map of the world which guarantees meaning and value through structures of congruity and conformity.

Students of religion have been most successful in describing and interpreting this locative, imperial map of the world—especially within archaic, urban cultures. It was first outlined by members of the Pan-Babylonian School at the end of the nineteenth century as centered in five basic propositions: "there is a cosmic order that permeates every level of reality; this cosmic order is the divine society of the gods; the structure and dynamics of this society can be discerned in the movements and patterned juxtapositions of the heavenly bodies; the chief responsibility of priests and kings is to attune human order to the divine order."[2] Subsequent inquiry by a succession of creative scholars such as Paul Mus, Stella Kramrisch, René Bertholet, Werner Müller, and Giuseppe Tucci has added further features culminating, for the present time, in the studies of Mircea Eliade on "primitive ontology" and the parallel work of Paul Wheatley on the city as a ceremonial complex. Yet, the very success of these topographies should be a signal for caution. For they are largely based on documents from urban, agricultural, hierarchical cultures. The most persuasive witnesses to a locative, imperial world-view are the production of well organized, self-conscious scribal elites who had a deep vested interest in restricting mobility and valuing place. The texts are, by and large, the production of temples and royal courts and provide their raison d'être—the temple, upon which the priest's and scribe's income rested, as "Center" and microcosm; the requirements of exact repetition in ritual and the concomitant notion of ritual as a reenactment of divine activities, both of which are dependent upon written texts which only the elite could read; and propaganda for their chief patron, the king, as guardian of cosmic and social order. In most cases one cannot escape the suspicion that, in the locative map of the world, we are encountering a self-serving ideology which ought not to be generalized into the universal pattern of religious experience and expression.

I find the same conservative, ideological element strongly to the fore in a variety of approaches to religion which lay prime emphasis upon congruency and conformity, whether it be expressed through phenomenological descriptions of repetition, functionalist descriptions of feedback mechanisms or structuralist descriptions of mediation. Therefore it has seemed to me of some value, in my own work, to explore the dimensions of incongruity that exist in religious materials. For I do believe that religion is, among other things, an

---

[2] C. Loew, *Myth, Sacred History and Philosophy* (New York, 1967), p. 13.

intellectual activity—and, to play upon Paul Ricoeur's well-known phrase, it is the perception of incongruity that gives rise to thought.

In our quest to distinguish cultural man from natural man, emphasis has rightly been laid on those activities of man which are unique, especially language and historical consciousness. But it has been one of the ironies of our intellectual history that we also use these faculties and this vision of human culture and creativity to dichotomize the world into human beings (who are generally like-us) and non-human beings (who are generally not-like-us), into the "we" and the "them" which are the boundaries of any ethnic map.

In classical Greek anthropology, this distinction was made on the basis of language. To be human was to be a Hellene, to speak intelligible, non-stuttering speech (that is to say, Greek). To be, in a cultural sense, non-human was to be a barbarian, to speak unintelligible, stuttering, animal or child-like speech (*bar, bar, bar* from which the word "barbarian" is derived). In the nineteenth and twentieth centuries, growing out of Western imperialist and colonialist experience and ideology, we have distinguished between those who have history and those who have no history—or, to put it more accurately, between those who make history whom we call human or visible beings and those who undergo history whom we call non-human or invisible beings.

This dichotomy (whether it be expressed in terms of primitive/modern, East/West, closed/open societies or what have you) has resulted in much mischief. It is frequently defended in terms of importance? But . . . important to whom? Judged by what criteria? Most of you would repudiate the declarations of the great art connoisseur, Bernard Berenson, when he wrote in *Aesthetics and History*:

> Significant events are those events which have contributed to making us what we are today . . . art history must avoid what has not contributed to the mainstream no matter how interesting, how magnificant in itself. [Art History] should exclude, for example, most German, Spanish, and Dutch art. It should dwell less and less on Italian art after Caravaggio and end altogether by the middle of the eighteenth century . . . [it may dismiss all art] from Western Kamchatka to Singapore, from Greenland's icy mountains to Patagonia's stormy capes, in Africa and on the islands of the sea . . . [it may ignore] all the arts of China and of India [for] they are not history for us Europeans . . . [they] are neither in the mainline of development nor of universal appeal to cultivated Europeans.[3]

---

[3] B. Berenson, *Aesthetics and History*, 2ed. (New York, 1954), pp. 257f.

You may laugh or you may be enraged by so Olympian and so myopic a vision. And yet anyone who is devoted to understanding cultural phenomena can testify to meeting variants of it daily, both within and without the academy.

You are all familiar with the usual portrait of the "mainstream" of world history (understood, of course, as 'our' history). It began in the Near East (need I emphasize the question: near to whom?) and flowed first to Greece, then to Rome, then to the Christians of Northern Europe. During the Middle Ages, Islam temporarily held in passive storage Western culture until it could be reclaimed by its rightful owners. Returned to Western Europe, the mainstream reached its culminating point in American civilization.

If the cartographer is sophisticated (and of liberal disposition), he will admit that India, China, Indonesia, Africa and Meso-America had ancient cultures; but these, he will maintain, were 'isolated' from the mainstream until 'opened' by the West.

The moral of this oft repeated tale is obvious. The West is active, it makes history, it is visible, it is human. The non-Western world is static, it undergoes history, it is invisible, it is non-human. At times, this contrast is revealed in telling semantic shifts, for example, the Classical Greeks are "Western"; the Byzantine Greeks are "Eastern".

The same sort of mapping occurs within the field of religious studies, especially with respect to the dubious category of "World Religions". A World Religion is a religion like ours; but it is, above all, a tradition which has achieved sufficient power and numbers to enter our history, either to form it, interact with it, or to thwart it. All other religions are invisible. We recognize both the unity within and the diversity between the "great" World Religions because they correspond to important geo-political entities with which we must deal. All "primitives," by way of contrast, may be simply lumped together as may be so-called "minor religions" because they do not confront our history in any direct fashion. They are invisible.

Let me emphasize that I do not mean this word "invisible" in any merely hyperbolic fashion. I mean, quite literally, that they may as well not exist. For example, a recent almanac gives the following statistics for members of the "principle religions of the world":

Christian	888 million
Muslim	430 million
Hindu	332 million

Confucian	300 million
Taoist	50 million
Shinto	50 million
Jewish	12 million
Primitive	121 million
Others or none	524 million

More than one fifth of the world's population has just been informed that religiously they have no identity and might as well not exist.

My colleagues in the academic study of religion have done much to address and counter this view of "importance" and the "mainstream" by exploring and, above all, by valuing the religious life of other men. But I grow increasingly troubled by the suspicion that we may not have truly advanced. We have set forth a new cartography, but it remains uncomfortably close to being a mirror image of the "mainstream" map I have just described.

In the nineteenth century it was common to speak of the "savage" as lacking all intellectual faculties and therefore being unable to make distinctions. Herbert Spencer summarized the general characteristics of the "savage" as one who lacks conceptions of generalized facts, who is unable to perceive difference, who lacks notions of truth, scepticism and criticism. He is, in short, a creature of rigid beliefs. James George Frazer employed a Biblical analogy: "haziness is the characteristic of the mental vision of the savage. Like the blind man at Bethsaida, he sees men like trees and animals walking in a thick intellectual fog."[4] There was even a technical German term coined to denote this "fog"—*Urdummheit*—primordial stupidity.

In the twentieth century, in conscious reaction against this portrait, it has become fashionable to insist on the holistic character of primitive culture. Religion for the primitive, we are told, includes everything and, therefore, to experience incongruity would be to deny existence itself.

The logic of this interpretation is inescapable—it is also circular. If, as W. E. H. Stanner declares, the mode, ethos and principle of primitive life are "variations of a single theme—continuity, constancy, balance, symmetry, regularity, system or some such quality as these words convey"—then there can be, by definition, no experience of the incongruous. If, to continue Stanner's oft-quoted statement, life,

---

[4] H. Spencer, *Principles of Sociology* (London, 1876), Vol. I, *passim*; J. G. Frazer, *Totemism and Exogamy* (London, 1910), Vol. IV, p. 61.

for the primitive, "is a one-possibility thing" where the myths "determine not only what life is but what it can be"— then there can be no discrepant experience and, hence, no theodicy or soteriology.[5] What was done in the mythic age must be good or it would not be paradigmatic; there can be no gap between ideal and real or repetition would be impossible. Indeed, Evans-Pritchard has gone so far as to declare:

> If in such a closed [primitive] system of thought a belief is contradicted by a particular experience this merely shows that the experience was mistaken or inadequate . . .[6]

What troubles me is that these two portraits of the primitive—the nineteenth century negative evaluation and the twentieth century positive (even nostalgic) appreciation—are but the two sides of the same coin. They are but variations on the even older ambivalence: the Wild Man and the Noble Savage. Both see the primitive as essentially not-like-us. To the degree that we identify change, historical consciousness and critical reason with being human (and we do), the nineteenth century interpretation maintained that the savage was non-human; the twentieth century interpretation suggests, at best, that the primitive is another kind of human. Both interpretations take the primitive's myths literally, and believe him to do the same, the nineteenth century holding that anyone who believes such stuff is a fool, a child or subhuman; the twentieth century arguing that the myths are true, although possessing another kind of truth than that which we usually recognize.

Such interpretations have severely limited our capacity for understanding the worlds of other men. On the conceptual level it robs them of their humanity, of those perceptions of discrepancy and discord which give rise to the symbolic project that we identify as the very essence of being human. It reduces the primitive to the level of fantasy where experience plays no role in challenging belief (as in the Evans-Pritchard passage just quoted), where discrepancy does not give rise to thought but rather is thought away.

I find the practical consequences of this consensus to be even more

---

[5] W. E. H. Stanner, "The Dreaming," in W. A. Lessa and E. Z. Vogt, editors, *Reader in Comparative Religion: An Anthropological Approach*, 2ed. (New York, 1965), pp. 161, 166.

[6] E. E. Evans-Pritchard, *Social Anthropology and Other Essays* (New York, 1962), p. 99.

severely limiting. It has skewed both our interpretive strategies and the formulation of our hermeneutic categories. Ernest Gellner has offered a devastating critique of what he terms the "liberal", "sympathetic", "tolerance-engendering contextual interpretation of indigenous assertions" in anthropological literature, declaring that the social-functional theory of religion appears to have as its chief aim: "to enable us to attribute meaning to assertions which might otherwise be found to lack it". He calls attention to the self-conscious use of verbal ambiguity, to the "logically illicit transformation of one concept into another", to those elements of verbal and conceptual manipulation and exploitation which are as characteristic of primitive as of more developed societies.[7] Gellner restores the capacity for thought, for rationality and rationalization to the primitive and, by so doing, restores their recognizable humanity. A similar critique should be made of the phenomenologist's preoccupation with replication.

Allow me to shift my mode of speech from the theoretical and critical to the anecdotal and homiletical. I should like to suggest some new possibilities for religious studies by narrating some stories. I do so to remind you that the work of the professional scholar of religions does not consist primarily of reading our colleagues works but in reading texts, in questioning, challenging, interpreting and valuing the tales men tell and the tales others have told about them. We are, at the very least, true anthropologists in the original Greek sense of the word—gossips, persons who delight in talking about other men.

My first story is about the Marind-anim of South New Guinea. Paul Wirz reported that it is a popular pastime among the Marind-anim to attempt to determine the relationship of a man to his clan by examining his belly-button. If the navel is slightly convex, then it resembles a betal nut and the individual is related to the betal clan. If the bearer possesses a bulging navel or hernia, it resembles a coconut and its owner is related to the coconut clan. Wirz goes on to state, without offering an explanation, that "all this is mere play" and describes the gales of laughter produced by each new identification.[8] It is, of course, play and laughter provoking. If there is one

---

[7] E. Gellner, "Concepts and Society," reprinted in D. Emmet and A. MacIntyre, *Sociological Theory and Philosophical Analysis* (New York, 1970), pp. 115-149. Compare my article, "I am a Parrot (Red)," *History of Religions*, XI (1972), pp. 391-413.

[8] P. Wirz, *Die Marind-anim von Holländisch-Süd-Neu-Guinea* (Hamburg, 1922-5), Vol. II, pp. 34f.

thing that is well known to the Marind-anim, it is the precise clan lineages of each individual. What is funny, what is interesting, what is provocative is the juxtaposition between the actual clan membership and the "theoretical" clan membership induced by the empirical science of navel-study.

A Dutch anthropologist, Jan van Baal, has recently confirmed Wirz's description and goes on to provide additional examples:

> When cattle were introduced rather recently into the region, the Sapi-ze, a pig clan, claimed the cow because of the verbal associations between their name (*Sapi*) and the Malay word for cow (*sapi*).[9]

Van Baal reports the same process of joking and punning accompanied by laughter, but within what appears to be a more "serious" situation. Something new has been encountered which must be related to the existing classificatory system if it is not to be rejected as a chaotic threat. The classification system depends on myths about objects produced by the ancestors in the beginning. The Marind-anim know very well that the ancestor of the Pig clan did not originally produce cows. At the same time, they know very well that, being divine, there is no reason why the ancestor of the Pig clan could not have originally produced cows. There is nothing more natural, more credible about pigs over against cows. The porcine limitation of the creativity of the ancestor was merely accidental. But, nevertheless, he did not originally produce cows. The pun, at once both serious and playful, asserts and denies the identification. And the discrepancy becomes the occasion for reflection upon the nature of divinity.

There is a leading school of scholarship which, drawing upon Romantic theories of language and survivals, has sought to maintain a distinction between the primal moment of myth and its secondary application, between its original expression and its "semantically depleted" explanation. I would propose, drawing upon the Marind-anim example, that there is no pristine myth; there is only application. Myth is (to slightly emend Gilbert Ryle's well-known formulation) a self-conscious category mistake. That is to say, the incongruity of myth is not an error, it is the very source of its power. Or (to borrow Kenneth Burke's definition of the proverb) a myth is a "strategy for dealing with a situation".[10] And, therefore, I expect that scholars of

---

[9] J. van Baal, *Dema: Description and Analysis of Marind-anim Culture* (The Hague, 1966), p. 196 quoting an oral report by Father J. Verschueren.
[10] K. Burke, *Philosophy of Literary Form*, rev. ed. (New York, 1957), p. 256.

religion in the future will shift from the present Romantic hermeneutics of symbol and poetic speech to that of legal-exegetical discourse.

My model of application has been much influenced by recent studies of African divination. The diviner, by manipulating a limited number of objects which have an assigned, though broad, field of meaning and by the rigorous interrogation of his client in order to determine his situation, arrives at a description of a possible world of meaning which confers significance on his client's question or distress. The diviner offers a "plausibility structure"; he suggests a possible "fit" between the structure he offers and the client's situation and both the diviner and client delight in exploring the adequacy and inadequacy, the implications and applicability of the diviner's proposal.

Myth, as narrative, is the analogue to the limited number of culturally determined objects manipulated by the diviner. Myth, as application, represents the complex interaction between diviner, client and situation.

There is something funny, there is something crazy about myth for it shares with the comic and the insane the quality of obsessiveness. Nothing, in principle, is allowed to elude its grasp. The myth, like the diviner's objects, is a code capable, in theory, of universal application. But this obsessiveness, this claim to universality is relativized by the situation. There is delight and there is play in both the fit and the incongruity of the fit between an element in the myth and this or that segment of the world or of experience which is encountered. It is this oscillation between "fit" and "no fit" which gives rise to thought. Myth shares with other forms of human speech such as the joke or riddle, a perception of a possible relationship between different "things". It delights, it gains its power, knowledge and value from the play between.

Some societies appear to have ritualized the perception of incongruity as part of their initiatory scenarios, as part of a process of education into the categories of mature thought. We have tended to understand initiation as a disclosure of sacred realities, a disclosure "earned" and reenforced by undergoing a series of ordeals. But there are other dimensions. There are elements in the initiation which remind me of that famous passage in *The Memoirs of Sherlock Holmes*:

> "Is there any point to which you would wish to draw my attention?"
> "To the curious incident of the dog in the night-time."
> "The dog did nothing in the night-time."
> "That was the curious incident," remarked Sherlock Holmes.

In religious disclosure, the unexpected is not only the surprising occurrence (a burning bush), it may be as well the lack of occurrence of an expected event which, as in the case of Sherlock Holmes, provides a "clue" to which ones thought and attention may be directed.

For example, among almost every Australian tribe the central act of initiation is the displaying of the bull-roarer, a little piece of wood with a slit in it that is whirled around at the end of a string to produce a loud humming noise that is identified as the voice of a deity.[11] Among the Aranda, the initiants had been previously taught that this sound was the voice of Tuanjiraka—a monstrous being who lived in a rock, walked with a limp carrying one leg over his shoulder, and eats little boys and girls. Tuanjiraka is responsible for all pain, including the pain of circumcision which the young boy has just undergone. Now that he has become a man, the tribal elders show him the bull-roarer and disclose its secret:

> We have always told you that your pains are caused by Tuanjiraka, but you must abandon belief in Tuanjiraka and understand that Tuanjiraka is only this piece of wood which you have just seen ... there is really no Tuanjiraka.[12]

We might argue that such rituals are degenerate and witness to a people who no longer remember the true meaning of what they do, that is to say, a religious experience has degenerated into a mere form of social discrimination maintained by deception. We might argue that the bull-roarer is apprehended as a real symbol by its believers—that it is only to the outside observer that it appears to be a fraud. We might argue that initiation, as a process of maturation, teaches the youth the difference between what is worthy of belief and what is make-believe. But I would want to insist that it is precisely the juxtaposition, the incongruity between the expectation and the actuality that serves as a vehicle of religious experience. The normal expectation has been suspended and the unexpected intrudes relativizing all previous modes of thought. The practical joke (and this, after all, is what most initiations are whether they occur in primitive societies or in college fraternities) structurally resembles that sudden breakthrough which scholars of religion have termed an epiphany or

---

[11] For a wide-ranging collection of examples, see A. M. di Nola, "Demythicization in Certain Primitive Cultures: Cultural Fact and Socioreligious Integration," *History of Religions*, XII (1972), pp. 1-27.

[12] C. von Strehlow, *Die Aranda und Loritja-Stämme in Zentral-Australien* (Frankfurt, 1913), Vol. IV, pp. 25f.

hierophany, but it does not, thereby, lose its character as a joke. The tradition has been applied, and the problematics of its application function as a religious experience and as an occasion for thought.[13] (Although space does not permit so complex a presentation, I would refer you to Victor Turner's monograph, *Chihamba, The White Spirit: A Ritual Drama of the Ndembu* [1962] for a stunning example of this process).

In my most recent work, I am attempting to develop this understanding of myth in two quite different groups of materials. I am working with a variety of Mediterranean religious texts from late antiquity in which incongruity is expressed through motifs of transcendence, rebellion and paradox.[14] I am also attempting to study a diverse collection of primitive materials—a set of traditions which are usually labeled "hunting magic" in which a discrepancy exists between what the hunters say they do when they hunt and what they actually do, a discrepancy that is raised to thought in rituals which enact a perfect hunt; a group of cargo cult materials in which the indigenous situation is rendered problematic by the incongruous presence of the white man; and a group of archaic myths which share the theme of a fundamental rupture between the world of the ancestors and the present human condition.[15] While it would be of some importance to indicate how these different sets of studies have reenforced each other as an indication of my commitment to the comparative enterprise, I shall obey the strictures of space and confine myself to one example drawn from the final group.

Perhaps the best known example of the mythologem of rupture is the story of Hainuwele, a tale that was first collected from the Wemale tribe of Ceram (one of the Moluccan islands, immediately west of New Guinea) in 1927. As this myth has been a favorite text for those who have insisted upon a radical separation of the primal myth from its application, its reconsideration will provide a test case for the adequacy of my proposal.

---

[13] I have been much influenced by M. Douglas' important article, "The Social Control of Cognition: Some Factors in Joke Perception" *Man*, III (1968), pp. 361-376.

[14] On this theme in Hellenistic literature, see J. Z. Smith, "Birth Upside Down or Right Side Up?," chapter 7, above and "Good News is No News: Aretalogy and Gospel", chapter 9, above.

[15] I have developed these themes at some length in my Arthur O. Clark Lectures for 1974 at Pomona College entitled "No Need to Travel to the Indies", which will be published in expanded form under the title, *The Disruptive Presence: Studies in Myth and Ritual*.

The text is too long to quote, so I shall offer only a brief summary. It begins "Nine families of mankind came forth in the beginning from Mount Nunusaku where the people had emerged from clusters of bananas" and goes on to narrate how an ancestor named Ameta found a coconut speared on a boar's tusk and, in a dream, was instructed to plant it. In six days a palm had sprung from the nut and flowered. Ameta cut his finger and his blood dripped on the blossom. Nine days later a girl grew from the blossom and in three more days she became adolescent. Ameta cut her from the tree and named her Hainuwele, "coconut girl". "But she was not like an ordinary person, for when she would answer the call of nature, her excrement consisted of all sorts of valuable articles, such as Chinese dishes and gongs, so that Ameta became very rich". During a major religious festival, Hainuwele stood in the middle of the dance grounds and excreted a whole series of valuable articles (Chinese porcelin dishes, metal knives, copper boxes, golden earings and great brass gongs). After nine days of this activity, "the people thought this thing mysterious ... they were jealous that Hainuwele could distribute such wealth and decided to kill her". The ancestors dug a hole in the middle of, the dance ground, threw Hainuwele in and danced the ground firm on top of her. Ameta dug up her corpse, dismembered it and buried the cut pieces. These pieces gave rise to previously unknown plant species, especially tuberous plants which have been, ever since, the principal form of food on Ceram.[16]

The chief interpreter of this myth, Adolf Jensen, has understood the tale to describe the origins of death, sexuality and cultivated food plants—that is to say, as a description of human existence as distinct from ancestral times. While I cannot within the scope of this lecture treat each detail, I find no hint in the text that sexuality or death is the result of Hainuwele's murder nor that the cultivation of plants are solely the consequence of her death.

Death and sexuality are already constitutive of human existence in the very first line of the text with its mention of the emergence of man from clusters of bananas. It is a widely spread Oceanic tale of the origin of death—found as well among the Wemale[17], that human

---

[16] See A. E. Jensen, *Hainuwele: Volkserzählungen von der Molukkeninsel Ceram* (Frankfurt, 1939); *Das religiöse Weltbild einer frühen Kultur* (Stuttgart, 1938) and, in English translation, *Myth and Cult among Primitive Peoples* (Chicago, 1963), esp. 83-115, 162-190.

[17] For the Wemale version, see Jensen, *Hainuwele*, pp. 39-43 (text 1).

finitude is the result of a choice or conflict between a stone and a banana. Bananas are large, perennial herbs which put forth tall, vigorous shoots which die after producing fruit. The choice, the conflict in these tales is between progeny followed by death (the banana) and eternal but sterile life (the stone). The banana always wins. Thus Jensen's interpretation collapses with the very first line. Man as mortal and sexual, indeed the correlation of death and sexuality, is the presupposition of the myth of Hainuwele, not its result. Ameta's dream, before the birth of Hainuwele, indicates that the cultivation of plants is likewise present. Jensen's interpretation rests on only a few details: that Hainuwele was killed, buried, dismembered and that from pieces of her body tuberous plants grew. This is a widespread motif, rendered more "plausible" by the fact that this is the way in which tubers such as yams are actually cultivated. The yam is stored in the ground, dug up and divided into pieces and these are then planted and result in new yams. That tropical yams can grow to a length of several feet and weigh a hundred pounds only furthers the analogy with the human body.

If Jensen's exegesis must be set aside, what then is the myth about? *Our* sense of incongruity is clearly seized by her curious mode of production—the excretion of valuable objects—and it is this act which clearly provides the motivation for the central act in the story, her murder. We share our sense of incongruity with the Wemale, for "they thought this thing mysterious ... and plotted to kill her".

There is, in fact, a double incongruity for the objects Hainuwele excretes are all manufactured trade goods—indeed they are all goods which are used on Ceram as money. Using the phrase literally, the myth of Hainuwele is a story of the origin of "filthy lucre", of "dirty money".

The text is not an origin of death or an origin of tubers tale. It is not primarily concerned with the discrepancy between the world of the ancestors and the world of men. It is, I would suggest, a witness to the confrontation between native and European economic systems. The text is important not because it opens a vista to an archaic tuber-cultivator culture but because it reflects what I would term a "cargo situation" without a cargo cult. It reflects a native strategy for dealing with a new, incongruous situation, a strategy that thinks with indigenous elements (the diviner's pot). The myth of Hainuwele is not a primal myth (as Jensen insists), it is rather a stunning example of application.

In Oceanic exchange systems, the central ideology is one of "equivalence, neither more nor less, neither 'one up' nor 'one down' " to quote a recent field report.[18] Foodstuffs are stored, not as capital assets, but in order to be given away in feasts and ceremonies that restore equilibrium. Wealth and prestige is not measured by either resourceful thrift or conspicuous consumption, but by ones skill in achieving reciprocity. Exchange goods are familiar. They are local objects which a man grows or manufactures. Theoretically everyone could grow or make the same things in the same quantity. The difference is a matter of "accident" and therefore must be "averaged out" through exchange.

Foreign trade goods and money function in quite a different way and their introduction into Oceania created a social and moral crisis that we may term the "cargo situation". How could one enter into reciprocal relations with the white man who possesses and hoardes all this "stuff"; whose manufacture took place in some distant land which the native has never seen? How does one achieve equilibrium with the white man who does not appear to have "made" his money? If the white man was merely a stranger, the problem would be serious but might not threaten every dimension of Oceanic life. But in Oceanic traditions, the ancestors are white and, therefore, the native cannot simply ignore the white man (even if this was a pragmatic possibility)—he is one of their own, but he refuses to play according to the rules or is ignorant of them. The problem of reciprocity cannot be avoided. What can the native do to make the white man (his ancestor who has returned) admit to his reciprocal obligations? His ignorance and refusal to recognize the rules and his obligations is a problem for native theodicy. The strategies for gaining his recognition of reciprocity is a question for native soteriology.

A variety of means have been employed to meet this "cargo situation". In explicit cargo cults, it is asserted that a ship or airplane will arrive from the ancestors carrying an equal amount of goods for the natives. Or that the European's goods were originally intended for the natives, but that someone has readdressed their labels. A native savior will journey to the land of the ancestors, correct the labels or bring a new shipment, or the ancestors will redress the injury on their own initiative.

In other more desperate cults, the natives destroy everything that they own as if by this dramatic gesture to awaken the white man's

---

[18] K. Burridge, *Mambu* (New York, 1970), pp. 82-85.

moral sense of reciprocity. "See, we have now given away everything. What will you give in return?" Both of these solutions assume the validity of exchange and reciprocity and appeal to it.

Other solutions, not part of cargo cults, but part of what I have termed the cargo situation appeal to mythic resources which underlie the exchange system rather than to the system itself.

Kenelm Burridge, in his classic studies *Mambu* and *Tangu Traditions*, has shown how, among the Tangu in the Australian Trust Territory of New Guinea, a traditional pedagogic tale concerning the social relations between older and younger brother has been reworked to reveal that the difference in status between the white man (younger brother) and the native (older brother) is the result of an accident and is therefore, in native terms, a situation of disequilibrium which requires exchange.[19]

I should like to make a similar claim for Hainuwele. That a "cargo situation" existed in the Moluccas is beyond dispute. After a period of "benign neglect", the Dutch embarked on a policy of intensive colonialist and missionary activities during the years 1902-1910 which included the suppression on ancestral and headhunting cults and (important for my interpretation) the imposition of a tax which had to be paid in cash rather than labor exchange. A number of nativistic, rebellious cults arose, known collectively as the Mejapi movements (i.e., "the ones who hide").

In traditional Moluccan society this term had applied to the gesture of a disaffected villager who would withdraw from his community and live alone in the forest in protest against a village chief. Such a gesture shamed the chief and upset the equilibrium of the village. A complex series of exchanges was required in order to restore harmony.

In their cargo form, the Mejapi movements constructed separate villages which sought to achieve direct contact with the ancestors and which would be fed by a "ship from heaven".[20]

The Mejapi cults represent an attempt to appeal to a traditional pattern of socio-political relations applied to a new, non-traditional

---

[19] Burridge, *Mambu*, pp. 154-176 and *Tangu Traditions* (Oxford, 1969), pp. 113f., 229f., 330, 400-411.

[20] For the classic description of the Mejapi, see A. C. Kruyt and N. Adriani, "De Godsdienstig-Politieke Beweging 'Mejapi' op Celebes," *Bijdragen tot de Taal-, Land-, en Volkenkunde van Nederlandsch-Indië*, LXVII (1913), 135-151; for a brief English description, see J. M. van der Kroef, "Messianic Movements in the Celebes, Sumatra, and Borneo," in S. L. Thrupp, ed., *Millennial Dreams in Action* (New York, 1970), especially pp. 80-91.

situation. But the white man failed to receive the "signal". He was not shamed and did not enter into exchange.

I would date the present version of the Hainuwele tale from the same period. Hainuwele disrupts a major ceremony which celebrates traditional values and exchange and produces imported objects, produces cash, in an abnormal way, objects which have so great a value that no exchange is possible.

But the Ceramese have a mythic precedent for this situation. "In the beginning", when Yam Woman, Sago Woman or some other similar figure, mysteriously produced a previously unknown form of food, the figure was killed, the food consumed and thereby acculturated. The same model, in the Hainuwele myth, is daringly applied to the white man and his goods.

I am suggesting that Jensen and others were essentially correct in calling attention to the theme of creative murder in these societies, but that their lack of sensitivity to incongruity and application has led them to ignore what is most creative in Hainuwele. They have been also led astray by Judaeo-Christian presuppositions. The murder of Hainuwele does not result in a loss of Paradise where food was spontaneously at hand (as in our Western Fall story)—spontaneity and endless productivity are not virtues in an exchange economy. The deed does not result in mortality, sexuality and agricultural labor (again as in the Fall story)—I have argued that these elements are presupposed by the myth. Rather murder and eating is a means of making something "ours", is a means of acculturation.

The myth of Hainuwele is an application of this archaic mythologem to a new "cargo" situation. The killing of Hainuwele does not represent a rupture with an ancestral age; rather her presence among men disrupts traditional, native society. The setting of the myth is not in the "once upon a time" but in the painful post-European "here and now".

The Ceramese myth of Hainuwele or the Tangu tale of the Two Brothers does not solve the dilemma, overcome the incongruity or resolve the tension. Rather it provides the native with an occasion for thought. It is a testing of the adequacy and applicability of native categories to new situations and data. As such, it is preeminently a rational and rationalizing enterprise, an instance of an experimental method. The experiment was a failure. The white man was not brought into conformity with native categories, he still fails to recognize a moral claim of reciprocity. But this is not how we judge the success of a science. We judge harshly those who have abandoned the novel and the incongruous to a realm outside of the confines of understanding and we value those who (even though failing) stubbornly make the attempt at achieving intelligibility, who have chosen the long, hard road of understanding.[21]

The position I have sketched in this lecture was an attempt to achieve what one of my old professors used to term "an exaggeration in the direction of the truth". It seemed worth undertaking at this juncture as there is no description about which so many different schools agree as the congruency of native thought and religion. I believe that this assumption has prevented us from seeing the craft, the capacity of thought and imagination, the impulse towards experimentation that is awakened only at the point where congruency fails.

I have suggested that myth is best conceived not as a primordium, but rather as a limited collection of elements with a fixed range of cultural meanings which are applied, thought with, worked with, experimented with in particular situations. That the power of myth depends upon the play between the applicability and inapplicability of a given element in the myth to a given experiential situation. That some rituals rely for their power upon a confrontation between expectation and reality and use of perception of that discrepancy as an occasion for thought.

All of this is to say that the usual portrait of the primitive (the nonhuman "them" of our cultural map)—whether in the nineteenth century negative form or our more recent positive evaluation—has prevented us from realizing what is human and humane in the worlds of other men. We have not been attendant to the ordinary, recognizable features of religion as negotiation and application but have rather perceived it to be an extraordinary, exotic category of experience which escapes everyday modes of thought. But human life—or, perhaps more pointedly, humane life—is not a series of burning bushes. The categories of holism, of congruity, suggest a static perfection to primitive life which I, for one, find inhuman.

To return to my starting point. Those myths and rituals which belong to a locative map of the cosmos labor to overcome all in-

---

[21] For a more complex analysis of Hainuwele in relation to Cargo Cult materials, see J. Z. Smith, "A Pearl of Great Price and A Cargo of Yams: A Study in Situational Incongruity," *History of Religions*, XVI (1976), 1-19 which introduces the key notion of *rectification*.

congruity by assuming the interconnectedness of all things, the adequacy of symbolization (usually expressed as a belief in the correspondence between macro- and microcosm) and the power and possibility of repetition. They allow for moments of ritualized disjunction, but these are part of a highly structured scenario (initiation, New Year) in which the disjunctive (identified with the liminal or chaotic) will be overcome through recreation. These values, within the great, urban, imperial cultures will frequently become reversed. What I have termed a utopian map of the cosmos is developed which perceives terror and confinement in interconnection, correspondence and repetition. The moments of disjunction become coextensive with finite existence and the world is perceived to be chaotic, reversed, liminal. Rather than celebration, affirmation and repetition, man turns in rebellion and flight to a new world and a new mode of creation. (The gnostic revaluation of ancient Near Eastern mythology, the yogic reversal of Brahmanic traditions would be good examples of such utopian cosmologies).

The dimensions of incongruity which I have been describing in this paper, appear to belong to yet another map of the cosmos. These traditions are more closely akin to the joke in that they neither deny nor flee from disjunction, but allow the incongruous elements to stand. They suggest that symbolism, myth, ritual, repetition, transcendence are all incapable of overcoming disjunction. They seek, rather, to play between the incongruities and to provide an occasion for thought.

Such are three maps of the worlds of other men. They are not to be identified with any particular culture at any particular time. They remain coeval possibilities which may be appropriated whenever and wherever they correspond to man's experience of the world. Other maps will be drawn as the scholar of religions continues his task. The materials described in this paper suggest that we may have to relax some of our cherished notions of significance and seriousness. We may have to become initiated by the other whom we study and undergo the ordeal of incongruity. For we have often missed what is humane in the other by the very seriousness of our quest. We need to reflect on and play with the necessary incongruity of our maps before we set out on a voyage of discovery to chart the worlds of other men. For the dictum of Alfred Korzybski is inescapable: "Map is not territory"—but maps are all we possess.

INDEX TO ANCIENT SOURCES

BIBLE; JEWISH AND CHRISTIAN APOCRYPHA

Abraham, Apocalypse of		33:3	50n.
10	52-53	40:9	50n.
18	52-53	54:6	50n.
Acts		71:8-9	50n.
14:11ff.	199	71:13	50n.
17:6	169	72:1	50n.
Adam and Eve, Life of		74:2	50n.
36:1	8n.	2 Enoch	
1 Baruch		22:4-10	64
3:36-37	45n.	22:6-7	42
3:37-38	56	29:2	52n.
2 Baruch		33:5-10	64
10	120	33:10-11	42
3 Baruch		67:2	64
11:1ff.	42	3 Enoch	
Ben Sirach, Wisdom of		10:3-4	64
24:8	45n., 55	10:48	64
2 Chronicles		47:2	52n.
34	176n.	Exodus	
36:23	73, 189	4:22	40
Colossians		19:4	62n.
1:15	40	20:26	3
1:17	40	26:7	14
3:9	11, 17	26:35	125
1 Corinthians		4 Ezra	
2:8	166	6:58	40
15:12-57	166	12	78
2 Corinthians		Genesis	
5:1-4	18	1	124
Daniel		1-3	2, 22
4:25	156	1:1	56n.
4:32-33	156	2:25	7
5:21	156	3:15	13n., 14
8:11	42	3:21	16-17
12:1	41	23:26	53
Deuteronomy		25:10-17	62n.
14	148	25:22-26	47
14:6-8	149	25:23	47
32:10	109, 136	25:26	48
32:11	62n.	25:29-34	47
Egyptians, Gospel of		27	47, 49
(f)	21	27:36	48
1 Enoch		28	29n.
9:1	66	28:10-27	57
10:1	34n., 66	28:12	58
20:2	50n.	28:12-19	94

28:13	58	20:5-6	6
28:19	62n.	20:30-31	201
32	43, 54, 65	21:18-19	204
32:24ff.	26, 49	John, Acts of (Greek)	
32:25-32	66	110	19n.
32:26-27	57	John, Acts of (Syriac, Wright)	
32:29	37, 49	2:39	9n.
32:30	42, 50n., 66	2:50	9n.
32:31	37	John, Apocryphon of	
36:1	47	30:7	36n.
36:8	47	65:11	34n.
36:9	47	72:4	164
36:43	47	Joseph, Prayer of	
48:18	27	1-18	28
48-49	26	2	37, 41
48-50	27	3	31, 36
49:1-2	30n.	4	36, 40
50:5	27	5	28n., 40
50:25	27	7-10	28n.
Hebrews		8-10	54
1:14	42n.	10-11	49
Hosea		11-12	28n., 51
9:10	39n.	13	29n.
12:3	48	14-18	28n.
Isaiah		15	40
20:2-3	7n., 10n., 11	17-18	43
34:9-15	109	18	29n.
34:12	109, 136	18-19	29n.
38:7-8	166	Joseph and Asenath, Prayer of	
49:3	58	14	42n.
65:3-5	149	Joshua	
Isaiah, Ascension of		5:13	42n.
4:22	26n.	Jubilees	
Jacob, Ladder of		2:2	41n.
4-5	37, 60n.	3:30-32	3n.
Jeremiah		32:21	30n.
2:2	109, 136	35-17	37n.
4:6-7	76n., 112	37-38	47n.
4:23-26	136	38:1-4	48n.
6:22-23	76n., 112	2 Kings	
17:9	48	20:8-11	166
19	82	22-23	176n.
Job		Leviticus	
25:2	51n., 53	11:3	149
32:26	109, 136	11:7	149
38:8-11	135	11:10-12	149
John		11:20-26	149
1:19-23	199	20:22	111
7:34	204	Luke	
7:35-36	204	13:30	166
8:58	40n.	24:12	6
10:9	62n.	1 Maccabees	
13:33	204	1:13-14	3n.

2 Maccabees		Revelation	
4:12-14	3n.	3:18	4
Malachai		16:15	4
4:5	189	Romans	
Mark		7	140, 163
1:1	197	7:10	140, 163
8	195	11:2	41n.
Matthew		Solomon, Odes of	
16:9	195	23:16	166
16:19	117	Solomon, Testament of	
18:3	18n.	10	50n.
19:30	160	Thomas, Acts of	
20:16	166	121	4n., 7n.
Moses, Assumption of		132-133	4n.
1:14	56n.	157	4n.
10:2	42n.	Thomas, Gospel of	
10:9-10	62n.	1	19
Obadiah		2	19
1:18	51	18	19
1 Peter		19	19
2:2	18n.	21	19n., 20, 23
Peter, Acts of		22	19n.
33-41	151-156	36	19n.
Peter and Paul, Acts of		37	1-2, 8, 19-23
60	155	51	19
Philip, Acts of		61	19
138-140	155-156	85	19
Philip, Gospel of		111	19
101	4	113	19
Proverbs		Twelve Patriarchs, Testaments of	
31	124	T. Benjamin	
Psalms		3:2-5	27n.
24:7-9	62n.	T. Judah	
30:11	10	9:3	48n.
48	112	9:4	47n.
88:27	40	T. Levi	
		3:5	42n.

OTHER ANCIENT SOURCES

Avot de R. Nathan		Apostolic Constitutions	
4	118n.	3.15-16	7n.
Aelian, Varia Historia		7.36.2	39n.
2.26	200	8.6.6	12n.
4.17	200	8.15.7	39n.
Aeschylus, Eumenides		Apuleius, Apologia	
616	183n.	42	180n.
Ammianus Marcellinus, Rerum Gestarum		Aristides, Hieroi Logoi	
22.16	251n.	3.48	61n.
Apollodorus, Epitome		Aristophanes, Clouds	
2.12	166n.	498ff.	2n.
Apollonius, Historia thaumasai		Aristotle, Fragments	
6	200	192	200

193	201n.	Shabbat	
Arrian, Anabasis		10a	3n.
7.1.6	102, 141	14a	3n.
Augustine		35a	29n.
De catechizandis rudious		116a	29n.
7	12	Sukkah	
De civitate Dei		10b	3n.
7.35	180n.	48b	117n.
15.20.4	14	Ta'anit	
De consensu evangelium		10a	115n.
2.14.3	14n.	23a	117
Sermons		Yevamot	
56-59	12-14	22a	18n.
212-216	12-14	47b	3n., 6n.
Ba, Man's Dispute with his		48b	18n.
103b-130a	77	62a	18n.
Ba'al and Anat 'nt		63b	3n.
3.26-28	112	97b	18n.
Babylonian Talmud		Yoma	
Bava Batra		21b	115n.
10b	166n.	38b	48n.
158b	114	39b	115n.
Bava Kamma		77a	51n.
82a	4n.	Baldr's draumar	
Bekharot		9.1-2	228
47a	18n.	Barnabas, Epistle of	
Berakhot		6.11	18n.
25b	3n.	Beowulf	
51a	50n.	4861-4875	230
Gittin		Berossus, Babyloniaka	
57b	48n.	1	69
Hagigah		4	69
12b	41	11	69
Hullin		21	69
91a	58n.	Book of the Dead, Egyptian	
91b	35, 57n.	30	176n.
Ketubbot		125	77
110b-111a	113-14, 120	Catalogus codicum astrologorum graecorum	
111b	12n.		
116b	231n.	IV.4, 254-58	173
Megillah		V.1, 149	184n.
8a	62n.	VII, 63	177n.
Niddah		VII, 231	173
66a-b	4n.	VIII.1, 190	184n.
Pesahim		VIII.3, 134-139	172-73
50a	166n.	VIII.4, 105	177
107a	3n.	Chaldean Oracles	
Rosh Ha-Shanah		213	185n.
23b	52n.	Chrysostom, John	
Sanhedrin		Catechesis	
57b	18n.	2.24	4n.
90b	12n.	Epistle to Innocent	
96a	33n.	4	4n.

Homily ad Colossians		Codex Parisinus	
6.4	7n.	510	155
Claudian, De raptu Proserpinae		BN Lat 919	6n.
2.277-293	221n.	BN Lat 8846	5n.
2 Clement		BN Arab 251	7n.
12.1-2	22	Codex Ms. Reims	
Clement of Alexandria		427	50n.
Eclogae ex scripturis propheticus		Codex Vaticanus graecus	
51	41n.	1144	173
Excerpta Theodoti		3550	5n.
10-12	39n., 47n.	Codex Vercellenses	
50	17n.	1	180n.
76	165	7	180n.
78	165	33-41	151-54
Paedagogus		Corpus Hermeticum	
1.9	38n.	1.4	184n.
Protrepticus		1.14	167n.
10	18n.	1.27	59n.
Stromateis		4.4-5	59n.
1.5	38n.	10.25	59n.
3.91	21	16 (title)	174n.
5.35.1-2	39n., 47n.	Asclepius	
Clementina		24-26	75, 85
Recognitiones		37-38	185n.
1.1	178n.	Fragments	
1.3	178n.	28	167n.
1.5-6	178n.	Cyprian, Testimonia	
Homiliae		1.20	45n.
1.1	178n.	Cyril of Jerusalem, Catecheses mystagogicae	
1.3	178n.		
1.5-8	178n.	2	4n., 7
1.10	178n.	(pseudo) Demokritos, Physika	
1.13-15	178n.	3	176n.
Codex British Museum		Didascalia apostolorum	
BM Add. 27201	5n.	16	4n., 6-7
BM Or 2884	5n.	Didymus Alexandrinus, de Trinitate	
BM Or 5987	35n.	3.4	41n.
BM Or 6794	34n.	Diodorus Siculus, Bibliotheke	
BM Or 6796	35n.	1.27	251n.
Codex Laurentinus		1.48-50	178n.
75.1	173-74	Diogenes Laertius, Bioi	
Codex Matritensis Bibl. Nat.		6.32	164
4631	172	8.1	198n.
Codex Montepessulanus Fac. med.		8.2-3	198n.
227	172-73	Dionysius Areopagita, De ecclesiastica hierarchia	
Codex Morgan			
724	5n.	2.2-3	4n.
Codex Nag-hammadi		Enuma elish	
2.5	36, 38n.	1-7	72-74
3.2	176n.	4.121-22	133, 160
4.2	176n.	4.135-40	135
5.5	x	4.139-40	133, 160
6.8	75-76	5.1-2	133, 160

6.78	133, 160	1.202	247n.
7.144	133, 160	1.215	247n., 248
7.149	133, 160	2.4	244n.
7.151-52	133, 160	2.10	245n., 247n.

Epiphanius, Panarion
26.5	3n.	2.12	247n.

Esaias, Orationes
		2.13	248n.
4.9	29n.	2.29	247n.
		2.33	247n.

Euripides, Iphigenia Taurica
		2.35-37	247n., 248
1254	183n.	2.42	248
1282	183n.	2.43	244n.

Eusebius
		2.43-45	248

Historia ecclesiastica
		2.49	244n.
3.1.2	152	2.50	244n.

Preparatio evangelica
		2.57	244n.
6.11.64	26n., 29n.	2.58	244n.
7.8	38n.	2.63	248
11.6	38n.	2.70	247n.
11.22	180n.	2.73	251

Firmicus Maternus, Matheseos
		2.75	251
4 (Praef. 5)	177n.	2.79	244n.

Galen, On Medical Simples
		2.80	247n.
10.19 (Kuhn, XII, 207)	177n.	2.81	244n.

Gedulath Moshe
		2.82	244n.
15	52n.	2.91	244n.

Gelasius Cyzicenus, Historia ecclesiastica
		2.105	247n.
2.16	41n.	2.123	248n.
2.18	56n.	2.142-146	248

Gilgamesh, Epic of
		2.146	248
1.9-19	135	2.167	247n., 248
11.303-307	135	3.8	248n.

Ginza (Lidzbarski)
		3.20	247n.
p. 98	31n.	3.37	248n.
p. 194	3n.	3.38	249
pp. 390-91	140, 163	3.102	251

Gregory Nazianzenus, Orationes
		3.105	251
40.4	12n.	3.106	247n.

Hekhaloth Rabbati
		3.111	248n.
9	58	3.124	248n.

Herodotus, Historiae
		3.125	248n.
1.65	183n.	4.17	247n.
1.74	247n., 248	4.23	247n.
1.94	247n., 248	4.28	251
1.131	248n.	4.44	247n.
1.134	247n.	4.45	248n.
1.135	244n.	4.53	247n.
1.140	247	4.59-76	246
1.142	247n.	4.59	248n.
1.149	247n.	4.61	247n.
1.173	247n.	4.79	248n.
1.193	248n.	4.99	247n.
1.195	247n., 248	4.104	247n.
1.198	247n.	4.105	247n.

INDEX TO ANCIENT SOURCES 317

4.109	247n.
4.168	247n.
4.170	247n.
4.171	247n.
4.172	247n.
4.180	248n.
4.186	247n.
4.187	247n.
4.198	247n., 248n.
5.80	248n.
7.26	248
8.55	248
8.144	246
9.51	248n.

Hermas
  Similitudines pastoris
    9.29.1-3 — 18n.
  Visiones pastoris
    3.4.1 — 40n.

Hesychius, Lexicon
  Dios kodion — 15

Hildefonse of Toledo, De cognitione baptismi
  14 — 14-15

Hippolytus
  Canones Hippolyti
    114 — 4n.
  Traditio apostolica
    21.3 — 4n.
  Contra haeresin Noëti
    5 — 38n.
  Refutatio omnium haeresium
    4.32 — 181n.
    5.7.3-9.9 — xi, 22n., 167n., 168
    5.7.15 — 22n.
    5.7.44 — 168n.
    5.8.13 — 168n.
    5.8.41ff. — 3n.
    5.8.44 — 22n.
    5.8.81-91 — 62n.
    5.26.2 — 34-35

Historia Lausica
  37 — 8n.

Homer
  Iliad
    1.403-4 — 31n.
  Scholia on Iliad
    1.340 — 200n.
    2.106 — 166n.

Horace, Satires
  2.5 — 178n.

Hromundar saga Greipssonar
  4-7 — 228n.

Iamblichus
  De communi mathematica scientia
    25 — 202n.
  De Mysteriis
    3.11 — 180n.
    3.18 — 188n.
    5.23 — 185n.
  De vita Pythagorica (Deubner)
    1, p. 5, 2 — 197
    3, p. 6, 5-7 — 198
    5, p. 7, 5-8 — 198
    5, p. 7, 9-23 — 198
    10, p. 8, 20-30 — 198
    15-17, pp. 11, 24-12, 26 — 199
    30, p. 18, 12-17 — 199
    31, p. 18, 12-16 — 200
    81-89, pp. 46, 22-52, 19 — 202n.
    135, pp. 76, 19-77, 13 — 201
    138-140, pp. 78, 14-79, 12 — 201
    139, pp. 78, 20-79, 3 — 201
    144, p. 80, 25-26 — 200n.
    148, pp. 83, 24-84, 7 — 201

Inscriptions and Amulets
  Calder, *Anatolian Studies Ramsay*
    76, no. 4 — 56n.
  Corpus Inscriptionum Latinarum
    14, no. 2213 — 225n.
  Dittenberger, *Sylloge Inscriptionum Graecarum*
    2, no. 653 — 3n.
  Merseburg Charm
    no. 2 — 231n.
  Mouterde, *Mélanges St.-Joseph*
    15, 56-57 — 33n.
  Newhall
    no. 35 — 33n.
  Palestine Museum
    no. 36-1856 — 35n.
  Ramsay, *Cities Phrygia*
    no. 404 — 35n.
  Southesk
    no. N 84 — 34n.
  Wycherley, *Athenian Agora*
    3, 198 — 136n.

Irenaeus
  Adversus haereses
    1.1.10 — 17n.
    1.4.1 — 167n.
    1.5.5 — 17n.
  Demonstration (Armenian)
    43 — 56n.

Isidorus Hispalensis, Etymologiarum libri
  7.5 — 51n.

8.9	192n.	Angad Rosnan 8	21n.
James of Edessa, Canons		fragment C	21n.
121	4n.	Psalms (Coptic)	
Jerome		2	21n.
Epistle to Fabiola		250	21n.
19	17	258	21n.
Liber Hebraicarum Quaest. in Gen.		Turfan Fragments	
	36n., 38n., 56n.	M.4	32n.
John the Deacon, Epistula ad Senarius		M.20	32n.
6	4n., 19-20	Mekilta	
John of Jerusalem, Homilies		Visha, 14	122
62	50n.	Methodius, Symposium	
Joannes Moschus, Pratum spirituale		8.15-16	165
3	6n.	Michael Glycus, Annales	
Josephus		2.171	25n.
Antiquities		Midrash Aggada	
12.241	3n.	Exodus 4.5	50n.
War		Midrash 'Asereth ha-dibberoth (Jellinek)	
2.148	3n.	1.66	52n.
2.161	3	Midrash Rabba	
Justin Martyr		Canticles	
1 Apologia		2.4	14n.
66.4	243n.	3.6.3	53n.
Dialogus cum Tryphone		3.11.1	52n., 53n.
125.5	37n.	Deuteronomy	
(pseudo) Justin		5.12	52n.
Cohortatio ad Graecos		5.15	52n.
37.3	68	Exodus	
Oratio ad Graecos		15.6	51n.
5	40	19.7	40, 56n.
Lactantius, Divinarum Institutionum		Genesis	
2.15.6	174n.	1.3	41n.
3.24	157	10.3	52n.
7	85	17.7	159n.
Lefafa Sedek		20.12	16-17n.
5a	44n.	47.6	57n.
(pseudo) Linus, Martyrium beati Petri apostoli		63.12	58n.
		68.12	57-58n.
12	155	68.13-69.3	57n., 58-60
Livy, Historiae		68.14	60n.
40,29	176n.	68.18	59n.
Lucian		77.1	63n.
Alexander		77.2	51
4	200n.	77.3	50
Necyomantia		78.2	53n.
3-6	148n.	78.3	50, 57n.
Macarius, Homiliae		79.8	63n.
47.5	38n.	82.6	57n.
Macrobius, Saturnalia		Leviticus	
5.19.2	216n.	9.9	52n.
Manichaean texts		29.2	60n.
Hymns (Parthian)		34	114
*Huwidagman 7	21n.		

Numbers		F.37-41	177n.
11.7	51n.	Origen	
12.3	113	Commentarii in Ioann.	
12.8	52n., 53n.	1.31	30n.
Midrash Tadshe		1.35	37n.
2	14n.	2.31	25, 27-28, 54-55
Midrash Tehillim		Contra Celsum	
18.159-60	48n.	6.21	61
78.6	60n.	Homiliae in Ezech.	
93.3	41n.	9.2	46n.
Mingana Manuscript 553		Homiliae in Gen.	
4b	19n.	15.5	55n.
Mishnah		Homiliae in Jer.	
Avot		20.2	46n.
1.2	118	Homiliae in Num.	
5.5	113	11.4	39n.
Gerim		13.5	46n.
1.4	3n.	17.4	30n.
Kelim		Philocalia	
1.6	113	22.15	25
Mikva'ot		23.15	25, 26n., 29
10.1-4	4n.	23.19	26n., 30, 54
Shabbat		De principiis	
6.1	4n.	4.3	38n., 55n.
Sanhedrin		4.12	55n.
7.8	29n.	Ovid, Fasti	
Sukkah		3.263-64	218n.
3.16	117	Palestinian Talmud	
Moses, Sword of		Avodah Zarah	
1	34n.	1.2	48n.
Moses Chorene, Historia		3.42	3n.
1.6	68	Kilayim	
Mota Muse (Leslau)		5.30a	231n.
p. 129	50	Nedarim	
Motif Index (S. Thompson)		38a	48n.
A 1371.1	159n.	Rosh Ha-Shanah	
A 2721.2.1	232	1.56d	29n.
E 34	159n.	1.58a	52n.
E 758	166n.	Sanhedrin	
F 167.4 (.1)	158n.	7.6	3n.
N 320	230	Yoma	
N 330	230	41d	115n.
Z 311	230	Papyrus British Museum	
Z 313	230	46	35n.
Z 352	232	Papyri Graecae Magicae (Preisendanz)	
Narsai, Homiliae		3.304	180n.
21-22	4n., 9-11n., 13n.	4.118	34n.
Nechepso, Fragmenta (Riess)		4.220-21	180n.
T.7	177n.	4.155-285	179n.
F.1	184n.	4.286-295	179n.
F.6	184n.	4.1345-80	139, 162
F.33	185n.	4.1735-37	33n.
F.35-36	184n.	4.1815-16	34n.

INDEX TO ANCIENT SOURCES

7.649	34n.
22b.1-3	63-64
36.310	35n.
Papyrus Graf	
29787	78, 81
Papyrus London	
121	34n.
384	34n.
6795	34n.
Papyrus Louvre	
2342	184n.
3284	176n.
Papyrus Magique Harris	
7.1	166
Papyrus Mimaut	34n.
Papyrus Oslo	
36	35n.
Papyrus Oxyrhynchus	
655	1-2
2332	78, 83
Papyrus Paris	
43	3n.
224	34n.
1736	34n.
1803	34n.
1884	177
3034	35n.
Papyrus Ranier	
19813	78, 83
Papyrus Societa Italiana, Florence	
982	79
Papyrus Trinity College, Dublin	
192b	82
Papyrus Turin	4n.
Pausanias, Periegeseos	
2.27.4	217
9.39.1	158n.
10.12.2	68
Philo	
De Abrahamo	
57	38n.
60-62	185n.
68-80	185n.
125	39n.
De Agricultura	
51	39n., 45n.
81	38n.
De Confusione Linguarum	
56	38n.
63	39n.
72	38n.
91	38n.
92	38n.
146	38n., 39n., 40, 45n.
148	38n.
159	38n.
174	39n.
De Congressu quaerendae Eruditionis gratia	
51	38n.
Quod Deterius Potiori insidiari solet	
118	39n.
159	17n.
Quod Deus immutabilis sit	
56	17n.
57	40n.
144	38n.
182	39n.
De Ebrietate	
111	38n.
De Fuga et Inventione	
108-110	40n.
208	38n.
De Gigantibus	
52	40n.
53	17n.
Legum Allegoria	
1.43	39n.
1.161	48n.
2.34	38n.
2.56ff.	17n.
2.89	48n.
3.15	38n., 48n.
3.82-88	40n.
3.93	48n.
3.172	38n.
3.175	39n., 45n.
3.177	39n.
3.186	38n.
3.212	38n.
De Migratione Abrahami	
6	39n., 45n.
14	38n.
18	38n.
54	38n.
102	40n.
113	38n.
125	38n.
176-96	185n.
192	17n.
201	38n.
De Mutatione Nominum	
81	48n.
87	39n., 40n.
109	38n.
189	38n.

203	38n.	75	17n.
209	38n.	De Vita Contemplativa	
258	38n.	34	180n.
De Plantatione		De Vita Mosis	
46-47	38n.	2.163	181n.
58	38n.	(pseudo) Philo, Liber Antiquitatum	
60	38n.	Biblicarum	
De Posteritate Caini		18.5	53n.
62	38n.	Philostratus	
92	38n.	Vita Apollonii	
137	17n.	1.3	196
Quaestiones et Solutiones in Exod.		1.4	196
2.22	38n.	1.6	196
2.38	38n.	1.18	195
2.47	38n.	1.21	197
2.64	39n.	2.37	180n.
2.66	39n.	3.15	195n.
2.68	39n.	4.24	195n.
Quaestiones et Solutiones in Gen.		4.43	195n.
1.53	17n.	5.7	195n.
2.69	17n.	6.11	195n., 197
3.48	38n.	6.32	195n.
4.1	17n.	7.15	196
4.233	38n.	7.30	197
Quis Rerum Divinarum Heres		7.38	195
78	38n.	8.15	197
205	39n.	8.31	196
252	48n.	Vitae Sophistarum	
279	38n.	590	193n.
De Sacrificiis Abelis et Caini		Picatrix	
42	48n.	3.6	182n.
120	38n.	3.9	181-182n.
134	38n.	Pirke de Rabbi Eliezer	
135	48n.	32	3n.
De Sobrietate		33	12n.
13	38n.	35	60n.
De Somniis		37	37, 53n.
1.40-60	185n.	Pirke Hekhaloth (Jellinek)	
1.68-71	185n.	3.161-63	36, 53n.
1.114	38n.	Pistis Sophia	
1.146-47	59n.	15-16	164
1.171	48n.	137	32n.
1.173	38n.	Plato	
1.230	39n.	Phaedrus	
1.240	39n.	253-54	97
2.44	38n.	Statesman	
2.173	38n.	269-74	165
2.265-67	39n.	Pliny, Historia naturalis	
2.279	38n.	7.6	68
De Specialibus Legibus		7.123	159
1.230	40n.	Plotinus, Enneads	
De Virtutibus		1.6.7	180n.
73	42n.	5.1.6	180n.

6.7.34	180n.
6.9.11	180n., 181, 185

Plutarch
Alexander
65.4	102

Numa
13.87	176n.

Porphyry, de Abstinentia
2.49	180n.
4.10	77n.

Priscillian, Liber de Fide
45-46	26n.

Proclus, in Platonis Timaeum commentarii
1.212	180n.

Procopius of Gaza, Commentarii in I Gen.
29	29n.

Psellus, Peri daimonen
881b-c	185n.

Qumran
1QS 7.12	3
1Qp (varia)	78
4Qp (varia)	78

Quodvultdeus, De symbolo
2	14

Saxo Grammaticus, Historia Danica
3.2	228

Seder Eliyyahu Rabbah
27	39n.

Seder Yizirat ha-Waled (Jellinek)
1.153-55	55n.

Sefer ha-Razim (Margalioth)
p. 97,19	34n.

Sefer Raziel
4b	34n.
6b	34n.
41b	34n.

Seneca, De consolatione ad Marciam
20	159n.

Servius, Ad Aeneida
3.46	216n.
6.136	215-16, 218n.

Sibylline Oracles
3.46-54	76
3.76-92	76
3.97-154	68
3.350-61	76, 85
3.809-829	68
4.165	4n.
5.512-632	76
11.245, 314	76

Sifre
Deuteronomy
320	3n.

355	63

Numbers
119	60n.

Silva Gaedelica
2	232n.

Snorri Edda
49-50	227

Sophocles
Oedipus Coloneus
337-38	251n.

Statius, Silvae
3.1.55-6	219n.

Strabo, Geographike
5.3.12	214, 267-69
17.1.27-29	178n.
17.1.46	178n.

Suda
to arnion	83
Dios kodion	15-16
Sibulla Delphis	68

Suetonius, Caligula
35	218n.

Sulpicus Severus, Chronica
2.50.8	19n.

Targum Neofiti
Gen. 32:25-32	66

Targum Yerushalmi
Gen. 28:12	57

Tatian, Oratio ad Graecos
9	165

Tertullian
Adversus Praxean
5	56n.

Adversus Valentianianos
24	17n.

De baptismo
9	6n.

De jejunio
7	180n.

De pudicitia
9	17n.

De resurrectione mortuorum
7	17n.

Testamentum Domini
2.8	4n., 19n.

Theodore of Mopsuestia, Homiliae
12-14	4n., 8-12

Theophrastus, Historia plantarum
1.3.4	231n.

Thessalos, Letter of
1-6, 7, 11	174-75
12-13, 21-23	177-81
25-27	183

25	185	7.761-82	218n.
Toledot Jeshu		Vitruvius, De architectura	
7	231-32	9.6.2	68
Tosefta		Voluspa	
Berakhot		31-32	227-28
2.14-15	3n.	Xanthippe and Polyxena, Acts of	
Sukkah		21	4n.
3.16	117n.	Xenophanes (Diels-Kranz)	
Valerius Flaccus, Argonautica		16(B)	244-45
2.305	218n.	Zohar	
Virgil, Aeneid		1.36b	16n.
6.136	215	1.138a	62n.
6.136-38	216	1.150b	58n.
6.138	221n.	1.173b	57n.
6.205-211	221, 224	2.4b	34n.
6.209	225	Hadash	120

GENERAL INDEX

Abaris, 201-203
Abraham, 27-28, 56, 185
Abydenos, 74
Adam and Eve, nudity and baptismal rites, 1-23
Aeneid, 208-39
African-Spanish exorcism, 12-13
Akiba, R., 122
Akitu festival, 72, 75, 79, 133, 161
Aldrich, C. R., 277-78
Alexander the Great, 73, 102, 137, 141, 163, 186
Alexander Polyhistor, 249
Alt, A., 70
Amenhotep, 81
Ammenemes I, 80-81
Amon-Re, 79
'Anath, 106
Anderson, B. W., 91
Angelological traditions, 31-37, 41-43, 51-53, 63-66
Anthropology and comparative religions, 240-64
Antigonus, 71, 73
Antigonus of Carytas, 251
Antiochus I, 73
Antiochus IV, 73
Apocalypticism, 68-87
Apollo, 198-99, 202-203
Apollonius of Tyana, 190-91, 195-97, 199-200, 203, 205
Apsu, 134
Apuleius, 193
Aranda, 301
Archimedes, 129, 289
Archontikoi, 34-35, 46
Aretalogy, 172-207
Aricia, priesthood, 208-39
Aristotle, 200, 202
Asclepius, 173, 180-81, 185
Ascent and descent, 57-64, 138-40, 166-68
Asenath, 27
Ashurbanipal, 73
Astarte, 105
Astral-botanical system, 172-89
Astronomy and astrology, 68-87, 172-89
Atreus, 166
Augustine, 12-14

Baal, 105, 134
Babylonian wisdom and apocalypticism, 68-87
Balder, 211, 222-23, 226-39
Baldus, H., 265-66
Baptismal rites and symbolism, 1-23
Bachelard, G., 104
Bastian, A., 255
Battas, 235
Berenson, B., 294
Berger, P., 145
Bergson, H., 10, 132, 178
Berkeley, G., 289
Berossus, 67-74, 84
Bertholet, R., 293
Best, E., 286
Betz, H. D., 67, 78, 190
Binswanger, L., 104
Boas, F., 248, 262-64
Bokcharis the Lamb, 75, 83-84
Bolos, 176
Bond of Heaven and Earth, 98-99
Book of Krates, 176
Bororo, 265-88
Boudreaux, P., 172
Box, G. H., 53
Brown, P., 86-87, 186-87, 192-93
Buber, M., 53
Buffon, G. L. L., 255, 259
Bulmer, R., 265
Bultmann, R., 205
Burch, V., 44-46
Burke, K., 299
Burridge, K., 142, 305-306
Butler, S., 241

Calanus, 102
Callimachus, 251
Callois, R., 104
Camus, A., 160, 170
Cargo cults, 142, 304-308
Cassirer, E., 144, 266
Castaneda, C., 268
Center, 98-99, 107-119, 186-89
Ceram, 302-307
Chaos, 79-81, 91, 97-98, 119-27, 308-309
Charles, R. H., 43-45
Childs, B. S., 104

Chnum, 82
Clement of Alexandria, 21-22
Clothing in baptismal rites, 21-22
Comparison, ix-xi, 240-64
Comte, A., 256
Cook A. B., 16
Creation myths, 88-103
Crocker, J. C., 288
Crucifixion, reverse, 147-71
Ctesias, 249
Cullmann, O., 1
Cumont, F., 173
Cunha, E. da, 170
Cuvier, Baron, 255, 259
Cyprian, 45
Cyril of Jerusalem, 7, 23
Cyrus, 73

Dahl, N. A., 172
Damis, 194-96
Daniélou, J., 23, 44, 46, 104
Darwin, Ch., 259, 263
Delphi, oracle at, 198-99
Demokritos, 176
Demotic Chronicle, 75, 78
Denis, A. M., 65
Desana, 270
Descartes, R., 129
Diana, 211, 215-16, 222, 225, 237
Dilthey, W., 242
Dinka, 281
Diogenes, 164
Dionysus, 235, 248
Dodd, E. R., 143, 161
Dositheus, 61
Douglas, M., 137, 148, 156, 206, 265, 291
Drijvers, H. J., 23
Dumézil, G., 147
Dumont, L., 102
Dumuzi, 72
Durkheim, E., 91, 145, 147, 192

Egyptian wisdom and apocalypticism, 74-85; magical traditions, 172-89
Eibschutz, J., 120
Eleusinian mysteries, xi, 16
Eliade, M., 88-100, 104, 106, 138, 150, 158, 170, 258-59, 283, 293
Emerald Tablet of Hermes, 176
Empedocles, 201
Enoch, 64
Enslin, M. S., 153

Enuma elish, 69, 72-73, 99, 133, 160
Epimenedes, 198, 201
Esagila, 73-74
Esau, 47-49, 65
Esfandiyar, 230
Eudoxus, 198
Evans-Pritchard, E. E., 279-81, 283-86, 297
Exchange system, Oceania, 141-42, 305-300
Exile, homeland and religion, xiii-xv, 104-128
Exorcism, 13-17

Feast of Water Drawing, 98
Fleece of Zeus, 15
Frankfort, H., 132, 160
Frazer, J. G., 147, 208-39, 251-52, 262, 266, 273, 285-86, 296
Friedrich, H-V., 174
Furetière, A., 130-31

Gabon pygmies, 119-20
Gabriel, 42-43, 49-50, 53
Garcia, S., 288
Gaster, Th. H., 106
Geertz, C., 282, 285
Gellner, E., 284-85, 298
Georgi, D., 190
Gifford, E. W., 169
Gilgamesh, 69, 133-36, 161, 232
Gillen, F. J., 278
Gnosticism, x, 1-2, 18-23, 47, 54-56, 59-60, 86, 122-26, 151-59
Goethe, J. W. von, 255-59
Gog and Magog, 137
Golden Bough by Frazer, 208-39; of Virgil, 210-26
Goldman, B., 194
Goodenough, E. R., 24, 31, 56, 63, 259
Gordan, A. D., 126
Gospel of Thomas, 1-2, 8, 19-23
Grant, R. M., 44, 47, 122
Graux, Ch., 172
Grimm, J., 256
Gurvitch, G., 102, 104
Guti, 71-72

Haedcyn, 230
Hainuwele, 302-307
Halder, A., 104
Ḥama b. R. Ḥanina, R., 50
Harpokration, 172-73

Harris, J. R., 55
Harsiesis, 82
Hays of Errol, 237
Heidegger, M., 104
Helios, 166
Helios-Re, 81-82
Hellanicus, 250
Hellenistic religions, central characteristics, xiii-xv, 60-62, 138-40, 160-66, 185-89
Hempel, Ch., 284
Henninger, J., 265
Herakles, 248
Herbert, G., 147
Herder, J. G., 258
Herebald, 230
Hermes, Hermes-Thot, 80-81
Herod the Idumenean, 48
Herodotus, 243, 245-49, 256
Hertz, R., 147
Hezekiah, 166
Ḥiyya, R., 58
Hobbes, Th., 130
Hobsbawm, E. J., 170
Hodgen, N. T., 245
Hodr, 227
Holy land, homeland and religion, 104-28
Honi the Circle-drawer, 117
Horus, 78-80, 82, 83, 122
Humboldt, W. von, 256
Hume, D., 273
Ḥuna, R., 51
Hyksos, 72, 74, 76
Hymn of the Pearl, 86
Hymns of Merneptah, 79
Hystaspes, Oracles of, 85

Iamblichus, 191, 193, 197-204
Imḥotep-Imouthes, 181
Ipu-Wer, Admonitions of, 77
Iriarte, J., 172
Isaac, 27-28, 48-49, 56, 157
Isaiah, 166
Isis, 80, 83
Island of Flames, 82
Israel, angel, 24-66; etymology, 36-42; homeland and religion, 104-28

Jacob, angel, 26-65
Jacobsen, Th., 132, 160
Jacoby, F., 62
James, M. R., 26-27, 43-45, 54
James, W., 242

Jaoel, 52-53
Jensen, Ad., 274, 303-304, 307
Jeremias, J., 104, 116
Jesus, 31, 37, 44-45, 61, 64, 122, 147-71, 195-96, 199, 202-205, 230
John, 61
John the Baptist, 28, 189, 196, 205
John the Deacon, 19-20
John of Pian del Carpine, 249
Johnson, S., 262, 289
Jonas, H., 161, 163
Jordan, L. H., 254
Josephus, 68
Jung, C. G., 259

Kalisker, A., 127
Kant, I., 91, 259
Karsten, R., 270-72
Keck, L., 193
Khakheperre-Soabe, Lamentations of, 77
Kingship, patterns of, xv, 72-73, 79, 132-37, 183-85
Klameth, G., 104
Knots, symbolism of, 138
Koenen, L., 78, 81, 83-84, 86
Koester, H., 190
Kook, A. I., R., 126
Koyré, A., 101, 132
Kramrisch, S., 104, 293
Krates, Book of, 176
Kroeber, A. L., 169
Kur, 134-35
Kyranides, 172-73, 179

Labib, P., 1, 4, 20
Lamarck, Chevalier de, 259
Lang, A., 224
Leah, 123
Leeuw, G. van der, 275
Lemminkäinen, 230
Lévi, E., 190-91, 197
Leviathan, 134
Lévi-Strauss, C., ix, 104, 137, 148, 156, 248, 265, 267, 272, 280, 287
Lévy-Bruhl, L., 274-81, 284-86
Lienhardt, G., 281, 283
Linnaeus, C., 256, 261
Livingstone, D., 255
Locative/Utopian ideology, 100-103, 130-42, 147-51, 160-66, 169-71, 185-89, 291-94, 308-309
Locke, J., 273
Loew, C., 132, 160

Loki, 227
Long, Ch., 106
L'Orange, H. P., 104
Lotan, 134
Lugbara, 158
Lukes, S., 285
Luria, I., 122, 124
Lycopolis, 80

Machiguengas, 288
McLennan, J. F., 258
Magic and magicians, 172-89, 190-207, 208-39
Malinowski, B., 248, 253, 266
Mallarmé, S., 144
Manetho, 74, 83-84
Mannheim, K., 253-54
Maori, 286
Marduk, 133-35, 160-61
Marind-anim, 298-99
Mark, Gospel of, 193, 195-96, 204
Marranos, 122
Marshall, J. T., 43, 45
Matrona, 121
Maui, 134, 161
Mauss, M., 142, 147
Meeks, W., 204
Megasthenes, 249
Meir, R., 16
Mejapi movements, 306-307
Melampous, 177
Menander, 61
Mercier, P., 264
Merkabah, 31, 61
Merton, R. K., 90
Metatron, 31, 35, 42-43, 50, 52, 59, 64
Michael, archangel, 31, 35, 37, 41-43, 48, 50, 53, 64, 117, 121
Midas, 200
Middleton, J. H., 222
Mill, J. S., 273
Mimingus, 228, 234
Mingana, A., 9-10
Miracle stories, 190-207
Misenus, 215
Mistletoe, 221-34
Mnesarchus, 198-99
Moluccan islands, 302-307
Morison, S. E., 141
Mountford, Ch. P., 108
Mowinckel, S., 96
Müller, W., 104, 293
Murray, G., 161

Murray, R., 23
Mus, P., 89, 104, 293
Mysticism, Hellenistic, 31-66, 151-56, 172-89
Myth, 190-207, 291-94, 299-309

Nachman, R., 114
Nathan, R., 40
Neanthes of Cyzicus, 196
Nebuchadnezzar, 73, 156
Nechepso, 175, 177, 183
Nefer-Rohu, 164
Neferti, 75, 80, 86
Nemi, priesthood at, 208-39
Neusner, J., 66, 264
New birth, baptismal rites, 18-23
New Guinea, 298-99
New Year festival, 72, 75, 79, 133, 161
Nicephorus, 25
Nichomachus, 202
Nicodemus, 205
Nilsson, M. P., 143
Ninurta, 134-35
Noth, M., 110
Nudity, 1-23
Nuer, 279-81, 284

Oannes, 69
Odin, 227
Orestes, 215
Origen, 24-25, 29-30, 44-46, 54-55, 57, 59-60, 65, 152
Orpheus, 134, 161
Ortiz, A., 99
Osiris, 122; and Horus, 79-80
Otto, R., 91

Pan, 248
Patai, R., 104, 109
Paul, 140
Pausanias, 217, 219
Penner, H., 284, 287
Percy, W., 282
Persius, 215
Peter, 195-96
Peter, Acts of, 151-56
Petosiris, 177, 185
Philo, 31, 38-39, 42, 45, 55, 65-66, 185
Philostratus, 191, 194-97, 204
Phlegon of Tralles, 251
Plato, 165, 258
Pliny, 68, 253
Plotinus, 181, 185

Poseidonius, 249
Posener, G., 80
Potter's Oracle, 75, 78, 81-82, 84-86
Poulet, G., 105
Prayer of Joseph, 24-66
Priebatsch, H., 66
Priesthood, 208-39
Primitive mentality, 265-88, 289-308
Proserpine, 215-16, 221
Proteus, 196
Psammetichus, 177
Pythagoras, 191, 193, 196-205
Pythias, 198-99

Queensland aborigines, 235

Rachel, 123
Rahab, 134
Ramses IV, 80
Rappoport, S. Z., 117
Re (Ra), 79, 81
Rebekah, 47
Redfield, R., 241
Reichel-Dolmatoff, G., 270
Reincarnation, 265-88
Resch, A., 24
Richelet, P., 131
Ricoeur, P., 128, 294
Riley, H. M., 23
Ritual repetition, 72, 98-100, 124-26, 169-71, 191
Rivers, W. H. R., 255
Rivet, P., 255
Roscher, W. H., 104
Rosetta stone, 80
Rostam, 230
Rostovtzeff, M., 143
Rubenstein, R., 105-106, 127-28
Ryle, G., 205, 299

Sabbatai Zevi, 123
Sabbē, 68
Sacred space, homeland and religion, 104-28
Sago woman, 307
Saint-Évremond, Seigneur de, 130
Sammael, 48
Samuel, M., 107
Sarana, G., 264
Sargon, II, 73
Sartre, J-P., 170
Saxo Grammaticus, 228-29, 234
Schärer, H., 108

Schenke, H. M., 21
Schlegel, Fr., 256
Schmidt, K. L., 104
Scholem, G., 52, 66, 122
Scribal wisdom and apocalypticism, 68-87
Sedlmayr, H., 104
Seleukos, I, 73
Seligman, C. G., 255
Sennacharib, 73
Servius, 215-19, 221, 223
Seth, 74, 79
Shamans, 90, 97
Shils, E., 99
Shmuel bar Nachman, R., 118
Simeon b. Lakish, R., 58, 62
Simeon Stylites, 186-87
Simon, M., 61
Simon Magus, 151
Smith, H. N., 131
Smith, M., 61, 190, 192-93, 264
Snefru, 80
Socrates, 190
Sophia, 55-56, 63
Space, sacred and time, 88-103
Spain, expulsion of the Jews, 122
Spencer, H., 228, 256, 296
Spinoza, B., 130
Stählin, O., 21
Stanner, W. E. H., 296
Stein, G., 208, 239
Steinen, K. von den, 255, 265-67, 269-76, 278-79
Steiner, F., 252-53
Stone of Foundation, 116
Storch, A., 277
Straus, E. W., 156
Symbolism and social change, 129-46
Syncretism, xiii, 67, 86-87

Tangu, 306-308
Temples, 112-26, 172-89, 293
Ternois, R., 130
Theodore of Mopsuestia, 8-9, 11-13, 23
Thessalos, 172-87
Thoas, 215
Thompson, S., 230
Tiamat, 134
Tiglat Pileser III, 73
Time, sacred and space, 88-103
Tocqueville, A. de, 131
Totemism, 265-88
Toynbee, A. J., 242
Transmigration, 265-88

Trilles, R. P., 119
Trumai, 266, 274
Tuanjiraka, 301
Tucci, G., 104, 293
Turner, F. J., 131
Turner, V., 148, 203
Tylor, E. B., 260-61, 273, 285
Typhonians, 81-82
Typhon-Set, 81

Utopian/Locative ideology, xii, 100-103, 130-42, 147-51, 160-66, 169-71, 185-89, 291-94, 308-309
Ur, Lamentation over the Destruction of, 71
Uriel, 30-66
Uruk, 71

Van Baal, J., 299
Van Baaren, Th. P., 270, 272, 287
Vermes, G., 66
Vesta, 225
Vikar, 230
Virgil, 211, 220, 222-24, 227
Visions, 5, 179-80, 190-207
Visions of Zosimos, 86
Voegelin, E., 101, 132, 160-61
Von Rad, G., 67-68, 110

Wagner, R-L., 101
Waika, 270
Weeden, T. J., 193
Wemale, 302-307
Weisstein, U., 264
Wensinck, A. J., 104
Wheatley, P., 293
Widengren, G., 61
Wiesel, E., 127-28
Wilson, B. R., 285
Winch, P., 285
Winckler, H., 102
Wirz, P., 298-99

Xenocrates, 198
Xenophanes, 244
Xerxes, 73
Xisuthrus, 69

Yakobel, 33
Yam woman, 307
Yannai, R., 58-59
Yoga, 89, 98, 158
Yoḥanan, R., 113

Zerries, O., 270
Zeus, 15, 166

www.ingramcontent.com/pod-product-compliance
Lightning Source LLC
Chambersburg PA
CBHW070808300426
44111CB00014B/2448